**BARRON'S
BUSINESS
REVIEW
SERIES**

Business Law SECOND EDITION

John W. Hardwicke
*LLB, George Washington University, Washington, D.C.
Chief Administrative Law Judge, Office of Administrative
    Hearings, State of Maryland
Instructor, Business Law, The Johns Hopkins University
Member of Maryland State Bar and U.S. Supreme Court Bar*

Robert W. Emerson
*JD, Harvard Law School, Cambridge, Massachusetts
Professor of Business Law, University of Florida
Member of Maryland State Bar and U.S. District Court Bar*

BARRON'S EDUCATIONAL SERIES, INC.

All inquiries should be addressed to:
Barron's Educational Series, Inc.
250 Wireless Boulevard
Hauppauge, New York 11788

Library of Congress Catalog Card No. 92-744

International Standard Book No. 0-8120-1385-9

Library of Congress Cataloging-in-Publication Data

Hardwicke, John W.
    Business law / John W. Hardwicke, Robert W. Emerson.—
2nd ed.
        p.   cm. —(Barron's business review series)
    Includes index.
    ISBN 0-8120-1385-9
    I. Business law—United States.   I. Emerson, Robert W.
    II. Title. III. Series.
    KF889.6.H37 1992 346.73'07—dc20
                                                92-744
[347.3067]   CIP

PRINTED IN THE UNITED STATES OF AMERICA
 45 800   98765 ·

CONTENTS

Preface   ix

1 ORIGIN AND NATURE OF LAW   **1**
The Origin of Law   *1*
Definitions of Law   *2*
Law and Morality   *2*
Development of Civil Law   *4*
Development of Common Law   *5*
Two Types of Law   *7*
Uniform Laws   *8*
Researching the Law   *8*
KNOW THE CONCEPTS   *9*
PRACTICAL APPLICATION   *10*
ANSWERS   *10*

2 GOVERNMENT UNDER LAW   **13**
Sources of U.S. Law   *13*
The U.S. Constitution   *14*
Federal Statutes   *16*
The State Constitutions   *19*
State Statutes   *19*
Local Ordinances   *21*
Rulings of Federal, State, and Local Agencies (Administrative Law)   *21*
Decisions by Federal and State Courts   *23*
KNOW THE CONCEPTS   *24*
PRACTICAL APPLICATION   *25*
ANSWERS   *26*

3 THE U.S. COURT SYSTEM AND THE LEGAL PROCESS   **28**
The Two Major U.S. Judicial Systems   *28*
Taking a Case to Court   *35*
Out-of-Court Procedures for Settling Disputes   *45*
Administrative Agency Proceedings   *47*
How Cases Are Cited   *48*
KNOW THE CONCEPTS   *49*
PRACTICAL APPLICATION   *50*
ANSWERS   *51*

4 CRIMES AND TORTS   **54**
Important Facts About Crimes   *54*
Important Facts About Torts   *59*
Comparison of Crimes and Torts   *62*
Examples of Torts   *62*
Examples of Business Crimes, with Tort Equivalents   *66*
The Businessperson as Criminal Defendant   *68*
General Defenses to Crimes and Torts   *69*
KNOW THE CONCEPTS   *72*
PRACTICAL APPLICATION   *74*
ANSWERS   *76*

5 CONTRACTS: NATURE, CLASSIFICATION, AND FORMATION   **81**
Nature of Contracts   *81*
Classification of Contracts   *83*
Negotiation   *85*

Forming a Contract 87
KNOW THE CONCEPTS 96
PRACTICAL APPLICATION 97
ANSWERS 98

6 REALITY OF THE CONTRACT: DID THE MINDS REALLY MEET? 100
Mistake 101
Fraud 103
Innocent (Nonfraudulent) Misrepresentation 106
Undue Influence 106
Duress 107
Unconscionability 108
KNOW THE CONCEPTS 109
PRACTICAL APPLICATION 110
ANSWERS 110

7 CONTRACTS: CAPACITY OF THE PARTIES AND LEGALITY OF SUBJECT MATTER 113
Capacity of the Parties 113
Legality of Subject Matter 117
KNOW THE CONCEPTS 121
PRACTICAL APPLICATION 121
ANSWERS 122

8 CONTRACTS: THE STATUTE OF FRAUDS; PAROL EVIDENCE RULE; PRIVITY 124
The Statute of Frauds 124
Parol Evidence Rule 128
Privity 129
KNOW THE CONCEPTS 133
PRACTICAL APPLICATION 134
ANSWERS 134

9 CONTRACTS: DISCHARGE; DAMAGES AND OTHER REMEDIES 136
Discharge 136
Damages 144
Other Remedies 148
KNOW THE CONCEPTS 150
PRACTICAL APPLICATION 151
ANSWERS 152

10 SPECIAL PROBLEMS RELATING TO SALES CONTRACTS 155
Article 2 of the Uniform Commercial Code 155
Principal Changes for Sales Contracts in Article 2 156
Nonsales Transactions 158
Definition of a Sale 159
Transfer of Title 159
Risk of Loss 160
Product Liability 163
Performance of the Sales Contract 168
Remedies for Breach of Sales Contracts 170
KNOW THE CONCEPTS 172
PRACTICAL APPLICATION 173
ANSWERS 173

11 COMMERCIAL PAPER: DEFINITIONS, CONCEPTS, AND   *176*
    NEGOTIATION

    The Negotiable Instrument as a Form of Commercial Paper   *176*
    Development of the Law Governing Negotiable Instruments   *177*
    The Uniform Commercial Code, Articles 3 and 4   *178*
    Elements of Negotiability   *178*
    Types of Negotiable Instruments   *183*
    The Parties to a Negotiable Instrument   *185*
    Advantages of Negotiable Instruments over Ordinary Contracts   *186*
    The Assignee of a Contract versus the Holder of a Negotiable   *187*
      Instrument
    Negotiation   *188*
    Indorsements   *189*
    KNOW THE CONCEPTS   *191*
    PRACTICAL APPLICATION   *193*
    ANSWERS   *194*

12 COMMERCIAL PAPER: THE HOLDER IN DUE COURSE,   *196*
    DEFENSES, LIABILITY, AND DISCHARGE

    Holder in Due Course   *197*
    Defenses   *202*
    Liabilities Among Parties   *207*
    Discharge   *213*
    KNOW THE CONCEPTS   *214*
    PRACTICAL APPLICATION   *215*
    ANSWERS   *216*

13 BANKING PROCEDURES AND THE BANK/CUSTOMER   *218*
    RELATIONSHIP

    The Contract Between Bank and Customer   *218*
    Rules Governing the Payment of Checks   *221*
    Certification of Checks   *222*
    Alterations   *223*
    Summary of Important Article 4 Rules   *224*
    Electronic Funds Transfer Act   *224*
    KNOW THE CONCEPTS   *226*
    PRACTICAL APPLICATION   *226*
    ANSWERS   *227*

14 AGENCY   *229*

    Nature of Agency and Agency Law   *229*
    Agency and Other Legal Concepts Whereby One Person May or   *230*
      May Not Perform Services for Another
    Creation of Agency   *231*
    The Agent/Principal Relationship   *233*
    Liability of Principal and Agent to Third Parties   *235*
    Termination of Agency   *241*
    KNOW THE CONCEPTS   *242*
    PRACTICAL APPLICATION   *243*
    ANSWERS   *243*

15 TYPES OF BUSINESS ORGANIZATIONS; PARTNERSHIPS; **246**
    FRANCHISES
    Types of Business Organizations   246
    General Partnerships   254
    Limited Partnerships   265
    Franchises   268
    KNOW THE CONCEPTS   270
    PRACTICAL APPLICATION   271
    ANSWERS   272

16 CORPORATIONS: NATURE, FORMATION, TYPES, AND   **274**
    POWERS
    Nature of a Corporation   274
    Background of Corporations   275
    Corporate Attributes   276
    Formation of the Corporation   277
    Types of Corporations   279
    Nature and Content of the Charter; Bylaws   282
    Corporate Powers and Limitations on Them   285
    Regulation of Foreign Corporations   287
    KNOW THE CONCEPTS   288
    PRACTICAL APPLICATION   289
    ANSWERS   289

17 MANAGEMENT OF THE CORPORATION; TERMINATION   **293**
    Corporate Overview   293
    Shareholders   294
    Board of Directors   301
    Officers   305
    Other Employees   306
    Termination of the Corporation   306
    KNOW THE CONCEPTS   308
    PRACTICAL APPLICATION   309
    ANSWERS   309

18 CORPORATIONS: FINANCIAL STRUCTURE; SECURITIES   **312**
    REGULATION; LIABILITY OF ACCOUNTANTS
    Corporate Financial Structure   313
    Securities Regulation   321
    Liability of Accountants   330
    KNOW THE CONCEPTS   332
    PRACTICAL APPLICATION   334
    ANSWERS   334

19 PROPERTY   **338**
    Property as a Legal Concept   338
    Personal Property   338
    Joint Ownership of Property   350
    Real Property   351
    Comparison of Major Property Arrangements   361
    Estates, Trusts, and Wills   361
    KNOW THE CONCEPTS   364
    PRACTICAL APPLICATION   366
    ANSWERS   367

20 CREDITORS' RIGHTS AND DEBTORS' PROTECTION;   **370**
   BANKRUPTCY; SECURED TRANSACTIONS
   Creditors' Rights: Collection of Debts   *371*
   Protection for Debtors   *374*
   Bankruptcy and Reorganization   *376*
   Secured Transactions   *382*
   KNOW THE CONCEPTS   *391*
   PRACTICAL APPLICATION   *392*
   ANSWERS   *394*

21 REGULATORY LAW AND OTHER TOPICS OF BUSINESS LAW   **398**
   Antitrust Law   *398*
   Environmental Law   *403*
   Employment Law   *405*
   Labor/Management Relations   *412*
   Insurance   *416*
   International Law   *418*
   Computers   *420*
   The Attorney's Many Roles and Ethical Responsibilities,   *423*
      Attorney/Client Conflict, and the Businessperson's Role
   KNOW THE CONCEPTS   *425*
   PRACTICAL APPLICATION   *426*
   ANSWERS   *427*
   Glossary   *430*
   Index   *474*

PREFACE

• PURPOSE AND SCOPE OF THE BOOK

Our purpose is to present both students and other interested persons with a simple and readily understandable explanation of essential and related business law and legal environment subjects.

For the citizen, corporate executive, and business manager, the book should serve as an independent explanation of fundamental law in both a practical and a technical setting. For the student, this overview should serve as a guide through the complex maze of the literally thousands of legal principles tossed out in a typical course on the law or legal environment of business.

Business law, including the legal environment of business, is a broad field; nearly every law school subject is covered or touched upon in this book. However, as experienced teachers and practicing attorneys, we have attempted to treat, in particular and adequate detail, the legal subjects that actually engage the attention of businesspersons and that are covered in university and college courses.

Legal theory is important in the "everyday business world" inhabited by corporate managers and all other businesspersons. We expect business professionals to be involved in major corporate decisions, as well as in buying and selling supplies and services. We expect them to know about tort responsibility and their duty to the public. Moreover, the modern business world now requires a general knowledge of governmental relations and activities, including the societal obligations described in the criminal and other statutory or regulatory law. This book deals with all of these concerns.

• CONTENTS OF THE BOOK: BOTH LEGAL ENVIRONMENT AND BUSINESS LAW

The text has been updated and expanded to include all relevant new topics and trends, as well as revisions of existing legislation, regulation, and case law. We examine the legal environment of business and delve at length into the conduct of litigation, the nature of governmental powers and individual rights, and specific areas of law with a strong impact on business. These include—in addition to "standard" business law topics—administrative and constitutional law, securities regulation, antitrust law, labor and employment law, consumer protection law, computer law, international law, insurance, attorneys and accountants, environmental law, and the general moral and social duties of business. Furthermore, the book contains an in-depth glossary of around 1,000 words, much more comprehensive and, we believe, more useful than the glossaries for other books of this size.

We consider the glossary to be a major asset of the book in that it can serve as an independent dictionary of legal terminology useful in the business world. Along these lines, a very thorough index also helps readers to find and understand legal topics in their overall context.

This book covers all of the material in the general business law course offerings (usually two semesters). Among these subjects are (a) an introduction to the law, (b) crimes and torts, (c) contracts, (d) business organizations (especially corporations and partnerships), (e) commercial paper, (f) agency, (g) property, (h) creditor rights and obligations, and (i) a full review of the Uniform Commercial Code.

The material presented is also designed to prepare accounting students for their future profession. It is in keeping with American Institute of Certified Public Accountants (AICPA) educational requirements. All AICPA law course topics are included and the book should serve as an excellent review for practicing accountants.

For the more general business law or legal environment student, our breakdown of the subject by chapter ties in with standard textbook treatment. This, and the comprehensive glossary and index, should be of help to the student who may need to key the class lectures or work assignments into explanations developed here.

• *VALUE TO TEACHERS AS WELL AS STUDENTS AND BUSINESSPERSONS*

Second only to our desire that readers receive a practical education in law suitable for the everyday business world is our desire that this book be eminently "teachable." We have tried to design a primary or supplementary text for the busy professors and lawyers who teach business law and the legal environment of business. We have endeavored to make the text presentation easy to summarize and readily tied to related legal concepts. We believe that this book is flexible enough to cover all subjects required in any current study of business law or the legal environment of business.

• *CONCLUSION AND ACKNOWLEDGMENTS*

This book embodies our respective teaching philosophies and teaching experience, as well as day-to-day advice to businesspersons. We welcome the comments and suggestions of our readers.

In closing, we especially thank two persons: Linda Stark, for her typing and organizational skills; and, for all her assistance, Heidi Hardwicke Emerson, who is the daughter of one of the authors and the wife of the other.

Baltimore, Maryland   John W. Hardwicke
Gainesville, Florida   Robert W. Emerson
April 1992

1 ORIGIN AND NATURE OF LAW

THE ORIGIN OF LAW

The origin of law is as obscure as the origin of society, since the existence of law is a precondition of society. In its most primitive, unreasoned form, law rests on brute power—the ability of one individual to control other individuals through strength. The *lex talionis*, the law of retaliation (an eye for an eye, a tooth for a tooth), arose from the natural impulse of individuals. As societies formed, this impulse was sanctioned by government as law. The law of damages is the substitution of monetary compensation for blood or retribution in kind.

As time passed, however, it became necessary to adopt rules governing the conduct of individuals toward one another and the conduct of a single individual toward the body of individuals as a whole (society). Certain laws were enacted, or evolved and developed, for different purposes:

1. To proscribe certain kinds of behavior that society finds objectionable. This is *public law* and concerns a citizen's relationship with society constituted as government. Public law includes constitutional, administrative, and criminal law.

1

2. To make an injured party (citizen, corporation, or other entity) whole. This is *private law* and concerns an individual's relationship with another individual. In this sense, private law includes tort law, the law of private injury.

3. To end disputes. This is again private law, specifically contract law, the law governing agreements. (If law is knowable, reasonable, fairly certain, and yet flexible, it may *prevent* disputes.)

YOU SHOULD REMEMBER

The origin of law s obscure; society cannot exist without law. Individual power and cunning constituted the first law, and primitive governments merely presided over the *lex talionis,* or law of private retribution.

As societies became complex, it became necessary to adopt rules of conduct for various purposes, (for example, to forbid objectionable behavior, to make an injured party whole, and to end disputes.)

DEFINITIONS OF LAW

Only if the total collective, the society, will enforce such rules can they have any meaning, or serve any purpose, in the regulation of conduct. One school of thought, sometimes called the school of American legal realism, considers that **law** is that which a judge will decide concerning matters properly brought before him/her; in a broader sense, law is defined as any rule that society will enforce. For our purposes, we prefer this definition of law. During the course of this book we will refer to law in terms of judicial decisions as well as statutory enactment.

However, there are other widely accepted definitions of law. A school of thought sometimes called "legal positivism" defines law as the command of a constituted political authority; "natural law" theorists argue that there is a higher law grounded in absolute moral rules and that any law contrary to such natural law is not law. The English jurist Blackstone (see page 5) defined law as "a rule of civil conduct prescribed by the supreme power in a state, commanding what is right, and prohibiting what is wrong."

LAW AND MORALITY

Law generally represents the developing, common **morality** of human beings. Government almost always seeks to ally itself with prevailing customs, to proclaim as right only that which most citizens already perceive to be right, to enforce as law the rules considered by the majority or by more powerful or vocal minorities to be moral and therefore just.

However law is defined, there is a close, although imprecise, relationship between morality and any rule that society will enforce. The majority of enforced rules are in agreement with the prevailing morality of the members of any given society. This agreement is necessitated by two major aspects of law: first, its origin, from the majority or from vocal, powerful minorities; second, its enforcement, the ease or practicability of which depends on the acquiescence of great numbers of people.

Since law is, or should be, reflective of prevailing morality, rigid societal control over all members of society should be unnecessary. The goal is self-control, based on the individual's own moral philosophy or "instincts."

The relationship between law and morality is not mere speculation. Contracts may be found illegal if in violation of "public policy," that is, contrary to the "public good," and some case law even refers to lawful action as consistent with that of "right-thinking members of the community." Juries are considered to be made up of ordinary people reflecting prevailing morality.

Important Principle: Conduct that a reasonable person conscientiously deems moral and just is unlikely to collide with law.

Even if supposedly moral conduct proves illegal, that is, in violation of a rule that society will normally enforce, society's enforcement in a specific case may be muted, otherwise restrained, or even suspended.

Example: Relationship Between Law and Morality

In criminal law (see Chapter 4), even when an action is criminal, a good motive is considered in mitigation of punishment. "Bad" motives can have the opposite effect, such as leading to punitive damages in tort cases.

YOU SHOULD REMEMBER

There is a close relationship between law and morality. Law not only has its origin in morality, but also is easier to enforce when citizens yield to government for moral reasons.

DEVELOPMENT OF CIVIL LAW

As society became increasingly complex, various "lawgivers" attempted to provide orderly systems of laws that would promote security and justice. There are four landmark "codes," each of which represents distinct progress in the development of law:

Lawgiver	Date	Noteworthy Aspects
Hammurabi (Babylonian)	2000 B.C.	Designed to promote "justice" but based on the *lex talionis*. A well-ordered system of 285 laws, arranged by titles.
Solon (Athenian)	594 B.C.	Established a stable government operating under a system of rules imposed by a consenting citizenry. "Citizens" were equal under the law.
Justinian (Roman)	A.D. 533	Summarized and systematized the civil law of Rome; remains the basis for the laws of most of western Europe.
Napoleon (French)	A.D. 1804	Preserved many democratic achievements of the French Revolution, such as civil equality and jury trial. Influenced modern law, for example, the modern law of the state of Louisiana.

Civil Law, or code law, is one of two major legal systems currently in use in the Western world. It is based primarily on the written codes of Justinian and Napoleon. The predominant feature of civil law is the attempt to establish a body of legal rules in one systematized code, a single comprehensive legislative enactment. In this system, judicial decisions, case law, are not a source of law, although judicial precedents may be useful in the decision of cases. Civil law remains the basis of the legal system in Italy, France, Spain, Germany, and other parts of the Western world that were once included in the Roman Empire.

YOU SHOULD REMEMBER

The progress of law through the centuries can be traced through the activities of four "lawgivers" who attempted to state the law in keeping with their perceptions of evolving civilization and to provide remedies for those wronged.

The laws of certain countries are still based on the principles set forth in these codes.

DEVELOPMENT OF COMMON LAW

One country did not follow the comprehensive code approach to law. In England, disputes were resolved on a case-by-case basis, binding the arbiter of a dispute to the rule elicited from the determination of an earlier, similar dispute—hence **common law**. Common law is the second of the two major legal systems currently in use in the Western world.

Today England (together with the United States and other former British colonies, including Canada, Australia, and New Zealand) follows the common law. An understanding of the concepts underlying the common law of England is thus vital to any discussion of American law, including American business law. Sir William Blackstone's **Commentaries**, published just before the American Revolution, are generally considered to be the best statement of English common law as it existed when the United States became an independent nation.

According to Blackstone, the common law is that "ancient collection of unwritten maxims and customs" which have "subsisted immemorially in this kingdom." These principles are revealed by the courts of law "through experience in the rendering of judicial decision." Common law is, therefore, the overall accumulation of judicial decisions, known as **case law** .

England has no written constitution. The basis of its constitution is the common law, derived mainly from precedent and incorporating also certain landmark documents, such as the Magna Carta (1215) and English Bill of Rights (1689).

American common law includes not only the "ancient maxims and customs" inherited from England, but also all subsequent and modern case law as developed and pronounced from time to time.

PRECEDENT AND COMMON LAW; *STARE DECISIS*

As common law developed, a judge confronted with a puzzling new case would search the literature for a similar case to determine whether a precedent had been established. If so, the judge would follow the prior decision.

Stare Decisis

The requirement that courts follow their own precedents is based on the legal principle of *stare decisis* or "stand by the decision." *Stare decisis* binds all of the lower courts of a jurisdiction to determinations rendered by the highest court in that same jurisdiction.

Stare decisis is not absolute; a decision of the highest court can be amended either by this court's changing its mind or by legislative mandate.

If a case arises for which no modern American or English precedent can be found, the court sometimes bases its decision on the Justinian code, from which some areas of the common law are derived. In the absence of a precedent, a court may follow its own sense of justice or fairness, with due regard for prevailing custom or morality.

LEGISLATION AND COMMON LAW CODES

Unless changes are constitutionally prohibited, Congress or the state legislatures may enact laws (**statutes**) that modify the common law. These statutes, also subject to judicial interpretation, are collected into codes: along with case law, the codes form the law generally applied in court. Unlike civil law codes, common law codes are not intended to be entire statements of the whole law.

EQUITY AND COMMON LAW

After the conquest of England by William the Conqueror (A.D. 1066), Norman kings created an independent, but parallel, system of justice alongside the developing common law, with ultimate judicial responsibility residing in the king himself. This system, the **equity** system, had exclusive jurisdiction over injunctive relief (court-ordered action) and the specific performance of a contract as well as certain contract modifications. Since the kings were not learned in the common law, they based their decisions on sensible principles of fair play (equity) embodied in "maxims" or commonsense rules of Solomon-like justice. As the equity system functioned alongside the common law courts, the two systems of law gradually merged. Equity maxims—"He who comes into equity must come with clean hands," "Equity regards that as having been done which ought to be done," and many other "fair play" principles—were adopted by the common law and are currently cited in judicial decisions.

Starting in the sixteenth century, before the equity courts merged into the common law system, the equity courts received responsibility for matters previously vested in the ecclesiastical (church) courts. Thus equity absorbed a number of functions involving the family (divorce, annulment, adoption). These equity responsibilities became part of the general legal system—and part of the common law—that developed in the United States.

Although law and equity are today merged into a common system in which equity principles are cited freely, the old equity domain (injunctive relief, specific performance of contract, contract modification, family law, divorce) is particularly influenced by the idea of fairness and is deliberately more relaxed in its concept of justice. Also, jury trial is not available in an equity-type proceeding, the jury having been a feature of the common law courts. Thus, although the equity court as a separate system of justice has ceased to exist, equity principles permeate all of the common law but are most diligently applied to traditional equity subject matter.

YOU SHOULD REMEMBER

England, the British Commonwealth, and the United States follow the common law. Whereas civil law attempts to state the whole law in a comprehensive code, the common law is found in the collected cases of the various courts of law. American common law began with the common law of England as summarized by Blackstone in his *Commentaries*. It includes the English common law and all subsequent legal developments, including the principle of *stare decisis*.

Common law codes should not be confused with civil law codes. In the common law, a code is a collection of statutes passed by a legislature; a civil law code is intended as a full and comprehensive statement of the whole law.

Equity began as an independent legal system based on concepts of fair play. It covers injunctive relief, specific performance of contract, and certain contract revisions, as well as parts of family law. Many of the principles and maxims of equity have been merged into the common law. There is no jury trial in an equity case.

TWO TYPES OF LAW

SUBSTANTIVE LAW

Substantive law refers to any body of law creating, defining, and regulating rights and obligations within the framework of a single subject, such as contracts, torts, crimes, or property.

PROCEDURAL LAW

Procedural law pertains to operating rules for obtaining substantive rights or defining substantive obligations in a court of law. Procedure may be as important as substance in obtaining justice, since access to the court and proper statement of the cause of action (basis for a lawsuit) are controlled by the rules of an orderly society.

In the federal legal system and in most state systems, procedural rules are promulgated by the judiciary, adopted after public hearings, and published along with editions of the various codes. The rules of procedure are intended to promote justice and are to be interpreted flexibly and broadly, in the interest of fairness. A trial attorney's basic skills center around his/her mastery of procedure.

Lesser courts, such as small claims courts or probate courts, have developed simplified procedures so that citizens may handle their own cases without benefit of attorneys.

YOU SHOULD REMEMBER

Substantive law defines legal rights and obligations in regard to a specific subject.

Procedural law is concerned with the enforcement of substantive law in a court of law.

UNIFORM LAWS

Theoretically there would be 50 bodies of common law (combined case and statutory law) among the 50 states. Actually, however, there is great interdependence, as well as conscious parallelism, among the various federal and state court systems. Moreover, there has long been a disciplined effort to develop uniform legislation, with states enacting the same set of statutes so as to reduce uncertainty about the laws of sister states, particularly in commercial law.

The **Uniform Commercial Code** (adopted in 49 states, and partly in Louisiana) is the most successful of the proposed uniform laws. This comprehensive statute covers numerous subjects within the framework of substantive commercial law, including sales, commercial paper, and secured transactions.

Uniformity has not been wholly achieved, however, by the Uniform Commercial Code. Various state legislatures can make changes, and courts are free to give varying interpretations to the same words and phraseology. Nevertheless, there is a general consistency (if not uniformity) of subject matter, sufficiently definite and ascertainable for the businessperson operating within several states.

RESEARCHING THE LAW

Modern attorneys operate in two main areas: the law office and the courtroom. All practicing attorneys bring to their profession a general working knowledge of legal principles. In addition, both sound office advice and courtroom skill require the *ability to find specific and detailed application of legal principles* within the large body of case law and statute law. Therefore a student of business law should have a general understanding of the kinds of legal materials needed to research the law.

Statutory law is found in a state code or in the federal code. These codes are published with annotations, footnotes, and cross references to other statutes and to key cases interpreting and applying the statute in question. A lawyer will instinctively turn to the statutes for information about criminal law, taxation, and govermental regulation of all kinds. Moreover, familiarity with the Uniform Commercial Code is essential for the student of commercial law.

Case law is collected in the opinions of the appellate courts of the states and of the United States. Opinions of trial courts are usually not published, except for federal trial courts.

Besides the statutory annotations, case law may be found in legal encyclopedias, textbooks, treatises, case digests, and computer data banks. All law books are based on principles developed and enunciated in the cases. Indeed, the cases themselves follow, distinguish, and discuss other cases, all of which are meticulously referenced and cited. Finally, most law books include comprehensive, easy-to-use tables of contents and indices.

KNOW THE CONCEPTS
DO YOU KNOW THE BASICS?

1. In what major way does the common law differ from civil law?

2. Why should a definition of law emphasize enforcement?

3. When we say that law "improved" or "progressed" from Hammurabi to Napoleon, what is meant by "improved" or "progressed"?

4. Are there any circumstances under which society could exist without law?

5. If the law requires that a person take some action (salute the flag, report or spy on an unpopular minority group or person) he/she considers immoral, should the person obey the law? Give other examples of such a conflict.

6. Why is it difficult to make law "uniform" by enacting uniform statutes?

7. Which is more important, procedural law or substantive law?

8. Why is it likely that the common law system will produce a greater number of lawyers than the civil law system?

9. Is it easier to know your "rights" in a civil law country or in a common law country?

TERMS FOR STUDY

case law	morality
civil law	procedural law
code	*stare decisis*
common law	statute
equity	substantive law
law	title
lex talionis	Uniform Commercial Code

PRACTICAL APPLICATION

1. If you were a citizen in the following societies at the times indicated, how would you conduct yourself in regard to a conflict between personal morality and the law?
   (a) Nazi Germany in 1937.
   (b) Boston, Massachusetts, at the time of the Boston Tea Party.
   (c) A slave owner in a southern state in 1850.

2. The right of appeal to a higher court usually expires 30 days after a decision is rendered in a trial court. Suppose that your lawyer forgets to "note" your appeal within that period of time, although you have instructed her to do so. Under the law, you lose your right to appeal under these circumstances. Do you agree with the law?

3. Under what circumstances would an American court consider the Justinian code in deciding a case?

4. Bernhard Goetz shot and wounded four young men who apparently were attempting to rob him in a New York subway in 1984. He had been robbed before under similar circumstances. Discuss.

5. In what sense is the "constitution" of England a "creature" of the common law?

ANSWERS
KNOW THE CONCEPTS

1. The common law emphasizes precedent; civil law emphasizes the wording of the applicable code. Common law codes are collections of statutes and do not attempt to set out the entire law on a particular subject.

2. If law is not enforced, it has no effect on society—it is ignored, a "dead letter" without meaning. If government passes many laws but does not attempt to police them, the citizenry loses its respect for government and law, and society is greatly weakened.

3. "Improvement" and "progress" are relative terms and must be evaluated in accordance with principles or criteria. If our evaluations are based on democracy or self-determination, then clearly there has been "improvement" and "progress." If, however, the criterion is order or governmental control, Justinian's code may have been the best of the codes.

4. To the extent that society necessarily involves several persons or millions of persons, it is hard to imagine common existence without enforced rules. Insofar as individuals are "self-enlightened" or "self-controlled," friction may be minimized, but will not be eliminated.

5. When the law conflicts with personal morality, the individual has a hard choice. When a person has strong feelings about the moral principle involved and enforcement of the conflicting law is weak, the individual may (at his/her peril) choose to ignore the law. However, there are many variations in regard to these conflicting forces, and no simple rule can be stated. Be wary of unlawful conduct that implies a gain or profit from the act, even though disobedience to the law (draft evasion; nonpayment of unjust, oppressive taxes) may be stated in moral terms.

6. Each of the 50 states is a "sovereign" state with the right to judge its own citizens and to define and carry out its own laws, subject, of course, to constitutional limitations. Even when uniform laws are uniformly enacted, judges may interpret them differently.

7. Substance is probably more important, but incorrect or improper procedures can deprive the individual of his/her substantive rights and remedies. Procedural law is (or should be) more flexible, but this flexibility is not without limits.

8. The fact that there are many precedents in the common law system, and hence, much scope for argument and disagreement, encourages litigation, which produces a need for lawyers.

9. The civil law, written in more comprehensive detail, may seem more definitive as to "rights." However, society's willingness to sustain these rights and the actual trial of cases involving rights may be more uncertain in civil law countries.

PRACTICAL APPLICATION

1. For the individual, the three situations presented involve moral conflicts between society and law, and many answers are possible. In your answer, consider the morality of (a) acquiescence, (b) feigned or actual ignorance of the

law, (c) patriotic activity that is unlawful, (d) the "right" to rebel against unjust government (note the Declaration of Independence), and (e) profit making in an immoral but "legal" situation.

2. The loss of the right to appeal after passage of a specified time is fairly rigid. The reason is that cases must end; it is unfair to the winning side to leave appeals open and unresolved. This is one of many examples of procedure superseding substance.

3. If there are no modern American or English precedents for a specific case, our courts can, and sometimes do, consider Justinian's code. Some areas of the common law, such as the law of negotiable instruments, are derived from Roman law.

4. This classic case of "taking the law into one's own hands" has been the subject of much discussion. As noted in this chapter, if Goetz acted in a way that seemed to him "moral" or "right," this may be considered in assessing his punishment, but guilt of the crime is still a fact. Even if society is failing in its duty to protect its citizens, a return to the *lex talionis* does not seem to be a workable solution.

5. The "constitution" of England is unwritten and is largely based on precedent; hence it is a true creation of the common law. Several documents, such as the Magna Carta and the English Bill of Rights, are incorporated into the precedent.

2
GOVERNMENT UNDER LAW

KEY TERMS

constitution a nation's or state's supreme set of laws, outlining the basic organization, powers, and responsibilities of the government and guaranteeing certain specified rights to the people

statute a law passed by the U.S. Congress or a state legislature

ordinance a law passed by a governmental body below the state level and dealing with a local concern

rule a regulation issued by a federal, state, or local administrative agency (or court) and governing procedure or conduct in a specific field

---

SOURCES OF U.S. LAW

There are eight important sources of law in the United States:

1. The U.S. Constitution.
2. Federal statutes and treaties.
3. Executive orders.
4. The 50 state constitutions.
5. State statutes.
6. Local ordinances.
7. The rules and rulings of federal, state, and local agencies
8. Decisions by federal and state courts.

THE U.S. CONSTITUTION

The U.S. Constitution (also known as "the federal **constitution**") outlines the organization, powers, responsibilities, and limits of the federal government. Federal and state judges are bound by the U. S. Constitution; any law that violates the Constitution is null and void.

The **supremacy clause**—Article VI, Section 2, of the U.S. Constitution— states that the federal constitution, laws made in pursuit of the Constitution, and treaties are "the supreme law of the land."

DIVISION OF POWERS AMONG THE FEDERAL BRANCHES OF GOVERNMENT

The U.S. Constitution sets forth a division of powers among the three major branches of government: legislative, executive, and judicial. Each branch of government has a *major area of responsibility:*

- Congress (the federal legislature) makes the laws. A bill may be introduced in either the Senate or the House of Representatives, where it is referred to the appropriate committee. After consideration and sometimes public hearings, the committee returns the bill with pro and con recommendations. The bill is then debated on the floor, often amended, and brought to a vote. A bill passed by both houses goes to a conference committee of the Senate and the House of Representatives to resolve any differences. If both houses approve the compromise bill, it is then sent to the President. If he signs it, the bill becomes a law. A bill vetoed by the President may become a law if repassed by a two-thirds vote of both houses.

- The President (the chief executive) enforces the laws. The modern President has broad powers in both domestic and foreign affairs. Domestically, he may sign or veto bills, issue pardons for federal crimes, and remove executive officials (e.g., cabinet officers) without legislative or judicial approval. Subject to the majority consent of the Senate, he makes appointments to the executive branch, to ambassadorships, to federal regulatory commissions, and to federal judgeships.

   In foreign relations, the President may recognize or withdraw recognition of foreign governments, enter into executive agreements with other nations without obtaining congressional approval, make treaties with the approval of two thirds of the Senators voting, and—as commander–in–chief—oversee military affairs.

- The courts (judiciary) pass on the constitutionality of laws enacted by Congress or a state legislature. They also interpret the law, using as guidelines:

  (a) the "plain meaning rule," that is, the obvious or customary meaning of the words in a law;

  (b) the legislative history of the bill, that is, the purpose for which it was enacted.

  Finally, the courts make law in the sense that, under the principle of *stare decisis*, judicial decisions in cases for which no legal precedent exists become binding, or at least serve as precedent, when similar cases arise.

THE SYSTEM OF CHECKS AND BALANCES

Fearing the accumulation of excessive power in any one person or group, the Founding Fathers established a system of **checks and balances**. Overlapping powers impinge upon each area. The President can veto bills passed by Congress and is responsible for selecting federal judges. Congress may override the President's veto, it may conduct hearings and compel the attendance of witnesses from the executive branch, and the Senate may refuse to confirm the President's nominees for federal judgeships or for certain high–level positions in the executive branch. The judiciary may limit or invalidate laws or other actions by Congress or the President. In turn, Congress may limit the scope of judicial review or increase the number of federal judges, including the number on the U.S. Supreme Court.

YOU SHOULD REMEMBER

The U.S. Constitution is the supreme law of the land. There are three branches of government: the legislature, executive, and judiciary. Each has certain powers, and there is a system of checks and balances among the three branches.

FEDERAL STATUTES

Congress has only such legislative powers as are granted to it by the U.S. Constitution, either expressly (enumerated powers) or implicitly; other powers (reserved powers) are granted to the states.

ENUMERATED AND IMPLIED POWERS

Article I, Section 8, of the U.S. Constitution expressly authorizes a number of Congressional legislative powers, including to tax, to regulate foreign and interstate commerce, and to provide for the nation's defense and general welfare. Section 8 also states that Congress may make laws "necessary and proper" for carrying out any of the government's enumerated powers under the Constitution. The implied powers under this **necessary and proper clause** have been interpreted to include any law not prohibited by or violative of the letter and spirit of the Constitution, so long as the law advances a legislative goal within the scope of the Constitution.

> Such a broad reading of the "necessary and proper" clause first occurred in *McCulloch* v. *Maryland* (1819), a key decision written by the great Chief Justice John Marshall. In *McCulloch*, the U.S. Supreme Court held that Congress had the power to incorporate the Bank of the United States; although such an incorporation is not an enumerated power under the Constitution, it is, the court found, appropriate to Congressional exercise of its enumerated fiscal powers.

• *POWER TO REGULATE INTERSTATE COMMERCE*

Congress has passed **statutes** that bar discrimination, regulate even small businesses, or are otherwise directed toward local commercial activities. In almost all cases, courts have refused to probe Congressional motives and have upheld the legislation under the **affectation doctrine**: as long as the activity sought to be regulated affects interstate commerce, it is within Congressional regulatory authority.

The term "affects" is quite broadly interpreted. For example, the Supreme Court has upheld (1) a federal ban on racial discrimination even in a small restaurant whose out-of-state purchases and customers were minimal; and (2) federal regulation of wheat production even when a particular crop was not placed in interstate commerce. (In the latter case the Court found that, in effect, this crop freed another crop to be used in interstate commerce.)

• *POWER TO TAX*

Courts generally uphold any taxing measure, even one that serves to regulate an activity, so long as the measure purports to be and is, in fact, revenue–producing. If, however, the measure is intended to punish rather than to raise money, it is likely to be judged an invalid penalty rather than a valid tax.

Example: Invalidating a Tax Law Passed for the Wrong Purpose

A statute placing a substantial tax on employers using child labor was found to be an invalid penalty because it applied only to employers who *knowingly* hired under–age children. (A valid tax would have applied to *all* employers of children rather than just the intentional wrongdoers whom Congress wished to punish.)

• *POWER TO SPEND FOR THE GENERAL WELFARE*

With its power to levy taxes for the general welfare, Congress has the implicit right to spend money for any general welfare purpose. In implementing this spending power, Congress may impose reasonable conditions on state and local governments, corporations, and individuals; failure to meet such conditions precludes participation in that spending program. Hence Congress can often induce compliance with a regulatory scheme by using a "carrot and stick" tandem: revenue–sharing and eligibility requirements.

Example: Inducing Compliance with Federal Regulation

Federal highway funds are made available to the states in return for their enforcement of a 55 mile–per–hour speed limit.

LEGISLATION TO PROTECT CIVIL LIBERTIES

Two fundamental rights in the U.S. Constitution are found in the Fourteenth Amendment: due process and equal protection. The amendment not only restricts governmental acts ("state action") infringing these rights, but also expressly authorizes Congressional legislation to enforce its provisions. Such authorization has been broadly interpreted to permit any legislation Congress rationally concludes is appropriate for enforcing the amendment. Probably the most important "enforcement" role, though, has been played by the courts. U.S. Supreme Court decisions have served to "incorporate" almost all of the fundamental rights in the Bill of Rights (U.S. Constitution, First through Tenth Amendments) into the due process clause of the Fourteenth Amendment, thus making these rights applicable to the states as well as the federal government.

The **due process** provision, and its case–law progeny, protect persons from being "deprived of life, liberty, or property, without due process of law" and outlines the steps that must be followed to ensure a "fundamentally fair" process. Under the **equal protection** provision no person may be denied "the equal protection of the laws"; "equal protection" does not prohibit all differences in the treatment of persons but rather requires that, at the very least, any distinctions be *reasonable,* not arbitrary or invidious. Corporations, as well as individuals, are covered under the due process and equal protection provisions. Moreover, via the Fifth Amendment's "due process" provision, the federal government also must not violate due process or equal protection.

Due Process and Equal Protection

Due process requires *procedural* protections: a fundamentally fair process including notice, a hearing, an unbiased factfinder, presentation of evidence and cross–examination, and appeals. Due process also encompasses fundamental *substantive* rights, including, but certainly not limited to, some of the "incorporated" Bill of Rights provisions.

For most cases involving regulation of business and for other "ordinary" cases, *equal protection* simply requires that differential treatment be reasonable and related to a permissible, governmental purpose (the "rational basis" test). For cases involving "suspect" classes (particularly racial, religious, or nationality minorities) or fundamental rights (voting, marriage, privacy, interstate movement, access to the courts), equal protection is violated unless the differential treatment is as narrow as possible and is necessary to achieve a compelling governmental interest (the "strict scrutiny" test).

Some important U.S. Constitutional rights for businesses as well as individuals are these:

1. Due process.

2. Equal protection.

3. Freedom of expression (First Amendment). Commercial speech (e.g., advertising) is not as well protected as political speech. However, governments may not prohibit commercial speech unless there is a substantial state interest in doing so **and** the governmental prohibition is as narrowly drawn as possible.

4. Protection from laws impairing contractual obligations (Article I, Section 10).

5. Compensation for the public taking of private property—eminent domain (Fifth Amendment).

6. Protection against some state regulations, including taxes, that discriminate against interstate commerce in favor of local businesses.

A few constitutional provisions that apply to individuals, such as the Fourteenth Amendment's privileges and immunities clause and the Fifth Amendment's protection against self–incrimination, do not extend to business entities.

YOU SHOULD REMEMBER

Legislative power must be expressly or implicitly delegated to Congress by the U.S. Constitution, or else it belongs solely to the states.

Many such Congressional powers are stated in Article I, Section 8, of the Constitution, including three whose expansive interpretation has permitted national regulation of numerous activities. These three powers are: (1) to regulate interstate commerce, (2) to tax, and (3) to provide (spend) for the general welfare.

The Fourteenth Amendment authorizes Congress to pass any legislation necessary to enforce the due process and equal protection provisions of the amendment.

THE STATE CONSTITUTIONS

Each of the fifty states has a constitution that establishes the general organization, powers, responsibilities, and limits of the state's government. The state constitution is the supreme law of the state, but it cannot contain any provision that violates a provision of the U.S. Constitution.

The state governments have their own spheres of power and do not look to the federal government as the source of their authority.

STATE STATUTES

State statutes constitute another important source of U.S. law. Just as some legislative powers are exclusively federal, others (reserved powers) remain exclusively or primarily within the domain of the states—for instance, divorce law and the common law of torts and contracts.

A third class of powers is shared by the state and federal governments. Sometimes the absence of Congressional action in regard to a shared power permits the states to act, even though Congress could preempt (bar) state action. (Preemption can be express, or it can arise implicitly from a Congressional legislative scheme intended to have uniform, national application.) *Regulation of commerce* tends to be such a shared power.

So long as a nonpreempted state regulation in regard to commerce:

(a)   concerns essentially local matters,

(b)   does not purposely discriminate against interstate commerce, and

(c)   is the least burdensome method for achieving legitimate state objectives,

it will usually be permitted *if* the state interest in maintaining the regulation outweighs any burdens imposed on interstate commerce. The courts ultimately make this determination.

Exception: Courts sometimes hold, that even without federal regulation, the commerce clause bars certain state legislation because an area requires national uniformity or is otherwise unsuited to state action. However, just as Congress may preempt state actions, so it may overturn these "negative implications" of the commerce clause and allow state regulation.

DETERMINING THE VALIDITY OF STATE STATUTES

In determining the validity of a state law involving a shared power, the court must first determine (1) whether the state law conflicts with a federal law, that is, whether a person obeying the state law would violate a federal law, and (2) whether Congress intended to preempt state legislation in that area. If the answer to either question is "yes," the state law is void.

TWO TYPES OF LAWS THAT CANNOT BE PASSED BY CONGRESS OR THE STATES

In addition to rights discussed previously, two other fundamental rights stated in the U.S. Constitution apply to the states as well as the national government. These rights, specifically set forth in Article I, Sections 9 and 10, are individual freedom from (1) *ex post facto* laws (laws making criminal past actions that were not defined as criminal when they occurred), and (2) **bills of attainder** (laws intended to single out an individual and/or punish him/her without benefit of a trial).

YOU SHOULD REMEMBER

Major legislative powers are divided between the state and federal governments. They are exclusively federal, exclusively or primarily state, or shared. Congress may preempt some areas that would otherwise be shared with the states.

The power to regulate commerce is an important example of a shared power, although certain areas are barred from state regulation.

Neither Congress nor the state legislatures may pass an *ex post facto* law or a bill of attainder.

LOCAL ORDINANCES

An ordinance is an enactment by a minor legislative body (a city counsel, a county legislature, a town board, etc.). Ordinances deal with local concerns such as zoning, on-street parking, area speed zones, and littering, and are designed to promote the safety and general welfare of the community to which they apply.

YOU SHOULD REMEMBER

An ordinance is a law passed by a governmental body below the state level and dealing with a local concern.

RULINGS OF FEDERAL, STATE, AND LOCAL AGENCIES (ADMINISTRATIVE LAW)

Legislation or case law cannot cover every actual or potential problem that arises in a dynamic, increasingly complex society facing numerous social, economic, and technological issues. Also, legislatures or courts cannot develop or retain the expertise to handle all specialties. Therefore administrative agencies have been created by legislative acts known as **enabling acts**, whereby the government—federal, state or local—**delegates** some of its authority to the agency.

A typical *enabling act* sets forth the objectives and standards by which an agency is to administer the law in a particular field. The agency then develops technical expertise in order to fill legislative gaps with detailed rules and to render sound decisions in individual cases.

Most important federal agencies have a mixture of legislative, judicial, and executive powers. (Administrative agency judicial proceedings are discussed in Chapter 3, pages 47–48.) Agencies perform some or all of seven functions, with certain functions being more important in some agencies than in others: (1) advising, (2) reviewing, (3) supervising, (4) rule making, (5) investigating, (6) prosecuting, (7) adjudicating.

Some agencies are directly under the supervision of one of the three branches of government, usually the executive. However, a large number are *independent* agencies, and their legislative hearings and the rules they make are generally free from outside control. Examples of independent federal agencies include the Federal Communications Commission, Federal Reserve Board, Federal Trade Commission, Interstate Commerce Commission, National Labor Relations Board, and Securities and Exchange Commission.

The actions of an administrative agency must conform with:

(a) constitutional law,
(b) relevant general acts governing administrative procedure (e.g., the federal Administrative Procedure Act),
(c) requirements in the agency's own enabling act, and
(d) rules of the agency itself.

When exercising its legislative (rule-making) powers, the typical agency does not need to hold a hearing. However, the *agency's own rules,* or *general statutes* such as the federal Administrative Procedure Act, *may require* that the agency give *notice of a proposed rule* and afford interested parties the opportunity to submit written or oral comments. The federal Negotiated Rulemaking Act (1990) is intended to foster cooperative rulemaking—rules negotiated between agencies and affected parties.

Courts have the power to review rules promulgated by regulatory agencies in much the same way as they are empowered to review legislative enactments. However, with respect to areas in which an agency presumably has expertise, its decisions (executive, legislative, or judicial) generally are overturned only if found to be clearly erroneous, arbitrary, based on bias, or exceeding the agency's authority.

However, with respect to areas in which an agency presumably has expertise, its decisions (executive, legislative, or judicial) generally are overturned only if found to be clearly erroneous, arbitrary, based on bias, or exceeding the agency's authority.

YOU SHOULD REMEMBER

Certain legislative, judicial, and/or executive powers have been delegated to federal, state, and local administrative agencies. Many agencies are not directly supervised by the legislature or executive; they are independent agencies.

An administrative agency may have to give interested parties both notice and an opportunity to comment before making a rule or regulation.

DECISIONS BY FEDERAL AND STATE COURTS

In the United States, as in England, decisions handed down by federal and state courts, that is, case law, constitute a primary source of the common law. New cases requiring the interpretation of statutes arise continually. When no precedent can be found, the judge's decision will produce a new legal principle.

A case may originate in either a federal or a state court, depending on the nature of the suit.

Under Article III of the U.S. Constitution, the federal courts' power is limited to actual "cases or controversies." This provision has prevented federal courts from furnishing advisory opinions, even if requested by another branch of government. (Many state courts can and do issue advisory opinions.) The case must be a real dispute between opposing parties with actual interests in the case (standing to sue, because of direct and immediate injury from, or other such connection with, the matter at issue). The proceeding must be in an adversarial format. Federal district courts have **original jurisdiction** (meaning that proceedings commence there) over federal criminal cases and certain specified civil cases.

The U.S. Supreme Court has original jurisdiction when the parties include ambassadors or other foreign officials, or when two states are the opposing parties. However, almost all of the cases heard by the Supreme Court arise out of its **appellate jurisdiction**: the *power to hear appeals from other courts' decisions*. Appeals generally involve interpretation of constitutional law and/or federal statutes.

The various types of courts and the cases they handle are discussed more fully in Chapter 3.

YOU SHOULD REMEMBER

Decisions by state and federal courts are a primary source of U.S. common law.

To originate in a federal court, a case must involve a real dispute between opposing parties.

The U.S. Supreme Court has original jurisdiction over certain cases, but its main function is to review lower court decisions that have been appealed.

KNOW THE CONCEPTS
DO YOU KNOW THE BASICS?

1. For each of the three branches of the federal government, name checks that it has on the powers of the other branches.
2. Name three Congressional powers specifically enumerated in the U.S. Constitution.
3. By what constitutional provision does Congress have the implied powers to take legislative action not specifically mentioned in the U.S. Constitution?
4. State the general test for determining whether a tax is constitutional.
5. How does Congress use its power to spend as a method for national regulation?
6. What two types of bills may neither Congress nor a state legislature pass?
7. Name the seven general functions that may be performed by an administrative agency.
8. State the two major standards for review in equal protection cases, including the type of cases that fall under each standard.
9. Name three independent federal agencies.
10. Over what types of cases does the U.S. Supreme Court have original jurisdiction?
11. Name two fundamental rights set forth in the Fourteenth Amendment to the U.S. Constitution.

TERMS FOR STUDY

affectation doctrine
appellate jurisdiction
bill of attainder
checks and balances
commercial speech
constitution
delegated authority
due process
enabling act

equal protection
ex post facto law
"necessary and proper" clause
ordinance
original jurisdiction
rule
statute
"supremacy" clause

PRACTICAL APPLICATION

1. Commerce–in–Claus is an interstate shipper of Santa Claus outfits. A neighboring state has passed a law raising fees on its toll roads for all trucks with out–of–state registration, but no one else. Is this constitutional? Discuss. What bearing does Santa Claus have on your answer?

2. Suppose that a dissatisfied customer brings his complaint against XYZ, Inc., to the state legislature, which passes a law making illegal XYZ's sales arrangement with the customer. Effective 30 days after the law's enactment, XYZ's sales license is to be suspended for 3 months. What should XYZ do? What arguments should XYZ make?

3. Congress has enacted a broad statutory scheme covering most aspects of labor/management relations. Fearing that unionization would increase operational costs for the town's private employers, Poor Town's board of commissioners wants to keep a national union from organizing any of the workers. What legislation may the commissioners enact?

4. A state statute prohibits businesses from contributing to election campaigns. This statute is challenged in court by a group of law students. What will be the outcome?

5. In Problem 4, on what grounds should the law be challenged?

6. Scott Sneaky wants the state legislature to pass a law that would provide his business with a series of windfall profits. A friend has convinced him to go to a state administrative agency to obtain a rule that would serve essentially the same purpose and, Scott hopes, would avoid the publicity that would probably kill the chance for a new law in his favor. Assuming that there are no constitutional problems with Scott's plan, will it succeed?

ANSWERS

KNOW THE CONCEPTS

1. *Executive*: veto legislation, appoint federal judges.
   Legislative: override veto, compel executive official's attendance at hearings, refuse to confirm appointments, limit scope of judicial review, increase the number of federal judges, impeach executive or judicial officials.
   Judiciary: limit or invalidate laws or executive actions.

2. To regulate foreign and interstate commerce, to tax, and to provide for the nation's defense and general welfare.

3. The "necessary and proper" clause of Article I, Section 8.

4. A tax may serve to regulate an activity. However, the more a tax acts as a punishment rather than as a source of revenue, the more likely it is to be judged an invalid penalty.

5. By placing conditions (compliance with a regulatory framework) upon participation in a federal program. Without compliance, the would-be participant—be it a state or local government, a corporation, or an individual—cannot receive the federal money.

6. An *ex post facto* law and a bill of attainder.

7. Advising, reviewing, supervising, rule making, investigating, prosecuting, and adjudicating.

8. "*Strict scrutiny*" (differential treatment constitutional only if (1) drawn as narrowly as possible, and (2) necessary to achieve a compelling governmental interest): cases involving adverse impact on racial, religious, and nationality minorities.
   "*Rational basis*" (differential treatment constitutional when reasonable and related to a permissible governmental goal): cases involving business regulation or "nonsuspect" classes.

9. Federal Communications Commission, Federal Trade Commission, National Labor Relations Board. For other agencies, see page 22.

10. Cases involving ambassadors or other foreign officials and cases in which two states are adversaries.

11. Due process and equal protection.

PRACTICAL APPLICATION

1. No. The state's action violates the commerce clause by purposely imposing a greater burden on interstate commerce than on local interests. Moreover, Congress may have preempted such state legislation.

The state's action also appears to violate the Fourteenth Amendment's guarantee of equal protection. The court may not believe that the state had a reasonable justification (rational basis) for the law.

Re: Santa Claus

A claim based on religious freedom, or one asking for the equal protection clause's "strict scrutiny" test because there is a suspect class (religion), would probably fail. Regardless of whether the Santa Claus aspect of the company gives it a religious affiliation, the legislation does not discriminate based on religion; the basis of the discrimination is whether or not a vehicle is an out–of–state truck.

2. Challenge the law in the courts. It seems to be both an *ex post facto* law and a bill of attainder, which are prohibited by Article I, Sections 9 and 10, of the Constitution.

3. None. The commissioners must follow the federal law. Inasmuch as the subject of unionizing has been preempted, no state, let alone a local government, can pass laws in this area (e.g., an ordinance prohibiting or limiting union activities).

4. The law students will be dismissed as plaintiffs. They are not members of the class affected by the statute (businesses), and therefore do not have standing to sue.

5. Violation of equal protection: the law treats businesses, including individuals and corporations, differently from other persons, and this differential treatment is neither reasonable nor related to a permissible, governmental purpose.

   Violation of due process: The Fourteenth Amendment's due process clause incorporates the First Amendment of the Bill of Rights, and thus protects persons from a state's infringement of their right to free speech. In *First National Bank of Boston v. Bellotti*, 435 U.S. 765 (1978), the Supreme Court held unconstitutional a Massachusetts statute that prohibited most corporate spending on political referendum proposals.

6. It is difficult to say. The agency rule–making process may indeed be less publicized, and thus Scott may be able to get a new rule promulgated. However, either of two factors may keep Scott from succeeding: (1) since this is an area apparently still open to the state's customary legislative oversight, it may *not* have been delegated to the agency in the enabling act; (2) the rule-making process usually requires notice to the public and an opportunity for comment. Thus publicity and/or opposition is, in fact, possible.

3

THE U.S. COURT SYSTEM AND THE LEGAL PROCESS

KEY TERMS

jurisdiction the power to hear and decide the issues in a case (subject-matter jurisdiction) and to bind the parties (personal jurisdiction)

pleadings the papers filed in court, with copies to other parties concerned, in preparation for bringing or defending a lawsuit before the court

discovery pretrial procedures by which the parties to a lawsuit obtain information from other parties and from potential witnesses

trial the proceedings before a competent tribunal in which a civil or criminal case is heard and adjudicated

---

Most of this book focuses on *substantive law*, such as contracts, business associations, and commercial paper. This chapter, though, concerns the places and methods for resolving disputes and applying the substantive law to individual cases.

THE TWO MAJOR U.S. JUDICIAL SYSTEMS

There are two main court systems in the United States, the federal and the various state systems.

STRUCTURES OF THE FEDERAL AND STATE COURT SYSTEMS

The hierarchical structure of federal courts is comparable to that of the various state court systems. Therefore, by way of example, we will look at the federal court system.

At the bottom rung are the U.S. *district courts*, which are trial courts. In each state there is at least one federal district court. Each district court may include any number of judges, one of whom will hear a particular case.

If a party wishes to appeal the district court's judgment, he/she brings the case before the *appeals court*, the circuit court, for that district. Each circuit generally covers the federal district courts in several states. (The one exception is Washington, D.C., which, because of its heavy volume of work, for example, in administrative law, has its own circuit.)

Lastly, appeals from circuit court decisions (or from holdings of the highest court of the state) *may* be heard by the *U.S. Supreme Court*. In a few cases, a party has an absolute right of appeal. *Supreme Court review by appeal* is a matter of right when:

(1) a state court declares a treaty or federal statute invalid or holds that a state law does not violate a treaty, the U.S. Constitution, or federal statutes; or
(2) a federal court
    (a) decides that a state law violates federal law; or
    (b) if the federal government or its employees are parties, rules that a Congressional statute is unconstitutional.

In most cases, however, it is within the sole discretion of the Supreme Court whether to hear an appeal. Usually the case must involve a federal question (e.g., about the U.S. Constitution and/or a federal statute).

Of course, there are other types of courts. For instance, many federal and state administrative agencies have their own judicial systems. There are specialized courts (e.g., federal bankruptcy courts), and states generally have special courts (ones without juries) for cases involving small amounts or special litigants, such as orphans or landlords and tenants. However, the general trial courts, with juries available, remain the crucial arena for most important cases.

The following diagrams show the structures of the federal court system and a typical state system.

JURISDICTIONS OF THE FEDERAL AND STATE COURT SYSTEMS

As discussed in Chapter 2, the national and state governments have different, but sometimes overlapping, spheres of power. This holds true also for their court systems. The power of a court system to hear and decide a case is called its **jurisdiction**.

THE FEDERAL JUDICIAL SYSTEM*

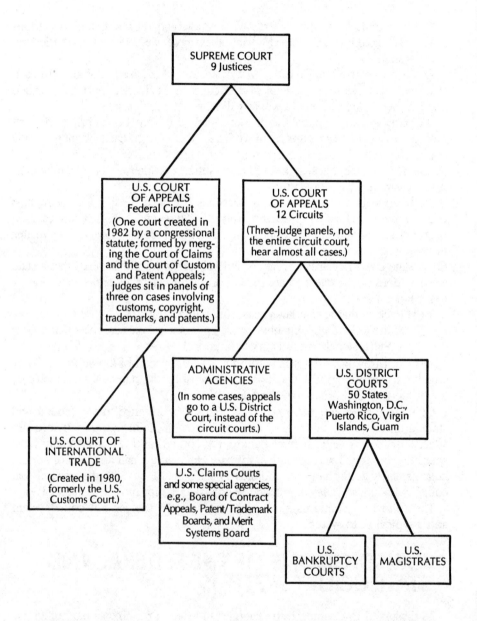

*Although federal administrative agencies are not part of the federal judiciary, they are included here because appeals from their decisions go to the federal courts.

A TYPICAL STATE JUDICIAL SYSTEM

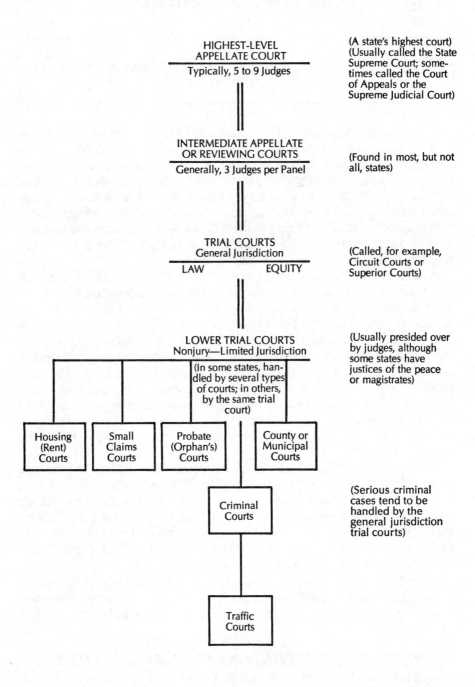

HIGHEST-LEVEL APPELLATE COURT
Typically, 5 to 9 Judges

(A state's highest court) (Usually called the State Supreme Court; sometimes called the Court of Appeals or the Supreme Judicial Court)

INTERMEDIATE APPELLATE OR REVIEWING COURTS
Generally, 3 Judges per Panel

(Found in most, but not all, states)

TRIAL COURTS
General Jurisdiction
LAW   EQUITY

(Called, for example, Circuit Courts or Superior Courts)

LOWER TRIAL COURTS
Nonjury—Limited Jurisdiction

(In some states, handled by several types of courts; in others, by the same trial court)

(Usually presided over by judges, although some states have justices of the peace or magistrates)

Housing (Rent) Courts

Small Claims Courts

Probate (Orphan's) Courts

County or Municipal Courts

Criminal Courts

(Serious criminal cases tend to be handled by the general jurisdiction trial courts)

Traffic Courts

• *SUBJECT-MATTER JURISDICTION*

> **Subject-matter jurisdiction:** judicial power to decide the issues in a case.

The federal courts are limited to hearing cases specifically placed within their power (subject-matter jurisdiction) by the U.S. Constitution or other laws. Numerous federal statutes, as well as certain exclusively federal areas under the Constitution (e.g., admiralty, bankruptcy, patents, copyrights), give the federal courts a vast array of subjects to decide; these areas are called **federal questions** (cases involving the federal constitution, statutes, or treaties). While sometimes federal court jurisdiction is exclusive (e.g., prosecution of persons charged with violating federal criminal laws), in some areas jurisdiction is concurrent, that is, state courts can also hear cases on these subjects.

In addition to federal questions, Congress has provided another form of subject-matter jurisdiction to the federal courts: **diversity jurisdiction**. This means that, when the opposing parties in a civil lawsuit are citizens of different states, a matter based on state law (and normally brought before a state court) can be heard in federal court *if* one of the parties requests it *and if* the amount in controversy is above $50,000. (Corporations are treated as being "citizens" of both their place of incorporation and their principal business location; for partnerships, however, courts look to the citizenship of each general partner.)

Note that diversity must be complete; that is, in cases involving multiple parties not even one party may have the same state citizenship as an opposing party. (It does not matter if parties on the same side, for example, two plaintiffs, come from the same state.)

If a defendant wishes to transfer a case from one state to another, or from state court to federal court, his/her request will be for *removal*. Such requests must be made at the beginning of the case and are premised on the claim that the correct jurisdiction lies in another court. In seeking a transfer from state to federal court, the defendant is often simply exercising a right to invoke diversity jurisdiction, or some other concurrent federal jurisdiction, which the plaintiff failed to use but the defendant also has a right to choose.

As for the state courts, they are generally open to hear any type of case unless it is precluded by the U.S. Constitution or federal statutes or treaties. *Most common law areas*—for instance, torts, contracts, crimes—*tend to be brought before state courts.*

• *PERSONAL (IN PERSONAM) JURISDICTION*
In addition to subject-matter jurisdiction, for each particular case a court needs jurisdiction over the litigants themselves.

Personal (*in personam*) jurisdiction: judicial power over the parties in a case.

By filing a lawsuit the *plaintiff* voluntarily submits to the court's personal jurisdiction. Personal jurisdiction over the *defendant* depends on: (1) his/her being properly served with the complaint and summons (see "Taking a Case to Court," pages 36-37); and (2) his/her having sufficient ties to the state in which the lawsuit was filed. Obviously, if the defendant resides or works in the state, personal jurisdiction is well founded. Also, states have passed "**long-arm statutes**," *which extend personal jurisdiction* over people or corporations that do business in the state, own real property there, or (in cases involving a tort or contract) committed the alleged tort in the state or entered the contract in the state.

There are many other grounds for "long-arm" personal jurisdiction. For each case, the *key constitutional question is whether the defendant has had enough "minimal contacts" within the state* so that requiring him/her to defend the lawsuit in that state does not violate due process of law (Fifth and/or Fourteenth Amendments) by offending "traditional notions of fair play and substantial justice" [*International Shoe Co.* v. *Washington*, 326 U.S. 310, 316 (1945).]

A defendant who does not challenge the court's personal jurisdiction over him/her is deemed to have consented to that court's determination of his/her rights and obligations. However, the defense, that *subject matter* jurisdiction is lacking, cannot be waived.

VENUE, CONFLICT OF STATE LAWS, AND FULL FAITH AND CREDIT

• *VENUE*

When a court has authority over the subject matter and parties of a lawsuit, it has jurisdiction. However, there still may be problems with **venue,** that is, the place (usually the county) where the case will be tried.

Generally, a lawsuit is to be brought in the judicial district where the parties work or reside, where the disputed interest in land is located, or where the occurrence leading to the lawsuit took place. Proper venue is defined by statute, and is usually based on the notion of convenience to the parties, especially the defendant. If there is to be a change in venue, it usually must be requested at the outset of the case. In rare instances, pretrial publicity or other factors may force a change of venue later in the case.

• *CONFLICT OF STATE LAWS*

Obviously, the law varies from state to state. The doctrine of *stare decisis* (see Chapter 1) does not require one state to follow another state's precedents.

What makes matters even more confusing is that disputes often arise out of transactions occurring in more than one state. Which state's substantive laws are to govern the resolution of such a dispute? This question is covered by a body of law known as **conflict of laws** (or choice of laws).

> While a court will almost always apply its own *procedural law* (rules as to form of pleadings, discovery, and the like), it must look to conflict-of-laws principles to choose between differing *substantive laws.*

Example: Conflict of Laws

A Colorado court is deciding a case involving a contract executed in New York, performed in Missouri, and involving Delaware corporations with principal offices in Colorado. So long as the lawsuit remains before a Colorado court, it will be governed by Colorado rules of procedure. However, interpretation of the contract may be based on the law of another state, such as New York or Missouri.

For *torts*, the applicable law is usually the *law of the state where the injury occurred.*

For *contracts*, the courts usually look to the *law intended by the parties* . A court ordinarily honors an express stipulation in a contract that the contract is to be governed by a particular state's laws. Even if no such express statement is made, courts will often look to the parties' *implied* intentions. At that point, though, the courts may turn to an earlier approach (still followed in some states) governing conflicts of law in contract cases: use of the law where the contract was made or performed. (In very complex tort or contract cases, some courts seek to determine, and then apply, the law of the state with the most significant ties to the parties and the matter in dispute.)

In *criminal cases*, conflicts of law simply do not arise. Courts apply their own substantive as well as procedural laws, even for acts committed elsewhere. Of course, if another jurisdiction's interests are paramount (i.e., because the crime took place on its soil), then the alleged criminal can be **extradited** (sent, via a legal process, to the other jurisdiction). Thus the accused is almost always tried in the place where the crime supposedly occurred.

• *FULL FAITH AND CREDIT*

Article IV, Section I, of the U.S. Constitution states, "full faith and credit shall be given in each State to the public acts, records and judicial proceedings of every other State." This **"full faith and credit" clause** does not mean that other states must adopt the reasoning on which a decision was based; one state's precedents are *not* binding on another state. It simply means that other states must recognize the validity of a civil or criminal judgment as it specifically affects the rights and duties of the parties subject to that judgment (i.e., involved as parties in the original case), provided, however, that the original court had personal and subject-matter jurisdiction.

YOU SHOULD REMEMBER

Although there are many types of courts, the main state and federal judicial systems involve general, trial courts, with appeals taken to one or more higher courts.

Federal courts have *particularized subject-matter jurisdiction*, usually based on "federal questions" or diversity jurisdiction.

State courts have *general subject-matter jurisdiction*.

Personal (in personam) jurisdiction requires that the defendant reside or work in the state in which the lawsuit was filed, or have other clear-cut ties to the state. *Long-arm statutes* grant courts power over out-of-state individuals and corporations in certain specified circumstances.

Courts follow their own procedural law. However, in some cases, they may apply the substantive law of another state.

For *torts*, the applicable law is usually that where the injury occurred.

For *contracts*, courts generally look to the law intended (expressly or implicitly) by the parties to the contract.

In *criminal cases*, courts apply their own substantive and procedural laws, regardless of where the acts were committed; however, almost all criminal prosecutions take place in the same state where the alleged crime occurred.

Once a court with jurisdiction renders a judgment, the U.S. Constitution's "full faith and credit" clause requires that, as between the parties to the lawsuit, the judgment must be honored by other states' courts.

TAKING A CASE TO COURT

Assume that Paul Plaintiff decides to sue Doris Defendant for breach of contract. Paul must file his lawsuit in an appropriate court and thereafter, since this is a civil case, meet the procedural rules governing civil litigation.

Procedural law is very complex and varies from court to court. There are federal rules of procedure, and each state court system also has its own set of procedures. Appellate courts have different rules from trial courts, and even the same type of courts, in the same jurisdiction (e.g., the same state), may have different local rules for each court. Moreover, criminal and civil cases follow different rules.

Nevertheless, it is also fair to say that, despite the differences, most cases follow a general pattern of procedure. In our case (*Paul Plaintiff* v. *Doris Defendant*), we will follow the general procedural pattern usually found in any American court of law.

THE PARTIES TO A LAWSUIT

The person who initiates a lawsuit is called the **plaintiff**. The person sued is the **defendant**. In equity cases (see Chapter 1), these parties are instead often called the **petitioner** and the **respondent**, respectively. In a criminal case, there is no "plaintiff"; rather, the criminal defendant is opposed by the state itself, often called "the prosecution" or even "the people." (Criminal cases are brought on behalf of the public as a whole.)

THE PLEADINGS

The papers required to bring the issues in a lawsuit before the court are termed the **pleadings**. Paul's lawsuit (action) against Doris starts when he or his lawyer files a **complaint** (sometimes called a declaration, petition, or bill of complaint) with the clerk of a trial court having proper jurisdiction and venue. The complaint should include a statement of facts, the basis of the suit (in this case, alleged breach of contract), and a request for one or more remedies (e.g., damages or an injunction). Often a complaint must also include information showing that the court has jurisdiction and venue. Paul's complaint might be as follows:

Example: Plaintiff's Complaint

Paul Plaintiff,	*	In the Circuit Court
Plaintiff	*	For Our County
v.	*	State of Bliss
Doris Defendant,	*	Civil Action No. AA-000
Defendant		

*   *   *   *   *

COMPLAINT

The plaintiff, Paul Plaintiff, by his attorney, Lucretia Lawyer, sues the defendant, Doris Defendant, and says:

1. Paul Plaintiff (hereinafter, "Plaintiff") and Doris Defendant (hereinafter, "Defendant") are both residents of the State of Bliss. This action concerns a

contract entered into in Bliss between Plaintiff and Defendant. The amount due and owing to Plaintiff by Defendant is more than $10,000.00

2. Based on the facts stated in paragraph 1, jurisdiction over this subject matter and over the person of Defendant is founded upon Bliss Code, Courts Article, Sections 21 and 22.

3. Defendant resides in Anytown, Our County, State of Bliss. Venue is thus founded upon Bliss Code, Courts Article, Section 31.

4. At various times in or around August, September, and October, 1987, Plaintiff, at the request of Defendant, delivered certain XYZ computers and ABC software programs to Defendant. The price agreed upon by Defendant was $29,000.00, and Defendant has only made one payment of $2,000.00.

5. Payment was to be made within thirty (30) days of delivery. Despite Plaintiff's repeated demands for payment, Defendant has refused and continues to refuse to pay the remaining amount owed.

WHEREFORE, Plaintiff demands judgment against Defendant for damages in the sum of Twenty-Seven Thousand Dollars ($27,000.00), plus prejudgment interest, costs of suit, attorney's fees, and such other relief as the Court deems just and equitable.

Lucretia Lawyer
Attorney for Paul Plaintiff
100 Lawyers Lane
Big City, Bliss

The sheriff or other such official then serves a **summons** and a copy of the complaint on Doris Defendant. Alternative methods of "service of process" include using a private process server or sending the summons and complaint by certified mail (receipt returned to sender); in either case, an affidavit is usually filed attesting to the fact that the defendant received the summons and complaint. In a case involving land or certain corporate defendants, service may be made by publishing notices in a newspaper or elsewhere and/or serving the summons and complaint upon an authorized state official, such as the state secretary of state or other registrar of corporations. There are many other variations on these procedures, which differ from state to state.

The summons notifies Doris Defendant that she must file her **answer** to the complaint with both the court and the plaintiff's attorney within a certain time period (usually 20 or 30 days, though often longer for out-of-state defendants). The summons also tells the defendant that failure to file an answer will lead to a judgment by default for the plaintiff.

An answer, though, is not Doris Defendant's only choice. She may file a **motion to dismiss**, sometimes called a **demurrer**, in which she contends that, even if the complaint's allegations are true, there is no legal basis for finding the defendant liable.

Major Reasons Why Dismissals May Be Granted

1. The court lacks subject-matter jurisdiction.

2. The time period to sue (statute of limitations) has expired.

3. The allegations do not set forth a breach of contract, tort, or whatever else could lead to a judgment for plaintiff.

In most jurisdictions, as in Doris's case, a motion to dismiss may be raised in lieu of an answer. Only if the court rules that part or all of the complaint remains viable, must the answer be filed.

The answer generally admits or denies each of the various allegations set forth in the complaint. It also may include **affirmative defenses**, that is, allegations of facts that, if proved by the defendant, defeat the plaintiff's claim.

Since the court does not uphold Doris's motion to dismiss, she files the following answer:

Example: Defendant's Answer

Paul Plaintiff,	*	In the Circuit Court
Plaintiff	*	For Our County
v.	*	State of Bliss
Doris Defendant,	*	Civil Action No. AA-000
Defendant		

*   *   *   *   *

ANSWER

Doris Defendant, by her attorneys, Atilla Attorney and Dewey, Cheatham & Howe, answers Paul Plaintiff's Complaint, and says:

1. Defendant admits the allegations in the first sentence of paragraph one of the Complaint, and denies the allegations in the second and third sentences.
2. Paragraph two of the Complaint is a legal conclusion rather than a factual allegation, and thus Defendant need not admit or deny said paragraph.
3. Defendant admits the allegations in the first sentence of paragraph three of the Complaint. Defendant need not admit or deny the second sentence, which is a legal conclusion.
4. Defendant acknowledges that, after she paid plaintiff $2,000.00, some computers and software were delivered to defendant by plaintiff on one occasion in or around September 1986. In all other respects, defendant denies the allegations stated in paragraph four of the Complaint.
5. Defendant admits that she has refused and continues to refuse to pay additional money to plaintiff. Defendant denies all other allegations in paragraph five of the Complaint, including any inference that defendant owes money to plaintiff.

Affirmative Defenses

1. There was no contract between the parties.
2. In the alternative, the contract was not as alleged by plaintiff.
3. Plaintiff failed to deliver goods promised.
4. Plaintiff delivered defective goods.
5. The court lacks jurisdiction over the subject matter.

Atilla Attorney
Dewey, Cheatham & Howe
5 Esquire Court
Big City, Bliss

(Generally, a complaint or answer may be amended unless a statute or rule specifically bars such amendment or unless the amendment is made at such a late date that its acceptance as a new pleading would be grossly unfair to another party.)

When answering the complaint, or shortly thereafter, a defendant generally has the option to file a **counterclaim**, which is, in effect, a "reverse" complaint: one by the defendant against the plaintiff. (Two other claims are *cross claims*, brought by a plaintiff against one or more coplaintiffs or, more likely, by a defendant against one or more codefendants, and *third-party claims*, whereby a defendant brings a new party into a lawsuit. In addition, large numbers of plaintiffs may join together in a *class action*.)

In our hypothetical case, Doris Defendant might file a counterclaim against Paul Plaintiff for return of the $2,000.00 already paid. The grounds for such a counterclaim would probably be the same as the third and fourth affirmative defenses raised in the answer: plaintiff breached the contract by failing to deliver goods and/or by delivering defective goods.

Besides the motion to dismiss, many other types of **motions**, that is, requests to the court, may be made before the case goes to trial. Such motions may ask for rulings on evidence, or may seek orders compelling a party or witness to provide discovery (see the next section). In fact, each party is generally free to make any motion that he/she wishes.

The most important motion is probably the motion for **summary judgment**. It may be filed at any time, by either party.

Summary judgment is to be awarded if the judge decides that:

(1) there is no genuine issue as to material (potentially determinative) facts, *and*
(2) when the law is applied to these facts, one party is clearly entitled to a verdict in his/her favor.

Summary judgment may be granted on all or part of a lawsuit. For instance, if a complaint sets forth different theories of liability (e.g., negligence and breach of warranty), the defendant may be able to get one of them stricken, even if the judge will not grant summary judgment on all counts. The summary judgment process may also be used to limit or eliminate certain types of damages, such as punitive damages. Of course, plaintiffs may also gain a partial summary judgment.

DISCOVERY

Before there is a trial, each party is entitled to obtain information from other parties and from other potential witnesses. These pretrial procedures are known as **discovery**.

Discovery may serve several purposes:
1. By providing parties with access to evidence that might otherwise be hidden, it prevents surprises at the trial.
2. It may narrow the issues at trial (i.e., some questions may be resolved).
3. It preserves witnesses' testimony prior to trial (important when witnesses may be unavailable at trial, their memories may fade, or their testimony may change).
4. It may place the case in a posture suitable for summary judgment.
5. It may lead to a pretrial settlement, as opposing parties come to see their strengths and weaknesses.

The main methods of discovery are depositions, interrogatories, requests for admissions, and the production of documents. Other methods include physical and mental examinations and, in cases involving land, inspections of premises.

A **deposition** is sworn testimony, by one of the parties or any other witness, usually recorded and transcribed by a notary public. The testimony is ordinarily taken in response to oral questions from the parties' attorneys, although it also can be in response to written questions.

Interrogatories are written questions, to be answered in writing, and under oath, by another party (generally, the opposing party). Unlike depositions, interrogatories can be directed only toward the parties themselves. Their usefulness is further limited by the fact that the answering party's attorney can, in effect, prepare the answers. However, interrogatories usually cost less (both in legal fees and other expenses such as transcripts) than depositions, and their scope can be broader.

Requests for admissions are, like interrogatories, made and answered in writing and can be directed only toward another party. The requesting party asks the other side to admit particular facts or acknowledge the genuineness of certain documents. Admissions are conclusive. Thus the requests, with the admissions they elicit, can save trial time because the parties have already agreed on some matters.

Finally, parties may be required to *produce*, for inspection and copying, all their *documents* that may be relevant to the case. Likewise, a deposition may include document production by the witness.

THE PRETRIAL CONFERENCE

The trial issues can be narrowed via a pretrial conference. Except for some smaller cases, such conferences may be called by the parties or the court itself; they are routinely held in most federal civil cases. Although judges may use these conferences to encourage settlement, the main purpose is to ensure that the trial will proceed as smoothly as possible: witnesses, exhibits, areas of dispute, and agreed upon facts are all identified ahead of time.

THE TRIAL

Aside from any pretrial motions (discussed previously), the next step is the trial itself.

Jury trial is available in criminal cases and most civil lawsuits. Major exceptions:

1. Certain types of cases (e.g., divorce) historically based on equity.
2. Administrative agency proceedings.

Plaintiff or defendant can ask for trial by jury; this right is usually waived if not requested in plaintiff's complaint or defendant's answer.

A jury trial involves a **petit jury** (usually 12 members, though some states allow as few as 6). The petit jury decides whether the defendant is guilty in criminal cases or is liable in civil cases; in federal courts and most state courts, the jury's decision must be unanimous. [The federal courts and most states also have **grand juries** (around 18 to 24 jurors), which, under the guidance of prosecutors, decide whether a person should be charged with a crime (indicted).]

In *jury selection*, the first step in the trial, prospective jurors are questioned by the attorneys for both sides and by the judge. This examination is known as **voir dire**. Any number of potential jurors can be kept off the panel "for cause" (e.g., bias), and the attorneys for each side also have the right to reject a few (generally about three) without offering a reason, that is, by *peremptory challenge*.

After the jury has been selected, the next step is the presentation of *opening statements*. These provide each attorney with the opportunity to indicate what he/she expects to prove.

The *plaintiff's* case is then presented. Witnesses, called by the plaintiff's attorney, testify in response to the attorneys' *questions: first, direct examination* by the attorney that called them, and then *cross-examination* by the opposing attorney. Also, exhibits, documents, and other evidence that may advance the plaintiff's cause are offered. At the close of the plaintiff's case, the defendant may file for dismissal of the case or for a **directed verdict,** that is, a judgment rendered by the court, in his/her favor.

If the trial is to continue, the next step is to present the *defendant's case*, following the same procedures as above but offering witnesses and evidence for the defense. When the defendant's case has been completed, the plaintiff, in turn, may move for a directed verdict in his/her favor. Also, in jury trials this may be the proper time for the defendant to request a directed verdict.

In the *summation*, each attorney has the opportunity to review the testimony and other evidence and make his/her closing arguments.

Throughout the trial, the *judge* makes legal rulings on evidence or other matters. Generally, only after the summations does he/she *instruct* the jury concerning the law that is applicable to the case and the various verdicts that the jury may render.

The jury then retires and attempts, in its deliberations, to resolve all factual (not legal) issues. As stated previously, in federal courts and in most states, it is only when all members agree that the jury renders a *verdict*. In a nonjury trial the judge makes the decision.

In reaching a verdict, consideration of evidence is governed by the *burden of proof*. This refers to:

1. A party's obligation, when asserting a fact, to *come forward* with evidence establishing this fact.

Example: Come forward

If party A alleges fact x, party A must produce evidence in support of x before opposing party B is expected to disprove x.

2. The necessity for one party (in civil cases, almost always the plaintiff) to *persuade* the trier of fact (judge or jury) that a preponderance of the evidence supports his/her contentions—that his/her version of the facts is, at the very least, slightly more credible than the opposing party's. If dead-even, the opposing party (generally the defendant) wins. ("Persuasion," not "coming forward," is the more common usage of the term "burden of proof.")

A few special types of allegations (e.g., fraud) may demand a higher standard of persuasion, such as "clear and convincing" proof; and, of course, in a criminal case, the prosecution has a much higher burden of persuasion: "beyond a reasonable doubt." (See Chapter 4.)

MOTIONS AFTER TRIAL

Under rare circumstances, in civil cases the judge may grant a *motion for judgment notwithstanding the verdict* (sometimes called "J.N.O.V.," for **judgment** *non obstante veredicto)*; there, after the jury has rendered a verdict for one party, the judge finds that there was insufficient evidence to support the jury's conclusions, and *enters a judgment for the other side*. This is a serious measure, and the judge's interpretation of evidence at the trial must meet very high standards.

Either attorney can request that the trial court grant a *new trial*, usually for one or more of the following reasons: (1) erroneous interpretations of the substantive law, (2) erroneous admission or exclusion of evidence, (3) insufficient evidence and/or a verdict contrary to law, (4) excessive or inadequate damages award, (5) jury misconduct or other irregularities, and (6) newly discovered evidence. Often these grounds, particularly (1) through (4), serve as the basis for an appeal requesting reversal or a new trial.

THE APPEAL

Each party to a lawsuit generally is entitled to one **appeal**, which is held in an appellate court. Consideration of further appeals (e.g., to the state or U.S. Supreme Court) is usually discretionary: such appeals can be, and often are, summarily denied (without any hearing).

Appellate courts do not hold trials. There are no witnesses or juries. The court simply reviews the record of the trial and the briefs submitted by the parties' attorneys. In an especially important case, a nonparty (usually a governmental or other institutional group) may file an *amicus curiae* ("friend of the court") brief.

A **brief** is a written *argument* supported by citations of prior court decisions, statutes, or other authorities. (Alas, briefs often are not brief.)

The attorneys may present oral arguments, which are usually not so much polished speeches as short statements of key points. They must also answer searching questions from the judges. When the court reaches a decision, it issues a written opinion that can provide future guidance in similar cases.

Opinions—in whole or in part—may affirm the original judgment, reverse it, instruct the lower court to issue a new judgment, and /or remand (i.e., send back) the case to the lower court for further proceedings. Appellate courts rarely reverse the trial court for its factual findings; to do so requires that the findings be unsupported or contradicted by the evidence. (Mere belief that the lower court, or jury, did not draw the right factual conclusions is insufficient grounds for reversal.) Any holding other than affirmance almost always must be based on errors of law.

ENFORCEMENT OF A JUDGMENT

A monetary judgment is a debt. If the losing party does not pay the judgment, the judgment creditor (winning party) may collect by using one or more of the debt-collection methods discussed in Chapter 20.

YOU SHOULD REMEMBER

Some of the more important pleadings are the complaint, answer, motion to dismiss, counterclaim, and motion for summary judgment.

There are four major types of discovery: *depositions*, *interrogatories*, *requests for admissions*, and *document production*. Each has its advantages and limitations.

The scenario for a lawsuit is as follows:

1. Alleged injury to plaintiff.
2. Complaint filed by plaintiff or his/her attorney.
3. Answer and/or preliminary motions by defendant or his/her attorney.
4. Discovery and pretrial motions.
5. Pretrial conference.
6. Trial.
7. Posttrial motions.
8. Appeal.

Summary judgment motions can occur from the time the complaint is filed until the trial. Attempts to settle the case are almost always possible, from before the case is filed through the appeals stage.

In a jury trial, the jury decides the factual disputes, while the judge interprets the law and instructs the jury on the law.

The plaintiff generally has the burden of proof (persuasion). In civil cases, he/she need only have a preponderance of evidence in

---

his/her favor; criminal cases require that the prosecution produce proof of guilt beyond a reasonable doubt.

A trial judge can overturn a jury verdict, but to do so requires much more than simply a belief that the jury drew the wrong factual conclusions.

An appeal does not entail a new trial. The appellate court must consider the law as a whole; its function is to furnish future guidance, not simply resolve an individual dispute.

An appellate court usually affirms the lower court's judgment. However, if the appeal is well founded in law, not merely a claim that the facts are different from what was decided by the jury or trial judge, an appeals court may reverse, instruct the lower court to issue a new judgment, or remand for further proceedings.

OUT-OF-COURT PROCEDURES FOR SETTLING DISPUTES

The vast majority of disputes are settled out of court. Most do not even reach the point where a suit is actually filed. If a complaint is filed, settlement usually occurs before trial.

Several factors may spur compromise, including (1) anxiety about going to court, (2) the time and expense of lawsuits, (3) concern about bad publicity, (4) the need for a speedier resolution, (5) uncertainty as to outcome, and (6) a desire to maintain good business or personal relationships with the other party.

Alternative Dispute Resolution (ADR)—rather than going to court—is a fast-growing phenomenon featuring such *private* approaches as "renting" retired judges or holding summary (expedited and nonbinding) jury trials or "minitrials." (It is also often sought in administrative disputes—e.g., the Administrative Dispute Act (1990) authorizes federal agencies to use ADR.)

The two most frequently used out-of-court methods of dispute resolution are mediation and arbitration. Both involve neutral third parties who often are familiar with, or even experts in, the contested subjects.

MEDIATION

In mediation, a third party (mediator) helps the disputing parties to settle the case. *Mediators cannot impose a settlement* on the parties, but often, by such means as separate, private consultations with each party and neutral recommendations to both sides, mediators can effect a compromise.

Mediation is increasingly used in settling labor disputes (the function of the National Mediation and Conciliation Service) and in resolving consumer complaints (via state or local governmental agencies or such private groups as the Better Business Bureau). Indeed, some laws mandate the use of mediation; for instance, when a business has an informal dispute-resolution system for complaints about its product warranties, an amendment to the Federal Trade Commission Act requires that parties first attempt mediation before filing a lawsuit for breach of warranty.

ARBITRATION

Of course, mediation can accomplish little when the parties themselves are unwilling to compromise. In such cases, **arbitration** may work. *Unlike a mediator, an arbitrator has the power to make a final, binding decision.*

A dispute usually goes to arbitration because a contract either requires it or permits a party to request it. In certain instances (e.g., medical malpractice), a law may mandate arbitration. Parties seeking to avoid arbitration, despite a contractual provision requiring it, may run headlong into either the federal Arbitration Act (1925) or the Uniform Arbitration Act (adopted by most states). Both Acts support arbitration and courts usually will compel parties to keep their agreements to arbitrate.

Arbitration is usually a shorter, cheaper version of litigation. Both sides present evidence and arguments, although often in a more informal manner than in court trials.

Once arbitration is completed, grounds for appeal are extremely limited. Courts are to overturn an arbitration award only *if* (1) it went beyond the matters submitted to the arbitrator(s), or (2) the arbitrator(s) failed to follow statutory requirements (e.g., acted in complete disregard of evidence), or (3) the award arose out of fraud or corruption. Clearly, an *arbitration award is even less susceptible to reversal than is a court judgment.* Because arbitration usually saves money and time, often promotes less hostile relations than litigation, and can, when necessary, submit complex issues to experts, arbitration clauses are routinely placed in many business contracts. Information about arbitration clauses, as well as experienced arbitrators, can be obtained from the American Arbitration Association, a nonprofit, private organization founded in 1926 to improve and promote arbitration techniques.

YOU SHOULD REMEMBER

The vast majority of cases never come to trial; they are settled beforehand. *Mediation* and *arbitration* entail the out-of-court use of third persons (mediators or arbitrators) to resolve disputes. A mediator cannot impose a settlement, but an arbitrator's decision is final (subject only to very narrow grounds for appeal).

ADMINISTRATIVE AGENCY PROCEEDINGS

All government, both state and federal, operates through agencies which are generally legislatively created. These agencies are given carefully drawn duties and responsibilities among which are the duties to promulgate rules and regulations, a quasi legislative function. The agency may also exercise a quasi judicial function since due process under the Fifth and Fourteenth Amendments requires that notice be given and a hearing held whenever a person is to be deprived of "life, liberty or property." Generally, this hearing must be held before the agency.

Examples: Administrative Deprivations of Liberty or Property (thus requiring a hearing)

- Revocation or suspension of a license to operate a motor vehicle.
- Revocation of a professional or business operating license.
- Cessation or reduction of welfare.
- Cessation or reduction of unemployment or social security benefits.
- Firing of a tenured teacher or—in most instances—a public employee.
- Revocation of parole.
- Termination of parental custodial rights.

The adoption of rules and regulations, as well as the holding of hearings, is governed by federal and state Administrative Procedure Acts. Under these Acts, the rules of evidence are relaxed (even hearsay evidence may be given some weight) and the hearing officer may play a more active, inquisitive role than is customary in U.S. courts. Nevertheless, basic fairness may not be disregarded. For instance, as in a court trial, each party has a right to counsel and is entitled to state his/her case and to cross-examine opposing witnesses. Moreover, although an agency may have considerable discretion in outlining the format of its hearings, it must, like a court of law, render decisions based only on the evidence presented. In cases involving administrative law, there is no right to a trial by jury. However, a dissatisfied party may appeal for judicial review of the case on the hearing record.

Many agencies have a staff of *administrative law judges* (hearing examiners) who are separate from the investigatory or prosecutory personnel. Most important federal agencies provide for intraagency appeals from the rulings of the administrative law judges to the board or commission at the top of the agency; some agencies also have intermediate review boards. Many states have created independent offices of administrative hearings to conduct agency hearings in order to separate the judicial function from the executive, enforcement function and better to assure the citizen of an unbiased due process hearing.

Exhaustion of remedies: The doctrine whereby court appeals are *not* permitted until administrative remedies are exhausted: the appellant must use all available agency procedures before complaining to a court of law.

In some areas of the law, the exhaustion of remedies doctrine may be discarded in certain rare circumstances:

1. An administrative procedure is unconstitutional, illegal, or otherwise exceeds agency authority.

2. The case involves fundamental constitutional guarantees (e.g., free speech).

3. The agency is deadlocked or hopelessly behind in its docket schedule.

4. Irreparable harm is likely to occur if court relief is not permitted.

5. An appeal within the agency is not required by agency rule or by statute.

YOU SHOULD REMEMBER

Due process under the Fifth and Fourteenth Amendments generally requires that notice be given and a *hearing* held before an administrative agency can render a decision that deprives a person of liberty or property. Administrative hearings are usually more informal than court cases but must be conducted fairly. In almost all cases, courts will not review an agency's decision until the administrative remedies have been exhausted.

HOW CASES ARE CITED

For the key case of *Marbury* v. *Madison*, 5 U.S. 137, 2 L. Ed. 60 (1803), in which Chief Justice John Marshall announced the doctrine of judicial review of federal and state actions, the citation means the following: 5 stands for the fifth volume of the U.S. Supreme Court Reports, and 137 is the page number of that volume on which the case begins; 2 stands for the second volume of the Lawyers Edition (L. Ed.), and 60 is the beginning page number for the case; 1803 is the year of the decision. To identify a quotation or point taken from a case, a second page number may be added to show the page(s) from which the quotation or point is derived. For instance, if a point in *Marbury* v. *Madison* were taken from page 176 of the U.S. Supreme Court Reports and page 73 of the Lawyers Edition, the citation would be 5 U.S. 137, 176, 2 L. Ed. 60, 73 (1803).

Federal circuit court of appeals cases are found in the *Federal Reporter*, 1st or 2nd series (F or F.2d, respectively, the latter being the more recent cases). Also, the *Federal Supplement* (F. Supp.) and *Federal Rules Decisions* (F.R.D.) contain federal district court opinions.

Cases from the state appellate courts, including the District of Columbia, are found in the National Reporter System of the West Publishing Company. The states are divided among seven regional reports: Atlantic (Atl. or A.), North Eastern (N.E.), North Western (N.W.), Pacific (Pac. or P.), South Eastern (S.E.), South Western (S.W.), and Southern (So.). Like the Federal Reporter, each of these reports has reached a second series (cited as A.2d., P.2d., S.W.2d., etc.) containing more recent cases.

YOU SHOULD REMEMBER

Published opinions by the U.S. Supreme Court, federal circuit courts of appeals, federal district courts, and state appellate courts are cited in U.S. Supreme Court Reports, the Federal Reporter, the Federal Supplement, and the National Reporter System, respectively.

KNOW THE CONCEPTS
DO YOU KNOW THE BASICS?

1. State the three main levels of courts in the federal system.
2. State the difference between the functions of a trial court and an appellate court.
3. What is the key constitutional question concerning "long-arm" personal jurisdiction?
4. Distinguish jurisdiction from venue.
5. What state's substantive laws usually govern a tort case?
6. (a) State the general order of pleadings filed before a trial.
   (b) What are the four main methods of discovery?
7. (a) Who usually has the burden of persuasion?
   (b) Who has the burden of coming forward?
8. Name at least four reasons why disputes are compromised.
9. What is the most important difference between mediation and arbitration?
10. Give at least four examples of administrative deprivations of liberty or property (thus requiring a hearing).

TERMS FOR STUDY

Administrative Procedure Act
affirmative defenses
alternative dispute resolution
answer
appeals
arbitration
brief
complaint
conflict of laws
counterclaim
defendant
demurrer
deposition
direct verdict
discovery
diversity jurisdiction
exhaustion of remedies
extradite
federal questions
"full faith and credit" clause

grand jury
interrogatories
J.N.O.V. (judgment *non obstante veredicto*)
jurisdiction
"long-arm statutes"
mediation
motions
motion to dismiss
personal (*in personam*) jurisdiction
petitioner
petit jury
plaintiff
pleadings
requests for admissions
respondent
summary judgment
summons
trial
venue
voir dire

PRACTICAL APPLICATION

1. Susie Sharp wants to sue Hap Hapless for breach of contract. Susie lives in New York, and Hap lives in Massachusetts. The contract was signed at a business meeting in Boston. Hap has not been outside Massachusetts for years, nor has he done any business elsewhere.
   (a) In what court can Susie sue?
   (b) In what court does Susie's right to sue depend on the amount in controversy?
   (c) Why is Susie unlikely to be able to sue elsewhere?
   (d) What happens if the contract specifies that it is to be governed by New York law? Discuss both personal jurisdiction and conflict of laws.
   (e) Assume that New York gives defendants a longer time to answer a complaint than does Massachusetts. Which time period can Hap use?
2. Hap refuses to answer Susie's complaint. Susie obtains a judgment, including a damages award, by default. Hap moves to another state, one which generally does not enforce the type of contract that Susie and Hap had. May Susie use the new state's courts to collect her money (damages) from Hap?

3. Hap does not leave Massachusetts. He answers and files a motion for summary judgment, with an affidavit saying that he has never met anyone named Susie Sharp, that there was no contract, and that the signature on the alleged contract is not his. Will he win? What is the standard for granting summary judgment?

4. On Monday, a dissatisfied customer files a complaint about Dew Processing, Incorporated (Dew). On Tuesday, an official at the State Board of Business calls the president of Dew and informs him of the complaint. On Wednesday, Dew receives notice that its consumer sales license has been suspended. What preliminary request for relief should Dew make? Discuss the problems of administrative procedure presented by this case.

5. At an administrative hearing, the Administrative Law Judge (ALJ) bases his decision on inadmissible evidence, unauthenticated records, and the ALJ's own knowledge of customs in the industry. He also talked about the case while on the telephone with one of the parties.

   The ALJ permitted testimony from all witnesses but allowed cross-examination of only the witnesses who were also parties. In an oral opinion announcing his holding, the ALJ did not clearly state the reasons for his decision. What problems, if any, are there with the ALJ's conduct of the case?

6. A case is cited as follows: 63 A.2d 221. Where would you find that case?

ANSWERS

KNOW THE CONCEPTS

1. District courts, circuit courts, U.S. Supreme Court.

2. In a jury trial, the judge interprets the law and instructs the jury on the law. He/she makes rulings on evidence and any motions. In a nonjury trial, the judge also assumes the jury's role and decides factual disputes.

   An appellate court does not retry the case. It does not hear witnesses. Rather, it reviews the lower court case for errors of law. Factual findings can be overturned only if they are not at all supported by the evidence.

3. The key question is: Has the defendant had enough "minimal contacts" within the state so that requiring him/her to defend a lawsuit there does not violate due process of law?

4. Jurisdiction involves a court's power to decide the issues in a case (subject-matter jurisdiction) and to bind parties (personal jurisdiction). Once jurisdiction has been established, the question of venue is merely a matter of deciding whether a particular locale (e.g., county) is the proper place to bring suit.

5. The state where the injury occurred.

6. (a) (1) Complaint, (2) motion to dismiss (optional), (3) answer, (4) counter-claim (optional). At any time, until shortly before trial, discovery requests, summary judgment motions, and other motions are possible.
   (b) Depositions, interrogatories, requests for admissions, and document production.

7. (a) The plaintiff.
   (b) Whichever party alleges the fact in question.

8. (1) Anxiety about going to court, (2) time and expense of lawsuits, (3) worries about bad publicity, (4) need for a speedy resolution, (5) uncertainty as to outcome, (6) desire to maintain personal or business relationship with other side.

9. Mediation cannot force a settlement; arbitration can. Arbitration, in essence, substitutes for a court trial.

10. Revocation of a professional or business operating license, cessation or reduction of welfare, cessation or reduction of unemployment or social security benefits, firing of a tenured teacher or (in most cases) another public employee, revocation of parole, termination of parental custodial rights.

PRACTICAL APPLICATION

1. (a) Massachusetts state court.
   (b) Susie can sue in the federal court in Massachusetts if the alleged contract was worth more than $50,000 (diversity jurisdiction).
   (c) It does not appear that Hap would be subject to another state's (e.g., New York's) long-arm jurisdiction; thus, no personal jurisdiction.
   (d) This probably would have no effect on personal jurisdiction. However, it should mean that the Massachusetts court must interpret the contract according to New York law, as that is the law intended by the contracting parties.
   (e) The one allowed by the court where he has been sued (presumably, Massachusetts). This is a matter of procedure, not substantive law.

2. Yes. The Massachusetts judgment is entitled to "full faith and credit."

3. Most unlikely because summary judgments can be granted only if there is (1) no genuine issue about the material facts, and (2) entitlement to judgment on the law applicable to the material facts.
   Susie's complaint probably sets forth enough facts to show that there is a material factual dispute between the parties as to whether there was a contract and whether Hap was a party to it. To be on the safe side (especially since Hap asserts that he never met Susie), Susie should probably file her own affidavit countering Hap's contentions and/or showing why his points are irrelevant (e.g., she acted through her agent and hence never met Hap).

4. Request that the suspension be lifted until a hearing has taken place. The State Board's action in suspending Dew's license without a hearing and perhaps without proper notice (telephone call enough?) may supersede agency authority and/or due process.

   Dew has a property interest in the license. Generally, administrative deprivations of property (or liberty) can only follow due notice and a hearing. The main exception is an emergency situation, which does not appear to be the case here.

   Dew may attempt to exhaust its administrative remedies before going to court, although on these facts some courts would not let the exhaustion of remedies doctrine operate to bar judicial relief.

5. ALJs usually have much more discretion than courts of law with respect to rules of evidence and the overall conduct of a trial. The improper activities were (1) talking about the case with one party while the other party was not present, and (2) not permitting cross-examination of all witnesses. Due process and, more likely, the enabling act and/or agency regulations would require that the ALJ's findings of fact (reasons for his decision) be stated to the parties.

6. In volume 63 of the Atlantic Reports (second series), starting on page 221.

4 CRIMES AND TORTS

KEY TERMS

crime a public wrong, committed with intent or by negligence, for which the law provides punishment or recompense to society

tort a private wrong against a person or his/her property. Aside from certain limited circumstances, all torts arise from either an intentional, wrongful action or from a negligent action.

burden of proof the degree of proof necessary for a criminal conviction (beyond a reasonable doubt) or for a successful civil suit (preponderance of evidence)

Most court cases fall within one of three major divisions of law: *crimes, torts,* or *contracts.* This chapter focuses on crimes and torts. Although these two broad subjects are not usually as important to business as are contracts, crimes and torts do frequently involve the businessperson. Therefore any serious student of business law must know about them.

This chapter gives important facts about crimes and torts, compares them, provides examples of business crimes and torts, and discusses defenses against them.

IMPORTANT FACTS ABOUT CRIMES

American criminal law is primarily codified law, based on statutes and regulations rather than merely on past judicial decisions. The same act or omission may be a **crime** *under both federal law and state law.* For instance, murder, a state crime, may also be a federal crime (e.g., a violation of the victim's civil rights) and thus be prosecuted in separate criminal cases in each of the two court systems. (Certain legal doctrines, as well as basic fairness, however, sometimes limit the use of such dual trials.)

THE U.S. CONSTITUTION AND AMERICAN CRIMINAL LAW

A fundamental premise of our criminal justice system is that it is *far worse to convict one innocent person than to let many guilty people go free*. The procedural guarantees for alleged criminals are thus much greater than for civil defendants. Many, if not most, of these guarantees are found in the state and federal constitutions, particularly the Fourth, Fifth, Sixth, and Eighth Amendments to the U.S. Constitution. Almost all *rights* in those amendments have been incorporated into the Fourteenth Amendment's *due process clause*, as described in Chapter 2. Thus, *criminal procedure* is now generally governed by nationwide standards of constitutional interpretation.

The *Fourth Amendment* protects against unreasonable searches and seizures and requires probable cause before a search warrant or arrest warrant is issued.

The *Fifth Amendment* prohibits compulsory self-incrimination; hence people sometimes "take the fifth" rather than testify. Other provisions include a prohibition against double jeopardy (trying someone twice for the same crime) and the federal due process clause (comparable to the Fourteenth Amendment's state due process clause; see Chapter 2).

The *Sixth Amendment* outlines the criminal defendant's right (1) to a speedy and public trial by an impartial jury, (2) to know the charge against him, (3) to confront and subpoena witnesses, and (4) to have a lawyer. Under the doctrine announced in *Miranda* v. *Arizona*, 384 U.S. 436, 86 S. Ct. 1602 (1966), any person about to be interrogated who "has been taken into custody or otherwise [significantly] deprived of his freedom" must be warned that (1) he has a right to remain silent, meet with an attorney before any questioning, and have a lawyer present during questioning; (2) anything he says can be used as evidence against him; and (3) if he wants a lawyer but cannot afford one, the state will provide one free of charge.

The *Eighth Amendment* prohibits excessive bail, excessive fines, and cruel and unusual punishment.

CLASSIFICATION OF CRIMES

The three classes of common law crimes are **treason, felonies,** and **misdemeanors.**

Treason against the United States, the only crime defined in the U.S. Constitution, is a comparatively rare charge.

The distinction between a felony and a misdemeanor is usually found within each state's criminal code. Felonies are more serious crimes, punishable by imprisonment. Murder (which can carry the death penalty in most states), arson, rape, armed robbery, and tax evasion are felonies. Misdemeanors are generally punishable only by fines or, at most, a brief stay in the local jail. Simple assault, disorderly conduct, and trespass are usually classified as misdemeanors. Certain minor offenses, such as violations of city ordinances or traffic regulations, may not even be considered misdemeanors in some jurisdictions (i.e., they are too petty to be labeled as crimes, and are often called "infractions" or "violations").

Three other ways of categorizing crimes are these:

1. **White-collar**: nonviolent crimes, perpetrated by people in positions of trust, usually against businesses or governments.
   Examples: embezzlement, mail fraud, bribery.

2. **Organized**: crime by groups in the "business" of crime, such as the Mafia.

3. **Victimless**: crimes that are sometimes considered to have no specific victims (just society as a whole).
   Examples: prostitution, gambling

Crimes can also be classified according to whom or what they are committed against: a person, the general public, the home, other property.

CRIMINAL INTENT AND CAUSATION

In most cases, a crime must include both a criminal act (*actus reus*) and a criminal intent (*mens rea*).

Example: No Actus Reus
Dave Deviant thinks about assaulting Veronica Victim, but does nothing about it. *No crime*, not even attempted assault.

Example: No Mens Rea
Ida Innocent, through no intent, negligence, or other fault of her own, collides with Veronica Victim and kills her. *No crime*.

Usually, a person is presumed to intend the natural consequences of what he/she knowingly does. Moreover, in a felonious action, the doer may be deemed responsible for even unwanted results, that is, *mens rea* is transferable from the intended felony to the one that actually occurred.

Example: *Unintended Harm*
Ed Evildoer, maliciously attempting to throw a brick through Ida Innocent's window, instead hits Ida. Ed is guilty of criminal assault and battery, although he intended a lesser, property crime.

Example: *Unintended Victim*
Betty Bad puts poison in Ivan Innocent's coffee. However, Todd Toughluck drinks the coffee instead and is injured. Betty is guilty of criminal assault and battery on Todd, although she meant *him* no harm. Her intent to injure Ivan is transferable.

Only certain *specific-intent* crimes (e.g., burglary and arson) require proof of intent to commit that particular crime.

In statutory law, unlike the common law, some crimes either presuppose or do not require criminal intent; the forbidden act is a *crime per se*. Such laws are most commonly found in state or municipal traffic codes.

Note that the law distinguishes between *intent* and *motive*. Intent involves an express or implied desire to perform a particular act; it is a state of mind preceding or accompanying the act. Motive is the overall goal that prompts a person's actions, and good or bad motives may be taken into account in assessing punishment.

CRIMINAL PROCEDURE

• *PRETRIAL STAGES*
A criminal case passes through several phases before trial. First, the crime is reported and investigated. Then, if there is **probable cause**, that is, reasonable grounds—something more than mere suspicion, to believe that a particular person committed the crime, that person can be arrested. A warrant for arrest is necessary unless the pressure of time requires immediate action (e.g., before the suspect flees).

Finally, criminal charges must be lodged against the defendant. Depending on the state, the charges, usually called either an **indictment** (by a grand jury) or an **information** (by a magistrate or police officer), must be based on probable cause, preponderance of evidence, or prosecutor's evidence that supports a belief in the defendant's guilt.

• *BURDEN OF PROOF*
At trial, there is a crucial difference between criminal and civil cases in the level of proof required.

A civil plaintiff merely needs a *preponderance of the evidence;* the judge or jury need only find that the evidence favors the plaintiff over the defendant.

A successful criminal prosecution requires proof of *guilt beyond a reasonable doubt.*

Absolute proof is not mandatory; the prosecution need not eliminate *all* doubts—merely all *reasonable* doubts.

A verdict of "not guilty" does not necessarily mean that the judge or jury believes the defendant to be innocent. It is simply a finding that there was insufficient evidence to prove guilt beyond a reasonable doubt.

• *EVIDENCE*

Criminal trial courts have numerous, complex rules about what evidence is admissible, and how it may be introduced. The rules are supposed to exclude irrelevant, unreliable, or unfairly prejudicial matters, especially in jury cases. (The system presupposes that a judge is less likely to be swayed by improper evidence.) The judge's or jury's verdict is to be based solely on the evidence properly brought out at trial. Otherwise proper, highly relevant evidence may be excluded because it was obtained in violation of a defendant's constitutional rights. Criminal appeals often are decided on such so-called technical issues.

YOU SHOULD REMEMBER

In both federal and state criminal cases, the most important aspects of the investigation, arrest, and trial are governed by guarantees contained in the U.S. Constitution, particularly the Fourth, Fifth, Sixth, and Eighth Amendments.

Crimes are generally classified as either *felonies* or *misdemeanors.* Felonies are the more serious crimes, with harsher punishments.

Other labels include white-collar, organized, and victimless crimes.

At common law, *actus reus* (criminal act) and *mens rea* (criminal intent) were the two necessary elements of a crime. These two concepts remain important, although some statutory offenses are crimes per se, with the *mens rea* requirement presumed or eliminated.

Arrests and searches must be based on probable cause, not mere suspicion. Criminal charges may have to meet an even higher standard. At trial, guilt must be proved beyond a reasonable doubt.

Rules of evidence, designed to exclude irrelevant, unreliable, or unfairly prejudicial matters, control the version of the facts presented at trial. Constitutional guarantees may necessitate further restriction of evidence.

Since the judge or jury is supposed to consider only the evidence properly introduced at trial, and since the prosecution must meet a high standard of proof, "not guilty" is not a synonym for "innocent."

IMPORTANT FACTS ABOUT TORTS

A **tort** is a private wrong, a trespass against a person or his/her property, for which a damages award or other judicial remedy may be sought. Most torts arise from either an intentional, wrongful action or from a negligent action. Many torts are also crimes, and most crimes involve tortious acts. Thus a single action may result in two trials: a criminal trial and a tort (civil) trial.

CLASSIFICATION OF TORTS

• *INTENTIONAL TORTS*

To constitute an **intentional tort**, the defendant's act must be expressly or implicitly intended; the resulting harm need not be intended, but must have been reasonably foreseeable. Examples of intentional torts are assault and battery, false imprisonment, slander, and invasion of privacy.

• *NEGLIGENCE*

In a tort case arising out of **negligence**, the plaintiff must show four things: (a) there was a duty imposed on the defendant in favor of the plaintiff, (b) the defendant breached (violated) that duty, (c) the breach was the proximate (natural and foreseeable) cause of the harm, and (d) plaintiff suffered damages.

Example: *Tort of Negligence*

Suppose that a building collapses, and X thus wants to sue architect Y for negligence. To win, X must prove that (a) Y designed or was responsible for the design of the building; (b) Y had a duty to design, or review the designs of, the building in accordance with reasonable standards of her profession; (c) this duty, owed to present and future passersby, people in the building, and persons with property in or near the building, covered X; (d) the duty was breached by Y; (e) if Y had exercised due care, the building would not have collapsed; and (f) the collapse damaged X or his property

DUTY AND "THE REASONABLE MAN"

The **duty** (standard of care) is that of a reasonable, prudent person acting with ordinary care and skill (the "reasonable man" standard). What would a reasonable person do in the situation faced by the defendant? This hypothetical person is given the defendant's physical attributes, including age, but is treated as having average intelligence and temperament. However, a highly educated or skilled defendant (e.g., a person accused of professional malpractice) may be held to a standard commensurate with his/her actual knowledge and ability.

CAUSATION

Breach of duty is not enough. The plaintiff must also prove **causation in fact**: that the damages would not have occurred but for the defendant's wrongful acts. An act need not be the sole or immediate cause of the damages. In fact, when two or more defendants act wrongfully, the defendants may be held *jointly and/or severally liable*; each defendant is liable for plaintiff's entire damages.

The second issue in causation, **proximate cause**, involves foreseeability. Were the plaintiff's damages the *natural and probable consequences* of the defendant's unreasonable acts? Although caused by these acts, the harm to the plaintiff may be so remote in time, distance, or chain of events that causation is not proximate. Alternatively, the plaintiff him-/herself may be unforeseeable.

Classic Case on Proximate Cause: Palsgraf v. Long Island R.R. Company, 162 N.E. 99 (Court of Appeals of New York, 1928)

A man carrying a package was rushing to board an already moving train. Two railroad guards helped to get him aboard, and the man dropped his package, which contained fireworks. Nothing about the package would have caused someone to discern its contents. The package exploded. The shock waves caused decorative scales to fall from the station's ceiling onto Mrs. Palsgraf, who was standing some distance from the three men and the exploding package. A divided court held that Mrs. Palsgraf was not a foreseeable plaintiff; hence there was no liability.

ADDITIONAL THEORIES OF TORT LIABILITY

• *RES IPSA LOQUITUR*

When a certain type of accident occurs ordinarily because of negligence, and the defendant had exclusive control of the instrument causing the injury (e.g., an airplane that crashed, a scalpel left in a patient's stomach), a presumption arises that the defendant was negligent. *Res ipsa loquitur* ("the thing speaks for itself") shifts the onus of coming forward and explaining the occurrence to the defendant. The ultimate burden of proof (looking at the *res ipsa loquitur* inference and all other evidence), however, remains with the plaintiff.

• *RESPONDEAT SUPERIOR*

Respondeat superior is the doctrine by which an employer may be liable for the tortious acts of an employee if the employee was acting in the scope of employment. Of course, regardless of *respondeat superior*, the employee is him-/herself liable for his/her actions. This concept is discussed further in Chapter 14. Incidentally, parents generally are *not* liable for torts by their children.

• *STRICT LIABILITY*

Under the doctrine of **strict liability**, the defendant is liable for the plaintiff's injuries despite the absence of negligence or intentional, wrongful acts. If the defendant was engaged in abnormally dangerous activities (e.g., blasting with dynamite, crop dusting, keeping wild animals), courts and legislatures have decided that he/she should bear the cost of any harm done. As in other areas of liability without fault (e.g., products liability, workmen's compensation), the strict liability of some manufacturers or employers is a matter of public policy based on the assumption that these defendants are in a better position to shoulder the costs of injury than are potential plaintiffs.

TORT PROCEDURE

Lawsuits involving torts are tried in civil courts and generally follow the procedures outlined in Chapter 3.

YOU SHOULD REMEMBER

An intentional tort involves intended acts, not necessarily intended harm.

In negligence, *duty of care* is breached if the defendant failed to act as a reasonable, prudent person would have acted in the situation the defendant faced. *Causation in fact* exists if, but for the defendant's wrongful acts, the damages to the plaintiff would not have occurred. However, if the plaintiff and/or his damages were unforeseeable, the defendant may successfully argue that the alleged tort lacks *proximate cause*.

Under *res ipsa loquitur*, there arises a presumption that the defendant was negligent.

When employees commit torts in the scope of their employment, *respondeat superior* places liability on employers as well as employees.

For reasons of public policy, defendants who engage in abnormally dangerous activities are held *strictly liable* for harm resulting from those activities.

COMPARISON OF CRIMES AND TORTS

The following table compares these two divisions of law.

Crime	Tort
1. A public wrong against society	1. A private wrong against individuals or businesses
2. "Plaintiff" (prosecutor) is the state (offended person is usually a witness)	2. Plaintiff is an individual or a business
3. Mostly statutory law	3. Mostly common law
4. Prosecutor's burden of proof: guilty beyond a reasonable doubt	4. Plaintiff's burden of proof: preponderance of the evidence
5. Consent rarely a defense	5. Consent usually a defense
6. No damages are necessary.	6. Damages must be shown.
7. Basis for criminal guilt: an intentional act, and sometimes gross negligence or recklessness	7. Basis for tort liability: an intentional act, negligence, or strict liability

EXAMPLES OF TORTS

Most torts are defined by common law precedent. Courts may (and occasionally do) define a new tort, such as infliction of emotional distress, invasion of privacy, or abusive discharge from employment—three twentieth century tort refinements. Courts and legislatures also abolish torts that no longer reflect concerns that society deems worthy of protection (e.g., alienation of affections).

NEGLIGENCE

Most common law torts arise out of negligence, that is, unintentional breaches of duty. *Examples*: poorly manufactured products, professional malpractice, traffic accidents.

INTENTIONAL TORTS

• *INTERFERENCE WITH THE PERSON*

Assault: arousing in another individual the apprehension of an *immediate* harmful or offensive contact with his/her body. Words alone are insufficient; they must be accompanied by some act. *Examples*: threats while raising fists, reaching toward what seems to be a concealed weapon.

Battery: unjustified contact with someone else's body or anything connected to it (purse, chair, cane, etc.). The contact may be direct (e.g., a slap) or due to a force put into motion by the defendant (e.g., shooting a bullet that strikes the plaintiff). It includes actions exceeding one's authority for physical contact. *Example*: a masseuse suddenly shaves a customer's head.

False arrest: detention of the plaintiff, without his/her permission, under the falsely asserted authority of the defendant. No physical barrier, force, or threat of force is necessary. *Example*: An insurance investigator posing as a police officer searches a person and detains him for questioning.

False imprisonment: wrongful use of force, physical barriers, or threats of force to restrain the plaintiff's freedom of movement. *Example*: A merchant forcibly detains a suspected shoplifter without reasonable cause for suspicion. Most states have "merchant protection" laws against suspected shoplifters, but the merchant must have reasonable grounds for suspicion, and the confinement must also be reasonable (accomplished without excessive force, and for no longer than necessary).

Intentional infliction of mental (emotional) distress: disturbance of the plaintiff's peace of mind by the defendant's outrageous conduct. Although damages are not limited to bodily injury, usually some physical harm must be shown. *Examples:* extreme actions by bill collectors, extensive cursing and threats of future violence, continued abuse about a sensitive person's stuttering or physical appearance, slipping a dead mouse into someone's lunch.

Invasion of privacy: interference with a person's right to be left alone. The right to solitude can be invaded in four different ways: (1) public disclosure of private facts; (2) publication of information placing a person in a false light; (3) intrusion upon a person's private life; or (4) unauthorized appropriation of name or likeness (e.g., picture) for commercial purposes. The first three must be disclosures or intrusions highly offensive to a reasonable person. Truth is no defense. *Examples*: publishing information obtained from the psychiatric files of a business competitor; making, and selling for profit, baseball cards without the permission of the ballplayers pictured.

• *INTERFERENCE WITH BUSINESS RELATIONS*

Abusive discharge: modification of the common law doctrine that "at will" employees (ones without a set term of employment) may be terminated for any reason. This tort occurs if a firing violates a clear mandate of public policy. *Also see* pages 407–411 including discussion of civil rights employment actions.

Example: a firing that stems from the worker's notifying authorities about criminal activities being carried on in the workplace.

Disparagement (trade libel): a business defamation that involves injurious falsehoods about a product or a competitor's reputation. *Example*: stating falsely to
customers that a competitor's products contain carcinogens.

Infringement of copyrights, patents, trademarks, or trade names: these will be
considered in the intellectual property section of Chapter 19.

Interference with contract: a tort requiring that (1) a valid contract exists between A and B; (2) C knows about the contract; (3) C intentionally causes A
or B to breach the contract, or C otherwise prevents performance. *Example*:
Interfering, Inc., persuades an employee who has another 6 months to run on
her year-long employment contract with Contract Company to breach that contract and work for Interfering. Contract Company may sue Interfering for the
tort (interference with contract) and sue the employee for breach of contract.

Interference with prospective economic advantage: a tort with roughly the same
three requirements as interference with contract (simply substitute "prospective economic advantage" for "contract"). *Example*: Gary Greedy has his employees stand outside a competitor's store to divert customers to Greedy's shop.

Unfair competition: a tort that, in its broad sense, overlaps other torts such as
infringement of intellectual property or interference with contracts or prospective economic advantage. In its more narrow application, this tort concerns
trying to "pass off" goods or services upon the public as if they were the goods
or services of another, more reputable business or product. *Other examples*:
deceitful advertising injures a competitor, secret rebates or concessions, bribery of a competitor's employees, use of a former employer's trade secrets.

• *INTERFERENCE WITH PROPERTY*

Conversion: unauthorized, unjustified exercise of control over another's personal
property. There are two requirements: defendant must (1) appropriate the
property to his/her own use, and (2) indefinitely withhold its possession from
the plaintiff and/or destroy it. A mistaken belief that one owns the property or
is entitled to keep or use it is no defense. *Examples*: acts of arson, robbery, or
embezzlement, taking someone else's umbrella, coat, or other personal property and keeping it after discovering that fact.

Nuisance (Liability for nuisances can be based not only on intentional acts but
also on negligence or strict liability): substantial interference with the individual plaintiff's right to use and enjoy his/her property (private nuisance) or with
rights common to all (public nuisance). Nuisance usually refers to wrongs
arising out of the defendant's unreasonable or unlawful use of his own property.
Examples: excessive noise, fumes or smoke; storing dangerous chemicals. *Private nuisance*—the defendant's watering his lawn so much that the plaintiff's
land is flooded. *Public nuisance*—interfering with the general right to health,
safety, peace, comfort, or morals, and including, for example, pollution, brothels,
and drag strips. There are "mixed" nuisances (both private and public).

Trespass to personal property: unjustified interference with the plaintiff's possessory interest (e.g., use) in personal property. *Example*: without permission, a person takes someone else's lawnmower, cuts her own lawn with it, and then returns the machine.

Trespass to real property: unauthorized entry onto the plaintiff's land, either by a person or by something the person caused to enter the land. This tort can also occur when presence on the plaintiff's property becomes unauthorized, but continues. *Examples*: building a dam so that water backs up onto someone's land, throwing rocks or trash onto another's land.

• *OTHER INTENTIONAL TORTS*

Abuse of process: the use of a court process (e.g., attachment, injunction) for a purpose for which it was not intended. *Example*: attachment on excessive amounts of X's property in one case so as to force X to dismiss an unrelated lawsuit.

Defamation: a false communication by the defendant to a third person (a "publication") that harms the plaintiff's reputation. *Slander* is oral; *libel* involves writing, broadcasting, or any other recorded medium. It is no defense that one was merely repeating what someone else wrote or stated. The media may claim in defense that the statement concerned a public figure and was made without malice. A plaintiff seeking to show malice must prove actual knowledge of falsity or a reckless disregard of the truth. *Example*: an employee tells his boss that another employee, whom he names, is a harlot, has repeatedly cheated on her income tax returns, and makes a practice of taking 3-hour lunches; the employee telling these tales knows or should know that they are false.

Fraud (deceit, misrepresentation): a very important intentional tort; depends on a false, material representation of fact that the defendant either knows to be false or recklessly makes knowing that the information is incomplete. The defendant must intend that the plaintiff rely on the representation, and the plaintiff must in fact justifiably rely upon the representation and thereby be damaged. Representations are usually by words, but can be by conduct (e.g., setting back an odometer). "Material" means any representation that would influence a reasonable person in the plaintiff's situation.

Opinions generally are not considered representations of fact, unless given by experts in their area of expertise. "Puffing" or other sales talk about the value of goods or services is usually treated as mere opinion unless a special, confidential relationship exists between buyer and seller.

Silence generally does not constitute fraud. A major exception involves silence when a defendant has a duty to speak (e.g., when the defendant knows that the plaintiff has misconstrued the silence).

Malicious prosecution: the instigation of criminal proceedings against someone for an improper purpose and without probable cause, with those proceedings terminating decisively in the criminal defendant's favor (e.g., by acquittal or dismissal for lack of evidence). When the improper proceedings are civil, the tort is called **malicious institution of civil proceedings**.

Negligent misrepresentation: Incorrect statements of opinion or fact made by persons who breached a duty to exercise reasonable care in ascertaining the truth; such persons may include accountants, lawyers, title examiners, or others supplying the plaintiff with business guidance. This tort generally has the same requirements as does fraud, except that negligence replaces fraud's *scienter* (knowledge of falsity or reckless disregard of truth or falsity).

Of the foregoing torts, *assault, battery, false arrest, false imprisonment, unfair competition, conversion, infringement of intellectual property, nuisance, trespass to personal or real property, libel, and fraud are also crimes or are directly related to particular crimes.*

YOU SHOULD REMEMBER

Duty, breach, causation, and damages are the crux of any tort case concerning negligence.

For intentional torts there are specific definitional requirements. For all tort cases, even those involving the same type of tort, the particular facts in the case remain crucial.

EXAMPLES OF BUSINESS CRIMES, WITH TORT EQUIVALENTS

The following are typical business crimes:

Arson: willfully setting fire to and burning a building. It is criminal fraud to burn a building in order to collect insurance. *Tort equivalent: trespass to real and personal property, conversion.*

Attempt: specific intent to do a criminal act, and—in furtherance of that intent—some action beyond mere preparation. *No tort equivalent.*

In the example on page 56, Dave Deviant could not be found guilty for merely thinking of, or even preparing a plan for, assaulting Veronica Victim. However, since Dave has the requisite intent to commit an assault, once he pours "knockout" drops into Veronica's glass of wine, once he drives her to a remote spot, or once he has taken some other affirmative action beyond "mere preparation," Dave can be criminally liable for attempted assault, if the assault itself does not occur.

Bankruptcy frauds: filing false claims by creditors or debtors, fraudulent transfer or concealment of assets, or obtaining credit with the specific intent to avoid paying debts. *Tort equivalent: fraud.*

Bribery: illegal payments or offers to pay, whether of money, property, or services, to a political campaign, to governmental officials, or to other persons such as the employees of a competing firm, for the purpose of receiving favorable treatment, proprietary information, or other assistance that the briber either is not entitled to receive or—at the very least—cannot lawfully receive by the method chosen (kickbacks or payoffs). *No direct tort equivalent: depending on the facts, a business competitor may have a claim for unfair competition, conversion, infringement of intellectual property, fraud, or tortious interference with a contractual or business relationship.*

Burglary: at common law, breaking and entering a dwelling at night with the intent to commit a felony, such as larceny. Modern statutes have tended to widen the definition by eliminating the requirements that the crime be at night, that there be an actual breaking, and that the building be a dwelling. *Tort equivalent: conversion, trespass to real and personal property.*

Compounding a crime: accepting money or anything else of value in return for not reporting or prosecuting a crime. *No tort equivalent.*

Computer crimes: a crime committed by using a computer. Common examples involve using computers to embezzle, to defraud, or to steal information. It may also involve damage to or destruction of computer systems. *Tort equivalent: depending on the facts, infringement of intellectual property, fraud, conversion, or trespass to personal property.*

Corporate crime: a crime by a corporation and/or its personnel. For a corporation to be guilty, intent either is no element or can be implied. Although a corporation cannot specifically intend a crime, its officers and employees can. Thus corporate personnel can be convicted of certain crimes (e.g., perjury) for which the corporation may not be liable. *Tort equivalent: depending on the facts, fraud, conversion, or trespass to personal property.*

Embezzlement: unlawful use of money or property for one's own purposes by a person with lawful possession or access to that money or property. Embezzlement may involve bank employees, company bookkeepers, or other money managers who decide to "borrow" the funds entrusted to them. In most jurisdictions, it is no defense to claim that the money or property would have been returned. *Tort equivalent: conversion.*

Forgery: falsely making or materially altering a legal document (e.g., a check or credit card) in order to defraud another person and/or otherwise affect rights. *Tort equivalent: fraud, conversion.*

Fraud against consumers: activities such as fraudulent solicitation in the mail, false advertising about products, and false labeling. *Tort equivalent: fraud.*

Larceny (theft): unlawfully taking personal property with the intent to deprive the owner of it. Two examples are shoplifting and theft of company property by employees. *Tort equivalent: conversion, trespass to personal property.*

Mail and wire fraud: use of mails, telephones, radio, or television to further or execute a scheme to defraud (the fraudulent scheme need not itself be a crime). These federal criminal statutes are used against a wide variety of crimes, including kickbacks to private employees and bribery of public officials. *Tort equivalent: fraud, conversion.*

Misappropriation of Trade Secrets: use of an employer's, a competitor's, or some other person's trade secrets (see page 350) for personal advantage and without the owner's permission. *Tort equivalent: unfair competition, perhaps infringement of intellectual property.*

RICO (Racketeer Influenced and Corrupt Organizations Act) violations: use of income from two or more racketeering actions (within ten years of each other) to create, acquire, operate, or have an interest in any type of "enterprise" (broadly construed to include not just any business, but also almost any other organization), or to conspire to do so. "Racketeering activity" is defined expansively to include any one or more of numerous types of "predicate acts"—federal crimes such as interstate transportation of stolen property, interference with interstate commerce via violence or threats of violence, various statutory frauds (e.g., as to securities, mail, currency reporting, and bankruptcy), and embezzling from pension, welfare or union funds; also, state felonies such as arson, bribery, drug dealing, extortion, gambling, insurance fraud, kidnapping, loan sharking, murder, and robbery. While intended to combat organized crime's "infiltration" into legitimate businesses, RICO reaches most white-collar crimes, whether by criminal organizations or by otherwise lawful enterprises. *Tort equivalent: fraud, conversion, RICO civil liability (treble damages and attorneys' fees), perhaps tortious interference with contract.*

Robbery: larceny accomplished by using force or threats of force. *Tort equivalent: assault, battery, conversion, trespass to personal property.*

THE BUSINESSPERSON AS CRIMINAL DEFENDANT

Business crimes include certain activities once thought to be simply "good business." For instance, price restraints, the division of markets, and reciprocal trade arrangements may be criminal, as well as civil, violations of antitrust laws. Failure to monitor industrial discharges can subject a company and its officers to fines and imprisonment under federal water pollution legislation. It may mitigate punishment, but does not alter criminality, that the offending monopolist or polluter did not intend to violate the law.

Most white-collar culprits, however, know full well that their actions are illegal. Using stealth rather than force, the white-collar criminal frequently makes money, or avoids paying debts, by violating the trust reposed in him/her.

> *White-collar crimes* include tax evasion, bribes, extortion, embezzlement, kickbacks, pilferage, forgery, computer crimes, antitrust violations such as bid rigging and price fixing, RICO offenses, and all types of fraud concerning consumers, credit cards, securities, insurance, bankruptcy, bank loans, and countless other areas.

Fraud is the essence of many, if not most, white-collar crimes. A criminally fraudulent act is any deceitful action or omission that (1) is intended to deprive another of his/her property or other rights, and (2) achieves this purpose.

The definition of **criminal fraud** is thus no more limited than the criminal mind itself; it stands ready to include the latest "scams" and the newest abuses of technology.

YOU SHOULD REMEMBER

There are numerous business crimes.
Fraud is often an essential element in white-collar crime. Criminal fraud is deceit that serves a purpose: the deprivation of another's property or other rights.

GENERAL DEFENSES TO CRIMES AND TORTS

Good **defenses** result from failing to comply with the definitional requirements of a specific crime or tort and/or from falling short of the level of proof required in any criminal or civil case. Furthermore, while all defendants have "due process" and other constitutional rights, the seriousness of criminal charges has led to additional procedural protections for criminal defendants, as outlined earlier in the section "The U.S. Constitution and American Criminal Law."

The following are some general defenses to crimes and/or torts:

Act of God is a defense to negligence when natural forces such as lightning, earthquakes, or hurricanes are the proximate cause of injury. However, when a person negligently created a situation whereby a foreseeable act of God could cause damage, no defense is available to foreseeable damages.

Assumption of risk, another defense to unintentional torts, means that a plaintiff who knowingly and voluntarily faced a dangerous situation may not recover for an injury arising out of the known risks inherent to that situation. An exception to this defense is a rescuer acting in an emergency situation.

Comparative negligence has replaced contributory negligence in almost all states. When the negligence of the plaintiff and the negligence of the defendant are concurrent causes of the plaintiff's damages, any damages awarded to the plaintiff are reduced by an amount proportionate to the degree of the plaintiff's fault. However, only some states, with "pure" comparative negligence, permit a plaintiff to recover any damages at all when his/her negligence exceeds the defendant's negligence.

Example: Comparative Negligence

If the plaintiff's damages are $100,000 and a jury finds that she was 30% at fault, while it assesses the defendant with 70% of the blame, then the plaintiff recovers $70,000. (Under the doctrine of contributory negligence, the plaintiff gets nothing.)

Consent is a defense to *all torts* and *few crimes*. When the criminal law forbids an act against the victim's will, consent makes the act no crime at all. If Ms. Able is a mentally competent adult who consented to sexual intercourse with Mr. Baker, no crime of forcible rape has occurred.

Most crimes are not negated by the individual victim's consent because the real plaintiff is society, which did not consent. Moreover, forgiveness after the crime occurs is not to be confused with consent: although it may affect the likelihood of prosecution and the severity of punishment, forgiveness is no defense. The same applies when stolen property is returned or a defendant pays for damages caused.

Contributory negligence is an absolute defense to negligence in a few states. If the plaintiff was negligent and that negligence contributed to his/her injuries, the defendant is absolved from liability even if the defendant's negligence was much greater than the plaintiff's.

Duress may excuse the commission of a crime while under an immediate and inescapable threat of serious bodily harm or death. The threatened harm must be more serious than the harm to be caused by the crime. Obviously, duress would negate the intent necessary for an intentional tort.

Entrapment is a criminal defense if the criminal act was induced by the government, with criminal intent originating from the police. If, however, the accused was predisposed to commit the crime, then entrapment is not a defense.

Immunity from prosecution is sometimes extended to actual or potential criminal defendants, usually to induce testimony and information from them. So long as the person receiving immunity cannot be prosecuted for his/her statements, that person cannot assert the Fifth Amendment privilege against self-incrimination.

Immunity is also a tort defense that may limit or outright bar recovery against governments, public officers, or other defendants specifically protected by statutes (e.g., charities).

Infancy bars criminal liability for children who are under a certain age and/or do not understand that a particular act is wrong. Children have no such immunity for torts: the law is more concerned with compensating the injured than with determining moral guilt. In negligence cases a child's standard of care (duty) is based on his/her intelligence and experience rather than the usual objective standard.

Insanity is a defense if the alleged crime occurred while the defendant lacked the mental capacity for the requisite criminal intent. As with duress or infancy, insanity may negate intent for some intentional torts. However, the mentally incompetent are generally held accountable for their tortious acts (including negligence) on the grounds that to deny compensation would be unfair to their victims.

Intoxication (use of alcohol or other drugs) is a complete criminal defense only when *involuntary*: a person, by force, by mistake, or by some situation beyond his/her control, ingests or has injected an intoxicating substance. *Voluntary* intoxication does not preclude the *mens rea* necessary for intentional crimes, nor does it excuse lesser crimes involving reckless behavior. For torts, intoxicated persons will generally be held to the same standard of care (duty) as if they were sober: intoxication is no defense.

Mistake of fact depends on whether the mistake negates *mens rea*.

Example: Mistake of Fact

If Nora Nearsighted walks off with Tammy True's child (who bears some resemblance to Nora's own tot), and Nora returns the child as soon as she discovers her mistake, Nora is not guilty of kidnapping.

Mistake of law is a criminal defense when a person honestly did not know that he/she was breaking the law, *and*: (1) the law was not published or otherwise made known to the public, or (2) the person relied on an erroneous but official statement of the law, such as a statute, court decision, or administrative order. Usually, ignorance of the law is no excuse.

Privilege is an immunity existing under law and sometimes constituting a defense in, for example, cases involving interference with contract, interference with prospective economic advantage, or defamation. Privilege involving the two interference torts frequently involves the concept of free competition (within bounds); for instance, strikes are usually privileged. For defamation, defenses include not only truth but also the absolute privilege extended to statements of attorneys and judges at trials and legislators during floor debate.

Self-defense (or defense of others) permits people to use the degree of non-deadly force that seems necessary to protect themselves (or others) from criminal force. Deadly force (likely to result in death or serious injury) is also permitted if (1) an attacker is using unlawful force, (2) the victim did not initiate or provoke the attack, and (3) the victim reasonably believes that he/she will otherwise suffer death or serious bodily injury. Some jurisdictions allow deadly force whenever it appears necessary to prevent a felony within a dwelling.

In tort cases, self-defense is judged by the "reasonable man" standard: if the defendant reasonably believes him-/herself to be in danger and responds reasonably, there is a defense. Defense of others is a similar tort defense, although some courts are more likely to find no defense for the actions of an "intermeddler" than for such actions taken in self-defense.

Statutes of limitations are statutorily defined periods of time within which a legal action must be brought. In civil actions, the stated time varies from state to state and depends on the subject matter—as little as 6 months or 1 or 2 years for certain defined torts, as much as 20 or more years for real estate actions. Generally, there is no period of limitation for crimes unless the statute creating the crime sets forth such a period.

The rationale for statutes of limitations is as follows:

1. People should not have to worry indefinitely about potential claims against them.

2. The law should encourage prompt prosecutions and lawsuits, which reduce the period during which memories fade, evidence is lost or destroyed, and witnesses die, disappear, or otherwise become unavailable.

Superseding (intervening) causes break the causal connection in torts between the defendant's act and the plaintiff's damages. As a general rule, they offer a defense based on lack of either causation in fact or proximate cause.

Example: *Superseding (Intervening) Cause*

Annie Absentminded leaves her grocery cart in a crowded, badly lit parking lot. Tom Thief places it in the back of his car and drives off. A half-mile later, the cart falls out and strikes Peter Pedestrian. Annie's negligence as to the cart would not render her liable to Peter; Tom's actions are a superseding cause of the accident.

YOU SHOULD REMEMBER

Even if a person has committed the act for which he/she is charged or is being sued, defenses may serve either to negate the crime or tort or—at the very least—to prevent a successful prosecution or lawsuit.

KNOW THE CONCEPTS
DO YOU KNOW THE BASICS?

1. What are the key guarantees for criminal defendants under the U.S. Constitution?
2. Discuss the levels of evidence necessary at each of the four phases of criminal procedure: investigation, arrest, lodging of charges, and trial.

3. (a) What are the rules of evidence intended to do?
   (b) What effect may U.S. Constitutional guarantees have on the introduction of evidence?
4. Name two methods by which crimes can be classified.
5. How is intent transferable?
6. Name the basic elements needed to prove negligence.
7. Distinguish between intent and motive.
8. Name (a) six intentional torts involving interference with the person, and (b) four concerning interference with property.
9. List some white-collar crimes.
10. Compare the law of crimes and torts with respect to burdens of proof, damages, consent, sources of the law, and types of acts required for guilt or liability.
11. *True* or *false*: If A does not disclose every problem he has had with a machine that he is selling to B, then B will probably win a suit against A for fraud. Explain your answer.
12. In a negligence case, a jury decides that plaintiff C suffered $250,000 damages and assesses the blame for C's injuries at 60% for C and 40% for defendant. How much would the plaintiff's damages award be (a) under contributory negligence; (b) under comparative negligence?
13. Name two crimes without tort equivalents.
14. Name nine crimes that may subject the culprit to tort liability for conversion.
15. Name four defenses to negligence that are not defenses to crimes.

TERMS FOR STUDY

actus reus	larceny
causation in fact	mail and wire fraud
burden of proof	misappropriation
crime	RICO
arson	robbery
attempt	defense
bankruptcy fraud	act of God
bribery	assumption of risk
burglary	comparative negligence
compounding a crime	consent
computer crime	contributory negligence
corporate crime	duress
criminal fraud	entrapment
embezzlement	immunity
forgery	infancy
fraud against consumers	insanity

intoxication
mistake of fact
mistake of law
privilege
self-defense
statute of limitations
superseding (intervening) causes
duty (of care)
felony
indictment
information
mens rea
misdemeanor
organized crime
probable cause
proximate cause
tort
  intentional tort
    abuse of process
    abusive discharge
    assault
    battery
    conversion
    defamation (libel, slander)
    disparagement

false arrest
false imprisonment
fraud
intentional infliction of mental
  (emotional) distress
interference with contract
interference with prospective
  economic advantage
invasion of privacy
malicious institution of civil
  proceedings
malicious prosecution
negligent misrepresentation
nuisance
trespass to personal property
trespass to real property
unfair competition
negligence
res ipsa loquitur
respondeat superior
strict liability

treason
victimless crimes
white-collar crime

PRACTICAL APPLICATION

1. You believe that wealthy Sam Sick has been molesting your 10-year old child. However, a jury has acquitted Sam of all criminal charges. (a) Can he be sued? (b) How would a civil trial be different from the criminal case?

2. For several months Derek Dirt has allowed his garbage to accumulate in his backyard, next to a school playground. Little Wendy Wanderer, age five, sees what to her promises to be a nice toy among the trash. Upon coming closer, she is bitten by a rat.
   Wendy screams and then faints. Her nearby mother calls an ambulance, which, on the way to the scene, jumps a curb and strikes Paul Pedestrian, seriously injuring him.
   Wendy requires a series of rabies shots. Except for some bad dreams, she apparently recovers.
   (a) Discuss the lawsuits based on negligence that Wendy and her parents may bring against Derek.
   (b) Discuss who might be liable to Paul.

(c) Discuss possible negligence by persons other than Derek.

3. Workers from a moving company are delivering furniture to an apartment. While Holly Hapless is walking by, a chair crashes through a window of the apartment and lands on her foot, causing injury. What two Latin terms may play key parts in Holly's case against the moving company?

4. Larry Loaded drove his 18-wheeler into the side of a schoolhouse. He destroyed the school cafeteria, frightened but left physically uninjured a number of children, and did serious harm to his own body. When the school principal pulled Larry out of the wreckage, she found a nearly empty bottle of bourbon under the front passenger seat. The school nurse treated Larry for shock and, for good measure, took a blood sample, which showed a high alcohol percentage. In a hearing before his criminal trial, Larry claims that evidence of the bottle and the samples should be excluded.
(a) On what grounds does Larry base this claim?
(b) What arguments would you make in response if you were the prosecutor?
(c) What would the judge decide?
(d) With what crimes should Larry be charged?
(e) For what torts may he be held liable?

5. One of your employees may have embezzled thousands of dollars from your company. What may you do to stop her, to investigate her, to convict her?

6. Sally Silly is or was your embezzling employee. Alas, she may not be "quite right in the head."
(a) In a criminal prosecution, what defense may her attorney raise?
(b) What if Sally's problems stemmed from alcoholism?
(c) What if Sally claims she stole from the company out of love for a man she thought was Albert Schweitzer, a man who gladly took most of her gifts of money and encouraged her to steal more?
(d) As a prosecutor, would you give her immunity to testify against "Albert"?
(e) What problems might you face?
(f) What torts have been committed?

7. (a) Should the finding "not guilty, by reason of insanity" be replaced by the verdict "guilty, but insane"?
(b) If so, how should such "guilty" defendants be punished?

8. Early one evening, Lucy Luscious stops Sidney Susceptible on a city sidewalk in the "red light" district. Hitching up her tight skirt a notch as she sits on a bench, Lucy asks for the time. Sidney gives it. Lucy asks Sidney to light her cigarette. He does. Lucy asks Sidney to sit down and join her for a smoke. He sits. While talking to Sidney, Lucy puts on rouge and more bright red lipstick. Sidney offers her money for sexual services. Lucy flashes her badge and arrests Sidney for solicitation.
(a) What defense might Sidney raise? Will he succeed?
(b) What tort has been committed?

9. Cory Criminal takes a bicycle left unattended on Vera Victim's front porch. Cory rides the bicycle all over town and fastens to the frame his own flashing neon bicycle license plate, emblazoned "CORY'S."
   (a) What crime has Cory committed?
   (b) What crime would it be if Cory broke through a window of Vera's house, entered, and then took the bicycle?
   (c) What if Cory put a knife to Vera's throat, made her get off her two-wheeler, and rode away with it?
   (d) In each case, name the torts, also.

10. Wally Worker suspects that his employer, Crass Conglomerates, Inc., may have rigged prices with its main supposed competitor. He raises questions with his superior, Brenda Boss, who fires him. Wally's union goes on strike in protest. The strike prevents Crass from meeting its existing contracts or making new ones. Furthermore, a shotgun, albeit unloaded, has been pointed at strikebreakers by union member Vera Vigilante.
   Crass management orders an investigation of the union leaders. Thus Crass manages to photograph and distribute pictures of the union's treasurer, Leo Leader, leaving a video club with several X-rated films, the titles plainly visible, in hand. Leo has countered by falsely telling Crass customers that certain Crass "super-balsam" products are actually made of papier-mâché. What torts have been committed, and by whom?

ANSWERS

KNOW THE CONCEPTS

1. Fourth, Fifth, Sixth, Eighth, and Fourteenth Amendments. Fourth: protection from unreasonable searches and seizures; Fifth: due process of law (federal) and prohibition of compulsory self-incrimination and double jeopardy; Sixth: speedy and public trial, impartial jury, information as to charges, calling and confronting witnesses, having a lawyer; Eighth: proscribes excessive bail, excessive fines, and cruel and unusual punishment; Fourteenth: due process of law (state).

2. Investigation: no level; arrest: probable cause; charges: probable cause, preponderance of evidence, or prosecutor's evidence supports belief in guilt; trial: guilt proved beyond a reasonable doubt.

3. (a) To streamline the trial, among other things. To exclude irrelevant, unreliable, or unfairly prejudicial matters. (b) Constitutional guarantees, especially their violation, may necessitate the restriction or outright barring of otherwise admissible evidence.

4. (1) Classification as either felony or misdemeanor; (2) classification according to the type of harm caused.

5. If one knowingly commits a criminal or tortious act, one is presumed to intend the natural consequences of that act. Moreover, if the consequences occur to someone not intended as the victim, or if the consequences are different from those intended, the law may transfer the *mens rea,* or tortious intent, from what was intended to what actually occurred.

6. Duty, breach of duty, causation, and damages.

7. Intent is the mens rea preceding or accompanying the act. Motive is the overall purpose, good or bad, for which the act is done.

8. (a) Assault, battery, false arrest, false imprisonment, intentional infliction of mental (emotional) distress, and invasion of privacy; (b) conversion, nuisance, trespass to personal property, and trespass to real property.

9. Tax evasion, bribes, extortion, embezzlement, kickbacks, pilferage, forgery, computer crimes, antitrust violations, RICO offenses, and fraud concerning consumers, credit cards, securities, insurance, bankruptcy, and bank loans.

10. Crimes: proof of guilt beyond a reasonable doubt, damages not necessary, consent usually no defense, mainly statutory law, and guilt requires intentional or grossly negligent acts.
    Torts: preponderance of evidence, damages needed, consent a defense, mainly common law, and liability based on intentional acts, negligence, or no-fault (e.g., strict liability).

11. False. In most cases, there is no duty to volunteer information. Even if, in this case, there were a duty to speak, it is not at all clear from the facts that (1) the nondisclosure was of a material fact; (2) A intended that B would rely on the nondisclosure; (3) B justifiably relied on the nondisclosure; and (4) B was damaged. All of those points would have to be proved, in addition to demonstrating that A had a duty to speak (e.g., because A knew that B had misconstrued A's silence).

12. (a) Nothing. (b) Under "pure" comparative negligence, 40% of $250,000 ($100,000); otherwise, nothing.

13. Attempt and compounding a crime. In some cases, other crimes (e.g., bribery) may also have no tort equivalents.

14. Arson, bribery, burglary, computer crimes, corporate crimes, embezzlement, forgery, larceny (theft), and robbery.

15. Act of God, assumption of risk, contributory or comparative negligence, and superseding (intervening) causes.

PRACTICAL APPLICATION

1. (a) Yes. Double jeopardy applies only to the filing of the same *criminal charges*.

   (b) The burden of proof for you, the plaintiff, would be only a preponderance of evidence, not—as it was for the prosecutor in the criminal case—proof of guilt beyond a reasonable doubt. There are, of course, other differences; for instance, some evidence may be more easily admitted in a civil trial.

2. (a) Certainly, Derek has acted negligently; he had a duty not to allow his garbage to accumulate over several months, and he breached that duty. The key issue is proximate cause.

   Wendy should be able to obtain a damages award against Derek for the physical and emotional harm suffered. It is foreseeable that rodents might gather in a festering pile of garbage, and that a rat might bite someone nearby. If Wendy were an adult or older child, she might be deemed contributorily negligent or to have assumed the risk, but for a five-year-old her actions appear to be reasonable. Moreover, the foreseeability of injury to a child is heightened by the close presence of a playground.

   Wendy's parents should be able to recover from Derek for their expenses in having Wendy transported, examined, and treated. Damages would include any of their costs that directly and proximately follow from the injury. Wendy's mother may also sue for trauma suffered, particularly if she actually saw her child being bitten; however, questions of duty, proximate cause, and actual damages may undermine such an action.

   (b) Although ambulances often have to travel rapidly, Paul may show that, in these circumstances, climbing the curb amounted to negligent driving. If, however, the ambulance company is part of a governmental or charitable agency, immunity may serve as a partial or absolute defense.

   Paul's claim against Derek appears to be too attenuated. Few, if any, courts would find proximate cause between Derek's negligence (accumulation of the garbage) and the force causing Paul's injuries (the moving ambulance). There is no foreseeability. Also, superseding cause may be a defense.

   (c) Derek may claim that Wendy's mother was herself negligent in supervising Wendy. That is a question of fact for the jury. Even if her mother was contributorily negligent, that defense would not bar Wendy's suit. [However, Derek might file a third-party claim (See Chapter 3, page 39) against the mother to receive a contribution from her for damages he must pay to Wendy.]

   As for Paul, Wendy's conduct (assuming she was negligent) and the mother's supposed negligent supervision of Wendy were no more the proximate cause of his harm than was Derek's negligent accumulation of garbage; the calling of an ambulance also did not foreseeably lead to Paul's injuries, nor was it breaching a duty of care in the first place.

3. *Res ipsa loquitur* and *respondeat superior*.

4. (a) Fourth Amendment protection against unreasonable search and seizure, Fifth Amendment protection against self-incrimination.

   (b) Actions taken were not by government (or, at very least, school officials are not police toward whom the amendments are really geared); search was reasonable; blood sample is not the sort of compulsory "testimony" that Fifth Amendment concerns.

   (c) Probably admit both the blood sample (more likely) and the bottle. May exclude bottle as unreasonable search (argument that bottle is unfairly prejudicial would probably fail; the fact that evidence is harmful does not make it inadmissible).

   (d) Among others, with drunken driving, reckless endangerment, destruction of public property.

   (e) Negligence, trespass to real and personal property.

5. Contact the authorities. Watch out not to be overzealous; this may lead to charges of malicious prosecution, abusive discharge, defamation, and so on. However, to countenance embezzlement by sending the embezzler on to another employer may amount to compounding a crime and may subject you to a civil suit from a subsequent employer.

6. (a) Insanity.

   (b) Does alcoholism constitute an involuntary or voluntary intoxication defense? Although intoxication may be a cause of personal anguish leading to embezzlement, it is hard to see how it can result in intentional acts of fraud, as opposed to mere recklessness. Even if it could, assuming that Sally has any moments of lucidity in which she realizes what she has done, she will probably be held accountable for failing to take corrective measures.

   (c) Sally's infatuation for "Albert" may be evidence of insanity, but it would not be duress.

   (d) If you, the prosecutor, consider Sally to be relatively innocent compared to Albert, you may decide that Sally's assistance is necessary to apprehend and convict Albert. Immunity may be deemed a necessary means to obtain Sally's full assistance.

   (e) Some problems: (1) before trial, how guilt should be apportioned between Sally and Albert; (2) how much leeway should a prosecutor have; (3) if immunity is given, how may Sally's credibility be ensured.

   (f) Sally: conversion; Albert: conversion (using Sally as his agent), perhaps fraud upon Sally.

7. (a) This question should induce much discussion, since there are many possible answers. One is that, since the insane person lacks *mens rea*, a finding of guilt would mean that the act is a crime *per se*.

(b) The punishment, if any, is generally a question of community standards: the range of choices deemed to be neither too lax nor too severe.

8. (a) Entrapment. The question is whether Sidney initially had the necessary predisposition or whether his *mens rea* was induced by Lucy. Was Lucy's conduct the sort that would have caused an "innocent" man, one without predisposition toward solicitation, to do what Sidney did?

(b) There is no tort equivalent to solicitation. Even if Sidney's act were tortious, could Lucy or any other individual prove damages?

9. (a) Larceny.

(b) Burglary (and larceny).

(c) Armed robbery (larceny is part of the crime).

(d) The first two crimes involve the torts of trespass to real property and conversion. The third crime's tort equivalents are assault, battery (assuming Cory or the knife touched Vera), and conversion; intentional infliction of mental (emotional) distress may also be raised, although assault, battery, and conversion should be easier to prove and each is a basis for complete recovery of compensatory as well as punitive damages.

10. If Crass has rigged prices, then it and the other price-riggers have engaged in antitrust violations and unfair competition. Depending on other facts, this activity may constitute interference with contracts or prospective economic advantages.

Wally may have an action for abusive discharge against Brenda and Crass (the latter under *respondeat superior*).

Strikes are privileged conduct; hence, they do not constitute tortious interference with contracts or prospective economic advantages. However, Vera's act is probably an assault upon the strikebreakers who saw it and—with reason—believed that the shotgun was loaded.

Concerning the distribution of photographs showing Leo with several X-rated films, Crass is probably liable for invasion of privacy (public disclosure of private facts, intrusion upon a person's private life), and perhaps also liable for intentional infliction of mental distress. Of course, so long as the photographs truly show the movies in Leo's hand, defamation is negated on the grounds of truth.

Lastly, Leo's statements to the customers appear to be disparagement (trade libel). That Crass has provoked Leo's ire is no defense; his remedy is to sue Crass, not counter its torts with his own.

Note that the individuals at Crass who authorize or carry out a tort are liable for that tort just as the company is.

5
CONTRACTS: NATURE, CLASSIFICATION, AND FORMATION

KEY TERMS

contract a legally enforceable agreement, express or implied.

agreement a meeting of the minds.

consideration something of value that is given in exchange for a promise.

statute of limitations a statute setting forth the period during which a lawsuit must be brought after a right to sue arises.

NATURE OF CONTRACTS

WHAT IS A CONTRACT?

A **contract** is a legally enforceable agreement, express or implied. There are four essential elements of a valid contract:

1. Capacity of the parties.

2. Mutual agreement (assent) or meeting of the minds (a valid offer and acceptance).

3. Consideration (something of value given in exchange for a promise).

4. Legality of subject matter.

Just as law is a rule that society will enforce, so a contract is also an enforced rule of society. That the rule to be enforced is derived from voluntary agreements between individuals does not make it any less a rule, or any less enforceable. Once a contract has been made, that contract is as binding upon the parties as any statute or any other law, and one party cannot withdraw without additional agreement by the other party or parties.

Most people make a number of contracts during each day. Every cab ride, purchase of a grocery item, use of a soft drink machine, appointment with a doctor involves a contractual relationship. It does not matter that these contracts are oral, or are based on gestures or even on a course of conduct. Mere informality does not render a contract less binding.

As defined above, a contract is a legally enforceable agreement; an **agreement** is a meeting of the minds. Since courts and juries are not mind readers, the existence of this mental condition must be manifest in words, oral or written, or in actions. ("Verbal" is not a synonym for "oral"; *verbal* includes all words, written as well as oral.) The mental condition that forms the agreement should be distinguished from the words or actions giving evidence of the mental condition. Although we sometimes call a written document a "contract," the document is only evidence of the mental agreement that constitutes the actual contract.

HOW MAY INTENT BE DETERMINED?

Let's assume that the words used, the action taken, or both the words and the actions would convince a reasonable person, such as a member of a jury, that there is a meeting of the minds and hence a contract. But suppose that there is trouble determining precisely what the agreement is, that the *intent* is clouded by ambiguity, contradiction, or vagueness. How can an observer arrive at an understanding of the real agreement existing in the minds of the parties?

Basic Principle of Contract Interpretation

Determine the *intent* of the parties from words or actions taken as a whole, not from isolated words, actions, or events.

Certain commonsense rules may be used to resolve contradictions and uncertainties. Fine print, obscurely placed, is given less weight than large, boldface type; handwritten interlineations, especially if initialed, are strong evidence of firm intention. Formal documents, diligently executed, may yield to conduct of the parties if that conduct clearly shows a mutual intent contrary to the written document.

YOU SHOULD REMEMBER

The four essential elements of a contract are competent parties, mutual agreement, consideration, and legality.

Contracts arise out of agreements that are purely mental; hence a contract really exists in the mind. This mental condition is shown by actions, by oral or written words, and rarely, by silence or inaction.

In interpreting a contract, a court tries to determine the *intent* of the parties from words and actions considered in their entirety.

CLASSIFICATION OF CONTRACTS

Contracts can be classified in several different ways.

BY TYPE OF FORMATION: EXPRESS VERSUS IMPLIED

An **express contract** is stated in words, written or oral, or partly written and partly oral. The express contract is overtly, consciously, and specifically arrived at.

There are two types of implied contracts: those implied in fact and those implied in law.

The existence and the terms of an **implied-in-fact contract** are manifested by conduct, rather than words. The proof of the contract lies in the conduct of the parties; a reasonable person aware of this conduct, including words, if any, would infer that a contract exists.

An **implied-in-law** or **quasi contract** is created by operation of law (i.e., a court implies a contract) in order to avoid *unjust enrichment* of one party at the expense of another. *There is no agreement, no meeting of the minds;* one party has rendered a benefit to another under such circumstances that fairness and equity require compensation.

Example: *A Quasi Contract*

Stanley Samaritan, M.D., renders assistance to an unconscious patient. When the patient recovers, he receives a bill for these services.

Since the patient received and benefitted from the services, he may be required to pay on grounds of quasi contract.

The amount of compensation due under a quasi contract is the current market price (called *quantum meruit*, "as much as he/she earned"), not a special price or even the performer's usual rate. In the example above, Dr. Samaritan is entitled to the ordinary rate of pay of a general physician rendering these services, even if Samaritan is a specialist ordinarily receiving thousands of dollars for his work.

BY TYPE OF PERFORMANCE

• *BILATERAL VERSUS UNILATERAL*

A **bilateral contract** is based on an exchange of promises—a promise for a promise.

A **unilateral contract** involves a promise by one party and an act by the other. If, however, the person receiving the offer promises to act before doing so, the contract may become bilateral.

Example: A Unilateral Contract

If a homeowner offers a youngster $5.00 to mow her lawn, this is an offer to make a unilateral contract. The offer is a promise (to pay $5.00) in exchange for the performance of an act (mowing the lawn).

• *EXECUTED VERSUS EXECUTORY*

An **executed contract** is one that has been fully performed by both parties; all promises have been fulfilled.

In an **executory contract** something remains to be done by one or both parties.

BY ENFORCEABILITY: VALID VERSUS UNENFORCEABLE, VOID, AND VOIDABLE CONTRACTS

A **valid contract** meets all legal requirements and can be enforced by either party.

An **unenforceable contract** does not meet one or more legal requirements and cannot be enforced by either party. Examples are promises to make a gift (no consideration), promises made in jest (no contractual intent), agreements that fail to meet Statute of Frauds requirements (see pages 124–28), and past breaches of contract now beyond the statute of limitations.

A **void contract** has no validity and cannot be enforced by either party. Examples are illegal agreements made under threat of physical force.

A **voidable contract** is binding on only one of the parties. The other party has the option to withdraw from the contract or enforce it. Examples are contracts made by minors and contracts made under mental duress.

YOU SHOULD REMEMBER

Contracts may be classified by type of formation (express or implied), performance (unilateral or bilateral, executed or executory), or enforceability (valid or unenforceable, void, or voidable).

NEGOTIATION

The word "negotiation" is derived from the Latin *negotium*, meaning "business" or, literally, "the absence of leisure." Since a contract (except a quasi contract) arises out of an agreement, and an agreement is a meeting of the minds, it is clear that most minds meet through the transaction of business, or through **negotiation.**

Step-by-Step Formation of an Agreement Between Two Parties

1. Negotiations begin with discussion or exchange of comments to determine mutual interest in making a deal.

2. Mutual interest is clarified and refined in terms of both parties' basic objectives. These objectives concern such things as description of goods to be sold, work to be performed, and price for goods or services.

3. The subject of the contract is defined, and a price is agreed upon.

4. The deal is now worked out in detail (e.g., cash or check, delivery tomorrow or next week, guarantees, fine points such as color and fabric).

5. The contract is formally accepted—a written agreement is prepared and executed, or the parties shake hands or otherwise express an intention to be bound.

Implied contracts are far more informal in their negotiation than are express contracts. Implied contracts may arise entirely from actions, but these actions must be so clear that no reasonable person (member of a jury, for example) would doubt the existence of a meeting of the minds. In the case of an implied contract, the performer is entitled to receive his/her current rate of pay for services rendered, since it is implied that the other party should have expected to pay that price. Under a quasi contract, as mentioned previously, the compensation is *quantum meruit*, the current market rate.

Express contracts are usually formal; certainly the fact that the contract exists is more formally expressed.

The express contract is often revealed through *words of contract*: "agree," "agreement," "promise," "offer," "accept," or even the very word "contract."

Most legal writers treat the negotiation of an express contract as though it invariably transpires through a formal offer and the acceptance of that offer. As a matter of fact, however, it may be difficult to say which party extends the offer (is the *offeror*) and which accepts the offer (is the *offeree*).

Example: Negotiation as Flirtation

Brown: "I like your car."
Jones: "Yes, Smith offered me $5,000 for it last week."
Brown: "That sounds like a good price. You should have sold it."
Jones: "I would not take less than $7,000."
Brown: "I would give you $6,000."
Jones: "It's yours for $6,200."
Brown: "Sold."

If the transaction is concluded at this point, most courts would construe the agreement as an express contract, *even without contract words*. In reality, it makes no legal difference that the offer and acceptance are not formally stated, or that the offeror or offeree cannot be identified or separated.

The Uniform Commercial Code defines an "agreement" as the bargain of the parties. This bargain is *always* derived from mutual assent, proved by outward actions or by spoken or written words. Subjective intent, not manifested by words or action, counts for little or nothing in a court of law.

YOU SHOULD REMEMBER

Most contracts are reached through negotiation, which may be formal or informal. Once there is a meeting of the minds on the fundamentals (an agreement), the parties are bound and neither party may withdraw without consent of the other.

FORMING A CONTRACT

Each of the four essential requirements—capacity of the parties, mutual agreement or assent, consideration, and legality—must be met in the formation of a valid contract.

CAPACITY OF THE PARTIES

Under the law, only a person who is legally competent has the power to make a binding contract and can be held to any promises contained therein. Persons who may be considered to be legally incompetent include minors, insane persons, and, sometimes under specified circumstances, intoxicated persons. This subject is discussed in detail in Chapter 7.

MUTUAL AGREEMENT (ASSENT): THE OFFER AND THE ACCEPTANCE

The mutual assent of the parties to a contract is manifested in two legal concepts, the offer and the acceptance.

• *THE OFFER*

The simplest way to form an express contract begins with a formal **offer**. This offer may be transmitted by acts or words, spoken or written, directly to the offeree, or in conversation, through the mails, by wire, by messenger, or through any medium whatsoever.

Requirements of an Offer

1. It must indicate a clear *intent* to make a contract.

2. It must be sufficiently *definite* so that a court can determine the actual intent of the parties.

3. It must be *communicated* to the other party.

The offer should contain the fundamental ingredients of the contract; then acceptance by the offeree will bind the deal. In communicating the offer, use of the word "offer" helps, but is not necessary, to show intent to make a contract. Even if the word "offer" is used, circumstances, actions, or other words may indicate that there is no real intent to enter into a valid contract. "Offers" made in obvious jest or under great emotional stress, for example, do not possess the requisite intent.

WHEN IS AN ADVERTISEMENT AN "OFFER"?

General advertisements, catalogs, brochures, and announcements are usually *not* offers because:

(a) they are not sufficiently definite,

(b) they are not communicated to a specific person or persons, *or*

(c) the circumstances of publication indicate lack of contractual intent.

Advertisements are usually considered to be "invitations to deal," that is, invitations to the public to make offers to the advertiser.

In the following circumstances, however, an advertisement *can* be construed to be an offer: *it is so specific to an identified or identifiable person or group* that contractual intent can be inferred.

Example: *An Advertisement Construed to Be an Offer*

A store places an ad in a newspaper that reads: "The first person in our store on Washington's Birthday will receive $100 toward the purchase of an appliance."

Courts would probably hold this to be an offer because it is addressed to an identifiable individual, not the general public. Therefore the first person in the store on the holiday named would be entitled to receive $100 toward his/her appliance.

HOW DEFINITE MUST THE OFFER BE?

Although an offer must state the essential terms of the proposed contract, modern common law, as well as the Uniform Commercial Code, assumes that many unstated terms may be understood by the parties, may be implied, or may be matters of common sense. With respect to the sale of goods, Article 2 of the Uniform Commercial Code specifically provides that one or more terms (including even the proposed price) may be left open so long as there is a clear intention to make a contract. Under the present common law also, if the offeror offers to sell his hat for $20, it is implied, or understood, (a) that the price is payable in cash, and (b) that delivery is to occur, and payment to be made, with reasonable promptness.

HOW LONG DOES AN OFFER LAST?

If an offer does not specify a period of time during which it is to remain open, it expires after the passage of a reasonable time. What constitutes a reasonable time depends on the implied intention of the offeror as shown by the property or goods offered, customs of the trade or business, and the like. An offer to sell or buy perishable goods, such as fresh fruit or vegetables, or goods having an unstable or fluctuating market, such as stock or other securities, is generally held not to remain open as long as an offer to sell or buy real estate, a far more stable item.

When the time during which the offer is to remain open is specified, that time then becomes the expiration date. An offer may expire at an earlier time than stated, however, because of *rejection, counteroffer*, or the *death* or *incompetency* of either offeror or offeree.

WHEN CAN AN OFFER BE REVOKED?

Fundamental Principle of Contract Law

An offer may be withdrawn at any time before it is accepted.

An offer is like an outstretched hand—it may be pulled back at any time before it is clasped by the outstretched hand of the offeree. Even a firm offer, that is, one expressly stated to remain open for a specified time, may generally be withdrawn. Thus a person who makes a firm offer to sell his hat for $20 and promises to leave the offer open for one week may withdraw the offer immediately, or any time before acceptance. If not accepted within one week, the offer will have expired.

There are three exceptions to the easy right to withdrawal.

Option contracts: The **option contract** (usually referred to as an "option") commits the offeror to keep his/her offer open in return for a specified price. In other words, the offeror makes a contract to hold the offer open for some specified period, and is paid a consideration for this agreement.

Example: An Option Contract

An offeror offers to sell a farm for $100,000, agrees to hold this offer open for 7 days, and is paid $100 for this agreement to be held open.

In this example, if the offeror withdraws the offer by selling the farm to some other person within the 7-day period, this would be a breach of contract. The offeree (also called the "optionee") has no obligation to buy; he has paid $100 for the right to accept the offer within the 7-day period. If he does not buy, his $100 is not refunded; if he does buy, the $100 is not credited to the purchase price unless the option contract expressly so provides.

An option is an excellent legal device to provide the opportunity to think a proposition over, investigate a deal, or raise money to go through with the deal.

Unilateral contracts: Since a unilateral contract depends on the performance of an act by the offeree, some courts consider that the offer can be revoked unless there has been substantial performance. According to this view, in the example on page 84, the homeowner could revoke the contract even though the youngster had already mowed half the lawn. Other courts, however, hold that the offer cannot be revoked once the offeree has clearly commenced to perform; the commencement is treated as consideration. (See further on page 91.)

The Uniform Commercial Code exception: Section 2-205 of the Uniform Commercial Code provides that a merchant's firm *written offer* to buy or sell goods cannot be revoked during the term specified in the offer, or, if no time is specified, for a reasonable period (but in either case the period of irrevocability shall not exceed 3 months).

YOU SHOULD REMEMBER

An offer must meet three requirements: it must be *communicated*, it must indicate a clear *intent* to make a contract, and it must be *definite*. However, many terms may be left unstated or may be implied or understood by the parties.

An advertisement is not an offer unless it is addressed specifically to an identified or identifiable person or group.

An offer lasts for the period of time stated or, if no time is stated, for a reasonable time. It may also expire by reason of rejection, counteroffer, or the death or incompetency of one of the parties.

Generally, an offer may be withdrawn at any time before it is accepted. There are three exceptions: option contracts, the UCC exception stated in Section 2-205, and, according to some courts, unilateral contracts if clear commencement to perform has occurred.

• *THE ACCEPTANCE*

Acceptance of the offer clinches the contract. However, the acceptance must meet certain standards.

First, the acceptance must be *clear* and *unqualified*; an "acceptance" that modifies the offer or attempts to get a better deal is treated in the law as a **counteroffer,** that is, a rejection of the original offer and the making of a new offer. Thus, if an offeror offers to sell his hat for $20, and the offeree says, "I can't pay $20, but I will give you $12," the offeree becomes the offeror for $12. If the original offeror rejects the $12 offer, the original offer is "dead" and cannot be revived by the original offeree.

Second, the offeree *must accept in any manner required by the offer.* If the offer states, "I must have your answer by 1 P.M. on December 1," then failure to have the answer in the hands of the offeror by that time is fatal to the contract.

HOW MAY AN ACCEPTANCE BE TRANSMITTED?

Prior to the Uniform Commercial Code, the common law gave special status to acceptance by the same medium as was used to transmit the offer. Thus, if the offer was mailed, the acceptance was good upon being *placed* with the mail carrier or in the post office—effective, as a matter of fact, more speedily than if made by wire, in which case the acceptance had to be received to bind the contract. According to UCC 2-206(1)(a), however, acceptance in any manner or by any medium, so long as reasonable and meeting the requirements of the offer (if any), is as effective as any other method.

WHAT CONSTITUTES ACCEPTANCE OF A UNILATERAL OFFER?

We have defined a unilateral contract as a promise in exchange for an act. Thus an order for 100,000 steel widgets for a price of $100,000 is unilateral: upon delivery of the widgets the contract will have been made. Under UCC 2-206(1)(b), an offer to buy goods to be shipped may be accepted either by performance (shipment of the goods) *or by a promise to act;* the latter effectively converts a unilateral offer to a *bilateral* contract, something the common law would not permit.

Since some courts, as well as the Uniform Commercial Code, Section 2-206(2), take the view that failure by the offeree to notify the offeror of acceptance of the order or offer gives the offeror the right to withdraw, good business dictates that the offeree of a unilateral offer transmit an acceptance *before commencing to act*, particularly when fulfillment of the contract will be expensive and laborious. Equitable principles of fair play may operate in many courts to favor an innocent party who has acted in good faith in reliance upon the unilateral offer and has clearly *begun* to do the requested act before the offer was withdrawn. Of course, substantially performing or completing the requested act constitutes acceptance in all courts.

DOES SILENCE CONSTITUTE ACCEPTANCE?

> Generally, silence is not acceptance, nor can the offeror impose a duty upon the offeree to speak.

"If I do not hear from you, I will assume that you have accepted my offer" does not operate to impose a duty of any kind on the offeree. Indeed, if such a statement, in writing or otherwise, accompanies goods that have not been ordered, no duty arises to pay, even if the goods are not returned and are consumed. There is no implied-in-fact contract because the circumstances do not give rise to the inference of an agreement; there is no quasi contract because there is no unjust enrichment.

There are, however, certain circumstances under which silence may give rise to acceptance.

1. If the offeror observes the offeree acting in response to the offer, and says nothing, there may be a contract.

2. The parties may mutually agree that silence will constitute acceptance by the recipient of goods that are shipped to him/her (record and book clubs use this approach).

3. If the parties, by previous dealings, have considered silence to be acceptance, the silent party must reject the offer if he/she wishes to change the customary practice.

Good business (if not good law) indicates that a written rejection should be sent to the offeror when silence could be reasonably considered ambiguous or the outcome doubtful.

YOU SHOULD REMEMBER

The acceptance of an offer should be clear and unconditional. A conditional acceptance is treated as a counteroffer, and is a new offer and, hence, a rejection.

Some courts hold that a unilateral offer is accepted by a clear commencement to perform the act requested. Since the offeror may withdraw his/her offer (and promise), however, the offeree should confirm acceptance and thereby bind the contract as a bilateral contract.

Silence does not constitute acceptance unless (1) the offeror, observing the offeree acting in response to the offer, says nothing; (2) the parties mutually agree that silence means acceptance; or (3) in previous dealings, the parties have considered silence to be acceptance.

• *LACK OF MUTUAL ASSENT*

Mutual assent may be lacking for a variety of reasons, including mistake, misrepresentation, duress, and undue influence. This topic is discussed in detail in Chapter 6.

CONSIDERATION

Consideration is something of value that is given in exchange for a promise. It is based on the idea of *quid pro quo* ("something for something"). In most contracts, consideration is required for enforceability.

It is not necessary that the thing promised be affirmative; it may be refraining from acting or promising not to act. A promise made to give $1,000 to a friend if she does not smoke (a negative unilateral contract) is mutual and binding.

A contract cannot be one-sided; it exists only if there is a promise or an action (or nonaction) on each side.

• *WHAT IS ADEQUATE CONSIDERATION?*

Usually a court will not evaluate the adequacy of consideration. In other words, if two parties make a deal, it will not be struck down because the court feels that the consideration is inadequate or unequal. Indeed, if a person contracts to buy a pencil or a piece of ordinary paper for $500, the agreement is enforceable, provided, of course, that there is intent to make a contract, the parties are competent, and there is no fraud or violation of other contract principles.

However, the agreement to pay a small amount of money in return for a larger amount of money is *not* enforceable; this is merely an agreement to make a gift of the difference. Thus, if a person were to agree to accept $10 for a $100 debt immediately due, the agreement would be to make a gift of $90. Usually a promise to make a gift is not consideration.

Suppose, however, that a property owner agrees to pay a contractor $150,000 to build a house in accordance with specifications. Suppose further that a dispute arises over the price after an agreement that the contract is to be modified by certain changes. The owner pays $145,000 "as full payment," which the contractor accepts. If there had been no dispute, the contractor could recover the remaining $5,000 since he received no consideration for this "gift"; here, however, since for $5,000 the owner gave up her disputed claim, the contract is considered real, and the benefits mutual.

WHEN DOES CONSIDERATION EXIST?

• *ILLUSORY PROMISES*

The mutual promises must be real. An *illusory promise* is not an actual promise; the promiser offers to do something only if he/she "wishes" or "needs" to.

Example: Illusory Promises

An employment agreement whereby the employee agrees to work for one year at a salary of $25,000, provided the employer has need of her services, is not a contract because the employer has no real obligation.

Agreements to buy all of a person's requirements, or to sell all of one's output, of a commodity may be illusory if no requirement or output has been established. Thus, if a homeowner heats his house with gas and expects to convert to fuel oil, the agreement to buy all of his fuel oil requirements from a particular supplier may be considered illusory, since no requirement for fuel oil has been established.

• *DOING WHAT ONE IS BOUND TO DO*

An agreement to do one's duty is not consideration. If a person already has a contract, an additional agreement to perform this same contract is lacking in consideration. An airline pilot who promises to land the plane safely for a frightened passenger who offers him $1,000 cannot claim the reward; he is already contractually obligated to land the plane safely. For the same reason, a sheriff is usually not entitled to a reward for capturing a wanted criminal—he is merely doing his duty, for which he is being paid.

• *MORAL OBLIGATION*

A moral obligation (what a person ought to do) has no *legal* substance; it is not measurable and not commercial. Under this heading are agreements to pay the obligations of others or agreements to provide for relatives. In addition, love and affection, as such, will not support a contract, although they be of the highest moral nature.

There is no consideration in such cases.

• *PAST CONSIDERATION*

Past consideration is something that was performed without expectation of obtaining something in return from the other party. If the latter should afterward promise some compensation for the benefit received, this promise would not be valid since it was not bargained for in the current transaction.

Example: Past Consideration

Susanna Swimmer rescues drowning Larry Landlubber, who thereupon promises to give Susanna $500 for her courageous act. Larry's promise is not contractually binding, however, since the act for which it was made—Susanna's rescue of Larry—has already been completed.

• *STATUTE OF LIMITATIONS*

Sometimes a contract is barred (no longer subject to legal action) by the statute of limitations. Periods of limitations vary from state to state but generally run from 3 to 6 years, except for sales contracts under the Uniform Commercial Code (4 years). An agreement to pay made years later, after the original obligation to pay is no longer binding, results, however, in a valid contract. No new consideration is needed; the old consideration is revived by the new promise to pay. Thus the law has arbitrarily created an exception to the "illusion" principle since concepts of fair play and equity do not favor the statute.

• *REQUIREMENTS AND OUTPUT CONTRACTS*

Consideration is found by the courts in rather vague contracts calling for the purchase of one's requirements or for the sale of a manufacturer's output. Frequently, a manufacturer will agree to buy all of his requirements for a material from a specified source, or he may agree to sell all of his output of a certain product to a single customer. Even though the quantity to be bought or sold is not specified, these contracts are good under modern case law, as well as under the Uniform Commercial Code, unless one side acts in bad faith or attempts to take advantage of the other by padding or understating the requirements or output.

Requirements and output contracts should be accompanied by an estimate of the quantities to be bought or sold. In most cases the facility buying or selling should have a record of needs or production so that contractual intent can be ascertained in the event of a dispute. If there is no such record, the contract could be "illusory," that is, no obligation to buy or sell could be demonstrated.

• *PROMISSORY ESTOPPEL*

Consideration may also be found where there is total reliance on the promise of another. This reliance gives rise to estoppel, which is a holdover from equity principles and appears in modern law in a number of different contexts. The word generally describes a situation in which a person, by reason of his/her actions, cannot assert certain legal defenses that are in contradiction of these actions.

Promissory estoppel occurs when a promise is made without any consideration, but the promisee, relying upon the gratuitous promise, takes certain action, or fails to take action, to his detriment. It is not sufficient that the gratuitous promise be made carelessly or thoughtlessly; the promisor should know, or reasonably expect, that the promisee will act in reliance. Unjustified reliance on a promise does not give rise to promissory estoppel.

Example: Promissory Estoppel

The promise to make a charitable contribution to a church, followed by expenditures or actions taken by the church in reliance upon the promise, would create a binding contract. Reliance should be expected and is surely reasonable, even though this simple promise to make a gift would ordinarily be unenforceable as lacking consideration.

YOU SHOULD REMEMBER

Consideration means "something for something"—one party promises to do something, or refrain from doing it, and the other party promises to give something of value in return.

The mutual promises must be real, not illusory.

A promise to do what one is already bound to do (one's duty) or to carry out a moral obligation is not consideration.

Usually the court is not concerned with the adequacy of consideration. An exception occurs when a small amount of money is given for a larger amount.

Past consideration is something that was done without expectation of receiving something in return. A subsequent promise of compensation for a benefit received in the past is not binding.

Promissory estoppel, a holdover from equity law, requires that a person who has made a gratuitous promise be held to it when the promisee, to his/her detriment, justifiably relied upon the promise.

LEGALITY OF SUBJECT MATTER

Contracts that are in violation of common or statutory law or are against public policy are generally held to be illegal. This topic is discussed in Chapter 7.

THE SEAL

Under the early English common law consideration was not required for a contract. To be binding, a contract had to be in writing and under **seal**. The seal was placed on the contract in heated wax, either on the signature or at the place of execution. Later, as wax seals fell into disuse, the word "Seal," *Locus Sigilli* (Place of the Seal), or the abbreviation "L.S." was substituted. Such "sealed" contracts did not require consideration, and the laws of many states extended the period of limitations for these agreements. Most states, as well as the Uniform Commercial Code, have now abolished the seal both as to consideration and extension of limitations, although a notary seal, corporate seal, or personal seal (including "Seal" and "L.S.") is still required for certain formal documents (e.g., deeds to real estate).

KNOW THE CONCEPTS

DO YOU KNOW THE BASICS?

1. In what sense is it incorrect to refer to a written document as a contract?
2. How would you go about proving (a) an express contract, (b) an implied-in-fact contract, (c) a quasi contract?
3. Why is a lawsuit based on an implied contract more likely to produce greater damages and a larger verdict than one based on a quasi contract?
4. How can a unilateral offeree convert the contract into a bilateral contract? When should he/she do so?
5. When is an advertisement an offer?
6. What are the three exceptions to the rule that an offer can be withdrawn at any time before it is accepted?
7. What is the effect of a conditional acceptance?
8. What is the meaning of the term "adequacy of consideration"?
9. What is the essential element of "consideration"?
10. What is the consideration for the promise in a unilateral contract?

TERMS FOR STUDY

acceptance	option contract
agreement	past consideration
bilateral contract	promissory estoppel
consideration	quasi contract
contract	seal
counteroffer	statute of limitations
executed contract	unenforceable contract
executory contract	unilateral contract
express contract	valid contract
implied-in-fact contract	void contract
negotiation	voidable contract
offer	

PRACTICAL APPLICATION

1. You enter an expensive restaurant and are seated by the hostess. A waiter brings you plates, knives and forks, napkins and other "setups" for dinner, including bread and butter, which you partly consume. When you read the menu, you realize that the prices far exceed what you can afford, and you then make it clear that you do not intend to order a meal. What kind of contract (obligation) do you have, if any?

2. In Problem 1, you read the menu and place an order. Nothing is said about agreement to pay. Is there a contract?

3. In Problem 1, there is fine print at the bottom of the menu: "15% gratuity, $25.00 cover charge." What is the effect, assuming that you order dinner but do not see the fine print?

4. You receive a letter from the General Moose Company containing an offer and concluding: "... and we will pay you for your services $50,000 for your first year." You respond by saying, "I like your offer, and would accept for $55,000." You hear nothing in response, so after 10 days you write and say, "I accept your offer of $50,000." Is there a contract? Suppose you hear nothing in response to this second letter. What is the result?

5. If a farmer agrees, in writing, to pay his wife $100 a month to keep farm accounts and perform farm chores "as you have always done," is this an enforceable contract?

ANSWERS

KNOW THE CONCEPTS

1. A contract is a mental condition expressed in a written document. The written document is only evidence of the mental condition.

2. (a) An express contract should be easy to prove since it is stated in words and generally in contract language.

   (b) An implied-in-fact contract is implied by the facts of the case. These facts include proof of the circumstances, actions of the parties, and their words, if any. All of these together should lead a "reasonable person" to believe that there was an agreement.

   (c) A quasi, or implied-in-law, contract involves proof of unjust enrichment, that is, proof of a benefit to an individual under circumstances requiring payment for the benefit. A quasi contract generally does not include benefits imposed upon someone who may or may not want them.

3. The implied contract is for the *usual charge* for services rendered, whereas the quasi contract is for the *going price* for such services in the marketplace. On the assumption that usual charges are higher than those in the marketplace, the implied contract is preferable.

4. If the offer is to buy goods that are to be shipped, the unilateral offeree can say, "I accept your offer and hereby agree to perform the requested services." This should be done before the offeree expends money and effort.

5. An advertisement is an offer only when definite and made very specifically to an identifiable person or groups of persons.

6. The option contract, the unilateral contract after substantial performance has taken place, and the UCC exception relating to a merchant's firm agreement to hold his offer open for the period specified or, if no time is specified, for a reasonable period (in either case, no more than 3 months).

7. A conditional acceptance is a counteroffer and a rejection of the original offer.

8. "Adequacy of consideration" relates to the value of the consideration or to its weight when compared with the consideration offered by the other party to the contract. Ordinarily, courts do not test the value or weight of consideration.

9. All contracts require "something for something," that is, a contract cannot be a "one-way street." There must be consideration on both sides.

10. In a unilateral contract, the consideration for the promise is the performance of the requested action.

PRACTICAL APPLICATION

1. There is a quasi contract for the food that you have consumed; the value of this food should be a subject of some discussion. Also, it could be argued that there is an implied unilateral contract for the price of a dinner, since you may have entered the restaurant knowing the kind of establishment it purported to be. However, a unilateral offer can be withdrawn before it is accepted if no substantial performance has occurred. Some courts, however, hold that clear commencement to perform constitutes acceptance.

2. Yes. Ordering food from the menu creates an implied-in-fact contract to pay the menu price.

3. In case of conflict between fine print and express contract language that contradicts the fine print, the fine print would be ignored. In this case the fine print is uncontradicted and becomes part of the contract. If the fine print is illegible or hidden in some manner, it could be argued that it is not part of the agreement and therefore not a part of the contract obligation. The fact that you did not see the fine print does not excuse your obligation if a "reasonable man" would have seen it.

4. Your response would probably be viewed as a counteroffer and a rejection of the General Moose offer. Consequently, your subsequent letter attempting to accept the rejected offer does not create a contract for the job in the $50,000 offer. However, failure of the original offeror to respond may lead a reasonable person to believe that General Moose has accepted the second reply. Usually, silence is not an acceptance, but there are exceptions to this rule, one of which relates to circumstances creating a duty to speak. Such a duty may arise when the first party opened the transaction by the original offer, and General Moose should now make some kind of response. This question should provoke discussion both pro and con.

5. If a person agrees to do what she already has a duty to do, there is no consideration for the agreement. Whether the wife has a duty to keep accounts and perform chores is the central question in this case. The fact that she has always done so without being paid, or as part of her wifely responsibilities, suggests that such a duty exists, and the new contract is not enforceable.

6 REALITY OF THE CONTRACT: DID THE MINDS REALLY MEET?

KEY TERMS

material mistake a mistake that goes to the very heart of the agreement.

fraud intentional misrepresentation of a material fact, made knowingly, with intent to defraud, that is justifiably relied upon by the other party and causes injury to him/her

undue influence taking advantage of another by reason of a position of trust in a close or confidential relationship

duress coercion, either physical or mental, that deprives a person of free will

unconscionability gross unfairness brought about by the superior position of one of the parties to the contract

As explained in Chapter 5, a contract is a legally enforceable meeting of the minds—a mental condition. This mental condition is manifested by words—oral or written—by actions, or by both words and actions. This chapter is concerned with situations where there is not really an agreement, even though words or actions seem to prove otherwise.

A meeting of the minds—mutual assent or agreement—is a necessary element of a contract. Without it, the contract may be void or voidable.

There are six reasons why mutual assent may be lacking: mistake, fraud, innocent misrepresentation, undue influence, duress, and unconscionability.

Theatre Authority, Inc.

16 EAST 42ND STREET, SUITE 202
NEW YORK, N.Y. 10017-6907
TEL: (212) 682-4215
FAX: (212) 682-8407

HELEN LEAHY
Executive Director

President
JANE POWELL

1st Vice President
JOHN H. SUCKE
Screen Actors Guild

2nd Vice President
TERRY WAXMAN
American Federation of
Television and Radio Artists

3rd Vice President
ROBERT J. BRUCE
Actors' Equity Association

4th Vice President
ROD McKUEN
American Guild of Variety Artists

Recording Secretary
THOMAS H. JAMERSON
American Guild of Musical Artists

Treasurer
JOAN GREENSPAN
Screen Actors Guild

Representative
FRANCES GAAR
American Guild of Variety Artists

MEMBER ORGANIZATIONS
Actors' Equity Association
Actors' Fund of America
American Federation of
Television and Radio Artists
American Guild of Musical Artists

October 25, 1995

Ms. Connie Simmons
Senior Vice President
Business Affairs
TV Food Network
New York, Avenue of the Americas, 31st floor
New York, NY 10036

Dear Connie:

Attached hereto is the Theatre Authority clearance agreement granting permission for members of our various unions to participate in the Nov. 19, 1995 cablethon, scheduled to emanate from your studio in New York City, New York, and airing live from Washington, D.C., and Los Angeles, California.

We understand Peter Kaminsky i

MISTAKE

> The most frequent circumstance barring a real meeting of the minds is mistake.

MATERIAL OR INCIDENTAL?

> A mistake concerning an incidental or trivial detail or insignificant matter will not affect the fact of agreement so long as there *is* agreement on the basic or material features of the transaction.

What is "incidental" or "trivial," and what is "material" or "basic"?

A basic or **material mistake** generally goes right to the heart of the matter; indeed it usually pertains to the existence or nature of the subject matter. If, for example, the parties agree that one will sell and the other buy a horse that, unknown to them, has died, the mistake is material and there is no contract.

In the preceding example, the parties believe that they know the facts—there is a live horse to be bought and sold—but both parties are mistaken. However, if the facts are not known *and* both buyer and seller take their chances, each believing that he/she has some advantage, there will be a contract. Purchase of land or chattels that prove to be more valuable, or less valuable, than anticipated by either party fall within this category. Such a contract is based, not on a common fallacy but on judgments about value. Such differing judgments and opinions about the bargain are present in practically all contracts, are considered incidental mistakes, and do not affect the validity of the contract.

MUTUAL OR UNILATERAL?

In general, there is no binding contract if a material mistake or fallacy is **mutual**. The contract is binding, however, if only one party is mistaken, that is, if the mistake is **unilateral**, except when the other party knows, or should have known, of the mistake.

Basic Philosophy of the Unilateral Mistake Principle

A person should not be allowed to benefit from his/her own ignorance or carelessness.

Persons who carelessly fail to read what they sign, fail to observe defects that are readily apparent, or fail to examine that which is displayed before them should not be able to claim lack of agreement in order to abandon contracts they do not like. In other words, a unilateral mistake usually does not provide the mistaken party with grounds for rescinding the contract.

But this result does not apply if the nonmistaken party knows of or suspects the mistake. Thus, if the buyer believes that a property contains 100 acres when in reality it contains only 65 acres, the seller should correct the buyer's misapprehension, if the seller is aware of it, even though the buyer might be able to discover the exact acreage without assistance from the seller. In such a case of *palpable unilateral mistake*, the contract may be voidable.

In the earlier common law, the principle of *caveat emptor* ("let the buyer beware") required buyers to inspect fully and carefully. Failure to do so was at their peril. Modern law, influenced by the equity concepts of fairness and the consumer-friendly provisions of the UCC, is more generous to unobservant or careless buyers and imposes on sellers a higher duty of speaking out. Indeed, it is sometimes argued that the law now enforces *caveat venditor* ("let the seller beware"). Mere failure by the seller to speak, in cases where he should have spoken, may permit the negligent, unobservant buyer to withdraw from the contract.

An agreement made as a result of a mutual mistake regarding a material fact can be made void by either party in the equitable action of **rescission** (cancellation). In this action, the supposed contract is rescinded, and the parties are restored to the respective positions existing before the agreement was formed, that is, any monies paid are returned and any goods delivered are restored to the original owner. Thus we say that all such contracts are *voidable*—they can be made void by the action of rescission.

Example: Rescission Due to Mutual Mistake of Fact

Sheila Steinway agrees to sell a painting generally thought to be a genuine Rembrandt to Angus Artlover for $2 million. Later a panel of experts determines at the painting was done by a pupil of Rembrandt, not by the master himself. ' contract is voidable because of a mutual mistake of fact.

YOU SHOULD REMEMBER

A material mistake usually pertains to a fact, not to a matter of value or opinion.

A voidable contract may be cancelled (is voidable) by the legal action of rescission. Unless such action is taken, however, the contract remains in effect.

In general, mutual mistake of a material fact is grounds to cancel a contract.

Unilateral mistake by one party, however, is not grounds for cancellation unless the other party knew about the mistake and said nothing.

FRAUD

If a person enters into a contract as a result of the **intentional misrepresentation** or deceit of the other party to the contract, there is no meeting of the minds, no agreement, and hence no legal obligation. In most cases of mistake, both parties are innocent of wrongdoing—the minds simply did not meet. In the case of **fraud**, however, the minds not only do not meet, but one party is guilty of deceptive, dishonest conduct.

REQUIREMENTS FOR A FINDING OF FRAUD

Five Requirements for a Finding of Fraud

(all five must be present)

(1) Misrepresentation of a *material fact*,
(2) made *knowingly*,
(3) with *intent to defraud*,
(4) justifiably *relied upon*,
(5) *causing injury* to the other party.

• *MISREPRESENTATION OF A MATERIAL FACT*

> To prove a case of fraud, the misrepresentation must concern a fact, and a fact that is *material.*

Examples: Misrepresentations of Material Facts

1. A painting is by a specified artist.
2. An air conditioner will adequately cool a certain-size room.
3. An automobile will pass state inspection.
4. Turkey poults are healthy and free from disease.

> Matters pertaining to *value* and matters asserted as *opinion* are generally not factual in nature and are not grounds for fraud.

As with simple mistake, the parties to a contract usually have different perceptions of the value of the chattel, land, or other object being bought or sold. Moreover, it is customary for the seller to "huff and puff" and to exaggerate the value of his/her goods, and many buyers, in turn, seek to diminish or deprecate the value of the goods in order to lower the price. Opinions are, of course, statements of judgment, not of fact, and do not constitute grounds for fraud.

There is, however, one major exception to this principle: an "opinion" by an expert—for example, a physician, a lawyer, an engineer, a financial advisor—or one claiming to be an expert may be the basis for fraud. The law treats the expert as a master of the facts; his/her judgments are to be relied on as skilled—and factual.

• *MADE KNOWINGLY*

The party misrepresenting the material fact must do so knowingly.

> **Scienter** is the legal word for "guilty knowledge."
> Nonlawyers frequently believe that they can claim ignorance of the falsity of a statement and thus defeat a claim for fraud. However, *scienter* goes beyond actual knowledge—it includes careless indifference to the truth, a lack of belief by the declarer in his/her statements. Whether *scienter* is present is a question for a properly instructed jury, and juries can be cynical about persons who "unintentionally" lie to gain an advantage.

• *WITH INTENT TO DEFRAUD*

The misrepresentation of a material fact must be made with intent to defraud. Obviously, every defrauding party will claim he/she had no intention to deceive, that the falsehood was innocent and not willful. *Unfortunately for such persons, the intent to defraud is presumed if the false statement is made knowingly—if* scienter *is present.*

• *JUSTIFIABLY RELIED UPON*

The party to whom the misrepresentation was made must rely on it. This requirement is of the greatest importance. *If the seller lies, knowingly and intentionally, and the buyer recognizes* (or should recognize) *the lie, but buys anyway, there is no fraud.* Thus, if the salesman says, "This pesticide will kill beetles on roses," but the container has a clear statement that the product will kill aphids and slugs but not beetles, an argument can be made that there is no reliance. (Some recent cases, however, have held that reliance is justified under these circumstances, and hence there may be fraud.)

• *CAUSING INJURY TO THE OTHER PARTY*

The party to whom the misrepresentation was made must have suffered injury as a result. Frequently, however, the false statement or concealment does not cause injury. In this case, there is no fraud.

Example: *Misrepresentation That Does Not Cause Injury*

Sam, the seller, tells Bill, the buyer, that Sam is the original and only owner of the 1985 Mustang Bill is purchasing. In fact, Sam bought the Mustang from his next-door neighbor.

In this case the car is in excellent condition, and there is doubt that any injury will result from the falsehood. Hence, there would be no basis for a claim of fraud.

As a matter of fact, many misrepresentations, although intentional and deceptive, are not bases of fraud, particularly if they pertain to other matters than the *use* intended of the goods by the buyer.

CONSEQUENCES OF FRAUD

In the case of fraud, the defrauded party can rescind the contract. However, he/she has an alternative remedy: to affirm the contract and bring an action in tort to recover damages for the deceit. For example, if a seller misrepresents the expired mileage of a second-hand automobile by turning back the odometer, the buyer may rescind the contract. Alternatively, she may keep the automobile and recover damages for the lessened value of the automobile.

Fraud is a grave offense in the eyes of the law. In any case where it can be proved, the victim has a real advantage over the perpetrator. Our analysis of business torts and crimes (Chapter 4) pointed out that not only is fraud a tort, it is also a crime. If the fraud is particularly aggravated, malicious, or oppressive, it can give rise to punitive damages (see Chapter 9).

YOU SHOULD REMEMBER

Fraud is intentional misrepresentation of a material fact, made knowingly, with intent to defraud, that is justifiably relied upon by the other party and causes injury to him/her.

A defrauded party has two choices: (1) rescind the contract and get back any consideration paid, or (2) retain the goods or value obtained and sue in tort for damages (the lessened value because of the fraud).

INNOCENT (NONFRAUDULENT) MISREPRESENTATION

Misrepresentation that lacks element 2 (knowing) and element 3 (intent to defraud) will result in a contract *voidable* by the innocent party.

Unlike fraud, however, **innocent misrepresentation** is not a tort and does not give rise to a claim for damages. The only remedy available to the plaintiff is rescission of the contract.

Example: *Innocent Misrepresentation*

Alice bought a rug for $1,000 at auction and was given a certificate stating that the rug was a genuine Aubusson. Shortly thereafter, Alice sold the rug, as an Aubusson, to Betty, whose insurance agent called in an appraiser. The expert pronounced the rug a fake worth at most $200.

Since Alice had been assured that the rug was an Aubusson and had innocently misrepresented it as such, with no intent to defraud, Betty could not win damages. The contract, however, could be rescinded; Betty returned the rug and Alice refunded the money.

UNDUE INFLUENCE

A contract entered into as a result of **undue influence**, although having the form and shape of an agreement, is *not* enforceable over the objection of the victim.

> **Undue influence** occurs when one party takes advantage of another by reason of a superior position in a close or confidential relationship.

There are many confidential relationships that may give rise to undue influence, in which the dominant party exercises control over the dominated person's will for the former's benefit. Attorney and client, doctor and patient, clergyman and parishioner, trustee and beneficiary, principal and agent, husband and wife (or wife and husband), guardian and ward—these are examples of such relationships. In each case, the person occupying a superior position, that is, one of trust, should be acting in the interest of the other person; hence any contract that is in reality for the former's benefit, and not for the latter's, is presumed to be tainted with undue influence and therefore voidable.

Examples: Undue Influence

A client wins a large judgment in a lawsuit and then lends a portion of the award to her attorney.

A dying patient deeds over valuable property to his doctor.

A husband, hospitalized because of a serious illness, signs insurance releases for the sole benefit of his wife, and upon her advice.

All these transactions would be suspect.

To overcome suspicion, the party in a position of trust should make full disclosure of his private interest and potential gain (in writing or before independent witnesses) to the other party, and if possible should assist him/her in obtaining independent advice concerning any proposed contract or gift.

DURESS

A contract that is in valid form and to all appearances is an agreement may be voided because of duress.

> **Duress** is coercion, either physical or mental, that deprives a person of free will.

A contract made at gunpoint or under other compelling *physical* force is simply *void*. No mental condition of agreement ever existed.

The more typical case of duress arises out of mental coercion. A contract made under mental coercion is *voidable*. Such coercion may come about by threats— a kind of blackmail. However, the threat must be *improper* or *wrongful*. A threat to sue in civil court on a just debt, thereby inducing a promise to pay, is not duress.

Four kinds of threats are generally considered duress in contract law:

1. Threat of physical violence or harm to the individual or to his/her family or property.

2. Threat of criminal prosecution; threat of civil prosecution *only if* the threat is made with actual knowledge that it is without basis or foundation.

3. Threat of personal or family social disgrace.

4. Threat of economic loss *if* the party claiming duress can show that the loss may occur because of actions of the one accused of coercion. *Note*: It is not wrong to threaten suit to recover a valid debt or even a supposedly valid debt.

UNCONSCIONABILITY

A contract in valid form may be voided because of gross inequality in the respective positions of the parties during the contract process. "Unconscionable" describes special situations in which an overbearing party in a superior position imposes outrageously unfair terms on some other party—a merchant to a consumer, in the case of an adhesion contract, through fine print and "fast talk." The **adhesion contract** is a standardized agreement tendered to a consumer on a "take it or leave it" basis, leaving him/her no opportunity to bargain or to obtain the desired goods or services without signing the printed form.

Unconscionability is not an "easy out" from contract obligations. The burden of proof is high; the law imposes a heavy duty to resist such high-handed, aggressive tactics before entering into the contract.

YOU SHOULD REMEMBER

Innocent misrepresentation is misrepresentation in a contract that is made unknowingly and lacks intent to deceive.

In *undue influence*, one party to the contract takes advantage of the other by reason of a position of trust in a close or confidential relationship.

Duress is coercion, either physical or (more commonly) mental, that deprives one party to the contract of his/her free will.

In *unconscionability*, the party to the contract who is in a superior position imposes oppressive or shockingly unfair provisions on the other party.

A contract made under any of the foregoing conditions may be voidable by the victim. In the case of physical duress, the contract is void.

KNOW THE CONCEPTS
DO YOU KNOW THE BASICS?

1. Explain the circumstances under which it may be possible to rescind a contract because of unilateral mistake.
2. Name a situation in which an opinion statement would give rise to rescission of a contract.
3. How have the old equity doctrines influenced the law of contract mistake?
4. How does the penalty for contract fraud differ from the right of recission in cases of simple mutual mistake?
5. Can a person's merely careless statements give rise to fraud when the person does not know for a fact that he/she is lying?
6. Name four confidential relationships where undue influence could exist.
7. When does duress cause a contract to be (a) void or (b) voidable?
8. Explain the meaning of an unconscionable contract.

TERMS FOR STUDY

adhesion contract
caveat emptor
caveat venditor
duress
fraud
innocent misrepresentation
intentional misrepresentation

material mistake
mutual mistake
rescission
scienter
unconscionability
undue influence
unilateral mistake

PRACTICAL APPLICATION

1. Fred Farmer is the owner of a 100-acre farm near a large city. Consider the following two situations:
    (a) An employee of the State Roads Department tells a friend, Lester Listener, that the state plans a major road relocation through Fred's property, including a cloverleaf and commercial interchange on the property. Lester persuades Fred to sign an option contract to sell him the farm for $125,000, a fair price for farm land.
    (b) Lester knows that XYZ Chemical Company is seeking a plant site near the city, and he gets an option contract from Fred, as before, for $125,000.
    If Lester says nothing to Fred about the plans outlined in (a) and (b), in either case is there mistake? Fraud?

2. Bruce Brown is seriously ill. While heavily sedated, he is persuaded by his wife Betty to sign some "papers" so she can pay the hospital bills. These "papers" include a bill of sale on Bruce's cabin cruiser. Actually, the hospital bill is amply covered by insurance, and Betty sells the boat to purchase expensive jewelry for herself. Is Betty's action lawful?

3. Marian Merchant discovers that her bookkeeper has embezzled $50,000 while working in Marian's store. Marian agrees not to report this theft if the bookkeeper will sign a 3-year, interest-free promissory note. Is the note valid?

4. Nellie Naive is an elderly, naturalized American citizen with a marginal knowledge of English and a meager education. She owns a boarding house but is having trouble making ends meet. One of her boarders, Sam Slick, a traveling salesman, is aware of her difficulties. He offers to lend her $10,000 "on her home" if she will sign a "paper." The "paper" turns out to be a deed, and Nellie now seeks to have an equity court set aside the conveyance. Should she be successful?

ANSWERS
KNOW THE CONCEPTS

1. Generally speaking, a unilateral mistake does not provide ground for rescinding a contract. The major exception covers situations where the other party is aware of the mistake and should have spoken up. In today's consumer-minded world, the unilaterally mistaken party has a substantial chance of rescinding the contract if (a) he/she could not easily have learned the facts, and (b) the other party had full control of the situation.

2. In a case involving fraud, an opinion given by a professional, such as an attorney or a physician, is a statement of fact giving rise to grounds for res-

cission. In addition, you should consider that opinions given by tradespeople, such as plumbers, electricians, and hairdressers (in cases concerning shampoos or brushes), will be given greater weight and should be discussed.

3. The equity concept of fairness controls the law of contract mistake. The old idea of *caveat emptor* favored an unscrupulous seller. The modern law tries to "balance the equities," so that neither side should be able to take unreasonable advantage of the other. This is basic equity law.

4. Contract fraud permits the defrauded party either to keep the contract and receive damages in tort (perhaps even punitive damages) or to rescind the contract; simple mutual mistake permits only the right of rescission.

5. Merely careless statements can give rise to fraud if they are made recklessly. The law does not protect those who show disregard for the truth, whether the disregard is shown by outright lying or lack of interest in presenting the facts accurately.

6. Undue influence can exist in the relationship of husband/wife, minister/parishioner, lawyer/client, doctor/patient, parent/child, trustee/beneficiary, political office holder/constituent and others involving trust and potential conflict of interest.

7. (a) Duress causes a contract to be void if it is the result of a physical threat, such as pointing a gun. (b) A contract is voidable when it is the result of mental coercion.

8. "Unconscionable" means grossly unfair. Gross unfairness occurs generally when one party is in an advantageous position in relation to the other party, because of either superior knowledge and power, or the inferior knowledge and power of the other. Disparities in skill, education, professional background, and economic status would be factors in determining unconscionability.

PRACTICAL APPLICATION

1. (a) This is an example of unilateral mistake on the part of Fred, where such mistake is known to the other party. Therefore Fred would have the right to rescind the contract. An argument could also be made that fraud exists since Lester has inside information that a judge or jury might hold he has a duty to share with Fred.

   (b) There is neither mistake nor fraud in this situation. XYZ Chemical Company may or may not be interested in Fred's property according to the statement of facts, and therefore Lester's failure to disclose this information is not nondisclosure of a material fact.

2. This is an example of undue influence practiced by a wife upon a husband. Betty is acting in her own self-interest while leading her ill husband to believe that she is acting either for him or for both parties.

3. The bookkeeper can rescind the obligation. The promise not to report a crime as consideration for a contract is duress. (*The promise not to sue generally would be okay.*)
4. This is a prime example of an unconscionable contract that will be set aside in an equity court. The one-sided nature of the bargain, combined with the lack of equality between the parties, is the essential characteristic of unconscionability. In addition, it could be argued that this is a case of fraud (check each of the five fraud elements) or even of undue influence (is there a relation of trust?).

7
CONTRACTS: CAPACITY OF THE PARTIES AND LEGALITY OF SUBJECT MATTER

KEY TERMS

capacity a legally defined level of mental ability sufficient to reach an agreement

insanity mental impairment sufficient to prevent one from appreciating the nature of an agreement or the consequences of his/her actions

public policy concepts of prevailing morality used by courts to determine the legality or illegality of contracts

Preceding chapters have dealt with consideration and mutual assent, two of the four elements necessary for a valid contract. In this chapter we consider the other two: capacity of the parties and legality of subject matter.

CAPACITY OF THE PARTIES

The technical requirement of capacity arises out of common sense. **Capacity is a legally defined level of mental ability sufficient to reach an agreement.** If one (or both) of the parties has a mind so immature or childish, so befuddled by mental illness or disease, or so stupefied by alcohol or other drugs that it cannot form an intent or know what is going on, there can be no agreement and no contract.

> Three categories of persons may lack capacity to make a contract: minors, insane persons, and intoxicated persons.

MINORS

In most states both parties must be at least 18 years old to make a legally binding agreement; a few states set the minimum age at 21.

• *DISAFFIRMANCE BY A MINOR*

> A person who deals with a minor does so at his/her peril. The adult party to the contract is bound by the bargain; the minor is not.

If one of the parties is under the age of 18—is a **minor**—that party has the right to declare the contract void. **Disaffirmance** is the cancellation or rejection of a contract made during one's minority. Disaffirmance may consist of returning goods bought (if they still exist or have not been consumed), in whatever condition they then may be, or of some other express or implied action of cancellation or rejection made known to the adult party. *This action must occur during minority or within some reasonable period after the minor reaches 18.*

If the minor has sold the goods in question to an innocent *third party*, that party will have acquired a good title with respect to third parties, but the minor can also disaffirm the contract and recover the goods. As for the original contract, if the minor still has the goods in his/her possesion at the time of disaffirmance, most courts hold that the minor must return the goods to the other party; if the goods are damaged, these courts hold that the damaged goods must be returned.

• *MINOR'S LIABILITY FOR FRAUD*

> **General Rule:** A minor is responsible for his torts down to a very tender age; however, a parent is not responsible for the torts of a minor child.

If a minor appears to be an adult and specifically represents him-/herself to be an adult, such fraud may be the basis of a tort suit if the minor then disaffirms the contract. Damages would be the loss sustained by the adult because of the minor's disaffirmance. Of course, if the minor is of such obvious youth that the adult party could not reasonably have *relied on* his/her misrepresentation of age, there would be no fraud (see Chapter 6).

Caution: *Many states do not follow the fraud principle set out above* since they see it as a subterfuge for circumventing principles of law designed to protect minors in their contracts.

• *CONTRACTS INVOLVING NECESSARIES*

Necessaries are items required to sustain existence, such as food, shelter, clothing, medical services, and some types of schooling (e.g., vocational training). A car may or may not be a necessary, depending on the minor's circumstances and intended use of the car. Indeed, the concept of "necessary" is flexible and may be defined in accord with circumstances and the minor's station in life.

A minor is legally liable for necessaries that he/she has used or consumed and that were provided by another person at the minor's request.

This liability is based on the quasi-contract (unjust enrichment) principle since a minor does not have the mental ability to make an express or implied-in-law contract. Since the obligation is based on a quasi contract, the liability is for the *reasonable* value of the goods, which may or may not be the agreed-upon value. Moreover, a quasi contract does not exist if the minor is living at home under the care of a parent or guardian.

Note that the unjust enrichment *is for goods used or consumed*. This principle does not apply to an executory contract (an exchange of promises not yet performed).

Example: *Contract for Necessaries*

If a 17-year-old enters into a 6-month lease agreement, at an exorbitant rental of $1,000 per month, and if she occupies the premises for 3 months, she would be responsible for the three months of actual usage but at a *reasonable* rental.

The express contract of lease is not relevant to the quasi-contractual obligation and is not binding on the minor. Of course, the minor has no liability for the unexpired 3-month remaining period in the lease.

• *RATIFICATION BY A MINOR*

Once a minor reaches the age of 18, he/she may accept the contract, and thus ratify it **ab initio** (from the beginning). *Such ratification may be express or* *implied*—an understanding of the kind required to have made a contract in the first place.

The courts are not agreed on what actions constitute implied ratification. In general, however, making payments when due, continuing to enjoy the benefits of the agreement, or other clear, unambiguous action within the scope of the contract usually implies acceptance.

INSANE PERSONS

By "insanity" the law does not necessarily mean insanity in the medical or extreme sense. Any temporary, oppressive condition affecting the mind and the ability to understand may amount to legal **insanity**, particularly if this condition is apparent to the other party.

A person who enters into a contract while unable to appreciate the nature of the agreement or the consequences of his/her actions may, upon recovery, declare the contract void. Such a person is in the same position as the minor (the contract is voidable) with one exception: *If the sane party acted in good faith, upon disaffirmance of the contract the mentally impaired party must restore whatever he/she received.*

If a person is "insane" in the medical sense *and* has been adjudicated insane (declared insane, upon medical evidence in a court of law), his/her agreements are void *ab initio* and of no effect. Such a person cannot contract for anything.

INTOXICATED PERSONS

For **intoxication** by drugs or alcohol to operate as a defense to a claim based on contract, the intoxication must (a) be such as to deprive the subject of the ability to understand the nature of his/her agreement, and (b) be apparent to the other party. If these two conditions are present, the contract is voidable, but the person under disability must restore the other party to the status quo by returning any goods or other consideration received.

ALIENS AND CONVICTS

Aliens have full access to state and federal courts and consequently have the right to bring suit on their contracts unless they are in the United States illegally or are citizens of a country at war with this nation.

Convicts, whether still in prison or restored to freedom after completion of their terms, are under no contractual disability, although other rights, such as the right to vote or hold political office, may have been forfeited.

YOU SHOULD REMEMBER

A minor, a person under the age of 18, lacks capacity to make a contract. Therefore a minor can cancel a contract at any time during minority and for a reasonable period of time after his/her eighteenth birthday. A minor is, however, responsible for necessaries consumed.

Although minors cannot be held to their contracts, they are responsible for their torts (down to a tender age), including frauds. Consequently, some courts hold a minor responsible for losses to the adult party to a contract because of the misrepresentation of age (fraud).

If a minor accepts the contract after reaching the age of 18, he/she is then bound by it because of ratification.

Insanity is grounds for cancellation of a contract. If, however, the "insane" person has not been adjudicated insane and if the other party acted in good faith, the mentally impaired party must restore value received if he/she wishes to cancel.

A contract made by a person so intoxicated by alcohol or drugs that he/she did not understand the nature of the agreement is voidable if the intoxication was apparent to the other party.

LEGALITY OF SUBJECT MATTER

If the subject matter of an agreement is not legal, the agreement is not enforceable in a court of law. In this respect, we do not use the expression "void" or "voidable"; *the illegal agreement simply has no existence in contemplation of law.* Generally, neither party has access to a court for the assistance of law with respect to any aspect of the agreement.

There are two reasons why the subject matter of a contract may be illegal: statute and public policy. Statutes are legislative acts; **public policy** is a judicial determination of prevailing morality.

In Chapter 1 we explored the close relationship between law and morality. We shall now see how law as statute and law as morality ("public policy") play identical roles in the law of contracts.

AGREEMENTS THAT VIOLATE STATUTES

Criminal statutes such as those dealing with murder or arson, and the criminal provisions of the antitrust laws, prohibit certain conduct. Any contract in furtherance of such activity (e.g., a wife's contract with a hired killer to murder her husband) would have no legal effect and be unenforceable.

In addition there are other statutes—for example, statutes requiring professionals or tradesmen to be licensed, statutes prohibiting betting or wagering, "blue laws" prohibiting purchases on Sundays, usury laws prohibiting exorbitant interest—that indirectly affect a contract and may render it unenforceable. Thus a person who is not a lawyer cannot enforce an agreement to be compensated for legal advice, and a faith healer cannot recover in contract for medical advice. For the same reason, an unlicensed person cannot collect in contract for a real estate commission, nor can an unlicensed contractor collect for home improvements in states where a license is required.

Betting and wagering contracts are generally illegal except where such activities are permitted by statute. *Public attitudes* (prevailing morality) *in these areas of the law, however, are influencing statute law,* so that many gambling activities, such as the bingo games conducted by churches or charities, are now lawful where only recently prohibited. Similarly, **blue laws**, prohibitions of trading contracts on Sunday, seem to be yielding to a more liberal morality in many states. However, one should be aware that Sunday sales of nonnecessity items are illegal in many states and contracts to pay consideration for such transactions may not be enforceable.

Usury (exorbitant interest) has historically been illegal. From the time of the Magna Carta (A.D. 1215) until the mid-1960s, usury was generally defined as interest in excess of 6%. For many years interest at such a low rate has been generally unavailable, and new ceilings, set by statute, vary from state to state. Moreover, a usury contract may be enforceable as to principal plus interest up to the legal rate in many states. Also, "interest" is usually defined as a charge for the use of money and does not extend to carrying charges or finance charges related to the sale of goods.

AGREEMENTS THAT VIOLATE PUBLIC POLICY

In this second ground for illegality of subject matter, general morality gives rise to public policy, but *this illegality is judicially declared* in cases as they appear before the courts.

We will now consider some instances of illegality created by public policy.

• *RESTRAINT OF TRADE*

Before the enactment of any antitrust laws, the common law found agreements that unreasonably restrained trade to be illegal. *Typical of such agreements were those unduly restricting a person in the pursuit of his/her livelihood.*

Example: *Agreements Restricting Persons in Pursuit of Their Livelihoods*

If a chemist agreed that, after any termination of her employment by a chemical manufacturer, she would not work for any other chemical manufacturer for an unlimited period of time, this agreement not to be employed might be found unduly restrictive and unenforceable.

If a barber sold his business and the agreement of sale provided that the seller would not thereafter work as a barber at any place in the state, such an agreement might be found unduly restrictive and unenforceable.

In determining the illegality of such restrictions, the courts consider the legitimate interests of the party that the agreement seeks to protect as well as the negative effect on the party being restricted. If there is a likelihood that the chemist in the example above may know technology and trade secrets useful to a competitor, or that the barber may be planning to work in a nearby shop, a court may be sympathetic to restriction upon her/his activity.

In *all* cases, however, the parties should refrain from total restriction—a person should be able to continue to make a living by practicing a trade, profession, or skill. Thus the restriction should be limited as to time (e.g., 2 or 3 years) and place (miles or a region) or as to specialty (organic chemist, woman's hair stylist). Otherwise, it may be vulnerable to attack as unreasonable.

> Some limit—by time and place or by specialty—should be placed on the restriction not to compete.

• *EXCULPATORY CLAUSES*

Many agreements contain **exculpatory clauses**, that is, provisions that disclaim liability for negligence or other actions. Thus a sign in a restaurant may warn customers that the restaurant has no responsibility for lost coats or a sign in a parking garage may deny liability for damages to vehicles. Exculpatory clauses are not against public policy per se, and disclaimers such as those in the restaurant or parking garage may genuinely warn the public or another party to a contract that one uses the premises at his/her own risk.

If, however, the parties are not in equal bargaining positions, or if the exculpatory clause attempts to excuse a party from his/her own negligence, such a clause may be against public policy and be illegal and unenforceable.

Such unequal bargaining positions are held, for example, by individual travelers with respect to public carriers, whose exculpatory clauses on tickets and claim checks may be found to be contrary to public policy and thus unenforceable.

In the case of the restaurant or parking garage mentioned above, the public has other options for obtaining the services offered and may refuse to be subjected to the risk implied by the disclaimer or denial of liability.

• *OTHER PUBLIC POLICY ILLEGALITY*

Some other types of contracts that are contrary to public policy and therefore illegal are those that would:

- Obstruct justice.

- Corrupt public officials.

- Impair public morality.

- Offend public concepts of decency.

- Discriminate because of race, religion, color, or national origin in the sale or rental of property or the use of public facilities.

EFFECT OF ILLEGALITY

As a general rule, a court of law will not admit into evidence any matter pertaining to an illegal agreement. Such agreements are not actionable and *do not even have legal existence* except as possible evidence of a crime or tort.

Exceptions to this general rule are primarily equitable in nature: the innocent public, the disadvantaged party, a repentant party, a party not as guilty of wrongful intent as the other party—all may be permitted to sue on the illegal agreement, and in many cases may obtain restitution and return of the status quo.

YOU SHOULD REMEMBER

An agreement may be illegal because it violates a statute.

An agreement may also be illegal because it violates public policy, that is, it is contrary to general morality as declared by a court of law. Two examples of such illegality are contracts in restraint of trade and contracts between parties not in equal bargaining positions that contain exculpatory clauses.

If an agreement is illegal, it does not have any legal existence and evidence of the agreement generally cannot be introduced into a court of law.

KNOW THE CONCEPTS

DO YOU KNOW THE BASICS?

1. Explain the sense in which the term "capacity" applies to both minors and insane persons.
2. Discuss the pros and cons of permitting a suit against a minor for fraud if he misrepresents his age.
3. What is the philosophical reason that an illegal contract is not enforceable in court?
4. Name a specific instance in which contract law attempts to protect general morality.
5. Why should an intoxicated person not be given the same right to disaffirm his/her contract as a minor?
6. Does the warning on cigarette packages that "Smoking by Pregnant Women May Result in Fetal Injury ..." operate as an exculpatory clause to the cigarette company?
7. If an action (e.g., murder) is a crime by reason of a statute, will it usually also be a crime by reason of public policy?

TERMS FOR STUDY

ab initio	intoxication
blue laws	minor
capacity	necessaries
disaffirmance	public policy
exculpatory clause	usury
insanity	

PRACTICAL APPLICATION

1. Just after his seventeenth birthday, Murdock Minor signs a contract with Scholarship Books, Inc., for a correspondence course in geology. The cost of this course is $1,000, payable in 20 monthly installments of $50.00 each. There are 20 units, each completed monthly. Murdock completes 14 units and makes monthly payments promptly. In the fifteenth month, he seeks to rescind the contract. Can he do so?

2. Fran Flighty, the 17-year-old daughter of wealthy parents, is visiting an aunt in Honolulu. While there, she signs a contract with the ABC Dancing School whereby she is to be taught "all sophisticated modern dances for young and old alike" in "12 easy lessons." Fran takes no lessons, makes no payments, and seeks to rescind the contract when the ABC Company threatens to sue.
   (a) What will be the result?
   (b) What would happen if she took the lessons and refused to pay just after her eighteenth birthday?

3. Dan Diver is a 22-year-old student at Ambiance Air Academy in Smalltown, Any State. He joins a parachute diving club to "experience the exhilaration of diving" and to "engage in the world's most exciting sport," according to a contract he signs with the club, Live-Long Divers, Inc. The contract also contains an exculpatory clause releasing the club for damages due to any reason whatsoever, "including negligence by the Club." While descending via parachute on his first jump, Dan collides with electric power lines and is seriously injured. Would the exculpatory clause excuse Live-Long Divers, Inc., if it should be found negligent?

ANSWERS

KNOW THE CONCEPTS

1. The term "capacity" relates to the ability of one mind to meet another mind. This ability may not yet be developed in a minor and may be clouded or confused by insanity.

2. A reason for permitting such a suit is that fraud is a tort, and minors are responsible for this kind of tort if all other requirements of fraud are met. A reason not to permit such a suit is that it indirectly permits the adult party to obtain the same benefits he/she would have received for the minor's breach of contract.

3. A court of law cannot be a party to that which is unlawful.

4. Public policy is "grounded" in common morality. Thus, an agreement contrary to public policy is simply one that is contrary to general morality. Restraint of trade is contrary to fairness and good morals. The same is true of an excessively broad exculpatory clause, as well as other illegality.

5. An intoxicated person becomes intoxicated by reason of his/her own freedom of action and is not within a class of persons whom society seeks to protect. Thus, unless the intoxication is evident to the other party, he/she is bound by a contract made while intoxicated.

6. In current cases, cigarette companies are attempting to use the Surgeon General's warning as an exculpatory clause. However, such a clause does not excuse their negligence, or active, intentional infliction of harm, if a jury finds such to be the case.

7. Actions made criminal by statute are usually contrary to prevailing morality and, hence, contrary to public policy. Murder, arson, robbery, and so forth are contrary to public policy. Some crimes—speeding, failure to file income tax returns, failure to register securities being offered to the public— arguably are criminal only because they are in violation of a statute.

PRACTICAL APPLICATION

1. Murdock has ratified the contract by continuing to take the course and making payments after his eighteenth birthday.

2. (a) This contract by a minor is not enforceable as an express or implied-in-fact contract. The dance studio might argue that it is a contract for necessaries and that there is a liability in quasi contract. However, since the lessons were never taken and no benefit has been received, there is no such liability.

   (b) If Fran had taken the lessons, she might be required to pay in quasi contract if the lessons could be considered necessaries. Whether "sophisticated modern dancing" lessons are "necessary" for the teen-age daughter of wealthy parents is a jury question.

3. Dan Diver does not have to take parachute diving lessons, and even if he did he could choose some other club—thus the parties are in equal bargaining positions. However, the clause should not operate to excuse the club from its own negligence, even though Dan proceeded to take the lessons at his own risk.

8 CONTRACTS: THE STATUTE OF FRAUDS; PAROL EVIDENCE RULE; PRIVITY

KEY TERMS

Statute of Frauds the statutory requirement that certain agreements must be evinced by a memorandum in writing

Parol evidence evidence concerning a written agreement that is not part of the writing

privity the requirement that a person be one of the parties to a contract in order to have a legal interest in the contract

Up to this point we have emphasized the mental nature of contracts—in fact, we have stated that written and oral words are mere evidence of the mental condition comprising the contract. However, some contracts require more than a provable mental condition.

THE STATUTE OF FRAUDS

In 1677, the British Parliament passed "An Act for the Prevention of Frauds and Perjuries," generally referred to as the **Statute of Frauds.** *This act was designed to prevent the perpetration of frauds arising out of purely oral agreements.* It required that there be specified evidence in writing (called a "memorandum") about certain kinds of contracts that the Parliament considered particularly subject to perjury, abuse, and frauds.

When the various states adopted the common law of England in 1776, this common law included the English statute law then in effect, including the Statute of Frauds. Many states, to this very day, follow the old English Statute of Frauds as part of their common law, and in addition follow the provisions of the Uniform Commercial Code that contain a statute of frauds provision relating to sales contracts. The British, however, have repealed the original Statute of Frauds.

The Statute of Frauds has two features: (1) it covers certain categories of contracts, and (2) it requires that there be a written memorandum about contracts within these stated categories.

SCOPE OF THE STATUTE OF FRAUDS AND THE UCC PROVISION RELATING TO SALES CONTRACTS

The Statute of Frauds and the UCC provision relate to six kinds of contracts that require written evidence:

1. A contract calling for the sale of land or an interest therein.

2. A contract not to be performed within one year.

3. A contract for the sale of goods for a price of $500 or more (Uniform Commercial Code).

4. A promise by one person to pay the debt of another.

5. A promise made in consideration of marriage.

6. A promise by the executor or administrator of an estate to pay a debt of the estate out of his/her own funds.

The meanings of specific words and phrases in contracts within these six categories are, of course, subject to judicial interpretation.

A brief explanation of each of these various contract categories follows.

1. **A contract for the sale of land or an interest in land.** This category covers real estate contracts, leases, and easements (rights of way and the like), as well as buildings, growing crops, trees, and other property attached more or less permanently to real estate. There is one important exception to the written evi-

dence requirement: most states, by statute, provide that an oral lease for one year or less is valid.

2. A contract not to be performed within one year.

> If it is *possible* for a contract to be performed within a year, a memorandum is not necessary.

A contract made January 1 for 2 years must have a written memorandum; a contract made January 1 for 1 year may be oral since the contract can be performed within a year. A contract to do work "for life" may also be oral, since the law acknowledges that a person may die within a year and thus fully perform the contract. Similarly, a contract for 5 years terminable at any time upon 90 days, prior notice (or some other notice provision of 1 year or less) is a valid oral agreement.

3. A contract for the sale of goods for a price of $500 or more. This requirement is now embodied in section 2-201 of the UCC. A further provision of Section 2-201 makes it clear that the statute covers only fully executory (unperformed) contracts. Once the goods have been delivered, the money can be recovered on an oral agreement; likewise, if the money has been paid, the goods can be demanded, again on an oral contract.

4. A promise by one person to pay the debt of another. This provision generally relates to *contracts of guaranty*, and is sometimes called the "suretyship provision." The contract of guaranty actually involves two contracts: (1) X is indebted to Y on a contract, and (2) A assures Y that, if X does not pay, A will pay. It is this second contract, a guarantee of one person's performance by another person, that is subject to the Statute of Frauds. Such contracts are generally not enforceable if oral.

5. and 6. A Promise made in consideration of marriage and executors' contracts. These two categories are somewhat archaic and narrowly technical. The category relating to marriage was not intended to be applicable to the promise to marry, that is, it does not involve an engagement to marry, which itself is not a legally binding contract. Rather, it was intended to involve **dowry**—the agreement of a woman (or her father) to pay consideration (money or land) to the intended husband. Although dowry agreements are not common in the United States, *prenuptial (or antenuptial) agreements are covered by the Statute of Frauds since such agreements usually involve a division of property upon death or separation and are made in consideration of marriage.*

The executors' contract relates to the promises of adminstrators or executors (sometimes called "personal representatives") to pay the estates' debts from their own pockets. This promise is like the agreement to pay the debts of another, and the memorandum in writing is required.

THE MEMORANDUM IN WRITING

Caution: It is misleading to say that the Statute of Frauds requires that certain contracts be in writing.

The Statute of Frauds requires, not that the entire contract be reduced to a written document, but only that there be some written evidence of the agreement. Several documents, letters, or notations may be read together as a memorandum if all clearly pertain to the disputed transaction.

The memorandum in writing must meet the following minimum requirements:

1. It must identify all the essential parts of the transaction. (This requirement is satisfied if only the *quantity of goods* is referred to in a sales contract subject to exceptions made by the Uniform Commercial Code).

2. It must have been signed by the party being charged (sued) in case of a dispute.

3. It must identify the other party to the agreement.

The contents of item 1 may vary from circumstance to circumstance, but usually a description of the price or consideration, as well as the nature or identification of the items being sold or the work to be done, is required. Note in items 2 and 3 that, although both parties must be identified, both parties do not have to sign; only the party against whom suit is being brought or against whom the claim is being made must have signed. Many legal writers and courts are critical of this one-sided requirement, since only one party (the signer) may be sued, not the other party. Moreover, in this rule, as well as most other rules of law pertaining to signing, *any* signing is sufficient: initials, a stamped or typed signature, a nickname, and the like.

Since the common law favors the enforceability of agreements, *the Statute of Frauds is strictly applied*, that is, if possible, a court will permit an agreement to stand if there is reasonable evidence that the written memorandum is adequate.

OTHER COMMENTS ON THE STATUTE OF FRAUDS

The Statute of Frauds relates only to executory contracts. Once an oral agreement has been carried out by both parties, the court will not nullify the performed agreement. Moreover, if the oral agreement has been partly or fully performed by one party, a quasi-contract action may be brought for the value of benefits rendered.

With regard to real estate contracts subject to the Statute of Frauds, an oral contract may be enforceable by the buyer even without the memorandum in writing if he/she has paid some or all of the purchase price *and* has taken possession of the property.

PAROL EVIDENCE RULE

The parol evidence *rule probibits either of the parties from contradicting or invalidating a fully written contract by means of evidence external to the contract.* If the parties have reduced their agreement to writing, why should they be permitted to introduce other evidence contrary to their own written understanding?

Although the word "parol" is derived from a Latin word meaning "oral," the rule prohibits *any* outside (extrinsic) evidence that contradicts or alters the written agreement. Great care should be used, however, in attempting to apply this broadly stated rule, beacause the exceptions are also broad and the courts are reluctant to withhold evidence of clear understandings freely assented to by both parties.

The following types of evidence may be introduced concerning matter *outside* the written contract:

1. *Evidence explaining,* clarifying, or elaborating upon the agreement.
2. *Evidence concerning later dealings* between the parties, particularly if there was mutual consideration, or reliance by either party, with respect to such dealings.
3. *Evidence tending to prove* that the parties did not intend the writing to be a contract, or that the transaction was signed under duress or tainted by fraud, or that other factors would render the agreement void *ab initio.*
4. *Evidence completing* an incomplete written agreement.
5. Evidence that a condition was to occur before the contract was to be enforced, and that condition did not happen.
6. For a sale of goods, explanatory or supplemental evidence of a custom (trade usage) or of the parties' prior repeated actions (course of dealing, course of performance) in similar situations (UCC 2-202).

YOU SHOULD REMEMBER

The Statute of Frauds requires that there be written evidence (called a "memorandum") for certain kinds of contracts: a contract for the sale of land or an interest in land, a contract not to be performed within a year, a provision by one person to pay the debts of another, a promise made in consideration of marriage, an executor's promise to pay a debt of the estate from his/her own funds. In addition, the Uniform Commercial Code requires written evidence for a contract for the sale of goods for $500 or more.

The memorandum in writing does not have to be a fully written contract, but it must (1) include all the essential parts of the transaction, (2) have been signed by the party being sued, and (3) identify the other party to the agreement.

The parol evidence rule prohibits any extrinsic (outside) evidence that contradicts or alters a written agreement. Exceptions to the rule, however, are very broad.

PRIVITY

Privity is the old common law requirement that *for a person to have a legal interest or right in a contract he/she must be a party to the contract.*

Exceptions to the Privity Doctrine

Modern common law has grafted two very important exceptions onto the privity doctrine: first, one party to the contract can assign his/her rights to someone else; second, sometimes an outside party intended to benefit by the contract may sue on the contract in order to obtain his/her benefit.

ASSIGNMENT OF RIGHTS

Each party to a contract enjoys a right but is also burdened with a duty. If A agrees to sell his hat to B for $20 and B agrees to buy A's hat for $20, A has a right (to receive $20) and A also has a duty (to deliver the hat); B has a right (to receive the hat) and B also has a duty (to deliver the $20).

Rights are freely assignable. Thus A could assign his right to receive the $20 to C; B could assign his right to receive the hat to D.

Example: Assignment of Rights

Smith gives Thompson an option contract to purchase his property, known as Blackacre, for $100,000. Thompson can freely assign the option (the right to buy

Blackacre) to Sanders, and Sanders can show up at the place of sale and purchase the property in the place of Thompson.

Whenever rights are assigned, the party to whom they are assigned (called the **assignee**) is simply substituted for the person making the assignment (called the **assignor**). In the example above, Thompson is the assignor, and Sanders is the assignee. This substitution of parties gives the assignee precisely the same rights and duties as the assignor, that is, the assignee is said "to stand in the shoes of the assignor."

This "standing in the shoes" principle is one of the most important rules of contract law and of commercial law generally.

Suppose that one purchases a boat and signs a contract of sale calling for making certain payments. If the seller of the boat assigns to any third party, such as a bank, the right to receive the payments under the contract, the assignee is substituted for the seller (assignor). If a dispute arises, *any defense (breach of contract, defects in the boat, or other claim of any kind) is good against the assignee to the same extent as against the seller* (assignor).

• *TWO RIGHTS THAT CANNOT BE ASSIGNED*
The right to receive personal services cannot be freely assigned. Thus, if Employee X agrees to perform clerical services in Y's store, and Y sells her store to Z, Z cannot claim the services of Employee X even though Y may have attempted to assign this employment agreement to Z.

Also, *the right to purchase goods on credit* generally cannot be assigned because it is based on a credit rating of the original party.

• *PROHIBITION OF ASSIGNMENT*
The contract *may expressly forbid assignment* by one or by both parties. A milder prohibition may require that the person wanting to assign must obtain the consent of the other party. To this requirement of consent is sometimes added the phrase "which consent shall not unreasonably be withheld."

In case of doubt, if you do not want your contract assigned, place a prohibition in the contract, or require consent of both parties for an assignment.

DELEGATION OF DUTIES

Whether duties to be performed under a contract can be delegated to someone else must be examined on a case-by-case basis. Routine duties, that is, duties that do not require any personal skill or reliability, can be delegated. Contrariwise, if the performing party was chosen because of talent, skill, reputation, standing, credit, or the like, such a performing party cannot assign or delegate the duty to perform to some other party. The person contracting to receive this performance is entitled to the work of this skilled or highly regarded person, be he/she a lawyer, doctor, engineer, artist, musician, actor, cabinetmarker, electrician, or other such person; this performer cannot delegate his/her duties to another.

A delivery service, messenger service, meter reader, storekeeper, or other party may perform routine duties that *can* be delegated, but a provision can be made in the contract prohibiting delegation.

NOVATION

A **novation** is an agreement among the two contracting parties and a third party whereby all parties agree that this third party shall perform the duties of one of the original parties to the contract. For example, if a patient agrees that a new doctor may assume the duties of a prior doctor under an original contract, and the new doctor accepts the delegation of these duties, this three-way agreement is a novation and the first doctor is relieved of the obligation.

THIRD-PARTY BENEFICIARIES

The rights of an assignee in a contract constitute one exception to the privity requirement; the other exception is the right of a third party beneficiary in a contract. A **third-party beneficiary** is a person for whose benefit a contract is made but who is not an actual party to the contract. Two categories of such beneficiaries can bring suit on a contract even though they are not parties to the contract: the creditor beneficiary and the donee beneficiary.

A **creditor beneficiary** is a person who is owed the performance of a contract. If X owes Y $1,000, which X agrees to pay by having Z pave Y's driveway, Y is the creditor beneficiary of the paving contract between X and Z. Y can sue Z to compel him to perform the paving agreement between Z and X. Of course, if Z cannot or does not perform, Y can still sue X for the $1,000 original debt.

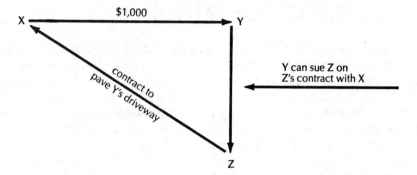

A common third-party creditor beneficiary is a bank holding, say, a mortgage of M that is assumed by a new party, A. Under the assumption contract, A agrees with M that she will take over (pay) M's mortgage. The bank is the creditor beneficiary of this assumption agreement and may bring suit against A even though the bank is not in privity with M and A on their contract. Of course, the bank may also sue the original mortgagor, M, if A does not pay.

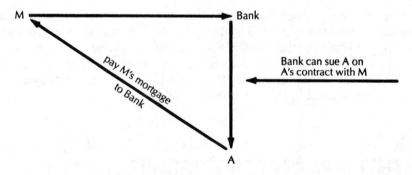

A **donee beneficiary** is the recipient, by gift, of a contractual performance agreed to by two other parties. Thus, if Mr. Smith makes a contract with an insurance company whereby Mrs. Smith will be given certain benefits upon the death of Mr. Smith, Mrs. Smith is a third-party donee beneficiary who can bring suit directly on Mr. Smith's contract with the company if payment is refused upon the death of Mr. Smith.

Beneficiaries of contracts other than creditor or donee beneficiaries cannot sue on the contracts of other parties. These "incidental" **beneficiaries** do not have a substantial interest in the contract. Although such a person may show a benefit under the contract, the contract was not made expressly *for* him/her or *for* his/her benefit. Thus, if a landlord were to employ security guards for an apartment complex and through the negligence of these guards a tenant's apartment was burglarized, the tenant would have no cause for action (under the lease) against the guards.

YOU SHOULD REMEMBER

Privity is the requirement that a person must be a party to the contract to bring suit on the contract. There are two major exceptions: the assignment of rights and third-party beneficiaries.

Most rights can be assigned, but as a rule certain others (e.g., the right to receive personal services) cannot.

Routine duties can be delegated, but duties requiring personal skill or reliability generally cannot.

Novation is a three-party agreement permitting one of the parties to be excused and another person to take his/her place.

There are two important types of third-party beneficiaries: creditor beneficiaries and donor beneficiaries.

KNOW THE CONCEPTS

DO YOU KNOW THE BASICS?

1. Does the Statute of Frauds require that certain contracts be in writing?
2. Is an agreement to work for a person for the lifetime of that person subject to the Statute of Frauds?
3. What is the meaning of the sentence "The assignee stands in the shoes of the assignor"?
4. Would the right to enter another person's property and pick fruit from fruit trees be subject to the Statute of Frauds?
5. Explain why an incidental beneficiary cannot sue on contracts to which he/she is a party.

TERMS FOR STUDY

assignee	novation
assignor	parol evidence
creditor beneficiary	privity
donee beneficiary	Statute of Frauds
dowry	third-party beneficiary
"incidental" beneficiary	

PRACTICAL APPLICATION

1. Evan Eager telephoned the Ardent Cosmetic Company asking for a job as manager of sales. Ardent had advertised this job in a trade publication, stating, in part, as follows: "Exciting opportunity for sales manager with leading cosmetics manufacturer. $75,000 per year; 2 years to make good."

   The president of Ardent, Amy Ardent, agreed on the telephone to employ Evan, and he reported for duty the following Monday. Amy also wrote Evan, stating, "Glad you saw our ad in *Cosmetics World*; welcome aboard!"

   Amy fires Evan after 6 months, and he sues for 18 months' compensation. What will be the result?

2. Guana Fertilizer Company made a written contract with Rufus Rural to mine phosphate from the "Rural farm in Boise County, Idaho." The contract required Guana to pay a royalty of $35 per ton for all mineable phosphate taken from the property.
   (a) Discuss whether parol evidence can be introduced for each of the following purposes: (1) to describe the location of the farm; (2) to define phosphate; (3) to state the depth to which Guana must dig to remove phosphate subject to the royalty.
   (b) Decide whether the royalty can be paid in Guana Company stock as opposed to cash.

3. Irene Instructor made an agreement to teach at a well-known university for a period of one year for a salary of $40,000 per year.
   (a) Discuss (1) Irene's right to delegate her teaching position to her friend, Smith, a highly qualified and respected teacher in the same field; (2) The university's right to assign this contract to a nearby university.
   (b) Discuss Irene's right to assign her salary to a bank as collateral for a large farm.

ANSWERS

KNOW THE CONCEPTS

1. The Statute of Frauds requires that there be written *evidence* of certain contracts. This written evidence is a so-called memorandum, not a full contract.
2. No. It is possible for this contract to be performed within one year.
3. The sentence simply means that the assignee has exactly the same rights as did the assignor. The other party to the contract does not have a better or worse position because the contract has been assigned.

4. Yes. Since the fruit is attached to trees, which are in turn attached to the real estate, and since the right to enter property is a right affecting real estate, a memorandum should be prepared as evidence of the agreement.

5. An incidental beneficiary's benefit is too indirect and too remote. When persons make a contract, they should not have to expect that any person in the world can bring suit on their private agreement.

PRACTICAL APPLICATION

1. This 2-year contract is covered by the Statute of Frauds. There is probably a good memorandum, since the ad contains the basic terms of the contract and Amy's letter is a signed document that can be read with the ad, thus meeting the requirements of the Statute of Frauds.

2. (a) Items (1), (2), and (3) are definable in court by parol evidence, since they do not contradict the terms of the contract. (b) Since the use of a dollar value suggests cash or the equivalent, Guana stock does not meet these requirements and would, therefore, contradict the writing.

3. (a) (1) The teaching position cannot be delegated, since teaching is a personal service and substitution is not permitted. (2) The same answer is true of the right to receive the teaching skill, since again the relationship between the employer and the employee is personal. (b) Irene can assign her salary, however, since this is the mere right to receive money.

9
CONTRACTS: DISCHARGE; DAMAGES AND OTHER REMEDIES

DISCHARGE

Discharge is a general legal term describing the termination or completion of a contract. This word is much broader than "performance," which denotes only one of several ways in which a contract is brought to an end.

DISCHARGE BY PERFORMANCE

When a contract is performed by both parties, it is said to be discharged by performance. By "performance" is meant substantial performance, not necessarily performance to the very last detail. Thus, if a contract to build a house and to grade and prepare the lot and lawn is fulfilled except for grading the lot, the contract is "performed," but the cost of completing the work can be subtracted from the agreed-upon price. On the other hand, if the contract is not substantially performed, that is, if the house itself is not completed, the contractor can recover, not on his unperformed express contract, but only in quasi contract for the quantum meruit ("going market value"; see Chapter 5) of his limited perform-ance. Of course, the contractor is responsible for his unperformed express con-tract. Moreover, in many states, a contractor who willfully departs from the contract cannot recover even in *quantum meruit*.

A contract may be "performed" even though minor aspects have not yet been completed. The performing party may bring suit on the contract, but the court will deduct the cost of completion.

DISCHARGE BY MEETING THE CONDITIONS

To recover for a performed contract (minus any minor omissions or costs of fully completing), all of the fundamental or essential parts of the agreement must have been completed. To determine whether the essential parts of the contract have been performed, one must usually look at the main provisions of the con-tract; if these have been achieved, the contract has been substantially performed.

These essential or fundamental parts of a contract are called **conditions**.

Conditions are the fundamental requirements that must be met by one party before the other party has an obligation under the con-tract.

It should be emphasized that, although failure to meet a condition may excuse performance by the other party under the express contract, the latter must re-spond in *quasi contract* for value received, that is, for the limited performance achieved. Of course, the failing party must still answer for the breached express contract.

There are a number of ways to classify conditions: (1) express conditions, (2) implied conditions, (3) conditions precedent, (4) conditions concurrent, and (5) conditions subsequent.

• *EXPRESS CONDITIONS*

Express conditions are conditions that the contracting parties *deliberately* cre-ate as such in making the contract. Usually, such phrases as "under the following conditions," "on condition that," "of the essence," and "subject to" are used to describe the agreed-upon essentials of the contract. In making a contract, each party should carefully state as essentials or conditions the things that must be done in order to call forth his/her obligation to perform.

• *IMPLIED CONDITIONS*

Most contracts, whether oral or written, contain **implied conditions**, some implied in fact or by the nature of the agreement, others implied by law.

Example: Implied Condition

If Arnold agrees to sell his hat to Bert for $25, it may be implied that the hat to be sold is the hat Arnold is wearing. This would be a condition implied in fact. The law implies that the $25 is to be cash and not a check.

The conditions set out in the example are implied from the nature of the transaction even though they are not expressly or consciously stated by the parties.

• *TIME OF PERFORMANCE*

Time of performance is usually not an implied condition; if one of the parties strictly requires performance at a certain time, express words of condition should be used. Thus, if a contract to have a house built for A provides "completion to be on or before September 1," failure to add such a phrase as "time being of the essence," or other words of condition, will require A to accept late completion, that is, September 20 or even October, as substantial performance. On the other hand, in the sale of highly perishable goods or of stocks and bonds having rapidly fluctuating values, time of performance could be implied as a condition because of the unusual or peculiar circumstances.

• *SATISFACTORY PERFORMANCE*

Satisfactory performance may be called for in the contract. Whether satisfaction is guaranteed as a condition depends on whether the "satisfaction" called for is subjective (a matter of personal taste) or whether the "satisfaction" can be objectively proved. If the satisfaction is subjective, the performer is saying, in effect, "I guarantee that the contract will be completed to your taste," and satisfaction *is* a condition. Thus, an agreement by painter P to paint C's portrait "to the satisfaction of C" sets up a subjective condition that must be met by P before C is obligated to pay under the contract.

On the other hand, an agreement by B to build a club basement for H "as per plans and specifications attached hereto, to the satisfaction of H," sets up an objective satisfaction for H. In other words, if the plans and specifications are complied with, H cannot unreasonably claim that he is not satisfied. In this case, satisfaction is not a matter of taste, and not a condition.

- ## *CONDITIONS PRECEDENT, CONCURRENT, AND SUBSEQUENT*

A **condition precedent** is one that must be complied with, or must occur, before the other party becomes obligated for his/her performance.

Example: A Condition Precedent

Tom agrees to buy certain property for commercial purposes, provided that Sheila, the seller, obtains proper zoning by an agreed-upon date. The zoning must be obtained before Tom becomes obligated.

Conditions concurrent require that performance by both parties take place at the same time. Most conditions fall within the concurrent category: the deed will be delivered when the price is paid or tendered, or the bank will make a mortgage loan when the buyer presents proof of credit.

A **condition subsequent** may abolish liability or obligation: for example, a clause that the seller will be liable for defective goods provided that the buyer gives notice within 30 days of delivery that the goods are defective. Failure to give such notice absolves the seller of any obligation for the defective goods.

DISCHARGE BY BREACH OF CONDITION

If one party to a contract *fails* in a material way *to perform a condition*, the other party has no obligation on the contract—the contract is discharged by breach. Bear in mind, however, that if the contract is substantially performed it is not materially breached. Also, remember that, even when the contract is not substantially performed, the nonbreaching party is responsible for value received (*quantum meruit*) in quasi contract. This value received may be subtracted from damages recovered from the breaching party.

DISCHARGE BY ANTICIPATORY BREACH

If one of the parties to a contract clearly states or implies that he/she cannot or will not perform as agreed, the other party does not have to sit idly by and await the due date of performance before declaring the contract breached and therefore discharged. Such a statement of nonperformance creates an **anticipatory breach**. Anticipatory breach may be implied by some clear, unambiguous action on the part of one of the parties: sale of goods under contract to the other party to some other person; failure to commence construction of a residence within several days or weeks of the date of completion.

Basic Principle of Anticipatory Breach

An anticipatory breach occurs if one party to a contract clearly states or implies that he/she cannot or will not perform as agreed, even though the time of performance has not yet arrived.

DISCHARGE BY AGREEMENT OF THE PARTIES

• *MUTUAL RESCISSION*

Since a contract comes into being by mutual agreement, it can be ended at any time by mutual agreement or mutual rescission. **Mutual rescission** *is a contract to end a contract.* If the contract is wholly executory, the mutual rescission requires no additional consideration.

Parties may orally agree to end a written agreement, regardless of the formality with which the written contract was made. Indeed, most courts hold that a written agreement providing "This contract shall not be modified except in writing, duly executed by a corporate officer of each of the parties hereto" may nevertheless be orally cancelled provided that the parties effecting the cancellation have the authority to do so.

• *ACCORD AND SATISFACTION*

Accord and satisfaction discharge a contract in that the parties agree to substitute a new performance in place of, and in satisfaction of, an existing obligation. An essential element is acceptance of the new performance, frequently the doing of an act, as full satisfaction for an obligation to pay money. The **accord** is the agreement to accept the substitution; the performance of the accord is the **satisfaction**.

Example: *Accord and Satisfaction*

Arthur owes Beth $1,000, which he cannot pay. Arthur agrees to repair the roof on Beth's house in lieu of paying the $1,000. The agreement to accept the repair is the accord; performance of the repair is the satisfaction.

Acceptance of a new performance in satisfaction of an existing obligation discharges the old obligation and operates as an accord and satisfaction.

• *RELEASE*

Another type of discharge of contract by agreement of the parties is a release.

A **release** is an agreement by one party to excuse the other party from performance of his contract. If A and B have a contract, and A is unable to perform or is in breach of contract, he may obtain a release from B by the payment of consideration, usually money, although anything of value will support the discharge. A release is valuable protection when a person has, or may have, breached a contract and wishes to avoid any possibility of suit.

In the case of claimed breaches by both parties, with claims and counterclaims by the contracting parties, mutual releases should be obtained in order to ensure the full discharge of the contract by both parties.

• *WAIVER*

Section 1-107 of the Uniform Commercial Code provides that "Any claim or right arising out of an alleged breach can be discharged in whole or in part without consideration by a written waiver or renunciation signed and delivered by the aggrieved party." A **waiver** is the voluntary relinquishment of a party's rights in a contract. A waiver may result in acceptance of defective or incomplete performance.

One should be careful, therefore, to object to incomplete performance and to serve notice that one's rights are *not* being waived when additional time is granted for performance or a defaulting party is afforded an opportunity for correction.

DISCHARGE BY OPERATION OF LAW

Four categories of occurrences will operate to discharge a contract as a matter of law: subsequent illegality, impossibility, bankruptcy, and the statute of limitations.

• *SUBSEQUENT ILLEGALITY*

Subsequent illegality is a rather narrow category of discharge. The principle applies to contracts that are legal when made, but become illegal by the subsequent passage of a statute. The example usually given pertains to alcoholic beverages; contracts to buy and sell become illegal by reason of the passage of prohibition laws.

Generally, legislation making certain acts or conditions illegal contains a **grandfather clause**, an exemption for conditions or circumstances (including contracts) existing before the legislation was enacted. Typical of such clauses are those found in zoning statutes: uses in existence before enactment of a law may continue thereafter as "nonconforming" uses even though contrary to the new statute.

A very real, but also narrow, subsequent illegality occurs with the declaration of war. Statutes making "trading with the enemy" illegal would nullify any executory contract requiring commerce with the enemy or even with a neutral if the "enemy" could be shown to benefit. There is a distinction, however, between executed and executory contracts: if the enemy had delivered goods or licensed patent rights (an executed contract as to him) but money was owing or not yet paid (an executory contract as to the buyer or licensee), payment would be suspended until the cessation of hostilities. After the war was over, the former "enemy" could collect!

• *IMPOSSIBILITY*

If performance becomes *"impossible,"* the contract is discharged by operation of law. There are a number of occurrences that may render performance impossible:

- In a personal service contract (e.g., services of a professional such as a lawyer or teacher), the death or incapacitating illness of the performer.

- Destruction of the subject matter of the contract (the property or goods being bought or sold).

- A law or administrative act of government (such as environmental controls prohibiting disposal of wastes or regulating the chemical or toxic content in goods to be manufactured and sold under a contract) that makes performance illegal.

- Acts of God (natural occurrences such as floods or hurricanes that render performance impossible).

"Acts of God" are frequently addressed in contract provisions called *force majeure* clauses. These clauses may excuse nonperformance (or permit delayed performance) because of a *force majeure*, that is, a superior force operating beyond the control of either party to the contract. Such clauses are highly desirable in contracts where performance is vulnerable to natural occurrences or to strikes, inability to obtain raw materials, or other outside "supervening" interferences. Reliance on the general legal principles of impossibility may not suffice, in that simple discharge of contract by the affected party would leave the other party in an unprotected, precarious position. It is best to define in the contract the *force majeure* occurrence in question and to anticipate possible delays and necessary make-up work, the need to purchase elsewhere, and other events occurring because of superior force intervention.

Some courts follow the principle of *strict impossibility*: the only impossibility excusing performance is absolute factual impossibility—the contract could not be performed *at any cost by anyone* under any circumstance. Other courts follow a rule of *commercial impracticability*, that is, if the contract cannot be performed except at excessive and unreasonable cost, the party subject to such cost is excused under the doctrine of impossibility. Courts following the impracticability rule require, however, that some unforeseen contingency occurred, that such contingency was not bargained for in the agreement, and that custom or usage in the business or trade of the contracting parties did not require that one of the parties assume the risk of the contingency.

Example: Commercial Impracticability

An excavator agrees to excavate a cellar under an existing building for a specified price. Upon commencing work, the excavator finds that underground springs at the site disproportionately multiply the anticipated costs. Even though it might be possible to do the job at enormous loss, many courts would excuse the contractor from performance on the grounds of economic impracticability, or impossibility.

The Uniform Commercial Code (see Section 2-615) also adopts the rule of commercial impracticability with regard to sales contracts.

• *BANKRUPTCY*

The Bankruptcy Act provides that certain contracts are discharged by compliance with the act (see Chapter 20). After a proceeding in a bankruptcy court, the debtor is released from all contractual obligations to his/her creditors.

• *STATUTE OF LIMITATIONS*

The statute of limitations was discussed in Chapter 5. It should be emphasized that, if the promise to perform is renewed following the period of limitation, the contract obligation is revived.

YOU SHOULD REMEMBER

"Discharge" means termination or completion of a contract.

A contract may be discharged by *substantial performance* of the obligation.

A contract may be discharged by meeting the fundamental *conditions* of the agreement. These conditions may either be agreed to in the contract specifically as conditions or be implied. It is important in making a contract to use words of condition to describe the things that are fundamental to the parties.

A contract may be discharged by *breach* if one party fails in a material way to perform his/her obligations.

If a contract is not working out to the satisfaction of both parties, it can be ended by *agreement*. In mutual rescission, this agreement may be written or oral: the only requirement is that there be a meeting of the minds to cancel.

In accord and satisfaction, the parties agree to substitute a new performance in place of, and in satisfaction of, the existing obligation. When one party has failed to perform a contract, or if there is dissatisfaction with his/her performance and fear of a suit by the other party, it is recommended that a release be obtained as protection from a later lawsuit. In a waiver one party voluntarily relinquishes his/her rights in a contract.

A contract may be discharged by *operation of law*. Four kinds of occurrences will operate to discharge a contract as a matter of law: subsequent illegality, impossibility, bankruptcy, and the statute of limitations.

Courts are not in agreement as to the meaning of "impossibility."

Since the terms of impossibility may be subject to argument, it is helpful to put into a contract a *force majeure* clause, which defines impossibilities that may occur during the life of the contract and states the consequences for the person claiming the impossibility. Generally, *force majeure* clauses relate to things beyond the control of the parties to the contract.

DAMAGES

The word **damages** refers to the compensation due the nonbreaching party to recover any financial loss or injury caused by a breach of contract. Damages are an essential ingredient in every contract case in a court of law.

Essential Elements of Plaintiff's Case in a Contract Action

1. Proof of the existence of a contract.

2. Proof that the contract was breached by the defendant.

3. Proof that, as a result of defendant's breach, the plaintiff has been injured or damaged.

Whether the contract action is brought by the plaintiff *pro se* (acting as his own lawyer) in a small claims court, or is a multimillion dollar suit between giant corporations in federal court, these three elements of proof are required.

Sometimes the injury or damage to the plaintiff is negligible, that is, the financial loss to the complaining party is so small as to be practically immeasurable. In that case, the plaintiff will receive only *nominal damages* ($1 or some other token amount), or plaintiff's case may be dismissed altogether for lack of proof of injury. *De minimis non curat lex* ("the law does not concern itself with trifles"), frequently abbreviated simply as *de minimis*, is an important principle of the law and should be carefully considered before a person goes to court to avenge some perceived violation of principle, hurt feelings, or embarrassment.

COMPENSATORY DAMAGES

If there has been a material breach of contract and this breach has caused measurable damages to the plaintiff, the court will try to compensate the plaintiff by awarding a sum of money sufficient to make him/her "whole." This sum of money is called **compensatory damages**. In Hammurabi's Code, society compensated the injured party by permitting him to injure the other party in the same manner; modern law places a money value on the injury and takes that money from the wrongdoer as compensation to the injured party.

Example: Compensatory Damages

Smith agreed to sell a new automobile, model X, to Jones for $10,000. If Smith fails or refuses to sell that automobile to Jones, or for any reason cannot deliver, and if Jones must pay $12,000 to some other seller for model X, the injury to Jones is $2,000, and that amount of money from Smith will make him "whole," or will compensate him.

Three principles operate to limit compensatory damages.

Limitations on the Ability to Be Legally Compensated for Damages

1. Damages must be proved to a *reasonable certainty*.

2. Defendant is liable only for damages that were *reasonably foreseeable* at the time the contract was made or at the time the breach occurred.

3. Plaintiff must use every reasonable effort to *mitigate*, that is, avoid or minimize, the damages.

Because of these three principles, proof of damages may be the most difficult part of the contract case.

• CERTAINTY

The first principle, *certainty*, eliminates speculative losses. Suppose, for example, that ABC Contractors, Inc., has a contract with Glass Manufacturing Company to build and have operative a glass factory by February 1, time being of the essence. Suppose that the factory is not completed on time, and the Glass Company claims that it would have made profits of over $1 million during the period of delay in completion. These profits are generally considered too speculative to support an award of damages.

• FORESEEABILITY

Foreseeability of damage at the time of making the contract or at the time of breach is the second limitation on compensatory damages. This principle is a reasonable guide for a party about to breach his/her contract: What will it cost to breach? This question can be answered only in terms of foreseen consequences. Suppose, for example, that a manufacturing company has a breakdown in its operations. It orders certain machinery parts from X Machine Company, such parts to be delivered in 24 hours. If the Machine Company is 3 days late in delivering the machine parts, the manufacturing company would have no basis for lost profits during the 3-day period if loss of these profits would not have been reasonably foreseeable by X Machine Company at the time of the breach.

• MITIGATION

The requirement of *mitigation* is the third limitation on compensatory damages. **Mitigation** means reduction to a minimum. It is the requirement that the injured party use reasonable efforts to minimize his/her loss.

If the plaintiff fails to mitigate damages, such failure may operate as a complete bar to his/her ability to recover in a breach of contract suit.

Suppose a tenant has a valuable piano under a leaking roof in a rented apartment. If the tenant has the opportunity to move the piano from the leaking area, failure to do so will defeat a contract case (for damages to the piano) against the landlord for breach of the lease provision requiring the roof to be kept in good repair.

Examples: Mitigation Requirement

1. The duty of a wrongfully fired employee to find comparable employment at the best salary possible.

2. The duty of a landlord to find a new tenant to replace a tenant who broke her lease by moving before the end of the lease period.

Of course, the mitigating plaintiff is entitled to compensation for the cost of mitigation. The fired employee is entitled to reasonable moving expenses to his new job; both the fired employee and the landlord whose tenant moved are entitled to reasonable advertising expenses. These direct costs of mitigation which can reasonably be anticipated by the parties are called **incidental damages** and are generally allowed to plaintiffs as part of their loss.

CONSEQUENTIAL DAMAGES

Consequential damages are also allowed as part of the compensatory damages if the breaching party knew or had reason to know that losses would result from the breach. These indirect damages *can* include injury and lost profits caused by faulty performance *if* the principles of foreseeability and certainty are met. If, for example, an automobile with defective brakes is delivered to a buyer pursuant to a contract, injuries to that buyer and other persons caused by this defect may be the responsibility of the seller. Lost profits may be allowed if the breaching party knew or should have known that the other party expected such profits at the time the contract was made.

It should be emphasized, however, that consequential damages are examined carefully under both the certainty and foreseeability tests; in any event, their inclusion in a specific case is usually a matter for the jury to decide.

LIQUIDATED DAMAGES

The question of damages is not always a simple one. *It is a good idea, therefore, to consider the inclusion of a damage clause in the contract itself as part of the meeting of the minds.* It is perfectly acceptable to insert a provision that the performing party shall (or shall not) be responsible for damages. A clause creating responsibility may be preceded by a statement that the parties understand and agree that profits in certain amounts are expected and are dependent on timely completion of performance.

Clauses specifying the dollar amount due upon breach are called **liquidated damage** clauses. When these clauses reflect reasonable efforts by the parties to calculate damages, they are enforced by the courts, particularly if the subject matter is such as to make the actual assessment of damages difficult. However, if the clause is found to be a *penalty* (i.e., an unreasonable or arbitrary amount) for nonperformance or breach, it is not judicially enforceable.

PUNITIVE DAMAGES

Punitive damages (to punish), sometimes called **exemplary damages** (to serve as an example), are recoverable in tort cases as punishment for the outrageous, malicious, and oppressive conduct of the defendant. Generally the amount of such damages is a matter for the jury, which may consider not only the oppressiveness or maliciousness of the conduct, but also the wealth (or lack of wealth) of the defendant, since wealth is a factor in assessing the degree of punishment.

A distinct majority of the states do not allow punitive damages for breach of contract. However, when a breach of contract is accompanied by an independent tort (e.g., fraud), this tort may give rise to punitive damages. Also, breach of contract may itself involve a tort, in which case the suit may have both contract and tort counts, the latter seeking punitive damages.

Example: *A Suit with Both Contract and Tort Counts*

Under a contract to deliver goods to the plaintiff's pier by barge, the defendant's barge captain negligently strikes the pier and destroys it. The suit may be both in contract (negligent performance) and tort (negligent destruction of property). If the captain were malicious (acted out of spite) or intoxicated (gross negligence), punitive damages may also be recovered.

OTHER REMEDIES

SPECIFIC PERFORMANCE

In Chapter 1, the equity courts first established in England by the Norman kings were discussed. Certain extraordinary relief requiring the power of the king, such as **specific performance** of contract or injunction, were reserved to the king's equity court; money damages were available in the regular English law courts. This division exists to this day as a matter of technical procedure; however, as in the old law, equity is used only as a matter of last resort. If damages will suffice, the plaintiff must seek them in a regular court of law.

Basic Principle of Law

Specific performance of a contract will not be granted if a money award of damages will make the plaintiff "whole."

Suppose X has agreed to sell a new automobile, model Z, to A for $10,000. If X refuses to perform her contract of sale, A cannot obtain specific performance in an equity suit. A must buy model Z for the best obtainable price and sue X for the difference in damages.

Two Kinds of Cases in Which Equity Can Be Counted on for Relief

1. The subject matter of the contract is unique (not available in the marketplace).

2. There is a contract for the conveyance of real estate.

   Since real estate is, in a sense, unique, the two categories can really be considered as one.

Suppose that, in the example of the new automobile, the car, instead of being new model Z, were an irreplaceable antique. Equity would then grant relief in specific performance. The same result would apply to parcels of ground, houses, and other items of realty: either buyer or seller can order specific performance in equity.

There is one kind of contract in which specific performance is *not* available: a personal service contract for the work of either a laborer or a professional. These personal service contracts are not enforceable in equity. Courts cannot supervise work to be done; moreover, they cannot be a party to involuntary servitude—a jail term for contempt of court arising out of breach of contract would be a giant step backward in modern law.

INJUNCTION

Injunction is a second form of relief available in equity in certain situations. An injunction is a court order to a person or party to do, or refrain from doing, a specific thing. The equity court order may prohibit a breach of contract that has not yet occurred if the prospective breach threatens "irreparable injury." For example, in an employment contract in which a person agrees not to work for a competitor in a specific area for a specific period of time after termination of employment, injunction may be obtained to block the person from violation of his/her agreement. In such a case, great injury may result if the employee works for a competitor even briefly, since the new employer may have full access to the first employer's business secrets through this breach of contract.

YOU SHOULD REMEMBER

The law does not concern itself with trifles, and litigation for abstract principles that have no financial implication should be avoided. An award of money damages is the general goal of contract litigation.

The courts will award compensation for damages only if (1) damages can be proved with reasonable certainty, (2) they were reasonably foreseeable when the contract was made, and (3) the plaintiff used every reasonable effort to mitigate damages.

To receive consequential damages for injury or lost profits, the principles of foreseeability and certainty must be met.

A liquidated damage clause should be considered as a provision in every contract. This is an attempt to specify the anticipated dollar loss should the contract be breached. If the amount is unreasonable, it is not enforceable.

Punitive damages are not generally available in a suit involving a simple breach of contract, since they represent a tort remedy. If, however, there is a tort aspect (e.g., fraud) to the contract suit, punitive damages may be claimed.

Equity actions—specific performance and injunction—are extraordinary relief and will not be allowed if money damages will make the plaintiff "whole." Specific performance may be obtained when the subject matter of the contract is unique or it is impossible to have satisfaction without the contract actually being performed. Injunction should be considered where "irreparable" damages will occur in the absence of a court order requiring performance.

KNOW THE CONCEPTS

DO YOU KNOW THE BASICS?

1. What is the difference between the words "discharge" and "performance"?
2. What damages can a plaintiff receive if:
   (a) a contract has been substantially, but not fully, performed, and
   (b) performance of a contract has barely begun and only a small benefit been given?
3. In a contract what words and phrases create express conditions?
4. When does the law consider "satisfaction" to be objective and not a matter

of taste? What difference does this distinction make in setting up a "condition"?

5. How can a contract be breached before the date of performance arises?
6. When should one obtain a release?
7. Discuss the legal significance of the word "impracticable."
8. Is an "act of God" the same as a *force majeure*?
9. Is a contract obligation "wiped out" by the passage of time provided in the statute of limitations?
10. There are three essential elements to a contract case in court. What are they, and which is most difficult to prove?
11. What limits are placed on compensatory damages?
12. When are consequential damages not allowed?
13. What prevents the parties, by mutual agreement, from placing any desired dollar amount of damages in their contract as the definition of liquidated damages if the contract is breached?
14. Why does the court permit a jury to hear about a defendant's wealth in a case involving punitive damages?
15. Name two equity remedies available in some breach of contract cases.

TERMS FOR STUDY

accord and satisfaction	express conditions
anticipatory breach	*force majeure*
breach	grandfather clause
compensatory damages	implied conditions
conditions	incidental damages
conditions concurrent	injunction
conditions precedent	liquidated damages
conditions subsequent	mitigation
consequential damages	mutual rescission
damages	punitive damages
de minimis	release
discharge	specific performance
exemplary damages	waiver

PRACTICAL APPLICATION

1. In a contract dated February 15, Wright agreed to build a drugstore on a lot owned by Peoples, near Washington, D.C. The drugstore was to be completed and ready for occupancy by January 1 of the following year. In September, a

hurricane struck the Washington area and flooded the work site, where excavations had just been commenced. No further work was done, and Wright walked off the job. On December 1, Peoples declared Wright to be in breach of contract and employed Turner to complete the job. What damages are available to Wright and Peoples, respectively?

2. Gunther, a German national, was the owner of a valuable patent covering dehydrated food processing filed in the U.S. Patent Office. In July 1936, he made a contract with Samson whereby Samson received exclusive rights to manufacture, market, and selll foodstuffs in the United States in accordance with the patent. Samson agreed to pay Gunther a royalty of 12% on all foodstuffs made and sold in accordance with the patent. Samson's payments were duly made until December 7, 1941, at which time Samson ceased these payments for "patriotic reasons." In July 1946, Gunther sued for an "accounting" (statement of sales and amounts due) and for back royalties. What would be the result?

3. Willis, a senior at Charlestown University, rented a room from Thomas by oral lease for a period of 10 months to expire June 1. On January 1, Willis moved from the room without notice to Thomas, but left the room occupied by Goldman, also a student. Thomas accepted Goldman's personal check for the January rent, but Goldman moved out on February 1. Thomas now seeks rent from Willis for the months of February, March, April, and May. Can he collect?

4. Singleton was transferred from employment in Dayton, Ohio, to Atlanta, Georgia. In June, he purchased an old house in Atlanta and made a contract with "We Fix It" to have the house ready for occupancy by September 1, "time being of the essence." The contract contained a "liquidated damage" clause providing for damages to Singleton in the amount of $100 per day for each day, after September 1, required for completion. The house was not ready until October 10. Is this damage clause enforceable if (a) the price of the work was agreed to be $10,000 and (b) Singleton had a family that included two teen-age children, and (c) the fair rental value of the house was $400 per month?

ANSWERS

KNOW THE CONCEPTS

1. "Discharge" refers to any of the ways in which a contract may be completed or ended; "performance" is one way to discharge.
2. (a) If a contract has been substantially, but not fully, performed, the plaintiff is entitled to the contract amount minus the cost of completion.

(b) If performance of the contract has barely begun, the plaintiff cannot recover on the express contract; he is entitled, however, to the fair value of the work performed based on quasi contract.

3. "Condition," "of the essence," "subject to," and equivalent words or phrases.

4. "Satisfaction" is considered to be objective if the contract contains a definition of performance, such as a reference to plans and specifications, or if performance is determined by ascertainable criteria. If satisfaction can be objectively proven, it is not a condition.

5. Anticipatory breach may occur before the date of performance arrives, if one party signifies or implies that he/she cannot or will not perform.

6. A release should always be obtained if there could reasonably be a question of performance of one's contract.

7. Many courts consider that a contract performance is "impossible" if it is commercially "impracticable." However, some unforeseen contingency must occur that was not bargained for and that custom or usage in the trade or business does not require one to assume.

8. *Force majeure* (superior force) is broader than "act of God" (natural forces), although it includes acts of God. *Force majeure* applies to any third force or action beyond the control or power of the contracting parties.

9. The statute of limitations does not "wipe out" the contractual obligation. This obligation may be revived by renewal of the promise.

10. These three elements are (1) that there was a contract, (2) that defendant breached it, and (3) that as a result of the breach, plaintiff was damaged. Depending on the nature of the case, difficulty of proof varies. An implied-in-fact contract is sometimes hard to prove; where performance is complicated, breach may be difficult to show; damages are difficult to prove when bills were not rendered or accounts not kept.

11. The limits are (1) reasonable certainty, (2) reasonable foreseeability, (3) mitigation of damage.

12. Consequential damages are not allowed if they were not reasonably foreseeable.

13. The parties cannot agree upon an unreasonable, unconscionable amount of damages under the guise of "liquidated" damages. To be enforceable, the agreed-upon damages should be related in some way to the expected or anticipated loss that would occur upon breach.

14. In order to assess an appropriate amount for such damages. A person of great wealth is not punished by a money damage award against him/her to the same extent as is a person of more modest means who is subject to the same award.

15. Specific performance of contract, and injunction to prevent breach of contract.

PRACTICAL APPLICATION

1. Peoples is entitled to a completed drugstore for the same price as agreed upon by Wright. This "make whole" principle governs this case. Wright is entitled to the value of the work performed in quasi contract, but this amount would no doubt be absorbed by People's greater damages. The September storm, an act of God, could be *force majeure*, excusing late performance, but Wright gave no notice—he merely walked off the job. Employment of Turner should have occurred early in order to mitigate damages; leaving the work unattended and uncompleted would conflict with the mitigation requirement. Compensatory damages are probably too uncertain; however, incidental damages caused by getting a new contractor to complete the work may well be allowable.

2. Gunther is entitled to the "accounting" and to back royalties during the war years. Samson's obligations were only suspended during this time.

3. Thomas is required to mitigate damages by finding a new tenant comparable to Willis, if possible. He found this tenant when he accepted Goldman and Goldman's rent for January—probably a novation. Willis has no further obligation on the oral lease.

4. Is $100 a day liquidated damages, or is it an unenforceable penalty? This $4,000 penalty for 40 days amounts to nearly half the price of the work. It is also too large when compared with the fair rental value of the house ($400 per month). In all events, there should have been a ceiling (e.g., $1,000) on the $100 per day penalty; moreover, it should have been tied to some other ascertainable dollar cost—rental of two hotel rooms, for example. Conclusion: this damage clause is an unenforceable penalty.

10
SPECIAL PROBLEMS RELATING TO SALES CONTRACTS

This chapter deals specifically with sales contracts and Article 2 of the Uniform Commercial Code. It serves also as a review of Chapters 5 through 9 on general contract principles. A comparison of the law of sales with the common law of contracts will be helpful in understanding both.

ARTICLE 2 OF THE UNIFORM COMMERCIAL CODE

Article 2 of the UCC deals specifically with contracts for the sale of personal property or movables, that is, **chattels**. In many cases the code does not change the common law of contracts, but merely restates or expands that law as it applies to sales. In other cases, although Article 2 is drawn only for sales contracts of personal property, the courts have tended to extend the code's principles to contracts generally, not just sales contracts.

YOU SHOULD REMEMBER

Sales contracts are singled out for special treatment in Article 2 of the UCC. However, much of Article 2 is the same as the common law or merely expands upon the general law of contracts. In addition, much of the general law of contracts is applicable to contracts of sale.

PRINCIPAL CHANGES FOR SALES CONTRACTS IN ARTICLE 2

HIGHER STANDARDS FOR MERCHANTS

Article 2 imposes higher standards of conduct on merchants than on nonmerchants. Section 2-104(1) defines a **merchant** as one "who deals in goods of the kind or otherwise by his occupation holds himself out as having knowledge or skill peculiar to the practices or goods involved in the transaction. . . ."

A number of provisions of the code implement the higher standards for merchants. For example:

(a) Section 2-103(1)(b): *Every* contract imposes on the parties an obligation of "good faith." "Good faith" in the case *of a merchant* means *both* "honesty" and the observance of "reasonable commercial standards of fair dealing in the trade."

(b) Section 2-201(2): A written confirmation *from one merchant to the other* of an oral agreement satisfies the Statute of Frauds unless the recipient, within 10 days, objects in writing.

(c) Section 2–205: A written firm offer of a *merchant* to buy or sell goods is irrevocable even without consideration, for up to 3 months. (See page 90.)

(d) Section 2-207(2): *Between merchants*, an acceptance may vary the offer, without being treated as a rejection, unless (i) the offer prohibits such varying, (ii) the proposed terms *materially* alter the offer, or (iii) the offeror objects within a reasonable time. Section 207(1) provides that, as to nonmerchants, an acceptance with new terms is an acceptance of the offer as made, not a rejection. The new terms are treated as proposals for additions to the contract unless the offeree specifies, as a condition, that they must be part of the agreement. This section attempts to solve a "battle of forms" in which each party tries to bind the other to his/her version of the contract by a last communication containing such a version.

(e) Sections 2-312(3) and 2-314(1): These provide for implied warranties of merchantability and ownership by merchants.

STATUTE OF FRAUDS

Under the UCC, an agreement for the sale of goods for $500 or more is subject to the Statute of Frauds. The requirement that the principal terms of the agreement be stated is satisfied if there is "some writing sufficient to indicate that a contract for sale has been made between the parties," but the contract is not enforceable for any quantity of goods beyond that shown in the writing. A reference to price is not required.

GREATER FLEXIBILITY

In general, *more relaxed, flexible rules* are permitted in the creation of sales contracts to carry out the intent of the parties. For example, the common law requires agreement on price before a contract can be said to have been formed. Under the code, a contract for the sale of goods may be silent about price, permitting the parties to set as a price whatever is "reasonable" at the time of delivery of goods. A clause permitting either party to fix the price is enforceable under the code, requiring the party setting the price to act in good faith.

INTERPRETATION OF THE AGREEMENT

To interpret a contract a jury or court tries to determine the intention of the parties. Section 2 of the code sets out certain criteria for determining the meaning of a sales contract. These principles, developed from the common law of contracts, are that intent is shown by (a) "the course of performance accepted or acquiesced in without objection" [Section 2-208(1)] and (b) "a sequence of previous conduct between the parties . . . as establishing a common basis of understanding for interpreting their expressions and other conduct," and (c) "practice or method of dealing . . . in a place, vocation or trade. . . ." These rules of interpretation, although specifically for sales contracts, are widely used by the courts to determine the meaning of any contract.

Caution: As stated above, Section 2 of the code is limited to *sales* of *personal property* (movables or chattels). It does not cover sales of real estate, nor does it apply to contracts for services or for employment. If personal property is conveyed along with real estate, or if the contract calls for both services and sales (such as supplying and installing automobile parts, or supplying blood for a blood transfusion), the courts attempt to determine whether the predominant factor, or primary purpose, of the contract is to supply services (not covered by the code) or goods (covered by the code). This primary purpose, of course, is shown by the intent of the parties, the nature of the transaction, the terms of the contract, and the like. Thus the sale of a residence, including furniture and lawn equipment, would *not* be covered by the code; a blood transfusion has been held by some courts to be covered by the code, although other courts disagree. However, a vaccination is generally considered a sale of vaccine and hence a transaction under the code!

YOU SHOULD REMEMBER

The principal ways in which the UCC changes sales contracts are as follows:

1. For merchants the code provides that
   (a) higher standards of conduct must prevail;
   (b) written confirmation of an oral agreement may satisfy the Statute of Frauds;
   (c) a firm offer to buy or sell goods may be irrevocable;
   (d) an acceptance may vary an offer without being considered a rejection;
   (e) implied warranties of merchantability and ownership are established.

2. The code establishes a Statute of Frauds for the sale of goods for $500 or more.

3. The code provides for more flexible rules in determining the existence of a sales contract.

4. The code lays down specific criteria for determining the meaning of a sales contract; these criteria are less technical and rely on performance, past conduct, and custom.

5. The sales contract changes in the UCC have influenced courts with regard to the conduct of sellers (courts have become buyer oriented) and the interpretation of contracts generally.

NONSALES TRANSACTIONS

Before sales transactions can be fully understood, it is necessary to understand nonsales transactions. The law sets up three important categories of nonsales: bailments, leases, and gifts.

BAILMENT

A **bailment** is a transfer of *possession, care and/or control* of personal property by the owner or possessor (**bailor**) to another (**bailee**) *for a limited time for a special purpose.* Bailments include temporary conveyance of goods for storage, repair, cleaning, and other such transfers of possession of chattels without transfer of title or ownership. There is a detailed discussion of bailments in Chapter 19.

LEASE

A **lease** is a transfer of *possession* by the owner (**lessor**) of real or personal property to another (**lessee**) *for that person's use during a period of time* for an agreed-upon consideration (rent). A new UCC article on the leasing of goods, Article 2A, applies many general UCC principles (course of dealings, trade usages, etc.) and has been adopted by a number of states since 1987.

GIFT

A **gift** is a transfer of *title* by the owner of goods (**donor**) to another person (**donee**) without consideration. Whereas an executory (promised) gift is not an enforceable agreement, a fully executed (completed) gift will not be legally disturbed. An executed gift requires (a) delivery, (b) donor's intent to make a gift, and (c) donee's acceptance.

YOU SHOULD REMEMBER

Transfer of possession of property by bailment or lease is a transaction arising out of contract.

Since there is no consideration, a gift transaction does not arise out of contract but it does convey ownership.

DEFINITION OF A SALE

Both the code (Section 2-106) and the common law agree that a **sale** of goods is the transfer of title from a seller to a buyer for a consideration known as the price.

TRANSFER OF TITLE

One of the cornerstone principles of the common law is that a seller can transfer only the title (rights) that he/she has. If the seller has no title (e.g., a thief) or has a defective title (e.g., subject to mortgage or lien) he/she transfers merely these limited rights, even though the parties may call the transaction a "sale."

The code, however, recognizes three exceptions to the common law, three circumstances in which a buyer may obtain a better title than the seller has had:

1. A person with a **voidable title** (i.e., title received by a buyer subject to cancellation by the seller) can pass a good title to a bonafide purchaser (a purchaser who has no knowledge of defect).

2. A person who in good faith buys goods from a retailer in the regular course of the retailer's business will get a good title even though the retailer *has transferred a prior interest to* others.

3. A person who in good faith buys goods from a dealer in such goods obtains a good title even though the goods in question may have been entrusted to the dealer by others.

In the first circumstance the seller's right to cancel under the code generally occurs because of some kind of fraud practiced by the buyer: giving a bad check, for example, or making some false representation. The buyer, thus in possession and with color (appearance) of title, *can* transfer title to a good-faith purchaser. The original seller who trusted the original buyer can sue only the buyer with whom he/she dealt.

The other two code exceptions to the common law rule against a buyer acquiring a good title from a seller having a less than perfect title involve *dealers in goods.* In the first, the dealer may have previously sold or committed the goods to another person, for example, on "layaway"; in the second, the goods were entrusted to the dealer or merchant for a special purpose—e.g., repair or storage (as in a bailment)—and the bonafide purchaser reasonably believes the dealer or merchant to be the rightful owner. In both of these dealer situations, the real owner's only remedy is against the dealer, not against the innocent buyer from the dealer.

YOU SHOULD REMEMBER

The common law provided that a seller could convey no more than he/she owned. The UCC permits three exceptions:
1. A person with a voidable title can pass a good title to a bona fide purchaser.
2. A person may get a good title from a retailer who has already sold the goods to others.
3. A person may get a good title from a dealer in goods even though the dealer is holding the goods for someone else.

RISK OF LOSS

Before the widespread adoption of the Uniform Commercial Code, the risk of loss of goods *in the process of being sold and delivered* hinged on the answer to the question, "Who had title at the time of loss?" Thus, if goods were lost during the process of delivery, that is, on the high seas, or were stolen from a warehouse, or were damaged while in rail cars, legal questions of title at the moment of loss or damage determined the liability for repair or replacement.

> Under the code, buyer and seller are expected to deal with the problem of potential loss, before or in the course of delivery, *by contract provisions.*

If there are no contract provisions, the code establishes general principles for determining risk of loss, depending on whether the contract of sale and delivery is a "shipment contract" or a "destination contract" (Section 2-509).

SHIPMENT CONTRACTS

A **shipment contract** passes the risk of loss to the buyer when the seller delivers the goods to a carrier. The carrier is deemed the agent (representative; see Chapter 14) of the buyer *in any situation in which the contract does not include a requirement for the seller to deliver the goods to a specified destination.*
Frequently, the use of certain shipping phrases creates a shipment contract:

1. *FOB (free on board),* sometimes with "point of origin," "seller's plant," or "manufacturing facility," together with the statement of FOB point, imposes the risk and cost of loss on the buyer at the FOB point, including the cost of shipment and loading at that point, the seller's factory. However, FOB car or vessel (statement of a different FOB point) requires the seller to load the goods into the buyer's carriage facilities.

2. *FAS (free alongside ship)* requires the seller to deliver the goods at his/her expense and risk to a specified ship and port. For example, "FAS *White Star,* Baltimore, Maryland" would require the seller to deliver the goods to the dock alongside the *White Star* in Baltimore. Cost of loading onto the ship is for the account of the buyer.

3. *CIF (cost, insurance, and freight)* means that the price of the goods includes the cost of shipping and insuring the goods to the buyer's delivery point. These costs are thus passed to the seller.

4. *C & F (cost and freight)* means the same as CIF *without* the insurance obligation falling on the seller.

DESTINATION CONTRACTS

A destination contract passes the risk of loss to the buyer when the goods are delivered to the specified destination. The following terms create destination contracts:

1. *FOB destination:* See item 1 above.

2. *Ex-ship:* This term does not require that the contract name a specific vessel; risk and expense of loss are borne by the seller until the goods have actually been unloaded from the ship.

3. *No arrival, no sale* (UCC, Sections 2-324; 2-613): If the goods do not arrive, there is no contract; and neither buyer nor seller has an obligation to the other unless the seller has caused the nonarrival. If the goods arrive damaged or in violation of the contract, the seller is responsible.

OTHER PRINCIPLES TO DETERMINE RISK OF LOSS

Sometimes it is difficult or impossible to ascertain whether the contract is a shipment or a destination contract *and* there may be no terms in the contract providing for risk of loss. *Section 2-509(3) provides that, if the seller is a merchant, he/she bears the risk of loss until delivery to the buyer; if the seller is not a merchant, risk of loss passes to the buyer when the goods are tendered for delivery, that is, become available to the buyer.* This is another example of the higher duty imposed by the code on merchants.

SALE ON APPROVAL/CONSIGNMENT

On occasion, a seller may deliver goods to a buyer for the buyer's inspection and approval (on trial) or for the buyer's resale (*consignment*), title remaining in the seller (*consignor*) and subject to the terms of a contract between the parties. *Until approval* (approval may be express, implied, or conveyed by silence after the passage of a contractually specified period of time), *risk of loss remains in the seller. However, if the goods are delivered on consignment, risk of loss passes to the consignee (person receiving delivery) and this person may convey title freely to others.*

Consigned goods may be seized or possessed by the consignee's creditors. The consignor may protect his/her interest in the goods by placing the public on notice of the consignor's ownership through proper filing of a notice of a security interest under the code, or placing a sign or other clearly visible statement of ownership where the goods are held for sale.

YOU SHOULD REMEMBER

Goods delivered for the buyer's approval remain titled in the seller and subject to his/her loss until the buyer approves.

If the goods are delivered on consignment (for the buyer to sell them), risk of loss passes to the buyer upon delivery of the goods to him/her.

PRODUCT LIABILITY
PRODUCT LIABILITY ARISING OUT OF CONTRACT

The general discussion in Chapter 6 of the law of contracts mentioned the movement of the law away from the old *caveat emptor* ("let the buyer beware") basis to a more balanced principle protecting the buyer from the seller's deceit, failure to correct misunderstandings, and the like. It was suggested that some courts may even go so far, in protecting buyers from unscrupulous or craftily silent sellers, as to lean toward imposing a rule of *caveat venditor* ("let the seller beware"). Much of this movement in favor of the buyer and against the seller is the result of "buyer-friendly" provisions of Article 2 of the code. Although Article 2 relates specifically to the sale of goods, it has tended to color the common law of all contracts.

Code provisions concerning warranty are at the heart of product liability imposed on sellers by contract.

• *WARRANTIES*

The word **warranty** is synonymous with "guarantee" (sometimes written as "guaranty"). Warranties are of two kinds: express and implied.

EXPRESS WARRANTIES

Like express contracts, express warranties arise out of words or actions that establish a promise.

Under the code [Section 2-313(1)], three kinds of representations *express* a promise of warranty (even though the word "warranty" or "guarantee" may not be used):

1. *An affirmation of the fact of conformance.* This affirmation may be simply a statement that the goods will do a specified thing or serve a specified purpose.

2. *A description of the goods.* Such a description is a warranty that the goods are as described or specified.

3. *Reference to a sample or model.* This reference may be by picture, diagram, drawing, standard, or prototype. It expresses a warranty that the goods are as shown in the sample or model.

   Note: Under general contract law, statements about value, statements of opinion, "huffing and puffing," sales talk, advertisements, and the like are not grounds for misrepresentation or fraud. *Moreover, they do not give rise to warranties or guarantees under the code.*

IMPLIED WARRANTIES

An *implied warranty* is implied by law and arises out of the buyer-seller relationship. *The implied warranty is the commonsense implication arising from the fact that the seller is selling goods to a buyer who has certain reasonable expectations.* This warranty can be disclaimed (denied) by a specific denial (see below). However, in the absence of a disclaimer, implied warranties arise under the code as a matter of law in two respects:

1. *Warranty of merchantability.* This warranty is imposed upon the *merchant* with respect to the goods that it is his/her business to sell. The code defines **merchantability** [Section 2-314(2)] by a number of stated rules, but the primary assurance is that the goods "are fit for the ordinary purposes for which such goods are used," and would thus pass without objection in the trade. The implied warranty of merchantability, however, does not form the basis of lawsuit without proof that: (i) the goods were not merchantable at the time of sale, and (ii) the plaintiff was injured because the goods failed to meet the merchantability standard (Section 2-314).

2. *Warranty of fitness.* The warranty of **fitness** differs from the warranty of merchantability in two major ways: first, it applies not only to merchants but also to any other sellers of goods, and second, it impliedly warrants that the goods will be fit for the buyer's *particular* purpose, which may or may not be the general purpose for which the goods were intended. Thus, if the seller knows that the buyer is purchasing a mower for a 10-acre field of weeds and undergrowth, the fitness warranty applies and is more severe than the merchantability warranty.

• *DISCLAIMERS*

The code and the common law permit a seller to avoid both express and implied warranties through general contract principles, that is, *through mutual agreement the parties may eliminate or modify the warranty obligation.* This avoidance of warranty is a **disclaimer.**

The best and simplest way for sellers to protect themselves from all warranty obligations is by use of the words "as is," or "without warranty of any kind, whether express or implied." "As is" is particularly recommended as a simple, direct, and unambiguous statement of contractual understanding with regard to used or second-hand merchandise or even new merchandise "on sale."

In addition to the "as is" disclaimer, Section 2-316 provides that there is no warranty if the buyer, before entering into the contract, examined the goods, or refused to examine the goods when such examination would have revealed the defect. (This is the common law principle of unilateral mistake referred to in Chapter 6.) Moreover, an implied warranty may be found not to have occurred because of some previous performance between the parties or because of usages of their trade [UCC, Section 2-316(3)(c)].

Caution: Disclaimers are most effective in contractual dealings between parties of approximately equal bargaining ability and equal skill and background. Merchants dealing with the entire public on a serve-one-serve-all basis *must lean over backward to make their nonexpressions of warranty just that: statements of value or opinion, with abundant exclusion and qualification. In addition, their written disclaimers should be in bold type or type of a different color, difficult for even the most uneducated or careless reader to miss or claim not to have seen.*

> For a contract to exist, minds must meet and language must be clear and discernible. Whether the buyer saw the disclaimer or should have seen the disclaimer may be a question for a jury to decide.

A careful seller, in short, takes pains to call attention to the disclaimer. Disclaimers in fine print, on tickets, and on the reverse sides of invoices are weak and may be ineffective to establish intent.

Even with all of the safeguards mentioned above, the disclaimer may be unenforceable if it is unconscionable because of the uneven bargaining powers of the parties or some other fundamental inequality in their respective circumstances.

• THE MAGNUSON-MOSS ACT

This federal statute, which became law on July 4, 1975, was intended to provide consumers with greater protection from merchants than was thought available under the code warranties. The act does not *require* that a merchant give warranties, nor does it alter the nature of implied warranties. It does provide that, for items purchased for amounts in excess of $10, any warranty by the merchant shall be conspicuously designated as either a "full (statement of time, for example, 24 months) warranty" or "limited warranty."

The "full warranty" is just that: it prohibits the merchant-seller from disclaiming, modifying, or limiting the duration of an implied warranty and requires the warrantor to remedy defects within a reasonable time and without charge. The "limited warranty" may clearly state any limitations on consequential damages or on the duration of implied warranties. However, the act provides that the substance of an implied warranty may *not* be disclaimed or modified if *in addition* the seller makes a written warranty or provides a service contract within 90 days of the time of sale.

• IS PRIVITY OF CONTRACT REQUIRED TO RECOVER FOR BREACH OF WARRANTY?

Privity, it will be recalled, is the requirement that a person be a party to a contract to bring a suit on that contract. From two entirely different points of view, privity of contract poses a problem with respect to breach of warranty.

From the point of view of the seller, does his/her responsibility for damages extend only to the buyer of the seller's goods, the party with whom he/she has privity? Or can other injured parties—a member of the buyer's family, a guest in the buyer's house, a customer in the buyer's place of business—bring suit against the seller of defective goods, even though there is no privity? Today most courts hold that persons on the same level of consumption as the buyer—guests, bystanders, family members—can sue the seller or manufacturer of the goods, even though there is no **horizontal privity** from the buyer or seller to these other persons, so long as the seller could reasonably anticipate that such persons would be exposed to, and might be injured by, the defective product. For example, exploding canned goods, defective cosmetics, contaminated foods—all subject their seller to claims for damages by *foreseeably* exposed persons (see UCC 2-318).

From the point of view of the buyer, can he/she seek redress not only from the person selling the goods but also from the manufacturer, the wholesaler, the distributor, and other persons in the chain of distribution with whom he/she had no contract, no privity? This question of **vertical privity** is answered in much the same way as that of horizontal privity. If these more remote persons could have foreseen the chain of sales placing the goods into the hands of the ultimate buyer, and could have reasonably foreseen that the persons subsequently injured by defects in the product would be exposed to the item, liability is established notwithstanding the absence of privity. This disregarding of privity, whether in contract/warranty or tort/negligence cases, began with the classic negligence case, *MacPherson v. Buick Motor Co.,* 111 N.E. 1050 (Court of Appeals of New York, 1916). Manufacturer Buick sold a car with defective wheels to a dealer who, in turn, sold the car to MacPherson. Buick was held directly liable to MacPherson for his injuries from a crash caused by the defective wheels; the court found this sequence of events foreseeable, and thus it extended Buick's duty of care to the remote, plaintiff consumer, despite a lack of privity between Buick and that consumer.

YOU SHOULD REMEMBER

The law has moved from *caveat emptor* toward *caveat venditor.* Part of this movement has been achieved by warranties.

Express warranties arise because the seller represents that the goods will do a specified thing, meet a certain description or specification, or be like a picture, drawing, or standard. An *implied warranty* arises from the implications of the fact that the seller is selling goods. If he/she is a merchant, the goods should be merchantable; if the seller (merchant or not) knows of some special use by the buyer, he/she implies that the goods will suit that purpose.

Warranty can be avoided by means of a *disclaimer,* such as the words "as is" or "without warranty of any kind, either express or implied." A disclaimer should be clearly evident by large, bold type and/or prominent position. Disclaimers are most effective between parties of approximately equal bargaining ability. They may be unenforceable if fundamental unfairness in circumstances exists.

The Magnuson-Moss Act sets certain requirements for warranties by merchants for goods costing over $10. The merchant-seller who gives a full warranty or a limited warranty is held to certain strict standards and must clearly identify the extent of the warranty.

Privity of contract is no longer required for suit based on warranty. In both horizontal and vertical privity, the usual test is *foreseeability,* that is, whether manufacturers, sellers, and distributors could reasonably foresee the kinds and groups of persons who would be exposed to the goods to be sold and thus possibly injured by them.

PRODUCT LIABILITY ARISING OUT OF TORT

So far the discussion of sales has dealt with product liability arising out of contract. We now turn to the tort liability of a seller of goods, that is, responsibility arising out of one of the following:

1. *Intentional* harmful action.

2. *Negligent* harmful action.

3. *Strict liability*, a relatively modern category.

Since intentional harmful action is rarely a factor in product liability cases, this discussion will deal with the *negligence* of a seller or manufacturer and with *strict liability.*

As discussed in Chapter 4, negligence is failure to follow some generally accepted standard of care. Thus, if manufactured goods explode, if cosmetics cause injury to the face or eyes, if plaintiff becomes ill upon consuming defendant's canned soup, a negligence case must demonstrate, first, some standard of care generally applicable in the manufacture of such goods, and, second, failure by the defendant to rise to the level of such standard of care.

Obviously, these requirements for proving negligence can be difficult if not impossible for a plaintiff to meet, and modern common law has devised principles to assist the plaintiff in certain carefully delineated kinds of situations.

One of these principles is *res ipsa loquitur* ("the thing speaks for itself"). Under this principle, negligence need not be proved by plaintiff if (a) the product was under the exclusive control of defendant at the time of its manufacture, and (b) injuries such as those suffered by plaintiff do not ordinarily happen in the absence of negligence. Thus, in the exploding bottle case—(a soft drink bottle exploding as it is being placed in a grocery cart), *res ipsa loquitur* may be used as a substitute for the requirement of proving negligence by the manufacturer when the drink was bottled. (*Res ipsa loquitur* is discussed in Chapter 4.)

Strict liability is another exception to the negligence requirement. This theory, a modern common law (not statutory) development, imposes liability on manufacturers and sellers *as a matter of public policy.* As set forth in the Second Restatement of Torts §402A (used by most courts), there are three requirements: (1) that the product was sold in a defective condition and as such was unreasonably dangerous to the user; (2) that the seller is in the business of selling such a product (a merchant); (3) that the product reached the user without substantial change.

The word "defective" does not have the literal meaning usually ascribed to it; rather, it means merely that the goods were not in such condition or of such manufacture as an ordinary consumer might reasonably expect. Thus, electric saws or drills without proper guards or protective devices, nightgowns that are readily combustible when exposed to the flame of a stove or oven, a child's toy that might easily cut or otherwise injure the child—all may be "defective" even though carefully manufactured.

The far-reaching effects of this tort doctrine are readily apparent. Cases abound dealing with the liability of automobile manufacturers and other dealers in a vast array of consumer products.

The seller's remedy for possible strict liability lies in full and adequately placed warnings. Even with such warnings, however, plaintiffs may have little or no difficulty framing a *prima facie* case—a case strong enough to reach a jury.

YOU SHOULD REMEMBER

Modern common law has developed certain principles to help plaintiffs in tort cases where negligence on the part of the seller or manufacturer would be difficult and perhaps impossible to prove. The most important of these are *res ipsa loquitur* and *strict liability*.

PERFORMANCE OF THE SALES CONTRACT

Peformance of the sales contract is governed by Part 5 of Article 2 of the Uniform Commercial Code. Before the provisions of Part 5 are discussed, it will be helpful to review both the common law of contracts and some other provisions of the code that touch on the question of performance.

As always, the performance obligations of parties to a contract are to be found, if possible, in the contract itself. At the beginning of this chapter we discussed the code requirement of "good faith"—"honesty" and, in the case of a merchant, observance of standards of "fair dealing" applicable to his/her trade. In truth, the code did not create the requirements of "good faith," "honesty," or "fair dealing"; they were, and are, part of the common law.

Unless specific provisions of the code affect or define the performance obligations of the parties, questions of performance are determined by the contract itself or by the general law of contracts.

TENDER

Section 2-507(1) of the UCC requires that the seller of goods "tender" their delivery as a condition of the buyer's duties to accept them and, unless otherwise agreed, to pay for them. Section 2-511(1) requires that, unless otherwise agreed, the buyer's "tender" of payment is a condition to the seller's duty to "tender and complete delivery of the goods."

The word "tender," as used here, means merely "to proffer" or "make available." However, "tender" is a legal term with specific shades of meaning as defined by the code and the general law.

• *WHO TENDERS FIRST?*

Although the code sections may seem to create an impasse as to whether the seller or the buyer makes the first tender, in practice an impasse rarely occurs. In most contracts, whether shipment contracts or delivery contracts, including FOB place of shipment or buyer's plant and FAS seller's or buyer's port, the first move must be made by the seller: he/she must tender (make available) the goods to the buyer unless the contract specifically requires that the buyer tender payment, or part payment, before the seller's tender is made.

• *SELLER'S TENDER; THE PERFECT TENDER RULE*

Under the common law of contracts, substantial performance of a contract is considered performance. The code changes this rule with regard to the seller's obligation to tender conforming goods; the goods must be made available strictly in conformity with the contract (the **perfect tender rule**). Substantial performance will not suffice. Section 2-601 of the code provides that, if the *tender of delivery or if the goods* "fail in *any respect* to conform to the contract," the buyer may do one of three things: (a) reject all the goods, (b) accept all, or (c) accept conforming goods and reject the rest.

> This rule of "perfect tender" is a hard rule, but the courts have held that it means what it says.

Other aspects of the seller's tender are also governed by the code, but these are generally mere codifications (statutory enactments) of the common law. The seller must hold the goods for the buyer for a reasonable time; the goods must be tendered within a reasonable time; if the contract does not specify or imply an obligation to deliver to a specified place, the place of tender is the seller's place of business. Here, also, such terms as "FOB," "FAS," "CIF," "C & F," and "No arrival, no sale," discussed earlier in this chapter, also apply.

• *BUYER'S TENDER*

In the absence of contract provisions to the contrary, once the seller has made the goods available to the buyer, the buyer must tender payment before taking possession. Section 2-511 provides that "payment" is sufficient if in accordance with the ordinary course of business. This permits payment by check; if the seller requires cash, the buyer must be given a reasonable period of time within which to procure it. Of course, if the check is dishonored, the buyer's title to the goods is voidable and the goods may be repossessed by the seller.

BUYER'S RIGHT OF INSPECTION

Section 2-513 of the UCC provides that the buyer has the right to inspect the goods before payment or acceptance. Cost of inspection must be borne by the buyer unless the goods do not conform to the contract; then these expenses revert to the seller. *A C.O.D. delivery does not provide the buyer with the right of inspection before payment of the price [Section 2-513(3)(a)].*

YOU SHOULD REMEMBER

The contract itself is the best guide to determine the performance obligations of the parties to a contract.

In the absence of express provisions in the contract, the seller has an obligation to tender (make available) the goods; the buyer is obligated to tender payment. Generally, the first move must be made by the seller. The code requires perfect tender (absolute compliance with the contract) by the seller.

The buyer generally has the right to inspect the goods before accepting or paying for them. Ordinarily the buyer may pay for the goods by check; if cash is required, he/she is entitled to a reasonable period of time to obtain it.

REMEDIES FOR BREACH OF SALES CONTRACTS

GENERAL PROVISIONS; THE "MAKE WHOLE" PRINCIPLE

Section 1-106(1) of the code provides that the remedies provided for shall "be liberally administered to the end that the aggrieved party shall be put in as good a position as if the other party had fully performed...." This code provision is a statutory confirmation of the general contract rule for damages (see Chapter 9). The expression "liberally administered" requires the courts to lean over backward in complying with the "make whole" principle in attempting to assess damages.

The code (Section 2-718) provides for liquidated damage clauses in sales contracts (if not unconscionable, penal, or excessive), as does the general law. Section

2-719 permits the parties to exclude or limit consequential damages (e.g., lost profits). However, such a limitation is considered *prima facie* unconscionable in the sale of consumer goods (where it would protect the merchant), but not so in the sale of commercial goods (sold to a merchant or in the course of trade).

There is one other important general provision in the code concerning remedies: *the statute of limitations for a sales contract (period within which suit must be filed) is 4 years* from date of breach (Section 2-725). The code goes on to state that the contract may provide for a shorter period down to 1 year, but may not extend the period beyond 4 years. Limitations for other kinds of contracts vary from state to state.

SELLER'S REMEDIES FOR BREACH BY BUYER

A buyer may breach a sales contract by (i) wrongfully refusing to accept the goods, (ii) wrongfully returning the goods, (iii) failing to pay for the goods when payment is due or (iv) expressing an unwillingness to go forward with the contract.

The code is quite detailed as to a seller's remedies (right to be made whole) upon the occurrence of a breach. Among other things, the seller may cancel the contract and hold up delivery, resell the goods to another buyer and recover damages for any difference in price (see Section 2-706 for this procedure), or recover damages for nonacceptance or repudiation. These rights are cumulative (the seller does not have to choose one to the exclusion of others). As stated, unless limited by contract, the seller is entitled to consequential and incidental damages. (See page 147).

BUYER'S REMEDIES FOR BREACH BY SELLER

A seller may breach a sales contract by (i) failing to deliver the goods as agreed, (ii) delivering goods that do not conform to the contract, or (iii) expressing an unwillingness to go forward with the contract.

As in the case of the seller's remedies, the code is detailed as to the buyer's remedies upon breach by the seller. The buyer (Section 2-712) may buy other goods (known as "covering") and recover damages for any difference in price plus additional expenses, recover damages based on the difference between the contract price and the current market price (Section 2-713), recover damages for goods that do not comply with the contract, or obtain specific performance if the goods are unique (see pages 148–149).

> The reader should compare the provisions of the code for breach of sales contracts with the general common law provisions already discussed. The code does not attempt to rewrite the law: it attempts to improve where appropriate and possible, and to make uniform.

YOU SHOULD REMEMBER

The UCC applies the "make whole" principle to damages incurred by buyer or seller when a sales contract is breached. The statute of limitations is set at 4 years after date of breach, but may by contract be reduced to a shorter term (no less than 1 year).

KNOW THE CONCEPTS
DO YOU KNOW THE BASICS?

1. Why is there a special article in the Uniform Commercial Code dealing with sales contracts but not an article dealing with contracts in general?
2. Give some examples of the higher standard of dealing imposed on merchants by the code.
3. Name two legal transactions that transfer possession, but not title.
4. In what ways does the code permit a possessor of property to convey a better title than he/she has?
5. Does the code rely entirely on contract terms in determining risk of loss during the process of sale and delivery of goods?
6. What is the basis of the seller's contract liability for defective goods? How can sellers protect themselves from this liability?
7. What is the basis of the seller's tort liability for defective goods? How can sellers protect themselves?
8. How did the Magnuson-Moss Act affect the law of warranty?
9. Is privity of contract required to recover for breach of warranty?
10. How does the perfect tender rule change the common law rule of performance?

TERMS FOR STUDY

"as is"	donor
bailee	fitness
bailment	gift
bailor	horizontal privity
chattel	lease
covering	lessee
destination contract	lessor
disclaimer	merchant
donee	merchantability

method of dealing
perfect tender rule
prima facie case
sale
shipment contract

tender
vertical privity
voidable title
warranty

PRACTICAL APPLICATION

1. Anderson, purchasing manager for Fast Kolor Paint Company, mailed a purchase order to AB Can Corporation for 100,000 cans. The order form contained 17 printed conditions on its reverse side. The third condition stated: "Buyer may reject any defective goods within 30 days of delivery." AB Can sent a letter confirming the order, but the letter stated: "Any objection to goods shipped must be made in writing within 5 days of receipt of goods." Anderson sought to object to 10,000 of the cans, as defective, on the seventh day after receipt. What would be the result?

2. AG Gas Wells, Inc., and Trans-American Pipelines Company enter into a contract whereby AG agrees to sell natural gas to Trans-American. The price is to be set by AG based on "the average price then being obtained by gas producers in the state of Oklahoma for sales of gas in interstate commerce." If all essentials other than price are established in the contract, is the contract binding as to price?

3. Smith takes an overcoat to XYZ Dry Cleaners to be dry cleaned. He inadvertently left a $20 gold piece in one of the pockets. XYZ sells this coin to Gould, a coin collector. Can Smith recover the coin from Gould?

4. Free State Fireworks Company, Silver Spring, Maryland, purchased a shipment of fireworks from Hercules Powder Company, FOB seller's plant, Wilmington, Delaware. While the shipment was in transit from Wilmington to Silver Spring, the fireworks exploded, killing three persons and causing a vast amount of property damage. There is some evidence of negligent manufacture of the fireworks. Discuss the possible liability of Free State and Hercules, respectively.

5. ABC Pharmaceutical Company manufactures drugs and medicines. In 1976 it was the producer of vaccine for the national swine flu immunization program. Speck, a vaccinee, was partially paralyzed after being vaccinated, and medical experts believe that the vaccine caused the paralysis. Does Speck have a valid claim against ABC? On what basis?

ANSWERS
KNOW THE CONCEPTS

1. Sales contracts involve both consumers and merchants, categories with high levels of visibility and concern in the law of business. Also, there is a greater need for uniformity of law in these categories.

2. Merchants must observe not only rules of honesty, but also reasonable standards of fair dealing in their trade; they are subject to an implied warranty of merchantability; their contracts are interpreted in accordance with methods of doing business in their trade; they have a high standard of duty to make disclosures to uneducated and untrained buyers; they may be subject to strict liability in tort; they have limited ability to disclaim liability for consequential damages in their sales contracts.

3. Bailment and lease.

4. A person with a voidable title can pass a good title to a bona fide purchaser; a purchaser from a retailer who had previously sold an interest in the goods to some other person can acquire a good title; a purchaser may get a good title from a dealer in goods even though the dealer is holding the goods for someone else.

5. If the contract terms are clear about risk of loss, these terms control. If the contract contains no provision, the seller bears the risk until delivery of goods to the buyer.

6. Seller's contract liability arises from express or implied warranty. The best defense is a disclaimer of warranty in the contract.

7. Tort liability in the sale of goods arises from negligent manufacture or from strict liability. The best defense is full warning about possible injury and the need of the buyer to use care.

8. The Magnuson-Moss Act sets certain requirements for warranties. They must be either "full warranties," without limitations, or "limited warranties," with clearly stated limitations.

9. No. Generally, parties may be sued if they could foresee the existence of, and possible injury to, the purchaser and others even though these injured persons do not have privity of contract with the seller, manufacturer, and others in the sales chain.

10. The common law rule of performance considers "substantial" performance as an acceptable performance. The perfect tender rule requires absolute compliance with the contract before the tender is considered to have been performed.

PRACTICAL APPLICATION

1. This is a "battle of forms" question. If Anderson objected to the 5-day notice-of-defect provision in the seller's letter of confirmation, he should have promptly notified the seller. Failure to object sets up the 5-day requirement as part of the contract, and the buyer cannot object after this period of time since the proposed term did not "materially vary the offer."

2. An agreement permitting one of the parties to set the price is enforceable if that party acts in good faith. The gas producer must make a genuine

effort, and document this effort, to determine an average price being charged for interstate gas sales in the state of Oklahoma.

3. Smith cannot recover the coin from Gould, a bona fide purchaser, from a party in possession with a voidable title. Smith can, however, sue XYZ Dry Cleaners for the value of the coin.

4. Free State is responsible for risk of loss in transit because of the term "FOB seller's plant," which designates the buyer's assumption of the risk. However, the *real cause* of the explosion, loss of the property, and damage to others may be negligent manufacture by Hercules. Free State could probably use *res ipsa loquitur* as a substitute for proof of negligence, or possibly strict liability in tort, depending on the circumstances of the sale.

5. Speck may have a *prima facie* case against ABC. Vaccines, properly tested and manufactured, should not cause paralysis; thus the doctrine of *res ipsa loquitur* or strict liability in tort may be applied.

11

COMMERCIAL PAPER: DEFINITIONS, CONCEPTS, AND NEGOTIATION

KEY TERMS

commercial paper in its broadest sense, documents used to facilitate the transfer of money or credit

negotiable instrument a type of commercial paper; a written, signed, unconditional promise or order to pay a certain sum of money to order or bearer either on demand or at a definite time

negotiation the process by which both possession of, and title to, an instrument are transferred from one party to another, with the transferee becoming a "holder"

holder a person who possesses a negotiable instrument issued, drawn, or indorsed to that person or his/her order or to bearer

---

The term "**commercial paper**" encompasses a variety of documents used to facilitate the exchange of money, including extensions of credit. There are two important types of commercial paper: a *promise* to pay money (e.g., the promissory note and the certificate of deposit) and an *order* to pay money (e.g., the draft and the check).

Chapters 11 through 13 will discuss the major forms of commercial paper and the uniform law governing those forms.

THE NEGOTIABLE INSTRUMENT AS A FORM OF COMMERCIAL PAPER

The development and use of commercial paper resulted from, and in turn helped to accelerate, the growth of trade. As the words themselves suggest only after the development of *commerce* did people need *commercial* paper. Once it became impracticable to pay always in cash or commodities, society needed a money substitute that would have the ready acceptability of cash, but would entail much less risk of loss or theft. Various types of commercial paper, including the check, have met these requirements.

Commercial paper, though, is not merely a substitute for cash. It can also serve as a means of extending credit. The borrower agrees in writing to repay his/her loan, and that document (e.g., a promissory note), like a simple money-substitute document (e.g., a check), is a special type of commercial paper: the **negotiable instrument**.

Negotiable instruments are constantly being used by businesses and consumers. Most major business transactions depend on credit. Without negotiable instruments, there would be no efficient, readily understood method of extending credit on such a grand scale. Likewise, consider the check: it is clearly the most common form of commercial paper (excluding money itself), and millions of checks are written every day.

YOU SHOULD REMEMBER

Commercial paper can serve as a substitute for cash and/or as a means of extending credit. Special types of commercial paper—negotiable instruments—play a fundamental part in most business transactions.

DEVELOPMENT OF THE LAW GOVERNING NEGOTIABLE INSTRUMENTS

In England, negotiable instruments law was part of a field of law known as the *law merchant*, which was first developed and enforced in special merchant courts. Based on the customs among merchants, this law's major concern was to aid, not hinder, the growth of trade.

The merchant courts were abolished in 1756. By then, the law merchant had been incorporated into the common law but remained incomplete and chaotic. Lord Mansfield, Chief Justice of the King's Bench from 1756 to 1788, extended the commercial law and refined the terms and rights of parties under that law.

Relying on Mansfield's work, the British Parliament formally codified the negotiable instruments law by enacting the Bills of Exchange Act in 1882. Many American lawyers, judges, and bankers realized that the United States needed a similar codification, and by 1924 all of the states had enacted a set of proposed uniform laws termed the "Negotiable Instruments Law."

By the late 1940s, changes in commercial practice, as well as divergent interpretations by state courts, led to the belief that negotiable instruments law had to be reformed and made truly "uniform."

YOU SHOULD REMEMBER

The American law of negotiable instruments originated in England. Despite previous efforts, by the late 1940s there remained a need to codify the law and make it uniform throughout the United States.

THE UNIFORM COMMERCIAL CODE, ARTICLES 3 AND 4

Negotiable instruments law is now a part of the Uniform Commercial Code, specifically Article 3 (Commercial Paper) and Article 4 (Bank Deposits and Collections). These articles, like the overall code, do not represent a brand-new approach to an old subject; rather they attempt to simplify, clarify, and make uniform the nation's commercial law. Indeed, a 1990 revised form of Articles 3 and 4 is before the states, but so far has been adopted by less than a dozen states. All of the discussion in Chapters 11–13 would apply to either the original or revised Articles. The original Articles still command the support of over three-fourths of the states, including all larger states but Illinois, so the UCC references in the text are to the original Articles.

Although some negotiable documents, such as documents of title and investment securities, are covered in other articles of the UCC, Articles 3 and 4 concern the two fundamental, omnipresent forms of commercial paper: promises to pay money and orders to pay money. As mentioned earlier, promissory notes and bank certificates of deposit are examples of promises to pay money. An order to pay money is called a draft. By far the most common type of draft is the check, which is an order directed to a bank.

YOU SHOULD REMEMBER

Articles 3 (Commercial Paper) and 4 (Bank Deposits and Collections) of the Uniform Commercial Code clarify and make uniform commercial law governing the two basic forms of commercial paper: promises to pay money and orders to pay money.

ELEMENTS OF NEGOTIABILITY

Section 3-104(1) of the Uniform Commercial Code states the requirements for negotiability. To be negotiable an instrument must:

(a) be written;

(b) be signed by the maker or drawer;

(c) contain an unconditional promise or order to pay a sum certain in money, and no other promise, order, obligation, or power given by the maker or drawer, except as authorized by Article 3;

(d) be payable on demand or at a definite time; and

(e) be payable to order or to bearer.

An instrument that meets all of these requirements except the last one (i.e., it is not payable to order or to bearer) is treated like a negotiable instrument except that there can be no holder in due course (HIDC) (UCC 3-805; a HIDC is defined in Chapter 12).

The five requirements given above are strictly construed. Ambiguities are resolved in favor of nonnegotiability; and, if an instrument is plainly nonnegotiable, the parties to that instrument cannot agree to make it negotiable.

Section 3-104(1) negotiability is thus restricted to drafts, checks, certificates of deposit, and notes. Other forms of commercial paper, including cash and investment securities, may be easily transferred, but are not negotiable instruments (UCC 3-103).

SIGNATURE OF MAKER OR DRAWER

A "signature" is any symbol that a party executes or adopts in order to authenticate a writing [UCC 1-201(3)]. It need not be handwritten, but must be on the instrument itself [UCC 3-401(1)].

The law presumes that a signature is authorized, that is, genuine, or made with the actual, implied, or apparent consent of the person who is to be bound by the signature [UCC 3-307(1)(b)]. Indeed, in some cases, even an unauthorized signature is treated as if it were authorized (UCC 3-404); for instance, if the person whose signature is unauthorized knew about it but failed to inform innocent parties who reasonably believed that the signature was authorized.

UNCONDITIONAL PROMISE OR ORDER TO PAY

The term "unconditional" generally means that the promise or order is not limited or changed by a clause or any other item contained within or incorporated into the instrument. Conditions include tying payment to the occurrence of an event or to the performance of an agreement.

• *INTACT NEGOTIABILITY*

Numerous statements can be placed on an instrument without destroying its negotiability. Such statements, which are not deemed to be conditions on the promise or order to pay, include mentioning:

(a) the transactions or agreements that gave rise to the instrument;

(b) the instrument's consideration;

(c) a separate agreement;

(d) that the instrument matures in accordance with a particular transaction;

(e) that acceleration or prepayment rights are in a separate agreement;

(f) that indorsement or cashing constitutes full satisfaction of the drawer's obligation;

(g) that the instrument is secured (but inclusion of the security agreement or mortgage in the instrument itself will make it conditional);

(h) that a confession of judgment is authorized upon default.

These statements are covered in UCC 3-105, 3-112, and 3-119.

• *DESTROYED NEGOTIABILITY*

Two types of statements make an instrument conditional, and thus nonnegotiable:

1. A statement that the instrument is subject to or governed by another agreement.

2. A statement that the instrument is to be paid only out of a particular fund or source (except for instruments issued by a government or its agencies). A provision limiting payment by a partnership, incorporated association, trust, or estate to the assets of that entity (but not one particular source within the entity) does not render the instrument conditional [UCC 3-105(2)].

SUM CERTAIN IN MONEY

To constitute a "sum certain," the amount must be expressly stated or readily verifiable from the terms of the instrument. A stated amount is not rendered uncertain by including a specified interest rate, installment payments, particular discounts or additions, collection costs, and/or attorney's fees (UCC 3-106).

The term "money" encompasses all means of exchange authorized by some government as part of its currency. Therefore an instrument payable in dinars, francs, or some other foreign currency can be negotiable.

PAYABLE ON DEMAND OR AT A DEFINITE TIME

To be negotiable, an instrument must be either payable on demand (UCC 3-108) or payable at a definite time (UCC 3-109).

• *ON DEMAND*

A negotiable instrument that either (a) does not state a time for payment or (b) expressly states that it is payable on demand, presentation, or sight, is a demand instrument (e.g., a check). It becomes due (is to be paid) simply upon being presented for payment.

• *AT A DEFINITE TIME*

A "definite time" instrument may be payable:

(a) on or before a stated date;

(b) at a fixed period after a stated date;

(c) at a fixed period after sight (presentment);

(d) at a definite time subject to acceleration (advancing the date of payment to a sooner, definite time);

(e) at a definite time subject to extension (postponing the date of payment) (i) by the holder; (ii) by the maker or acceptor, to a further, definite time; or (iii) automatically, upon or after a specified act or event, to a further, definite time.

The payment time cannot be based on a special act or event that is uncertain as to time of occurrence, *even though the act or event has in fact occurred or is certain to happen some time* [UCC 3-109(2)]. Thus an instrument is nonnegotiable if it is payable on Mr. X's death; although death is a certainty, when Mr. X's death will occur is uncertain.

PAYABLE TO ORDER (UCC 3-110) OR TO BEARER (UCC 3-111)

"To order" includes:

(a) pay to the order of A;

(b) pay to A or his/her assigns;

(c) pay to A or his/her order;

(d) pay to the order of A and B;

(e) pay to A as the agent of B;

(f) pay to the order of A or B.

"To bearer" includes:

(a) pay bearer;

(b) pay to the order of bearer;

(c) pay A or bearer;

(d) pay to the order of cash.

A person can indorse an instrument in such a way as to convert it from order to bearer paper, or vice-versa.

RULES OF CONSTRUCTION

Negotiable instruments may be postdated, antedated, or undated (UCC 3-114), and need not state the place where the instrument is drawn or payable (UCC 3-112). The dates on the instruments are presumed correct.

Rules of agency (see Chapter 14) are applicable. Thus authorized agents may complete an instrument (UCC 3-115).

If it is unclear whether a negotiable instrument is a draft or a note, the holder may treat it as either (UCC 3-118).

When there are disputes as to the terms of an instrument, the following rules govern:

1. Handwriting takes precedence over typewriting and print.
2. Typewriting takes precedence over print.
3. Words take precedence over figures, but vice versa if the words are ambiguous.
4. An unspecified rate of interest is treated as being the same as the judgment rate (interest rate earned on unpaid judgments) for the place where the instrument is paid. Interest runs from the date of the instrument or, if undated, from the issue date.

Two or more persons may sign in the same role (e.g., as comakers or codrawers). Unless otherwise specified, each such person is fully responsible for any liability charged to that "role," be it maker, drawer, or whatever.

REMEMBER: The fact that an instrument is nonnegotiable does not mean it is worthless. It still may evince a valid, enforceable contract.

YOU SHOULD REMEMBER

To be negotiable, an instrument must (a) be written; (b) be signed by the maker or drawer; (c) contain an unconditional promise or order to pay a sum certain in money, and no other promise, order, obligation, or power given by the maker or drawer, except as authorized by UCC Article 3; (d) be payable on demand or at a definite time; and (e) be payable to order or to bearer. The four types of negotiable instruments are promissory notes, certificates of deposit (a type of note), drafts, and checks (a type of draft).

Signatures need not be handwritten, can consist of any symbol used to authenticate a writing, and are presumed (as are the dates on an instrument) to be authorized. "Sum certain" generally means that the amount is expressly stated or readily verifiable from the terms of the instrument. "Unconditional" means that the promise or order is not limited or changed by a clause or anything else within the instrument; however, UCC Article 3 specifies numerous statements that do not render an instrument "conditional."

If an instrument does not state when payment is due, the instrument is deemed to be a demand instrument. A "definite time" can include acceleration or extension, but payment cannot be contingent upon an act or event uncertain as to when it will occur (even though the act or event has in fact occurred or is certain to happen sometime).

A person can indorse an instrument in such a way as to convert it from order to bearer paper, or vice versa. Authorized agents may complete an instrument, and two or more persons may sign in the same role (e.g., as comakers or codrawers). If there is a dispute as to the terms of an instrument, handwriting takes precedence over typewriting and print, typewriting takes precedence over print, and words take precedence over figures (unless the words are ambiguous).

A nonnegotiable instrument may still be evidence of a valid, enforceable contract.

TYPES OF NEGOTIABLE INSTRUMENTS
PROMISSORY NOTE

The **promissory note** is a two-party instrument in which one person (the **maker**) makes an unconditional, written promise to pay another person (the **payee**), or a person specified by the payee, a certain sum of money either on demand or at a particular time in the future.

$ ___10.02___   Date ___May 30, 199–___

___Ninety days___ after the date above ___I___ promise to pay to

the order of _____ Larry Smith _____

------------------ten dollars and 02/100------------------

No. ___8165___   Due: ___August 28, 199–___   ___Jim Jones___

Jim Jones is the maker, and Larry Smith is the payee.

CERTIFICATE OF DEPOSIT (CD)

Issued by a *financial institution* (e.g., a bank) as an acknowledgment that the institution has received the deposit of a particular sum of money, the **certificate of deposit** contains the institution's written promise to pay the depositor that sum of money, plus a stated rate of interest, at a specified time in the future.

```
┌─────────────────────────────────────────────────────────────────────┐
│                        Certificate of Deposit                         │
│                                                                       │
│                                          Date ___August 22, 199–___   │
│                                                                       │
│  This is to certify that ____Sybil Caesar____ has deposited in        │
│                                                                       │
│  PLEBEIAN NATIONAL BANK ___$20.00___                                  │
│                                                                       │
│  Twenty and no/100------------------------------------------ dollars  │
│                                                                       │
│  Payable to __Sybil Caesar__ or order __6__ months after date above   │
│  with interest at the rate of 7% per annum from date above.           │
│                                                                       │
│  Due: __February 22, 199–__                     ____/s/____           │
│                                             President, Plebeian National │
└─────────────────────────────────────────────────────────────────────┘
```

Plebeian National Bank is the maker, and Sybil Caesar is the depositor/payee.

DRAFT

A **draft** is a three-party instrument in which one person (the **drawer**) orders a second person (the **drawee**) to pay a certain sum of money to a third person (the **payee**), or another person specified by the payee, either on demand or at a particular time in the future.

```
┌─────────────────────────────────────────────────────────────────────┐
│  $ __76.54__              _____  Washington, D.C.   April 17, 199–   │
│                                                                       │
│   __60 days after date__ Pay to the order of                         │
│                                                                       │
│   Pseudo Manufacturing Company                                        │
│                                                                       │
│   Seventy-six dollars and 54/100----------------------------------    │
│                                                                       │
│  Value received and charge the same to account of:                    │
│                                                                       │
│  To: Erstwhile Services, Inc.                                         │
│                                                                       │
│   Anytown, U.S.A.  12345          _____Tom Thompson_____            │
│                                              Drawer                    │
└─────────────────────────────────────────────────────────────────────┘
```

Thompson is the drawer, Erstwhile is the drawee, and Pseudo is the payee.

CHECK

A **check** is a special type of draft in which the *drawee* is always a *bank* and the instrument is *payable on demand.*

	Date ____ September 2, 199– ____
Pay to the order of _____ Mary Merchant _____	$ 2.00
Two -- dollars	
NAME OF BANK	
For: ____ Memorandum ____	____ Bob Buyer ____
012345666 70 114679	

Mary Merchant is the payee, Bob Buyer is the drawer, and Name of Bank is the drawee.

A check drawn by a bank upon itself is a *cashier's check.* The *traveler's check* is likewise a check in which the financial institution is both drawer and drawee. *Certified checks* are checks that have been "accepted" by the drawee bank, that is, the bank certifies that there is money in the drawer's account to cover the check.

THE PARTIES TO A NEGOTIABLE INSTRUMENT

A promissory note and a certificate of deposit originate with two parties:

1. The maker, who promises to pay.

2. The payee (depositor), who will be paid by the maker.

All drafts start with three parties rather than the two initial parties for promissory notes:

1. The drawer, roughly comparable to the note's maker.

2. The drawee, the party ordered by the drawer to make payment

3. The payee, essentially equivalent to the note's payee.

> Whereas the maker of a note simply promises to pay, more or less directly, the payee, the drawer of a draft states that a third-party, the drawee, will actually pay the payee. The drawee pays with funds from an account the drawer maintains with the drawee.

Both notes and drafts may have additional parties known as indorsers. Although indorsements come in different forms, they all have a common feature: the signature of the indorser.

YOU SHOULD REMEMBER

A note has two initial parties: a maker and a payee. A draft has three initial parties: a drawer, a drawee, and a payee. Both notes and drafts may have additional parties who are indorsers.

ADVANTAGES OF NEGOTIABLE INSTRUMENTS OVER ORDINARY CONTRACTS

Negotiable instruments are frequently preferred over nonnegotiable types of commercial paper or ordinary contracts. *The major reason for this preference is that, in exchange for greater formal requirements, the negotiable instrument conveys to its holder rights superior to those of someone trying to enforce an ordinary contract* (e.g., a nonnegotiable instrument). (See page 188 for the definition of "holder.") Also, rights, duties, and liabilities of the parties are generally clearer under Article 3 of the UCC than under the common law of contracts.

In the ordinary contract, consideration must be proved. With a negotiable instrument, consideration is presumed unless evidence to the contrary is introduced. Even if the other party proves that there was no consideration, the holder's case will generally not be affected if he/she is deemed to be a *holder in due course* (HIDC) defined in Chapter 12. Whereas past consideration (e.g., a pre-existing debt) is not usually an enforceable basis for ordinary contracts, it is sufficient for negotiable instruments. Most important, the assignee of an ordinary contract is subject to personal defenses (see Chapter 12), but a HIDC generally is not (i.e., many defenses ordinarily available under contract law are not as readily available against some holders).

YOU SHOULD REMEMBER

Negotiable instruments are often easier to enforce than ordinary contracts because (1) consideration is presumed, (2) past consideration is sufficient, (3) a HIDC usually need give no consideration, and (4) a HIDC is generally not subject to personal defenses.

THE ASSIGNEE OF A CONTRACT VERSUS THE HOLDER OF A NEGOTIABLE INSTRUMENT

ASSIGNEE OF CONTRACT

In the "ordinary" contract, one party may be able to assign to someone else his/her rights under the contract (e.g., the right to receive money or goods). The party to the contract is called the **assignor**, and the person to whom the assignor assigns his/her contractual rights is the **assignee**. Although not usually a party to the original contract, the assignee "steps into the shoes of the assignor" and not only gains all of the assignor's contractual rights, but also is subject to all of the contractual defenses to which the assignor was subject.

Example: Rights and Risks of an Assignee

Otto's Outerware Outlet (OOO) contracts with Brenda's Bikini Boutique (BBB); OOO is to supply BBB with 25 specially designed "OOO-La-La outfits" at $40 per outfit. If OOO later assigns to a third party, Inga, its rights under the OOO-BBB contract, then Inga has whatever rights OOO had at the time of the assignment. Inga would be entitled to receive $1,000 from BBB if the 25 outfits were delivered to BBB in proper condition and on time. The money would properly belong to Inga because OOO had performed as promised, was thus entitled to the money from BBB, and had assigned to Inga the right to receive the money from BBB.

But what if OOO failed to conform to the terms of the contract, perhaps by not delivering the outfits or by delivering cheap imitations of the "OOO-La-La" line? Then Inga would be subject to BBB's defense against payment to OOO.

The assignee takes a risk, particularly if he/she cannot verify the rights and defenses that are being assumed. For this reason, the potential assignee may request a "premium" (high or extra payments) for taking assignments, and may instead insist on taking a negotiable instrument whenever possible.

HOLDER OF NEGOTIABLE INSTRUMENT

For commercial paper to be readily accepted as a safe substitute for cash, the potential "acceptor" must be confident that the commercial paper does not entail many of the risks assumed by the assignee of an ordinary contract.

A holder possesses an instrument passing to him/her via an unbroken chain of negotiation, if transferred, (see below) and (1) issued, drawn or indorsed to him/her or to his/her order, or (2) payable to bearer. To qualify as a **holder in due course** (HIDC), the holder must have good title to an instrument for which he/she paid value, against which the holder had no notice of any claims or defenses, and which the holder acquired in good faith. See Chapter 12 for a detailed discussion of the holder in due course.

Example: *Advantages of a HIDC*

If Hollis is the HIDC of a check issued by Baker Co. to pay for an industrial appliance sold by Smith, then Hollis is not subject to Baker's claim against the seller for breach of warranty or for fraud inducing the sale. These are personal defenses against payment on the instrument, which the buyer, Baker, cannot assert against a HIDC. However, these defenses can be used against Smith and any assignee of Smith.

YOU SHOULD REMEMBER

A holder possesses an instrument passing to him/her via an unbroken chain of negotiation (if transferred) and issued, drawn, or indorsed to the holder or to his/her order, or payable to bearer. If the instrument is negotiable, and the holder is a HIDC, then the HIDC generally can defeat personal defenses that would work against an assignee.

NEGOTIATION

The inherent value of negotiable paper rests largely on the easy, relatively safe manner in which possession of such paper and title to it can be transferred. The transfer process is called **negotiation**. The negotiable instrument is "negotiated" (transferred) to a **holder**.

Bearer paper, such as checks made out to "Cash" or indorsed in blank (the holder's name is signed on the back without any accompanying instruction, such as "Pay to the order of X" or "For deposit only"), can be *negotiated merely by a change in possession*, that is, by "delivery." Holders of such instruments may not be the lawful owners; for instance, a thief may take bearer paper.

Order paper negotiation, on the other hand, requires not only delivery but also the proper indorsement(s).

An instrument payable to the order of Joe Smith is not negotiated to Barbara Brown until delivered to her with Joe Smith's indorsement. Without the indorsement, Barbara (and anyone else who acquires the instrument from her) is a mere transferee.

To have rights under an instrument (e.g., obtain payment), a mere transferee (someone to whom the instrument was transferred, but to whom there was no effective negotiation) must prove that the instrument is valid and that he/she has title to it. There are no presumptions in favor of the transferee's claim.

A holder, though, benefits from negotiation. Opposing parties have the burden of proving that the holder is not entitled to payment.

YOU SHOULD REMEMBER

For negotiation to occur, an instrument must be negotiable. Negotiation involves transfer of possession of the instrument and title to it. Bearer paper is negotiated by mere delivery; order paper negotiation requires delivery *and* the proper indorsement(s).

A holder is not necessarily the "owner" of an instrument. A holder can obtain payment on an instrument, however, unless the opposing party proves a defense to payment. Mere transferees, though, must prove their right to payment.

INDORSEMENTS
DEFINITION

Written on a negotiable instrument by or on behalf of the holder, an **indorsement** is the signature of the holder, with or without additional or qualifying words, so that title to the instrument and the holder's property interest in the instrument are transferred to a new holder. An instrument may be indorsed on its front or back, or on an **allonge** (a paper physically attached to, and made a part of, the instrument). When the role of a signatory is ambiguous, his/her signature is treated as an indorsement. Moreover, if a name is misspelled in the instrument, the indorsement may be made in either the correct name, the name as misspelled, or both. (Dual indorsement can be demanded by the person taking the instrument.)

TYPES OF INDORSEMENTS

There are several different types of indorsements.

Blank (general) indorsements specify no particular indorsee; a mere signature constitutes a blank indorsement. The effect is to make the instrument payable to bearer.

Special indorsements specify the person to whom, or to whose order, the instrument is payable. Such an indorsement makes the instrument order paper.

Example: Special Indorsement

John Smith, the payee of a check, specifically indorses the check to Mary Jones by writing on the instrument "Pay to the order of Mary Jones [signed] John Smith."

John Smith could simply indorse "Pay Mary Jones," and it would still be a special indorsement. It renders the instrument order paper (to Mary Jones), even though the front of a negotiable instrument should not be made out that way (see page 181 and UCC sections 3-104(1) and 3-805).

An instrument may have any number and combination of blank and special indorsements. The last (most recent) indorsement determines whether the instrument is bearer or order paper.

A third type of indorsement is the **restrictive indorsement**. There are four main types of restrictive indorsements:

1. Those that are conditional. Indorsements can contain conditions that would destroy negotiability if they were in the instrument itself. However, despite its negotiability, no holder (except a bank handling or paying instruments in the normal course of collection) has any right to enforce the conditionally indorsed instrument until the condition is met.

Example: Conditional Indorsement

John James, the payee of a check, indorses it as follows:

"Pay Jane Jones when she delivers 250 shares of Blue Chip Stock to me [signed] John James."

John then delivers the check to Jane, who in return promises to transfer the stock to John. Jane could negotiate the check to another holder. However, until she met the condition, most subsequent holders could not enforce payment.

2. Those that attempt to prohibit further transfer of the instrument. Like a conditional indorsement, an indorsement prohibiting further transfer has no effect on the instrument's negotiability. An example is: "Pay to the order of Joe Doe only." In effect, the UCC [Section 3-206(1)] converts such an indorsement to "Pay to the order of Joe Doe."

3. Those that include the words "for collection," "for deposit only," "pay any bank," or similar expressions. Like conditional indorsements, those made

to facilitate deposits or collections have no effect on negotiability. However, the holder who first receives such an indorsed instrument must obey that indorsement, although subsequent holders need not. "Pay any bank" also means that only a bank may be a holder of the instrument unless it is specially indorsed by the bank or returned to the indorser.

4. Those that state that they are for the benefit or use of the indorser or another person. An example of this type of indorsement is: "Pay X in trust for Y." The instrument's first new holder must take any money transferred to him/her via the instrument and apply the money in accord with the indorsement. Subsequent holders have no such constraints unless they know that the terms of the indorsement were violated.

Regardless of type, the indorsement can have a **disclaimer**. Such an indorsement places subsequent holders on notice that the indorser disclaims liability on the instrument if it is not paid. The most frequent disclaimer is the phrase "without recourse."

YOU SHOULD REMEMBER

An indorsement can be blank (which makes the instrument bearer paper), special (to a particular person or his/her order), or restrictive. Restrictive indorsements can be conditional, can try to proscribe further transfer, can be designated for deposit or collection, or can be for the benefit of—or in trust for—the indorser or someone else. Indorsements can create conditions and impose certain requirements that, if originally placed in the instrument, would render it nonnegotiable.

Any indorsement may have a disclaimer of liability on the instrument ("without recourse").

KNOW THE CONCEPTS
DO YOU KNOW THE BASICS?

1. Name two purposes of commercial paper.
2. (a) Name the parties to a promissory note.
   (b) Name the parties to a draft.
3. (a) What article of the UCC covers the law of negotiable instruments?
   (b) What article of the UCC covers the law of bank deposits and collections?

4. How is a check different from other drafts?

5. The role of consideration is different when one attempts to enforce a negotiable instrument rather than an ordinary contract. State the differences.

6. What advantage does a holder-in-due-course have over the assignee of a contract?

7. Which usually requires greater formality (adherence to specific requirements for proper formation): a negotiable instrument or an ordinary contract?

8. What are the requirements for an instrument to be negotiable?

9. *True* or *false?*
   (a) Ambiguities are to be resolved in favor of negotiability.
   (b) By agreement of the parties, a nonnegotiable instrument can become negotiable.

10. What types of statements may affect the amount due under an instrument, but do not create a *sum uncertain?*

11. What types of statements do not make a promise or order conditional?

12. *True* or *false?*
    (a) An instrument "payable upon drawer's death" is negotiable.
    (b) Agents may complete an instrument for their principals (e.g., employers).
    (c) Dates and signatures on an instrument are presumed correct.

13. In disputes about the terms of an instrument, which usually takes precedence?
    (a) Handwriting or typing
    (b) Typing or print
    (c) Handwriting or print
    (d) Words or numerals

14. How are negotiable instruments negotiated?

15. What is the effect of a blank (general) indorsement?

TERMS FOR STUDY

allonge	holder
assignee	holder in due course
assignor	indorsement
bearer paper	maker
blank (general) indorsement	negotiable instrument
certificate of deposit	negotiation
check	order paper
commercial paper	payee
disclaimer	promissory note
draft	restrictive indorsement
drawee	special indorsement
drawer	UCC Articles 3 & 4

PRACTICAL APPLICATION

1. Weaver, who had an account at Boris's Bank & Trust, borrowed money from Porter. In an attempt to repay Porter, Weaver sent him to Boris, Sr., President of Boris's, with this writing:

September 26, 199–

To: Boris's Bank & Trust
From: W. Weaver

I would be very appreciative if you would pay to the order of J. B. Porter $100.00 (one hundred dollars).

(signed)
W. Weaver

Is this a negotiable instrument?

2.

January 20, 199–   78-84
                                                    1397
  BANK OF MAYFLOWER

Pay _____ Wallace Wimpy _____ $ 58.70

Fifty eight and 70/100--Dollars

For _____ Career Counseling _____   /s/ _____
                                            Eddie Eager

  :1585::0045::802:5

Is this a negotiable instrument?

3. (a) Miss O'Hara obtains a loan of $300 from Mr. Butler, to whom she dates and signs a written "I owe you" (IOU) for $300.00. Soon thereafter, Butler expresses to O'Hara his resolute apathy as to her future whereabouts and seeks recovery of the $300 from O'Hara. Is the IOU a negotiable instrument? Is the IOU crucial, merely helpful, irrelevant, or in fact harmful to his case?

   (b) Suppose Butler, in order to get some cash quickly, discounts his IOU from O'Hara and transfers it to Mr. Dashing Silkes for the sum of $200, with Butler placing his "indorsement" on the back of the IOU. May Silkes collect from O'Hara on the IOU?

4.

LAST COUNTY BANK OF KINGSVILLE

$2,500.00   October 1, 199–

Arnold Anonymous has deposited in this bank

Two thousand five hundred and no/100 dollars payable to
Arnold Anonymous at maturity __6__ months from date upon return of this
instrument properly indorsed, with interest at 9¼% per annum from date.

E. Moneybags
Cashier

Is this a negotiable instrument? If so, what type?

5. A promissory note states that one year from the instrument's date the maker
will pay the amount set out in the note "with interest at the current rate." Is
this a negotiable instrument? If so, what type?

6. (a) Jerry Joker makes a note payable to Kid Kooke "five days after Nate
Nerd's first kiss." Is the note negotiable?
(b) What if Kid gets tired of waiting and plants one, that is, a kiss, on Nate?

7. An instrument from A to the order of C is handed by C to B.
(a) What should B request from C?
(b) What may B do if he is afraid that A may not be good for the money
and a subsequent holder may seek the money from B, instead?

ANSWERS
KNOW THE CONCEPTS

1. Extension of credit, money substitute.
2. (a) Maker, payee.—(b) Drawer, drawee, payee.
3. (a) Article 3.—(b) Article 4.
4. The drawee of a check is always a bank, and a check, unlike some drafts,
   is payable on demand.
5. Ordinary contract: consideration must be proved; past consideration generally insufficient.
   Negotiable instrument: consideration presumed; consideration unnecessary for holder-in-due-course; past consideration sufficient.
6. A holder-in-due-course is usually not subject to personal defenses, as an
   assignee is.
7. The negotiable instrument. Some special contracts (e.g., land transactions)
   must meet formal requirements to be enforceable. Generally, though, contracts do not require such formality.

8. It must be (1) in writing, (2) signed by the maker or drawer, (3) an unconditional promise or order to pay a sum certain in money, (4) without any other promise, order, obligation, or power except as permitted by UCC Article 3, (5) payable on demand or at a definite time, and (6) payable to order or to bearer.

9. (a) False. (b) False.

10. Specified interest rate, stated installments, collection costs, attorney's fees, particular discounts or additions.

11. Statements that mention: the underlying transaction or agreement; the instrument's consideration; a separate agreement; that maturity, acceleration, or prepayment arises out of a separate transaction or agreement; that indorsement or cashing constitutes full satisfaction of the drawer's obligation; that the instrument is secured; that upon default a confessed judgment is permitted.

12. (a) False. (b) True. (c) True.

13. (a) Handwriting. (b) Typing. (c) Handwriting. (d) Words.

14. Bearer instrument: by delivery.
    Order instrument: by delivery and proper indorsement.

15. It makes the instrument bearer paper.

PRACTICAL APPLICATION

1. No. The instrument does not contain a promise to pay or an order to pay. It merely says that Weaver would be very appreciative.

2. No. It is not to bearer or to order. It should read: Pay *to the order of* Wallace Wimpy. Note, however, that, because this instrument would otherwise be negotiable, under UCC 3-805 it is treated as negotiable except that there can be no HIDC.

3. (a) The IOU should be helpful. Although not a negotiable instrument, it is evidence of a loan to O'Hara from Butler.
   (b) Perhaps. Silkes is, at best, an assignee of Butler's rights and duties under Butler's contract with O'Hara (the IOU). Silkes is subject to personal defenses O'Hara may have had against Butler.

4. Yes. A certificate of deposit.

5. No. A "current" interest rate is unclear. Thus there is no sum certain. (If the interest rate were not specified at all, then the judgment rate could be used, so as to render a sum certain.)

6. (a) No. It is not payable at a definite time.
   (b) The note is still not a negotiable instrument. The happening of an uncertain event does not convert an indefinite as to time (hence nonnegotiable) instrument into a negotiable instrument. However, such a triggering event could make enforceable the contract that may underlie the nonnegotiable instrument.

7. (a) An indorsement.
   (b) When B cashes the instrument, he should indorse it "without recourse."

12

COMMERCIAL PAPER: THE HOLDER IN DUE COURSE, DEFENSES, LIABILITY, AND DISCHARGE

The holder in due course (HIDC) of a negotiable instrument is not generally subject to claims or personal defenses that could be raised by the original parties to the instrument. This protection from claims or defenses is the central tenet of negotiable instruments law.

In Chapter 11 you learned what negotiable instruments are and how their title and possession can be transferred (negotiated). This chapter mainly concerns

HIDCs, other holders, defenses, and liability among parties. In essence, Chapter 12 covers what happens when something goes wrong.

HOLDER IN DUE COURSE

A holder, you have learned, possesses a negotiable instrument drawn, issued, or indorsed to the holder or his/her order or to bearer. The **holder in due course** (**HIDC**) is a special type of holder, one who takes possession and title free of most personal defenses (see pages 203-204) that could be raised against the HIDC's transferor.

The Uniform Commercial Code expressly includes payees as possible HIDCs. However, a HIDC is protected against (exempt from) only personal defenses raised by a "party to the instrument with whom the holder has not dealt" (UCC 3-305). Since payees have usually dealt with the drawer or maker, it is a very rare case in which the payee can use his/her HIDC status to block personal defenses.

REQUIREMENTS FOR A HIDC

To be a HIDC, the holder must:

(1) take a negotiable instrument for value,
(2) in good faith, and
(3) without notice that it is overdue, has been dishonored, or has defenses or claims against it (UCC 3-302).

• *TAKING FOR VALUE*

EXTENT OF CONSIDERATION, SECURITY INTEREST, OR LIEN ON INSTRUMENT

A holder takes an instrument for "value" to the extent that (1) the agreed-upon consideration has been performed, or (2) he/she acquires a security interest or lien on the instrument. "Value" does not arise, however, from security interests or liens obtained via legal proceedings, such as deficiency judgments. (For more on security interests or liens, see Chapter 20.)

Example: Taking for Value

Carrie is to pay Bart $500 in order to receive a check from Anne to Bart in the same amount. If Carrie pays Bart $500, then Carrie can be a HIDC for the full amount of the check. If Carrie gives less than $500, however, then she can be a HIDC for *only* that amount for which she actually gave value to Bart. It does not matter what consideration, if any, passed between prior parties, such as Anne and Bart.

Although an executory promise (to do something in the future) is generally good consideration for contracts, including those under the UCC, it does *not* constitute the "value" necessary to make a HIDC.

PREEXISTING CLAIMS, RECIPROCAL NEGOTIABLE INSTRUMENTS, AND IRREVOCABLE COMMITMENTS

There is also HIDC "value" when a person takes an instrument as security or payment for a preexisting claim, whether or not that claim is due. If Baker claimed that Connor owed him money, an instrument from Connor to pay Baker's claim would be for "value." HIDC "value" also occurs when, in order to take an instrument, a person gives a negotiable instrument or makes an irrevocable commitment to a third party. For instance, Smith gives "value" by giving Jones a check in return for taking Jones's promissory note.

The following are not HIDC "value": (1) gifts, (2) inheritances, (3) promises (except binding ones to third parties), (4) purchases pursuant to legal proceedings such as foreclosures; and (5) bulk transfers not made in the ordinary course of business (UCC 3-302).

• *GOOD FAITH*

A person takes an instrument in **good faith** if he/she acts honestly [UCC 1-201(19)]. The test is *subjective*: Did the holder actually believe that the instrument was regular (genuine, authorized, and conforming with the law)? It is usually irrelevant that a reasonable person (the "objective" test) might have acted differently.

Obvious defenses may, though, lead to a presumption against subjective good faith. In addition to the size of any discount from the instrument's face amount, courts will look at the parties' relationship, the instrument's appearance, the time remaining before the due date, and the time and place of the instrument's transfer.

• *ABSENCE OF NOTICE*

Most disputes about HIDC status concern alleged notice of a claim or defense; whether "value" was given is generally easy to determine, and good faith is usually assumed.

"Notice" includes both what the holder actually knew and what he/she should have known from all of the facts and circumstances [UCC 1-201(25)]. Under this *objective* test, obvious forgeries, alterations, or blanks in material terms are themselves sufficient to suggest potential claims or defenses to the instrument; hence nothing else is necessary to show notice. In most other cases, the court will have to look beyond the instrument itself to determine notice.

UCC 3-304 covers the defects about which a holder, in order to be a HIDC, must not have had notice.

1. *The instrument is overdue.* For *time* instruments (those with a specific due date), "overdue" means that some or all of the amount of the instrument remains unpaid after the due date. Unless the holder knows that acceleration has occurred, there is no notice of an overdue instrument merely because an installment note or draft contains an acceleration clause.

   For *demand* instruments, "overdue" means either that a demand for payment has been made, yet money remains due, or that the instrument has been outstanding for an unreasonable period of time (more than 30 days, presumably, for certified checks; longer for other instruments).

2. *The instrument has been dishonored.* To **dishonor** an instrument is to refuse payment on, or acceptance of, the instrument. For drafts the dishonoring is generally by the drawee, while for notes it is usually by the maker.

3. *There are defenses against, or claims to, the instrument.* Aside from obvious forgeries or alterations, notice of claims or defenses arises from awareness that the obligations of one or more parties are voidable or that the parties have been discharged.

   Merely filing a document or recording it (e.g., in the land records, with a governmental agency or the like) does not provide notice to a holder. Courts look beyond such "constructive" (legally implied) notice to determine whether the holder actually knew or should have known about that defense or claim.

Example: Notice of a Defense

If Gary Gullible pays Skippy Skunk $10,000 in cash to obtain a check payable to Skippy in the amount of $11,000 and with the words "trustee for Molly Minor" written in bold face in the memorandum section of the check, Gary may be deemed to have notice of a defense to payment. The words in the memorandum section seem to indicate that payment is intended to be for the benefit of Molly Minor, but from the $1,000 discount and the fact that payment is in cash a person could reasonably infer that Skippy will keep the money for himself.

Without the discount or the cash payment, Gary probably could argue successfully that he neither knew nor should have known that Skippy was violating his duties as Molly's trustee.

Notice of a Claim or Defense?

Generally Yes	Generally No
1. *Instrument Itself:*	
a. Incorrect indorsements	a. Antedated or postdated
b. Material omissions	b. Originally incomplete and later completed
c. Important alterations	

Notice of a Claim or Defense?

<u>Generally Yes</u>   <u>Generally No</u>

2. Knowledge of Facts:

a. Party's obligation void or voidable	a. Parties to the instrument include accommodation parties or fiduciaries (trustees)
b. Parties discharged	
c. Transferor's title defective because of fraud, illegality, theft, etc.	b. Instrument issued or negotiated for an executory promise
d. Unauthorized completion of the instrument	c. Instrument accompanied by separate agreement
e. Default in principal payments on this instrument	d. Default in interest payments on this instrument
f. Default on any other instrument that is part of a series with this instrument	e. Default on another instrument [except (f) in left column]

Notice is effective only if received early enough to give a potential holder time to respond.

Example: Inadequate (Untimely) Notice

If Company X's branch manager in one store receives notice 30 seconds before Company X's branch manager in another store accepts the instrument in question, Company X may still be a HIDC. Notice was not timely.

Obviously, later notice cannot serve to undo HIDC status; however, it can limit such status to cover only the amount already given for an instrument. Thus the HIDC is not an HIDC for subsequent, postnotice value provided on that instrument.

Lastly, in most cases no connection need exist between (a) whatever deprives a person of HIDC status, and (b) the defense or claim being asserted against the would-be HIDC.

Example: Personal Defenses Against Holder Need Not Be Related to the Notice That Deprived Holder of HIDC Status

If holder Harry takes a note that Harry knows or should know has been dishonored, maker Mike can assert personal defenses against Harry not necessarily related to the reasons for dishonoring the note. In other words, "A miss is as good as a mile"; if Polly Smith is not a HIDC, it does not matter how close she came to being one—she is subject to the same personal defenses as are other mere holders.

THE SHELTER RULE
• *WHO IS COVERED?*

Non-HIDCs usually take whatever rights their transferors had. Thus a transferee who is not a HIDC (e.g., a donee—there is no "value"; the instrument is a gift), but who takes the instrument from a HIDC, acquires all the rights of a HIDC [UCC 3-201(1)]. This **shelter rule** furthers the transferability of instruments and the benefits of HIDC status; HIDCs and potential transferees know that the latter will acquire HIDC status.

Example: The Shelter Rule

Maker is induced by Payee's fraud to issue Payee a promissory note. Payee negotiates the note to Course, who takes it for value, in good faith and without notice that it is overdue, has been dishonored, or has defenses or claims to it. After the note becomes obviously overdue, Course negotiates it to Safehaven.

Although Safehaven is clearly not a HIDC (he has notice that the note is overdue), Course was. Therefore Safehaven takes all the HIDC rights that Course had, and Safehaven is free of Maker's personal defense (fraudulent inducement).

The shelter rule covers anyone who can trace his/her title back to a HIDC. Thus, in the preceding example, once Course takes the instrument, all subsequent transferees, no matter how far down the line, also have HIDC rights.

• *WHO IS EXCEPTED?*
Two types of transferees cannot use the shelter rule:

1. Those who participated in fraud or illegality affecting the instrument.

2. Those who, as prior holders, had notice of a defense or claim.

In these two cases, it would be unseemly to let a party acquire HIDC status by "laundering" an instrument through one or more transferees and then reacquiring it. In the preceding example, the fraudulent Payee cannot become a HIDC no matter how far down the chain of title he reacquires the instrument; Course's and the subsequent transferees' HIDC rights will not pass to Payee.

YOU SHOULD REMEMBER

A holder has all of the rights of an assignee. A HIDC is a holder who takes a negotiable instrument for value, in good faith, and without notice that it is overdue, has been dishonored, or has defenses or claims against it. Although a mere holder is subject to all defenses, the HIDC is free of personal defenses raised by a party with whom the HIDC has not dealt.

HIDC "value" includes presently performed or past consideration, most security interests or liens, negotiable instruments, and irrevocable commitments to third persons. Gifts, inheritances, mere promises, purchases pursuant to legal proceedings, and most bulk transfers do not constitute HIDC "value."

HIDC "good faith" is tested subjectively: Did the holder believe that the instrument was regular (genuine, authorized, and conforming with law)? The "without notice" issue is measured objectively: besides the holder's actual knowledge, notice also arises whenever a reasonable person would have known. Notice of claims or defenses usually arises when the instrument has incorrect indorsements, material omissions, or important alterations, or the holder knows or should know that a party's obligation is void, voidable, or discharged, that title is defective, or that the instrument's completion was unauthorized. There is usually no such notice for antedated or postdated instruments, for knowledge that persons are accommodation parties or fiduciaries, or for knowledge that the instrument came with a separate agreement or a mere executory promise.

Once HIDC status has occurred, it is not removed by later notice. Personal defenses raised against a holder need not be the same as the defense or other factor that deprived the holder of HIDC status.

The shelter rule extends HIDC benefits to all transferees in the chain of title after a HIDC. The exceptions are transferees who (1) were parties to fraud or illegality affecting the instrument, or (2) as prior holders, had notice of a claim or defense to the instrument.

DEFENSES

The key to understanding the HIDC's special status is to distinguish between **"real" defenses**, which work against even HIDCs, and **personal defenses**, which do not.

"REAL" DEFENSES

These include:

1. **Fraud in the execution (factum).** Before signing an instrument, the maker, drawer, or indorser is led to believe (with no reasonable opportunity to discover otherwise) that he/she is signing something else, not an instrument.

2. **Forgery** (writing another person's name as if that person had done so) or an **unauthorized signature** (a signature indicating that the signer has authority to bind another person when such is not the case) wholly inoperative for passing title, unless the person whose name is signed ratifies the signature (consents or acquiesces to it) or is estopped to deny it (conducts him-/herself in such a way that another party reasonably assumes that the

signature is authorized, and then relies on this assumption). However, a good-faith, paying transferee always has the right to enforce the instrument against the actual forgerer.

3. Other defenses sufficient to render a contract *void*, including extreme duress, illegality, some cases of incapacity and, in some states, infancy (being a minor).

4. Discharge of the instrument, if the holder knew or should have known about the discharge.

5. Discharge in bankruptcy.

6. Statute of limitations.

7. Material alteration (important changes in one or more terms) of the instrument. Such alteration would give the instrument a different legal effect (e.g., change the liability, duties, and/or rights of one or more parties to the instrument). (Nonmaterial alterations, e.g., crossing an uncrossed "t" or changing the date of a note without any effect on its maturity, are not even personal defenses.) The HIDC can still enforce the instrument's terms as they existed before alteration. Also, as with forgeries or unauthorized signatures, a party can ratify or be estopped to deny an alteration.

Example: Material Alteration as a "Real" Defense

If Cora Careless signs a check for $10 and a transferee erases the period and otherwise changes the amount to $1,000, Cora may have a real defense against a HIDC for all but the original $10. The HIDC's hopes for collecting the additional $990 would depend upon estopping Cora—showing that she carelessly left large gaps in her writing or in some other manner made it easy for someone else to change the amount without being detected.

PERSONAL DEFENSES

These include the following:

1. Lack or failure of consideration.

2. Fraud in the inducement. The maker, drawer, or indorser knows that he/she is signing an instrument for *x* amount; the fraud concerns misrepresentation about the consideration or other matters. If fraud in the execution (factum) could reasonably have been discovered, it is treated as merely a personal defense, like fraud in the inducement.

3. Ordinary contract defenses, such as another party's breach of contract (nonperformance, failure to pay, or the like).

4. Undue influence, mistake, slight duress, infancy (in some states), or other defenses rendering the contract voidable.

5. Violation of a restrictive indorsement (e.g., a prior transferee's cashing a check indorsed "for deposit only").

6. Illegality or incapacity that render a contract *voidable*, but not void.

7. Nonbankruptcy discharges of which the holder has no notice.

8. Lack of agency.

9. Nondelivery or unauthorized delivery of an instrument.

10. Acquisition of lost or stolen bearer instruments.

Example: Acquisition of a Stolen Instrument

Thad Thief picks the pockets of Abner Obtuse and discovers among his ill-gotten gains a bearer check, which Thad indorses to the order of Harry Holder. The theft operates as a personal defense; Abner's title remains good against all but a HIDC or someone taking possession of the check under the HIDC shelter rule. There can be a holder, and even a HIDC, because the bearer paper does not require Abner's forged signature.

11. Unauthorized completion of an instrument. Because the UCC generally permits authorized persons to complete instruments on behalf of others, the burden of paying for unauthorized completions is placed on the person who might have been more careful, rather than the HIDC.

Example: Unauthorized Completion of an Instrument

If Barry Bumbler signs a blank check and then loses it, with the finder filling in x amount, a HIDC could collect x from Barry. Of course, if Barry's signature were forged or the check's material terms were altered, the defense would be "real."

12. Certain "real" defenses when the party asserting the "real" defense was negligent. Defenses involving material alterations or fraud in the execution can thus be converted from "real" to merely personal and cannot then be asserted against a HIDC.

RESTRICTIONS ON THE HIDC CONCEPT

HIDC status encourages the use of negotiable instruments. It makes such instruments almost as transferable as money, yet safer. To paraphrase the words used by Lord Mansfield, the negotiable instrument is a "courier" not bogged down with any luggage. This is especially the case for a HIDC.

• *STATE LAWS TO PROTECT CONSUMERS*

The HIDC's special status sometimes runs counter to the modern law's emphasis on consumer protection. For instance, if Connie Consumer buys a refrigerator from Manny's Manufacturers, the usual law of commercial paper would allow a HIDC to enforce payment from Connie on her check to Manny; it would not matter that Manny is not entitled to payment from Connie because of numerous problems with the refrigerator.

Many state laws are now designed to protect people such as Connie Consumer. State legislatures and courts have reduced or eliminated the HIDC's right to collect from consumers who have personal defenses. Another approach is simply to eliminate HIDC status in certain cases. The Uniform Consumer Credit Code (UCCC), enacted by several states, does that for most consumer transactions involving negotiable instruments other than checks; and courts often deny HIDC status to finance companies closely tied to sellers of consumer products. (For more on the UCCC, see Chapter 20.)

• *THE FEDERAL TRADE COMMISSION RULE*

To make consumer protection more uniform, as well as to cover states which had failed to act, the Federal Trade Commission (FTC) in 1976 adopted a rule requiring that a consumer credit agreement include the following statement in very bold type:

NOTICE

ANY HOLDER OF THIS CONSUMER CREDIT CONTRACT IS SUBJECT TO ALL CLAIMS AND DEFENSES WHICH THE DEBTOR COULD ASSERT AGAINST THE SELLER OF GOODS OR SERVICES OBTAINED PURSUANT HERETO OR WITH THE PROCEEDS HEREOF.

Thus HIDC status is impossible with respect to the debtor's/consumer's defenses and claims against the seller; these defenses and claims can be asserted against all subsequent holders. (However, HIDC status may still arise and serve to overcome other personal defenses, i.e., defenses and claims by parties other than the debtor/consumer, or by the debtor/consumer against someone other than the seller.)

If a party other than the seller lends the money needed for a consumer purchase, the loan documents must contain the same bold-type statement (without the words "pursuant hereto or") *if* the lender is affiliated with the seller by common control, contract, or business arrangement *or if* the seller otherwise referred the consumer to the lender.

Of course, if the bold-type statement is missing, the holder could become a full-fledged HIDC. However, that situation is extremely unlikely; those who violate the FTC rule are subject to such severe fines that compliance is usually assured.

YOU SHOULD REMEMBER

The HIDC, or someone taking possession under the shelter rule, is usually free of personal, but not "real," defenses. Others take an instrument subject to both types of defenses.

Real Defenses	Personal Defenses
a. Fraud in the execution (factum).	a. Fraud in the inducement.
b. Forgery or other unauthorized signature, unless ratification or estoppel.	b. Stolen or lost bearer instruments.
c. Defenses rendering contract *void*.	c. Defenses rendering contract *voidable*.
d. Discharge of instrument, if holder knew or should have known.	d. Ordinary contract defenses (breach, etc.).
e. Discharge in bankruptcy.	e. Nonbankruptcy discharges of which holder has no notice.
f. Statute of limitations.	f. Material alteration or fraud in the execution, when accompanied by negligence of party asserting the defense.
	g. Unauthorized completion of instrument.
g. Material alteration ("real" as to the altered amounts or other altered terms).	h. Lack or failure of consideration.
	i. Violation of a restrictive indorsement.
	j. Lack of agency.
	k. Nondelivery or unauthorized delivery of instrument.

Concerns about consumer protection have led to restrictions on the HIDC concept. State courts and legislatures have permitted consumers to raise personal defenses, not merely real defenses, against a HIDC.

The FTC requires, in consumer credit agreements and related loan documents, a bold-type statement informing any holder that he/she is subject to all claims and defenses that the buyer/debtor can make against the seller.

LIABILITIES AMONG PARTIES

Heretofore, we have assumed that a person being sued on an instrument was liable unless he/she could successfully assert a defense. We now consider liability in the absence of a defense.

Liability may be based on either the underlying contract or on the instrument itself. A third type of liability, warranty liability, is discussed later in this chapter.

No one is liable on the instrument, however, unless it contains his/her signature or the signature of an authorized agent.

PRIMARY AND SECONDARY LIABILITY ON THE INSTRUMENT

The parties to an instrument are either primarily or secondarily liable. **Primary parties** are makers and acceptors (usually drawees), while **secondary parties** are drawers and indorsers.

The primary party must pay on an instrument (1) as it existed when drafted by the maker or accepted by the drawee, or (2) for an incomplete instrument, as it was ultimately completed (if the completion was authorized). A secondary party usually can assume that the primary party will pay on the instrument.

If the primary party has not paid, the secondary party has an obligation to pay, provided that (1) the person seeking payment first demanded payment from the primary party, and (2) the secondary party received notice that the primary party dishonored (refused to pay) the instrument.

Drawers are secondarily liable for the amount of the draft. The indorser's secondary liability, however, is for the amount stated at the time of his/her indorsement. These contractual liabilities can be avoided by signing with the words "without recourse." The indorsement or drawer's signature is then "qualified." The drawer or indorser is saying, "I make no guarantee that the primary party will pay; if he does not, I will not pay, either." (When multiple, unqualified indorsements are on an instrument, the indorsers are generally liable to one another in the order in which they indorse (i.e., each indorser is liable to the subsequent indorser); that chronological order is presumably the order in which signatures appear on the instrument.

Aside from these contractual liabilities (which can be qualified), secondary parties also may face liability on warranties (see pages 211–212).

THREE MAIN TYPES OF LIABILITY BASED ON THE INSTRUMENT

Three main types of liability problems involve negligent persons, impostors or fictitious payees, and signers lacking capacity or authority.

• *NEGLIGENT PERSONS*

Under UCC 3-406, any person whose negligence substantially contributes to the material alteration of an instrument or the making of an unauthorized signature is precluded from asserting such alteration or signature against a HIDC or anyone else who pays the instrument in good faith and in accordance with reasonable commercial standards (i.e, the payor is not negligent). Most states define UCC 3-406 negligence in the same way as is done for the common law tort of negligence: failure to exercise ordinary care.

Remember: To preclude a claim because of UCC 3-406 negligence, the negligence must be significant ("substantially contributes"), not just remotely responsible.

Examples of UCC 3-406 negligence include the following:

1. Upon receiving notice that forgeries are occurring, failure to act to prevent more forgeries.

2. Negligence in controlling access to, and use of, a signature stamp.

3. Drawer's failure to include a corporate designation (e.g., Co., Corp., Inc.) after a corporate name.

4. Delivery of an instrument to the wrong person.

5. Failure to audit corporate books.

• *IMPOSTORS OR FICTITIOUS PAYEES*

UCC 3-405 says that indorsements in the payee's name are effective for negotiation purposes under the following circumstances:

1. An impostor induced the drawer or maker to issue the instrument to the impostor or his/her accomplice. (This usually involves bona fide payees, with an impostor obtaining the instrument directly from the drawer or maker.)

2. The payee was never intended to have an interest in the instrument, and an agent of the maker or drawer supplied the latter with the payee's name or simply signed the instrument on the maker's or drawer's behalf. (This generally entails "fictitious payees"—made-up accounts actually controlled by dishonest employees.)

With negotiation effective, there can be holders and even HIDCs down the chain of title. Thus the duped drawer or maker cannot raise the personal defense of fraudulent inducement against someone shielded with HIDC status. (Of course, for what it is worth, the drawer or maker could proceed against the person(s) who duped him/her.)

UCC 3-405's underlying policy is plain: it encourages the ready transfer of instruments, and it discourages carelessness by makers and drawers.

• *SIGNERS WITHOUT CAPACITY OR AUTHORITY*

Negotiation is effective even though it may be subject to rescission because of incapacity, illegality, duress, fraud, mistake, or breach of duty (UCC 3-207). Furthermore, negotiation cannot be rescinded against a HIDC if the problem amounts to merely a personal defense, not a "real" defense. Like UCC 3-405, this provision of UCC 3-207 is to be distinguished from blatantly unauthorized signatures (forgeries), which simply do not constitute negotiation and thus cannot create holders, let alone HIDCs.

EXAMPLES OF LIABILITY PROBLEMS

By way of review and example, let us look at two liability problems involving forgery: (1) the drawer's forged signature, and (2) the indorser's forged signature. Then we will examine a hypothetical case involving rescission.

Example: Drawer's Forged Signature

Ira Innocent loses a check that he has not yet written. Fanny Forger finds the check. She fills it out, making it payable to the order of Paula Payee for $2,000, and signing Ira's name as drawer. Fanny, using her fake identification cards as Paula Payee, obtains payment from Tammy Transferee, who takes it for value, in good faith, and without notice of the forgery.

May Tammy recover from Fanny? Yes. An unauthorized signature still operates as the signature of the unauthorized signer [UCC 3-404(1)]. Fanny is also liable for breach of warranties.

May Tammy recover from Ira? Probably not. Ira's signature would be necessary to make the check negotiable and to make him liable on the instrument. Since Ira did not ratify the signature, it remains unauthorized and, having failed to receive a duly negotiated instrument, Tammy is not a holder, let alone a HIDC. Only if Ira was negligent *and* if this negligence "substantially contributed" to what Fanny did, could Tammy recover from Ira (UCC 3-406). To make such a case, Tammy would need more facts.

Example: Forged Indorsement

Mary Maker issues a note to the order of Pam Payee for $3,000. Donald Devious steals the check, forges Pam's blank indorsement, and then himself indorses "without recourse" and to the order of Trudy Transferee. Trudy takes it for value, in good faith, and without notice of the forgery. She in turn gives an unqualified indorsement to Troy Transferee, the note being a gift to Troy.

May Troy recover from Donald Devious? Yes. It does not matter that Donald himself indorsed "without recourse." Donald's forgery of Pam's signature leaves him accountable as if he were Pam (UCC 3-404). Furthermore, Donald is liable for breach of warranties.

May Troy recover from Trudy? Yes, if Troy indorses the instrument and the primary party (Mary Maker) refuses to pay. Aside from any breach of warranties, Trudy is secondarily liable on the instrument because she failed to qualify her indorsement.

May Troy recover from Mary or Pam? No. As in the preceding example, Trudy is not a holder, let alone a HIDC. (The note was "order paper" to Pam, not properly negotiated by Pam.) Thus Troy (a non-HIDC for the same reason as Trudy and also because of the fact that he did not "take for value") cannot acquire HIDC rights under the shelter rule. Furthermore, there is no indication that either Mary or Pam acted negligently and thus permitted Donald to steal the check and forge Pam's signature (i.e., no recourse under UCC 3-406).

Example: Rescission

Ignatius Insane issues a note to the order of Pat Payee. Pat knows that Ignatius is insane. The note is then indorsed without qualification by Pat and given to Arnie. In turn, Arnie indorses "without recourse" to Sue, who pays value in good faith and without notice of Ignatius's condition or any other defense or claim. By the time that Sue transfers the note to Sam, it has, on its face, become overdue.

Can Sam collect from Ignatius? It depends on whether Ignatius's insanity is a "real" defense. If it is merely a personal defense, then Sam wins, for he took possession from a HIDC, Sue, and thus acquired rights under the shelter rule. Sam acquired Sue's rights even though he could not himself become a HIDC. (The note was, by the time he took it, obviously overdue.)

Can Sam collect from Pat? Yes, if the primary party, Ignatius, refuses to pay. Pat is secondarily liable; her indorsement was unqualified.

Can Sam collect from Arnie? No, unless Arnie breached a warranty. On the instrument itself, Arnie qualified his indorsement.

What about rescission (cancellation) in order to discharge the instrument? If Ignatius or his guardian rescinded at any time before the formation of a HIDC, then Ignatius probably would be free from paying. (Discharge is a "real" defense when the holder knows or should know about it; otherwise, it is still a personal defense.) But what if, after hearing about the rescission, a holder went ahead and transferred the instrument? The holder's actions appear to be in bad faith, and he would probably have to reimburse Ignatius for any amount Ignatius has to pay to a subsequent HIDC.

WARRANTIES ON PRESENTMENT OR TRANSFER

Negotiable instruments are often issued or transferred as part of an underlying contract (e.g., a sale of goods or services). The law governing such matters is the law of contracts, discussed in preceding chapters.

A second type of contractual liability, which we have just finished examining, is based on the negotiable instrument itself. In this case, a signer to the instrument is either primarily or secondarily liable. By signing, having someone else sign on his/her behalf, or ratifying a signature, the primary or secondary party has, in the absence of a qualified signature, made a type of contract to pay according to the instrument's terms.

There is another basis for liability: *warranties*. Any person who obtains payment or acceptance of an instrument, or who transfers an instrument and receives consideration, makes warranties. Under these, like other warranties (e.g., sales warranties under UCC 2-312, 2-313, 2-314, and 2-315), a party may be liable for damages if they are breached.

Some warranties are imposed on both the person who obtains payment or acceptance [in negotiable instruments law, acceptance is "the drawee's signed engagement to honor the draft as presented" (UCC 3-410)] and all prior transferors. There are three such **presentment warranties:**

1. That the person has good title to the instrument or is authorized to act for someone else with good title.

2. That the person has no knowledge that the maker's or drawer's signature is unauthorized. HIDC exceptions: the warranty is not given by a HIDC to an acceptor (if the HIDC acquired the instrument after acceptance or discovered the lack of authorization only after obtaining acceptance) or to the maker or drawer himself. These exceptions are consistent with Lord Mansfield's decision in *Price* v. *Neal* (1762): the drawee (e.g., acceptor), let alone the drawer him-/herself, should know the drawer's true signature and thus be able to prevent payment on a forged signature.

3. That the instrument has not been materially altered. Exceptions: not given by HIDCs to makers, drawers, or—in most cases—drawees.

These presentment warranties are given to any person who in good faith pays or accepts the instrument.

The other warranties are **warranties on transfer.** They are made by any person who transfers an instrument and receives consideration. This group includes sales agents or brokers, unless they have disclosed that they are acting solely on behalf of someone else. If they make such a disclosure, then they warrant only their good faith and authority.

The five warranties on transfer are as follows:

1. That the person has good title to the instrument or is authorized to act for someone else with good title, and the transfer is otherwise rightful.

2. That all signatures are genuine or authorized.

3. That the instrument has not been materially altered.

4. That no party's defense is good against the transferor. [A qualified indorsement ("without recourse") not only negates contractual liability on the instrument, but also limits this fourth warranty on transfer to simply a

statement that the transferor does not *know* of a party's defense good against him/her]

5. That the transferor has no knowledge of any insolvency proceeding concerning the maker, the acceptor, or (for an unaccepted instrument) the drawer.

These transfer warranties are given to the immediate transferee and, if the transfer is by indorsement, any subsequent holder who takes the instrument in good faith. This means, in effect, that a remote holder can sue the indorser-warrantor directly without having to sue intermediate transferors also.

There are no Article 3 provisions detailing warranty damages. Generally, damages are the difference between the instrument's value had the warranty not been breached and the instrument's actual worth because of the breach. That difference usually translates into damages equaling the face amount of the instrument.

OTHER AVENUES OF LIABILITY

Article 3, in addition to providing specifically for warranty liability and contractual liability on the instrument, also provides that a person may be sued for the tort of conversion (UCC 3-419). (For further discussion of conversion, see Chapter 4.) Also, as already discussed, negligence may preclude a person from recovering on, or maintaining a defense on, an instrument (UCC 3-406).

Aside from possible remedies or legal theories outside of Article 3 (e.g., recovery on the underlying contract), there is one other major form of liability: that of accommodation parties or guarantors.

• *ACCOMMODATION PARTIES*

An **accommodation party** signs an instrument in some capacity (e.g., maker, drawer, indorser, or acceptor) to lend his/her credit status to another party to the instrument. (Generally, an indorsement not in the instrument's chain of title is an accommodation indorsement.) The accommodation party is essentially a surety for the accommodated party; therefore, without first seeking recourse from the accommodated party, subsequent holders for value can enforce the instrument against the accommodation party, who can assert only the defenses available to the accommodated party as well as general surety defenses. (For more on sureties, see Chapter 20.) Of course, the accommodated party has no right to enforce payment from the accommodation party. That right is held by other parties to the instrument.

• *GUARANTORS*

Indorsement with the words "payment guaranteed" or their equivalent converts an indorser's secondary liability to primary liability. The holder may proceed directly against the indorser (**guarantor**) once the instrument falls due and is unpaid.

Another type of guarantor, though, is not liable until it is clear that proceeding against the primary party (maker or acceptor) is useless. Such a guarantor has indorsed with the words "collection guaranteed" or their equivalent.

If the words of guarantee do not specify their nature, they are deemed to guarantee payment, not just collection.

Example: Guarantor

If Guarantor Smith does not want to be primarily liable for a note signed by Dead-Beat Dingham, Smith should plainly indicate that the guarantee extends simply to collection.

YOU SHOULD REMEMBER

Liability on an instrument requires a person's signature or the signature of an authorized agent. Primary parties are makers and drawees; secondary parties are drawers and indorsers. Secondary parties can avoid potential liabilities on an instrument (except for some warranties) by indorsing "without recourse."

If a person's negligence substantially contributes to a material alteration or an unauthorized signature, that person cannot use the alteration or signature as a defense against a HIDC or anyone else who in good faith pays for the instrument. Although a drawer or maker issues an instrument to an impostor or fictitious payee, the negotiation remains effective; usually, the drawer's or maker's only recourse is against the impostor or other persons who got him/her to issue the instrument.

Presentment warranties cover title, signature authorization, and lack of material alteration.

Transfer warranties cover these three areas as well as (1) lack of good defenses and (2) absence of knowledge about the insolvency of the maker, acceptor, or (for an unaccepted instrument) drawer.

Accommodation parties, who serve as sureties for the accommodated parties, and guarantors may become liable on instruments they sign.

DISCHARGE

A party's liability to pay an instrument may be discharged (terminated). **Discharge** *usually arises by payment or other satisfaction.* However, some or all of the parties may be discharged of their liabilities by any of these other methods:

1. Tender of payment (even though unaccepted).
2. Cancellation.

3. Impairment of reimbursement rights.

4. Fraudulent, material alterations.

5. Check certification.

6. Reacquisition of instrument by maker or drawer.

7. Unexcused delay in presentment

8. Unexcused delay in notice of dishonor.

9. Draft varying acceptance.

10. Any act that discharges a simple contract to pay money.

Discharge is generally effective against all parties except a HIDC who lacked notice of the discharge when he/she took the instrument.

YOU SHOULD REMEMBER

Liability on an instrument is usually discharged by payment, but other methods of discharge are also available.

KNOW THE CONCEPTS
DO YOU KNOW THE BASICS?

1. Define a HIDC.
2. (a) Name three characteristics of an instrument that usually indicate notice of a claim or defense.
   (b) Name two that do not.
3. (a) Name at least three facts that, if known by the would-be HIDC, usually indicate notice of a claim or defense.
   (b) Name at least three that do not.
4. Name at least five "real" defenses and seven personal defenses.
5. Which type of defense works against even a HIDC?
6. In regard to consumer protection versus the HIDC concept, one approach has been to reduce the HIDC's power to evade personal defenses, while another approach has been to make it more difficult for someone to become a HIDC. Which approach has been followed by many state legislatures? By the FTC?
7. Name at least three types of negligence that can so substantially contribute to unauthorized alterations or signatures that they preclude recovery against persons paying in good faith.

8. (a) State the three main types of liability between parties to a negotiable instrument.
   (b) What tort is expressly listed as a remedy (e.g., for wrongful payment of an instrument) in UCC 3-419?
9. Name the areas covered by the three presentment warranties.
10. Name the areas covered by the five transfer warranties.

TERMS FOR STUDY

accommodation party
discharge
dishonor
forgery
good faith
guarantor
holder in due course (HIDC)
personal defenses

presentment warranty
primary party
"real" defenses
secondary party
shelter rule
unauthorized signature
warranty on transfer

PRACTICAL APPLICATION

1. Jim pays Joan $50 for a check in the amount of $75. Can Jim be a HIDC? If so, for what amount?
2. Fred Fraud owes Helen Holder $500. Fred fraudulently induces Tom Taken to buy a worthless stereo system for $500. Helen knows nothing about Fred's misdeeds but is told that, if she releases Fred from his debt to her, Fred will have Tom issue a check to her for $500. Two weeks later, Helen takes the check to the bank. By then, however, Tom has discovered Fred's fraud. Tom asserts that payment may be refused because:
   (a) Helen is a payee, not a HIDC.
   (b) Helen did not act in good faith.
   (c) Tom can successfully raise Fred's fraud against Helen.
   (d) The check was overdue.
   Discuss each reason.
3. Paul Payee indorses a negotiable instrument "to the order of Julia Jumper," who takes the instrument for value, in good faith, and without notice of claims or defenses to it. The instrument is not overdue, nor has it ever been dishonored, when Julia indorses it and gives it to Debbie Dole. Apparently, however, Paul has still not performed the services for which the instrument was issued. Now the issuer refuses to pay Debbie. Discuss.
4. What is meant by the statement, "A negotiable instrument is a courier without any luggage?"

5. Having performed services for Poe Credit, you are concerned about the check that you received as payment: Is Poe really "good for the money"? You owe Jane an amount somewhat less than the face value of Poe's check. Jane is willing to take the check as complete payment of the debt. She seems to be impressed by the amount of Poe's check, while you are more concerned about whether one can really collect on the check. In indorsing the check to Jane, what can you do to protect yourself if Jane or a subsequent transferee has trouble collecting?

6. M issues a note payable to P's order. C steals the note, forges P's indorsement, and sells the note to X. M pays X. On the assumption that M has to pay P for conversion (UCC 3-419), may M recover from other parties?

7. In Problem 3, what warranties, if any, have been breached?

8. John drafts a check on Bank Y, payable to the order of Pat. For money, Pat negotiates the check to Viola. Pat has been declared insolvent in a federal bankruptcy court. What warranties, if any, have been breached?

ANSWERS
KNOW THE CONCEPTS

1. A holder who has taken a negotiable instrument for value, in good faith, and without notice that it is overdue, has been dishonored, or has defenses or claims against it.

2. (a) Incorrect indorsements, material omissions, important alterations.
   (b) Antedated or postdated, originally imcomplete and later completed.

3. (a) Party's obligation void or voidable, parties discharged, defective title, unauthorized completion of instrument, default in principal payments or on series instruments.
   (b) Parties include fiduciaries or accommodation parties, instrument issued or negotiated for an executory promise, existence of separate agreements, default on interest payments or on different instruments.

4. "Real" defenses: fraud in the execution (factum), forgeries and unauthorized signatures, defenses rendering a contract void, bankruptcy discharges, other discharges about which the holder knew or should have known, statutes of limitations, material alterations.
   Personal defenses: lack or failure of consideration, fraud in the inducement, ordinary contract defenses, defenses rendering a contract voidable, violation of a restrictive indorsement, nonbankruptcy discharges about which holder has no notice, acquisition of lost or stolen bearer paper, nondelivery or unauthorized delivery of an instrument, unauthorized completions, some "real" defenses in which party asserting defense was negligent.

Chapter 20 discusses the concepts of creditor and secured party in much greater detail.

Because the bank owes money to the customer, it is subject to garnishment by the customer's creditors. (For information on garnishment, see Chapter 20.) Likewise, because the customer does not actually "own" the bank funds, he/she cannot assign the funds. All a customer can do is order the bank to make payment (by writing a check: "Pay to the order of ..."). Since the order is not an immediate "assignment," a customer may die, issue a stop-payment order, or otherwise undermine the order before it takes effect; and, unless the check is certified, the holder has no recourse against the nonpaying bank. (The holder would instead sue the drawer and/or indorsers.)

THE BANK'S DUTY TO THE CUSTOMER

The bank's primary duty to its customer is to honor his/her checks when the customer has sufficient funds on deposit. Banks are thus liable to their customers for **wrongful dishonor**. If the wrongful dishonor was a mistake (i.e., not intentional), the customer's recovery is limited to his/her actual damages, which are, however, liberally defined as including harm to credit or reputation, arrest for writing bad checks, or other proved, consequential damages.

Note that dishonor must be *wrongful*. For instance, banks are not liable for refusing to pay on insufficient funds or on improper or missing indorsements.

A second duty of the bank is to maintain customer signature cards and to be familiar with the depositor's authorized signature, so that forgeries can be detected before any payment is made.

Rules under the federal Expedited Funds Availability Act (1988) limit the maximum length of holds a financial institution may place on the funds from local and non-local checks deposited at the institution. The Act also requires disclosure of hold policies and of the specific hold placed on a deposit.

THE CUSTOMER'S DUTY TO THE BANK (SECTION 4-406)

The first duty of the customer is to maintain sufficient funds in an account to cover the checks that he/she expects to write. In addition, under section 4-406, the customer has a second important duty.

As mentioned above, banks are supposed to maintain customer signature cards and thus be able to verify the authenticity of a customer's signature, whether as drawer or indorser. As a practical matter, however, the enormously high volume of checks frequently renders it impossible for a busy bank to examine the authenticity of every check in every account. Therefore, while the drawee bank is charged with knowing its drawer's signature (*Price* v. *Neal*, briefly discussed in Chapter 12) and with otherwise avoiding payment on altered or forged instruments or indorsements, the customer is also expected to do his/her part in preventing or correcting unauthorized transactions.

Section 4-406 of the Uniform Commercial Code requires that the customer review his/her bank statements and any other documents (e.g., canceled checks) sent by the bank. Generally, if failure to do so results in his/her not discovering and reporting an alteration or unauthorized signature, the customer is precluded from asserting a claim against the bank in the following situations:

1. The bank suffered a loss because of the customer's failure to discover and report.

2. The bank paid in good faith and without notice of the type of problem that the customer should have discovered by the time payment was made.

Example: Failure of Customer to Review Bank Statement

If Customer Carol had reviewed the bank statements sent to her by Big Bank, she could have told Big Bank about a check forged by Fanny Fraud. Carol is thus precluded from having her account recredited if prompt reporting to Big Bank would have spared the bank a loss (item 1 above).

More importantly, if Fanny Fraud continues to practice her deceit, Carol is barred from asserting against Big Bank these later forgeries by Fanny; simply put, Carol's diligence could have prevented these later problems because she would have put Big Bank on notice (item 2 above).

Preclusion under 4-406, as well as preclusion under 3-406 (drawer's negligence) and 3-405 (impostor/fictitious payee), is discussed in Chapter 12. However, note that, *as under Sections 3-405 and 3-406, the bank cannot take advantage of 4-406 unless the bank itself was not negligent.* Customers who review their bank statements and are not otherwise negligent are entitled to have their accounts recredited not only for checks bearing their own forged signatures, but also for checks containing other persons' forged indorsements.

Example: Bank Customer Rights

Agnes writes a check for $700 "to the order of Tim." Chris forges Tim's indorsement and cashes the check. So long as Agnes is not precluded by her own failure to inspect or other negligence, she is entitled to have the bank recredit her account for the $700. The bank failed to carry out Agnes's order to pay "to the order of Tim."

Besides going after Chris, Agnes's bank can recover its loss from the bank that cashed the check; The cashing bank breached its warranty that there were no forged indorsements. (Warranties were discussed in Chapter 12.) For a forged drawer's signature, though, the drawee bank can recover only from the forger unless others were negligent or actually knew that the signature was unauthorized. Again, the drawee bank is charged with knowing its drawer's signature (*Price v. Neal*).

YOU SHOULD REMEMBER

Banks are debtors to the account-holders/creditors.

Checks are not assignments.

The primary duty of a bank is to honor the depositor's checks when sufficient funds are on hand; a bank is liable for wrongful dishonor of a check. A second duty is to be familiar with the customer's authorized signature in order to detect forgeries.

The customer is responsible for maintaining sufficient funds in an account to cover the checks written and for reviewing bank statements, canceled checks, and other documents for alterations or unauthorized signatures. UCC 4-406 precludes a customer from asserting an alteration or unauthorized signature against a nonnegligent bank when (1) the bank suffered a loss because of the customer's failure to examine his/her bank statements promptly and then report the alteration or unauthorized signature, or (2) the bank paid in good faith and without notice of the type of problem that the customer should have noticed by then.

A customer who promptly reviews his/her bank statements and is not otherwise negligent has the right to have his/her account recredited for checks bearing the customer's forged signature or another person's forged indorsement.

RULES GOVERNING THE PAYMENT OF CHECKS

The drawer's bank is the primary agent in the collection process, that is, the sequence of events through which a check goes before final settlement. Article 4 of the UCC sets forth specific rules governing the payment of checks:

1. The bank need not (but may) pay **overdrafts** (checks for more than the amount in the customer's account). If the bank has specifically agreed to pay overdrafts, then it must do so.

2. The bank can charge the customer's account for the full amount that it pays on an overdraft.

3. The bank can refuse to pay **stale checks** (uncertified checks drawn more than 6 months before presentation for payment).

4. In the check-collection process, a bank may supply necessary indorsements for a customer, except when the missing indorsement is that of the payee and the check expressly requires the payee to sign.

5. If a customer dies or is adjudged (declared by a court) to be incompetent, the bank may continue to honor his/her checks (pay them from the customer's account) until it receives notice of the death or incompetence and has had a reasonable opportunity to respond. Even with notice, the bank may pay or accept checks during the first 10 days after death (unless it receives a stop-payment order from someone claiming an interest in the decedent's account).

6. The customer can order the bank not to pay a particular check, provided that the bank has enough time to act on the **stop-payment order**. Such orders can be either oral or written, with oral orders effective for 14 days and written ones effective for 6 months. Stop-payment orders can be renewed. If the bank fails to comply, it is liable to the customer for his/her actual losses.

These rules, as well as other Article 4 requirements, are not absolute. A bank and its customer may, by their contract, alter these rules. The only unchangeable terms are these: a bank's responsibility for its lack of good faith or ordinary care (dishonesty or negligence), and the measure of damages resulting from such lack of good faith or ordinary care. Indeed, so long as the terms are not plainly unreasonable, the bank and its customer may even state in their agreement the standards by which bank responsibility is to be decided.

YOU SHOULD REMEMBER

Article 4 has rules specifically governing overdrafts, stale checks, missing indorsements of customers, dead or incompetent customers, and stop-payment orders.

A bank and its customer may, by their contract, alter most of the Article 4 rules. However, they cannot void the bank's responsibility for its own dishonesty or negligence, or the measure of damages for such dishonesty or negligence.

CERTIFICATION OF CHECKS

Initially, a check is only as good as the credit of the drawer. To ensure payment, a payee or subsequent holder should have the check certified. Certification prevents the drawee bank from denying liability; the **certified check** is the bank's guarantee that sufficient funds (presumably from the drawer's account) have been set aside to cover the check.

The drawee bank is not required to certify a check. Refusal to certify is not dishonor; the bank merely refuses to agree in advance to cover a check.

Once the check is certified, the drawer and all indorsers prior to certification are released from liability on the check. If, when payment is later sought, the drawee bank discovers that there was not in fact a "hold" on sufficient funds in the drawer's account, the drawee must make up the difference. Furthermore, the bank can never revoke certification against someone with HIDC rights or any other good-faith holder who changed position in reliance on the certification. It is thus easy to see why banks are generally very cautious about certifying checks. As is the case for cashier's checks (where the account-holder has the bank issue a check to a particular payee, the bank being both drawer and drawee), the bank tends to subtract the amount of the check from the customer's account immediately.

YOU SHOULD REMEMBER

A certified check serves as a guarantee that sufficient funds have been set aside to cover the check.

A bank is not required to certify a check, and most banks are very cautious about doing so, because certification releases the drawer from liability on the check and makes the drawee responsible for payment.

ALTERATIONS

If the drawer was negligent (e.g., left unreasonably large spaces in writing the check), then Section 3-406 may completely bar bank liability for payment if the check was altered (generally, the amount was increased). If the drawer was *not* negligent, however, then these are the general rules:

1. The bank bears a loss to the extent of the raised amount.

2. The bank may charge the drawer's account for the original amount of the check.

3. The bank may recover from the person who presented the check for payment (warranty liability).

For certified checks, the crucial question on alterations is "when?" Alterations before certification are deemed to have been accepted by the certifying bank, whereas alterations after certification could not, of course, have been accepted by the bank when it certified the check. Therefore, unless the drawee bank negligently goes ahead and pays the altered amount, the drawee bank will be liable only for the check as it stood when certified.

YOU SHOULD REMEMBER

If a check has been altered, the bank can charge a non-negligent drawer only for the original amount of the check, but may seek to recover from the person presenting the check the loss it incurred by paying the larger amount.

For an altered certified check, the drawee bank is liable only for the amount before certification.

SUMMARY OF IMPORTANT ARTICLE 4 RULES

UCC 4-401: *Charge Against* *Account*	Bank may charge customer for every properly payable item even if an overdraft.
UCC 4-402: *Wrongful* *Dishonor*	Bank is liable to customer for wrongful dishonor. Unless more than just a bank "mistake," damages are limited to damages actually proved, but can include consequential damages (e.g., loss of credit, arrest and prosecution).
UCC 4-403: *Stop-Payment* *Orders*	Bank is liable for payment over a timely stop-payment order. Oral orders bind for 14 days, but can be confirmed (and extended) by putting the order in writing. Written orders last for 6 months and are renewable.
UCC 4-404: *Stale Checks*	Bank has no duty to pay uncertified checks more than 6 months old, but may in good faith pay them.
UCC 4-405: *Death or* *Incompetence*	Bank may pay checks as long as it does not know of customer's death or incompetence. Despite knowledge, bank can honor or certify checks in first 10 days after customer's death (unless a stop-payment order is issued by a person claiming an interest in the dead customer's account).
UCC 4-406: *Customer's Duty* *to Examine Bank* *Statements*	Customer must examine account statements and notify bank of unauthorized signatures or alterations. Bank exercising reasonable care is not liable to customer if (a) customer's failure to examine and report results in bank's loss or (b) customer fails to examine and report within 14 days of receipt, in the case of continuing unauthorized signatures or alterations by the same wrongdoer.
UCC 4-406: *Statute of* *Limitations*	More than one year after receiving relevant bank statement, customer is precluded from asserting against bank unauthorized customer signatures or alterations. Time limit is 3 years for unauthorized indorsements. These time limits can be enforced even if bank was negligent.

ELECTRONIC FUNDS TRANSFER ACT

Most banks have sought to substitute, when possible, electronic communications for a time- and paper-consuming check-collection process. Electronic funds transfer (EFT) is practically instantaneous. No checks are needed, with payment being by electronic signal. The most common methods of EFT are automated teller machines, paycheck direct deposits/withdrawals, pay-by-phone systems, and point-of-sale terminals (e.g., direct transfers from consumers' accounts to store accounts).

Since 1989, over half of the states have adopted a new UCC Article, 4A, which governs fund transfers between the bank accounts of large, highly sophisticated businesses. Much more comprehensive in scope (covering *consumer* EFT) and applicable in all states, is the federal *Electronic Funds Transfer Act* of 1978. This act includes the following provisions:

1. Limits are placed on customer liability for charges on a lost or stolen bank card (e.g., a "debit card" used to transfer funds directly from the customer's bank account to the account of a merchant from whom the customer makes a purchase). The limits, though, increase or even disappear entirely if the customer fails to tell the bank about the loss or theft.

2. Banks must furnish receipts for computer terminal transactions, but not for telephone transfers.

3. Banks must furnish a statement for each month that an electronic funds transfer occurs. Such statements have to show amounts, dates, names of retailers, locations of terminals used, and any fees. An address and telephone number for customer inquiries and error notices must also be included.

4. The customer must discover any errors on the monthly statement and notify his/her bank within 60 days. If the bank takes longer than 10 days to investigate, it must, for the time being, credit the disputed amount to the customer's account. (Obviously, if there was no error, the bank gets this money back.)

5. Information about rights and duties under the act must be given to customers opening an EFT account.

Several federal agencies are empowered to enforce the Electronic Funds Transfer Act. Customers can sue for violations of the act. They may recover their actual damages as well as statutory penalties. There are also criminal provisions.

YOU SHOULD REMEMBER

The Electronic Funds Transfer Act includes provisions specifying limits on customer liability for charges on lost or stolen bank cards, requiring receipts for computer terminal transactions (but not for telephone transfers), and mandating monthly statements of amount, date, name of retailer and so forth, for each electronic fund transfer.

As with regular bank statements, customers have a duty to examine the statement and notify the bank of errors.

> Several federal agencies enforce parts of the act, and customers can sue their banks directly for violations.

KNOW THE CONCEPTS
DO YOU KNOW THE BASICS?

1. Are checks assignments?
2. Are banks subject to garnishment by a customer's creditors? Why?
3. Give at least three proper reasons for dishonoring a check.
4. State the two ways of making stop-payment orders and the length of time for which each is effective.
5. What Article 4 legal requirements can a bank and its customers *not* change via the bank/customer contract?
6. When can certification of a check be required?
7. (a) What does Section 4-406 require of bank customers?
   (b) If the customer fails to meet the 4-406 requirements, what can happen to him/her?
8. What is the statute of limitations for a customer's claim against his/her bank on (a) unauthorized customer signatures or alterations and (b) unauthorized indorsements?
9. Name at least four areas covered by the Electronic Funds Transfer Act

TERMS FOR STUDY

alterations	stale check
certified check	stop-payment order
Electronic Funds Transfer Act	UCC Articles 4 & 4A
Expedited Funds Availability Act	wrongful dishonor
overdraft	

PRACTICAL APPLICATION

1. Horace Holder presents to Big Bank a check, drawn by Big Bank account-holder Cory Careless to the order of Horace for the amount of $900, and containing all of the proper signatures. Big Bank pays it, although Cory's account contains only $750. Cory says that Big Bank should not have paid Horace.
   (a) Is Cory correct?
   (b) What may the bank do in regard to Cory and to Horace?
2. Assume that Big Bank refused to honor the check, and Cory therefore lost a major business contract. Could Cory win a lawsuit against Big Bank?

3. Sharon Survivor's uncle has just died, leaving Sharon as his next of kin. Sharon believes that her uncle wrote several "crazy" checks in the last few days of his life. She is concerned that her uncle's bank will honor these checks. What should she do?

4. Gary Greedy wants to bring a certified check to his meeting with Robert Reelistate. However, Gary feels that he needs every last cent of interest he can get from his account. Are these conflicting goals?

5. During a 3-month period, Boris Baddie forges Dudley Dewgood's signature on several checks, makes Dudley's supposed checks payable to Boris, and then cashes them. Dudley takes each month's bank statement and simply puts it in a box. Six months later, Dudley discovers Boris's fraud.
   (a) May Dudley recover from the bank?
   (b) What if the checks were themselves inartfully drawn copies, not the ones actually sent by the bank to its customers?

ANSWERS
KNOW THE CONCEPTS

1. No.

2. Yes. In essence, the bank is a debtor of the customer/account-holder.

3. Insufficient funds, improper or missing indorsement, unauthorized drawer's signature, stale check (over 6 months old).

4. Written and oral. Written last 6 months and can be renewed. Oral last 14 days, but can be confirmed in writing (and thus extended to 6 months).

5. The bank's responsibility for its lack of good faith or ordinary care (dishonesty or negligence) and the measure of damages resulting from such dishonesty or negligence.

6. Generally, never. It is the bank's option whether to certify.

7. (a) That the customers promptly examine bank statements and report any unauthorized signatures or alterations.
   (b) The customer can be precluded from recovering for unauthorized signatures and alterations that he/she could have discovered, unless the bank was itself negligent.

8. (a) One year after receiving relevant bank statements.
   (b) Three years after receiving relevant bank statements.

9. Customer liability limits on lost or stolen bank cards, receipts for transactions, monthly statements, customer examination of monthly statements, bank investigation of alleged errors, information about the act for new customers.

PRACTICAL APPLICATION

1. (a) No. Banks generally have the option to pay overdrafts.

    (b) Big Bank may seek reimbursement from Cory for the remaining $150 (plus perhaps a penalty). It may charge Cory's account directly, assuming that more money is deposited.

    As for Horace, once Big Bank honored the check, its only recourse against him would be claims arising under Article 3. However, Horace may well be a HIDC.

2. Not ordinarily. However, checking account arrangements can specifically provide for the payment of overdrafts. If Cory had such a contract with Big Bank, then he could hold the bank liable.

3. Sharon should immediately contact the bank to inform it of her uncle's death and her status as next of kin. She should also demand that it stop payment on any checks in her uncle's account and thus give the estate time to determine the propriety of the "crazy" checks.

4. Probably. When a check is certified, the bank usually withdraws the amount from the account *immediately*. Unless Gary's bank has some other arrangement (or somehow continues to credit interest until the certified check is actually cashed), Gary will lose further interest on the amount of the check once he has the check certified. Of course, with ordinary checks, interest earnings are unaffected until the check is collected.

5. (a) Unless the bank was itself negligent, Dudley certainly cannot recover for checks drafted toward the end of the 3-month period; by that time, if Dudley had examined his bank statements, he could have detected the fraud and put the bank on notice in order to prevent further forgeries. Even for the earlier checks, Dudley cannot recover if his prompt review of the bank statements would have left the bank able to prevent a loss (e.g., by getting the money back from Boris or some other party to the instrument).

    (b) If the bank was negligent, as in this case, Dudley's failure to examine does not matter. The bank's cashing of inartfully drawn copies constitutes the type of bank negligence that eliminates 4-406 preclusion of Dudley's claim.

14
AGENCY

KEY TERMS

agency a legal relationship whereby one person acts for another

agent a person authorized to act for another (principal)

principal the person for whom an agent acts and from whom the agent derives authority

independent contractor a person hired to undertake a contractually defined result (not an employee and usually not an agent)

NATURE OF AGENCY AND AGENCY LAW

Agency is of fundamental importance to all business. An **agency** is a legal relationship in which one person represents another and is authorized to act for him/her. The person who acts is the **agent**; the person for whom the agent acts is the **principal**.

Agency law consists of all the rules, recognized and enforced by society, whereby one person acts for another. Without the body of agency law, every person would have to act directly for him-/herself and could not send a representative, a salesman, or a messenger. Since corporations can act only vicariously though employees, officers, and agents, corporations could not function at all and would cease to exist.

Without the ability of a principal to act through an agent, business would be severely crippled.

By and large, agency law is state common law. Neither federal law nor the Uniform Commercial Code deals expressly with the subject of agency.

YOU SHOULD REMEMBER

Agency is a legal relationship in which one person (the agent) represents another (the principal) and is authorized to act for him/her.

Agency law is largely the common law of the various states. It consists of the rules that society recognizes and enforces in regard to situations in which one person acts for another.

AGENCY AND OTHER LEGAL CONCEPTS WHEREBY ONE PERSON MAY OR MAY NOT PERFORM SERVICES FOR ANOTHER

1. *Agency includes employment.* An agent may be an employee since an employee frequently serves in a representative capacity. An employee is under the full control and supervision of his/her employer, who determines not only what is to be done, but also how it is to be done as well as other details of performance. The discussion of agency will include the employment relationship, called "master/servant," which is one very important kind of agency. The master/servant relationship is defined by the contract of employment.

2. *Agency includes and may be created by a power of attorney.* In its broadest sense, the word "attorney" denotes a representative or agent. An **attorney-at-law** is a legal representative, employed to represent a client in lawsuits and other legal matters. An **attorney in fact** may represent another person as an agent for general or special purposes other than legal ones. An attorney in fact is named as representative or agent in a **power of attorney**, a written document setting out the appointment of the attorney. The appointment may be general, that is, for broad agency purposes ("to do any act for me"), or special ("to sell my real estate known as "Blackacre") for named and limited purposes.

3. *Agency generally does not include independent contractors.* An **independent contractor** is hired (or chosen), not to represent, but to achieve a purpose, to do a job, to undertake a contractually defined result. How the contractor achieves the end result and what tools and techniques are used are his/her responsibility.

The tort or contractual responsibility of a principal for the acts of his/her agent moves from very great, when the agent is an employee, to almost zero in the case of an independent contractor, where there usually is no agency relation at all.

---

4. *Personal service obligations cannot be performed by an agent.* As discussed in Chapter 8, a number of personal service obligations cannot be delegated to another. These nondelegable obligations require the special skill of a designated person who cannot send a representative (agent) to act in his/her place. Thus, without the approval of the benefitted third party, a doctor or lawyer, for example, cannot name an agent to act in his/her place. Similarly, a member of a corporation's board of directors, charged with the personal responsibility of a fiduciary (trustee), cannot act through an agent but must discharge his/her board duties in person. *What can be delegated* to an agent or subagent? Administrative, clerical, or mechanical duties—almost anything in which the delegating party's special skills or judgment are not involved.

YOU SHOULD REMEMBER

The categories of agents include employees and agents under power of attorney. An independent contractor generally is not an agent, and personal service obligations cannot be delegated to an agent.

CREATION OF AGENCY

BY EXPRESS CONTRACT OR CONSENSUAL AGREEMENT

Usually, but not always, agency is created by contract, oral or written. The contract element that *may* be lacking is consideration; the relation is, however, always consensual. For example, the power of attorney creates a consensual, noncontractual agency. The attorney in fact makes no promise to act, nor does the power granted necessarily provide for his/her payment or compensation. In some states, the power of attorney to sell real estate must be in writing, signed by the principal.

If the agency is consensual and not contractual, either party can terminate it at any time without liability to the other for failure to continue performance of the agency. However, there is contractual responsibility for tasks completed, undertaken, or underway.

Even if there is no contract, the parties are bound by all of the general duties and responsibilities of principal and agent.

BY THE CONDUCT OF THE PARTIES

Implied contracts of agency may be judicially determined because the words or actions of the parties would lead others to believe that an agency existed, that one party was acting for another. This is the test for implied contracts, generally.

Indeed, because of the way persons act, third parties may depend upon there being an agency relationship even though the parties, as between themselves, may deny the existence of an agency.

BY RATIFICATION OF AN UNAUTHORIZED ACT

Even though there is no contract of agency, either express or implied, at the time an "agent" performs an act that implies a contract for another person, that person may ratify the act by accepting the results of the act or contract after the fact.

Example: Implied Contract by Ratification of an Unauthorized Act

Tara Tenant employs an interior decorator to install draperies and rugs in a residence owned by Larry Landlord. Larry will be responsible on the contract by ratification if he accepts the benefits of the work knowing of the transaction and knowing that the decorator expects to be compensated.

Since the ratification can be express or implied, in order to avoid responsibility Larry should repudiate the action as soon as he learns of it.

BY ESTOPPEL

Estoppel is conduct by one person that causes another person, reasonably relying on this conduct, to act to his/her detriment or to change his/her position. An agent is given apparent authority by his/her principal if the principal, by his/her conduct, leads another to believe that the agent is in fact authorized to act on the principal's behalf. If a corporation permits an office manager to exercise general supervision over office employees, the office manager may have apparent authority to discipline these employees or to increase their compensation, even though secret or confidential limitations may have been placed upon this authority.

BY NECESSITY

There are a few special situations in which one person, for example, a parent, is responsible for the necessities of another, a child. In such a case, the parent may be responsible as a principal for a contract made by the child for his/her necessities (e.g., for medical treatment when away from home). The contract, of course, must be reasonable, and the provider of the service will be liable to the parent (principal) for failure to perform the contract with proper care.

YOU SHOULD REMEMBER

Agency can be created by contract (express or implied, oral or written), by ratification (assent is given either to an act done by someone who had no previous authority to act or to an act that exceeded the authority granted to an agent), by estoppel (a person allows another to act for him/her to such an extent that a third party reasonably believes that an agency relationship exists), or necessity (a person acts for another in an emergency situation without express authority to do so).

THE AGENT/PRINCIPAL RELATIONSHIP
DUTIES OF THE AGENT TO THE PRINCIPAL

When the agent is appointed by contract, the terms of the contract determine the duties of each party to the other. However, the duties of an agent may be modified by express agreement. In the absence of specific terms or modifications by contract, these duties are as described in this section.

The law considers that an agent acts in a fiduciary capacity to his/her principal. The obligations of a **fiduciary** are very strict; failure of the fiduciary to account for monies collected for his/her principal, **commingling** of such monies with the fiduciary's own, or appropriation of the principal's property to the fiduciary's own use may be not only a breach of the agency contract, but also a criminal act (embezzlement, larceny after trust).

In keeping with this high degree of fidelity, the following duties are required of the agent (unless modified by contract):

1. *Duty to obey instructions.* This duty is self-evident; it involves no more than might be expected from any contract obligation. Bear in mind, however, that the agent may be undertaking duties of the highest and most complex nature: buying and selling, entering into contracts, and the like, all as an **alter ego** (other self) for the principal. The agent is *personally liable* to the principal if he/she (a) causes the principal to become responsible for unauthorized contracts, (b) improperly delegates his/her duties to another, or (c) commits torts for which his/her principal may be responsible.

2. *Duty to act with skill.* An agent undertakes to act with the degree of skill ordinarily expected from others undertaking such employment. A business agent, a stockbroker, a manufacturer's representative—all undertake their agencies with the understanding that they will perform with skill. Any case for breach of contract requires proof (a) of the proper standard of care or skill and (b) of failure of the agent's performance to rise to that level.

3. Duty to avoid conflict of interest (duty of loyalty). An agent who is acting for a principal cannot act for him-/herself with respect to the same matter. An agent buying property for a principal cannot purchase property in which he/she has some personal or private interest; an agent selling the principal's goods cannot sell to him-/herself or to friends or relatives at a special or lower price. An attorney cannot act for conflicting parties in a lawsuit, or represent conflicting interests in any business transaction. On occasion a conflict, or possibility of conflict, can be resolved by full disclosure of all facts to both principals, followed by their fully informed consent to such double representation.

The disclosure of conflict or possible conflict must be complete, and the consent of the principal must be given with realization of all consequences.

---

4. Duty to protect confidential information. Obviously, the principal must be free to disclose all necessary information to his/her agent, including trade secrets and proprietary information. The agent must protect this property from the general public, third persons, and the principal's competitors. Also, such proprietary and confidential information must be restored to the principal upon termination of the agency.

5. Duty to notify. Since the agent is, in some respects, an extension of the principal, he/she is, by this extension, the eyes and ears of the principal. Consequently, the agent must notify the principal of all information that is or may be useful to the principal in evaluating the matter at hand. In this way, the principal can make further choices with respect to his/her business and continue to give the agent proper guidance.

6. Duty to account. The contract of agency will specify times and manner of accounting. In all cases, the agent must maintain "an open book" for the principal so that the principal may assess the progress of the work. At termination of the agency, all property must be accounted for and all income turned over to the principal in accord with the agency agreement. *Commingling of funds is a violation of the agent's duty of fidelity*

Failure to account and breach of the relation of trust may be criminal.

DUTIES OF THE PRINCIPAL TO THE AGENT

The duties of the principal to the agent are governed by the contract of agency. The primary duty is to compensate the agent for his/her services If the contract is implied, the compensation is the agent's fee as understood, or generally understood. If there is no contract, express or implied, the agent is entitled to compensation in quasi contract calculated at the reasonable value (*quantum meruit*) of the services performed. If, however, the agent agreed to perform the agency gratuitously, no compensation is due.

The principal is obligated to pay all costs and expenses of the agent reasonably incurred by the agent in furtherance of the principal's business.

If the agent is an employee, he/she is entitled to a place to work and to the equipment, supplies, and accessories necessary to perform the employment.

YOU SHOULD REMEMBER

An agent is a trustee, and this trust relation requires a high degree of loyalty. The law implies a number of duties of performance, but these may be modified by contract.

The primary duty of the principal to the agent is to compensate the agent according to the terms of the agency agreement or, if no agreement exists, at the reasonable value of the services performed.

LIABILITY OF PRINCIPAL AND AGENT TO THIRD PARTIES

LIABILITY OF THE PRINCIPAL FOR CONTRACTS MADE BY THE AGENT

The agent is a representative of the principal. In regard to the business of the principal, the agent is an extension of the principal, an alter ego. Thus, when an agent is acting within the authority granted by the principal, he/she can bind the principal to the deal; otherwise, creation of agents would serve no purpose, would make no sense. Justinian's code stated it this way: *Qui facet per alium, facet per se*, that is, "Who acts through another, acts himself."

The principal is bound contractually if the agent has either the *actual authority* to make a contract for the principal or has the *apparent authority* to do so.

> **Actual authority** is either *express* (based on oral or written words to the agent) or *implied* (inferred from words or conduct manifested by the principal to the agent).
>
> Implied authority to make contracts for the principal is a commonsense fulfillment of the agent's job, a going forward with the purposes of the principal's business.

If the agent can buy goods, manage real estate, or set up a branch office, he/she has the implied authority to make contracts to achieve these purposes. Remember that almost every business transaction involves a contract, and the authority to transact the principal's business usually carries with it the authority to make contracts in furtherance of that business.

> **Apparent authority** is a communication or signal directly from the principal to a third party.

Apparent authority, unlike implied authority, arises out of actions or conduct of the principal which causes a third party to believe that the agent has the authority to make contracts for the principal. Lawyers and judges sometimes say that an agent is "clothed" with apparent authority, that is, the principal has "dressed" the agent in such a way as to lead others to rely on his/her authority. If the agent is given an office, a title, and a staff, third parties may reasonably believe the agent can bind his/her employer or principal. Indeed, any trappings or other evidence of agency may create apparent authority.

Actually, unknown to the third party, there may be a private order or memo to the agent that he/she is *not* to bind the principal, that the agent has no authority. Even so, if the third party relies on the appearance of authority, the principal is bound by the agent's contracts and is estopped (precluded) from denying the agent's authority.

LIABILITY OF THE PRINCIPAL FOR TORTS OF THE AGENT

• *DIRECT LIABILITY*

A principal is directly responsible for his/her agent's torts under any of the following circumstances:

1. The principal gave the agent improper orders or instructions that caused the tort to occur.

2. The agent was improperly or negligently chosen or employed.

3. The principal failed properly to supervise or oversee the work when he/she had a duty to do so.

This direct liability of the principal for tort does not derive from the agency relation. Rather, it is the very act of the principal that is negligent.

Examples: Direct Liability of the Principal

An agent hired by the principal to drive the principal's bus has a record of drunken and negligent driving.

A company car to be driven by an agent has defective brakes.

An agent is given chemical pesticides with improper instructions for application to the fruit trees of a third person.

• *INDIRECT LIABILITY*

Even though the principal has committed no act of negligence, the agent's negligence is imputed (charged) to the principal if the agent is acting for the principal *in the scope of his/her employment.*

This liability is founded on the common law doctrine of **respondeat superior**: "Let the superior respond."

The key requirement of indirect liability, *respondeat superior*, is that the agent be acting in the scope of his/her employment. The expression "scope of employment" is a technical legal phrase, and the concept must meet four tests:

Tests for *Respondeat Superior*

1. The conduct must be of the kind the agent was employed to perform.

2. The conduct must occur at the authorized place and time of employment.

3. The conduct must be motivated, at least in part, by service to the principal.

4. The use or means employed by the agent could have been anticipated by the principal.

If a night club "bouncer" evicts a drunken patron with such force as to cause death, the club owner is indirectly liable under the doctrine of *respondeat superior*. If, however, an elevator operator pulls a knife from his/her jacket and seeks to carve up a passenger, this tort would *not* be imputed to the building owner, the principal, under the doctrine of *respondeat superior* since the first, third and fourth tests above are not met. (*However, the negligent employment of this operator might give rise to direct tort responsibility.*)

The principal is responsible for such torts as fraud and misrepresentation since they clearly meet the *respondeat superior* tests. Note that liability for fraud and misrepresentation is present notwithstanding the fact that the agent has no authority to misrepresent the product he/she is selling.

The vicarious responsibility of the principal arises out of the fact that the agent is an extension of the principal. The agent was chosen by the principal; and it is the action of making the choice, holding the agent out to the public as the transactor of the principal's business, that creates liability for the principal.

• *TORTS OF INDEPENDENT CONTRACTORS*

An independent contractor does not act under the supervision and control of the person who hired him/her. The contractor is chosen to accomplish a result by his/her own means. Consequently, the doctrine of *respondeat superior* does not apply to the torts of an independent contractor.

It is not always possible, however, to avoid liability by delegating work to an independent contractor. Under the law of torts, strict liability is imposed in regard to certain "ultrahazardous activities," such as blasting and the transport of volatile chemicals or wild animals. Responsibility for mishaps arising from such activities cannot be delegated to an independent contractor.

The person hiring the independent contractor may be *directly* responsible, however, if the contractor is negligently chosen, or if other conditions of direct liability are present.

PERSONAL LIABILITY OF THE AGENT FOR THE PRINCIPAL'S CONTRACTS

• *DISCLOSED PRINCIPAL*

If a third party knows, or should know, that the agent is acting for a principal *and* if the third party knows the identity of this principal, the principal is a disclosed principal.

If these conditions are met, the agent has *no* personal responsibility for a contract made on behalf of this principal.

The fact of the agency and the identity of the principal are usually disclosed in any contract with a third party. If the contract is between P, the principal, and T. P., the third party, A, the agent who negotiates the contract and signs P's name, is obviously the agent. Nevertheless, *some word of agency should be used when A signs*; such words as "by" or "for" or "agent for," or, if A signs in her employment capacity, "President," "Sales Manager," or "Secretary"— all of these indicate the representative capacity and bind the principal, not the agent.

Failure to identify the principal and to use agency words upon signing may create personal liability for the agent.

Even if a principal is disclosed, however, the agent may have personal liability *if, in fact, he/she had no authority*. Obviously, if agent A merely claims to act for principal P, but P has not given her authority or clothed her with any appearance of authority, A is on her own and is bound by the contract, not P. Indeed, such a case gives rise to a tort by A (fraud and misrepresentation) and possibly a crime.

On the other hand, if A, the agent, frequently acts for P and has the apparent authority to do so, but in fact P has either not given authority or has withdrawn it, *both* A and P may be liable to the third party. If the third party sues P and recovers, P may in turn recover from A, who had no authority in fact. In all cases where an agent discloses a principal, the agent is deemed to make an implied warranty that he/she has the authority to make a contract for that principal.

• *PARTIALLY DISCLOSED PRINCIPAL*

In this case the third party knows that the agent is acting for a principal but does not know the identity of the principal. This **partially disclosed principal** situation occurs when a principal wishes privacy or seeks for financial reasons to conceal his/her identity. For example, a wealthy developer, seeking to accumulate a large commercial tract of land from a number of small landowners, may send his agent to obtain contracts with these owners. The *fact* of the agency is disclosed but *not the name or identity of the principal*. In such a situation the agent is liable on the contract. If the principal's identity can be determined and the agent cannot satisfy the contract, the principal may be liable on the contract also.

• *UNDISCLOSED PRINCIPAL*

If neither the fact of agency nor the identity of the principal is disclosed (**undisclosed principal**), the agent is liable on the contract since the third party was led to believe that the agent was the real party on the contract. Of course, the agent may recover from the undisclosed principal; if the third party learns of the agency, he/she, too, may recover directly from the principal, not just the agent.

TORT LIABILITY OF AGENTS

An agent who commits a tort, whether acting within the scope of his/her employment or not, is personally liable for the tort. If the agent is acting within the scope of employment, both he/she and the principal are simultaneously liable for the tort. In cases of such **joint and several liability**, the injured party may sue either principal or agent, or both. Of course, the victim may not have a double recovery, and any recovery from one party is deducted from the recovery from the other. The agent, the party who actually committed the tort, is liable to reimburse the principal for the latter's loss to third parties because of the agent's tort.

Example: Joint and Several Liability

Charlie Careless, a truck driver for the XYZ Hauling Co., while hauling a load of goods for the company, negligently runs over a child riding her bicycle. Both the principal (XYZ Hauling Co.) and the agent (Charlie Careless) are liable to the child for the tort. Technically, Charlie is liable to XYZ Hauling Co. for any judgment obtained by the child or her parents.

LIABILITY FOR CRIMES

If a principal directs, approves, or participates in a crime of his/her agent, the principal is criminally liable, as is the agent. An employer whose employees are violating criminal statutes in furtherance of their employment may be liable if the employer knows, or *should know*, of the criminal acts. Employees who violate pollution laws or antitrust laws create criminal liability both for themselves and for their employers if the employers fail adequately to supervise their job performance or negligently delegate work that the employees perform in a criminal manner.

Scienter, knowledge, is imputed to the employer if the employer fails to learn what he/she has a duty to know.

YOU SHOULD REMEMBER

The agent may have actual authority or apparent authority to make contracts for the principal. *Actual authority* is either express or implied. *Apparent authority* arises from a signal to a third party that the agent is clothed with authority to bind the principal in contract.

The principal has direct or indirect responsibility for the torts of an agent. *Direct responsibility* involves a negligent act of the principal him-/herself, including negligence in the choice of agents. Indirect responsibility arises from torts committed by the agent while acting within the scope of his/her employment.

The agent has no personal responsibility for contracts made for his/her principal if the principal is fully disclosed, provided, of course, the agent has authority to make the contract. If the principal is undisclosed or partially disclosed, the agent is responsible (and, once discovered, the principal is, also).

An employer who knows, or should know, of criminal acts by his/her employees is jointly responsible with the employees for these acts.

TERMINATION OF AGENCY BY ACTS OF THE PARTIES

The parties may terminate the agency by any act that would terminate a simple contract. If the agency was created for a specified time or for a specified purpose, it terminates upon the passage of that time or the accomplishment of that purpose. If no time is specified, the agency is terminated by the passage of a reasonable time.

The agency can also be terminated by mutual rescission, by revocation of authority by the principal, or by renunciation by the agent. Both revocation and renunciation are achieved by a simply communication, oral or written, manifesting withdrawal of consent. (*Remember that agency is consensual; in the absence of a contractual obligation to continue the agency, the consent may be freely withdrawn by either party.*)

To assure that there is no *lingering apparent authority,* the principal generally must give actual notice of termination to third persons who previously dealt with the agent; for other third parties, the former agent's apparent authority may arise only if there was not even **constructive notice** of the termination (e.g., an announcement in a trade publication that the agency had ceased would suffice as notice to these third parties, whether they actually read it or not.)

BY OPERATION OF LAW

The agency relation is terminated by any of the following:

1. The death or permanent incapacity of either the principal or the agent.

2. The bankruptcy of either party.

3. Frustration of the purpose of the agency. This frustration may occur because of the destruction of the subject matter (e.g., fire damage or loss to goods or property being bought or sold), changes in business conditions, or changes in the value of property being bought or sold.

4. Subsequent illegality of the business or of the business venture. This would occur, for example, if the business were prohibited, or if the agent were required to have a license which he/she could not reasonably obtain, or if the property were rezoned so as to prevent the legal operation of the business.

5. Impossibility of performance by either principal or agent. This is an example of termination of a contract by impossibility (see pages 142–143).

6. Material breach of the agency contract by either principal or agent.

YOU SHOULD REMEMBER

An agency may be terminated by acts of the parties (any act that would terminate a simple contract) or by operation of law (e.g., death, permanent incapacity, or bankruptcy of either party; material breach of the agency contract by either party).

KNOW THE CONCEPTS
DO YOU KNOW THE BASICS?

1. Why would corporations be unable to function without agency law?
2. What is the difference between an employee and an agent?
3. How does an attorney in fact differ from an attorney-at-law?
4. Is the agency relationship always created by contract?
5. Why is an independent contractor usually not an agent?
6. Give examples of obligations that cannot be delegated to an agent.
7. Can a person further his/her own goals and objectives while acting for a principal?
8. How does the term *alter ego* play a part in the agency relation?
9. What is meant by "commingling" of funds?
10. Does insanity of the principal make a power of attorney void?
11. Why do lawyers and judges say that an agent may be "clothed" with apparent authority?
12. Explain the difference between the principal's direct and indirect liability for his/her agent's torts.
13. When can the hirer of an independent contractor be liable for the contractor's tort?
14. What does the expression "partially disclosed principal" mean?

TERMS FOR STUDY

actual authority	agent
agency	alter ego

apparent authority
attorney at law
attorney in fact
commingling
disclosed principal
fiduciary
implied authority
independent contractor

joint and several liability
lingering apparent authority
partially disclosed principal
power of attorney
principal
respondeat superior
scienter
undisclosed principal

PRACTICAL APPLICATION

1. XYZ Oil Company, a corporation that owned and operated a number of gasoline filling stations in northern California, hired Tom's Tank Company to dig up and replace underground tanks at one of its stations in San Francisco. While this work was being done, Cora Endicott, a customer, fell into the open and unprotected hole and was severely injured. The hole was left open and unattended by Sam Jones, an employee of Tom's Tank Company, who was drunk at the time. Cora sues both XYZ Oil and Tom's Tank in tort. What will be the result?

2. Jim Mason, a janitor at the Celestial Trade Center in Dallas, Texas, ordered 500 cartons of paper products from MX Toilet Supply Company. Celestial Trade Center duly paid the invoice rendered for this merchandise. A year later, Jim ordered 1000 cartons of goods from the same supplier. Celestial Trade Center refused to pay this bill, citing a memorandum to Jim after the last order forbidding him to order supplies. What would be the result?

3. Seedy Apartments employed Melvin Malefactor as a painter for the interior of its apartments in Kansas City. Unknown to Seedy, Melvin had been convicted of assault 3 years previously and of indecent exposure 17 years ago. Seedy checked Melvin's references and found that he was an excellent painter on his last two jobs. Three weeks after his employment, Melvin raped a tenant while painting her apartment. Is Seedy liable for this tort?

4. Pollutant Company operates a large manufacturing facility in Factory City, Anywhere. Stuart Smedley, its plant manager, has caused sulfuric acid from the manufacturing operations to be dumped into an adjacent river for years. Is Pollutant (a) criminally liable for this violation of the environmental laws, and (b) liable in tort to downstream property owners whose wells have been contaminated by the acid?

ANSWERS
KNOW THE CONCEPTS

1. A corporation has no "arms and legs" of its own. It can act only through agents.

2. "Agent" is a broader term than "employee" and includes representatives of various kinds. An employee is an agent who is under stricter control and supervision than other agents.

3. The word "attorney" designates a representative. An attorney in fact represents his/her principal for general or special purposes other than legal purposes; an attorney-at-law represents his/her principal for legal purposes only.

4. No. The agency relationship is consensual. The element of consideration is not present in every case.

5. An independent contractor usually is not a representative, but is employed to achieve a specific purpose or to do a specific job.

6. Obligations that require relationships of personal trust, skill, or confidence cannot be delegated to some other person. These can be performed only by the principal.

7. The principal's purpose must always come first; therefore any person who also helps him-/herself while helping the principal is open to a charge of conflict of interest. If agents believe that they can accomplish their own personal ends as well as the goals of their principals, they should advise the principals in advance and obtain their approval.

8. The term *alter ego*, meaning "other person," describes the agency relationship in that the agent serves as an alternate person for a principal and acts in his/her place.

9. "Commingling" of funds refers to mixing of the agent's funds with those of the principal. Agency law prohibits such a mixing since the agent's creditors might attempt to reach this money; moreover, the agent may be spending the principal's money on personal obligations—an action that is a breach of the agent's duties and probably criminal.

10. As a rule, insanity of the principal voids a power of attorney. Under the law in many states, however, the power may contain an express provision permitting it to survive insanity or incompetence of the principal.

11. Apparent authority is a kind of outward appearance causing others to believe that the agent can make a contract for the principal. The word "clothed" is appropriate to express this outward appearance.

12. Direct responsibility of the principal arises out of personal participation in the negligent act, that is, his/her own negligence is involved, instead of or in addition to the agent's negligence. Indirect liability arises from negligence of the agent, which is charged or imputed to the principal.

13. When the hirer of an independent contractor has a direct (but not indirect) responsibility for a negligent action of the contractor. If, for example, a contractor is improperly chosen or erroneously instructed, his/her hirer may be liable.

14. "Partially disclosed principal" refers to the situation where a third party knows that the agent is acting on behalf of some other person, but does not know the identity of that person.

PRACTICAL APPLICATION

1. Tom's Tank Company is an independent contractor, hired to do a job, not to represent XYZ Oil Company. Unless there was some kind of direct negligence by XYZ Oil Company, XYZ has no responsibility for the tort. Sam is an agent for his employer, Tom's Tank Company, and his employer is liable for this tort, which was committed in the scope of Sam's employment. Of course, Sam is personally responsible also, but is probably without funds to pay a judgment.

2. Since Celestial Trade Center has paid at least one previous bill arising out of its employee's contract, MX Toilet Supply Company is entitled to rely on the "apparent authority" of Jim, the employee. The private memorandum between master and servant does not negate the appearance that has already been created.

3. Seedy is liable for the tort since it is directly responsible for its negligent employment of Melvin. However, a good argument can be made that the reference check of previous employers was the only precaution Seedy should have been required to take in hiring a painter. The counterargument is that an employer should check police records before exposing apartment house tenants to strangers.

4. (a) Pollutant is liable for criminal acts committed by its plant manager in furtherance of his employment if the company knows or should know of these actions. The company has a duty to supervise, and it would appear that failure to do so may have permitted the wrongdoing.

   (b) As to the tort liability, Stuart is clearly acting within the scope of his authority as plant manager, and consequently Pollutant is responsible for this tort, which is inflicted on persons whose existence is known and the harm to whom can be foreseen.

15
TYPES OF BUSINESS ORGANIZATIONS; PARTNERSHIPS; FRANCHISES

KEY TERMS

sole proprietorship the simplest form of business, in which a sole owner and his/her business are not legally distinct entities, the owner being personally liable for business debts

partnership the association of two or more persons who have expressly or implicitly agreed to carry on, as co-owners, a business for profit

corporation an artificial being created by operation of law, with an existence distinct from the individuals who own and operate it

franchise a contractual arrangement in which the owner (franchisor) of a trademark, trade name, copyright, patent, trade secret, or some form of business operation, process, or system permits others (franchisees) to use said property, operation, process, or system in furnishing goods or services

---

TYPES OF BUSINESS ORGANIZATIONS

There are three basic types of business organizations:

1. The **sole proprietorship,** the simplest form. The sole owner and his/her business are not legally distinct entities. The owner has unlimited liability for debts of the business.

2. The **partnership.** Two or more individuals are the owners, having expressly or implicitly agreed to establish and run a business for profit. The two types of partnership, **general** and **limited,** are discussed in this chapter.

3. The **corporation.** A distinct legal entity having an existence separate from its shareholder owners is created, usually under state law. Corporations are discussed in detail in Chapters 16, 17, and 18.

There are many subtypes: limited partnerships, general partnerships, S corporations, close corporations, professional corporations, nonprofit corporations and general corporations, to name a few. Even organizational forms not strictly classified as either partnerships or corporations—for instance, syndicates, business trusts, joint ventures, and cooperatives—rely on partnership and/or corporate law for most, if not all, of their governing principles.

Comparison of Sole Proprietorships, Partnerships and Corporations

Item	Sole Proprietorship	Partnership	Corporation
1. Creation	Few, if any, requirements (easiest to organize)	By agreement of partners (generally should be written, but can be implied; limited partnerships, though, must complete and file a statutory form)	By statutory authorization (must meet state requirements to receive a state charter)
2. Formality required	Little	Some (more for limited partnerships)	The most
3. Governmental regulation of the business structure	Almost none	Little, except for limited or other special partnerships	The most
4. Governmental regulation based on the type of business (products, markets, etc.)?	Yes	Yes	Yes
5. Owners	The proprietor	The partners	The stockholders

Item	Sole Proprietorship	Partnership	Corporation
6. Transfer of an owner's interests	By sale of business, inheritance, or any other lawful means chosen by proprietor	Buyer can receive some but not all rights of a partner unless remaining partners agree; limited partner's interest is freely transferable	In most cases, stock is freely transferable, subject only to limits that might be placed in contracts between stockholders
7. Legal entity separate from owners?	No	Generally no, but most states recognize the partnership as a legal entity for a few purposes, such as owning property in the firm's name	Yes for almost all purposes; e.g., a corporation can acquire and transfer property and sue or defend lawsuits, and it has a domicile, duration, and tax status distinct from owners
8. Agency	If business has employees (agents), proprietor is principal	Except for limited partners, each partner is both a principal and an agent of the other partner(s)	Officers are the corporation's agents; stockholders and directors are not
9. Division of labor	Usually the least conducive to such efficiencies of scale		Usually most conducive
10. Liability of individual owners for business debts or actions	Unlimited	Unlimited except that in a limited partnership the limited partners usually can lose only their investments	Limited; stockholders generally can lose only their actual investments
11. Access to specialists	Usually, the least		Usually, the most

Item	Sole Proprietorship	Partnership	Corporation
12. Use of business funds to pay personal debts	Generally permitted	Usually barred	Prohibited
13. Profits	Solely the proprietor's	Shared equally by partners, unless partnership agreement states otherwise	Calculated after paying salary to employees, including officers; profits are retained by corporation and/or distributed pro rata to stockholders as dividends
14. Management	The proprietor	General partners—equal votes unless expressly stated otherwise in partnership agreement; limited partnership—limited partners have no management rights	Management distinct from owners; officers are appointed by directors, who are elected by stockholders (generally each stockholder's number of votes equals the number of common shares he/she owns)
15. Changes in business formation documents	Need not file	Need not file, unless a limited partnership	Must file and perhaps must obtain state permission (which is usually a mere formality)
16. Organizational fee, annual licensing fee, and annual reporting requirements?	No	Generally no	Yes

Item	Sole Proprietorship	Partnership	Corporation
17. Requirements for doing business in other states	Usually none	Usually none, but limited partnerships must file copies of a completed statutory form	Generally must qualify to do business and obtain state certificate of authority
18. Ability to raise capital	Although dependent on many factors (size, type of business, profitability), often difficult	May be difficult without adding new partners, to which all general partners must agree	Relatively easy; may just issue (and sell) additional stock
19. Income taxes	Profits part of personal income; no separate tax for the proprietorship	Each partner's share of profits (whether distributed or not) is part of his/her personal income; no separate tax for the partnership	"Double taxation"— corporation pays income tax on net profits (no deductions for dividends); each stockholder's dividends are part of his/her personal income and thus are taxed
20. Termination	By sale, insolvency, or voluntary cessation of business; or by death or incapacity of proprietor	By terms of partnership agreement; by subsequent agreement of partners; by death, incapacity, or withdrawal of one or more partners; or by sale, insolvency, or voluntary cessation of business	Can have perpetual existence, as provided by statute and/or articles of incorporation; can continue despite death, incapacity, or withdrawal of officers, directors, and/ or stockholders

Item	Sole Proprietorship	Partnership	Corporation
21. Size of business	Can be substantial, but tends to be small	Can be substantial, but tends to be small	Varies from small to the largest business entities in existence: although most corporations are *not* large, the biggest, most significant businesses are or become corporations

A 1989 Internal Revenue Service regulation deems a business entity to be a corporation rather than a partnership only if the entity has at least three of the following four traits: limited liability, centralized management, continuity of life, and free transferability of interests.

Advantages and Disadvantages of the Two Major Business Forms

General Partnership's Advantages over the Corporation

Formation: Easier

Organizational costs: Usually less

Taxes:
- (a) No "double taxation"
- (b) No tax on exempt interest (e.g., from municipal bonds) partner receives from partnership
- (c) Share of business operating losses more easily and immediately deducted from partner's personal income
- (d) In many states, no state income tax on the partnership itself
- (e) No social security tax for partners (Disadvantage: may have a self-employment tax)

Owners' voice in management: A more direct role

Multistate operations: Few legal formalities

Governmental regulation: Generally less

Flexibility of decision making: Generally greater

General Partnership's Disadvantages

Taxes:	(a) Partners required to pay tax on undistributed income
	(b) Missing many of the other tax advantages of a corporation
Control:	Unless changed to a limited partnership, cannot raise capital by increasing number of "owners" without affecting actual or potential control of business
Number of owners:	As a practical matter, there are limits
Ability to raise capital:	Usually more difficult
Duration:	Depends on good relationships of partners; withdrawal or death of a single partner can unhinge the entire partnership
Owners' liability for entity:	Unlimited
Owners' liability for other owners' acts:	Often liable
Ability to transfer ownership interest:	Usually more difficult

Corporation's Advantages over the General Partnership

Taxes:	(a) No personal tax on undistributed profits (sometimes, though, a corporate tax penalty for accumulations of undistributed income)
	(b) Favorable tax treatment of some expenses or benefits
	(c) Employee stock option purchase plans are available.
	(d) For some corporations with a limited number of stockholders, Subchapter S status is available: this permits the favorable tax treatment that a partnership sometimes has (no double taxation, immediate deductibility on personal income for business losses), while allowing corporate form in other respects.
Control:	By use of nonvoting or preferred stock, can raise capital and increase number of "owners" without affecting control of business
Number of owners:	Unlimited

Ability to raise capital:	For medium or larger corporations, generally easier and can obtain larger amounts
Duration:	Can be perpetual; not structurally dependent on individual owners' good relationships or health
Owners' liability for entity:	Limited (However, lenders or other parties contracting with a small corporation often require that the corporation's stockholders furnish personal guarantees)
Owners' liability for other owners' actions:	Usually none
Ability to transfer ownership interest:	Generally easier

Corporation's Disadvantages

Formation:	More complicated
Organizational costs:	Usually more
Taxes:	(a) "Double taxation": corporate tax on the corporation's income (no deduction for dividends) plus a personal tax on the stockholder's income (including dividends)
	(b) Exempt interest distributed by corporation is fully taxed income for stockholders.
	(c) Subject to state income tax (deductible on federal income tax)
	(d) Missing some of the tax advantages of a partnership
Owners' voice in management:	May have little or no role even if actively sought
Multistate operations:	Generally must qualify to do business and register in each state as well as make other filings
Governmental regulation:	Generally more
Flexibility of decision making:	Generally less

YOU SHOULD REMEMBER

For businesses owned by more than one person, the major types of organizations are partnerships and corporations. The decision as to which organizational form to use depends on numerous factors, such as costs, relationships among owners, desirability of linking ownership and direct management, need to limit potential individual liability, raising of capital, size of the business, and (often most important) tax consequences.

> A general partnership should require fewer legal formalities and afford a more direct tie between ownership and management. However, individual liability is unlimited, and duration is less assured, more dependent on continued good relations among all owners.
>
> A corporation can increase ownership and (usually) capital without drastically affecting management, the duration is more definite (can be perpetual), and ownership interests are more easily transferred. Disadvantages for corporations include "double taxation," greater formal requirements and costs, and greater potential for separation and estrangement of persons into either owners or management, but not both.

GENERAL PARTNERSHIPS
INTRODUCTION

Partnerships are one of the oldest forms of business. Laws on partnerships can be found in Hammurabi's code as well as in early Hebrew and Roman texts. Although corporations, a more recent phenomenon, are the prevailing form among medium-sized and larger American businesses, and corporate law now involves an extensive body of statutes and case law, the law of partnerships remains very important. Without a knowledge of partnership law, a businessperson may be unable to decide intelligently what organizational form to use for a new, expanding, or recently acquired business.

Moreover, a businessperson will encounter partnerships in many of his/her personal and business activities and certainly should know something about their nature: for instance, how are partnerships created, what is their structure, how are they run, who is responsible for their contracts, their debts, their torts?

CREATION OF PARTNERSHIPS

Unlike corporations, partnerships usually require no special formalities in order to be created. All that is needed is a partnership agreement.

Like most other contracts, the partnership agreement can be express or implied, and no writing is necessary except for contractual matters generally covered by the statute of frauds. Thus, for example, a partnership agreement that permits partners to transfer real estate, or that has a set term exceeding one year, must be written to be enforceable, at least with respect to these matters.

From a practical point of view, a written document is usually the best way to assure that partners, from the outset, understand the nature of their agreement. The absence of such writing probably increases the chances of disputes between partners; in many cases, it makes disputes harder to settle.

• *BY EXPRESS AGREEMENT*

Some typical provisions in an express partnership agreement include the following:

1. The partnership's name.

2. A description of the partnership's business.

3. A listing of the present partners.

4. A statement of the contributions made and/or to be made by the present partners.

5. A means of determining what constitutes partnership expenses rather than personal expenses.

6. A method for dividing profits and losses (otherwise, the assumption is that partners share profits and losses equally).

7. A statement of the general powers of individual partners and the limitations on their authority.

8. A system for quickly managing routine matters while bringing more serious issues before a management committee and/or the full partnership.

9. Allocations of salaries and/or drawing accounts among partners.

10. Treatment of a partner's outside business interests.

11. Conditions on an individual's withdrawal from or addition to the partnership.

12. The term of duration.

13. The closing out or selling of the business upon the partnership's dissolution.

• *BY IMPLIED AGREEMENT*

Is there an implied partnership?
Key issue: Did the alleged partners intend to be co-owners of a business?

If Jones, Smith, and Gray *jointly* own property, contribute money to run a business on the property, decide how to conduct the business, and share the profits or losses from the business, a court would probably decide that Jones, Smith, and Gray have formed a partnership. In reaching this decision, the court would look to *three factors*:

1. Joint ownership of a business.

2. Sharing of profits or losses.

3. Equal management rights.

Generally, there must be some evidence of all three factors. That A and B merely own property together and receive rent for it will usually be insufficient. Likewise, the mere fact that C's payments to D are pegged at a percentage of C's business profits does not mean that C and D are partners. In each case, at least one of the three crucial factors is missing. (Note that installment payments on loans, as well as interest payments, wages, rents, annuities, or money from the sale of business goodwill do *not* constitute profits.)

The *Uniform Partnership Act* (UPA), adopted by every state but Louisiana, furnishes guidance on partnership issues (including whether a partnership exists) *when* there is *no partnership agreement or* the *agreement does not cover the issues in question*. Thus, the UPA permits partners to fashion their own rules, bound only by the law of contracts and little else (except for limited partnerships).

• *BY ESTOPPEL*

Although almost all partnerships are based on consent, there is one important exception: the partnership by estoppel. When a person represents, or allows someone else to represent, that that person is a partner when in fact he/she is not, the law estops (prevents) that person from denying that he/she is a partner with respect to third persons who reasonably relied on the misrepresentation. The partnership to which the "partner" allegedly belonged may be fictitious, or it may be a real partnership, but one in which he/she is not a partner. In either event, the alleged partner is liable to the third persons.

Example: Partnership by Estoppel

Suppose that Sam Slick tells Big Bank that he is a partner with Rick Rich, and Big Bank thus extends credit to Sam because of Rick's good reputation and extreme wealth. If Rick knew about Slick's falsehood but did nothing, then most courts would treat Rick as a partner for purposes of Sam's dealings with Big Bank; therefore Big Bank could come to "partner" Rick for money owed.

Of course, this partnership by estoppel works only for third parties such as Big Bank; between Sam and Rick themselves, no partnership rights exist. Rick may have to pay Big Bank, but—since he owes Sam no duty (as a partner) to contribute toward the loan payments—Rick can seek complete reimbursement from Sam for any money Rick paid to Big Bank.

YOU SHOULD REMEMBER

Partnerships are created by express or implied agreement. Oral agreements are permitted, although written agreements are preferable. For implied partnerships, the court generally must find: (1) joint ownership of a business, (2) sharing of profits or losses, and (3) equal management rights.

The typical partnership agreement usually covers many subjects (e.g., the partnership's name, type of business, individual partner contributions, division of profits and losses, and authority of partners). The Uniform Partnership Act (UPA) provides guidance on partnership issues not covered by the partnership agreement.

Partnership by estoppel occurs when a person misrepresents or allows someone else to misrepresent that he/she is a partner in a fictitious or a real partnership. The alleged partner is liable to third persons who reasonably relied on the misrepresentation. Between the purported partners themselves, though, no partnership rights exist.

RIGHTS AND DUTIES OF PARTNERS
• *MAKING DECISIONS*

Each partner has both a right and a duty to help manage the partnership (UPA Section 18). Unless the agreement provides otherwise, each partner has one vote, with ordinary business decisions being decided by majority vote. (As in most voting arrangements, a proposal does not pass if there is a tie vote; however, especially for small partnerships, for example, two partners, the partnership agreement may make special provisions for resolving a deadlock.) Certain very important actions usually require unanimous consent:

1. Amending the partnership agreement.
2. Changing the essential nature of the partnership's business.
3. Altering the partnership's capital structure (e.g., partnership contributions).
4. Adding an entirely new line of business.
5. Admitting new partners.
6. Confessing judgment (admitting partnership liability on a debt *and* agreeing to have a court judgment entered against the partnership on that debt).
7. Submitting to arbitration.
8. Transferring the partnership's goodwill.
9. Placing partnership assets in a trust or assignment for the benefit of creditors.
10. Conveying or mortgaging property, unless that is the usual business of the partnership.
11. Any other act that renders impossible the continuation of the partnership's business.

• *OTHER RESPONSIBILITIES AND RIGHTS*

Other important UPA rules are as follows:

1. Each partner must *work* only on behalf of the partnership, except perhaps for noncompetitive activities that do not infringe on the partnership's time.
2. Although partners are entitled to *profits* (and to reimbursement/

indemnification for personal expenses or liabilities incurred on behalf of the partnership), they are *not generally paid a salary* for partnership work, except for services in winding up the affairs of a dissolved partnership.

3. Each partner may examine and make copies of some or all of the partnership's *records,* which should be maintained at the partnership's main place of business.

4. Each partner has a duty to produce, and a right to receive, *complete information* on all aspects of the partnership's business.

5. Partners are entitled to an *accounting* of partnership assets (including profits) and liabilities whenever partners are excluded from the business or from the partnership records (perhaps in violation of item 3, above), whenever profits or other benefits have been wrongfully withheld or diverted, or whenever else such accounting would be "just and reasonable."

6. Each partner has a *property interest* in the partnership equal to (a) a proportionate share of the profits and (b) a return of capital contributions upon dissolution (partners can assign or creditors can attach that interest without dissolving the partnership itself).

7. Partners are *tenants in partnership* of all partnership property; this means that each partner has full possessory rights, that the property can be used only for partnership purposes, that none of the partners can assign, have attached, or in any way transfer specific partnership property (such as equipment, real estate, or office supplies), and that a deceased partner's rights in partnership property passes to the surviving partners, not to the deceased partner's heirs (although his/her heirs have a right to both an accounting and compensation for the value of the deceased partner's property interest).

Partners may also have implied authority to: hire personnel; pay partnership debts with partnership funds; buy and sell inventory; borrow money and issue commercial paper; settle claims; receive notices on behalf of the partnership. These and other implied powers depend on the nature of the partnership.

• *PARTNER AS AGENT AND FIDUCIARY*

Each partner is an agent for the other partner(s). As such, he/she owes the other(s) a high, fiduciary duty of care similar to that required in any principal/agent relationship. See Chapter 14.

A partner must act in good faith for the benefit of the partnership.

Example: Partner as Fiduciary

When the interest of partnership PR conflicts with Polly Partner's personal interest, Polly must remain loyal to PR's interest. Polly must not keep pertinent information from her fellow partners, and she must account to the entire partnership for any personal gains made while using PR property or otherwise acting in her role as a partner.

AUTHORITY OF A PARTNER TO BIND OTHER PARTNERS

• *APPARENT AUTHORITY*

Each partner also has a responsibility to third persons.

Example: Authority of a Partner to Bind Other Partners

Suppose that partner Pam transacts business with a third person, Theo, and Theo reasonably believes that Pam is engaged in ordinary partnership business. Theo is then entitled to treat the transaction as being one with the partnership itself, regardless of whether Pam had actual authority.

From this example we see that the agency concept of *apparent authority* applies to partnerships. (See Chapter 14.) In fact, a partner's implied authority is usually broader than the authority of other agents. Third persons know that the partner is an "owner"/principal, not simply an employee/agent.

• *THREE OTHER MEANS OF BINDING THE PARTNERSHIP*

Aside from apparent authority, a partner's acts may bind the partnership to a contract because he/she has (1) express actual authority stemming from the partnership agreement; (2) implied actual authority based on the partnership's business and/or the law of partnerships; or (3) ratification by the other partners after the fact. In the last case, any unauthorized action, even one that would not bind the partnership under a theory of apparent authority, may be expressly *or* implicitly ratified by the entire partnership.

Note that, whereas any one of these four approaches (including apparent authority) permits a third person to hold the partnership accountable, only three of them allow the acting partner to do so. A partner with apparent, but not actual or ratified, authority not only has no rights against his/her fellow partner(s), but also may have to indemnify the partnership for binding it to an unauthorized transaction.

Express actual authority and ratification are fairly straightforward. Implied actual authority, however, requires an assessment of various criteria, based mainly on the nature of the business and any industry customs. If the partner's activities were reasonably necessary to conduct ordinary partnership business, and if the partnership agreement did not prohibit such actions, the partner's powers are implied. For example, a partner in a sales business generally can buy or sell goods of the type customarily traded in the business, and can make warranties on the goods. In most partnerships, a partner can hire and fire employees, pay and collect debts, and acquire personal property needed to conduct the business. However, as stated earlier, there are restrictions on implied authority—some actions require the express consent of all partners.

LIABILITIES OF PARTNERS TO THIRD PARTIES

Because of their broad powers, partners can bind the entire partnership to admissions or other statements made during the course of ordinary partnership business. Moreover, once a partner learns of facts relevant to running the partnership or its business, these facts are imputed to the partnership as a whole. Finally, because partners are principals for each other and their employees, they are civilly *liable* under *respondeat superior for breaches of trust* and/or *torts* committed by a partner or employee acting within the scope of his/her authority. (*Respondeat superior,* though, does not apply in criminal law. Therefore a partner who has committed no wrongful acts or omissions will not be held *criminally* liable for another partner's crimes.)

Whereas partners are jointly *and* severally liable for torts and breaches of trust (the plaintiff may sue all the partners together or any one or more of them separately), partners are jointly, but *not* severally, *liable for contracts.* Therefore any lawsuits based on a contract (including partnership debts) must be brought simultaneously against all partners.

YOU SHOULD REMEMBER

In most ordinary business matters, a partner's actions may bind the entire partnership. Routine partnership decisions are usually decided by majority vote, with each partner having one vote. Certain fundamental decisions usually require unanimous consent; two examples are (1) to change the essential nature of the business, and (2) to take action that renders impossible the continuation of the business.

Partners are tenants in partnership. They have *duties* to furnish partnership information to other partners, work on behalf of the partnership, and not compete with the partnership. They have the *right* to examine partnership documents, be provided complete information on the partnership's business and finances, and retain a property interest in the partnership itself.

Partners are principals and agents for each other. Each partner must act in good faith for the benefit of the partnership.

Third persons may bind the entire partnership to the actions of a single partner if the partner had (1) express actual authority, (2) implied actual authority, or (3) apparent authority, or if the partnership otherwise ratified the partner's actions. Apparent authority depends on the reasonableness of a third person's belief in the partner's authority. Because apparent authority involves unauthorized actions, the partnership may have a right to proceed against the partner for unjustifiably binding it to a transaction with a third person.

PARTNERSHIP AS EITHER A DISTINCT ENTITY OR A MERE AGGREGATE OF INDIVIDUAL PARTNERS

For a few limited purposes, partnerships are treated as entities; in these cases, the partnership, like a corporation, has a legal existence distinct from its individual owners (the partners). In most situations, though, a partnership is considered to be simply a collection (aggregate) of individual partners, with no separate status for the partnership entity itself.

Entity	Aggregate
1. In the case of bankruptcy, liquidation proceedings may be brought in the name of the partnership and thus limited to exclusively partnership assets and liabilities, excluding the nonpartnership assets and liabilities of individual partners.	1. Under federal income tax laws, the partnership is not separately taxed (as the corporation is); the partnership is generally considered to be an aggregate of the partners' interests, and the individual partners are taxed on their shares of the profits. (Partnerships, though, must file informational tax forms.)
2. Judgments against the partnership entity usually must be collected from partnership property before collection remedies are instigated against individual partners.	2. Generally, partners cannot disclaim personal liability for the partnership's acts or omissions; the partnership is not a separate entity.
3. The partnership usually can sue or be sued, have accountings performed and property owned in the partnership's name, and enforce judgments; some states, though, will not allow such actions.	3. In many situations, the partnership itself has no power or distinct status, but must depend on the sum of individual efforts by partners.

TERMINATION OF PARTNERSHIPS

Partnerships are terminated upon their dissolution and liquidation (winding up).

• *DISSOLUTION*

Dissolution is a change in the partners' relationship caused when one partner ceases, generally because of death or voluntary or involuntary withdrawal, to be associated with the partnership business (UPA Section 29). There are three methods of dissolution: (1) acts of the parties, (2) operation of law, and (3) court decree.

BY ACTS OF THE PARTIES

"Acts of the parties" can dissolve the partnership by several different means:

1. The partners agree to dissolve the partnership.

2. The partnership's term of duration expires, or its purpose for being formed is completed. (Either eventuality is usually covered in the partnership agreement.)

3. A partner is expelled or withdraws voluntarily from the partnership.

4. A new partner is admitted to the partnership. (The admission not only dissolves the existing partnership, but also creates a new one.)

When the partnership is at will (there is no set term of duration), a partner's expulsion or good-faith withdrawal leaves neither the departing partner nor the remaining partners liable for breach of the partnership agreement. When expulsion or withdrawal occurs before the end of a specified term of duration, however, such an action is a breach *if* not done for good cause.

Departing partners remain liable for partnership obligations existing at the time of their departure. (A withdrawing partner who fails to notify the remaining partners of his/her withdrawal may continue to be bound as a partner for *future* partnership obligations.) In fact, no partner can cancel existing partnership obligations by dissolution. Of course, the remaining partners and any partnership creditor may agree not to hold a departing partner accountable for the debts to that creditor; this type of agreement is inferred when there have been past such arrangements and the creditor, knowing that a partner is leaving, has done nothing to alert the partner that he/she remains liable. As for the partnership *liabilities of a new partner,* they extend *only* to *partnership debts incurred after* the incoming *partner joined* the partnership.

Note that, although a partnership interest may be assigned or attached, such assignment or attachment does not dissolve the partnership. The assignee or attaching party may acquire rights to profits or other rights, but not the right to a voice in management (UPA Sections 27–28).

BY OPERATION OF LAW

"Operation of law" arises in one of the following ways:

1. Illegality (it would be unlawful to continue the partnership's business or to conduct such business with one of the partners).

2. Bankruptcy of the partnership or of a partner (*most* cases serve as a dissolution).

3. A partner's death.

The partnership obligations of a dead partner pass to his estate. This rule follows the general requirement that dissolution not eliminate a partner's partnership liabilities. However, creditors for other debts have claim to the partner's estate before the estate pays claims from partnership creditors.

BY COURT DECREE

A court decree dissolving a partnership can be applied for by a partner or a third person. The partner's grounds for dissolution [UPA Section 32(1)] are as follows:

1. A partner is insane or otherwise incapable of participating in management.

2. A partner has acted improperly, either by a breach of the partnership agreement, another act severely harmful to the partnership's business, or still other conduct rendering it impracticable to continue the business with that person as a partner.

3. The partnership's business can be operated only at a loss.

4. Other circumstances, such as strong personal conflicts between partners, make dissolution equitable.

The third person's grounds are fewer: if he/she is a partner's assignee or is the recipient (creditor) of a judicial charging order (in essence, attachment) upon a partner's interests, then the third person may obtain a dissolution decree for a partnership at will or for a partnership whose set term or purpose of formation has been completed.

GIVING NOTICE OF DISSOLUTION

No matter how dissolution occurs (except for illegality or bankruptcy), notice of the dissolution must be given to third persons to ensure that the entire partnership is not held accountable for future obligations. *Actual notice* (by mail, telephone, or the like) must be extended to all partnership creditors; *public (constructive) notice* (via a statement in the community newspaper) is all that is needed for others who knew about the partnership. Of course, there is no duty to give notice to third persons who did not know about the partnership or (in cases of withdrawal) were unaware of the withdrawing partner's involvement with the partnership.

Example: Importance of Giving Notice

Proper notice serves to eradicate the potential for apparent authority to bind the partnership. Although dissolution removes partner X's actual authority to bind her partners, third person Z, who does not know about the dissolution, might see X as still having authority. Therefore, without proper notice of dissolution, X probably has the apparent authority to bind the dissolved partnership to transactions with Z.

• *LIQUIDATION*

After the partnership is dissolved, it must be liquidated. This **liquidation** process is often called "winding up"; the dissolved partnership retains authority to complete unfinished business and do whatever else is necessary to terminate the partnership. Winding up typically involves: (1) collection, preservation, and sale or other liquidation of partnership assets, including collection of money owed to the partnership; (2) paying or otherwise settling partnership debts; and (3) accounting to each partner for the value of his/her partnership interest.

• *DISTRIBUTION OF ASSETS*

Once the winding up is completed, distribution of assets takes place. Distribution proceeds in this order:

1. Payment of third-party debts.

2. Return of a partner's advances (loans) to the partnership.

3. Return of each partner's capital contribution.

4. Distribution of remaining assets to partners in accordance with the division of profits stated in the partnership agreement (if there is no such provision, the surplus is divided equally).

Of course, among themselves, partners can always agree to alter the order of payments they are to receive.

Creditors' Priorities in Looking for Payment from the Assets of:

A Dissolving Partnership	An Individual Partner
Higher priority: the partnership's creditors	*Higher priority:* the individual partner's creditors
Lower priority: individual partners' creditors	*Lower priority:* the partnership's creditors

These are the general approaches in nonbankruptcy cases.

Only after individual and partnership creditors are paid may partners seek contribution from another partner (payment of that partner's partnership obligations).

A partner's personal creditors have no claim against the personal property of other partners.

YOU SHOULD REMEMBER

Termination of partnerships requires dissolution and winding up.

The three methods of *dissolution* are acts of the parties, operation of law, and court decrees. Notice of dissolution is necessary except for cases of illegality or bankruptcy.

Winding up involves collecting the partnership assets, paying partnership debts, and accounting to each partner for his/her interest in the partnership.

Upon completion of winding up, final *distribution of assets* takes place. Partnership creditors generally have first priority as to payment from partnership assets, while a partner's individual creditors have first priority as to his/her personal (nonpartnership) assets.

LIMITED PARTNERSHIPS
INTRODUCTION

A **limited partnership** (LP) must conform to state statutory requirements, including the filing of a LP certificate. In this respect, as well as the limited liability of limited partners, the LP is similar to corporations.

Special laws on LPs have existed since the Middle Ages, and the first LP statutes in the United States were enacted during the early nineteenth century. In this century, the Uniform Limited Partnership Act of 1916 (ULPA) became law in nearly every state, but the Revised ULPA of 1976 (RULPA) has since superseded it in all but a few states. The RULPA really comes in two formats, as about half the states have adopted a 1985 amended version of the 1976 Act. (Unless stated otherwise, references to the RULPA apply to both versions.)

Limited partnerships can conduct almost any business that could be carried on by a general (ordinary) partnership. Exceptions include banking, insurance, and most professional partnerships, such as law firms.

TWO TYPES OF PARTNERS

The key feature of a LP is that there are *two distinct types of partners, general and limited.* A **limited partner** contributes capital and receives a specified share of the LP's profits, but does not participate in management and is not held personally liable for partnership obligations beyond the amount of his/her capital contribution. A **general partner** in a LP has essentially the same rights and duties as do partners (i.e., general partners) in a general partnership (GP).

STATUTORY REQUIREMENTS

The LP certificate must state the following information:

1. The partnership's name.
2. Its location.
3. The name and address of its agents for service of process.
4. The names and addresses of its general partners.
5. The term of duration.

Under the 1976 RULPA or the ULPA, *additional* information is required:

6. A description of the LP's business.
7. The names and addresses of limited partners.
8. The cash amount or description and value of initial and subsequent (if any) contributions by each partner.
9. A description of all partners' rights to receive distributions, including return of contributions. (The ULPA even requires a statement of the share of profits to be received by limited partners.)
10. The method (if any) for withdrawing/changing partners and continuing the business.

Other provisions may also be included. The certificate can be amended, and it tends to resemble both a GP agreement and a corporate charter.

Because limited partners are free from any liability beyond what they have contributed to the LP, *statutory requirements must be carefully followed.* If a LP fails to file in the state (RULPA) and/or county (ULPA) office(s) required, third persons dealing with the partnership but having no actual notice that it is a LP will usually be permitted to treat the limited partners as if they were general partners. Moreover, a LP properly certified in one state may not expect to be treated as such in another state unless it makes the necessary filings there, also. (Most corporations must likewise register in other states where they do business.)

In every LP, there must be at least one general partner. As with the GP, the one or more general partners are personally liable for partnership debts. (However, in states where general partners can be corporations, the ultimate effect could be to have a LP in which no *individual* could be held personally liable for partnership debts in any amount above that paid into the LP. Although the general partner that happens to be a corporation has unlimited liability, if this general partner/corporation becomes insolvent, its "owners" (stockholders) are not personally liable for these corporate obligations.)

A LP likewise needs at least one limited partner. Ordinarily, there is no specified maximum number of limited partners. Since the limited partners do not participate in management, having numerous limited partners should not prove nearly as unwieldy as having large numbers of general partners, whether in a GP or a LP.

THE LIMITED PARTNER'S ROLE

The limited partner's exemption from personal liability depends on his/her abstinence from any role in management.

1. Under the ULPA, the LP's partnership contribution—whether by general or limited partners—must be money or other property, not services. The RULPA, however, also permits the contribution to be services, a promissory note, or another obligation.

2. His/her last name must be excluded from the partnership name. The RULPA also requires that the partnership name include, without abbreviation, the words "limited partnership."

3. He/she must not misrepresent, or allow others to misrepresent, his/her role as being anything other than that of a limited partner.

4. He/she will probably have to withdraw from the LP, or at least renounce any future profits, upon learning that the partnership certificate contains false statements or that the LP was formed defectively. Good faith, substantial compliance with LP legal requirements is sufficient; a minor defect does not destroy the LP.

If any of these requirements are violated, the "limited partner" becomes just as liable as a general partner. The RULPA, however, protects the limited partner if the partnership creditor seeking to hold him/her liable did not have a reasonable belief, based upon the limited partner's conduct, that the limited partner was, in fact, a general partner. Under the RULPA, limited partners who engage in managerial activities retain the limited liability if their participation in the control of the business is unknown to the partnership creditor. Also, the RULPA, especially the 1985 version, lists a number of "safe harbor" activities in which limited partners may engage without opening themselves to general, unlimited liability. These activities include consultation with general partners about the LP's business, being a contractor or surety for the LP, and proposing—and voting on—various fundamental or structural changes to the LP.

The *limited partner* obviously has *no right to bind the partnership,* as a general partner can, *but* does have *almost all of a general partner's other rights.* Some of the more important rights of a limited partner include suing (either individually or for the partnership), reviewing all partnership records, obtaining an accounting of partnership assets and liabilities, deciding whether to admit new partners, assigning his/her partnership interest, and participating in the dissolution process for terminations by court decree.

TERMINATION AND DISTRIBUTION OF ASSETS

Dissolution and winding up occur for the same reasons and by the same methods for a LP as for a GP. A limited partner's withdrawal, expulsion, or death, though, does not dissolve the partnership.

The order in distributing a dissolved LP's assets is dramatically different between the ULPA and the RULPA. Under the ULPA, the LP's repayment of limited partners' loans to the LP (except partnership contributions) has the same, top priority as for other LP creditors, and is far ahead of that for loans made by general partners. Remaining ULPA priorities are in this order: limited partners' profit shares, limited partners' capital contributions, general partners' loans to the LP, general partners' profit shares, general partners' capital contributions. While the ULPA leaves limited partners more protected than general partners, *the RULPA treats all partners in a dissolving LP the same.* All creditors, including limited and general partners, are paid first. Unless the LP agreement specifies otherwise, the LP next pays to both general and limited partners any accrued profit shares, then returns *all* partners' contributions, and lastly, if LP assets still remain, it pays *all* partners in accordance with the LP's profit-distribution scheme.

REASONS AGAINST AND FOR FORMING LIMITED PARTNERSHIPS

On the negative side, the LP is not as effective as the corporation in shielding "owners" from personal liability. Moreover, LP agreements and certificates tend to require formal amendment more frequently than do articles of incorporation, which can be very broadly drafted.

Two reasons for forming a LP are these:

1. Tax laws sometimes make a LP more profitable than a corporation, which is subject to "double taxation." Tax laws may also favor R&D (Research and Development) LPs. (However, the 1986 federal income tax reforms reflect a continuing effort to prevent the use of LPs that make little or no economic sense except as tax shelters.)

2. A GP is in the works (and is preferred over a corporation), but (a) one or more important, potential partners are unwilling to assume unlimited liability and/ or do not wish to participate in management; (b) the general partners seek a large infusion of capital without giving up actual or potential control of management. [In case (b), securing a bank loan might make more sense than forming a LP.]

YOU SHOULD REMEMBER

The LP must meet state statutory requirements, including certificate filing. Forty-four states have adopted the Revised Uniform Limited Partnership Act (RULPA).

Limited partnerships have at least one of each of the two types of partners: general and limited. General partners have essentially the same role in a LP as in a GP. Limited partners have almost all of the rights held by a general partner, except the right to bind the partnership to their actions. In most cases, limited partners simply contribute money, property, or (under the RULPA) services and receive a specified share of the profits; by not participating in management, the limited partner's partnership liability is limited to his/her actual contributions to the partnership. Inappropriate management participation or other noncompliance with statutory requirements may render a "limited partner" generally liable if the partnership's creditor reasonably believed, because of the limited partner's conduct, that the limited partner was actually a general partner.

In distributing a dissolved LP's assets under the ULPA, limited partners come after outside creditors but before general partners. Under the RULPA, for distribution of assets the limited and general partners are treated the same.

Tax laws or other factors favoring a partnership may make a LP preferable to a corporation.

FRANCHISES

A **franchise** is a contractual arrangement in which the owner (**franchisor**) of a trademark, trade name, copyright, patent, trade secret, or some form of business operation, process, or system permits others (**franchisees**) to use that property, operation, process, or system in furnishing goods or services. Usually, the franchisee conducts a business in accordance with conditions and procedures prescribed by the franchisor, who in turn advertises, advises, perhaps lends capital, and/or otherwise assists the franchisees.

Note that the franchise is a relationship. The parties to that relationship— the franchisor and franchisees—are business entities whose individual structures, like those of other businesses, tend to be in the form of sole proprietorships, partnerships, or corporations.

BENEFITS OF FRANCHISING

Typical advantages to *franchisors* are as follows:

1. Franchisees together provide much capital, as well as entrepreneurial skills.

2. Franchisees provide a set distribution network and (usually) **greater** efficiency in limiting costs and expanding sales.

3. Franchisees absorb much of the risk of losses.

These are typical advantages to *franchisees:*

1. They can start a business despite limited capital and experience.

2. They can rely on the goodwill generated by a regionally or nationally known trade name or product.

3. They can rely on the franchisor's business expertise in such areas as marketing, research, and the training of personnel.

4. They are assured access to supplies and to prices based on volume buying.

A franchise may be based on an agency relationship between franchisor (principal) and franchisee (agent). If, however, the franchisee is able to run the business with few outside controls, he/she will probably be viewed as an independent contractor. (See Chapter 14 on Agency.)

TYPES OF FRANCHISES

Franchises fall into three main categories:

1. Distributorships (a manufacturer licenses dealers to sell products).

2. Chain-style businesses (franchisees conduct a particular type of business under the franchisor's trade name and customarily follow the franchisor's standard method of operation).

3. Manufacturing or processing arrangements (the franchisor provides its franchisees with the ingredients or formula for making a product and then marketing it in accordance with the franchisor's standards).

THE FRANCHISE AGREEMENT

The franchisor usually prepares the franchise agreement, which ordinarily contains these provisions, among others:

1. The franchisee's payment to the franchisor for receiving the franchise and/or for obtaining the franchisor's assistance in running it.

2. The franchisor's controls over business territory, structure, purchases, and operations.

3. The duration of the franchise and grounds for termination.

CASE LAW AND STATUTES GOVERNING FRANCHISES

The franchisor usually has much more bargaining power than does the franchisee. Therefore the *case law* on franchises recognizes the occasional need to protect franchisees. Courts will find obligations of good faith and commercial reasonableness in any franchise agreement, and they will not enforce grossly unfair ("unconscionable") provisions.

As for *statutory law,* most states have passed statutes specifically designed to govern franchises. Some statutes, like the UPA for partnership agreements, set forth guidelines in the absence of provisions within the franchise agreement; and many statutes forbid certain franchisor practices, such as franchise termination without "good cause." Even more state statutes require the filing of a franchise registration statement, with mandatory disclosure of pertinent facts about the franchisor.

The Federal Trade Commission (FTC) also mandates disclosure of detailed information about the franchisor and its business. Although there is no franchise registration with the FTC, the government can prosecute for failure to comply with the FTC's disclosure requirements or its rules on establishing and terminating franchises.

Finally, federal and state laws also protect franchisees in special industries. Two examples are the Automobile Dealers' Day in Court Act and the Petroleum Marketing Practices Act, both federal laws. In addition, federal antitrust laws may prohibit restrictions on sales territories, sales prices, or dealings with others.

YOU SHOULD REMEMBER

Franchises are based on contractual arrangements between franchisers and franchisees. The franchisee may be an agent or an independent contractor.

Franchises involve (1) distributorships, (2) chain-style businesses, or (3) manufacturing or processing arrangements.

Because franchisors usually have much more bargaining power than franchisees, the courts and legislatures have provided special protections for franchisees (e.g., forbidding franchise termination without "good cause"). Good faith and commercial reasonableness are imputed in any franchise agreement, and the Federal Trade Commission, as well as some states, require the disclosure of rather detailed information about the franchisor.

KNOW THE CONCEPTS
DO YOU KNOW THE BASICS?

1. What are the three basic types of business organization?
2. Compare these types with respect to manner of creation, formality, governmental regulation, ownership, transfer of ownership, legal entity, agency, division of labor, owner's liability, access to specialists, payment of personal debts, management, profits, changes in business formation documents, fees, multistate businesses, raising capital, income taxes, termination, and size of businesses.
3. Name 13 typical provisions in a partnership agreement.
4. To what three factors do courts look for evidence of an implied partnership?
5. What actions generally require the partners' unanimous consent?
6. List some duties and rights of partners.

7. Name the four bases for binding a partnership to a contract between third persons and a partner.
8. Name three ways in which a partnership is a legal entity.
9. Name the three methods of dissolution of a partnership.
10. Name up to five reasons why a supposedly limited partner may be held generally liable for partnership obligations.
11. Between general partners, limited partners, and creditors, state the basic order of distribution of assets for a LP and for a GP.
12. State three customary provisions in a franchise agreement.
13. Federal and state statutes, as well as court cases, have sought to furnish additional disclosures from whom (franchisors or franchisees) and protection from unfair creation and termination of franchises for whom (franchisors or franchisees)?

TERMS FOR STUDY

corporation	general partnership (GP)	tenants in partnership
dissolution	limited partner	Uniform Limited Partnership
distribution of assets	limited partnership (LP)	Act (ULPA)
franchise	liquidation (winding up)	Uniform Partnership Act
franchisee	partnership by estoppel	(UPA)
franchisor	Revised ULPA (RULPA)	
general partner	sole proprietorship	

PRACTICAL APPLICATION

1. John wants to control a business completely, knows nobody else with whom he wishes to work, and dislikes formalities, paperwork, and lawyers. What type of business organization would he probably prefer?
2. Mary has the time and expertise to put into a new bakery, but little money. Sally has a substantial sum of money to invest, but no interest in the day-to-day operations. What business form would you recommend?
3. There are six partners in a LP: general partners A, B, C, and D, and limited partners E and F. Under the LP agreement, E and F are each entitled to 20% of the profits. E and F each contributed $20,000. A, B, C, and D are each entitled to 15% of the profits, each having contributed $2,500 and also having assumed managerial duties. C assigns his interest in money receivable from the LP to Ms. C on January 1. On February 1, E sells her partnership interest to Bank E. On March 1, G is added as a new general partner; he has made no capital contribution. On April 1, D dies. Assets and liabilities are as follows:

   January 1 to February 14 $95,000 in assets, and no liabilities
   February 15 and thereafter $95,000 in assets (minus a new liability—
                                    judgment of $20,000 against the LP)

   The LP is now dissolved. It made no profits this year, but the previous year's profits were $60,000, which has not been divided among the partners.

   Assume that the LP agreement does not alter the RULPA or ULPA rules. Discuss (a) the changes in the partnership. (b) the judgment liability, and (c) distribution of the remaining $75,000.

ANSWERS
KNOW THE CONCEPTS

1. Sole proprietorships, partnerships, and corporations.
2. See charts on pages 247-253.
3. Name, description of business, list of partners, statement of contributions, delineation of partnership and personal expenses, division of profits/losses, statement of individual partner's powers and limits, management system, allocations of salaries/drawing accounts, treatment of outside business, membership withdrawals and additions, term of duration, and closing out.
4. Joint ownership, sharing of profits or losses, equal management rights.
5. Amending partnership agreement, changing essential nature of partnership's business, altering capital contributions, adding a new business or new partners, confessing judgment, submitting to arbitration, transferring goodwill, placing assets in trust or assignment for creditors, conveying or mortgaging property (usually), other acts rendering business impossible.
6. *Duties:* uncompensated work for, and noncompetition with, partnership, producing information on partnership for other partners, accounting for any personal gains while acting as partner or using partnership property.
   Rights: examination of books, receipt of information on partnership from other partners and accounting of partnership assets and liabilities, property interest in partnership, tenant in partnership, and other implied rights.
7. Express actual authority; implied actual authority; apparent authority; ratification.
8. Bankruptcy can be brought by partnership; judgments against partnership are first enforceable only against the partnership; in most states, it is possible to sue, having accountings, and own property in partnership's name.
9. Acts of parties, operation of law, and court decree.
10. He participated in management; his last name was part of the partnership's name; he misrepresented or allowed others to misrepresent that he was a general partner; the LP certificate contained falsehoods; the LP was defectively formed.
11. *LP:* under the RULPA all creditors are repaid, then the limited and general partners are paid together, according to various priorities (unless the LP agreement states otherwise)—(a) accrued profit shares, then (b) contributions, then (c) remaining assets in accord with the LP's profit-distribution scheme; under the ULPA all creditors other than general partners are repaid, then limited partners, and then general partners.
    GP: third-party creditors are repaid, then general partners (loans, then capital contributions, then remaining assets according to the division of profits in the partnership agreement). There are no limited partners in a GP.

12. Franchisee's payment to franchisor; franchisor's controls over aspects of the business; franchise's duration and grounds for termination.
13. Franchisors; franchisees.

PRACTICAL APPLICATION

1. Sole proprietorship.
2. General partnership seems inappropriate because of disparity in wealth and interests of Mary and Sally. Limited partnership might be suitable, especially since Mary's contribution could come in the form of property other than just money (e.g., rent-free use of her house as the business location) or—under the RULPA—it could even be services or a promissory note. Mary would be the general partner, and Sally the limited partner.

   However, a corporation is by no means out of the question. There the decision depends more on the tax consequences, Mary's concerns about her unlimited liability in a partnership, and Mary's and/or Sally's desires as to transferability of ownership. Unless Sally's stock was nonvoting, though, Mary would probably face a situation in which ultimate control would rest with Sally.

3. (a) Ms. C can collect the profits due C; she just cannot participate as a general partner. If there is no agreement to the contrary, E may transfer her entire limited partner interest and status to Bank E without dissolving the partnership. G may be added as a new general partner with the other general partners' permission. D's death dissolves the new LP (the one with G in it).

   (b) G is not personally responsible for a debt incurred before his admission, except for an amount no greater than his capital contribution, which is nothing. All of the other partners, however, would be responsible, with even the limited partners liable to the amounts of their capital contributions.

   (c) After the liability of $20,000 is paid off, $75,000 remains. There appear to be no other creditors, so the next priority under the *RULPA* is to pay the $60,000 in accrued profits. A, B, Ms. C, and D's estate each are entitled to 15% of the profits of $60,000, and F and Bank E are entitled to 20% each. The remaining $15,000 is distributed *pro rata* according to the partners' contributions. Thus F and Bank E get most of the $15,000, but A, B, Ms. C, and D's estate each get 5% (because each is credited for a contribution of $2,500 out of a total capital outlay of $50,000). G, of course, gets nothing because he made no capital contribution.

   Under the *ULPA*, the $75,000 is first distributed to limited partners—here F and Bank E, with each getting a 20% share of the $60,000 in profits ($12,000 apiece) and each getting back its $20,000 capital contribution. Thus, F and Bank E receive $32,000 each. The general partners (or their assignees) have only $11,000 to split, with each receiving one-fourth. Each is entitled to $9,000 in profit shares—15% of $60,000—but there is only $11,000 *in toto* to distribute; the general partners get only $2,750 in profit shares, and nothing is returned from their capital contributions.

16

CORPORATIONS: NATURE, FORMATION, TYPES, AND POWERS

NATURE OF A CORPORATION

A corporation is an artificial being created by operation of law. This artificial being, or entity, is entirely separate from its shareholders, directors, officers, and employees. This separation gives the corporation a life of its own and the responsibility and accountability to the law that are attributable to a natural person.

If all the shareholders, directors, officers, and employees of corporation A were to die simultaneously in a common accident, corporation A would continue to exist: stock ownership would pass to heirs of the deceased shareholders; these new shareholders would name new directors and hire new officers and employees.

A corporation has a totally independent existence apart from the persons who own and operate it.

BACKGROUND OF CORPORATIONS

Although the imperial government of Rome suppressed private societies and associations of every kind, it permitted individuals to form *collegia,* that is, non-profit, membership clubs for such diverse purposes as education, fire control, and burial of members. In the late Middle Ages and early modern period (the twelfth through the sixteenth centuries) the Roman model was expanded in France and Germany to permit merchants to form trading societies and craft guilds for investment and larger business purposes.

In the late 1500s the English government began to grant monopolies to individuals, or groups of individuals, for trading and for revenue purposes, with the Crown receiving a share of the monopoly profits. Colonization of the New World was undertaken by such monopolies, which, when granted a charter for the colonization and development of specified territories, operated as governments under the general supervision of the king. Trading ventures such as the *Massachusetts Bay Company, Hudson's Bay Company,* and the *East India Company* were established for exploitation and development of the New World and other foreign lands.

During the colonization period corporate charters were granted to private individuals by special acts of the colonial legislatures. When the United States became a nation, corporations were created by grant of charter by the several states, first by legislative enactment, and later by special state agencies or commissions created for this purpose. *In all of the states, corporations are created by state corporation commissions, although the management of corporations is left to internal controls within the corporate structure.*

Most states now follow, to some degree, the Model Business Corporation Act (MBCA), which was first proposed in 1950 and since has been frequently amended (including a completely overhauled Revised Model Business Corporation Act—RMBCA—in 1984). Still, the state corporation commission, by whatever name it may be called, is little more than the issuer of the corporate charter at the beginning of the corporate life; in practice, the state rarely takes any interest in the actual corporate function. Nevertheless, a corporation must be a good citizen. It may be punished for its crimes, sued for its torts, and held accountable for its contracts. *At all times it must be operated for the benefit of its shareholders, who are its owners.*

YOU SHOULD REMEMBER

The idea of the corporation originated with the Romans, who permitted the formation of private clubs, or *collegia,* for certain non-profit purposes. The Europeans expanded the Roman concept to permit incorporation for business purposes; the English used corporations for colonization and trading.

> Modern corporations, although created mainly through state corporation commissions, are controlled internally through the corporate structure. They must be good citizens, though they are operated for the benefit of their owners (shareholders).

CORPORATE ATTRIBUTES

A LEGAL PERSON

For most legal purposes a corporation is a person. Like any citizen, it can sue and be sued, make contracts, own property, and perform other personal acts. Moreover, it can be charged with almost any crime except crimes the sole punishment for which is imprisonment. For most purposes, a corporation is entitled to the protections afforded citizens under the Bill of Rights except the right against self-incrimination provided for in the Fifth Amendment.

CREATION BY STATUTE

A corporation is created under the provisions of applicable statutes by contract with the state. The evidence of this contract is the corporation's charter. Under modern corporation law most state statutes provide that, as a condition to the grant of charter, the state may, by regulation or statute, unilaterally modify the terms of charters already granted. [In the case of *Dartmouth College* v. *Woodward,* 17 U.S. 518 (1819), the Supreme Court held that, without such statutory permission, a state could not modify or revoke a corporate charter without "impairing the obligation of contracts" as forbidden by Article I, Section 10, of the United States Constitution.]

LIMITED LIABILITY OF SHAREHOLDERS

Since a corporation is a legal entity separate from its shareholders, it, and not the shareholders, is liable for its debts. However, the courts will disregard the corporate entity, that is, will **"pierce the corporate veil,"** if the corporate name is used as a false front or "stalking horse" behind which the owners or operators perpetrate fraud upon creditors or others dealing with them.

> The "corporate veil" may be pierced if two conditions are present:
> (1) a fraudulent purpose, and
> (2) operation of the corporate business as though the corporation does not exist.

Thus the principal creates a corporation and uses a corporate name; however, the principal holds no corporate meetings, keeps few corporate books or records, and disregards the corporation that he/she has created. In addition, the principal fraudulently permits or causes others to believe that he/she is, in fact, responsible for the corporate business.

> Although the courts will do so reluctantly, they may *pierce the corporate veil* and hold the principal liable as though the corporation did not exist.

PERPETUAL EXISTENCE

As previously indicated, a corporation has a life of its own, independent of its shareholders and managers. Modern corporations are usually granted *perpetual existence* as a routine charter provision, although corporate existence may also be for a stated or limited period of time.

YOU SHOULD REMEMBER

For most legal purposes a corporation is a person.
A corporation is created by statutes and is granted a charter, usually by the state.
A corporation is liable for its debts.
A corporation is usually granted perpetual existence.

FORMATION OF THE CORPORATION
THE PROMOTER

> A **promoter** is the person who conceives of, organizes, and begins the corporation.

Not only is the corporation his/her "brain child," but also the promoter finds others who are willing to participate in the development and exploitation of the idea.

Although the promoter is not an agent of the corporation to be created, he/she occupies a fiduciary relationship (position of trust) in regard to the proposed corporation and its investors, shareholders, and creditors. Basically, this trust relation requires that the promoter make full disclosure of his/her anticipated personal gain, the nature of the business, its prospects, and the promoter's plans with regard thereto.

In the course of forming the corporation, the promoter may incur costs, make contracts, and do other acts in furtherance of the corporation. Since the promoter is not an agent, the corporation is not automatically responsible or liable for these obligations and contracts; however, *it may ratify, adopt, or accept them, provided that there is full and open disclosure by the promoter to the corporation.* The promoter remains obligated with respect to such obligations or contracts unless released by the obligee or unless the corporation is substituted for him by a novation (see Chapter 8).

OBTAINING THE CHARTER

The persons wishing to form a corporation (the **incorporators**) make application to the state corporation commission for a charter by presenting to the commission a form of the charter they want to have granted. Although the charter is usually prepared by an attorney, this is not strictly necessary. A detailed discussion of the nature and content of the charter follows later in this chapter.

> A requested charter is reviewed by the commission; and if provisions of the law are complied with, the charter along with a certificate of incorporation will be issued by the appropriate state official.

The **certificate of incorporation** is the state's official authorization for the corporation to commence to do business.

FIRST ORGANIZATIONAL MEETING

The incorporators, after receipt of the certificate of incorporation, call a meeting of the interim board of directors named in the charter to be held, at which time bylaws are adopted, officers are elected, and other necessary business is transacted. *Once stock is issued and sold, the shareholders duly meet and name the regular board of directors.*

DE JURE AND *DE FACTO* CORPORATIONS

A **de jure** corporation *is one that has been formed in accordance with all of the requirements of law; a* de facto corporation *is one that has not been properly formed, even though the incorporators made a good-faith effort to do so.* The defect in the formation of the *de facto* corporation is technical—there is some omission, for example, in the charter—but the certificate of incorporation is nonetheless granted.

The status of the *de facto* corporation can be challenged only by the state; third parties must accept it as a valid, authentic corporate entity.

YOU SHOULD REMEMBER

A corporation is created through the grant of a charter. This charter, although prepared by the incorporators, is officially approved and certified by the state corporation commission. Even if the corporation is imperfectly created, it may function as a *de facto* corporation.

TYPES OF CORPORATIONS
PUBLIC OR PRIVATE

A **public corporation** is formed to meet a governmental or public purpose.

Generally, a public corporation is created for the direct function of government—town, city, or county.

Most corporations fall into the category of **private corporations**—corporations created for private purposes. In the context of commercial law, the word "corporation" generally connotes a private entity. Public utilities have some features of both public and private corporations.

There is an important group of corporations that might be considered "hybrids," that is, they have features of both public and private corporations. These **quasi-public corporations** are *public utilities*—privately owned businesses created for public purposes. Although these monopolies, or partial monopolies, are strictly controlled both as to services and as to prices (rates), they are permitted a reasonable return on investment, established during the course of a regulatory rate case.

FEDERAL OR STATE

Although the federal government has the right and power to create corporations, the United States has shown great restraint in entering the incorporating field. Since the exercise of this power must be solely within the scope of legitimate constitutional authority, most **federal corporations** are created for narrow and specific purposes. The systems of national banks and of federal savings and loan institutions are examples of federally created corporations, all of which are federally chartered and supervised.

In general, this discussion is limited to state-chartered corporations. Note, however, that within the limits of legitimate constitutional purposes, the United States can readily enter this field.

PROFIT OR NONPROFIT

Business law primarily concerns corporations organized for profit. *However, nonprofit, charitable, or eleemosynary corporations are of great importance,* even in the business world, not only because of the important tax benefits and concessions accruing to such corporations but also because of the importance of permitting these charitable groups to own property, form contracts, and otherwise engage in business without individual members having personal liability for business matters. Such corporations may be stock corporations, or **membership corporations** (owned by their members without issuing stock).

DOMESTIC OR FOREIGN

A corporation is said to be **domestic** in the state of its incorporation, the state of its "birth." In respect to all other states, it is a **foreign corporation**. Thus, in Delaware, a Delaware corporation is a domestic corporation; in all other states it is foreign.

Corporations formed in foreign countries are called **alien corporations**.

CLOSE CORPORATIONS

A **close corporation** is a stock corporation whose shares are held by a relatively few persons, frequently members of a family. Such a corporation may be operated like a partnership, sometimes with no board of directors, or with other informalities not permitted to general stock corporations for profit.

To permit such loose organization, the laws of most states limit the number of stockholders and permit restrictions on stock transfer by agreement among the shareholders or by charter provision.

S CORPORATIONS (formerly "Subchapter S" of the Internal Revenue Code)

S corporations are organized to minimize the effect of federal income taxes on small businesses, principally by doing away with corporate "double taxation." This double taxation, as explained in Chapter 15, is taxation applied first to the corporation's income, and second to the individual shareholders' income in the form of earnings and dividends.

> The S corporation does not pay a corporate income tax on earnings; the entire income is taxed to the shareholders, whether distributed or not.

S corporations must meet a number of requirements. The principal one is that they have 35 or fewer shareholders, all of whom own the same class of stock and none of whom can be a corporation, partnership, or other non-natural person.

LIMITED LIABILITY COMPANIES

Because S corporations have so many restrictions, the **limited liability company (LLC)** is an alternative. A 1988 IRS ruling that, for tax purposes, LLCs are to be treated like partnerships has led some states to authorize the LLC. Unlike the S corporation, the LLC has no restrictions on the number of owners, the class of stock, the owning of subsidiaries, and the like; unlike general or limited partnerships, the LLC permits investors to *manage* the business yet not be personally liable for the business debts. The LLC thus is a partnership-corporation hybrid, with the corporate shield protecting against personal liability, but with LLC "members" like partners in that (1) death or a decision to pull out probably dissolves the LLC, and (2) transfer of a membership requires the other members' approval. Legal analysis, though, must be tentative: LLC law is in its infancy.

PROFESSIONAL CORPORATIONS

Professional corporations are created by lawyers, doctors, accountants, architects, engineers, and other professionals in order to gain corporate tax advantages for traditional partnership or proprietorship activities. These corporations, organized under state law enacted in conformity with internal revenue code requirements, are generally identified by abbreviations: P.A. (Professional Association), P.C. (Professional Corporation), or S.C. (Service Corporation).

> Although it is a corporation for most purposes, the professional corporation cannot shield its shareholders and members from individual tort liability for professional negligence.

Most states leave the individual professional within the corporation free from personal liability for the professional negligence of another member of the organization, unless the individual was, in fact, supervising that negligent member or otherwise participating in the tortious acts.

> ### Basic Principle of
> ### Common Law Partnership
> Each partner is responsible for the torts and contracts of the other partners within the scope of the partnership venture.

Courts have not decided whether this principle is applicable to the professionals comprising a professional corporation.

YOU SHOULD REMEMBER

Most corporations are created under state law; federal corporations can be, and are, created for specific federal purposes.

Business law is generally concerned with profit corporations; however, nonprofit corporations are also important, because of (a) tax considerations and (b) protection of their members from personal liability in the course of corporate business.

A corporation is domestic in the state of its creation; foreign, in all other states.

Professional corporations are created strictly for tax sheltering purposes. They do not have the general attributes of corporations.

Corporations are subject to a corporate income tax. In addition, the shareholders are also taxed on distributions or dividends received from the corporation.

S corporations and limited liability companies are exceptions; they do not pay a separate tax.

NATURE AND CONTENT OF THE CHARTER; BYLAWS

THE CHARTER

The **charter** (also sometimes called the **articles of incorporation**, or **articles**) is the grant of corporate existence, the birth certificate of the corporation. This formal document, executed by the state through its corporation commission, is the source of corporate authority. Also, the charter is a public document.

Although the charter may contain any number of provisions, drawn formally or informally, modern charters tend to cover only the minimum provisions required by law. *The charter is more or less a "form" document; however, the required coverage may vary from state to state.*

The following information is usually required in the charter:

1. Incorporators

2. Corporate name

3. Corporate address and name and address of resident agent

4. Duration

5. Purpose

6. Capital structure

7. Internal organization

8. Other permissible provisions

• *INCORPORATORS*

The incorporators are the persons who make application for the charter. Their only function is to lend their names and signatures to the incorporating documents. By so doing, they acquire no special legal liability. Generally, the only requirement is that an incorporator be old enough to make a contract, that is, at least 18 years of age. Usually, there must be at least three incorporators. Many states do not require that these incorporators be residents of the state.

• *NAME*

Any name may be chosen for the corporation provided that:

(a) the name indicates that the entity is a corporation by inclusion of one of the following words, or by one of these words abbreviated: Company (in most states), Corporation, Incorporated, Limited, and

(b) the name is not the same as, or misleadingly similar to, the name of any other domestic corporation, or corporation doing business in the state.

In addition, many states limit, in corporate names, the use of certain words closely associated with particular types of businesses or industries. For example, a manufacturing concern would not be allowed to include in its name a word such as "insured," "finance," or "fiduciary."

• *CORPORATE ADDRESS AND NAME AND ADDRESS OF REGISTERED AGENT*

The corporate address is the principal address of the corporation in the state of its incorporation.

The registered agent is a person or another corporation authorized to receive service of process and other legal and official papers. The requirement that a legal agent be named is of more than passing importance: the state is concerned that persons having business with a corporation, or interested in bringing suit against it, be able to discover a way of finding the corporation in order to hold it accountable for its actions.

• *DURATION*

As stated above, the duration may be perpetual or limited to a stated period of time.

• *PURPOSE*

Modern statutes permit a corporation to be organized for any legal purpose, and the charter may contain merely a broad statement of purpose. Usually, however, the charter states the specific purpose for which the corporation is being formed—for example, "to operate a restaurant business"—followed by very broad grants of power and usually a statement of purpose to do any legal act.

Charters that fail to contain the "for any legal purpose" provision are nevertheless granted such broad powers as a matter of right, unless the charter contains restrictions or limitations on certain powers or rights.

• *CAPITAL STRUCTURE*

Requirements concerning charter statements about capital vary from state to state. Generally, state incorporation statutes require information about the number of shares of stock of all classes that the corporation has authority to issue, the number of shares of stock of each class, the par value, and other matters concerning both equity and capital.

• *INTERNAL ORGANIZATION*

State statutory requirements about organization are quite minimal: usually the only requirements are a provision as to the number of directors (e.g., "not more than seven") and the names and addresses of those who will serve as an interim board until the shareholders meet and name the first board.

Other organizational and detailed day-to-day matters are usually left for the bylaws.

• *OTHER PROVISIONS*

The charter may include other provisions, not inconsistent with law, defining, limiting, or regulating the powers of the corporation, its directors and shareholders, or classes of shareholders. Included may be restrictions on the transferability of stock (creating a close or S corporation), requirements of a concurrence of shareholders greater than a majority for certain actions, provisions for minority shareholder representation by cumulative voting, provisions relating to preemptive rights (see Chapter 18), and other provisions that may be included in the bylaws.

BYLAWS

Generally, the charter should be a lean, sparse document and the bylaws should be more detailed. The reason is that charter amendments must be approved by the state as well as the shareholders. Bylaws are generally adopted by the directors and may or may not be approved by the shareholders.

Bylaws contain specific provisions for the organization and operation of the corporation, including such matters as election of the board of directors, quorum and voting requirements for shareholders, and places for meetings.

The bylaws may not contain a provision contrary to, or inconsistent with, the charter.

CORPORATE POWERS AND LIMITATIONS ON THEM

POWERS

Modern corporations are granted very broad powers by law; indeed, in most states they can perform any act not inconsistent with law. Thus it should be assumed that for most purposes a corporation has all of the rights and powers of action accruing to a natural person.

The MBCA and RMBCA list a number of general powers for a corporation, including the power—

> to sue and be sued;
>
> to have a corporate seal, which may be altered at will;
>
> to make and amend bylaws, not inconsistent with the articles of incorporation or with law;
>
> to purchase, lease, and otherwise acquire real and personal property;
>
> to sell or dispose of its property;
>
> to purchase, own, hold, vote, or pledge stock;
>
> to make contracts and guarantees, incur liabilities, and issue notes and bonds;
>
> to lend money and invest and reinvest its funds;
>
> to be a promoter, partner, member, associate, or manager of a joint venture or partnership;
>
> to conduct its business and exercise the powers granted by law within or outside the state;
>
> to do any act, not inconsistent with law, that furthers the business of the corporation.

LIMITATIONS ON POWERS

> Powers are, however, sometimes limited by statute, by the corporation's charter, by the bylaws, or by a resolution or other action of the board of directors.

• *BY STATUTE*

A number of statutory limitations may be placed on the power of corporations. By way of example, one very common statutory limitation, a limit on the power of the corporation to make a gift, will be discussed.

All corporate property is owned by the shareholders. At the common law, no gift of this property could be made without unanimous shareholder approval. Consequently, *any* gift of corporate property not unanimously approved by the shareholders was illegal. This illegality is preserved in the corporate law of some states. Most states now permit corporate gifts, but place statutory limits on their nature and object. Typically, gifts may be permitted without shareholder approval provided that they are (a) reasonable in amount, (b) approved by the directors, (c) made from profits, and (d) made for charitable purposes.

• BY CHARTER, BYLAWS, OR ACTION OF THE DIRECTORS

Further limits and restrictions on corporate power can be placed in the charter or bylaws. These may include such restrictions as limits on the borrowing power of officers, on pensions or salaries, on the purchase of real estate, and on the sale of assets.

Other limits may be established from time to time by resolution or other specific action of the board of directors.

• BY THE ULTRA VIRES DOCTRINE

A corporate action beyond the charter powers of the corporation or of the person purporting to act for the corporation is ultra vires, "beyond the powers." If the action is appropriate and lawful, it is *intra vires,* "within the powers."

Because of the broad-power concepts of modern law, the *ultra vires* doctrine is not a problem of major consequence. However, *ultra vires* acts can be enjoined by shareholders in a suit against the corporation, or by a derivative suit for damages in favor of the corporation against an officer or against the board because of the unauthorized action; or the state itself may seek to block the unauthorized action (see Chapter 17). Of course, if a third party dealing with the corporation knew of the *ultra vires* nature of the corporate act, the act may be set aside. Moreover, if a proposed *ultra vires* act is still executory (not yet performed), the corporation may refuse to proceed with the action unless the third party can demonstrate specific injury through his/her reliance on the corporate proposal.

YOU SHOULD REMEMBER

Under modern law corporations are granted very broad powers. These powers may be limited, however, by statute, by the corporation's charter or bylaws, or by a resolution or other action of the board of directors.

An act of the corporation that exceeds its charter powers is an *ultra vires* act. The *ultra vires* doctrine is no longer of major importance in modern corporate law because of the broad grant of powers to corporations, permitting them to do any and all lawful actions.

REGULATION OF FOREIGN CORPORATIONS

If a corporation wishes to *"do business" in a state other than the one in which it was incorporated, it must register or qualify in that other state as a foreign corporation.* Although registration or qualification may be a mere formality, the corporation must pay a fee, sometimes post a bond, and always designate a registered agent in that state to receive service of process and other legal papers.

The out-of-state corporation, having subjected itself to the laws of the state in which it seeks to do business, is vulnerable to the expense and difficulty of suit in a more remote or inconvenient location. Penalties for failure to qualify or register can be severe: loss of privilege of using state courts for the purpose of suit; a fine for every day of failure to register while doing business; and personal liability of officers, directors, and agents for actions in the foreign state.

The key phrase is "doing business."

Under the federal constitution, a state cannot restrict or regulate interstate commerce. Therefore a state cannot require registration or qualification for a foreign corporation doing an *interstate* business, that is, coming through on its way to another state. Indeed, cases dealing with the meaning of the phrase "doing business" abound.

It is generally held that a foreign corporation is "doing business" within a state if it:

(a) maintains sufficient contacts or ties within a state,
(b) on a continuous or regular basis,
(c) so as to make it fair and equitable that the corporation be accountable in the foreign state.

(See the discussion of personal jurisdiction on page 33.)

YOU SHOULD REMEMBER

If a corporation is "doing business" in a state other than that of its incorporation, it must register in that state as a foreign corporation.

The phrase "doing business" means that the corporation maintains sufficient contacts in the foreign state on a continuous or regular basis as to make it accountable to that state for its actions.

KNOW THE CONCEPTS

DO YOU KNOW THE BASICS?

1. List some ways in which a corporation is treated as a person and some ways in which it is not treated as a person.

2. Is there any reason why a democratic society would be more likely to foster the corporate form of business than a totalitarian society? Discuss.

3. Why is it possible for corporations to function with little or no policing and supervision by the state?

4. Discuss the ways in which a public utility is a public corporation and the ways in which it is a private corporation.

5. What is meant by corporate "double taxation"? Explain several ways in which double taxation may be avoided.

6. What is the meaning of the expression "pierce the corporate veil"? Is this a "moral" as well as a legal principle?

7. Why should the charter be a "lean" document?

8. What is meant by the phrase "misleadingly similar to" in establishing a corporate name?

9. What is the underlying philosophy in requiring stockholders to approve a corporate gift? Why have many states found it necessary to relax this philosophy?

10. Why is the common law doctrine of *ultra vires* not as important to the modern corporation as it was in earlier times?

11. Why is it necessary that a foreign corporation "do business" within a state in order to be subject to the registration requirements of that state?

TERMS FOR STUDY

alien corporation
articles of incorporation
bylaws
certificate of incorporation
charter
close corporation
corporation
de facto corporation
de jure corporation
domestic corporation
federal corporation
foreign corporation

incorporators
intra vires
limited liability company
membership corporation
pierce the corporate veil
private corporation
professional corporation
promoter
public corporation
quasi-public corporation
S corporation

PRACTICAL APPLICATION

1. Doctors Hacksaw, Smith, and Spurgeon operate a general medical practice as a professional corporation, known as HSS, P. C. While performing a tonsillectomy on one Samuels, Hacksaw is allegedly negligent, as a result of which Samuels is left partly paralyzed. Each of the doctors is quite wealthy, but the corporation is without substantial assets.
   Advise Samuels as to whether he can expect to win a case against each of the doctors as individuals.

2. In 1970, Soper and his two adult sons, Sam and Steve, created a corporation, Soper and Sons Electrical Company. During the first year or so, they maintained corporate bank accounts, had the name printed on trucks and stationery, and held annual stockholders' meetings. After the elder Soper died in 1975, Sam and Steve forgot about the corporation and failed to hold meetings or otherwise follow the corporate formalities. In 1982, Sam's allegedly negligent electrical wiring caused a disastrous fire at a local elementary school, in which several children and school personnel were injured.
   Are there legal theories under which Steve and Sam can be personally liable to the injured parties?

3. Snyder wishes to create a corporation under the name "First National Liquor Stores, Inc." Should this name be permitted as a good corporate name over the objection of First National Food Stores, Inc.?

4. Good Times Candy Company, an Illinois corporation, is a large manufacturer and distributor of confections and candies in the Midwest. It has never qualified or registered in the state of Iowa as a foreign corporation, although it has passed through Iowa in the course of making sales in other states. Most sales of the company and all of the sales that involve passing through Iowa are made in response to orders shipped FOB Chicago. If Good Times sells its products directly in Iowa at Christmas, 1985, should it register as a foreign corporation before doing so again at Christmas, 1986?

ANSWERS
KNOW THE CONCEPTS

1. A corporation has all of the constitutional rights of a person except protection from self-incrimination, provided for in the Fifth Amendment to the Constitution. This protection against self-incrimination has been construed to be "a human protection," and the courts have refused to extend

it to a corporate entity. Other constitutional rights, such as the protection of property rights, extend to the corporation. A corporation cannot commit a crime the only punishment for which is a jail sentence. Bear in mind, however, that the mere fact that a corporation may be guilty of a crime or liable for a tort does not protect the corporate employee, agent, or officer; these individuals may also be concurrently guilty of a crime or liable for a tort, along with their corporate employer.

2. There are several reasons why a democratic society fosters the corporate form. First of all, the shareholders vote for directors, and the voting power is distributed among the stockholders in equal measure to their actual ownership of stock. These are democratic concepts. Also, the protection of stockholders' property rights is in accord with democratic principles.

3. Since corporations exist for the benefit of their shareholders, it is presumed that the shareholders will protect their interests through regular corporate procedures. Shareholder rights are discussed in the next chapter.

4. A public utility is public in the sense that it performs a public function. Its prices are fixed by regulatory authorities. The rate of return allowed to its investors is set by regulation. Its service territories are determined by regulators. Another public aspect is its right of eminent domain or condemnation.

   As a private matter, a public utility is owned by private investors; its stock may be freely traded. Within legal constraints, some of which are discussed in this chapter, the investors may make a profit. The utility's stockholders have the usual legal rights of shareholders generally.

5. "Double taxation" is taxation on the corporation's profits and further taxation on these profits when they are distributed to shareholders.

   The S corporation and the limited liability company provide a direct way of dealing with this problem: professional corporations permit professionals such as doctors, lawyers, and accountants to incorporate without double taxation and receive a number of tax benefits through corporate planning. Of course, in a small "mom and pop" corporation, the principals, who are usually the shareholders, may pay themselves reasonable salaries, expense monies that are not taxed to the corporation.

6. "Piercing the corporate veil" has a moral aspect in that the shareholders are not directly responsible for corporate losses unless the corporate form is abused: the corporation is operated as a "front" for a fraudulent purpose, and the corporate business is operated as though the corporation does not exist.

7. The charter is more difficult to amend or change than bylaws or other documents. Approval of the state corporation commission may be required, as well as that of the shareholders and directors.

8. Members of the public should not be misled by the name into believing that they are dealing with some other corporate entity. Many corporations spend vast sums establishing an identity or a reputation for excellence; it would not be fair to permit a new enterprise to adopt a similar name and thus benefit from the older company's established identity or reputation.

9. The underlying philosophy is that all corporate property belongs to the shareholders; their assets cannot be given to another without their approval.

   Corporate giving may be necessary and appropriate in the modern world. There may be tax, advertising, and goodwill advantages to the corporate gift. Moreover, several shareholders, or perhaps a single shareholder, might otherwise thwart a gift giving against the wishes of a vast majority.

10. The modern view of corporate powers is more relaxed and trusting than the earlier common law view. Most modern corporations are permitted to consummate any lawful act.

11. A state cannot interfere with interstate commerce; hence it is necessary that the state have legitimate control over foreign corporate activity in order to prohibit it or police it in some manner. The state has legitimate interests of its own citizens to protect. If a corporation's business is not interstate (and subject to federal control), but is performed on a continuous and regular basis within the state, it becomes accountable to the state.

PRACTICAL APPLICATION

1. The creation of a professional corporation does not protect the individual doctor from professional torts. Hacksaw is personally responsible. Unless Smith or Spurgeon were personally involved with the tonsillectomy, most states would not hold them responsible for Hacksaw's tort (although if the doctors had held themselves out as general partners each would be liable for the torts of the others). A few courts might hold both Smith and Spurgeon responsible for Hacksaw's negligence on the theory that professional corporations do not alter the old partnership obligations of the members to each other.

2. This question has broad implications beyond the subject matter of this chapter. However, one obvious problem, that of piercing the corporate veil, is covered in the current chapter. The veil would not be pierced in the absence of a showing of a fraudulent purpose; hence this theory is not adequate to reach the individual stockholders or principals. However, in Chapter 14 (Agency) we dealt with the personal responsibility of employee agents for their torts while undertaking company business. Under agency law, Sam and Steve may well be liable if they, or others acting under their supervision, personally committed the tort.

3. "First National Liquor Stores, Inc." is probably not confusing or misleadingly similar to "First National Food Stores, Inc." Not only are the product lines different; the name "First National" is not strongly identified with any special or unusual type of business.

4. Good Times may need to qualify in Iowa as a foreign corporation before doing an intrastate business for the second Christmas in a row. It could certainly be argued that twice is not "regular and continuous"; however, it seems that a pattern of doing business is beginning to emerge. Good corporate practice should be conservative, and doubt should be resolved in favor of complying with the registration requirement. Note that going through the state is an interstate activity and does not constitute "doing business." Note also that an "FOB Chicago" sale causes the title to pass in Chicago; consequently, the sale did not take place in Iowa, and the seller has not entered that state on an intrastate basis.

17

MANAGEMENT OF THE CORPORATION; TERMINATION

CORPORATE OVERVIEW

THE CORPORATE STRUCTURE

The owners of the shares of stock issued by the corporation are the owners of the corporation. These **shareholders** elect a board of **directors**, who oversee the management of the corporation. The directors, in turn, name and employ the **officers**, who are responsible for the operation of the business.

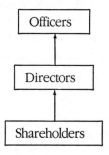

CORPORATE OBJECTIVES

Theoretically, the modern corporation has the power to accomplish any lawful purpose. However, the corporation is owned by its shareholders and exists solely for their profit and benefit.

Broad corporate powers must be exercised strictly in furtherance of the interests of the corporate shareholders.

The managers of the corporation (the board of directors) have wide discretion to determine precisely the best way to funnel corporate powers into shareholder gain. Corporate profits will result in shareholder gain; corporate losses become shareholder losses.

Gain or loss is not necessarily measured solely in financial terms. A good corporate image created by conformity with environmental laws, charitable acts of kindness, and good neighbor policies within the larger community may foster profits and serve the shareholder. On the negative side, a corporation with uncaring and hardened management, a polluter of air and water, an enterprise that neglects its employees or imposes on their loyalty may inhibit profits and harm its shareholders.

To say that a corporation exists solely for the profit and benefit of its shareholders is also to say that it cannot act for the profit and benefit of others, to the neglect of its shareholders. In other words, while the community at large, or the poor, or certain charities, may benefit by corporate action, all such benefit must somehow contribute to the ultimate good of the corporation and therefore of the shareholders.

YOU SHOULD REMEMBER

The corporate structure consists of shareholders, the owners of the corporation; directors, elected by the shareholders to oversee its management; and officers, named by the directors to operate it.

Although the corporation must be operated for the benefit of its shareholders, good corporate operation considers also the larger community welfare and the public interest.

SHAREHOLDERS

Shareholders may own either preferred or common stock. The classes of stock are discussed in Chapter 18.

SHAREHOLDER FUNCTIONS

• *ELECTION OF DIRECTORS*

Although the shareholders are the owners of the corporation, this ownership does not carry with it the right of management.

> The primary right of the shareholder is to attend meetings of the shareholders and to vote on matters properly brought before such meetings, including the election of directors and other fundamental matters affecting the corporation and required by statute or by the charter.

Except for attending the shareholders' meetings and casting votes in favor of directors, a shareholder cannot directly interfere with the directors or with their management of the corporation, even though he/she may own or control a majority or all of the outstanding shares.

• *AMENDMENT OF THE CHARTER*

At common law, a corporate charter was considered to be a contract between the state and the corporation, on the one hand, and between the corporation and the shareholders, on the other. Change of this contract required unanimous shareholder approval.

Under modern corporate law a change can be accomplished by a less than unanimous shareholder vote. The percentage of shares required for approval of a charter amendment varies among the states in accordance with the nature of the proposed amendment. Generally, minor changes, such as dropping the word "The" from the corporate name or changing the registered agent, do not require *any* shareholder approval but can be done by the directors.

Drastic changes in the nature of the corporate business, however, or changes affecting the value of the stock or voting rights may require approval of

(a) two thirds of the shares outstanding and entitled to vote, or

(b) a majority of the outstanding shares entitled to vote, or

(c) a majority of the shares present and voting,

depending on the applicable state statute.

Procedures for charter changes require that any change be first proposed by a resolution of the board of directors. Certain changes may specifically require that dissenting shareholders be given the right to sell their stock to the corporation at its appraised value.

• *MERGER AND CONSOLIDATION*

Corporations merge when the stock of one is purchased by another; they are consolidated when a third corporation (generally created for that specific purpose) purchases the stock of both. In a **merger**, corporation A buys all of the stock of B; A continues to exist, but B will be dissolved or continued as a subsidiary of A. In a **consolidation**, corporation C buys the stock of A and B; A and/or B will be dissolved or continue as subsidiaries of C.

In a merger, approval is required in all cases by the shareholders of B, the merged corporation; approval is also required by the shareholders of A, the continuing corporation, unless that corporation already owns most of the stock of the merged corporation, or unless the surviving corporation is so much larger than the merged corporation that the acquisition of the smaller corporation will have no effect on the business of the survivor or on the value of its stock.

Example: Merger

If corporation A, with assets in excess of $50 million, merges with corporation B, with assets of $100,000, approval of the shareholders of A would not be required. The shareholders of B, however, must approve.

In most states, two thirds of the outstanding shares eligible to vote must approve a merger or consolidation.

• *SALE OF ASSETS*

Sale of all or substantially all of the assets of a corporation other than in the regular course of business requires shareholder approval. The meaning of the phrase "substantially all" varies from case to case, but the principal test is whether the sale affects the corporate business to the extent that the nature of the shareholders' investment has changed.

Shareholder approval not required: The corporation owns five fertilizer plants; two are sold and the proceeds are used to repair and remodel the remaining three.

Shareholder approval required: Two of the five fertilizer plants are sold, and the proceeds are used to invest in facilities and technology for the manufacture of ice cream.

Cautious and prudent business practice dictates that the approval of the shareholders be obtained in any doubtful or borderline case.

As with consolidations and mergers, most states require that two thirds of the shares outstanding and eligible to vote approve the sale of all, or substantially all, of the assets of a corporation.

SHAREHOLDER MEETINGS

The functions described in the preceding section are carried out by the shareholders at their meetings.

• *NOTICE OF MEETINGS*

Notice of both the annual meeting and of special meetings must be given to shareholders of record, that is, shareholders whose names appear on the share transfer books of the corporation at the time of notice. The notice must state the purpose of the meeting, such as amendment of the charter, sale of all or substantially all of the assets, or other extraordinary matter.

> Failure to give notice, or giving a defective notice, will *void* any shareholder action unless the shareholder waives his/her objection by attending the meeting without objection, or by signing a written waiver.

• *CONDUCT OF THE MEETING*

A **quorum** (usually defined by state law as a majority of shares outstanding) must be present in person or by proxy. The president or chairman of the board usually presides, and minutes are kept by the secretary of the corporation. Many states, by statute, permit shareholder action without a meeting, provided that all (in some states, a majority) of the shareholders give their consent in writing to the action or actions taken.

• *VOTING*

Most matters are decided by a majority of the votes cast. If there is more than one class of stock (see Chapter 18) and approval of all classes is required, a majority of each class is necessary. In the election of directors, each share has one vote for each director. This mode of director election is usually referred to as straight voting. If, for example, 7 directors are to be elected, the holder of 100 shares may vote these 100 shares for each of 7 nominees.

CUMULATIVE VOTING

Cumulative voting is permitted by law, or by special provision in the corporate charter in most states. In the example just given, in cumulative voting the holder of 100 shares has a potential of 700 votes and may distribute them among 7 nominees as she chooses. If this shareholder "accumulates" her votes and casts all 700 in favor of a single nominee, this nominee may very well be elected when there are, for example, a total of 1000 shares present and voting.

> By cumulative voting, a minority shareholder may be assured of some representation on the board of directors and a voice (albeit a minority voice) in management.

PROXIES

A **proxy** is a limited power of attorney whereby a shareholder names an agent or a representative (a proxy) to vote his/her shares. Several shareholders may join forces, name a proxy, and control the corporation. A proxy may be revoked at any time, as is the case with powers of attorney in general (see Chapter 14).

VOTING TRUSTS

Most states permit shareholders to transfer their shares to a voting trustee for the limited purpose of electing directors and for voting on other matters to be decided by shareholders. Alternatively, shareholders may enter into a contract creating a voting agreement or stock-pooling agreement whereby they combine forces in order to gain a voice or exercise control. Such **voting trusts**, voting agreements, or stock-pooling arrangements are governed by the law of contracts unless state statute imposes a special restriction or limitation.

SHAREHOLDER RIGHTS

• *APPRAISAL RIGHTS (SOMETIMES CALLED "DISSENTERS' RIGHTS")*

If shareholders object to certain corporate actions that may diminish the value of their stock holdings, most states give these objectors (dissenters) the right to receive the fair value of their stock from the corporation. "Fair value" may have to be determined by appraisal if it is not otherwise ascertainable.

This right of dissenters is usually provided for following two kinds of majority action: (1) consolidation or merger of the corporation, and (2) sale or transfer of all or substantially all of the corporate assets in other than the usual course of business. In addition, appraisal rights may be provided for with regard to any charter amendment that adversely affects the value of the stock or the rights of shareholders.

The appraisal procedure varies from state to state. If the stock is traded on a recognized securities exchange, the fair value is readily ascertainable. Otherwise, statutes provide for a judicial determination, or for the appointment of an appraiser by the corporation and by the dissenter, respectively, and for the two appraisers to name another one if they cannot agree.

The dissenting shareholder must follow a strict procedure in order to avail him-/herself of the appraisal right: the shareholder must file a written objection to the proposed action, must vote against the proposal (or, in some states, abstain from voting), and must make a written demand for appraisal and buy-out within some specified time.

• *RIGHT TO SHARE IN DIVIDENDS*

The decision to pay dividends is within the business judgment of the board of directors. In the absence of an agreement to the contrary, however, holders of a particular class of stock have the right to share in a dividend on a parity with other holders of the same class.

• *RIGHT TO APPROVE GIFTS; OTHER MATTERS*

Since the assets of the corporation belong to the shareholders, these assets cannot be given away or transferred to others without shareholder approval.

Most states statutes have special procedures for shareholder approval of eleemosynary gifts from profits approved by the board. Furthermore, bonuses, stock option plans, and incentive plans not tied into contract payments for specific work performed may require shareholder approval since such payments may be judicially construed as gifts.

Conflict of interest questions involving members of the board of directors may be resolved by the shareholders. Indemnification of directors and officers, as well as all other matters pertaining to benefits and potential benefits to the corporate managers, may be subject to stockholder approval.

Prudent corporate management favors obtaining shareholder approval for major, fundamental decisions vitally affecting the corporation.

• *RIGHT OF INSPECTION*

Statutes in practically all states permit shareholders to inspect corporate books and records. However, this right of inspection may be limited with respect to the nature of the records sought, depending on the number (or percentage) of shares making the request and, in some states, the purpose of the request.

As a general rule, any shareholder (even one with a single share out of 100,000 shares outstanding) may inspect and copy the annual reports to shareholders, minutes of the shareholders' meetings, the bylaws, the charter, and the list of shareholders, together with their names and addresses. In addition, some percentage, frequently the holders of 5% or 10% of the outstanding stock (along with or through their attorneys and accountants), may inspect and copy all books and records, including books of account.

Whether the broad right of inspection accorded the holders of some specified percentage of stock will be permitted without showing good cause varies from state to state. Some courts, arguing that the corporate property belongs to the shareholders, and that the state does not closely police the corporate business, permit unlimited inspection unless the corporation can demonstrate an improper motive, such as proof that these shareholders are "fronting" for a competitor or seeking to discover trade secrets. *Other states take a contrary view: unless a proper purpose or motive is shown by the shareholders, inspection is not permitted.*

• *PREEMPTIVE RIGHTS*

Existing shareholders may have the right to preempt, or come ahead of, other purchasers of stock of the same class in order to protect their percentage interest in, or control of, the corporation. Thus, if 100 shares of common stock are outstanding, the owner of 20 of these shares has a one-fifth interest in the corporation. If the corporation were to sell 100 additional shares to a new party or to the other four-fifth owners, the ownership of 20 shares would be diluted to a one-tenth interest. However, with a right to preempt, the owner would have the ability to maintain his one-fifth interest (by purchasing 20 of the additional 100 shares).

In most states, in the absence of a charter provision granting preemptive rights, shareholders do not have these rights.

Even when such rights are granted, they do not attach to treasury stock (stock previously issued, but not outstanding) or to shares issued for a merger or consolidation or in noncash transactions.

SHAREHOLDERS' LAWSUITS

• *DERIVATIVE SUITS*

Derivative suits are suits brought by one or more shareholders on behalf of the corporation and for its benefit. Since these suits are not for the benefit of the suing party, any recovery belongs to the corporation, and in such event the corporation must pay the stockholder's reasonable attorney's fees. A shareholder who loses the suit, on the other hand, may be required to reimburse the defendant for his/her expenses, including attorney's fees.

Derivative suits are usually brought against individual officers or directors for waste or conflict of interest. There are certain strict requirements for such a suit. The shareholder must first demand that the directors bring the suit (demand may be excused if the shareholder can show that it would have been futile), and that demand must be refused. Some states and the Federal Rules of Civil Procedure also require that the shareholder notify other shareholders of his/her intent to bring a derivative suit in order to give them an opportunity to ratify or confirm the alleged wrongful action.

• *INDIVIDUAL SUITS*

A shareholder may sue the corporation individually to protect his/her personal rights or property in the corporation. Such a suit may seek to enjoin an *ultra vires* act or to protect the right to inspect the books of the corporation.

SHAREHOLDERS' LIABILITIES

Basically, the only loss that a shareholder may sustain is his/her investment in the corporation's stock. This limitation on liability for stock ownership is one of the primary reasons for the existence of the corporate form. As Chapter 16 pointed out, however, if the shareholders themselves disregard the corporate entity, and use the corporate form for fraudulent purposes, the "corporate veil" may be pierced and the shareholders may be personally responsible for corporate obligations.

YOU SHOULD REMEMBER

Although shareholders own the corporation, their ownership does not give them the right of direct management, a function of the board of directors. Shareholders have the right to elect directors, control major charter amendments, and approve mergers, consolidations, and the sale of all or substantially all of the corporate assets.

Shareholder functions are exercised chiefly at meetings of shareholders, either general or specially called pursuant to proper notice. A quorum of shareholders must be present, in person or by proxy. In the election of directors, straight voting is generally required, although state law or the charter may permit cumulative voting.

In addition to the right to attend meetings and to vote on directors and other corporate business, shareholders have other rights: appraisal rights if they dissent from corporate acts that may affect the value of their stock; right to share in dividends, to approve corporate gifts, and to inspect and copy the corporate books; and, if permitted by the charter, preemptive rights.

Shareholders may bring legal action against the corporation by derivative suits (suits for the corporate benefit and on its behalf) or by direct suit.

BOARD OF DIRECTORS

TERM

Directors are elected to hold office until the next shareholders' meeting at which directors are elected or until their successors are elected and qualify.

The MBCA and RMBCA provide that one or more directors can be removed by the shareholders "with or without cause" unless the charter permits removal only for cause. The common law (case law) and some statute law different from the Model Acts permit removal only for cause. "Cause" includes conflicts of interest or other violations of fiduciary functions, violation of the charter or bylaws, or legal actions.

FIDUCIARY FUNCTION

The board of directors is chosen by the shareholders to manage the corporation.

In this management function the directors are neither employees nor agents of the shareholders; rather, they occupy a position of trust to the shareholders. This trust relation is legally described as that of a **fiduciary**—a position of loyalty to the corporate interest and well being, superior to the director's self-interest or desire for personal gain.

In general, this fiduciary relationship applies to the officers, as well as the directors, of the corporation.

Four important aspects of the fiduciary relationship are as follows:

1. *Duty of loyalty.* This fiduciary function requires an uncompromising duty of loyalty by the directors and officers to the corporation and to its shareholders. Above all, the corporate manager must make full disclosure of any personal interest in a matter involving the corporation or its business and in any doubtful case should refrain from voting upon, or taking any action regarding, any such matter. Corporate loans, bonuses, and gifts to directors and officers are *prima facie* colored by a conflict of interest and should have prior shareholder approval.

2. *No usurpation of corporate opportunity.* Directors or officers violate their fiduciary duty if they personally avail themselves of a business opportunity that should have been reserved for the corporation.

Example: Corporate Opportunity

A director or officer of a corporation owning and operating mineral lands cannot purchase other, similar lands for his/her own private purposes without first giving the corporation the opportunity to make the purchase, or without first making a full disclosure of the private objective.

3. *No personal use of corporate assets.* Obviously, a director or officer cannot use corporate property or personnel to conduct personal business or to achieve his/her own ends. Moreover, directors and officers cannot divulge company secrets or technology without breach of their fiduciary obligations.

4. *Restrictions on transactions in shares.* Directors and officers cannot deal in corporate stock if they receive such stock at an unfair price or on advantageous terms. Moreover, federal statutes require certain disclosures of insider transactions affecting stock values or transpiring in interstate commerce.

BUSINESS JUDGMENT RULE

> Both directors and officers of the corporation must govern its affairs with reasonably good judgment.

The phrase "reasonably good judgment" is somewhat difficult to define, but is intended to describe a standard of care lower than that applicable to a sharp, well-trained, prudent businessperson but higher than that of a casual, disinterested outsider. Three standards are generally applied to director or officer actions to determine compliance with the **business judgment rule**:

1. Exercise of due care.

2. Action in good faith.

3. Reasonable belief that the action is in the corporate interest.

A court is understandably reluctant to substitute its wisdom or judgment for that of a director—after all, directors are chosen by the shareholders, and they are familiar with the business and with the overall corporate objectives. However, a court may be compelled to substitute its judgment for that of a director who, in effect, forfeits responsibility by breach of his/her fiduciary or loyalty duties.

NUMBER AND QUALIFICATIONS OF DIRECTORS

> Generally, the bylaws determine the number and qualifications of directors.

The number can reasonably be any number, but for obvious reasons should be an odd number. The board should be of such size as to function well as a committee, although many large corporations, banks, and other widely held corporate entities may have boards of 25 members or more.

In most states, any person who can make a simple contract can be a director. A director is generally not required to own stock.

COMPENSATION OF DIRECTORS

At the common law, directors did not receive compensation for their services, although they were reimbursed for their expenses. Today most state statutes permit directors to set their own reasonable compensation; extraordinary compensation must be approved by the shareholders.

MEETINGS OF THE BOARD

Since a director is a fiduciary, he/she can act only in person. In other words, a director cannot delegate his/her duties or attend board meetings by proxy.

A director can act only as a member of the board, not individually. Meetings are held at the times and places designated in the bylaws or at special times and places as indicated in the notices of meetings. *It is important that a director attend director meetings, that minutes be kept of such meetings, and that the director's vote be recorded.* Failure to attend meetings or to use business judgment are acts of negligence that may create personal liability to shareholders who sustain loss as a result of such negligence.

The bylaws usually establish the number of directors required for the transaction of business. A majority of the members is ordinarily designated as a quorum.

Most state statutes permit action without a meeting or upon telephone or other oral approval, provided that all of the directors consent in writing to the action.

COMMITTEES

Although board members cannot delegate their responsibilities and duties, committees of board members may be designated to perform a number of board-type activities under the general supervision of the whole board. The executive committee, the finance committee, the audit committee, and the like may meet on a daily or weekly basis to attend to management affairs on a more intimate basis. Such committees keep agendas and minutes of business transacted for the information and ratification of the entire board where appropriate or necessary.

DECISIONS REGARDING EARNINGS

The decision to declare dividends, or to invest and reinvest profits, or to expand the plant or otherwise dispose of earnings and profits are matters for the board of directors, acting within the business judgment rule. In the absence of proof of negligence or bad faith, all such decisions are immune from shareholder attack.

YOU SHOULD REMEMBER

Directors are chosen by the shareholders to manage the corporation. They occupy a fiduciary (trust) relationship to the shareholders. This trust relationship requires an uncompromising duty of loyalty to the corporation, no usurpation of corporate opportunity, no personal use of corporate assets, no unfair dealing in the corporation's stock, and the exercise of reasonably good judgment in managing corporate affairs.

The bylaws generally provide for the number and qualifications of directors. Most state statutes permit the directors to provide reasonable compensation for themselves. Directors must personally attend board meetings; they cannot attend by proxy.

Committees of board members may be appointed to supervise day-by-day functions, but these committees must report to the full board.

Declaration of dividends is subject to the discretion of the board, acting within the business judgment rule.

OFFICERS

The officers are named and hired by the board of directors. Designation of the various offices and the duties of each office are set forth in the bylaws. As a rule, the officers are the president, one or more vice presidents, the secretary, and the treasurer.

PRESIDENT

The president is the chief executive officer (CEO) of the corporation. He may be a member of the board of directors and preside at meetings of the board and of the shareholders. Frequently, all or some of these functions are performed by a chairman of the board, as the bylaws determine.

VICE PRESIDENT

The vice president usually fills the office of president in the absence of the latter. In most corporations, vice presidents are given responsibility for various line activities—manufacturing, sales, administration, and the like. Sometimes executive or senior vice presidents are designated to supervise one or more vice presidents in order to relieve undue burdens that may otherwise fall on the president. Quite often, at least one vice president is a member of the board of directors.

SECRETARY

The secretary is in charge of the corporate books and records. As such, he/she is responsible for keeping the minutes, giving notices, and affixing the corporate seal. (The seal attests to (witnesses) the corporate validity of action and to the authority of the individual signing the document on behalf of the corporation.) Because of the need for knowledge of corporate functions and of director and officer responsibilities, many corporations, especially large ones, require that the secretary be an attorney. Other than responsibility for books and records, the secretary generally exercises no executive functions, such as executing contracts.

TREASURER

The treasurer is responsible for management of the corporation's funds. The treasurer can bind the corporation by his/her checks, indorsements, and disbursements, but performs no other executive functions.

OTHER EMPLOYEES

The corporation's other employees are hired by the officers and given such duties at such compensation as is within the authority of the officers. The bylaws may designate specific duties to one or more employees.

Note: The law of agency governs the authority of these corporate agents. Chapter 14 (Agency) should be reviewed with respect to the corporation's responsibility for contracts, torts, and crimes committed by its employees, either in its name or while acting in a representative capacity. Moreover, the general law of agency governs the personal liability of the agent for acts committed in furtherance of corporate business.

YOU SHOULD REMEMBER

The officers are named and hired by the board of directors. The officers and their duties are prescribed by the bylaws.

Officers usually include the president (chief executive officer), one or more vice presidents (generally with responsibility for line activities), a secretary (with responsibility for maintaining books and records), and a treasurer (with responsibility for management of corporate funds). The secretary and treasurer generally do not have other executive responsibilities.

TERMINATION OF THE CORPORATION

Although most corporations have perpetual existence, the law contemplates both nonjudicial and judicial **dissolution**.

> Corporate existence is terminated by dissolution followed by (a) winding up of its affairs, and (b) liquidation of its assets.

NONJUDICIAL DISSOLUTION

Shareholder approval is usually required for nonjudicial dissolution, although an act of the state legislature, as well as expiration of the period of existence stated in the charter (if a period is stated), will result in nonjudicial dissolution without shareholder action. Voluntary dissolution is achieved by (a) passage of a resolution by the board of directors and (b) approval of the directors' resolution by a majority of the shares entitled to be voted at a shareholders' meeting called for that purpose.

JUDICIAL DISSOLUTION

There are three methods of judicial dissolution:

1. The shareholders may petition for judicial dissolution upon their claim that the directors are hopelessly deadlocked, or that the shareholders themselves are deadlocked with regard to election of directors or to some other matter requiring shareholder approval, or that the directors are operating the corporation in an illegal or fraudulent manner.

2. Creditors may implement court action if (a) the corporation cannot pay its debts in the usual course of business *and* a creditor has obtained a judgment against the corporation that the corporation cannot satisfy, or (b) the corporation has stated in writing that it cannot pay the claim of a creditor.

3. The state itself may bring about judicial dissolution if the corporation fails to file its annual report with the secretary of state, fails to pay its annual franchise tax, abuses its corporate authority, or fails to maintain a registered agent in the state.

In the case of failure to file an annual report or pay the annual franchise tax, the secretary of state usually dissolves the corporation by *administrative action*. After giving the corporation notice and after the passage of a specified period of time (and generally publication of proposed dissolution), the secretary dissolves the corporation by signing a certificate of dissolution. *Many, if not most, small and insignificant corporations, and corporations merely created but allowed to languish without conducting any business, are dissolved by administrative action in this manner and without penalty.*

WINDING UP AND LIQUIDATION

After dissolution, the board of directors liquidates the assets of the corporation and distributes the proceeds, first to creditors, second to preferred shareholders (if any), and finally to common shareholders.

YOU SHOULD REMEMBER

Termination is achieved by dissolution, followed by winding up and liquidation.

Dissolution is effected judicially (by court action) or nonjudicially (voluntarily by shareholder action, expiration of charter period, or act of the the state legislature). Administrative dissolution occurs by action of the secretary of state following the corporation's failure to report and pay the annual franchise tax to the state.

KNOW THE CONCEPTS

DO YOU KNOW THE BASICS?

1. Can a majority shareholder, acting alone, dismiss an officer of the corporation?
2. Should a charitable donation be considered, in all cases, a corporate gift subject to the approval of shareholders?
3. Why are the directors of a corporation having assets of over $100 million not required to submit to their shareholders a proposed merger with a corporation having assets of less than $1 million?
4. What advice should be given to someone who strongly objects to the consolidation of a corporation in which he owns a stock interest with another corporation?
5. How can you determine the necessity of attending a special meeting of shareholders?
6. What is cumulative voting?
7. Why can a shareholder attend a shareholders' meeting by proxy, but a director must attend in person?
8. Can the president of a corporation conduct a telephone poll of the members of the board of directors and use the result of that poll as the basis of a board decision?
9. Do shareholders have the right to compel the board to declare a dividend?
10. Why should a vice president of a corporation also be a member of the board of directors?
11. What is one relatively effective and inexpensive way to cause a corporation to be dissolved?

TERMS FOR STUDY

attest	merger
business judgment rule	officer
committee	preemptive right
consolidation	president
cumulative voting	proxy
derivative suits	quorum
director	secretary
dissolution	shareholder
fiduciary	voting trust

PRACTICAL APPLICATION

1. You own about 1% of the outstanding stock of XY corporation. A number of shareholders believe that the management is paying a grossly exorbitant salary to Ms. X, secretary to the president of the company and believed to be his mistress. Ms. X and the president are known to take trips to Europe and other places on "corporate business" and at corporate expense. What course of action should be considered to protect your rights as a shareholder?

2. The vice president of corporation AB, a jewelry company, attends an auction at the direction of the corporation. She is directed to bid up to $100,000 for the Omega diamond. The bidding reaches $125,000, and the vice president then buys the diamond for her own account for $126,000. Is this action proper?

3. MM Corporation has received an order of the state department of health to cease the discharge of acid into the waters of the state. The board of directors has before it the proposal of a management team to spend over $50 million for capital equipment that will correct the effluent discharge. The company has operated at a loss for the past 2 years. Director Q and a majority of the board vote against the proposal. Later the corporation is fined $1 million for acid discharge, and shareholders ultimately bring a derivative suit against Q, claiming violation of the business judgment rule. What will be the result?

ANSWERS

KNOW THE CONCEPTS

1. A shareholder, even the owner of all of the outstanding stock, cannot directly dismiss an officer or other employee. The shareholder can only

elect a board of directors that will consider his/her wishes with regard to corporate management, including the hiring and firing of officers.

2. Charitable gifts are usually subject to state statutes and, if reasonable in amount and approved by the board of directors, do not require shareholder approval (see Chapter 16). A small or reasonable donation for a good cause may also be good business and inure to the benefit of the corporation and the shareholders. As such, it may be a proper business expense and not require submission to shareholders.

3. The purchase of such a disproportionately small business would not affect the nature of the business of the larger corporation or the value of its stock. Shareholder approval is, therefore, not necessary.

4. He must file a written objection to the proposed consolidation, attend the shareholders' meeting in person or by proxy, vote "no," and promptly demand a "buy-out" of his shares. If the stock is traded on a national exchange, the value will have been set by the board of directors as of some previously specified date. If the stock is not traded, the shareholder will proceed to have "fair value" determined by the appraisal routine.

5. You are entitled to a notice of the meeting, which will set out its purpose and other matters to be voted upon.

6. Cumulative voting is the right to concentrate all of your voting rights on fewer than all of the directors being elected. Thus, if you own 10,000 shares and 5 directors are being elected, you have 50,000 votes, all of which may be voted for 1 or 2 directors.

7. A director is in a fiduciary relationship to the shareholders and cannot delegate his/her duties to a proxy or agent. Failure of the director to attend to his/her duties in person may give rise to a charge of neglect. Shareholders are exercising a right when they attend shareholder meetings and vote their shares; rights, unlike fiduciary duties, may be assigned to others by proxy.

8. In most states, telephone action of the board is permissible if all of the directors consent in writing to the action. This consent should be given promptly and affixed to the corporate resolution pursuant to which the action is taken.

9. Declaration of a dividend is usually regarded as a question for the board, not the shareholders. Of course, the decision is subject to the business judgment rule.

10. Generally, a vice president should be a member of the board so that he can preside over board meetings in the absence of the president.

11. If the corporation fails to file an annual report with the state, or fails to pay its annual franchise tax, the state may cause it to forfeit its charter by administrative action.

PRACTICAL APPLICATION

1. So far, you have only hearsay and suspicion as a basis for objection to improper payments and corporate expenditures for Ms. X. Assuming that your state permits shareholders freely to inspect the corporate books but that some minimum percentage of shares is required (e.g., 5%) in order to make demand, you should join with other shareholders in order to develop the requisite percentage.

   If inspection rights are obtained without litigation (filing a petition in court), you should inspect the corporate expense records, probably with an attorney or an accountant. If waste or impropriety is discovered, you may consider a derivative suit. This, of course, will be preceded by a demand on the directors to take action to stop the waste and to cause the president to account for the misappropriation of funds. State law should be checked to determine whether other shareholders must be notified of the wrongdoing and planned lawsuit.

2. The question is one of corporate opportunity. Has the vice president seized for herself an opportunity belonging to the corporation? Probably not; she had no authority to exceed $100,000. To have purchased the stone for a price in excess of that amount for the corporation would have violated the terms of her employment. She was impliedly authorized, therefore, to act for her own account and for her own opportunity.

3. The shareholders would probably lose their suit against Q. If he acted in the reasonable belief that his negative vote was in the corporate interest, if he acted in good faith, and exercised due care, he acted properly. We are not told of his other options; we do not know what other competent advice he may have received. We do not know the history of the violations or the reasonableness of the corporation's course of action.

18

CORPORATIONS: FINANCIAL STRUCTURE; SECURITIES REGULATION; LIABILITY OF ACCOUNTANTS

KEY TERMS

share (of stock) a proportionate ownership interest in a corporation or in its equity

stock a term used synonymously with "share"; also, the physical evidence of share ownership, the share certificate; also, the aggregate of corporate shares

dividend a distribution of cash or stock to the shareholders

blue sky laws state laws regulating the intrastate issuance and sale of securities

Up to this point we have thought of shareholders as the ultimate source of power in the corporate structure. In this chapter we consider their role as investors. Also, we distinguish and define the various sources of corporate financing and investigate the issuance, trading, and regulation of corporate securities.

CORPORATE FINANCIAL STRUCTURE

SOURCES OF CORPORATE FUNDS

> Funds to operate the corporation are derived in three principal ways:
> **1.** By the issuance or sale of corporate debt securities (debt).
> **2.** By the issuance of equity securities (equity).
> **3.** Through retained earnings.

• *CORPORATE DEBT SECURITIES*

The corporation may raise money by borrowing. Unless there is a special limitation or other provision in the charter, the decision to borrow is a matter for the board of directors and does not require shareholder approval. When the corporation borrows, it becomes a debtor; the holder of the security that it issues as evidence of this debt is a creditor.

Short-term borrowing is generally accomplished by the issuance of promissory notes or other commercial paper subject to the general principles of negotiable instruments law. **Debt securities** are of two main types: notes and bonds.

NOTES

The corporation's **notes** are promissory notes subject to the Uniform Commercial Code (see Chapters 11 and 12). These notes may be secured or unsecured.

BONDS

Bonds are written promises to pay a fixed sum of money at a set maturity date, with specified interest paid, at stated intervals. Bonds may be secured by real or personal property. Bonds may be **debentures**, which are *unsecured*. If the corporation can redeem (pay off) the bond early, it is a **callable bond;** and a **convertible bond** may be converted by its holder (at such time as he/she believes most favorable) into other securities of the corporation, such as preferred or common stock.

An indenture is a contract stating the terms under which debt securities are issued. For secured bonds, the indenture may describe, along with other contract provisions, the collateral and conditions of default. For debentures, the indenture may restrict other corporate borrowing or declaration of dividends, and place various other limitations on management in order to protect the debenture holder.

• *EQUITY SECURITIES*

Funds to operate the corporation may be generated by the sale of shares of stock, that is, **equity securities**. *The equity in the corporate enterprise, that is, the residual value of the assets after the payment of all debts following dissolution, belongs to the shareholders.*

Equity financing may open up participation in corporate ownership (and, indirectly, management) to additional investors. Sound corporate structure attempts to maintain a fair balance between debt and equity.

There are two classes of equity stock: common shares and preferred shares.

COMMON SHARES

In Chapters 16 and 17 all references to "shareholders" were to common shareholders (or stockholders). Holders of **common shares** participate in management control; however, these owners of the corporation are in for the "ride"—losses or gains in the value of their holdings follow the vicissitudes of the corporate enterprise. Common shareholders have a threefold interest in the corporation: (a) to vote for directors and on other fundamental matters (b) to participate in the distribution of dividends, and (c) to share in the distribution of net assets (equity) after dissolution and liquidation.

PREFERRED SHARES

Preferred stock may be cumulative or noncumulative, participating or nonparticipating.

Advantages of Owning Preferred Shares

Preferred shareholders are "preferred" to common shareholders in two respects:

1. *In the distribution of dividends.* If the directors determine that a dividend is to be paid, holders of **preferred shares** may receive a specific percentage share of the dividend before the common stockholders are paid.

If the preferred stock is **noncumulative**, the preferred shareholders lose their dividend rights for years in which no dividend is declared; if the preferred stock is **cumulative**, unpaid dividends accumulate for years of nonpayment, and these accumulated dividends, plus current ones, are paid before common shareholders receive any dividend. Moreover, not only does **participating preferred stock** receive preference when dividends are declared, but also holders of these shares may "double dip," that is, share also in the dividend to common stock on a pro-rata basis. Holders of **nonparticipating preferred stock** do not share in the distribution of surpluses.

2. *In distribution upon liquidation.* The preferred shareholders may also be owners of part of the equity; upon dissolution and liquidation, after the payment

of debt, they may receive the first distribution of the net assets, before payment to the common stockholders, provided that such precedence is expressed in the articles of incorporation. Otherwise, the preferred shareholders participate pro rata with the holders of common stock upon liquidation.

Other Aspects of Preferred Shares

1. *Redemption.* The corporation may be given the right to purchase (redeem) preferred shares, even over the objection of their owners. The right of redemption by the corporation, as well as the price to be paid (the **call price**), is set out on the share certificate. The articles of incorporation provide for the right of redemption, if such right exists.

2. *Conversion.* If the articles of incorporation so provide, the corporation may, at its option and under the terms stated, convert preferred stock into common stock or convert from one class of preferred to another.

3. *Voting rights.* Generally, preferred shareholders have no voting rights. However, the articles of incorporation may give them such rights or may permit them to vote for directors in the event that the corporation fails to pay dividends.

CLASSIFICATION OF SHARES

- Authorized **shares**   shares issued in accordance with the number of shares that the articles of incorporation permit the corporation to issue.

- Issued shares   authorized shares that have actually been sold to shareholders.

All authorized shares may or may not be issued.

- Outstanding shares   the same as "issued stock," except that some shares may have been repurchased by the corporation after issuance. Such repurchased stock ceases to be "outstanding."

- Treasury shares   shares repurchased by the corporation.

- Canceled shares   shares that have been repurchased by the corporation and canceled. Such shares then cease to exist.

STOCK OPTIONS

Stock options grant their holders the right to purchase stock, at such time and price as are specified in the option. Stock options may be granted to employees, directors, and officers as incentive payments, and to purchasers of other classes of securities as an added inducement to buy.

• *RETAINED EARNINGS*

Retained earnings are earnings and profits not distributed to shareholders as dividends, but held back to be invested or "plowed back" into the corporate enterprise.

YOU SHOULD REMEMBER

There are three sources of corporate funds: debt, equity, and retained earnings. Debt securities consist of notes, bonds, and debentures. Notes are short-term promissory notes. Bonds are *secured* long-term securities; debentures are *unsecured* long-term securities.

Equity securities consist of common and preferred shares. Common shareholders participate in the election of directors and in other fundamental matters; preferred shareholders may be preferred over common shareholders in regard to dividends and to distribution upon liquidation. Preferred stock may be subject to redemption and conversion into other securities.

DIVIDENDS AND DISTRIBUTIONS

The expectation of a dividend or distribution is one basic reason for an investor to purchase the shares of a corporation.

A distribution of *cash* or *stock* is usually referred to as a **dividend**; distribution of *corporate assets*, while also a dividend, is generally referred to as a **distribution**. (Stock or shares of stock are not corporate assets.)

• *DECISION TO DECLARE A DIVIDEND*

The decision to declare a dividend or distribution is within the business judgment of the board of directors. This decision may not be "second guessed" by shareholders in the absence of director abuse or a wrong motive, such as deliberate withholding of accumulated cash without good business reasons. Once a dividend is declared by a proper resolution of the board, it is a legal debt of the corporation and is enforceable in a court of law.

• *FORM OF DIVIDEND*

The dividend may take the form of cash, other property or assets, or shares of stock. Real estate, merchandise, or other tangibles may be distributed to the shareholders. A **stock split** is not a stock dividend, but merely an across-the-board substitution of additional shares for shares already held. It does not alter the total value of an individual stockholder's investment.

• *RESTRICTIONS ON DIVIDENDS*

If a corporation has borrowed large sums of money, creditors may have restricted (by means of "loan agreements") its ability to declare dividends, particularly without the prior approval of the creditors. Moreover, all states prohibit the payment of a dividend or other distribution if such payment would render the corporation insolvent, that is, unable to pay its debts as they become due in the ordinary course of business. Further statutory restrictions vary among the states; most states require that dividends be paid from earned surplus. A few states (including Delaware) permit the payment of **nimble dividends**, that is, payment from current earnings even though there are debts outstanding from prior years.

• *EFFECT OF ILLEGAL DIVIDEND OR DISTRIBUTION*

Directors who vote in favor of an illegal dividend are jointly and severally liable for the illegal portion of the dividend, that is, the amount by which the dividend exceeds the legally permissible limit. ("Joint and several" means that each director is fully responsible, but a director who pays is entitled to contributions from the others.) Directors who rely in good faith upon the financial data and statements of accountants and financial officers of the company are not liable. Only shareholders who know, or ought to know, that the dividend is illegal can be made to return it.

CONSIDERATION FOR SHARES

• *PRESENT VERSUS FUTURE CONSIDERATION*

Stock may be paid for in cash, by check, with tangible or intangible property, or by services *previously* rendered. The value to be placed on noncash items (property or services) is usually considered to be a matter for the good-faith judgment of the members of the board fixing the value, although some states consider this value to be a question of fact to be determined by a jury in the event of litigation.

In most states, contracts for future services or benefits or for promissory notes (including postdated checks) are not good consideration for shares. The trend, though, may be to permit such "future consideration"; MBCA amendments (1979) and the RMBCA both allow it.

• *PAR AND NO-PAR SHARES*

A *par share has a specific dollar amount indicated on the share certificate.* The par value can be any amount chosen by the board (or by the incorporators), and may or may not reflect the actual value, but the par value must be set out in the articles of incorporation.

> The corporation must receive, as a minimum, the par-value price for each share it sells.

No-par shares are issued for any amount that the board assigns to such shares, arbitrarily or otherwise. Consideration received for shares in excess of the par value is **capital surplus**. With respect to no-par shares, the directors may arbitrarily assign a designated portion of the consideration for such shares to capital surplus, that is, surplus that may be used in the calculation of dividends. The excess of consideration over par value, or the designated portion of the consideration assigned to capital surplus in the case of no-par value, is an important factor in determining the lawfulness of a dividend.

• *TREASURY SHARES*

Treasury shares (shares issued and then repurchased by the corporation) may be reissued for an amount equal to their fair value even though this amount may be less than the par or stated value.

• *DISCOUNT SHARES*

"Discount shares" are shares issued for less than par value or stated value.

> A shareholder who purchases shares at discount from the corporation is liable to the corporation for the amount of the discount.

A shareholder buying discounted shares from another shareholder is liable for the amount of the discount only if he/she knew that the shares had been originally purchased at discount.

SHARE SUBSCRIPTIONS

A **subscription** is a promise to buy shares at a specified price. Although such a promise may be made after the corporation has been formed and is a going concern, most of the legal problems associated with subscriptions involve preincorporation subscriptions.

> Since the promoters require assurance that sufficient equity capital will be raised to support the corporate venture, it is important that subscribers be bound to their promises to purchase stock that the corporation (not yet formed) will issue.

Section 6.20 of the RMBCA deals fully with share subscriptions and should be consulted as authoritative even though its provisions may not have been adopted in a specific state. *This section provides that, if the corporation is yet to be organized, a subscription is irrevocable for a period of 6 months unless the subscription agreement provides otherwise or unless all subscribers consent to revocation.* The section also provides that, unless the subscription agreement specifies otherwise, the price shall be paid in full at the time of the agreement or in installments at times determined by the board of directors.

Under the MBCA, RMBCA, and the other corporate law of most states, preincorporation subscription may result in a binding contract if all conditions for a contract are present. This contract may be enforced by promoters and creditors relying on it. This may be true even though the corporation is not yet formed, since the *promoters and their creditors* may legally enter into agreements looking toward the formation of the corporate enterprise and the creation of its underlying capital. Preincorporation share subscribers should expect that persons extending credit to the venture may seek redress from subscribers if obligations are not paid by the promoters.

ISSUANCE OF SHARES

A **share** in a corporation is a fractional interest in the ownership of the corporate entity.

The share interest may be physically represented by a share certificate (a stock certificate), or it may be uncertificated under general state corporate law or under the provisions of the MBCA.

In the modern electronic, computerized world documentary transfer is not always practicable. Article 8 of the Uniform Commercial Code, dealing with investment securities, specifically recognizes that such securities may be uncertificated but states that the share or participation must be "registered upon books maintained for that purpose by or on behalf of the issuer" (Section 8-102).

The issuer of a certificated security (which, of course, includes stock or share certificates) must maintain, or cause to be maintained, books of registration of share ownership.

Section 8-207 of the Uniform Commercial Code provides that the issuer may treat the registered owner as the person "exclusively entitled to vote, to receive notifications, and otherwise to exercise all rights and powers of an owner." Section 8-405 permits the owner of a lost, destroyed, or stolen certificate to obtain a new certificate provided that he/she notifies the issuer within "a reasonable time."

TRANSFER OF SECURITIES

Article 8 of the UCC also governs the transfer and registration of investment securities. Share certificates, bonds, debentures, and corporate notes are covered by its provisions. Article 8 provides that, even though a certified security (certificate) meets the requirements of Article 3 (Negotiable Instruments), a security is nevertheless governed by the provisions of Article 8.

Securities certificates are either in registered form (registered with the issuer, usually the corporation, in a specific name) or in blank (payable to the holder). A registered certificate is transferred by delivery plus indorsement or by delivery plus the execution of a stock power (or assignment).

If a share certificate is transferred without designating a transferee by name, the certificate is a **street certificate** and may be further transferred by delivery only, without indorsement.

The free transfer of a certificate may, however, be restricted. Restrictions may be intended to maintain voting controls, to preserve an S corporation or a close corporation, or to maintain exemption from federal or state securities laws requiring registration for *public* offerings. Restrictions on transfer are accomplished by a number of legal devices. Section 8-204 of the UCC requires that the restriction be noted conspicuously on the certificate or—for uncertificated securities—in the initial transaction statement, unless the transferee has actual knowledge of the restriction.

YOU SHOULD REMEMBER

The decision to declare a dividend is within the business judgment of the board of directors. The dividend may take the form of cash or of other property or assets.

A dividend cannot be paid if the corporation is insolvent or if the payment would make the corporation insolvent. Most states require that the dividend be paid from earned surplus.

In most states, shares must be paid for in cash or other valuable present consideration, or by services previously rendered. If the shares have a par value, that value establishes a minimum price. No-par shares are issued for an amount established by the board of directors. Shares may not be sold at a discount; otherwise, the purchaser may be liable for the discount.

Share subscriptions obligate the subscriber to purchase the stock at the time of the subscription agreement or in installments as determined by the board. Promoters and creditors who rely on the subscription agreement may enforce its terms.

Share interest may be shown by a share certificate, or the share may be uncertified. Names of both certified and uncertified owners of securities are registered in books maintained by the issuer, and these persons are treated as the owners for all legal purposes.

Free transfer of securities may be restricted, but the restriction must be noted on the share certificates.

SECURITIES REGULATION

Statutory regulation of securities operates within three broad categories (although there are other important but more specifically directed statutes):

1. The Securities Act of 1933.

2. The Securities Exchange Act of 1934.

3. Securities regulation within the various states.

THE SECURITIES ACT OF 1933

The Securities Act of 1933, a federal "consumer protection law" for investors, requires that the public be given complete and full disclosure about *new securities* being offered for sale. This act is administered by the Securities and Exchange Commission (SEC), established in 1934.

Congressional investigation during the early 1930s into the stock market crash led to passage of the Securities Act of 1933. The goal of this act is twofold: (1) to assure the investor of the opportunity to make informed decisions, and (2) to protect honest enterprises seeking capital through public investment.

• *DEFINITION OF "SECURITY"*

The Securities Act defines "security" not only as a note, stock, bond, debenture, or evidence of indebtedness, but also as an "investment contract," or a "fractional undivided interest in oil, gas, or other mineral rights, or, in general, any interest or instrument commonly know as a 'security'." This broad statutory reach is designed to prevent circumvention of the law by the *form* of the document; rules of contract and statutory construction such as *ejusdem generis* ("of the same kind or class") or *noscitur a sociis* (words are explained "by their company with other words") require that general words and phrases be construed in their broad generality within the scope of Congressional goals and purposes. Statutes enacted to remedy widespread abuses or alleviate large societal concerns are liberally construed to achieve their legislative objectives.

In the 1946 case of *Securities and Exchange Commission v. W. J. Howey Co.*, 328 U.S. 293, the Supreme Court laid down three requirements to bring an "investment contract" within the definition of "security": (1) an investment of money (2) a common enterprise, and (3) the expectation of profits solely from the efforts of a promoter or third party. In the *Howey* case, contracts offering investors acreage in orange groves to be cultivated and marketed by others were held to be "investment contracts" and consequently "securities" within reach of the 1933 act.

However, the Securities Act has been held not to apply to warranty deeds to real property, to an interest in a joint venture to sell real estate, or to distributorship agreements or franchise agreements (unless the distributor or franchisee has no obligation and merely reaps profits).

Although the reach of the 1933 act must be fully understood, most of the cases, both at the Securities and Exchange Commission (SEC) level and in the courts, pertain to stocks, bonds, debentures, and traditional securities.

• *SECURITIES EXEMPT BY STATUTE*

Section 3(a) of the Securities Act exempts a number of securities (although administrative agencies other than the SEC impose regulation in some cases):

1. Any security issued or guaranteed by the United States, by any state, by any political subdivision of any state, or by a public instrumentality of any state. Municipal bonds and industrial revenue bonds, as well as "authority" bonds and securities are excluded under this exemption.

2. Short-term commercial paper, that is, paper having a maturity date at time of issue not exceeding 9 months.

3. Securities issued by an organization operated exclusively for religious, educational, benevolent, fraternal, charitable, or reformatory purposes, and not for profit.

4. Securities of domestic banks, savings and loan associations, building and loan associations, cooperative banks, and the like.

5. Securities whose issuance is regulated by the Interstate Commerce Commission.

6. Securities issued by a receiver or trustee in bankruptcy.

7. Any insurance or endowment policy or annuity contract issued by a regulated insurance company.

8. Securities issued for conversion or exchange with existing shares of a security holder where no commission or other remuneration is paid or given, directly or indirectly.

9. Securities issued for local (intrastate) investment only. This exemption applies to issues for the local financing of local industry or business. To qualify, the offering must be made solely to investors in a single state by a resident doing business within the state. In-state purchasers cannot buy for the purpose of reselling to persons outside the state; however, delivery to a resident temporarily out of the state is not an interstate sale. SEC Rule 147 requires that the security not be sold out of the state for at least 9 months. One sale or offer to sell to a nonresident (even a friend or relative) will vitiate the exemption status.

• *REGISTRATION OF SECURITIES*

Registration is the heart of the 1933 Act.

THE TWO ASPECTS OF REGISTRATION

Registration Statement

The registration statement, filed with the SEC, *contains all relevant information* about the securities to be offered, the issuer and the business involved, and plans for use of the dollar proceeds of the issuance. The registration statement makes the party executing it (chief executive officer, financial officer, board of directors) liable for errors in the statement, which becomes effective on the 20th day after its filing with the SEC, although this date may be advanced by the SEC. Substantive amendments may require a recommencement of the 20-day period.

Statutory Prospectus

The statutory prospectus for potential investors is derived from the registration statement. It is a comprehensive and detailed booklet concerning the security, its issuers, the use of monies to be generated, the terms of reimbursement to the investors if minimum financing (as defined) is not obtained, the prospects of success of the venture, financial statements, and other matters, including special items that may be required by the SEC and as provided for in SEC Regulation C.

> The prospectus is an informing, not a promoting, document, and is intended to enable the prospective purchaser fully to evaluate the prospects, both good and bad, of the proposed venture.

The booklet must state the following on its outside cover in boldface roman type:

"THESE SECURITIES HAVE NOT BEEN APPROVED OR DISAPPROVED BY THE SECURITIES AND EXCHANGE COMMISSION, NOR HAS THE COMMISSION PASSED UPON THE ACCURACY OR ADEQUACY OF THIS PROSPECTUS. ANY REPRESENTATION TO THE CONTRARY IS A CRIMINAL OFFENSE."

COMMUNICATION WITH INVESTORS

Before the filing date there should be no communication with the public or potential investors concerning the planned offering, although Rule 135 of the SEC permits the publication of a limited informational notice of anticipation of the issue and prospectus (**tombstone advertisement**). After the filing date, but before the effective date (i.e., during the waiting period), the securities may be offered orally (in person or by telephone) but not sold.

A *preliminary prospectus*, tentatively reviewed by the SEC, must accompany any *written* offer. This preliminary prospectus is known as a **red herring prospectus** because of a mandatory red-ink warning on its cover that the registration is incomplete and that the securities are not yet available for sale. Even though the SEC may finally allow the prospectus, such allowance is not a "blessing," and the issuer is responsible for the fullness and accuracy of the document.

> After the effective date, the securities, accompanied by the final prospectus, may be freely offered to investors.

• EXEMPTED TRANSACTIONS

Section 4 of the Securities Act exempts transactions (a) by any person other than an issuer or underwriter (or persons acting under the control of an issuer or underwriter) and (b) transactions by an issuer that are not public offerings (private offerings).

BROKERS AND DEALERS

The Securities Act is intended to cover the issuance and original distribution of securities.

> The Act does not cover *trading transactions* or transactions involving persons other than issuers and underwriters (persons dealing with the issuer as part of the plan of original distribution).

Brokers' and dealers' transactions are exempt to the extent that these transactions are not part of the plan of distribution.

PRIVATE OFFERINGS

In differentiating a public offering from a private offering, the SEC follows general guidelines permitting, as exemptions, offerings to no more than 25 persons, *provided that such a small offering is not a scheme to promote a wide distribution in circumvention of the Securities Act.* Also, the exemption pertains *to the number of offerees and not to the number of purchasers.* Thus a meeting with 40 persons to promote a small "private offering," of whom only 3 persons actually consummate a purchase, would constitute a violation of the 1933 act.

> The burden of proof is upon the issuer that *any* offering is not a public offering, no matter how few the offerees or how small the dollar amount of issue.

• *SECURITIES EXEMPTED BY THE SEC*

Section 3(b) of *the Securities Act provides that the Securities Exchange Com mission may prescribe exemptions applicable to issues of limited dollar amounts* Section 4 of the act provides, however, that there can be no advertising or public solicitation in connection with such a dollar-exempt transaction. Furthermore, the issuer must file "such notice with the Commission as the Commission shall prescribe."

The SEC has issued, among others, the following regulations under this section

REGULATION A (SMALL PUBLIC OFFERINGS)

This regulation permits a simplified and limited registration for public offerings of up to $1.5 million of securities in any 12-month period. The issuer must notify the SEC at least 10 days before the initial date of offering, furnishing general information concerning the issuer, the nature of the securities, the purpose of the issue, and a description of the arrangement (if any) to return investors' funds if the financial objectives are not met. The issuer must also distribute to potential investors an offering circular, containing essentially the same information as the notification to the SEC.

REGULATIONS B & C

Regulation B covers oil and gas securities. Regulation C deals with general registration requirements, registration by foreign governments and other rules

REGULATION D (PRIVATE SALES OFFERINGS)

This regulation is intended to simplify offerings to *informed, sophisticated investors* and to *accredited investors* such as banks, insurance companies, investment companies, and other persons clearly defined in the regulation. *Several SEC rules, requiring SEC notification of an offering, are issued under this regulation.*

Rule	Amount	Period	Resale	Offering
504	Up to $1 Million (no more than $500,000 of which can be without registration under a state's securities laws)	12 mo.	Restricted, unless in compliance with state blue sky law	No limit on number of purchasers, but offering may not be publicly promoted unless in compliance with state blue sky law requiring pre-sale delivery of disclosure documents.

Rule	Amount	Period	Resale	Offering
505	Up to $5 million	12 mo	Restricted	No limit on number of accredited purchasers; permits up to 35 additional nonaccredited purchasers, provided they receive an offering circular; no public promotion
506	Unlimited	No limit	Restricted	No limit as to accredited investors, and up to 35 non-accredited investors that the issuer reasonably believes have sufficient experience to evaluate the risks; no public promotion

• RESALE OF RESTRICTED SECURITIES

SEC Rule 144 allows the purchaser to resell restricted securities only after full beneficial ownership (free from debt) for 2 years, and provided that information about the issuer is publicly available and that the seller may thereafter sell only a limited amount of the securities in any 3-month period during the next year Rule 144A, adopted in 1990, provides further resale rights for sales to qualified institutional buyers (large-scale securities investors such as financial institutions, registered broker-dealers, and major corporations)

• CIVIL LIABILITY

Section 11 of the 1933 Security Act provides for civil liability for the following

1. The sale of an unregistered security required to have been registered

2. Sale of a registered security without delivery of a statutory prospectus

3. Offer of a sale before the filing (or approval) of a registration statement

4. Inclusion of a false statement in the registration statement

5. Omission of a material fact from the registration statement

In the event of an improper offer or sale (item 1, 2, or 3 above), the purchaser's remedy is recission of the transaction or damages The penalty for inadequate information or a false registration statement is damages. Damages may be assessed against the issuer, the chief executive officer, the chief financial officer, the chief accounting officer, the directors, the underwriter, and the experts (auditors or lawyers) who certified the statement or rendered an opinion with regard to its sufficiency. The *issuer* has no defense to a civil suit; other parties have the burden of proving exercise of reasonable due diligence with regard to failures and omissions in the registration.

• *CRIMINAL LIABILITY*

Willful violation of the Securities Act of 1933 or of rules and regulations promulgated by the SEC pursuant to the act carries a maximum fine of $10,000 and up to 5 years' imprisonment.

• *ANTIFRAUD PROVISIONS*

Section 12 of the Securities Act imposes broad liability *for any person offering or selling any security (whether registered or not)* by means of an oral statement or a prospectus containing a false statement of a material fact or an omission of a material fact. This liability requires privity, however; that is, the right of private legal action extends only to the immediate purchaser. The seller may defend on the grounds of lack of knowledge of the falsity or omission.

YOU SHOULD REMEMBER

The Securities Act of 1933 requires that the public be given full information about new securities being offered for sale. This information is provided by filing a registration statement with the SEC and by preparing and furnishing a statutory prospectus for all persons to whom the securities are offered.

The 1933 act does not cover:

1. Securities exempt by statute.

2. Exempted transactions: (a) trading transactions and (b) private offerings.

3. Securities in issues of limited dollar amounts under SEC-defined exemptions.

The Securities Act provides for both civil and criminal penalties.

THE SECURITIES EXCHANGE ACT OF 1934

The Securities Exchange Act of 1934 is a federal statute concerned with *existing securities* in the marketplace. This statute established the Securities and Exchange Commission to administer federal securities laws, including the 1933 Securities Act.

• *PURPOSES OF THE ACT*

There are four major goals:

1. To regulate the securities market and securities exchanges.

2. To make available to persons who buy and sell securities information relating to the issuers of such securities.

3. To prevent fraud in trading in securities.

4. To prevent the use of insider information for the private gain of a privileged few, to the detriment of outsiders.

• *IMPORTANT PROVISIONS*

REGULATION OF EXCHANGES AND BROKERS

The Securities Exchange Act created the SEC and charged it with responsibility for administering the 1933 Securities Act and other federal securities laws. It requires that all stock exchanges, over-the-counter brokers, and dealers register with the SEC.

REGISTRATION OF TRADED SECURITIES

Any security that is to be traded on an exchange must be registered with both the SEC and the exchange. If an issuer has gross assets in excess of $1 million and at least 500 stockholders, securities traded in the over-the-counter market must be registered with the SEC.

REGISTRATION REQUIREMENTS

Registration requires disclosure of financial and organizational information concerning the business; terms governing outstanding securities; names of underwriters and security holders with at least 10% of any class of registered security; and balance sheets and profit and loss statements for each of the 3 preceding fiscal years.

UPDATING REPORTS

1. *Annual report.* The 10-K report to the SEC includes audited financial statements for the year of filing, together with certain required information about the business, its management, and its outstanding securities.

2. *Quarterly report.* The 10-Q report is a quarterly, unaudited operating statement with an updated statement covering capitalization and shareholders' equity.

3. *Monthly report.* The 8-K report is a monthly update covering any change in the amount of securities, any default under the terms of any issue of securities, and details concerning any other materially important event relevant to the larger aspects of the business.

STATEMENTS BY 5% SHAREHOLDERS

Pursuant to Section 13(d) of the Securities Exchange Act, the SEC requires the beneficial owner of more than 5% of any class of security registered under the act to file a notification statement with the commission, with the issuer, and with each exchange on which the security is listed. The purpose of this statement is to inform potential investors of a possible attempt to take over corporate management.

• *PROXY SOLICITATIONS*

The SEC has established rules for the solicitation of **proxies** by management, those opposing management, and other persons involved in solicitations, consents, and authorizations directed toward holders of registered securities or of debt securities. The proxy rules establish disclosure requirements to be met before solicitation, and mandate full disclosure of material facts to stockholders before any meeting to enable them to make informed decisions on matters to be raised at the meeting. SEC Rule 14a-3 requires that the statement be accompanied by the annual report if the election of directors is to come before the meeting.

• *INSIDER TRANSACTIONS AND FRAUD*

An **insider** is a director, officer, or owner of 10% or more of the corporate stock of an issuer listed on a national stock exchange. Section 16(b) of the Securities Exchange Act prohibits an insider from engaging in "short-swing" trading based on inside information not available to the public. The Securities Exchange Act provides that any profit realized by the insider within any period of less than 6 months shall be recoverable by the issuer.

For purposes of the regulations, "insider" includes not only "top management" and controlling shareholders, but may include also any employee or consultant with access to special information. It may include close relatives and friends of directors and executives, brokers, and dealers, as well as "tippees" who receive confidential, inside information that materially affects the value of the corporation's stock or securities such as the planned sale of the corporation or its assets, the issuance of dividends, mineral discoveries, or know-how and technological breakthroughs.

Under 1984 and 1988 federal statutes, persons convicted of insider trading now face substantially harsher maximum penalties: up to $1 million in fines ($2.5 million for corporations), prison sentences up to ten years, and civil penalties that, in effect, could require payments of four times the profits gained or losses avoided. SEC Rule 10b-5 permits the SEC and private parties to sue those who have knowingly engaged in fraud and thereby gained an unfair advantage in buying or selling securities.

• *MARGIN REQUIREMENTS*

Margin requirements are restrictions placed on the percentage of the value of securities that may be borrowed to purchase the securities. The term **margin** refers to the amount that must be paid in cash. These restrictions are created to prevent the excessive, large-scale use of credit for the purchase of, and investment in, securities. The Securities Exchange Act provides that the Board of Governors of the Federal Reserve System shall prescribe rules and regulations with respect to margins and may set lower or higher margins (up to 100%) for securities investment.

STATE SECURITIES REGULATION (BLUE SKY LAWS)

Many states regulated the *intrastate* sale of securities long before the 1933 Securities Act; indeed, Kansas enacted such legislation in 1911. Since these statutes were enacted to protect unsophisticated investors from unscrupulous securities salespersons often peddling "the blue sky," these state statutes are sometimes referred to as "blue sky laws."

Every U.S. jurisdiction now has in effect a blue sky law. A Uniform Securities Act has been enacted in most of the states and by the District of Columbia. The blue sky laws, together with the Securities Act of 1933 and the Securities Exchange Act of 1934, completely cover the intrastate and interstate regulation of securities.

YOU SHOULD REMEMBER

The Federal Securities Exchange Act of 1934 established the Securities and Exchange Commission and is concerned with *existing* securities. It provides for the regulation of stock exchanges, brokers, and dealers; the registration of traded securities; the updating of reports; and the imposition of margin requirements.

The blue sky laws are state statutes and are similar in scope and purpose to the Securities Act of 1933. They require full-disclosure registration and a statutory prospectus.

Generally, private offerings (offerings to no more than 25 persons) are not subject to registration requirements under the state securities laws.

LIABILITY OF ACCOUNTANTS

Lawyers and accountants, acting as employees or consultants (independent contractors), are an integral part of every corporate team having responsibilities for finance and securities. In addition, both attorneys and accountants are subject to professional **malpractice suits** founded in the law of torts, have strict professional codes governing their performance and behavior, and have extraordinary liability exposure in some instances under statutory law.

LIABILITY UNDER THE SECURITIES LAWS

• *CIVIL LIABILITY*

Section 11 of the *Securities Act of 1933*, imposing civil liability upon issuers of new securities for misstatements or omissions of material fact in registration statements, specifically includes accountants and financial officers within its sweep. A complaint against an accountant or financial officer under Section 11 is sufficient if it alleges (a) that the investor purchased the security pursuant to a registration statement that (b) contained a materially defective financial statement (c) certified by the accountant or financial officer, and (d) that as a result of the material defect the plaintiff suffered damages. Under Section 11, there is no requirement that the plaintiff relied on the materially defective financial statement. *The plaintiff is not required to prove negligence; the accountant has the burden of proving due diligence (lack of negligence).* The 1933 act also contains a statute of limitations: suit must be brought within 1 year after the omission or error was discovered or 3 years after the securities were offered to the public.

The Securities Exchange Act of 1934 imposes civil liability on accountants who furnish false or misleading statements in reports or documents filed with the SEC. Unlike a suit based on the 1933 act, in a Securities Exchange Act suit the accountant is faced with a lawsuit from a purchaser *acting in reliance* on the alleged false or misleading statement. As is the case with civil suits under the 1933 act, however, the plaintiff must prove damages proximately caused by the false or misleading statement.

The accountant's usual defense is that he/she acted in good faith and without knowledge that the information was misleading.

• *CRIMINAL LIABILITY*

The 1933 Securities Act provides that a participating accountant may be criminally liable for a fine of not more than $10,000 or imprisonment of not more than 5 years, or both; the 1934 Securities Exchange Act provides for a fine of up to $1 million ($2.5 million for corporations) and/or imprisonment of up to 10 years. *Violations of state securities laws carry similar criminal sanctions.*

COMMON LAW TORT LIABILITY

Malpractice suits against professionals (doctors, lawyers, accountants, etc.) are based on three claims:

1. There is a professional standard of care applicable to the services rendered by the professional.
2. The professional employed by the plaintiff failed to conform to the standard.
3. As a direct and proximate result of this failure to conform, the plaintiff suffered compensable damages.

Proof of the applicable standard of care is generally deduced in court by the testimony of other professionals who state the standard that they consider applicable to the circumstances of the case. *With regard to accountants*, this standard is usually said to be GAAS (generally accepted auditing standards) or GAAP (generally accepted accounting principles). Of course, the defending professional, although not necessarily disagreeing with plaintiff's experts regarding the applicable standard of care, may disagree as to whether the defendant conformed to the standard. *The applicable standard, as well as defendant's conformity to the standard, is a question of fact to be determined by a jury.*

LIABILITY TO THIRD PARTIES

In preceding chapters we discussed the *foreseeability standard* in determining tort and contractual responsibility for damages to secondary and remote persons. In the case of product liability, for example, a manufacturer of defective goods is responsible to all persons in the chain of distribution whom he/she could foresee as a user and hence to any party who could reasonably be expected to suffer damages.

In a leading case (*Ultramares Corp.* v. *Touche*), 174 N.E. 441 (N.Y. Ct. App. 1931), the New York Court of Appeals refused to apply the foreseeability principle to damages based on an accountant's alleged negligence. The court limited claims for damages to persons receiving the *primary benefit* of the accountant's services (the **Ultramares principle**), not creditors and other third parties who might incidentally rely on statements and documents certified to be correct. *The primary benefit test is still used by many courts, but other courts hold the accountant responsible to any injured party whose existence and injury he/she might reasonably have foreseen, even though that party may not have been the primary beneficiary of the accountant's services.* A recent decision by the U.S. Supreme Court *(United States* v. *Arthur Young & Co.)*, 104 S. Ct. 1495 (1984), reveals a judicial tendency to hold the accountant responsible for serving a broad public interest and having a duty "to preserve the integrity of the securities market."

KNOW THE CONCEPTS

DO YOU KNOW THE BASICS?

1. What are some advantages and disadvantages of raising corporate capital by equity financing vis-à-vis debt financing?
2. What is the principal difference between a bond and a debenture?
3. In what three ways do common shareholders have an interest in the corporation?
4. In what sense may shareholders influence the directors' decision to declare a dividend?
5. What is a nimble dividend? What general dividend requirement does a nimble dividend violate?
6. Under what theory of contract law can creditors sue subscribers to the stock of a corporation not yet formed? Does this violate the privity rule?
7. What evidence does the corporate issuer have of uncertified ownership of shares?

8. What are some reasons for restricting the free transfer of share certificates?

9. Which came first, state or federal regulation of the issuance and marketing of securities?

10. Why are the common law rules of fraud and misrepresentation insufficient to protect investors from unscrupulous securities salespersons? In any case, does the modern day rule of *caveat venditor* ("let the seller beware") not afford the gullible investor sufficient legal protection?

11. Does allowance by the SEC of a statutory prospectus constitute SEC approval of the securities described or of the prospectus?

12. What rationale underlies various exemptions to the federal securities laws based on private offerings or on the size of offerings?

13. Is the term "insider" limited to a defined group?

14. Why should accountants receive special attention for civil and criminal liability under the securities laws?

15. Is a professional malpractice case merely a "swearing contest" between two sets of professional "experts," with one set claiming that the defendant's professional work did not conform to the standard of care, the other set claiming that the work did conform?

TERMS FOR STUDY

authorized shares	nimble dividend
call price	noncumulative preferred stock
canceled shares	nonparticipating preferred stock
capital surplus	no-par shares
common shares	note
convertible bond	par shares
cumulative preferred stock	participating preferred stock
debenture	preferred shares
debt security	proxy
discount shares	red herring prospectus
distribution	share
dividend	stock option
equity security	stock split
indenture	street certificate
insider	subscription
issued shares	tombstone advertisement
malpractice suit	treasury shares
margin	Ultramares principle

PRACTICAL APPLICATION

1. ABC Gulf Investment Co. owns 1000 acres of gulf-front property in Manatee County, Florida. In December 1986, it flies 35 persons of "substantial" means from various parts of the country to Tampa to tell them of the "opportunity of a lifetime." The "opportunity" is the offer of a contract with ABC to buy 20-acre tracts of "prime" undeveloped land, designated on a property plat, for a price of $100,000 each, payable over 30 years. Twelve persons, including Shuster, sign contracts. If the only written information concerning the property was a promotional brochure, can Shuster void this contract on grounds of illegality?

2. Sawyer is the owner of a large, unincorporated country estate on which is located an established golf course. Approximately 100 persons regularly play golf on the course, paying semiannual dues for the privilege.

   Sawyer needs to raise $1 million to build a club house and put the course in "first-class" condition. He proposes to create a corporation and issue $1 million of $10-par-value capital stock. Each of the 100 present members signs a stock subscription agreement for 1000 shares of stock, and Sawyer enters into contracts with builders and developers for the work. Sawyer defaults on these contracts, and the contractors bring suit on the subscription agreements. What should be the result?

3. In Problem 2, suppose that Sawyer wishes to form a corporation in Kentucky (where the golf course is situated) and sell the capital stock, all as described, to the present members, under Kentucky's blue sky law, which has essentially the same registration and prospectus requirements as the federal Securities Act of 1933. However, the capital to be raised is $2 million of which $1 million (100,000 $10-par-value shares) will be issued to Snead, for which Sawyer will deed the country estate to the corporation.

   Discuss the following:
   (a) The liability of Jones, CPA, for errors in Sawyer's financial statements leading to an overstatement of the value of Sawyer's estate in the amount of $300,000.
   (b) The liability of Sawyer for violation of the Securities Act of 1933 if 12 of his members, residents of Ohio, resell their shares in Ohio within 6 months.

ANSWERS
KNOW THE CONCEPTS

1. Equity financing does not have to be repaid; however, ownership and control of the business enterprise must be shared with equity investors.

Although issuance of debt securities may not require sharing ownership or control, the necessity of repayment may limit the scope and freedom of corporate activity.

2. Both are long-term debt securities; however, a bond is secured, whereas a debenture is unsecured. Both bonds and debentures are subject to the terms of indenture agreements.

3. Common shareholders may vote for directors and on other fundamental matters; they may participate in the distribution of dividends; they may share in the distribution of net assets after dissolution and liquidation.

4. Shareholders may influence the directors' decision to declare a dividend only through their power to elect or reject directors. Unless the directors abuse their discretion with respect to dividends, shareholders play no role in the dividend process.

5. A nimble dividend is a dividend payable from current earnings even though *there are debts outstanding from previous years.* Such dividends are not permitted in most states because of the general requirement that dividends be paid only from earned surplus.

6. The privity rule states that only a person who is a party to a contract can sue on that contract. However, there are two classes of third-party beneficiaries who can bring suit without privity: donee beneficiaries and creditor beneficiaries. If it is assumed that the subscriber could reasonably anticipate that creditors of the embryonic enterprise would extend credit in reliance on his/her promise to purchase stock, the subscriber should be legally responsible to such "creditor beneficiaries."

7. Section 8-102 of the Uniform Commercial Code requires that uncertificated shares be "registered upon books maintained for that purpose by or on behalf of the issuer."

8. To retain voting controls within a defined group, to preserve an S corporation or a close corporation, or to maintain exemption from federal or state security laws requiring registration for *public* offerings.

9. The state of Kansas was the first regulator of securities, passing its underlying statute in 1911. However, many states did not enter the field of intrastate regulation until many years after the passage of the basic federal laws in 1933 and 1934.

10. Modern law places a great burden on sellers to make full disclosures to buyers, particularly where there is a disparity of education and training between them. However, the 1933 Securities Act not only requires full disclosure of all relevant facts, but also defines the nature and extent of that disclosure. Reliance on general principles of *caveat venditor* would leave the parties uncertain of their rights and duties without resorting to litigation in every case.

11. The SEC explicitly takes no position with respect to the securities or to the accuracy or adequacy of the prospectus. The SEC has no duty or responsibility to investigate the contents of the registration statement or of the prospectus, even though these documents are in complete statutory and regulatory form. Both civil and criminal liability attach to the issuer for omissions and inaccuracies in these documents. The SEC cannot lead the public to believe that such omissions and inaccuracies do not exist.

12. The primary purpose of the federal securities laws is to protect the investing public. To the extent that an investor is sophisticated or informed, he/she requires less protection. The evils that the legislation was designed to prevent involve large-scale promotion of dubious and ill-designed plans or of schemes for the secret profit of their promoters.

13. Although the term "insider" basically means "top management" and controlling shareholders, it extends to any party with inside knowledge or information giving him/her an unfair advantage over ordinary members of the investing public. Included are employees, consultants, and total outsiders who are "tipped off" directly or indirectly by insiders.

14. As the compilers and preparers of financial data, accountants are in a unique position to mislead or deceive (intentionally or carelessly) not only regulators but also issuers and their managers, as well as the investing public.

15. Almost every case in a court of law turns on the credibility of conflicting witnesses. In Chapter 3 we learned that the strengths and weaknesses of both defendant and plaintiff are explored in pretrial discovery. If experts cannot be found to testify truthfully and conscientiously for one side or the other, litigation may not proceed to trial or the case may be settled without trial. In any event, the jury will have full opportunity to evaluate both sides as presented by opposing experts.

PRACTICAL APPLICATION

1. The question presented is whether the contracts to purchase the real estate tracts are "securities" within the meaning of the Securities Act of 1933. Of the three tests laid down in the *Howey* case, the third—the expectation of profits solely from the efforts of a promoter or third party—is clearly lacking. As a matter of fact, this contract is an ordinary real estate contract. Such contracts have been treated by the courts as a mere interest in a joint venture to sell real estate. Of course, the offer to sell to 30 persons and the interstate nature of the transaction might bring the matter to the attention of the SEC. However, since the contract is not a "security," there is no violation of law.

2. Persons relying on the subscription agreements would be able to sue subscribers who had not paid the agreed-upon subscription price. On the assumption that the contractors know of the subscription agreements, they should be successful in their litigation.

3. (a) On the assumption that the Kentucky blue sky law and any application of professional liability thereunder would follow the Securities Act of 1933, Jones, CPA, would be liable not only to the Kentucky authorities, but also to Sawyer and other persons with whom he had a direct contract. He may also be liable to investors who may have relied on his erroneous financial statements. Under the broader interpretation of accountant liability, he would be responsible to *all* persons whose injury or loss he could have foreseen. The Kentucky blue sky law would be applicable since the offering is to 100 persons and would be a public sale subject to the Securities Act.

(b) If the securities were sold to residents of Ohio who came to Kentucky to purchase these securities, the out-of-state residency would not itself cause the transaction to be an "interstate sale" unless there is a "scheme" to violate the federal statute. The facts given do not suggest such a scheme, and there would appear to be no violation of federal law in failing to file a registration statement under the 1933 act. However, the securities cannot be sold by the Ohio residents or by other purchasers outside the state of Kentucky for at least 9 months.

19
PROPERTY

In law, property is a collection of rights and interests, generally associated with the idea of ownership. There are two main types of property: (1) **real property**, which is land, the buildings, trees, or other items attached to the land, and the rights of land ownership and use; and (2) **personal property**, which is all other property, tangible or intangible, except real property.

PROPERTY AS A LEGAL CONCEPT

The law of contracts has an enormous influence on property. Unless a contract involves solely services, it probably has property (goods, land, etc.) as its subject matter. Indeed, a contract itself may be a form of property; the contractual rights and interests are owned by the parties to the contract, and generally are both transferable and enforceable in court.

Using this broad perspective, one sees that, for example, a negotiable instrument is a form of both a contract and property. Under the broad definition of property as a "bundle of rights," property is anything capable of ownership, whether individually, collectively, or for the benefit of others.

PERSONAL PROPERTY
TANGIBLE AND INTANGIBLE

Personal property (also called "personalty") can be tangible or intangible. **Tangible personal property** is subject to physical possession. It can include almost

338

anything that takes up space and is movable (nonmovables would be real estate or fixtures).

Intangible personal property consists of rights in something that lacks physical substance. Examples include contracts, stocks, bonds, computer software (programs), employment, utility services (telephone, electricity, etc.), and intellectual property (copyrights, patents, and trademarks). Documents or other materials related to such property are really just evidence of the property; they are *not* the property with which we are concerned.

For instance, a written agreement evinces a contract, but the rights under the contract are the important property interest. Likewise, it is not the stock certificate, the computer disk, the employment card, or the certificate of copyright registration that is the key property interest; these are evidence of property, but the property itself is not capable of physical possession. One cannot control a portion of IBM equal to a 10-share interest in that company; nor can one simply pick up job tenure and put it in one's pocket; nor can one physically possess the exclusive right to publish the latest "great American novel." All such rights (stock ownership, employment, copyright) are real, but intangible.

FIXTURES

Another class of property is called a **fixture**. Consisting of personal property that has become attached to real property, the fixture is generally treated as part of the real property. Once personal property has become so incorporated into real property that it is difficult, costly, and/or impossible to remove, the personal property is considered a fixture. The main question is often whether an item's value is intrinsically related to the surrounding real property; the more closely the two are connected, the more likely the item (be it a backyard swing, a clothes dryer, a chandelier, or the like) is a fixture.

In the absence of agreement by the parties, courts often look to the parties' apparent intent to have, or not have, a fixture. This "intent test" considers:

(1) the item's purpose;

(2) the way in which it was attached; and

(3) the usual practice and custom with respect to such an item.

An exception is the **trade fixture**, placed on leased premises by a tenant for use in his/her business. Unlike the situation for other would-be fixtures, the tenant can continue to treat a trade fixture as personal property. However, if removal causes damages, the tenant must reimburse the landlord. (If removal would cause severe damage, the trade fixture may have to stay.)

YOU SHOULD REMEMBER

Personal property can be *tangible* (subject to physical possession) or *intangible* (e.g., stocks, contracts, intellectual property).

> Fixtures are personal property that have become incorporated into real property to such an extent that they are treated as part of the real property. Trade fixtures usually may be removed, however.

ACQUIRING TITLE TO PERSONAL PROPERTY

• *CONTRACTS, SALES OF GOODS, AND TRANSFERS OF COMMERCIAL PAPER*

Contracts in general, as well as UCC Article 2 (sale of goods), have already been discussed in Chapters 5–10.

The transfer of negotiable instruments under UCC Articles 3 and 4 was covered in Chapters 11–13.

• *GIFTS*

A **gift** is a voluntary transfer of property from its owner (**donor**) to another person (**donee**) without any compensation for the donor. When the donee is a minor and the property is held in trust (see page 361), the Uniform Gifts to Minors Act often outlines the custodian's (trustee's) duties and the minor's rights.

ELEMENTS OF A GIFT

The three elements of a gift are as follows:

1. Donative intent (language or circumstances indicate that the owner intended to give away the property).
2. Delivery [the property was actually or symbolically (e.g., keys to an automobile) placed in the donee's hands, with the owner giving up control].
3. Acceptance by the donee (usually presumed).

Because delivery is essential, there are no "executory" gifts; in the absence of consideration, a mere promise to give something is unenforceable.

TYPES OF GIFTS

The three categories of gifts are *inter vivos*, *causa mortis*, and *testamentary*.

Gifts inter vivos are made during the donor's lifetime, when he/she is *not* facing imminent death. The three elements are those listed above.

Gifts causa mortis are a type of conditional gift, which places a precondition on permanent retention of the item. When the donor, believing that his/her death is imminent, conveys property with the intent that the donee keep it after the donor's death, that is a gift *causa mortis*. The property must be returned to the donor if (1) the donor recovers, or dies from a cause quite different from that contemplated by the parties; (2) the donee predeceases (dies before) the donor; or (3) the donor revokes the gift.

A **testamentary gift** is stated in a will. It serves to transfer property when the maker of the will dies. Because wills are freely revocable until death, the effect is to make testamentary gifts likewise revocable. There is no actual gift until after death.

• *ACCESSION*

Accession is an addition to the value of personal property, by labor, materials, and/or natural process (e.g., growing fruit).

Examples: Accession

>   1. Adding an air conditioner to an automobile.
>   2. Turning an uncut diamond into a finished gem.

The property owner has a right to the increased value. Typically, he/she has paid for or performed the accession.

If ownership is at issue, these principles control:

1. Accessions performed by a thief or otherwise done in bad faith and without the owner's consent: The original property's rightful owner is entitled to the accession.

2. Accessions performed in good faith: The more the accession increases the value of the property, the more appropriate it becomes to place title with the person responsible for the accession. If the original owner keeps the property, he/she must (unlike the situation above) compensate the improver for the accession. If the improver gets the property, he/she must pay the original owner for its preaccession value.

Example: Accession Performed in Good Faith

Bobby Booby, thinking that a beat-up chair in his late Aunt Esmerelda's house was left to him, does extensive work to refinish it. A formerly $20 chair is now worth about $100. Actually, the chair was left to cousin Kate.

Bobby probably will be allowed to keep the chair, after giving Kate $20 for what it was originally worth. If, instead, Kate takes the chair, Bobby should be compensated for the accession.

• *CONFUSION*

When the personal property of different owners is commingled, there is **confusion** of goods: the various owners' properties can no longer be distinguished. For collective warehouses, silos, storage tanks and the like, confusion is avoided by maintaining thorough records showing how much of a fungible good (e.g., a particular grade of oil or grain) is held by each owner.

If the confusion was the intentional or otherwise wrongful act of one of the owners, then title rests exclusively with the innocent owner(s). On the other hand, all owners share equally if the confusion occurred by the owners' consent or agreement, through an accident or honest mistake, or by an act of God or a third party. The only way for one owner to obtain more than an equal share (or, perhaps for insurance purposes, to show a disproportionate share of loss) is to produce records that adequately support such a claim.

• *POSSESSION*

> When personal property is lost, mislaid, or abandoned, or clearly had no prior owner, a person may obtain title simply by taking possession of it.

Property is **lost** when it is accidentally left somewhere by its owner, who cannot find it but does not intend to give up ownership. The finder of lost property is a gratuitous bailee for the true owner, with title against all other persons but the true owner. (A "gratuitous bailee" has a right of possession, but the owner retains superior title interests. This bailee usually must take measures, but only those reasonable under the circumstances, to protect the property and locate the owner. Bailments are discussed later in this chapter.)

There are, however, two exceptions: if the property is found by a *trespasser* or by an *employee at work*, then the owner of the premises on which the item was found, not the finder, acts as bailee and has the title interest.

Property is **mislaid** when it is intentionally put somewhere, but then forgotten. In most states, the owner of the premises, not the finder, becomes the gratuitous bailee with good title against everyone but the true owner.

Property is **abandoned** when the owner discards it without intending to reclaim it. Title passes to the first person who takes possession of the property and intends to keep it. Valuable items, however, presumably are mislaid, not abandoned.

According to the **treasure trove rule** followed in most states, a nontrespassing finder has title to money or other treasure buried for so long a time that it is unlikely a prior owner will return. (Otherwise, the landowner usually has the rightful claim.) More important are the **estray statutes** found in most states: they provide the procedures (including publication of notice) whereby the finder/holder of lost or mislaid property may claim full title to it if it is not reclaimed by the true owner within the statutory period.

• *OPERATION OF LAW*

Federal, state, and local laws provide for transfer of property title via intestate succession or escheat (see the discussion of wills, pages 363–364), via bankruptcy or execution on judgments (see Chapter 20), or via lawsuits for conversion (see torts, Chapter 4). Except in certain limited instances (e.g., a UCC "bona fide purchaser" of goods; see Chapter 10), even innocent third persons cannot obtain title to stolen property; the thief never obtained title, which remains with the true owner.

• *CREATION*

The final method of gaining title—by invention, art, or other intellectual endeavor—is considered in the section on intellectual property later in this chapter.

YOU SHOULD REMEMBER

Title may be acquired by sales contract, by the proper taking of a negotiable instrument, or by gift, accession, confusion, possession, operation of law, or creation. Except for certain specific exceptions (e.g., UCC bona fide purchasers), a person who takes from a thief does not acquire title.

BAILMENTS

A **bailment** involves a transfer of personal property possession, but not title. The **bailor** (owner) transfers possession to the **bailee**.

The requirements for a bailment are as follows:

1. Bailor retains title.
2. Bailee obtains possession:
   (a) delivery by bailor,
   (b) acceptance by bailee.
3. Possession is for a specific purpose.
4. Possession is temporary; property ultimately reverts to bailor or bailor's designee.

• *TYPES OF BAILMENTS*

There are three general categories of bailments: (1) bailments solely benefitting the bailor; (2) bailments solely benefitting the bailee; and (3) bailments beneficial to both parties.

Bailments are generally express or implied agreements, but they can be imposed by operation of law (**constructive bailments**).

BAILMENT TO BENEFIT SOLELY THE BAILOR

Example: Only the Bailor Benefits

Barbara Bailor leaves her cat with Boris Bailee while Barbara is on vacation; Boris is to take care of the cat, with no compensation expected or received.

Also known as a **gratuitous bailment**, this bailment is really a favor performed by the bailee. Thus the bailee usually *owes just a slight degree of care*; only gross negligence will leave him/her responsible for damages to, or loss of, the bailed property.

Constructive bailments usually fall into this category. The constructive bailee has found lost or stolen property, has received a misdelivery, or has otherwise had the property "thrust upon him/her." Once the constructive bailee takes control of the property, he/she is held to the standard of care (that is, slight care) associated with a gratuitous bailment.

BAILMENT TO BENEFIT SOLELY THE BAILEE

Example: *Only the Bailee Benefits*

Bob Bailor lends his car to Barry Bailee, with Bob neither expecting nor receiving compensation for the "loan."

Because here the bailor is doing the bailee a favor, with the bailee passing nothing in return to the bailor, it seems only fair to hold the bailee to a *duty of great (extraordinary) care.* Unless he/she was exceedingly careful, the bailee may be held accountable for damages to, or loss of, the bailed property.

BAILMENT OF MUTUAL BENEFIT

Example: *Both the Bailor and the Bailee Benefit*

Goods are left with a firm entrusted to packing and storing them. The bailors pay for the bailee firm's services.

Here the bailee owes a *duty of ordinary care*. In effect, he/she is held to the "reasonable person" standard found in the tort law of negligence.

Note that parking lot bailments involve transfer of the keys of the vehicle and physical control of it. If a person parks the car and retains the keys, he/she has merely rented parking space. There is no bailment because delivery and acceptance of possession are lacking.

• *MODERN TREND IN DETERMINING THE BAILEE'S DUTY OF CARE*

As just discussed, most courts decide the bailee's duty of care according to whom the bailment benefits. An increasing number of courts, however, treat the issues of whether the bailment benefits only one of the parties, and whether the bailee is compensated, as being two important, but not necessarily decisive, factors in determining the duty of care. The question is simply: What was reasonable care, given all the circumstances present in a particular case? Obviously, the overall effect may not be different from the older three-tiered standard; for instance, most judges and juries will hold that the degree of care reasonable when the bailee is simply doing a favor for someone is lower than when the bailee is compensated for his/her services.

• *THE BAILOR'S DUTIES*

Just as the bailee has a duty of one of three levels of care, so the bailor also has duties. He/she must deliver to the bailee property safe and fit for the bailment's purpose, must defend against any third party's wrongful claim to title in the property, and must tell the bailee about property defects of which the bailor has or should have knowledge.

• *LIMITS ON THE BAILEE'S LIABILITY*

Express, written bailments can expand or (more typically) limit the bailee's potential liability. For bailees bearing a special, public interest (e.g., parking garages, hotels), liability limits may be forbidden by state statute or municipal ordinance; even if not prohibited, limits must be reasonable. For purely "private" bailments, liability limits are usually permitted unless they defeat the bailment's purpose. The modern law's emphasis on consumer protection has led to most states' requiring that liability limitations be clearly expressed, via a method that would be noticed by a reasonable bailor before, or at the outset of, a bailment.

• *BAILMENT TERMINATION AND THE RETURN OF PROPERTY*

Bailments are terminated by performance, time, destruction of bailed property, acts of the parties, or operation of law.

Performance arises when the bailment's purpose has been fulfilled or when the agreed-upon duties of bailor and bailee have otherwise been completed.

Time terminates the bailment when the period expressly provided or implicitly agreed to by the parties has lapsed.

Destruction of bailed property can occur through a third party or by an act of God (e.g., a hurricane). It also arises when the bailed property is no longer appropriate for the bailment's purpose.

Acts of the parties include (a) the parties' subsequent agreement to terminate; (b) *either* party's decision to terminate a bailment that is for the sole benefit of one party and/or has an indefinite duration; (c) the "innocent" party's choice to terminate and, if applicable, to seek damages, because the other party has materially breached the bailment agreement (e.g., the bailee used the property in a way not agreed to by the bailor).

Operation of law concerns the bailee's death, incompetence, insolvency, or other such event that renders performance impossible.

Upon termination, the bailee must return the bailed property to the bailor *unless*:

(a) it was lost, stolen, or destroyed through no fault of the bailee;

(b) it was delivered to someone with a better claim to it than the bailor has;

(c) it was taken by legal process (e.g., attachment); or

(d) the bailee has an unpaid lien on it.

Most states have statutes permitting a *bailee's lien* on the bailed property if the bailee has not been paid for services performed on the property. After notice, the property is sold to pay off the lien (see discussion of liens in Chapter 20). Usually the lien is solely possessory (if the bailee gives up possession, the lien ends) and cannot be used for work done on credit.

YOU SHOULD REMEMBER

Bailments involve transfer of the possession of personal property, but not title to it, from a bailor to a bailee. Possession is temporary, for a specific purpose.

The three main types of bailment are (with bailee's duty of care in parentheses): bailments solely to benefit bailor (slight), bailments solely to benefit bailee (great), and mutual benefit bailments (ordinary).

Bailments are usually express or implied agreements, but can be imposed by law (constructive bailments). If a bailee's liability limits are clearly and noticeably expressed, they will generally be upheld.

Bailments are terminated by performance, time, destruction of bailed property, acts of the parties, or operation of law. In the absence of a justifiable excuse, the bailee is liable for failure to return bailed property.

• *THE COMMON CARRIER AS A SPECIAL TYPE OF BAILEE*

A **common carrier** holds itself out to the public as available for transporting goods or passengers.

A common carrier may be regulated by state agencies or, if an interstate carrier, by federal agencies such as the Interstate Commerce Commission. Although this discussion will focus on carriers of goods, note that carriers of passengers are also subject to extensive state and federal regulation. *Passenger carriers* are *not insurers* of their passenger's safety (hence not strictly liable), but they are usually *held to a high duty of care*—more than just avoiding ordinary negligence.

When *transporting goods*, the *common carrier is a special type of bailee*, strictly liable for property damaged, lost, or taken while in its possession unless the damage, loss, or taking resulted from one of the following:

1. The shipper's actions, such as improper packing, if the resulting problem was not obvious to the carrier. (The "shipper" is the party sending the goods via the carrier; e.g., the owner or seller of the goods.)

2. Governmental acts, such as attachment or confiscation pursuant to legal processes.

3. An act of God, such as a severe flood, tornado, earthquake, or other unforeseeable natural catastrophe.

4. An act of a "public enemy," a term that includes nations, groups, and individuals seeking the violent overthrow of the government.

5. The inherent nature of the property, such that the shipper should have made special carrying arrangements. The nonnegligent carrier is thus not responsible if, for example, perishable goods spoil.

It is usually the common carrier's burden to prove that the damages arose from one of these exceptions.

Once transportation is completed, the common carrier is considered a "warehouse" for goods still in its possession. Thus strict liability (with just the five exceptions listed above) ends when (a) the goods are unloaded from the common carrier and placed in a storehouse; or (b) the consignee (the person to whom the shipment was sent) has had reasonable time to inspect and take possession of the goods (with some states also requiring that the consignee receive notice of the goods' arrival).

The common carrier as warehouse owes a duty of ordinary care. Like warehouses generally, the carrier is then held just to a negligence standard, not one of strict liability.

COMMON CARRIER'S LIABILITY LIMITATIONS

Intrastate commerce: most states permit limits except for gross negligence.

Interstate commerce: federal law [and UCC 7-309(2)] allows limits if the shipper can obtain a higher amount of liability by paying increased rates.

YOU SHOULD REMEMBER

Common carriers of goods are, in effect, bailees. They are strictly liable for goods damaged in transport unless a particular exception intervenes (e.g., the shipper's negligence or third-party acts caused the damages).

Once the transportation is completed, or shortly thereafter, the common carrier owes only a duty of ordinary care (a negligence standard).

INTELLECTUAL PROPERTY

A special type of intangible property, arising from the creative endeavors of the human mind and known as **intellectual property**, is evinced by patents, copyrights, and trademarks and trade names.

• *PATENTS*

A **patent** is the 17-year exclusive right to make, use, and sell a new and useful process, machine, manufacture, or other composition, or any new and useful improvement on it. Besides such *invention patents*, there are special, *plant patents* (17 years, for asexual reproduction of new plants) and *design patents* (14 years, for the appearance of a manufactured article, not its use or operation).

Key point: to be patented, something must be novel, useful, and nonobvious.

Patent law is exclusively federal. The U.S. Patent Office searches prior patents to determine whether a proposed patent conflicts with a previously issued or pending patent.

Patents cannot be renewed. Once a patent lapses, the invention enters the public domain; this means that anyone can make, use, or sell it without obtaining a license from the inventor. However, a person can combine or add to unpatented or lapsed works in such a way as to create a new, patented invention.

• *COPYRIGHTS*

A **copyright** is the exclusive right to print, reproduce, sell, and exhibit written material, musical compositions, art works, photographs, movies and television programs, data systems, and other creations placed in a tangible, preserved medium of expression.

Copyright law is almost exclusively governed by federal statutes. A copyright lasts for the life of the creator, plus 50 years. Copyrights predating the revised federal copyright law (effective January 1, 1978) do not have that time frame, but may last for as long as 75 years.

Unlike the situation for patents, the exclusivity of copyrights (as to use, etc.) is subject to a number of exceptions. The two most important are these:

1. The *fair use* exception includes, among other things, limited reproduction for classroom purposes. To determine whether the use is fair, these four factors are considered: (a) purpose and nature of the use (e.g., nonprofit or educational vs. commercial); (b) proportion and importance of the part used in comparison to the work as a whole; (c) the nature of the work; (d) the use's effect on the value of the work, including its potential market.

2. *Libraries and archives usually can reproduce single copies for noncommercial purposes.* Wholesale copying of large works or periodicals, though, is not allowed.

Like other forms of intellectual property, copyrights protect, not ideas, but only the tangible *expression of ideas.*

• *TRADEMARKS AND OTHER TRADE SYMBOLS*

A **trademark** is a distinctive symbol, word, letter, number, picture, or combination thereof adopted and used by a merchant or manufacturer to identify his/her goods.

The law of trademarks and other trade symbols is meant to keep businesses from "cashing in" on the goodwill and reputation of a competitor's products or services. It helps to prevent or punish the fraudulent marketing of goods or services as being those of another, presumably more reputable, business. Obviously, if unchecked, such unfair competition deceives the public and steals trade from honest businesspersons.

Although not required to do so, the owner or user of a trademark may seek to register it in the U.S. Patent and Trademark Office. A trademark not yet in use may still be registered if it is to be put in use within 6 months. (This pre-use protection can be extended for up to 30 more months.)

If approved, a registration lasts 10 years from the first use and can be renewed for any number of additional 10-year periods. Infringement of the registered trademark may be enjoined (ordered stopped by a court) and damages awarded.

To be protected, a trade symbol (1) must not lapse from disuse; and (2) must remain associated with the business or its products and services (not becoming a generic term). Immoral, deceptive, confusing, or merely descriptive "marks" are not protected.

Besides trademarks, other types of trade symbols include *service marks* (similar to trademarks, but concerning services rather than goods) and *trade names* (may act as trademarks or service marks, but serve mainly to designate the business entity itself). Although trade names cannot be federally registered, infringement is still subject to injunction and damages.

Some former trade names now in common public use (thus, no longer protected) are aspirin, cellophane, and thermos.

Like the law of trade symbols generally, this area of law permits extensive state statutory, regulatory, and case law development, a far cry from the federal pre-emption of almost all patent and copyright law.

• *TRADE SECRETS*

Even after the termination of a job, employees owe their employers a duty of loyalty not to disclose trade secrets. Note that leaving an employer to work for a competitor is generally permitted unless explicitly barred in the employee's written contract with the first employer. The nondisclosure loyalty is not so narrowly based. Although an explicit, more extensive protection of trade secrets can be included in a written employment contract, a general duty of nondisclosure implicitly arises out of, and continues beyond, almost any employment relationship.

What is a **trade secret?**
Perhaps customer lists. Certainly any formula, process, or method of operation used in the production of goods or services, meant to be held in the employee's confidence, and needed by the employee to perform his/her job.

JOINT OWNERSHIP OF PROPERTY

Both personal and real property may have more than one owner. The four main categories of co-ownership are joint tenancy, tenancy by the entirety, tenancy in common, and community property.

A **joint tenancy** is established when equal interests in property are conveyed by an instrument expressly stating that the parties acquire the property as joint tenants. Four "unities" are preconditions to the joint tenancy: the owners must all have received their interests in the property (a) at the same time (unity of time), (b) from the same source (unity of title), (c) in equal interests (unity of interest), and (d) with each owner having a right to possess the whole (unity of possession).

Perhaps the most important aspect of joint tenancies is that the owners have a **right of survivorship**: when one of the joint tenants dies, his/her interest passes equally to the surviving joint tenants. Moreover, just as a joint tenancy interest cannot pass by inheritance (it goes to the surviving joint tenants, not the deceased joint tenant's heirs), so it cannot be transferred by one of the joint tenants; such a transfer destroys the unity of time and converts the tenants' ownership to that of a tenancy in common (see below).

A **tenancy by the entirety**, which only a married couple can create, is similar to a joint tenancy in that there are four unities and a right to survivorship. Unlike the situation in a joint tenancy, though, a unilateral action of one tenant (e.g., an attempt to transfer his/her interest to a third party) cannot turn a tenancy by the entirety into a tenancy in common. Only death, divorce, or agreement by both spouses terminates this tenancy. Many states, including all community property states no longer recognize this tenancy.

A **tenancy in common** requires only one of the four unities: unity of possession. There is no right of survivorship; a deceased common tenant's heirs receive his/her interest in the tenancy. If the type of co-ownership is unspecified or otherwise unclear, a conveyance to two or more persons is treated as creating a tenancy in common.

Lastly, some southwestern and western states (plus, to a certain extent, Wisconsin) follow a system known as **community property**. Almost all property acquired by the husband or wife during the marriage, except for gifts or inheritances, is owned equally by both spouses. Property acquired before marriage is not included, unless it becomes so "commingled" with community property that it can no longer be traced.

A special form of real property, the **condominium**, features sole ownership of individual office or apartment units, with joint ownership (by all the sole owners) of the land and common areas. The owners' management participation and their shares of expenses are governed by state law and the terms of the condominium agreement. Condominium owners typically have the right to enjoy free and equal use of the common areas, and to transfer their units subject only to lawful restrictions in the condominium agreement.

YOU SHOULD REMEMBER

The major forms of joint ownership are joint tenancy (with survivorship rights and the four "unities"—time, title, interest, and possession) and tenancy in common (with no survivorship rights and only one "unity," possession).

Many noncommunity property states still permit tenancy by the entirety, which is similar to joint tenancy, but harder to terminate and available solely to married couples.

Two other forms of joint ownership are community property and condominiums.

All of the above forms of ownership can apply to both personal and real property, except for condominiums, which are real property.

REAL PROPERTY

Real property interests center around ownership, use, and possession.

ACQUISITION OF TITLE

Ownership (title) may be acquired in many ways.

• *VOLUNTARY TITLE TRANSFER BY DEED*

The transfer, by sale or gift, is formally accomplished by delivering to the grantee a **deed**, which customarily includes the following:

1. Names of the grantor and grantee.

2. Consideration paid, if applicable.

3. "Words of conveyance," stating the parties' intent to convey.

4. A precise, formal description (metes, i.e., measures, and bounds, i.e., directions) of the property.

5. Exceptions or reservations, such as easements or profits (both described shortly).

6. Quantity (acreage).

7. Covenants or other warranties.

8. The grantor's signature.

General warranty deeds include all of the usual covenants (title, no encumbrance, quiet enjoyment, i.e., possession without disturbance). The grantor warrants title against defects or encumbrances arising *before* or *during* his/her ownership.

Special warranty deeds include the general warranty's covenants, but warrant only against defects or encumbrances arising *after* the grantor acquired the property.

Deeds (whether general warranty or special warranty) usually warrant the grantor's "good and merchantable title." If disputes over title arise later, the grantor may be subject to a breach of title lawsuit.

A **quitclaim deed**, however, contains no warranty of title; it simply grants all of the grantor's rights in the property, whatever these rights may be. Unless the quitclaim and the grantor's actions were fraudulent, he/she is not liable to the grantee even if it turns out that the grantor had no title at all and hence conveyed none to the grantee.

Recording the deed in the local records office is not needed to transfer title. However, recording provides notice to others, and in many states establishes priority over unrecorded deeds involving the same property.

FACTORS INVOLVED IN REAL PROPERTY SALES

The sale of real property generally involves the following:

1. Contract of sale, which must be in writing to be enforceable (Statute of Frauds).

2. Title search, generally performed to determine if the grantor has a marketable title.

3. Mortgage(s), when money is borrowed to purchase the property.

4. At closing, delivery of the deed to the buyer, who pays the purchase price. The money may then be disbursed to, among others, the broker or agent (if any), the title company (if applicable), the seller's mortgagee (if money is still owed), and the seller.

MORTGAGES

Mortgages are a type of security transaction involving real property. (See Chapter 20.) The mortgage is a document, and a conveyance, from the mortgagor (debtor) to the mortgagee (creditor), with real property described and given as security for the loan made by the mortgagee to the mortgagor. The loan itself is usually evinced by a promissory note.

Most states consider the mortgagor to have title, even if in default, until court action has resulted in a foreclosure; in essence, the mortgagee simply has a lien on the property. Some states, though, treat title as resting with the mortgagee, whose interest is subject to a condition subsequent (payment of the debt), which would place title with the mortgagor; in effect, this "title theory" makes little difference, as the mortgagor retains possession and other property interests, as well as such duties as paying taxes. (For a discussion of foreclosures, see Chapter 20.)

ALTERNATIVES TO THE MORTGAGE

Two alternatives to the mortgage are as follows:

1. Deed of trust. The property is conveyed to a third person (the trustee), who holds it in trust as security for the debt. The debtor retains possessory and other property rights (see pages 354–355). Foreclosure is generally along the same lines as for mortgages, but the trustee, not the sheriff, may conduct the public sale.

2. Installment land contract. The seller retains a security interest until the total purchase price is paid. The buyer possesses the property, with forfeiture conditions (such as for default in payments) stated in the contract.

• *INVOLUNTARY TITLE TRANSFER BY OPERATION OF LAW*

1. Foreclosure sale. Title may pass because of an unpaid mortgage or a mechanic's lien. For more, see Chapter 20.

2. Judgment sale. Title may pass because of an unpaid judgment, leading to a writ of execution for the judgment creditor. For more, see Chapter 20.

3. Eminent domain. The right of the federal and state governments, as well as some other entities with governmental powers, to take privately owned real property for the public benefit is called **eminent domain**. The Fifth

Amendment to the U.S. Constitution requires that the owner be compensated for the property taken; the amount awarded is generally the property's fair market value before the taking occurred.

4. Adverse possession. If a trespasser actually occupies property continuously, exclusively, openly, and in a manner hostile to the owner's rights (without permission), and if this state of affairs lasts for the period of time required by state statute (it varies from about 5 to 20 years), then the owner's title passes to the trespasser by **adverse possession**. Some states require that the trespasser have had at least some claim of title beforehand, and most states look to whether the would-be adverse possessor paid taxes on the property. Neither government land nor land occupied by permission of the owner can be acquired by adverse possession.

• *TRANSFER BY INHERITANCE*

Title to real property may be transferred either through a will or intestate succession.

YOU SHOULD REMEMBER

Real property title can be acquired via voluntary transfer (sale or gift), formally accomplished by delivery of a deed. There are general warranty, special warranty, and quitclaim deeds.

Sales of realty must be in writing to be enforceable (Statute of Frauds), generally involve a title search, and often are accomplished by a mortgage. In return for borrowing money to purchase the realty, the mortgagor (debtor) conveys to the mortgagee (creditor) a security interest in the real property. Alternatives to mortgages are deeds of trust and installment land contracts.

Involuntary transfer of real property title can be accomplished by foreclosure sale, judgment sale, eminent domain, or adverse possession.

Title to real property can also be acquired by will or intestate succession.

RIGHTS ASSOCIATED WITH LAND OWNERSHIP

The law has long held that certain rights naturally accompany land ownership.

1. *Surface rights.* A landowner holds the exclusive right to occupy the surface of a piece of land.

2. *Subterranean rights.* A landowner has the exclusive right to oil, minerals, and other substances found beneath the land's surface. He/she is also entitled to a reasonable use of percolating (subsurface) waters; this last right is often treated as a riparian right (see 8, below).

3. *Air rights*. A landowner has the exclusive right to the air above his/her land, to that height over which control is reasonable. (Obviously, absent zoning restrictions, a landowner cannot prevent airplanes from flying over his/her property at a safe altitude.)

4. *Right to trees, crops*, or *other vegetation* on the land.

5. *Right to fixtures* on the land (e.g., a shed or a patio).

6. *Right to lateral and subjacent support*. A landowner's neighbors may not excavate or otherwise change their own land to such an extent that the owner's lands or buildings are damaged.

7. *Right to be free of public or private nuisances*. A landowner may request a court order to abate pollution, noxious odors, excessive noise, or other interference with his/her enjoyment of the land. (If governmental actions make the land uninhabitable, the owner may seek "inverse condemnation"—an order that the government take the property by eminent domain and compensate the owner.)

8. *Riparian rights*. A landowner may use a natural waterway within his/her property. (Title to navigable streams extends only to their low water mark, with the federal government owning the rest.)

In conjunction with these rights comes the obvious duty not to interfere with other landowners' rights. For example, an owner's riparian rights do not permit the owner to pollute or divert a waterway passing through his/her property. Most states also do not allow the owner to diminish unreasonably a waterway's flow.

RESTRICTIONS ON LAND-USE RIGHTS

• *GOVERNMENTAL CONTROLS*

The owner's right to use his/her land is now usually subject to many governmental controls, including zoning and building codes.

Zoning is legislative action, usually at the municipal level. It regulates the use of property, including the types of construction permitted within different zoning districts.

Like other administrative rulings, zoning decisions are subject to judicial review but are presumptively valid. Courts are extremely reluctant to overturn decisions unless they were *clearly* arbitrary or otherwise violated due process.

Unlike eminent domain, zoning changes generally do not afford landowners an opportunity to receive compensation from the government. Typically, to qualify for compensation, some or part of the land must actually be taken, not merely adversely affected by land-use regulation.

• *PRIVATE RESTRICTIONS*

So long as they are not unlawful or otherwise contrary to public policy, private restrictions may also be placed in deeds, subdivision plans, or the like; such restrictions are usually upheld if they benefit the landowners as a whole. Examples of use restrictions include limits on the size and design of houses or other buildings, and prohibitions of commercial establishments or certain other buildings.

YOU SHOULD REMEMBER

Rights naturally accompanying land ownership include surface, subterranean, air, riparian, and lateral/subjacent support rights; the right to trees, crops, or other vegetation; the right to fixtures; the right to be free of nuisances.

Duties also come with land ownership. For example, owners generally may not abuse their riparian rights to the detriment of others. Also, of course, owners have the duty to conform with zoning and building codes and other governmental controls. There may also be private restrictions on land use.

POSSESSORY AND NONPOSSESSORY (USE) INTERESTS

• *POSSESSORY INTERESTS*

There are three main types of possessory interests in real property:

1. **Fee simple estate.** The highest form of ownership and possession, fee simple estate includes all rights in the land. Owners in fee simple may pass to others rights in the land without giving up absolute ownership.

Besides fee simple absolute (FSA), there are **fee simple determinable** (FSD; ownership automatically ends if a specified action occurs) and **fee simple subject to a condition subsequent** (FSSCS; ownership is subject to a grantor's right of repossession if a specified action occurs). In either case, ownership and possession are absolute until and unless the specified action occurs.

Example: FSA

Land is granted to X. There are no conditions and no possibility of reversion.

Example: FSD

Land is granted to a university "so long as the land is used for educational purposes." If the educational purpose ceases, the land automatically reverts back to the grantor or his/her heirs.

Example: FSSCS

Land is granted to a museum, but "if a painting by Pablo Picasso is ever exhibited on the premises, the grantor or his/her heirs may re-enter." If a Picasso is shown, it is up to the grantor or his/her heirs whether to have the land revert.

2. **Life estate.** Here the term of a person's possessory interest in land is the duration of one or more human lives as specified in the granting instrument. Usually the estate is for the life of the grantee (the person receiving the life estate). Upon the death of the life tenant, the land either reverts to the grantor or his/her heirs (a reversionary interest) or passes to another party designated in the granting instrument. In the latter case, the remaining estate is called a "remainder," with the ultimate recipient being the "remainderman."

Life tenants may generally do anything with their property, including leasing or transferring it, that will not cause permanent damage to it. Of course, if A has a life estate for the life of B, she cannot give to C a fee simple estate or any other estate that exceeds the lifetime of B, that is, A cannot transfer more than she herself has.

3. **Leasehold.** Both fee simple estates and life estates are labeled "freeholds"; in both cases, the estates are of uncertain duration. A leasehold, however, generally has a set term. Unlike the freehold situation, the property's owner is distinct from its occupant, because a leasehold grants only possession, not title. (See the discussion of leases later in this chapter.)

• *NONPOSSESSORY INTERESTS*

Three nonpossessory interests are easements, profits, and licenses.

1. **Easements.** Created either by agreement (express) or by operation of law (implied), the easement gives to its holder a limited right to use, or forbid the use of, another person's land for a specific purpose. Although most easements are *affirmative,* that is, they grant the use of another person's property (e.g., a farmer's driving on his neighbor's private road to get to a second parcel of land that he owns), they can also be *negative,* that is, they restrict a property owner's use of his/her property, the servient estate, because such a use would affect an adjoining, dominant estate (e.g., servient estate S cannot build in such a way as to deprive dominant estate D of access to sunlight). (The effect of negative easements is similar to that of **restrictive covenants.** The latter are express provisions, usually placed in deeds, that attempt to restrict the transfer or use of property.)

Deeds transferring title, or documents accompanying deeds, are the usual means of creating express easements. One main type of express easement is the **appurtenant easement,** which concerns adjoining land: the dominant estate holds a negative or affirmative easement over the neighboring, servient estate. Appurtenant easements, intended for holders of particular property, "run with the land." Thus, when the dominant estate is transferred, the appurtenant easement also passes to the new owner.

The other main type of express easement, an **easement in gross,** is given for a specific purpose. There is no adjoining, dominant estate. At common law, this "personal" easement could not be transferred. However, most states now allow such transfers, especially for easements necessary for commerce or other public purposes.

Example: Easement in Gross

A utility company's right to run lines on private property.

Implied easements, like implied contracts, are based on the parties' presumed intent. Other nonexpress easements include **easements by prescription** and **easements by necessity.** The former is similar to title by adverse possession; it results from actual, open, continual, and nonpermissive easement use of another's land for the statutory period of time needed to establish adverse possession. (Like adverse possession, prescriptive rights typically cannot be acquired in public lands.) An easement by necessity arises if a land conveyance makes such an easement necessary for the use and enjoyment of granted or retained land.

Example: Easement by Necessity

Olive Owner transfers some land to Bill Buyer. Bill's tract has no access to a public road except through Olive's retained land. Thus there is an easement by necessity through Olive's land.

2. **Profits.** A profit is the right to obtain a possessory interest in some aspect of another's land, such as crops, timber, or minerals. An easement usually accompanies the profit, so that the profit holder can enter the land to remove the particular crop, mineral, or whatever.

3. **Licenses.** The owner permits someone to use his/her land, generally for a limited, specific purpose (e.g., to camp, hunt, hike, or fish). The license is subject to revocation at any time.

YOU SHOULD REMEMBER

The three main possessory interests in real property are (1) fee simple estate (can be absolute, determinable, or subject to a condition subsequent); (2) life estate; and (3) leasehold. Absolute ownership vests with fee simple. Leaseholds convey only possession, not title.

Three major nonpossessory interests are easements, profits, and licenses. Easements can be affirmative (to use another person's property) or negative (restricting the use of property). They can be appurtenant ("running with the land") or in gross (to a particular person). Besides arising by express or implied agreement, easements can be by prescription (similar to adverse possession) or by necessity.

TENANT/LANDLORD RELATIONSHIP

The owner of real property may be a **landlord**, having put possession in the hands of a **tenant**.

• *THE LEASE*

The rental agreement, a **lease**, is between the lessor (owner) and lessee (tenant). Although most leases should be express and stated in writing, most states permit short-term leases (one year or less) to be oral or simply implied. The Statute of Frauds, however, bars enforcement of an unacknowledged, unwritten lease covering more than one year. Also, federal, state, and local fair housing laws bar discrimination in renting based upon race, color, religion, national origin, sex, handicap, or familial status.

TYPES OF LEASEHOLDS

There are four main types of *leaseholds* (nonownership, possessory interests in realty):

1. **Estate for years.** Tenancy is for a definite period of time, and usually ends on or by a date stated in the lease, although termination may instead occur because of the parties' mutual agreement, a condition stated in the lease, operation of law (e.g., bankruptcy), or merger (lessee acquires fee simple title to the property).

2. **Periodic tenancy.** Tenancy is for a definite period of time, often month to month, which automatically renews until a contrary notice is given by the lessor or lessee (usually one rental period, e.g., a month, in advance).

3. **Tenancy at will.** Either party may end the tenancy at any time, although most states require a termination notice.

4. **Tenancy at sufferance.** Tenancy continues after the lease has expired, with most jurisdictions holding that this leasehold implicitly becomes a periodic tenancy.

COVENANTS

Most written lease agreements contain covenants, that is, statements about the parties' rights and duties. Covenants customarily cover security deposits, rent (e.g., requiring payment in advance), lease assignments or subleases (e.g., whether, and in what circumstances, they are permitted), and restrictions on use of the premises (e.g., as solely a retail store—no manufacturing allowed). Even if not in writing, there generally are implied covenants that (1) the landlord has the right to transfer possession to the tenant; (2) the tenant will not cause "waste," that is, damage the property beyond normal wear and tear; (3) the landlord grants "quiet enjoyment," that is, will not disturb a lawful tenant's use and enjoyment of the premises; and (4) the property is livable—in good repair (warranty of habitability).

TERMINATION OF THE LEASE

Before its term has run, a lease may be terminated for the following reasons:

1. Frustration of the lease's purpose due to zoning changes, eminent domain, or the like. Also, if a mortgage predates a lease, its foreclosure ends the lease.

2. Tenant's breach of covenants. The landlord must generally serve notice and follow other statutory provisions before evicting a breaching tenant.

3. Constructive eviction. When a landlord materially impairs the tenant's ability to enjoy the premises, the tenant may terminate the lease. (The law considers the landlord's conduct to be, in effect, an eviction.) Other breaches of covenant by the landlord usually permit the tenant just to collect damages, not terminate the lease.

A tenant's unilateral abandonment of the premises does not terminate the lease. He/she remains liable for the remaining rent, with the landlord usually subject to a statutory duty to mitigate damages (attempt to get a new tenant).

• *MAINTENANCE OF RENTED PROPERTY*

The common law left maintenance completely up to the tenant. Now, though, statutes, case law, and leases themselves may place maintenance responsibility on the landlord, tenant, or both. Obviously, landlords are in charge of common areas (facilities used by all tenants, such as parking lots, halls, and shared electric and plumbing systems).

YOU SHOULD REMEMBER

The four main types of leaseholds are estates for years, periodic tenancies, tenancies at will, and tenancies at sufferance. Leases may contain express covenants, and almost all leases have implied covenants, such as: (1) landlord has the right to transfer possession, (2) tenant will not cause "waste," (3) landlord grants "quiet enjoyment," (4) the property is in good repair (warranty of habitability).

Before its term has run, a lease can end because its purpose has been frustrated, the tenant has breached covenants, or there has been a constructive eviction.

TORT LIABILITY FOR REAL PROPERTY CONDITIONS CAUSING INJURY

A landowner may be liable in tort for a visitor's personal injuries resulting from property conditions.

The traditional approach is to label the visitor an *invitee* (e.g., someone entering the premises to engage in business, such as shop or make repairs), a *licensee* (e.g., a social guest or household member), or a *trespasser*. The property owner's duty to invitees extends beyond the issuance of warnings to the exercise of reasonable care in protecting invitees against all dangerous conditions they are unlikely to discover; his/her duty to licensees is to warn them of known, dangerous conditions they are unlikely to discover; his/her duty to trespassers is merely not to injure them intentionally, simply for trespassing. When the landowner knows or should know that children, attracted by a swimming pool or some other feature or artificial condition, are likely to trespass, he/she generally has a higher duty of care (the "attractive nuisance" doctrine).

Most states no longer look only at the status of the injured party. Instead, the test of due care is the overall reasonableness of the landowner's acts or omissions, considering all facts and circumstances. Therefore, status as an invitee, a licensee, or a trespasser is only one consideration out of many.

Some other general principles in establishing liability are as follows:

1. Tenants, as occupants of the premises, have the primary potential liability to injured persons.

2. Most states have **recreational use** statutes: when real property is used for recreation, and without charge, then these statutes remove from the landowner any duty to make property safe or to post warnings.

3. Case law and statutes have increasingly held landlords responsible under fitness warranties customarily involved in land sales. Thus a landlord may be responsible to third parties injured because of the landlord's failure to (a) repair defects as required by the lease; (b) reveal known defects to the tenant; and (c) keep the premises in accord with the local building code. Indeed, landlords and tenants may both be held accountable for injury-causing failure to maintain the premises.

4. A lease may provide that the landlord is not liable for injury to anyone on the premises. However, such **exculpatory clauses** often are not upheld, particularly if the circumstances indicate that it would be inequitable to do so (e.g., the landlord knew or should have known about an extremely dangerous defect in a stairway, while the injured person had no such actual or constructive knowledge).

COMPARISON OF MAJOR PROPERTY ARRANGEMENTS

The following table shows the comparative characteristics of the major arrangements governing property.

ESTATES, TRUSTS, AND WILLS

ESTATES

A person's real and personal property is his/her **estate**. When the person dies, the estate passes to others by trust, will, or state statute.

TRUSTS

To establish a **trust**, one party (the settlor, donor, creator, or trustor) transfers property to another party (the trustee), who administers it for the benefit of a third party (the beneficiary). The settlor can create a trust while still alive, or provide for one through a will.

Property Arrangement	Characteristic					
	Transfers Title	Transfers Possession	Right to Use*	Right to Assign Possession or Use*	Consideration Necessary to Be Enforceable	Right to Sell/Keep Property to Pay Owner's Debts*
Bailment	No	Yes	Rarely	No (although may create a subbailment)	No (can be gratuitous)	If permitted by statute
Lease	No	Generally, yes	Yes	Generally, yes unless lease specifically prohibits	Yes	No**
Sale (see Chapter 10)	Yes	Yes	Yes	Yes	Yes	Already completely has the property
Security interest (see Chapter 20)	No	Generally no (except for pledges)	Generally no	Generally no	"Value" given—cannot be gratuitous	Yes

*Such right would be by the person that acquired this property interest (i.e., the bailee, lessee, buyer, or secured creditor).
**Tenant cannot "convert" a leasehold to fee simple even if landlord owes tenant money.

Requirements for Creation of an Express Trust (the usual type)

1. Capacity of settlor to make a contract or will
2. Intention to create a trust
3. Adherence to any formal, statutory requirements
4. Conveyance to trustee of specific property that settlor has right to convey
5. Clearly identified beneficiary
6. Trust not violative of law or other public policy

Implied Trusts (imposed by law to remedy unjust situations)

Constructive trust. This is used to require the return of wrongly obtained property. Corrects fraud or other misconduct.

Resulting trust. When the person receiving property was not intended to receive it, he/she is made a resulting trustee for the intended beneficiary. Corrects mistakes.

WILLS

A **will** is an instrument, executed by a **testator** (male) or **testatrix** (female) with the formalities required by statute, setting forth how that person's estate is to be distributed after death. It may also specify guardians of the person and/or property of minors or others for whom the testator/testatrix acts as guardian.

Most states require that a will be (1) in writing; (2) made by someone who is an adult and of sound mind; (3) signed by the testator/testatrix in the presence of two or three witnesses, who also sign in the presence of each other and the testator/testatrix.

To amend a will, the testor/testatrix completes a **codicil**, which must meet the same formalities of procedure as a will itself. Although a will can be revoked by the testor's or testatrix's simply destroying it, the clearest expression of revocation—rather than worrying about possible "unrevoked" copies—is to execute a new will, which, as a matter of course, revokes all previous wills.

Wills are submitted and approved by a court according to the process known as **probate**. An **executor** (sometimes referred to as a personal representative) is usually named in the will itself; if not, the probate court names an administrator, usually a close relative or friend of the decedent. The executor or administrator takes inventory of the estate, settles debts and taxes, oversees sales or other liquidation of assets, and (if there is a will) distributes the estate in accordance with the decedent's intentions as expressed in the will.

INTESTATE SUCCESSION BY STATE STATUTE

To die **intestate** is to die without leaving a valid will. Distribution of the estate is then governed by intestate succession laws. Each state has its own such law, specifying the order in which the estate is divided among surviving relatives. Only if there are no surviving relatives does an intestate's estate pass over (**escheat**) to the state.

YOU SHOULD REMEMBER

A deceased person's estate passes to others by trust, will, or state statute.

In a trust, the trustor (settlor) transfers property to a trustee, who administers it for the benefit of a third party (the beneficiary). A trust can take effect while the trustor is still alive, or upon his/her death (through a will). Trusts can be express or imposed by law.

Wills generally must be written, by a competent adult, and signed in the presence of two or three witnesses. A will is freely revocable by the person who makes it (the testator/testatrix). The executor administers the deceased testator's estate: paying debts and expenses and distributing the property in accordance with the terms of the will.

If a person dies intestate (without a valid will), state law determines the distribution of his/her property among surviving relatives. Escheat occurs only if there are no surviving kin.

KNOW THE CONCEPTS

DO YOU KNOW THE BASICS?

1. Name at least five forms of intangible personal property.
2. What are the three basic elements of a gift?

3. What are the four requirements for a bailment?

4. Name four types of bailments and the bailee's duty of care for each.

5. (a) For each of the three main types of intellectual property that can be registered, state its duration (assume the property was created after 1978), two examples (or its definition), and the degree to which the law is federal (not state).

   (b) Name two elements needed to show the existence of a trade secret.

6. If your state follows the community property system, where in the United States do you live?

7. Is it necessary to record a deed? If not, why do it?

8. (a) Name two examples of voluntary transfer of real property, and name the document that must be delivered in order to make such transfers.

   (b) Name three types of deeds.

   (c) Name four methods of involuntary transfer of real property.

9. Name eight rights associated with land ownership.

10. Name three possessory and three nonpossessory interests in real property.

11. (a) What are the four main types of leaseholds?

    (b) Name four implied covenants.

12. In most states, what is the test of the landowner's due care toward visitors?

13. Name three general requirements for a will to be effective.

TERMS FOR STUDY

abandoned property
accession
adverse possession
air rights
appurtenant easement
bailee
bailment
bailor
codicil
common carriers
community property
condominium
confusion
constructive bailment
copyright
deed
donee
donor

easement (affirmative or
    negative)
easement by necessity
easement by prescription
easement in gross
eminent domain
escheat
estate
estate for years
estray statutes
exculpatory clause
executor
fee simple determinable
fee simple estate
fee simple subject to a
    condition subsequent
fixture
general warranty deed

gift
gift *causa mortis*
gift *inter vivos*
gratuitous bailment
intangible personal property
intellectual property
intestate
joint tenancy
landlord
lease
leasehold
license
life estate
lost property
mislaid property
mortgage
patent
periodic tenancy
personal property
probate
profit
quitclaim deed
real property
recreational use statutes

restrictive covenant
right of survivorship
right to lateral and
   subjacent support
riparian rights
special warranty deed
subterranean rights
surface rights
tangible personal property
tenancy at sufferance
tenancy at will
tenancy by the entirety
tenancy in common
tenant
testamentary gift
testator (testatrix)
trade fixture
trademark
trade secret
treasure trove rule
trust
will
zoning

PRACTICAL APPLICATION

1. Daryl Dentist leases an office from Laura Landlady. He has hung several abstract paintings on the walls, and has strongly bolted and attached his dental equipment to the walls and to plumbing and electric outlets. Now that his lease is expiring, Daryl wants to take all of this property to a new location. Laura claims that he cannot do that; the paintings and equipment are now hers. Discuss.

2. Joe suffers a heart attack. Believing he hears the "flapping wings of the Angel of Death," he gives his prized sports trophies to Herb. Joe recovers. When he asks for the trophies back, Herb says, "Sorry, Joe; they're mine now."
   (a) Can Joe get the trophies back?
   (b) What if Joe recovers, thinks about asking for the return of the trophies, and then dies in a car accident?

3. While you are in a restaurant, you find a diamond-studded hat under your chair. Is it now yours? Discuss.

4. Shipper's goods are damaged during transit by a common carrier. No one can show why. Who will probably be liable?

5. (a) Husband Harry and wife Wilma own property P as tenants by the entirety. Without telling Wilma, Harry transfers his interest in P to Otherwoman Olive. Harry dies. Wilma then dies, with her will leaving each of her heirs an equal interest in P. How much of P do the heirs own, and how much does Olive own? What type of tenancy now exists?

(b) Same questions as (a), but assume that husband and wife held P as joint tenants.

6. A fee simple owner conveys a life estate to L, with the remainder to R. L wants to lease his interest. May he do so?

7. Carrie Kiddie passes through Nellie Neighbor's yard every school day in order to catch the bus, and to return home after getting off the bus. This use continues for several years, during the school year. When Carrie's parents sell their house, the new owners start to use Carrie's former pathway to walk to and from a local store. Nellie asks them to stop. If she goes to court, who will win?

ANSWERS
KNOW THE CONCEPTS

1. Contracts, stock, bonds, computer software (programs), employment, utility service, and intellectual property.

2. Donative intent, delivery, and acceptance.

3. Bailor keeps title, bailee obtains possession (delivery and acceptance), possession is for a specific purpose, possession is to be temporary.

4. (1) Bailment solely for bailor's benefit (gratuitous bailment)—slight
   (2) Bailment solely for bailee's benefit—great
   (3) Mutual benefit bailment—ordinary
   (4) Constructive bailment—usually slight

5. (a) Patents—17 years (design patents, 14 years): examples: a new type of mechanical process, a new industrial cleaning formula; exclusively federal.
   Copyrights—creator's life plus 50 years; examples: a song, a novel; almost exclusively federal.
   Trademarks—no set term—10 year registrations can be renewed any number of times; any distinctive mark used by a business to identify its goods; little preempted—state law plays an important role.

   (b) Formula, process, or method to produce goods or services that is (1) meant to be held in employees' confidence, and (2) needed by employees to perform their jobs.

6. Probably in the Southwest or the West.

7. No. To provide notice to others and to establish priority over unrecorded deeds to the same property.

8. (a) Gift and sale; deed.
   (b) General warranty, special warranty, and quitclaim.
   (c) Foreclosure sale, judgment sale, eminent domain, and adverse possession.

9. Subterranean, surface, air, riparian, and lateral support rights; the right to fixtures; the right to trees, crops, or other vegetation; the right to be free of nuisances.

10. Possessory: fee simple estate, life estate, and leasehold. Nonpossessory: easement, profit, and license.

11. (a) Estate for years, periodic tenancy, tenancy at will, tenancy at sufferance.
    (b) Landlord has right to transfer possession, tenant will not cause "waste," landlord warrants habitability, and landlord grants quiet enjoyment.

12. Reasonable care given all facts and circumstances, including but not limited to the visitor's status as invitee, licensee, or trespasser.

13. In writing, by a competent adult, and signed by the testator or testatrix in the presence of two or three witnesses (who also sign, as witnesses).

PRACTICAL APPLICATION

1. Laura evidently claims that the various properties are fixtures. However, if the dental equipment is a fixture, it is obviously a trade fixture. Thus Daryl can take it, although he will have to reimburse Laura for any costs or damages associated with detaching the equipment.
   The paintings probably are not fixtures. Only if they were attached in such a way as to make removal difficult and costly, or only if other circumstances indicate they were intended to remain on the premises, will Daryl be barred from taking them.
   If the paintings are fixtures, Daryl may claim that they are subject to the trade fixture exception. However, unless the paintings are actually pictures of bicuspids or otherwise oriented toward dentistry, a court may well hold that they are not crucial to Daryl's business. Even if they are trade fixtures, removing them might be, on balance, too costly to be permitted.

2. (a) Yes. First, a gift *causa mortis* is freely revocable. Second, Joe recovered, so the trophies revert to him anyway.
   (b) It does not matter. Even though merely thinking about asking for return would not constitute revocation, Joe's recovery automatically rescinds the gift. To be effective, the death must be of the type contemplated; the car accident certainly is not.

3. It appears unlikely that the hat was abandoned; valuable items are presumably mislaid. In most states, the restaurant owner would become a gratuitous bailee. After following the mandates of the estray statute (found in

most states) and otherwise reasonably attempting to locate the owner, the hat would become the restaurant's. However, if the property were deemed to have been lost rather than mislaid, or if there were a specific statutory provision on this point, you, the finder, might get the hat (after attempts to locate the owner have failed).

4. The common carrier. Usually a strict liability standard is applied, with the carrier having the burden of proving an exception to liability.

5. (a) Heirs—all; Olive—none. The present tenancy could be joint or in common, depending on how the will sets it up.

   (b) Heirs—half; Olive—half. Unlike situation (a), the transfer to Olive is effective, although it does convert the tenancy to one in common (no longer joint).

6. Yes. However, because L can rent out the land only for as long as he is alive, prospective tenants should be informed of that fact, including the possibility that R may suddenly become their new landlord. Depending on landlord/tenant law, the rental agreement may have to make the lease subject to early termination upon a condition subsequent: L's demise.

7. Probably Nellie. The question appears to be whether the new owners have an appurtenant easement. Carrie's use, if it constituted an easement, was probably an easement in gross—to Carrie personally, for purposes of catching and leaving a school bus. At such, it would not pass on to the new owners. There are no facts which show that the owners have to use the pathway (easement by necessity), or that the previous use was long or frequent enough (note that the pathway was used only when school was in session) to constitute an easement by prescription.

   Actually the judge may well decide that Carrie's use was merely a license, not transferable and, in any case, freely revocable by Nellie.

20
CREDITORS' RIGHTS AND DEBTORS' PROTECTION; BANKRUPTCY; SECURED TRANSACTIONS

KEY TERMS

surety a person who has expressly or implicitly agreed to be liable for another's debts even if the creditor has not exhausted all remedies for collection

guarantor a person who has expressly or implicitly agreed to be liable for another person's debts if the creditor cannot collect directly from the debtor

bankruptcy a legal procedure for settling the debts of individuals or business entities that are unable to pay debts as they become due. The debtor's business may be reorganized; a set payment may be arranged, or the debtor's nonexempt assets may be liquidated and distributed to creditors. Proper completion of the bankruptcy procedures leaves the debtor free from liability on some or all of the remaining debts.

secured transaction any transaction involving a security interest, which generally is an interest in the debtor's personal property (or fixtures). The security interest is held by the secured party (the creditor) as a means to ensure payment or performance of the debtor's obligation.

History has not been kind to debtors. In various places and at various times, debtors have faced prison, slavery, torture, dismemberment, and/or death because they were unable to pay in full their creditors. For good measure, a debtor's relatives were often punished.

Under modern law, the creditor is not the only one with rights. In fact, the emphasis on consumer protection and on giving people a "second chance" (or more) has led to creditors' complaints that debtors now receive *too much* protection. However, the law generally reflects society's choices; as long as society cannot definitively decide the relative worths of competing values, neither can the law. In the meantime, both creditors and debtors have many rights or remedies available through statutes, the law of contracts, and the common law.

CREDITORS' RIGHTS: COLLECTION OF DEBTS

There are several major debt-collection mechanisms. A creditor may:

1. *Place a lien upon the debtor's property.* When real estate owner Red receives services or materials intended to repair or improve his premises, a *mechanic's lien* on the real estate may develop if Red does not fully pay his bill. A lien is an encumbrance upon Red's property—if the lien remains unpaid, the security held by the creditor can be sold to satisfy the debt (lien). In Red's case, the real property itself is security; after following the mechanic's lien procedures outlined in the relevant state statutes, including a filing of notice, the lien holder may foreclose (force a sale).

Other liens include *artisan's liens* and *hotelkeeper's liens*, both of which involve personal property. As long as the lien holder retains possession of the debtor's personal property, he/she may have a lien on that property for unpaid services or for unpaid repairs, improvements, or care of the debtor's property.

2. *Obtain a prejudgment attachment.* A **prejudgment attachment** entails a court-ordered seizure of the debtor's property before the creditor's claim and the debtor's defenses have been fully adjudicated. It is designed to prevent the wasting or removal of assets pending the completion of a lawsuit. Obviously, this remedy carries the potential for abuse, including deprivation of property based on claims that the "debtor" later successfully refutes; therefore Fourteenth Amendment due process considerations limit the scope and use of prejudgment attachments.

Generally, the creditor must strictly comply with the state statutes governing such attachments. For instance, the creditor must file an affidavit, as well as post a bond covering court costs, loss of use of the property, and the value of the property itself. Seized property is not sold immediately, but remains under the sheriff's control until a judgment is entered.

3. *Take a security interest in the debtor's property.* See the sections on secured transactions later in this chapter.

4. Recover the debt before or during the course of a bulk transfer. A **bulk transfer** occurs when (1) a business sells or otherwise disposes of a substantial portion of its materials, supplies, merchandise, or other inventory, and (2) this sale or other disposal does not occur "in the ordinary course of business." Although the sale of a service operation or of a nonretail manufacturing concern is not covered, UCC Article 6 governs most bulk transfers; it requires that the would-be transferor list both its creditors and the property to be transferred, and that the would-be transferee notify the creditors of the proposed transfer, tell creditors whether debts will be fully paid, and provide other information.

Article 6 then gives creditors at least 10 days before the transfer to take steps necessary to protect their rights (eg., levying of execution on property, suing for an injunction on the sale.) If Article 6 procedures have not been followed, the creditors have 6 months after learning about the bulk transfer to file suit and/or to levy against the transferred property. (Some states have repealed Article 6 or have adopted a 1989 revision.)

5. Proceed against property fraudulently conveyed to a third party. Just as improper bulk transfers may be set aside, so the law does not permit other transfers by debtors trying to avoid debt payment by selling or giving away their assets. Such a transfer is termed a **fraudulent conveyance.**

6. Seek payment from a surety or guarantor, who has expressly or implicitly agreed to be liable for another person's debts. A **surety** is *primarily* liable—the creditor need not exhaust all of his/her remedies against the debtor before holding the surety liable. A **guarantor** is *secondarily* or collaterally liable—the creditor can seek payment from the guarantor only after first trying to obtain relief directly from the debtor. Suretyships need not be in writing, but usually are. All guaranty agreements, though, fall under the Statute of Frauds requirement of a written contract.

Some guaranty agreements are *general* (applying to all creditors who agree). Others are *special*; they apply only to a named creditor and are usually not assignable.

Performance bonds and *fidelity bonds* are examples of suretyship contracts. Performance bonds cover the costs of a party's failure to meet the terms of a contract, such as one for construction of a building. Fidelity bonds protect against losses from the dishonest acts of employees or others. In either instance, payments under the bond cover the costs or losses up to a maximum amount stated in the bond.

Both sureties and guarantors "step into the shoes of the debtor," and may thus raise any claim or defense that the debtor might have advanced, except infancy, bankruptcy, and—in some cases—the statute of limitations. Two other major defenses for sureties or guarantors are that (1) the debtor tendered payment; (2) the debtor's obligations were materially altered without the consent of the surety or guarantor.

Upon paying the creditor, most sureties and guarantors are entitled to reimbursement, if possible, from the debtor. This right is sometimes referred to as

subrogation. In subrogation (also frequently invoked by insurance companies that have paid a claim), the surety or guarantor is substituted for the original creditor, thus acquiring the latter's right to collect from the debtor.

7. *Foreclose on real property.* If a loan is secured by real property, there is a **mortgage** agreement between creditor (mortgagee) and debtor (mortgagor). Upon mortgagor's default, mortgagee may initiate **foreclosure** procedures.

A few states permit the mortgagee to acquire absolute, immediate title to the foreclosed property ("strict foreclosure") or to take immediate possession and then gain title after a waiting period. Most states allow foreclosure and sale to occur pursuant to terms within the mortgage agreement. The *customary method* of foreclosure, though, is a **judicial sale**; after proper notice, the sheriff or other court official takes control of the property and sells it. As with forced sales arising from liens, writs of execution, or otherwise, the sales proceeds are applied first toward the costs of the foreclosure (advertising, court filing fees, etc.) and then toward payment of the debt. Any surplus goes to the debtor. In most states (California is one exception), if the proceeds do not cover the debt, the mortgagee can obtain a "deficiency judgment" against the mortgagor for the remaining amount owed and then collect from other, nonexempt property owned by the mortgagor.

From the time of default until the foreclosure sale, the mortgagor has a right, called **equity of redemption**, to redeem (recover) the property by fully paying the debt, plus the foreclosure costs to date and any interest. Most states also allow mortgagors to redeem within a brief, specified time after the sale ("statutory period of redemption"); this type of redemption serves to cancel the sale, but usually requires the debtor to cover yet another set of costs, namely, the nonrefundable expenses incurred in the sale.

8. *Obtain a writ of execution and/or a garnishment.* After obtaining a judgment in a lawsuit on a debt, an unpaid creditor ("judgment creditor") may seek a court order that (a) a sheriff or other authorized official seize and sell the debtor's nonexempt property (**writ of execution**); (b) third parties holding property of (owing money to) the debtor send to the judgment creditor the nonexempt portion of that property (**garnishment**). After costs have been paid, the proceeds go to the creditor until the judgment debt is satisfied. For garnishment, common third parties are employers (who hold wages due) and banks (who hold checking or savings accounts).

9. *When there are two or more creditors, accept a composition and/or extension agreement or an assignment to a trustee.* In the first situation, the debtor and creditors agree that each creditor will receive a certain percentage (less than 100%) of the amount owed (the composition) and/or extend the payment period (the extension). The debtor's full compliance constitutes a **discharge**, that is, a release from obligation, of the entire debt. In the second situation, the debtor transfers to a trustee the title to some or most of the debtor's property. The trustee in turn sells or otherwise disposes of that property for cash and then distributes the proceeds *pro rata* among the creditors. A creditor accepting such payment discharges the entire debt owed to him/her.

YOU SHOULD REMEMBER

Creditors have numerous methods for collecting debts. The major such methods are liens (mechanic's and artisan's), prejudgment attachment (requires strict statutory and constitutional compliance), security interests, the preventing or setting aside of bulk tranfers or fraudulent conveyances, payment from sureties or guarantors, mortgage foreclosures on real property, writs of execution, garnishment, composition and/or extension agreements, and assignments to a trustee.

PROTECTION FOR DEBTORS

Both state and federal laws provide certain measures of protection for debtors.

EXEMPTION STATUTES

State law exempts certain types of property from being seized and sold to satisfy debts. Most states provide for a **homestead exemption**. When a home is sold to pay a judgment, a specific amount may be retained by the debtor, free of the judgment debt. Although mortgages are not subject to this exemption, it is generally meant to provide a debtor with sufficient funds to protect his/her family and find another home.

Example: *Homestead Exemption*

X owns a house with a $50,000 mortgage on it, and Y has a judgment against X for $25,000. If the mortgage agreement antedates the judgment, proceeds from the sale of the house must go first to pay the mortgagee, not Y.

If the state homestead exemption is $10,000, and X's house sells for $75,000, the mortgagee receives $50,000, X then gets $10,000 (the exemption), and Y takes the remaining $15,000. Y can, of course, collect the remainder of the debt from other nonexempt property that X may own.

Exemption statutes also cover personal property. Most states protect up to a *specified dollar value* for household furnishings, clothes, personal possessions, motor vehicles, livestock, pets, and veterans' pensions.

LIMITS ON GARNISHMENT

A provision in the federal Consumer Credit Protection Act (commonly known as the Truth-in-Lending Act) limits garnishments in any week to the *lesser* of either (1) 25% of that week's disposable earnings, or (2) the amount by which that week's disposable earnings exceed 30 times the federal minimum hourly wage. (Disposable earnings are net income after withholding for federal and state income taxes and social security.) The federal law permits states to substitute, in effect, an even larger exemption of disposable earnings; many states have done so. Some even permit judges to set a higher exemption rate so as to prevent undue hardship.

CONSUMER PROTECTION STATUTES

Numerous federal consumer protection statutes apply to the debtor/creditor relationship.

1. The *Truth-in-Lending Act* (1968) states that a lender, or a seller who is extending credit, must comprehensively disclose credit terms, including finance charges. The act covers all transactions in which the creditor, during the ordinary course of business, makes a loan or extends credit in an amount less than $25,000; the loan or credit must go to an individual or individuals and must concern real or personal property used for personal, family, household, or agricultural purposes.

2. The *Fair Credit Billing Act* (1974) (an amendment to the Truth-in-Lending Act) requires the prompt posting of payments and a notice of prospective finance charges on new purchases, prohibits credit card issuers from forbidding merchants to offer cash discounts, and provides procedures for disputes about credit statements, billings, or purchases.

3. The *Fair Debt Collection Practices Act* (1977) prohibits certain abusive practices by debt collectors.

4. The *Fair Credit Reporting Act* (1970) (part of the Truth-in-Lending Act) provides for debtors' access to credit reports and sets forth procedures for correcting misinformation or otherwise protecting a consumer's credit reputation.

5. The *Equal Credit Opportunity Act* (1976) prohibits discrimination in the extending of credit.

6. Credit card rules in the Truth-in-Lending Act (a) limit the liability of a cardholder to $50 per card upon notifying the creditor about a lost or stolen card, and (b) prohibit outright billing a consumer for unauthorized charges (e.g., on a card never accepted by the consumer).

In addition to these federal measures, the states have their own laws and regulations, which may set maximum interest rates (usury laws) or otherwise protect consumers who have been extended credit. For example, approximately ten states have adopted some form of the *Uniform Consumer Credit Code* (UCCC), which establishes maximum interest rates and requires a full disclosure of facts to buyers on credit in almost any situation. The UCCC is an attempt to systemize the law; it thus serves to replace particular laws on such matters as usury, credit advertising, small loans, retail installment sales, and service, delinquency, or deferral charges. Perhaps most important, the UCCC forbids (1) multiple agreements in order to obtain higher interest rates, (2) "balloon" payments more than twice as large as the average payment, (3) assignments of a debtor's wages, and (4) in most cases, judgments for money beyond that obtained by repossessing goods purchased on credit. Criminal as well as civil penalties are provided.

LENDER LIABILITY

Lenders increasingly have been sued by debtors and others for damages allegedly resulting from lender misconduct in revoking credit, foreclosing on security, administering a loan, refusing to extend credit, or *even for extending credit*. Liability theories include: breach of contract, fraud, excessive control (e.g., interference with the debtor's contractual relations with others), negligence, economic duress (which may make a loan settlement voidable), breach of fiduciary duties or implied duties of good faith and fair dealing, and even statutory bases such as state consumer fraud legislation and federal environmental, bankruptcy, securities, RICO, and tax laws.

YOU SHOULD REMEMBER

State law exempts some property from seizure to satisfy debts. After the proceeds on the sale of a home have paid the mortgage, most states exempt a specific amount of the remaining proceeds. For personal property, state law tends to exempt up to a specified dollar value for household furnishings, clothes, personal possessions, motor vehicles, livestock, pets, and veterans' benefits.

The federal Consumer Credit Protection Act (known as the "Truth-in-Lending-Act") limits garnishment to 25% of disposable earnings or even less in the case of low-income wage earners; state law may further limit garnishment. Numerous federal and state statutes regulate creditor practices, prohibit abuses, provide dispute-resolution mechanisms, or otherwise protect debtors.

BANKRUPTCY AND REORGANIZATION

Bankruptcy is a method for settling the debts of individuals or business entities that are unable to pay debts as they become due.

Under court supervision, all or most of the debtor's assets are used to pay his/her creditors, with creditors of equal status (priority) each receiving the same proportion of the amounts owed to them. Once the liquidation, reorganization, or adjustment plan is judicially approved and then properly completed, the bankruptcy serves to relieve the debtor from all or most of his/her debts even though these debts have not been fully paid.

The U.S. Constitution, Article I, Section 8, empowers Congress to make "uniform laws on the subject of bankruptcies throughout the United States." Congress has structured a system of *federal bankruptcy courts*, with judges appointed to 14-year terms and serving the same or similar geographic areas as do federal district court judges. Appeals go either to the U.S. District Court or (as some U.S. circuits provide) to a bankruptcy appellate panel consisting of bankruptcy judges from within the circuit.

Although matters of state law may arise during a bankruptcy proceeding, the essential issues in the bankruptcy itself are governed by *federal* law as stated in the Bankruptcy Code and interpreted in federal court opinions. For instance, while orders about legal fees and costs in conjunction with a divorce case are matters of state law, it is up to the federal bankruptcy court to decide whether, under federal law, these orders are, in effect, part of a debtor's obligation to pay alimony or child support and thus cannot be discharged in bankruptcy.

CHAPTERS 7, 11, AND 13 OF THE BANKRUPTCY CODE

The Bankruptcy Code provides for three main alternatives: proceedings under Chapter 7 (Liquidation), Chapter 11 (Business Reorganization), or Chapter 13 (Adjustment of an Individual's Debts). A fourth type of proceeding, to adjust the debts of a municipal corporation, is available under Chapter 9 when authorized by the state where the municipal corporation is located.

Under any of these four alternatives, the debtor may file a voluntary petition for bankruptcy. Creditors may initiate only a Chapter 7 or a Chapter 11 proceeding; this is done by filing an involuntary petition. A *filing* under any of the four chapters *creates an "estate" consisting of all of the debtor's property.*

• CHAPTER 7

In a *Chapter* 7 case, the bankruptcy court appoints a trustee to take charge of the estate. The trustee sells ("liquidates") the debtor's nonexempt property, and the proceeds are then distributed to the creditors according to their priorities under law—for example, taxes are usually paid before general creditors are paid.

A Chapter 7 discharge covers debts, including judgments, arising before the bankruptcy order granting the discharge. Just as a bankruptcy petition operates temporarily to prevent most creditors from trying to collect their debts pending the bankruptcy proceedings, the discharge makes this prevention permanent.

Because Chapter 7 discharges cover only individuals, business entities such as corporations and partnerships remain technically liable for their debts. However, the lack of discharge does not matter unless the entity later acquires assets. The effect is to prevent the resurrection of that same entity (e.g., as a "shell" business) after a Chapter 7 liquidation. (Under Chapter 11, a type of discharge is granted.)

Some businesses, though, are simply denied the right to file for bankruptcy. Railroads, banks, savings and loan associations, credit unions, insurance companies, and other financial institutions are regulated in all matters, including insolvency, by administrative agencies, not the Bankruptcy Code. However, railroads are permitted to file for a Chapter 11 reorganization.

• *CHAPTER 11*

Chapter 11 is mainly intended to allow on-going businesses to restructure their debts. Before restructuring occurs, a court-appointed trustee or examiner conducts an investigation, files reports with the court, and may submit a reorganization plan (if the debtor has not) or (instead) recommend conversion to a Chapter 7 liquidation.

Whether for an individual proprietorship, a small firm, or a large corporation, successful reorganization requires a detailed plan covering all aspects of the organization's business operation and its assets and debts. Then the plan must be accepted by the bankruptcy judge and by two-thirds in amount, and more than half in number, of the claims in any particular class of creditors. Each creditor must receive at least as much as the creditor would be entitled to obtain under Chapter 7 liquidation.

• *CHAPTER 13*

Chapter 13 is available only to individuals with regular sources of income, unsecured debts not exceeding $100,000, and secured debts of no more than $350,000. The debtor files a payment plan, with payments beginning no more than 30 days after the bankruptcy petition is filed and continuing for up to 5 years. Payments are made to a court-appointed trustee, who begins paying creditors after the court approves the plan. Upon completion of the plan, and even for "hardship" cases in which plan payments are incomplete, a Chapter 13 discharge (comparable to, but in some ways broader than, a Chapter 7 discharge) is granted.

Usually about one fourth of the debtor's disposable earnings goes to his/her creditors, although the specific amount is somewhat dependent on the debtor's level of income and family responsibilities. As in Chapter 11, payments cannot be any less than a creditor would receive under Chapter 7 liquidation. At any time, the debtor or the court may turn the case into a Chapter 7 proceeding.

PROCEDURE AND EXEMPTIONS

A debtor must file a financial statement (including income and expenses) and must list assets, creditors (with addresses and amounts owed), and exempt property. Exemptions under federal law include the following:

1. Equity in a home and burial plot up to $7,500.
2. Interest in one motor vehicle up to $1,200.
3. Trade or business items up to $750.
4. Prescribed health aids.
5. Unmatured life insurance policies (other than credit life insurance.)
6. Federal and state benefits such as social security, local public assistance, and veterans', disability and unemployment benefits.
7. An interest in jewelry not to exceed $500.

8. Alimony and child support, as reasonably necessary for the debtor.
9. Certain pensions, stock bonuses and annuities.
10. An interest in household furnishings or goods, clothes, books, appliances, pets, or other items of a personal, family, or household nature (up to $200 for any one item, with the total not exceeding $4,000).
11. Criminal victim restitution payments, wrongful death benefits, life insurance payments to a dependent beneficiary, and—up to $7,500—personal injury payments.
12. Any other property worth altogether (a) no more than $400, plus (b) up to $3,750 of the unused portion, if any, of the $7,500 homestead exemption (item 1, above).

THE TRUSTEE'S ROLE IN BANKRUPTCY

The **trustee** acquires title to all of the debtor's property ("the estate") and administers the estate by collecting and liquidating assets as well as deciding claims. The trustee may sue, accept or reject executory contracts, revoke unperfected property transfers, and negate preferential or fraudulent transfers.

> Preferential transfers favor one creditor over others (i.e., the favored creditor gets more than he/she would under the Bankruptcy Code). Such transfers are prohibited when they concern preexisting debts and are made during the 90-day period before the bankruptcy petition is filed.

Creditors with liens on or security interests in the debtor's property may sell or otherwise dispose of the property in order to collect the debt secured by that property. If a sale generates more than is owed, the excess goes into the debtor's estate. If, after disposition of the secured property, the debtor still owes money, the creditor becomes an unsecured, general creditor for the remaining amount owed (category 7, immediately below).

The trustee distributes the debtor's estate (pays costs, claims, or other expenses) in this order:

1. Costs of administering, collecting, and maintaining the estate, including attorneys' fees.

2. Claims arising in the ordinary course of business, after the bankruptcy petition was filed but before a trustee was appointed or an order for relief was made.

3. Claims up to $2,000 per employee for wages earned 90 or fewer days before the bankruptcy petition was filed.

4. Claims up to $2,000 per employee for contributions to employee benefit plans arising from services rendered 180 or fewer days before the bankruptcy petition was filed.

5. Claims up to $900 for deposits with the debtor that were to pay for consumer purchases or leases of property or services, if the property or services remain unprovided.

6. Taxes and penalties due in the 3 years before the bankruptcy petition was filed.

7. Claims of general creditors (almost all other unsecured debts). Those parts of claims that exceed the money or time limits in categories 3, 4, or 5 above fall within this category.

NONDISCHARGEABLE DEBTS, DENIAL OF OVERALL DISCHARGE, AND LIMITS OF DISCHARGE

• *NONDISCHARGEABLE DEBTS*

Five types of debts are considered to be too important to be discharged by bankruptcy:

1. Alimony.

2. Child support.

3. Some government fines and penalties.

4. Taxes owed for the 3 years before bankruptcy.

5. Student loans received within 5 years of bankruptcy.

The main reason for not discharging a debt may be the debtor's misconduct. These other nondischargeable debts are as follows:

1. Intentional tort claims.

2. Judgments based on drunk driving.

3. Claims to money or property obtained by fraud, false pretense, embezzlement, or misuse of funds.

4. Criminal restitution obligations.

5. Claims not listed in the bankruptcy petition.

6. Debts exceeding $500 for luxury goods/services purchased within 40 days before the bankruptcy filing and certain cash advances exceeding $1,000 within 20 days before the filing.

Moreover, if in a prior bankruptcy action the debtor was denied a discharge of a particular claim (for reasons other than the 6-year waiting requirement between bankruptcy discharges), he/she cannot later get a discharge on that claim. (Nor, as discussed earlier, can the debtor use a fraudulent or preferential transfer to avoid his/her responsibilities or favor certain creditors.)

• *DENIAL OF OVERALL DISCHARGE*

Overall bankruptcy discharge may be denied in these cases:

1. The debtor has: (a) in writing waived his/her right to a discharge; (b)

destroyed, concealed, or transferred his/her property and/or records in order to hinder or defraud a creditor; (c) unjustifiably failed to maintain records from which his/her financial status could be determined; (d) not adequately explained a supposed loss of assets; (e) committed a bankruptcy "scam" or other such crime; or (f) refused to obey a bankruptcy court order to answer the court's questions or to appear at scheduled bankruptcy meetings or hearings.

2. A bankruptcy court granted the debtor a discharge within 6 years of the filing of his/her present petition (not applicable when the prior proceeding was a good-faith Chapter 13 plan paying at least 70% of unsecured claims).

3. A prior bankruptcy petition was dismissed 180 days before the present petition was filed.

4. A Chapter 7 discharge by a consumer debtor would be a "substantial abuse" of the system.

In most, if not all of these cases, the debtor's nonexempt assets are still distributed to creditors; but, instead of receiving a discharge, the debtor remains liable for the unpaid portion of his/her debts.

• *LIMITS OF DISCHARGE*

A discharge does not affect the liability of a codebtor, a surety, or a guarantor. Moreover, within one year of a discharge the bankruptcy court may revoke its discharge decree because of evidence that the debtor committed fraud or lied during the bankruptcy proceedings.

Debtors may reaffirm a dischargeable debt; such a **reaffirmation agreement,** though, must be in writing and contain a statement to the effect that the debtor knows of his/her right to rescind the reaffirmation before discharge or within 60 days, whichever is later. The reaffirmation agreement must be filed in bankruptcy court, along with an affidavit by the debtor's attorney that the agreement would impose no undue hardship on the debtor or a dependent of the debtor, and that the debtor was fully informed of his/her rights and entered into the agreement voluntarily. If the debtor was not represented by counsel, a reaffirmation agreement usually requires the bankruptcy court's approval; it must find that the reaffirmation does not impose undue hardship on the debtor and is in the debtor's best interest.

Of course, a debtor may simply volunteer to repay a discharged debt. Such payments cannot be compelled, however, in the absence of a binding reaffirmation.

YOU SHOULD REMEMBER

The test for bankruptcy is: Can the debtor pay debts as they become due?

The Constitution empowers Congress to make uniform laws on bankruptcy. Thus bankruptcy is governed by federal law, with a system of U.S. bankruptcy courts.

The Bankruptcy Code has three main alternatives: Chapter 7 (Liquidation), Chapter 11 (Business Reorganization), and Chapter 13 (Adjustment of an Individual's Debts). Petitions for bankruptcy may be voluntary (filed by the debtor) for all three chapters or involuntary (filed by creditors) for Chapters 7 and 11.

Chapter 7 is the traditional, "straight" bankruptcy. Certain regulated businesses cannot obtain such a bankruptcy. Chapter 11 involves a reorganization of business debts, with a plan requiring the approval of the bankruptcy judge and most creditors. Chapter 13 permits individuals with a regular source of income, and debts not exceeding a statutory amount, to seek court approval of a payment plan lasting up to 5 years.

The Bankruptcy Code exempts certain property, or amounts of property, from being used to satisfy creditors' claims.

A court-appointed trustee administers the debtor's property ("the estate") and distributes the debtor's nonexempt property according to the priority of claims outlined in the Bankruptcy Code.

The Bankruptcy Code prohibits the discharge of certain debts and also allows the bankruptcy judge to deny discharges because of the debtor's misconduct.

Discharges do not remove the liability of codebtors, sureties, or guarantors; and a debtor may, in writing, reaffirm a discharged debt.

SECURED TRANSACTIONS

A **secured transaction** is any transaction in which a debtor gives a creditor a security interest in personal property or fixtures.

INTRODUCTION

Article 9 of the UCC governs secured transactions. In a typical case the debtor has borrowed money (often a purchase on credit), with the creditor expecting the debtor's performance (e.g., payments) in compliance with the terms of the loan. As additional protection of his/her right to repayment, the creditor requires that the debtor give a security interest in personal property; if the debtor fails to perform, the *secured creditor* can use that personal property (known as **collateral**) as a substitute for, or a means to collect, the debtor's performance.

Security interests are commonly given in the very property for which a business or consumer has borrowed money (received financing) in order to buy. Secured credit thus permits a consumer or business to make large-scale purchases while assuring the sellers and lenders that they can obtain complete, or at least partial, payment from the secured property if necessary.

PLEDGE

The oldest and simplest type of secured transaction is a **pledge**; there the debtor provides the creditor with physical possession of some of the debtor's property. This collateral may consist of tangible items, such as jewelry or machinery, or intangible personal property, such as stocks. If the debtor defaults, the creditor sells or uses the collateral to satisfy the debt.

Example: Pledge

Ellen Extravagent owes a credit card company $500. She borrows the money from Paul Pawnbroker and leaves a diamond ring worth $800 with Paul as collateral.

One obvious problem with a pledge is that the debtor frequently will not or cannot turn over possession of his/her property. In fact, a pledge contradicts the underlying purpose of many credit transactions, that is, to help the debtor acquire *and use* property, not merely buy property (on credit) and then pledge away its possession.

SECURITY INTEREST

Because of problems with the pledge, the law has long permitted the use of security devices that do not require transfer of possession. Such devices include chattel mortgages, trust receipts, and assignments of accounts receivables· the UCC now labels all of these **security interests**.

• *COLLATERAL*

Article 9 of the UCC states that any of the following types of property can be **collateral** (i.e., property subject to a security interest):

- Goods (including equipment and inventory).

- Documents evincing rights (e.g., commercial paper, securities, bills of lading, receipts).

- Accounts receivable.

- Most other personal property or fixtures.

Excluded are such items as real estate, mortgages, insurance, deposit accounts, landlord's or mechanic's liens, and claims arising from lawsuits.

Even "after-acquired property" (personal property acquired by the debtor after the security agreement was executed) may be collateral, although UCC 9-204(2) sets limits on after-acquired interests in consumer goods (only permitted for accessions or for property acquired within 10 days after the secured party gave value). Collateral may even secure future credit, not just past or present loans.

• *REQUIREMENTS FOR AN EFFECTIVE SECURITY INTEREST*

ATTACHMENT

To make the security interest effective between the debtor and creditor, the interest must "attach" to the secured property (the collateral). The three requirements of an **attachment** are as follows:

1. A written agreement sets forth a security interest, describes the collateral, and is signed by the debtor.
2. Value is given by the secured party to the debtor.
3. The debtor has rights in the collateral.

"Value" arises from commitments to extend credit, from consideration sufficient for a contract, or from preexisting consideration. When the secured party obtains possession of the collateral (a pledge), no written agreement is necessary.

PERFECTION

To make the security interest effective against third parties, it must be "perfected." **Perfection** gives the secured party priority over other parties seeking to attach or otherwise use the collateral. In short, if C perfects a security interest in D's equipment, most third-party creditors will not be permitted to seize and sell that equipment in order to satisfy D's debts to them.

The method for obtaining a *perfection* depends on the type of collateral. The three methods are possession, attachment, and the filing of a **financing statement**.

1. *Possession* constitutes perfection for pledges. It is the required method for negotiable instruments or other documents (e.g., stocks, bonds, promissory notes, warehouse receipts, bills of lading), *except* for purely intangible collateral such as (a) paper evincing a right to accounts receivable, or (b) chattel paper (documents evincing both a monetary obligation and a security interest in, or lease of, specific goods).

2. *Automatic perfection (perfection by attachment) usually involves a purchase-money security interest (PMSI)* in consumer goods other than fixtures or motor vehicles. Section 9-107 of the UCC defines a PMSI as a security interest that is: (a) held by the seller of the collateral in order to secure all or part of the sales price, *or* (b) held by a person lending money or otherwise giving value that the debtor uses to acquire or use the collateral.

Without automatic perfection, filing offices would be swamped with financing statements concerning PMSIs in consumer goods. Most authorities believe that such increased filing would provide little added protection to other creditors, and might only confuse matters.

The other typical instance of automatic perfection involves assignments of accounts or contract rights that do not, alone or with other assignments to the same assignee, amount to a "significant part" of the assignor's outstanding accounts or contract rights.

3. The third and *most common method of obtaining perfection* is to *file a financing statement*. Such a statement must contain the debtor's signature, the addresses of both the debtor and the secured party, and a description of the collateral. Filing is necessary for perfection if possession is not the required method for perfection, as it is, for example, for negotiable instruments; if the secured party does not in fact have possession; and if the transaction does not involve automatic perfection (usually via a consumer PMSI).

The secured party has the duty of filing the financing statement. Section 9-401(1) of the UCC provides three alternatives on where the financing statement should be filed. Each state has chosen one of these alternatives, with about half adopting some form of the second alternative:

1. A central filing with a state office, except for local filings for timber, minerals and some fixture collateral.

2. Local filings for farm and/or consumer goods, timber, minerals, and some fixtures, and central filings for other collateral.

3. Same as 2, above, but requiring a local filing in addition to the central filing requirements (e.g., the county where the debtor resides, or where the collateral is located). The additional filings are if the debtor has a place of business in just one county or has no in-state place of business but resides in the state.

Just as a person in doubt as to whether he/she needs to file a financing statement should—to be safe—file one, so anyone in doubt as to *where* to file should file in every possible county or state. The costs are usually nominal.

Do not confuse the financing statement with the security agreement. The former cannot replace the latter.

Indeed, the financing statement simply furnishes the minimal information needed to put other parties on notice of a security interest. (In some cases, the security agreement itself may be filed as the financing statement.) To obtain further information, the debtor or secured party may have to be contacted directly.

A proper filing will be good for 5 years, unless it indicates a shorter maturity date. Continuations may be filed in order to extend the financing statement for another 5 years. The number of such extensions is unlimited, and the secured party need not obtain the debtor's signature.

RIGHTS AND DUTIES OF SECURED PARTIES AND DEBTORS

• *WHAT IS A DEFAULT?*

A **default** on a debt is not defined in UCC Article 9. The parties usually state in their security agreement the conditions that will constitute a default. The typical default is failure to make timely payments on the loan. Another type of default may be to breach a warranty that no liens or other security interests cover the same collateral as that relied on in the security agreement.

• *RIGHTS AND DUTIES BEFORE DEFAULT*

Before default, the parties have certain rights or duties, unless specified differently in the security agreement.

The *secured party*:

(a) may release or assign all or part of the collateral;
(b) may file an extension or amendment of a financing statement, although the latter also requires the debtor's signature;
(c) if in possession of the collateral, must use reasonable care to preserve it.

The *debtor*:

(a) may periodically request and receive from the secured party a written statement as to the current amount of the unpaid debt, and perhaps a full listing of the collateral;
(b) bears the risk of loss or damage to the collateral;
(c) must pay for all reasonable expenses incurred in taking care of the collateral.

• *RIGHTS AND DUTIES AFTER DEFAULT*

Upon default, the secured party may sue on the underlying obligation or enforce the security interest directly. These remedies are not exclusive, and can be cumulative if need be [UCC 9-501(1)].

UCC Section 9-503 states the secured party's right to take possession after default, unless prohibited by the security agreement itself. Although the secured party may take possession without a court order, such conduct must not lead to a breach of the peace. As is the case before default, the secured party has to exercise reasonable care over any collateral it now possesses.

As an alternative, a secured party may require the debtor to assemble the collateral at a place designated by the secured party. In fact, the secured party may choose not to remove collateral equipment, but simply to make it unusable and then dispose of it (e.g., sell it) on the debtor's premises.

SPECIAL PROVISIONS IF THE SECURED PARTY CHOOSES TO KEEP THE COLLATERAL

The secured party may decide to keep the collateral in satisfaction of the debtor's obligation. However, if the debtor has paid over 60% of the price or the loan for collateral that consists of consumer goods, the secured party may *not retain* these goods *unless after default* the debtor signs a statement permitting such retention rather than a sale. In cases not involving an over-60% payment on consumer goods, the secured party must notify the debtor, unless a signed statement permits retention.

For collateral other than consumer goods, the secured party must also notify other secured parties who have given written notice of an interest in the collateral. If within 21 days a person entitled to notification (e.g., the debtor or another secured party) objects to the secured party's retention of the goods, a sale must take place. Otherwise, the secured party may keep the collateral (UCC 9-505).

SALE OF THE COLLATERAL

The secured party may choose to sell the collateral or, as provided in UCC 9-505, may be forced to conduct such a sale. In either case, the disposition may be by any method so long as it is "commercially reasonable." It is not enough to show that a different type of sale could have produced a better price; for example, the sale is "commercially reasonable" if it was conducted in the usual manner for a recognized market in the goods, or if it obtained the current market price, or if it conformed to the practices of merchants selling the same type of property.

The debtor, of course, has a right to redeem the collateral before the sale by fully paying the debt, plus the additional expenses incurred by the secured party. Moreover, another secured party may, in effect, substitute his/her payment for that of the debtor so as to secure the collateral. Once sold, the purchaser takes the collateral free of claims by the debtor or by secured parties.

Upon sale, the proceeds are distributed in this order to pay:

(a) reasonable expenses related to possessing, preserving, and selling the collateral, including attorney's fees;

(b) the debt owed to the secured party;

(c) claims of other secured parties who gave written notice of an interest in the collateral.

The surplus, if any, goes to the debtor.

As with other debt-collection mechanisms, if the sale does not give the secured party all that he/she is owed, then the secured party (unless barred by the security agreement itself) usually retains a right to collect the deficiency by other means. (The exceptions involve accounts or chattel paper, in which a deficiency is non-recoverable unless the security agreement specifically provides otherwise.)

TERMINATION STATEMENT

Once the debtor's obligations are satisfied, he/she may require that the secured party file a termination statement wherever a financing statement was filed. For financing statements concerning consumer goods (a rarity because of automatic perfection), the termination statement is mandatory even if the former debtor does not demand it. Failure to file subjects the secured party to fines and also liability to the debtor for any resulting losses.

PRIORITY OF CREDITORS

Obviously, one major purpose of the secured transaction is to ensure that the secured party can use the collateral to collect the debt before other creditors may do so. Thus one creditor has *priority* over another creditor (*who has an interest in the same collateral and/or is owed money by the same debtor*). The following table shows the major priority controversies and their usual outcomes.

Opposing Creditors		Priority Creditor
	General Rules	
Perfected security holder	Another perfected security holder	The first to perfect [UCC 9-312(5)]
Perfected security holder	Unperfected security holder	The perfected security holder, regardless of whose security interest arose first [UCC 9-312(5)]
Unperfected security holder	Another unperfected security holder	The first party whose security interest attached [UCC 9-312(5)]
Unperfected security holder	Unsecured creditor or unlevied judgment creditor	The unperfected security holder [UCC 9-301]
	PMSI and Crop Exceptions to "First to Perfect" Rule	
Perfected PMSI in inventory	Earlier perfected non-PMSI	PMSI (and also as to PMSI cash proceeds if notice was given to non-PMSI on or before debtor takes possession) [UCC 9-312(3)]
Perfected PMSI in noninventory collateral	Earlier perfected non-PMSI in the same collateral	PMSI, if perfected within 10 days after debtor obtains possession [UCC 9-312(4)]
Perfected security interest in crops	Earlier perfected interest in crops that secures obligations due over 6 months before crops began	Later perfected security interest if, within 3 months before planting, new value was given to enable debtor to grow the crop [UCC 9-312(2)]
	Lien Creditors	
Lien creditor	Unperfected or later perfected security holder	Lien creditor, except if pre-existing PMSI is perfected before or within 10 days after debtor possesses the collateral [UCC 9-301(1)-(2)]
Lien creditor	Perfected security holder	Lien creditor, but subject to the perfected security interest inasmuch as (1) it secures advances the secured party made before or within 45 days after the lien creditor obtained the lien, or (2) it secures advances made without knowledge of the lien [UCC 9-301(4)]

Opposing Creditors		**Priority Creditor**
Other Exceptions to "First to Perfect" Rule:		
Purchasers of the Debtor's Collateral and Trustees in Bankruptcy *		
Purchaser of negotiable instruments, documents of title, and/or securities	Earlier perfected security holder	The purchaser [UCC 9-309]
Purchaser of chattel paper	Earlier perfected security holder	The purchaser, if gave new value, took possession in the ordinary course of business, and had no actual knowledge of the security interest (last requirement unnecessary when chattel paper claimed as proceeds of inventory) [UCC 9-308]
Purchaser of goods in the ordinary course of business	Earlier perfected security holder for a security interest created by the goods' seller	The purchaser, even if purchaser knows of the security interest [UCC 9-307(1)]
Purchaser of consumer goods	Earlier PMSI or other security interest perfected without filing a financing statement	The purchaser, if gave value, had no knowledge of the security interest, and used the goods for personal, family, or household purposes [UCC 9-307(2)]
Trustee in bankruptcy	Earlier perfected security holder	Trustee, if the security interest was given for antecedent debt no more than 4 months before bankruptcy petition was filed
Fixtures to Real Estate and Accessions to Personal Property		
Perfected security holder in a fixture	Conflicting real estate claimant (e.g., mortgagee)	First to file, except that PMSIs filed within 10 days of affixation always have priority [UCC 9-313]

*Of course, a purchaser or trustee may not, in fact, be a "creditor." Nonetheless, priority disputes often arise between purchasers (or trustees) and creditors.

Opposing Creditors		Priority Creditor
Fixtures to Real Estate and Accessions to Personal Property		
Unperfected security holder in a fixture	Conflicting real estate claimant	Conflicting real estate claimant [UCC 9-313(7)]
Security holder in an accession	Security holder in the chattel to which the accession is added	Generally, the security holder in the accession, whether perfected or unperfected, if security interest attached to accession before accession was added to the chattel. [UCC 9-314(1)]

YOU SHOULD REMEMBER

UCC Article 9 governs secured transactions. A security interest may be taken in almost any type of personal property.

To make the security interest effective between the debtor and the creditor, it must "attach" to the secured property (collateral). Attachment requires (1) a written agreement stating a security interest, describing the collateral, and signed by the debtor; (2) value from the secured party to the debtor; and (3) rights of the debtor in the collateral.

To make the security interest work against third parties, it must be "perfected" by (1) possession, (2) attachment, or (3) the filing of a financing statement. The proper method depends on the type of collateral, with the financing statement being the most common method.

Parties to a security agreement have numerous rights or duties with respect to collateral, financing statements and debt information. Upon default, the secured party may sue on the underlying obligation or enforce the security interest directly; these remedies can be cumulative.

In *some* cases, the secured party may keep the collateral as satisfaction of the defaulting debtor's obligations. In *all* defaults, the secured party may sell the collateral by any "commercially reasonable" method, with the debtor having a right to redeem up to the time of sale. Proceeds are distributed first to cover expenses, then to pay (1) the secured debt, (2) other secured parties, and (3) if any money remains, the debtor.

Satisfaction of the debtor's obligation is evinced by the secured party's filing of a termination statement.

The order in which creditors are paid follows an established system of priorities, in which the first to perfect a security interest usually takes precedence.

KNOW THE CONCEPTS
DO YOU KNOW THE BASICS?

1. Name ten lawful methods for collecting debts.

2. Name five or more types of personal property that may be at least partly exempted from debt-collection enforcement.

3. (a) Name at least four federal statutes that regulate creditor practices, prohibit abuses, provide dispute-resolution mechanisms, or otherwise protect debtors.
   (b) Would you include the UCCC in your list?

4. Which law, federal or state, governs bankruptcy proceedings?

5. Under the Bankruptcy Code, what is the test for insolvency (the "bankruptcy test")?

6. Name the three main chapters of the Bankruptcy Code, the type of relief under each chapter, and the party that may ask for that relief.

7. Name at least four types of assets (property) *totally* exempt from being liquidated or otherwise disposed of to help pay claims against a bankrupt debtor.

8. Name at least four types of nondischargeable debts, as well as the main other reason for not discharging a debt.

9. Does a bankruptcy discharge affect the liability of a codebtor, surety, or guarantor?

10. What is the simplest type of secured transaction?

11. Name four types of property that can be subject to a security interest.

12. (a) What are the requirements for an attachment?
    (b) What does an attachment accomplish?

13. (a) What are the three methods for making a security interest "perfect"?
    (b) What does perfection accomplish?

14. Upon default, what may a secured party do with the collateral?

15. What is the general rule governing priority between two conflicting security holders?

TERMS FOR STUDY

attachment	discharge
bankruptcy	equity of redemption
bulk transfer	financing statement
collateral	foreclosure
default	fraudulent conveyance

garnishment
guarantor
homestead exemption
judicial sale
lender liability
lien
mortgage
perfection
pledge

prejudgment attachment
reaffirmation agreement
secured transaction
security interest
subrogation
surety
trustee
writ of execution

PRACTICAL APPLICATION

1. Sure-Thing Surety has entered into suretyships with the following debtors. Coincidentally, in each case the creditor is Wanda Wealthy.
   (1) Dirk Debtor owes $10,000 on a loan. Payments are in default. Dirk is 15 years old.
   (2) Daphne Delinquent purchased a number of items on credit. Wanda demands payment. Daphne says a check is in the mail.
   (3) Ollie Obligor persuaded Wanda to extend the duration of his loan, in return for Ollie's agreeing to pay a higher interest rate. Ollie now defaults.
   (4) Karen Komitted goes bankrupt. She receives a discharge of her debt to Wanda.
      (a) For each case, state whether, on the limited facts given, Wanda can obtain payment directly from Sure-Thing Surety.
      (b) What additional two defenses might be raised if Sure-Thing were a guarantor, not a surety?

2. Harry Homeowner owes $50,000 on a mortgage for a house, owned solely by Harry and lived in by the entire Homeowner family. Harry also owes $5,000 to unsecured creditor A, as well as $3,000 to creditor B, the latter debt being secured by a perfected security interest in Harry's sailboat. Harry is in default on all three debts. The house would sell for $69,000 with costs of sale being $2,000. The state homestead exemption is $9,000.
   (a) If the mortgagee conducts a foreclosure sale, what will happen to the sales proceeds?
   (b) If Harry files for bankruptcy, what will happen to the boat and the home, and what will be the distribution of proceeds?

3. Betty's Boutique (BB) has filed for a Chapter 7 liquidation. BB's creditors are as follows:
   Corporation A: $7,000 claim for business deliveries (similar to previous deliveries) occurring between time of bankruptcy petition and appointment of trustee.
   Ms. B and Mr. C: Deposits of $400 and $1,900, respectively, for purchases of consumer goods not yet provided.
   State D: Unpaid taxes of $10,000 for the past 2 years.

Workers E, F, and G: $500, $2,000, and $3,000, respectively, owed for the last 2 months of work as BB's employees.

Secured creditor H: $5,000 owed on a car loan (perfected security interest in the car).

Unsecured creditors J and K: $8,000 owed to each.

(a) Assume that the proceeds, after costs, from a sale of BB's car are $3,000. Assume that the liquidated value of the estate is $37,800 with costs of administration, collection, and maintenance being $5,000. State the distribution to each creditor.

(b) If BB proposes a Chapter 11 reorganization, name one creditor whose lone objection would not render the plan inoperative. How much must that creditor receive under the plan?

4. Delia Debtor purchased an automobile on credit. May her creditor take priority over a previously perfected security holder who took a security interest in Delia's present and after-acquired motor vehicles?

5. A lends money to B. As collateral, A takes possession of stocks and promissory notes owed to B. B subsequently receives a business loan from C, with a security agreement (and properly filed financing statement) specifying a security interest in (among other things) B's stocks, promissory notes, and other documents. Who has priority as to the stocks and promissory notes, A or C?

6. (a) Don Debtor is lent money by Bob Bucks, who takes an unperfected security interest in a number of items, including the word processor Don has owned for 3 years. If Telly's Type Shop (TTS) obtains a lien for repairs on Don's typewriter, does Bob or TTS have priority?

(b) What if Bob now perfects his security interest?

7. Joe, for money lent to Kay, receives a signed agreement stating a security interest and describing the collateral (Kay's accounts receivable). Kay already has a judgment against her in favor of A. She also already owes money to B, although no collateral or security interest is in effect. After Joe lends Kay the money and takes her security agreement, C also lends Kay money and gets her to sign a security agreement almost identical to the one with Joe (it, too, covers Kay's accounts receivable). C follows up by filing, in the correct location(s), a financing statement containing Kay's signature, the full names and addresses of Kay and Joe, and a description of Kay's accounts receivable.

In each of the following, who has priority?
(a) Joe or A   (b) Joe or B   (c) Joe or C

8. (a) Mary has a perfected security interest in Nancy's inventory of 100 widgets. Nancy regularly sells widgets, and soon sells 8 widgets to Opal. Opal knows about Mary's security interest, but knows nothing that would indicate the sale to her violates that security interest. If Nancy defaults, can Mary enforce her security interest against the 8 widgets that Opal bought?

(b) Assume that the widgets are consumer goods. Further assume that Mary has a PMSI perfected by attachment, not filing. If Nancy is not ordinarily in the business of selling widgets, can Walter, a widget purchaser, be free of Mary's security interest?

ANSWERS

KNOW THE CONCEPTS

1. Lien (mechanic's, artisan's, or hotelkeeper's), prejudgment attachment, use of security interests, preventing or setting aside bulk transfers or fraudulent conveyances, payment from sureties or guarantors, mortgage foreclosure, writ of execution, garnishment, composition and/or extension agreement, and assignment to a trustee.

2. Homes, household furnishings, clothes, personal possessions, livestock, pets, and veterans' pensions.

3. (a) The Consumer Credit Protection Act (Truth-in-Lending Act), the Fair Credit Billing Act and Fair Credit Reporting Act (both part of the Truth-in-Lending Act), the Fair Debt Collection Practices Act, and the Equal Credit Opportunity Act.

   (b) The Uniform Consumer Credit Code (UCCC) is not a federal statute, but has been passed by some states.

4. Federal.

5. Inability to pay debts as they become due.

6. Chapter 7, Liquidation (straight bankruptcy), voluntary or involuntary (debtors or creditors); Chapter 11, Reorganization of a Business, voluntary or involuntary (debtors or creditors); Chapter 13, Readjustment of an Individual's Debts, voluntary (debtors).

7. Criminal victim restitution payments, prescribed health aids, unmatured life insurance policies, alimony and child support, pensions and annuities, and federal and state benefits such as social security, disability, and unemployment benefits.

8. Alimony, child support, some government fines and penalties, taxes owed for the 3 years before bankruptcy, student loans received within 5 years of bankruptcy. The other main reason is the debtor's misconduct

9. No.

10. A pledge.

11. Almost any type of personal property, goods (including equipment and inventory), documents evincing rights (e.g., commercial paper, securities, bills of lading), accounts receivable, after-acquired property.

12. (a) Requirements are that (1) a written agreement sets forth a security interest, describes the collateral, and is signed by the debtor; (2) value passes from the secured party to the debtor; and (3) the debtor has rights in the collateral.
    (b) It makes the security interest effective between the secured party and the debtor.

13. (a) Possession, attachment, and the filing of a financing statement.
    (b) It makes the security interest effective against most third parties.

14. Either (1) take it in satisfaction of the debtor's obligation (although the debtor or another secured party may prevent such action), or (2) sell the collateral and apply the proceeds toward payment of the debtor's obligation.

15. The first to perfect has priority.

PRACTICAL APPLICATION

1. (a) (1) Yes. Dirk's infancy is not a defense for Sure-Thing.
    (2) Perhaps. It depends on whether Daphne has indeed mailed a check. If Daphne has tendered payment, then Wanda's claim against Sure-Thing would be reduced (by the amount of a partial payment from Daphne) or eliminated (if the payment was complete or otherwise settled the debt).
    (3) No. Ollie's obligations were materially altered (higher interest rate, longer loan) without the consent of Sure-Thing.
    (4) Yes. Karen's bankruptcy is not a defense for Sure-Thing.
    (b) Guaranty agreements must be in writing, and the creditor must first try to obtain relief from the debtor. Neither is necessary for a suretyship.

2. (a) First, $2,000 to pay the foreclosure costs; second, $50,000 to the mortgagee; third, the remainder to Harry. There is no indication that creditor A or B has obtained a judgment or otherwise acquired a right to some of the remaining proceeds. If the creditors had, they would take only after Harry exercised his homestead exemption.
    (b) The boat and home will be liquidated.
    Proceeds from the home sale will be applied first to costs of sale and second to the mortgagee, with Harry then being entitled to the state homestead exemption of $9,000. (Unless precluded by state law, Harry could instead choose the federal list of exemptions; although the federal homestead exemption is only $7,500, other exemptions may make the federal list altogether better than the overall state exemptions.)
    Proceeds from the boat sale will go first to sales costs and then to B. If there is a deficiency, B will become an unsecured creditor for the remainder. If there is a surplus, that goes into the estate.

In summation, the mortgagee and house sales costs will be paid in full. Of the remaining $17,000, either $9,000 (state) or $7,500 (federal) will be kept by Harry. The rest goes to the estate, for distribution according to priority of claims. As an unsecured creditor, A is at the bottom of the priority list. B is in the same position with respect to any deficiency after the sale of the boat.

3. (a) The easiest way to answer this problem is to proceed in order of priority, from top claims down to the lowly "general creditors." Also, note that H would receive $3,000 from the car sale and become a general creditor for the remaining $2,000 owed.

Payments, in order of priority, would be as follows:

1. Costs of $5,000 for administering the estate.
2. Corporation A: $7,000.
3. Workers E, F, and G: $500, $2,000, and $2,000, respectively. (For his remaining $1,000, G becomes a general creditor.)
4. Ms. B and Mr. C: $400 and $900, respectively. (For his remaining $1,000, C becomes a general creditor.)
5. State D: $10,000.

General creditors and amounts of claim would be as follows: C, $1,000; G, $1,000; H, $2,000; J, $8,000; K, $8,000; (total $20,000).

Liquidated value $37,800 minus total amounts in categories 1–5 ($27,800) equals $10,000. Because the amount left in the estate is $10,000, whereas the general creditors' claims total $20,000, each general creditor will be paid half of his/her claim. Thus C and G each get $500 to add to the $900 and $2,000, respectively, already received; H gets $1,000 in addition to the $3,000 received from the sale of her collateral (BB's car); and J and K get $4,000 apiece.

(b) Worker E. At least $500.

4. Yes, *if* the creditor perfects before or within 10 days after Delia, the debtor, takes possession of the automobile.

5. A. Here possession generally constitutes perfection. In fact, for stocks and promissory notes, possession is the *only* means of perfection. Since A apparently retains possession, C cannot perfect. Even if C's actions could make perfection, A's perfection by possession has occurred before C's attempted perfection by filing; thus A wins under the general "first to perfect" rule.

6. (a) TTS. Lien creditors prevail over *unperfected* security holders, except for some PMSIs. Because Don had owned the word processor for 3 years, clearly his loan from Bob did not enable Don to purchase the typewriter (so *not* a PMSI).

(b) Bob has priority, at least inasmuch as his security interest concerns a loan made before or within 45 days after Telly's lien.

7. (a) Joe. Unperfected security holders have priority over unlevied judgment creditors.
   (b) Joe. Unperfected security holders have priority over unsecured creditors.
   (c) C. Unperfected security holders lose to subsequent *perfected* security holders [UCC 9-312(5)].
8. (a) No. UCC 9-307(1) provides that a purchaser of goods in the ordinary course of business prevails over a perfected security holder.
   (b) Yes. Walter's ownership would not be subject to Mary's PMSI if Walter gave value to Nancy, did not know about Mary's security interest, and used the widgets for personal, family, or household purposes [UCC 9-307(2)]. Nancy's filing of a financing statement, although not needed to perfect a PMSI in consumer goods, would prevent this type of outcome: Walter could not then take the 8 widgets "free and clear" of Mary's security interest.

21
REGULATORY LAW AND OTHER TOPICS OF BUSINESS LAW

KEY TERMS

antitrust law statutory, regulatory, and case law, the most important being federal, designed to prevent and correct unreasonable restraints on trade

employment law most law on the individual rights of employees and employers (e.g., as to hiring, firing, promotion)

environmental law statutory, regulatory, and case law, the most significant being federal, designed to protect and clean the environment

international law law governing relations between nations; derived from custom, past court cases, treaties, texts, and all other sources used in national law.

labor relations law statutory, administrative, and case law, almost exclusively federal, dealing with labor/management relations

Chapters 2 and 3 included a discussion of administrative law and procedure. This chapter considers some special areas of administrative law: antitrust, environment, employment, and labor relations law. It also considers four other topics of significance to the businessperson or business student: insurance, international law, computers, and the role of attorneys.

ANTITRUST LAW

Because the U.S. economic system is generally based on capitalism and free enterprise, the common law has traditionally sought to protect open competition in the marketplace. Sometimes, however, economic changes outpace the law. Thus America's industrial revolution led to the pyramiding of economic interests in "trusts" or other monopolies, and state legislatures and courts could not control these vast new concentrations of power. In response to this problem, beginning

398

with the Sherman Act of 1890, the most important antitrust laws have been enacted by the federal government, not individual states.

This body of federal **antitrust law** is designed to promote free competition by regulating the various activities of businesses engaged in interstate commerce. The four main statutes are the Sherman Antitrust Act, the Clayton Act, the Robinson-Patman Act, and the Federal Trade Commission Act.

SHERMAN ACT

This act prohibits contracts, combinations, or conspiracies in "restraint of trade" as well as monopolization or attempted monopolization. Courts, however, look at this seemingly absolute prohibition through a "rule of reason"; only unreasonable monopolies are actually outlawed. Reasonableness depends on all of the surrounding circumstances.

Under the **rule of reason**, most unintentional, reasonable restraints of trade are lawful if tied to a valid business purpose. However, some types of agreements among supposed competitors are automatic *(per se)* violations:

1. *Price fixing:* setting prices (e.g., a rate schedule) for products and/or services.

2. *Group boycotts:* excluding other businesses from dealing in their product(s).

3. *Production quotas:* arbitrarily restricting the supply of certain goods in order to increase prices.

4. *Tying arrangements:* requiring the purchase of one product in return for a contract involving another product. (A **tying arrangement** is illegal if the seller has a unique advantage over competing sellers with respect to the product actually sought by the buyer.)

5. *Horizontal territorial limitations or market divisions:* competitors dividing up and keeping exclusive certain geographic areas for the sale of products.

Not all monopolies are violations of antitrust laws. A monopoly is ordinarily lawful if it is simply the result of business skills, patented or otherwise protected products, or sheer luck.

If, however, the monopoly is the result of intentional restraint of trade (a conspiracy to acquire monopolistic powers), then it probably violates the Sherman Act. The act sets forth *criminal penalties* (up to 3 years' imprisonment and fines of up to $350,000 for individuals, $10 million for corporations) and *civil sanctions* (treble damages). A plaintiff who proves direct damages because of antitrust violations recovers three times the actual damages. These civil remedies, including injunctions, attorneys' fees, costs of suit, and interest, are also available in antitrust actions under the Clayton and Robinson-Patman Acts.

CLAYTON ACT

The "rule of reason" and apparent loopholes in the Sherman Act led to the passing of the Clayton Act 1914 in an effort to control continued monopolization.

Under this act, injunctions can be obtained in federal court by either the government or private parties against certain expressly declared, unlawful practices:

1. Exclusive dealing and tying arrangements for the sale of commodities when these contracts tend to reduce competition or to create monopolies.

2. Interlocking directorships, whereby the same person serves as director of two or more significantly competing companies, both of which has capital, surplus, and undivided profits altogether exceeding $10 million (this threshold rises with inflation since 1990).

   "Significant competition" means that competing activities account for more than $1 million in sales and 2% of total revenue for each company, and 4% or more of total sales for at least one company.

3. Monopolistic mergers, that is, mergers that substantially lessen competition or tend to create monopolies in either a product market or a geographic market. The three types are:

   (a) Horizontal: the merged entities operated the same type of business at the same level (e.g., both were widget manufacturers)—*usually illegal.*
   (b) Vertical: the merged entities operated in the same business, but at different levels (e.g., a manufacturer merges with his/her supplier of raw materials)—*generally permitted.*
   (c) Conglomerate: the merged entities are in unrelated businesses (e.g., a restaurant chain and an airline), geographic areas, or both—very likely allowed.

The test for Clayton Act violations is whether there is a *probable* adverse impact on competition, unlike the Sherman Act's higher standard—*actual* adverse impact, as interpreted in the court doctrine "rule of reason."

ROBINSON-PATMAN ACT

Enacted in 1936, the Robinson-Patman Act forbids sellers in interstate commerce to have different prices for the same commodity if that may substantially lessen competition, tend to create monopolies, or otherwise harm or prevent competition. Price differentials are allowed only if the seller demonstrates that they result from differences in costs (e.g., shipping expenses), from a good-faith reduction in price to meet competition in a particular region, or from changing market conditions. Buyers may also be liable for inducing or knowingly receiving a forbidden price differential.

FEDERAL TRADE COMMISSION ACT

Enacted in 1914 and amended several times since, this act prohibits "unfair or deceptive [business] practices" and "unfair methods of competition"; the meanings of those terms are left for the courts to decide. As the enabling act for the Federal Trade Commission (FTC), the act creates and empowers the FTC to investigate possible violations and to enforce the law.

The FTC generally considers the following factors when deciding whether a business activity violates the act:

1. Is it against public policy?

2. Is it immoral, oppressive, unscrupulous, or otherwise unethical?

3. Does it substantially harm customers?

The FTC enforces the act via:

- *Advisory opinions*: The FTC counsels businesses about the legality of a proposed business activity.
- *Consent decrees*: A business agrees to stop doing something, in return for the FTC's agreeing not to impose penalties.
- *Cease and desist orders*: The FTC may tell businesses to stop violating particular laws. (Violations can subject the offending business to fines of up to $10,000 per day.)
- *Extreme measures*: These include (a) requiring divestiture (selling off) of assets, subsidiaries, or the like, and (b) ordering the dissolution of a business.

While state attorneys general may sue Sherman Act violators on behalf of injured state residents, it is the FTC and the U.S. Justice Department (Justice) that are mainly responsible for enforcing the federal antitrust laws. Each has issued guidelines setting forth enforcement policies: Justice's discusses when it will oppose mergers, and the FTC's covers certain industries. In addition to the Sherman, Clayton, and Robinson-Patman Acts, the FTC and Justice enforce other, lesser known laws such as the section of the Lanham Act that prohibits deceptive trademarks.

The FTC's role continues to be controversial. In promulgating trade regulation rules, the FTC has sometimes stirred the ire of powerful business groups. Conversely, like most other administrative agencies, the FTC has also been accused of being "not tough enough." Clearly, the extent of antitrust regulation is related to the political climate. When the public is upset with a particular industry or problem, heightened regulation and enforcement tend to follow, whereas regulation—or, at least, enforcement—sometimes decreases when the predominant concerns are governmental interference and the stifling of would-be entrepreneurs.

EXEMPTIONS FROM ANTITRUST LAWS

The actions of governmental officials, fishermen, agricultural cooperatives, export associations, and labor unions usually are exempt from the antitrust laws. Also generally exempt are business activities required (and/or exclusively regulated) by state law, industries directly regulated by a federal agency, and—to the extent already regulated by the states—insurance companies.

Currently controversial are the extent to which state actions can be subject to antitrust laws (sometimes), the special role of professional sports (only baseball has an overall exemption), and the FTC's treatment of professions. Doctors, lawyers, and other professionals can no longer establish minimum fee schedules or otherwise forbid competitive pricing. However, traditions of self-policing, federalism, and professional independence have been advanced as reasons to leave regulation to the profession itself and to the individual states. In any case, FTC regulation is subject to Congressional and court review.

YOU SHOULD REMEMBER

Federal statutes dominate the antitrust field.

The *Sherman Act's* prohibition of any "restraint of trade" has been judicially modified by a "rule of reason." Thus an unintentional, reasonable trade restraint tied to a valid business purpose is usually legal unless it is a *per se* violation (e.g., price fixing, group boycotts, production quotas, tying arrangements, territorial limitations or market divisions). Monopolies are not *per se* violations: they probably are lawful if simply the result of business skills or luck.

The *Clayton Act* declares unlawful the following: exclusive dealing and tying arrangements for commodity sales, interlocking directorships, and monopolistic mergers. Vertical mergers are usually allowed; horizontal mergers generally are not. The Clayton Act test for violations is a probable adverse impact on competition (as opposed to the "rule of reason" standard—actual adverse impact).

The *Robinson-Patman Act* allows only those price differentials that do not substantially lessen competition <u>or</u> that result from differences in costs, changing market conditions, or a good-faith reduction in price to meet competition in a particular region.

The *Federal Trade Commission Act* empowers the FTC to determine whether a business practice is "unfair or deceptive." It considers public policy, ethics, and harmful effects on customers. The FTC responses are advisory opinions, consent decrees, cease and desist orders, or extreme measures (e.g., ordering divestiture or dissolution).

The FTC and the U.S. Justice Department enforce the antitrust laws; both have issued enforcement policy guidelines. (States and private persons may also bring actions.)

Government officials, farm cooperatives, fishermen, export associations, and labor unions usually are exempt from antitrust laws. Also exempt are state-regulated activities and subject areas governed by particular federal agencies. FTC regulation of professionals is a continuing controversy that Congress and the courts may ultimately resolve.

ENVIRONMENTAL LAW

In the past 25 or so years, Congress and state legislatures have responded to the increased presence and awareness of pollution with many statutes (**environmental law**) intended to protect air, water, and land. At common law, an individual or a government could seek a court-ordered abatement of pollution (under, respectively, the tort doctrines of private or public nuisance), but with these recent statutes court access and available remedies have been dramatically expanded.

Some statutes have tended to expand the types of lawsuits, and the prospective plaintiffs, for private actions based on violations of state environmental standards by businesses. Typical common civil or criminal remedies are injunctions, damages, statutory fines, and—on occasion—jail sentences.

The most important federal statutes are as follows:

1. *The National Environmental Policy Act (NEPA)*. Enacted in 1969, NEPA created the Council of Environmental Quality to monitor and report annually on the condition of the nation's natural resources. The council also reviews conservation plans or other programs (e.g., construction) affecting the environment, and it proposes legislation.

NEPA requires an environmental impact statement (EIS) on any action that may significantly affect environmental quality and that involves federal funds, approval, licensing, or supervision. The EIS requirement thus especially affects the construction, maintenance, or abandonment of power plants, transportation facilities (railroads, highways, harbors, etc.), leases of federal land, and many other activities. While a federal agency will actually prepare the EIS, it must consult concerned businesses and other agencies in order to report adequately (a) the proposed action's environmental impact, including unavoidable adverse effects on, and commitments of, resources; (b) the tie between local short-term environmental uses and maintenance; and (c) alternatives to the proposed action.

Federal enforcement of environmental regulations rests with the Environmental Protection Agency (EPA), created in 1970, which also establishes national pollution standards.

2. *The Federal Water Pollution Control Act (FWPCA)*. Enacted in 1965, FWPCA strengthens earlier federal water pollution statutes. In essence, this act expanded the federal government's power to limit dumping in navigable waterways.

3. *The Clean Water Act (CWA)*. Passed in 1972, CWA sets forth timetables (pushed back by 1977 amendments) for cleaning up the nation's waters. Congress authorized the EPA to promulgate "water quality criteria" (statements about the concentration of pollutants allowed in a particular body of water), and "effluent limitations" (statements about the concentration of pollutants discharged from a particular source).

To oversee these criteria and limitations, CWA has established a permit system, called the "National Pollutant Discharge Elimination System." The permit specifies each pollutant that can be discharged and the average and maximum daily limits on each. Permit holders must monitor their discharges and furnish reports to the authorities. Violations (e.g., failure to obtain a permit or to obey permit standards) can result in fines and, for grossly negligent or wilful offenses, jail terms.

CWA enforcement is controlled by the EPA. However, in some states, the EPA has delegated enforcement to the state government, which has agreed to meet EPA specifications. Citizens also may initiate civil actions against CWA violators.

4. *The Clean Air Act (CAA).* Enacted in 1963, CAA places air pollution control responsibilities mainly with the states. The EPA investigates, sets and revises standards, and intervenes when necessary (e.g., with injunctions and fines of violators).

Via a 1977 amendment, CAA permits states to issue permits for noncomplying pollutant emissions, provided that certain conditions (e.g., the polluter's reaching the lowest achievable emission rate) are met. A 1990 amendment provides stricter emission limits for cars, requires phasing out the use of ozone-depleting chemicals (to a total ban after the year 2000), calls for tougher emission standards at coal-burning plants and other producers of "acid rain," dramatically expands both the list of toxic air pollutants and the EPA's role in curtailing them, and creates a Chemical Safety Board to determine why chemical accidents occur. As with CWA, enforcement entails injunctions, fines, potential imprisonment, and citizen suits.

5. *The Resource Conservation and Recovery Act (RCRA).* Passed in 1976, RCRA covers solid/hazardous waste management (ambient air standards, groundwater quality, waste collection, open dumps, resource recovery, and markets for recovered materials); and it requires handlers of hazardous waste to meet specified standards. According to the EPA, hazardous wastes, which pose significant health risks if improperly managed, are characterized by toxicity, corrosiveness, reactability, and ignitability. In line with RCRA, Congress passed the Comprehensive Environmental Response, Compensation, and Liability Act of 1980 CERCLA which created the "Superfund" to help clean up hazardous waste contamination. Both RCRA and CERCLA provide for criminal and strict civil liability.

6. *The Federal Environmental Pesticide Control Act (FEPCA)*—amending the Federal Insecticide, Fungicide, and Rodenticide Act of 1947. Enacted in 1972, FEPCA prohibits misuse of pesticides and extends the protections of previous federal legislation governing the content and adequate labeling of pesticides involved in interstate commerce or manufacturing. The EPA oversees enforcement of the act. Manufacturers must file reports. Fines, injunctions, seizures of pesticides, and even jail are possible penalties for noncompliance.

7. *Noise Control Acts.* Passed in 1970 and 1972, these acts require the EPA and Federal Aviation Administration to set standards and to regulate aircraft noise.

8. *The Endangered Species Act* (1973). It authorizes the Secretary of the Interior to protect certain plants, fish, and wildlife, as well as their habitat, from extinction. There are fines for persons who violate the Act, and a cabinet-level review committee ultimately determines whether federal projects may be exempted from the Act.

9. *The Oil Pollution Act.* Enacted in 1990, it increases the maximum liability of persons causing oil spills, establishes a fund to pay for clean-up expenses when the liable person is unknown or has paid the maximum amount of liability, mandates thick, double hulls for all newly-built oil tankers, and, after the year 2015, requires such hulls for every tanker in use.

Other environmental statutes include the Toxic Substances Control Act (1976), Surface Mining Control and Reclamation Act (1977), and Nuclear Waste Policy Act (1982).

YOU SHOULD REMEMBER

Many states and federal statutes concern the protection and cleaning of the environment. The most important laws are federal, with enforcement responsibilities vested in the Environmental Protection Agency, although private lawsuits are also usually allowed. Major federal laws include the *National Environmental Policy Act* (NEPA), the *Clean Water Act,* the *Clean Air Act,* the *Resource Conservation and Recovery Act,* and the *Endangered Species Act.* Under NEPA, environmental impact statements are required for proposed actions that may significantly affect environmental quality and that involve federal funds, approval, licensing, or supervision.

EMPLOYMENT LAW

The states and the federal government have many statutes concerning employment (**employment law**). For example, all states have workers' compensation statutes, and many states have minimum wage and maximum hour laws that mirror or approximate federal statutes (e.g., the Fair Labor Standards Act) and apply to employees not covered by the federal laws. Also, state laws may foster a similar national law: e.g., after much state legislation forbidding lie-detector tests (polygraphs), Congress enacted in 1988 the Employee Polygraph Protection Act (EPPA) prohibiting most private employers from using polygraphs, but not proscribing paper and pencil honesty questionnaires—civil penalties, injunctions, and private lawsuits are all authorized remedies for EPPA violations.

The goal of legislation affecting employment is to protect workers' health and safety, provide them with a minimum level of economic protection, and—overall—foster an employment setting free from both discrimination and disruptive labor/management "wars."

HEALTH AND SAFETY LEGISLATION

Each state has a workers' compensation statute requiring many types of employees to relinquish their right to sue their employers for accidental death, injury, or disease arising from or during the course of their employment. In exchange, the employee gains the right to receive financial benefits regardless of fault: common law tort defenses are eliminated, and the employer is held strictly liable to pay an amount of compensation defined in, and limited by, a statutory schedule of benefits.

Many states also have legislation on health and safety in the workplace. The primary statute in this area, however, is the federal Occupational Safety and Health Act (1970). This act states that workplaces are to be "free from recognized hazards" which could cause death or serious injury. Employees are to comply with safety and health rules, and their employers are bound by the regulations, including health and safety standards, promulgated by the Occupational Safety and Health Administration (OSHA), a federal agency created by the act. OSHA conducts various inspections and investigations; therefore employers must keep comprehensive records on employees' illnesses and accidental deaths or injuries.

FAIR LABOR STANDARDS ACT

As noted at the beginning of this section, the Fair Labor Standards Act (FLSA), first enacted in 1938, has been, in effect, adopted by many states to cover employees exempt from federal laws. FLSA does the following:

1. Establishes a minimum wage.

2. Mandates payment of "time and a half" (150% of normal wage rate) for overtime work, with a regular work week being 40 hours.

3. Exempts from coverage professionals, executives, and administrative or outside sales personnel.

4. Generally forbids any employment of children under 14 years old.

5. Prohibits employment of persons under age 18 in hazardous occupations, and further restricts the employment of 14- and 15-year-olds to nonschool hours.

INCOME PROTECTION

• *FOR WORKERS DISCHARGED WITHOUT CAUSE*

Under a joint federal-state program (both governments making contributions, along with employers), a tax on employers is paid into unemployment insurance plans. Workers in the covered (taxed) businesses, if discharged "without cause" (through no fault of their own), can draw unemployment compensation. The unemployed worker must have worked for at least a minimum time period or have earned at least a minimum amount of wages, with the threshold periods or amounts varying from state to state. The length of time for which unemployment compensation may be drawn also varies according to state, and at all times the discharged worker must be ready, willing, and able to accept another job.

Another protection is the federal WARN (Worker Adjustment and Retraining Notification) Act that took effect in 1989. WARN requires large business enterprises (those with over 4,000 total work hours per week) to give workers at least 60 days' notice before a plant closing or mass layoff. A shorter notice period is allowed only if due to *unforeseeable* business circumstances.

• *FOR DISABLED OR RETIRED WORKERS*

The two main federal statutes on retirement income are the Social Security Act of 1935 (SSA) and the Employee Retirement Income Security Act of 1974 (ERISA). Both have been frequently amended.

SSA provides money when incomes from employment are reduced or cease because of death, disability, or retirement. The Federal Insurance Contributions Act (FICA) requires that the employer withhold a specified percentage of each employee's wages and contribute a matching sum on all earnings up to a statutory maximum amount (now over $40,000 per annum). Employers must keep detailed records, file quarterly reports, and (usually) make monthly payments of the amounts withheld and matched.

ERISA sets standards for the adequate funding of private pensions. It established a Pension Benefit Guaranty Corporation, as well as additional, statutory bases for governmental or private civil actions based on pension mismanagement or fraud. Regulations are promulgated by both the Department of Labor and the Internal Revenue Service.

PROTECTION AGAINST DISCRIMINATION

• *THE DOCTRINE OF ABUSIVE (WRONGFUL) DISCHARGE*

At common law, a worker without an employment contract was termed an "at-will" employee: just as the employee could quit at any time, for any reason, so the employer could fire him/her at any time, for any reason. Federal and state statutes, including those on discrimination, have qualified the **at-will doctrine.** Now, for instance, most at-will employees may not be fired because of their race, sex, or religion. Court cases have also undermined the at-will doctrine: some state courts have ruled that certain reasons for firing a person are so pernicious as to be disallowed, and others have abolished the doctrine altogether.

Examples: Unacceptable Reasons for Firing

1. A worker asks his superiors to obey securities or environmental laws.
2. An employee is about to become entitled to a bonus.
3. A worker exercises a statutory right (e.g., files a worker's compensation claim).
4. An employee refuses to participate in antitrust violations.
5. A worker seeks to have his/her employer comply with consumer protection laws.
6. An employee reports criminal activity by his/her employer.

In short, the at-will doctrine has been replaced, in many areas, by broad statutory schemes and by case-law requirements that employers obey the law and common notions of public policy. (Apart from this tort doctrine, at-will employment has also been restricted by finding implied contracts of good faith and fair dealing—e.g., implied or even express contracts based on statements in a company's Employee Handbook.)

• *FEDERAL STATUTES*

Although cases on abusive (wrongful) discharge have rapidly increased in importance, federal statutes still dominate the law regarding individual employment disputes. The most important statute on discriminatory employment practices is Title VII of the Civil Rights Act of 1964. Under the Equal Employment Opportunity Act (1972) and subsequent amendments in 1979, the Equal Employment Opportunity Commission (EEOC) enforces Title VII and other federal statutes such as the Equal Pay Act, the Age Discrimination in Employment Act, and the Americans with Disabilities Act. Complaints may be filed by individuals, state human rights (fair employment) commissions, or the EEOC itself. Of course, as with other administrative proceedings, appeals may be taken to the courts. (Also, under federal statutes predating Title VII, if a claim includes constitutional rights allegedly deprived "under color of a state law or custom," i.e., with the state's explicit or implicit approval or condonement, a plaintiff can bypass the EEOC and proceed directly to federal court.)
hiring halls) and any business or labor organization that affects interstate commerce and has at least 15 workers/members.

> Title VII prohibits discrimination in hiring, firing, promotion, compensation, terms of employment, granting of privileges, or any other aspect of employment, because of an individual's race, color, religion, sex, or national origin; or because of a person's opposition to a Title VII violation or his/her making a charge, testifying, assisting, or in any other manner participating in a Title VII investigation or proceeding.
>
> Certain exemptions are permitted when religion, sex, or national origin is a bona fide occupational qualification (e.g., a seminary may consider the religion of teaching applicants).

Title VII not only prohibits expressly discriminatory policies and actions—cases where discriminatory motives are clear—but it also proscribes discrimination under the judicially-created theories of **disparate treatment, adverse impact,** and **pattern or practice.**

To win under **disparate treatment,** the plaintiff shows what on its face (*prima facie*) seems to be discrimination (e.g., she sought a job for which she was qualified, she was not hired, and the employer then continued to seek applicants), and the defendant/employer must then state legitimate, nondiscriminatory reasons for its challenged employment decision. If the employer states its reasons, it is then up to the plaintiff to show that these reasons were only a *pretext* for a decision actually based upon discrimination (e.g., defendant's alleged hiring criteria were only applied to women, not similarly situated men).

Under **adverse impact,** plaintiffs must show that the challenged employment practice (tests, educational degree requirements, height and weight limits, etc.), while neutral on their face, have a disproportionate, adverse effect on one or more groups protected by Title VII. The employer must then prove that the practice is justified by "business necessity" (e.g., a test is job-related because it predicts a worker's ability to perform essential tasks). The plaintiff may still succeed if he/she demonstrates that other criteria would achieve the employer's purposes with less impact on the protected group(s).

In some cases, government or private plaintiffs use the fact that a protected group's representation in the local labor market greatly exceeds the group's representation in an employer's work force. That may indicate a Title VII violation through a pervasive **pattern or practice** of discrimination, but the employer is free to rebut any inference of discrimination by introducing its own evidence.

Sexual harassment is also a violation of Title VII, whether it is **quid pro quo** (linking salary, promotion, or other employment conditions to an employee's submission to sex-related behavior—e.g., sex with the boss in return for retaining one's job) or **work environment** (sexual behavior so severe or pervasive that it affects work performance or creates an intimidating, hostile, or offensive working environment—e.g., a barrage of unwelcome sex-related jokes, comments and/or touchings from co-workers). Employers tend to be strictly liable for quid pro quo harassment by supervisors and also liable for work environment harassment if higher-level managers knew or should have known about the harassment and did not take appropriate corrective action.

As for *affirmative action,* the concerted effort to improve hiring and promotion of minorities or women under-represented in the work force, employers who are government contractors or otherwise receive federal funds are required to have affirmative action programs. These programs may also be part of a consent decree or other court order against an employer, and employers may opt to have such programs as a matter of choice. *Quotas* — e.g., requiring that certain numbers or percentages of racial minorities or women be hired or promoted regardless of their qualifications when compared with those persons not hired or promoted — usually subject an employer to "reverse discrimination" charges. The passed over persons (e.g., white males) can also bring Title VII actions, such as claims of race or sex discrimination.

Besides Title VII, several additional statutes cover discrimination in employment.

1. *The Equal Pay Act* (1963), an amendment to FLSA, prohibits differences in pay between the sexes for employees performing substantially equal work. The "equal" jobs must involve substantially the same skill, effort, responsibility, and working conditions.

The **comparable worth doctrine** involves a different issue: although two jobs are quite different—including, at the very least, distinct skills and working conditions—are they essentially worth the same? While the wage disparity between a predominantly male job (e.g., driving a truck) and a predominantly female job (e.g., doing secretarial work), for the same employer, certainly does not violate the Equal Pay Act (the two jobs are not substantially the same type), some have argued that the disparity violates Title VII. Courts generally have rejected this notion; therefore battles over comparable worth should now center around proposed state and federal legislation.

2. *The Age Discrimination in Employment Act* (1967) ("ADEA") outlaws job discrimination against people ages 40 and over. The business entities covered by this act are somewhat fewer than for Title VII; here the employers must have at least 20 employees, and the labor organizations without hiring halls must have at least 25 members. In some cases, age can be a bona fide occupational factor, just as there are such exemptions for Title VII. Furthermore, in some instances an employer may provide a lower level of fringe benefits (e.g., life insurance) for its older workers if such treatment is justified by the costs involved (i.e., older workers' benefits cost much more to provide).

3. *The Americans with Disabilities Act* (1990) ("ADA") covers essentially the same employers as does Title VII, with the minimal number of employees for a covered employer being 25 (in July 1994, coverage will extend down to employers with 15 or more employees). ADA forbids employment discrimination against qualified individuals with mental or physical impairments, records of such impairments, or a perception—albeit false—of such impairments. Many situations or conditions are **not** covered disabilities: e.g., illegal drug use, work place alcohol use, various sexual behaviors (including homosexuality), compulsive gambling, kleptomania, and pyromania. (Note: persons with AIDS may be protected under this Act.) Employers may not discriminate against a qualified, disabled person if he/she could perform the job with "reasonable accommodation" by the employer (e.g., modified work

schedules, making facilities accessible, retraining or job restructuring). Employers, though, are not required to accommodate when to do so poses significant difficulty or expense (*undue hardship*). As under Title VII, tests or standards that are job-related and a business necessity are permitted even if that reduces or eliminates employment opportunities for persons protected under ADA. Also, most testing for drug or alcohol abuse has been upheld in court.

4. *The Pregnancy Discrimination Act* (1978) amended Title VII to require that employers treat pregnancy and childbirth like other medical conditions similarly affecting an employee's ability to work.

5. Section 1981 of the Civil Rights Act of 1866 bars discrimination on account of race, color, and occasionally national origin with respect to the making and enforcing of private contracts. As such, it can cover areas of discrimination **beyond simply employment contracts.** Unlike Title VII, there are no small employer exemptions. Compared to Title VII, the Section 1981 time periods to sue generally are longer, the procedures simpler, and the available types of cash damages more expansive (e.g., juries—available under Section 1981 but not Title VII—can award punitive damages).

6. *Civil Rights Law amendments* (enacted in November 1991) provide that Title VII or ADA plaintiffs claiming discrimination based on disability, religion, or sex (including sexual harassment) can receive punitive damages, although amounts are capped at between $50,000 and $300,000, depending on the employer's size. While still not as broad as Section 1981, the amendments reduce some of the differences in treating Section 1981 racial discrimination compared to other forms of discrimination under Title VII.

7. Most states have laws comparable to Title VII and ADEA, and many have ADA-like statutes. Some impose higher standards on employers than do the federal laws, and some go beyond federal law by forbidding discrimination against persons based on marital status, sexual orientation, political affiliation, and—with a specificity not found in ADA—persons with AIDS. The state laws cover governmental units and/or small business entities often exempted from the federal employment laws.

For all proceedings before the EEOC or comparable state agencies, time is often critical and the maze of required procedures can be very complex. For this reason it is essential that all covered employers, unions, and employment agencies, regardless of whether they are currently involved in an investigation or proceeding, keep abreast of all record-keeping, reporting, and other EEOC requirements.

YOU SHOULD REMEMBER

There are numerous federal and state acts concerning workers' health, safety, and income protection. All states have workers' compensation statutes. Federal laws include OSHA, FLSA, WARN, SSA, FICA, and ERISA.

Under common law, "at-will" employees could be fired for any reason, or no reason at all. Via the doctrine of abusive (wrongful) discharge, many states have greatly reduced this power to fire.

Title VII of the Civil Rights Act of 1964 (as amended) prohibits discrimination in hiring, firing, promotion, compensation, employment terms, privileges, or any other aspect of employment because of race, color, religion, sex, or national origin. Moreover, an employee must not suffer retaliation because of involvement with a Title VII investigation or claim.

Other important antidiscrimination in employment statutes are the *Equal Pay Act,* the *Age Discrimination in Employment Act,* and the *Americans with Disabilities Act.* These and other federal or state statutes are enforced by the EEOC, comparable state commissions, and private lawsuits.

LABOR/MANAGEMENT RELATIONS

Until 1932, American unions had few recognized rights. Injunctions against organizing activities, strikes, or other union actions were almost always granted under common law notions of conspiracy and restraint of trade. However, in the 1930s a substantial body of **labor relations law** came into being.

In 1926 Congress passed the **Railway Labor Act** (requiring good-faith bargaining between railroads and their employees' elected representatives). The **Norris-LaGuardia Act** (1932) withdrew from federal courts the power to issue injunctions in nonviolent labor disputes and declared a federal policy that employees are free to form unions.

NATIONAL LABOR RELATIONS ACT

A comprehensive labor statute, the **National Labor Relations Act of 1935** (NLRA, also known as the **Wagner Act**), created the National Labor Relations Board (NLRB). Section 7 of the act strengthened the Norris-LaGuardia statement of policy into a federally protected right to organize and to engage in collective bargaining. Section 8 prohibited certain specific acts (**unfair labor practices**) by employers:

1. Interference with rights to unionize and to bargain collectively.
2. Domination of, or contributing to, unions.

3. Discrimination against employees because of their union activities or because they filed charges or testified under the NLRA.

4. Refusal to bargain in good faith with the employees' elected representatives.

As part of these prohibitions, employers cannot completely prohibit any union activities on company property. Also, employers are not free to relocate a business simply to discourage or "bust" a union. Economic reasons for relocating are lawful, however, even if the effect is to destroy a union.

An NLRA amendment, the *Taft-Hartley Act* (1947), set forth unfair labor practices by unions. These include:

1. Refusing to bargain in good-faith with the employer.

2. Having employers pay for work not actually performed (feather-bedding).

3. Charging excessive or discriminatory fees or dues.

4. Interfering with employees' choice of a labor union.

5. Discriminating against certain employees and/or seeking the employer's discrimination against certain employees (e.g., to encourage or discourage membership in a particular union).

6. Picketing, striking, and carrying out boycotts against businesses other than the employer involved in the primary labor dispute. These *secondary* boycotts and the like are forbidden except for (a) businesses joined with the employer in a common business purpose ("the ally doctrine"), or (b) truthfully advising the public, via limited activities, that the secondary business has ties with the employer.

7. Strikes or boycotts designed to make an employer assign work to a particular craft group or to recognize a union without NLRB precertification.

In addition, Taft-Hartley (also known as the *Labor-Management Relations Act)* established the notion of "employer free speech." In essence, for an employer's actions to constitute an unfair labor practice he/she must do more than simply state an opinion or present an argument. Speech, to be unprotected, must be accompanied by a threat of reprisal.

An additional amendment to the NLRA, the Landrum-Griffin Act (1959) prohibits "hot cargo" contracts, in which the employer agrees not to use, handle, or purchase products from a specified business. Likewise, Landrum-Griffin (also known as the Labor-Management Reporting and Disclosure Act) established a "bill of rights" for union members. In line with these rights, Landrum-Griffin provides for federal regulation of union internal operations, including NLRB supervision of union officer elections, which must be regularly scheduled and use secret ballots. Landrum-Griffin further requires that union officers be bonded and accountable for union property and funds. Also, they must permit the attendance and participation of union members at union meetings.

THE ROLE OF THE NATIONAL LABOR RELATIONS BOARD

In general, the NLRA and subsequent amendments are intended to *promote good-faith bargaining* between employer and union. Although both sides must bargain, the NLRB cannot force an agreement. (The Federal Mediation and Conciliation Service, a U.S. agency, has a panel of recommended arbitrators for labor disputes.) Rather, the NLRB investigates and attempts to remedy unfair labor practices, with one of its main functions being to ensure that labor elections are fair. Undue interference with union solicitation of, and communication with, employees, as well as campaign statements deemed to be misrepresentations, coercive offers of reward, and/or threats, are Section 8 unfair labor practices.

The NLRB resolves disputes about what constitutes an appropriate employee bargaining unit (e.g., supervisors and managerial employees, as well as government workers and independent contractors, are not covered by the NLRA). Besides union officer elections, the NLRB supervises (1) representative elections, whereby employees choose the union that will represent them, and (2) certification or decertification elections, in which employees decide, respectively, whether to have a union or whether to decertify (remove) their union. A certified union has the exclusive right to bargain on behalf of the employees it represents. Thus individual employees *within the represented group* are not permitted to enter into separate agreements with the employer.

UNIONISM AND ANTIUNIONISM

One of the more commonly alleged unfair labor practices brought before NLRB administrative law judges is the claim that an employee suffered discrimination because of his/her union affiliation or activity. Just as this form of antiunionism is unlawful, so are some types of compulsory unionism. Taft-Hartley bans the **closed shop**, which forces all employees to belong to the union before being hired and to remain members throughout their employment. It also prohibits preferential hiring schemes, whereby employers agree to hire only union members so long as the union can supply them.

Taft-Hartley does not ban union shops. The **union shop**, instead of requiring union membership before a worker obtains employment (the closed shop concept), simply mandates that membership must come within a specified time after employment begins.

Taft-Hartley, though, permits states to outlaw union shops. In states with **right-to-work laws**, union membership cannot be required for continued employment. Right-to-work states include the 11 states of the Old Confederacy, plus Arizona, Idaho, Iowa, Kansas, Nebraska, Nevada, North Dakota, South Dakota, Utah, and Wyoming.

YOU SHOULD REMEMBER

The law of labor/management relations is governed by three major federal statutes: the *NLRA* (Wagner Act), *Taft-Hartley Act,* and *Landrum-Griffin Act.*

Businesses may not (1) interfere with the right to unionize and bargain collectively; (2) dominate or contribute to unions; (3) discriminate against employees because of their union activities or other actions under the NLRA; (4) refuse to bargain in good faith with the workers' elected representatives.

Labor unions may not (1) refuse to bargain collectively with an employer; (2) require "feather-bedding" (pay for unperformed work); (3) charge excessive or discriminatory fees or dues; (4) interfere with employees' choice of a union; (5) discriminate against particular employees; (6) conduct secondary boycotts, picketing, or strikes (except against a business "ally" or (via limited methods) to inform the public); (7) strike or boycott to obtain improper work assignments or union recognition.

Labor laws are enforced by the National Labor Relations Board. It oversees union officers' elections, and workers' elections as to union certification or decertification. Once a union is certified, all members of the group(s) represented by the union are barred from making separate agreements with the employer; the union's duty is to bargain collectively (for all of the represented workers).

Taft-Hartley permits either union shops or state right-to-work laws. In a union shop, the employee must join the union within a certain time period after being hired. States with right-to-work laws forbid union membership as a requirement for continued employment.

Strikes are generally allowed unless they violate a collective bargaining agreement or a cooling-off period, involve public employees and are prohibited by law, or are wildcat strikes (not called by the union) or sitdown strikes (occupation of employer's premises).

STRIKES

United States labor law recognizes a right to strike. If the strike concerns an employer's unfair labor practices, upon the strike's settlement the employer must rehire the striking employees. If the strike is over economic issues (e.g., wages, hours), however, upon its conclusion the employer does not have to rehire the strikers or to discharge substitute employees hired during the strike.

Employers may use **lockouts** to fight strikes. Thus, when a single union bargains throughout an industry by striking one or more plants and employers, but not all, nonstruck employer(s) may respond with a defensive lockout: preventing members of the striking union from entering the premises. Sometimes, an offensive lockout is allowed, that is, keeping workers out in anticipation of a strike.

Finally, four types of strikes are disallowed:

1. Those in violation of a collective bargaining agreement.

2. Those not called by the representative union (wildcat strikes).

3. Those involving occupation of the employer's premises (sitdown strikes).

4. Those involving government employees (e.g., police, firefighters, air traffic controllers) and prohibited by law because of the severe adverse affects they would have on the public.

5. Strikes in violation of a court-ordered "cooling off," further negotiating period (no more than 80 days altogether) if a labor disruption in that industry would, the President finds, "imperil the nation's health or safety."

Of course, strikes must remain peaceful. Taft-Hartley reinstated the federal courts' right to issue injunctions in certain situations.

INSURANCE

Insurance is intended to transfer and allocate risks. The insurer (insurance company) issues a policy covering certain events (risks) that, if they occur, will result in a loss (generally, economic). The policy is a special kind of contract between the insurer and the insured (the person obtaining the insurance). For the insurance agreement to be enforced, (1) it must meet the usual requirements of a contract, and (2) the insured must have an insurable interest in the subject matter (e.g., property, health, life) that is insured.

> An **insurable interest** is a legal or equitable interest in the subject matter such that the insured benefits from its preservation and/or incurs a loss if it is destroyed or damaged.
>
> (a) For *property* (real or personal) *insurance,* the insurable interest is usually ownership. However, many states also permit any lawful economic interest. The interest must exist when the loss insured against actually occurs.
>
> (b) For *life insurance,* the insurable interest may be the insured's own life; the lives of his/her spouse, parents, or children; the lives of debtors, partners, and (for shareholders in close corporations) other shareholders; for business entities, the lives of their key personnel. The interest must exist when the policy is issued.

Insurable losses are fortuitous, that is, occur by chance. If intentional, or if the result of wear and tear or other occurrences certain to take place, then the loss is uninsurable.

There are numerous types of insurance, such as term life, whole life, health, and disability. Property insurance includes automobile (commercial or personal), homeowners', fire, and theft insurance. *Liability insurance, which pays for damages that the insured is legally liable to pay to a third person*, is often a component of property insurance policies. Workers' compensation insurance is a special type of liability insurance.

Businesses generally have commercial liability policies. They may also have interruption insurance, which covers losses due to equipment malfunctions or other covered risks that interrupt a business. A policy may include coinsurance provisions: the insured business agrees to have other insurance on a certain percentage of the property's value; if not done, there would be a *pro rata* reduction in insurance proceeds paid for a loss.

Property and liability insurance policies usually cannot be assigned without the insurer's permission. As for policy interpretation, ambiguities are interpreted most strongly against the contract's preparer (almost always the insurer). *Insurers must act in good faith*; failure to do so (e.g., by denying a legitimate claim) may lead to liability for compensatory *and* punitive damages.

Via **subrogation**, an insurer "stands in the shoes of" the insured. Having paid for an insured's loss, the insurer may seek reimbursement from a third party whose intentional or negligent act caused the loss. There is, however, no subrogation right against a third person who causes the death of someone covered by life insurance.

Like most written contracts, insurance policies may be canceled by either party upon giving required notice (generally in writing). Most policies contain grace periods (to allow for delinquent payments or to prevent a coverage lapse). Besides failure to pay premiums, a policy also loses enforceability if: (1) important contractual sections, such as those on notice of loss (promptly informing the insurer about a loss) and on proof of loss (demonstrating the insured's damages) are ignored; (2) the policy was procured by fraud; (3) there is no insurable interest; or (4) certain acts are illegal or otherwise violate public policy.

YOU SHOULD REMEMBER

Insurance transfers certain defined risks from the insured to an insurer (insurance company). The insurance policy is a special contract that must meet the ordinary requirements of a contract, and the insured must have an insurable interest.

Types of insurance include life, health, disability, property, and liability. Many types of insurance policies, including property and liability, generally cannot be assigned without the insurer's permission.

Insurers must act in good faith, and willful denial of a legitimate claim or other misconduct may leave the insurer liable for punitive as well as compensatory damages. Once the insurer has paid for a loss, it usually may proceed against third parties responsible for the loss (exception: life insurance). This right is called "subrogation."

INTERNATIONAL LAW

INTERNATIONAL LAW AND U.S. LAW

International law is derived from custom, past court cases, treaties, texts, and all other sources used in national law. It is recognized in U.S. courts as a part of the common law or as an outside body of legal doctrines that common law courts will enforce.

Nations generally recognize other nations' sovereign immunity; this recognition leads to judicial restraint (**comity**) toward another nation's sovereign immunity. However, with the Foreign Sovereign Immunities Act of 1976 (effective 1977), Congress provided that another nation is not immune from suits in U.S. courts for its commercial activities pursued in this country.

Federal courts have exclusive jurisdiction over cases involving foreign officials or admiralty (maritime) law. Also, most other "international" cases can go to U.S. District Court under diversity jurisdiction. (For more on diversity jurisdiction, see Chapter 3.) Lastly, note that treaties are fundamental federal law, superior to all state laws and antecedent federal statutes.

TRADE AND IMMIGRATION

All nations regulate trade. A key U.S. statute mandating export licenses and placing controls on the outflow of goods and technical data is the Export Administration Act (1979; amended 1985). Violations of the Bureau of Export Administration's regulations are subject to both civil and criminal penalties. As for facilitating exports, the Export Trading Company Act (1982) created a Department of Commerce "Office of Export Trade" to promote exports, and the Act permits applicants to seek a certificate of antitrust immunity for their export activities. Two later Acts, in 1984 and 1988, let American *foreign sales corporations* and *shared foreign sales corporations* take tax exemptions or other benefits related to their export income. Another law, the Foreign Corrupt Practices Act of 1977 (FCPA), prohibits U.S. companies from, in effect, bribing or trying to bribe foreign officials in order to obtain special contracts or other favors. FCPA also requires strict accounting standards and internal control procedures to avoid the hiding of improper payments. The FCPA provides steep fines and even imprisonment for its violators.

There are numerous economic "unions" of countries for purposes of trade. The most important is the European Common Market. In effect, these unions have expedited trade by providing a common geographical area, much larger than an individual nation, where the same or quite similar rules operate with respect to outside tariffs, trade within the union, and usually other economic matters (e.g., international movement of capital and labor).

Nearly 100 countries, including the U.S., have assented to the General Agreement on Tariffs and Trade (GATT). Via a series of regular meetings called "rounds," it has reduced tariffs. GATT also sets forth procedures for reciprocation in, and attempted resolution of, trade "wars." Of course, important bilateral or regional trade pacts are also significant, such as the United States—Canada Free Trade Agreement that took effect in 1989. Moreover, a number of countries, including the U.S., are signatories to the United Nations Convention on Contracts for the International Sale of Goods (CISG), which draws on principles from UCC Article 2. CISG governs sales contracts for goods (*not* services or warranty work) between businesses from two different signatory nations, unless the parties' contract excludes CISG provisions. Note that trade occurs not just through direct exports or foreign agents/distributors; joint ventures, franchises, subsidiaries, and licensing arrangements are among the other methods.

The *Immigration Reform and Control Act of 1986* (IRCA), with 1990 amendments, was intended to discourage aliens from illegally entering the United States by eliminating job opportunities. Employers with **actual knowledge** that an employee was unauthorized to work in the U.S. may be fined and—in the case of repeated offenses—even imprisoned. Employers must verify that each new employee is a U.S. citizen or is an alien authorized to work in the U.S. Good faith compliance with IRCA verification requirements shields the employer if, in fact, a worker is an illegal alien.

IRCA has no effect upon **business visas**, which may be obtained by aliens investing in the U.S., working at multinational businesses, performing seasonal work, or qualifying professionals of "distinguished merit and ability."

NATIONALIZATION

Occasionally, a firm with operations overseas may face **nationalization**, which involves converting a private (usually foreign) business into a government-owned business. The nationalizing country, almost always a developing one, considers this action to be legal. However, if the nation does not have a proper purpose or does not pay just compensation, then nationalization is termed "confiscation" (illegal), not "expropriation" (legal). Of course, the nationalized firm's only real hope for redress may be from insurance (e.g., if it used the Overseas Private Investment Corporation to make the now-nationalized investment).

INTERNATIONAL DISPUTE RESOLUTION

Obviously, there is no sure international method for resolving disputes peacefully. For instance, the International Court of Justice (a U.N. agency) depends on the consent and cooperation of the nations involved. (Since only nations may appear before this court, an aggrieved private business must get its government to espouse its claim.) Also, many nations refuse to enforce a U.S. court judgment. Therefore, rather than appearing before an international tribunal or a national court, businesses often choose arbitration.

The United Nations and many countries provide procedures whereby courts can enforce arbitration decisions. International business contracts increasingly include arbitration clauses, with statements as to where arbitration will occur and what body of law will apply; and national courts increasingly recognize the validity of these clauses. (For more on arbitration, see Chapter 3.)

YOU SHOULD REMEMBER

International law is derived from numerous sources. Although U.S. courts and other courts usually recognize (give "comity" to) another nation's sovereign immunity, the Foreign Sovereign Immunities Act takes away comity in U.S. courts for commercial activities pursued by another nation in this country.

Some key U.S. trade or immigration statutes are the Export Administration Act, Export Trading Company Act, Foreign Corrupt Practices Act, and Immigration Reform and Control Act. There are numerous economic unions of nations with the same or quite similar trade rules, including the tariffs charged for outside commerce. The General Agreement on Tariffs and Trade (GATT) has reduced some tariffs and provided methods for dealing with trade "wars." Moreover, an international convention (CISG) governs international sales of goods.

Nationalization of business is illegal if done without a proper purpose or without just compensation. However, effective redress for illegal nationalization is often impossible, with insurance being the only means of recovering losses.

The three major methods of peacefully resolving an international business dispute are the International Court of Justice, national courts, and arbitration.

COMPUTERS

The most serious legal problem posed by computers is their encroachment upon the individual's right of privacy. With their incredible power to store and transmit information, and with national and worldwide information networks that can draw upon much of the available data, computers have furnished businesses and governments with the means to amass a vast amount of information about numerous individuals.

In 1974, Congress passed a Privacy Act restricting the types of computerized records that the government may maintain and its uses of those records. This act also gives individuals access to the data on themselves, as well as the right to copy, challenge, and correct what they find in these records. In many cases data may not be disseminated unless the individual concerned is notified. Further refinements in protecting against release of U.S. government computer data came with the Computer Security Act of 1987 and the Computer Matching and Privacy Protection Act of 1988; and the Counterfeit Access Device and Computer Fraud and Abuse Act of 1984 (with 1986 amendments) prohibited the unauthorized use of computers to obtain certain restricted information, as well as banned trafficking in U.S. government computer passwords.

Many states have passed similar privacy laws affecting their governmental agencies. Regulation has lagged, however, in regard to record-keeping and data dissemination by private businesses.

Two other federal acts involving electronic data systems were discussed in prior chapters. The *Electronic Funds Transfer Act* (1978) is covered in Chapter 13. The *Fair Credit Reporting Act* (1970), discussed briefly in Chapter 20, has the following provisions:

1. Credit information may be shared only in these permitted cases:
   (a) credit, insurance, and employment applications;
   (b) relevant business transactions (those involving the person whose credit now matters);
   (c) governmental license applications;
   (d) sharing consented to by the person concerned or ordered by a court.

2. The use of out-of-date adverse information is prohibited (generally, data older than 7 years; 14 years for bankruptcies; 3 months for specially prepared investigative reports; there is no time limitation on information used in deciding applications for life insurance worth at least $50,000 or jobs paying at least $20,000).

3. Governmental use of information is limited.

4. Credit-reporting agencies are required to:
   (a) follow reasonable procedures for assuring maximum accuracy;
   (b) disclose to a requesting consumer the information in his/her file (except medical information or the sources of information) and the identities of those who have received credit information.

5. Those who order an investigative report must inform the consumer and, if rejection stems from a credit report, tell the consumer the reasons and the name of the reporting agency.

6. Consumers may dispute the information on file, force a reinvestigation, and even include a statement (no more than 100 words) in the file, with copies going to businesses that received the disputed information.

7. Violations of the act are punishable by fines or even jail, with civil actions open to persons who can prove financial damages.

In addition to privacy concerns, there are also intellectual property problems. In 1980, Congress passed the Computer Software Act, which corrected a copyright law oversight by specifically stating that computer programs can be copyrighted. A copyright, however, only prohibits copying; there is no infringement if another person independently develops the same or a quite similar program (and certain, limited uses of copyrighted materials are permitted, particularly for those who have purchased software—that is why software producers usually market it through licenses, not outright sales). A patent, on the other hand, grants, in effect, a monopoly. Thus many commentators believe that computer software will not be adequately protected until Congress expressly states that it can be patented.

An important example of intellectual property piracy concerning computer technology involves semiconductor chips, whose design and manufacture may entail huge sums of labor and money. In 1984, Congress enacted the Semiconductor Chip Protection Act (SCPA), which provides a 10-year copyright protection for the masks used in producing semiconductor chips. SCPA remedies for infringement include injunctions, disgorgement of the wrongdoer's profits, or statutory damages up to $250,000.

YOU SHOULD REMEMBER

A federal Privacy Act (1974), other federal statutes, and similar state laws restrict governmental record-keeping and data dissemination. The U.S. Fair Credit Reporting Act (1971) provides numerous limits on, and prohibitions of, the use of adverse credit information, and sets forth procedures whereby customers may dispute what is on file. The federal Computer Software Act (1980) explicitly permits copyright protection for computer programs, but the stronger patent protection is still not generally afforded.

THE ATTORNEY'S MANY ROLES AND ETHICAL RESPONSIBILITIES, ATTORNEY/CLIENT CONFLICT, AND THE BUSINESSPERSON'S ROLE

THE ATTORNEY'S ROLES

Businesses increasingly rely on attorneys not only when they are sued or encounter other crises, but also to prevent problems. The hope is to improve business practices and thus reduce the risks of lawsuits, fines, or other legal penalties or expenses.

Lawyers do not so much "know the law" as they are familiar with general legal principles and able to find specific cases, statutes, or other law applicable to a particular set of facts. A lawyer often has several functions: investigator, drafter, negotiator, advisor, and advocate. A lawyer has a duty to advise against illegal actions, but also must maintain confidences shared with him/her during the course of the attorney/client relationship.

THE ATTORNEY'S ETHICAL RESPONSIBILITIES

Although U.S. Supreme Court decisions permit advertising by lawyers, there still are restrictions on an attorney's individual solicitation of clients. Therefore, except for "in-house" counsel (lawyers who are employees of a business, perhaps in a company's "legal department"), the businessperson usually contacts an attorney rather than vice-versa. Only if a business has already had dealings with outside counsel can it sometimes expect these attorneys to take the initiative concerning new legal problems.

The **attorney/client privilege** permits clients to keep confidential matters discussed by or with their attorneys. This privilege can be waived by the client; for instance, he/she may subsequently disclose attorney/client communications to a third party. Also, because the attorney/client privilege depends on *confidential* communications, it does not extend to statements made in the presence of, or letters sent to, persons in addition to the attorney and client.

Each state has ethical codes of conduct governing lawyers. These concern the attorney's responsibilities, sometimes conflicting, both to the client and to the legal system. In general, the attorney must:

(a) only take cases that he/she can handle competently;

    (b) zealously advocate the client's cause, while remaining faithful to the attorney's own obligation, as an officer of the court, not to undermine the overall purposes of the system itself;

    (c) keep the client reasonably informed (e.g., concerning settlement offers);

    (d) abide by the strictures of attorney/client privilege; and

    (e) when withdrawing from a case, take measures to protect the client's interests (e.g., try to obtain new counsel for the client).

These rules help to delineate duties in specific situations Published opinions of courts and bar association panels, as well as telephone "hotline" services, may also furnish guidance. Violation of the rules can result in disciplinary action, with punishment ranging from reprimand to disbarment.

ATTORNEY/CLIENT CONFLICT

As a professional, the attorney cannot always be expected to do the client's bidding; the attorney may believe that the client's interest would best be served by another course of action. But occasionally attorney/client differences stem from what the attorney perceives to be his/her professional, ethical obligations. Whenever differences arise, no matter what the reason, frank discussions are usually necessary and may, in fact, resolve the differences.

THE BUSINESSPERSON'S ROLE

The businessperson, armed with some knowledge of the legal system, the role of lawyers, and the substantive and procedural law, can play an active role in the lawyer's endeavors to resolve problems and/or prepare cases for litigation. Although taking a few courses, reading law books, and participating in past cases are no substitute for professional advice, the businessperson's basic, if limited, knowledge of the law should help him/her to realize when the services of a lawyer are necessary, and what assistance the attorney and the client can provide one another.

YOU SHOULD REMEMBER

    Attorneys can be used not only to resolve problems, but also to prevent them. Familiar with general legal principles, the lawyer directs his/her knowledge toward finding and applying the law to a particular set of facts.

    A lawyer may have several roles: investigator, drafter, negotiator, advisor, and advocate. Each state's code of attorney conduct governs the lawyer's duties to his/her client and to the legal system.

The attorney/client privilege protects communications between attorney and client. The client may waive the privilege, and it arises only for confidential communications (ones not shared with third parties).

KNOW THE CONCEPTS
DO YOU KNOW THE BASICS?

1. Name five *per se* antitrust violations.
2. What sanctions are available under (a) the Sherman Act; (b) the Clayton Act?
3. Name three practices expressly declared unlawful in the Clayton Act.
4. (a) What are three factors that the FTC considers in determining whether business practices are unfair or deceptive? (b) What are the available FTC responses?
5. Name at least five federal environmental statutes.
6. State the insurable interest a person can have in (a) property insurance; (b) life insurance.
7. *True* or *False*: Workers' compensation law does not generally involve questions about fault.
8. Does Title VII apply to all businesses?
9. Name the federal commission that oversees the enforcement of several antidiscrimination statutes.
10. Name (a) at least three unfair labor practices by businesses; (b) at least four by unions.
11. Name the three major means of peacefully resolving an international business dispute.
12. Can computer programs be (a) copyrighted; (b) patented?
13. Which of the following may waive the attorney/client privilege: (a) the attorney; (b) the client; (c) a third party; (d) a judge?
14. Name at least four general, ethical duties of an attorney.

TERMS FOR STUDY

abusive (wrongful) discharge
Americans with Disabilities Act
attorney/client privilege

at-will employment doctrine
Clayton Act
Clean Air Act

closed shop
comity
comparable worth doctrine
environmental impact statement
Fair Credit Reporting Act
Fair Labor Standards Act
Federal Trade Commission Act
Immigration Reform and Control Act
insurable interest
lockout
National Labor Relations Act
nationalization

per se violations
right-to-work laws
Robinson-Patman Act
rule of reason
sexual harassment
Sherman Act
subrogation
superfund
Title VII
tying arrangement
unfair labor practices
union shop

PRACTICAL APPLICATION

1. Amalgamated Bigshot Company (ABC) controls 80% of the market in retail sales of buckshot. ABC wants to acquire (1) Diddly Squat Sales (DSS), which controls 7% of buckshot retail sales; (2) Mid-Sized Manufacturers (MSM), which has no retail sales but manufactures approximately 30% of all buckshot; and (3) Little-Of-Both Operations (LOBO), which has about 1% each of retail buckshot sales and buckshot manufacturing. Which merger is most likely to be permitted? Which is least likely?

2. You are the chief executive officer of a nationwide, Fortune 500 Company. A pesky little firm in the Midwest keeps underselling your company's product P. Can you lower product P's price in response, doing so only in the Midwest?

3. You are in charge of a construction project that uses federal funds and will necessitate discharges into waterways and the atmosphere.
   (a) What three types of documents should you develop or obtain?
   (b) If you fail to do so, what are the possible consequences?

4. (a) Ignatius Insured has a liability insurance policy covering all negligent acts by employees. One of his employees behaves negligently, and Ignatius is sued. The insurer refuses to provide Ignatius with a defense because it believes that the employee was not meant to be covered by the policy. Ignatius wants to file a claim for bad faith. Discuss.
   (b) Assume that the insurer pays on the policy. Is subrogation possible? If so, against whom?

5. Corky Creep fires Fanny Fitz, age 50, because he "just doesn't like that dame." What legal actions may Fanny bring (a) without any specific employment statute to rely upon; (b) with respect to federal statutes?

6. An executive at Heavy-Handed, Inc. tells employees that unionization may lead to higher costs and force the shutdown of factories, resulting in unemployment for many workers. Is that statement a violation of labor laws?

7. Big Business has two groups of unionized workers on strike. Union A's workers are protesting the discharge of their union president from her job with Big Business. Union A claims, and an NLRB administrative law judge ultimately agrees, that the discharge stemmed from the president's union activities. Union B's workers simply want better wages. Big Business has replaced the striking workers. When the strikes are settled, must it rehire the strikers from union A and/or union B?

ANSWERS

KNOW THE CONCEPTS

1. Price fixing, group boycotts, production quotas, tying arrangements, and territorial limitations.

2. (a) Criminal penalties (up to 3 years' imprisonment and fines of $10 million) and civil sanctions (treble damages). (b) Injunction.

3. Exclusive dealing and tying arrangements for the sale of commodities; interlocking directorships; monopolistic mergers.

4. (a) Is the practice (1) in violation of public policy; (2) immoral, oppressive, unscrupulous, or otherwise unethical; (3) substantially harmful to customers?
   (b) Advisory opinions, consent decrees, cease and desist orders, or extreme measures (e.g., ordering divestiture or dissolution).

5. National Environmental Policy Act, Federal Water Pollution Control Act, Clean Water Act, Clean Air Act, Resource Conservation and Recovery Act, "Superfund," Federal Environmental Pesticide Control Act, Noise Control Acts, Endangered Species Act, and Oil Pollution Act.

6. (a) Usually ownership, but can be any legal, economic interest existing when the loss occurs.   (b) The insured's own life or that of his/her spouse, parent, child, debtor, or partner, or other shareholder in a close corporation, and (for business entities) lives of key personnel.

7. True.

8. No. It applies just to businesses affecting interstate commerce and having at least 15 workers.

9. The Equal Employment Opportunity Commission.

10. (a) Businesses: interference with unionization, domination of or contribution to unions, discrimination because of an employee's union activities, refusal to bargain in good faith with workers' elected representatives.

    (b) Unions: refusal to bargain with employer, feather-bedding, excessive or discriminatory fees or dues, interference with choice of a union, discrimination against employees (or requesting employer to discriminate), most secondary boycotts, picketing, or strikes, and strikes or boycotts to obtain improper work assignments or union recognition.

11. Bringing claims in (1) the International Court of Justice (must be espoused by a nation), (2) a national court, (3) arbitration.

12. (a) Yes.   (b) Generally not.

13. (a) No.   (b) Yes.   (c) No—if a communication was made in the presence of a third party, then no confidentiality existed and no privilege ever arose in the first place.   (d) Generally, no.

14. Handle cases competently, zealously advocate the client's cause, remain true to his/her duties as an officer of the court, keep the client reasonably informed, abide by the strictures of attorney/client privilege, and try to protect a client from problems caused by the attorney's withdrawal from a case.

PRACTICAL APPLICATION

1. The DSS acquisition would be a horizontal merger; the MSM would be vertical; and the LOBO would be a mixture of both. MSM seems most likely to pass muster. DSS is clearly least likely (it would remove 35% of the remaining competition in a field already dominated by ABC).

    An argument could be made that the LOBO acquisition should be the easiest to approve because, although involving some "horizontal" elements, its overall acquisition should have the smallest probable adverse effect on competition.

2. The resulting price differential will probably not violate the Robinson-Patman Act if it is simply a good-faith attempt to meet the particular competition with respect to the Midwest firm's product. (Query: Is selling at a loss "in good faith"?) Robinson-Patman is not directed at such cases, but at price differentials intended to wipe out competing, regional entities so as to leave the underselling company with a monopolistic share of the market.

3. (a) An environmental impact statement, a Clean Water Act permit (under the National Pollutant Discharge Elimination System), and a Clean Air Act (1977 amendment) state permit.

    (b) Failure to obtain these documents may bring the project to a halt and/or lead to fines, injunctions, imprisonment, and/or citizen suits.

4 (a) Presumably the insurer prepared the policy. Unless it can point to language in the policy supporting its construction, the insurer will be bound by these facts: (1) the policy appears to cover all employees, and (2) any ambiguities should be resolved in favor of the insured (nonpreparer of policy). A claim for bad faith could succeed if Ignatius shows the usual elements necessary to receive punitive damages, including willful or incredibly reckless acts by the defendant and resulting harm to the plaintiff.

(b) The only person we know about is the employee. Unless barred by the policy itself, or by a separate policy between that particular employee and the insurer, or by virtue of public policy, the insurer might proceed against the employee. Note, however, that if the employee had a right to indemnity from his employer (Ignatius), the insurer's claim would be self-defeating.

5. (a) In many states, Fanny must still point to a specific breach of contract. Otherwise, as an "at-will" employee, she can be fired without cause. Some states, though, might consider this to be an abusive discharge, wrongly based on her age, sex, or appearance or on other illegitimate reasons.

(b) Fanny could sue for damages and, if she chooses, reinstatement. The statutes that she might invoke include Title VII and ADEA.

6. Probably not. Under Taft-Hartley, employers have a right to free speech. Unless the statement was accompanied by something else (also, the tone could be important), the executive's statement would usually be seen as simply an opinion regarding the potential problems of unionization, not a threat of reprisal.

7. Yes as to union A, whose strike was about an unfair labor practice. No as to union B, whose strike was over economic issues.

GLOSSARY

abandoned property personal property that the owner has voluntarily relinquished, as to both possession and any claim of title

abandonment surrendering control of property with the intention to relinquish all claims to it. This is a voluntary act; losing property is involuntary. When used in regard to duty, "abandonment" means repudiation.

abatement of nuisance removal or cessation of that which is causing a nuisance. Also, a suit seeking to terminate a nuisance.

ab initio (Latin) "from the beginning"

abuse of discretion failure to exercise reasonable, legal discretion. Referring to errors of law and plainly erroneous conclusions of fact, this is a standard that usually must be met in order to overturn decisions of administrative agencies and trial courts

abuse of process the use of a court process (e.g., attachment, injunction) for a purpose for which it was not intended

abusive (wrongful) discharge a modification of the common law doctrine that "at-will" employees (those without a set term of employment) may be terminated for any reason. This tort occurs if a firing violates a clear mandate of public policy.

acceleration clause in a mortgage or a promissory note payable in installments, a provision that default in payment of a single installment makes the entire debt immediately payable.

acceptance 1. for contracts: an assent to an offer in accordance with its terms. 2. for commercial paper: the drawee's signed agreement to pay a draft upon presentment

acceptor the person accepting a draft and thus agreeing to be primarily responsible for its payment. See also **drawee.**

accession an addition to personal property by labor and/or materials. The property owner generally has the right to increased value, although compensation may be required for an accession added in good faith by another person.

accommodation paper a negotiable instrument in which an accommodation party has, in effect, agreed, usually without consideration, to share liability or potential liability on the instrument with another, accommodated party. See also **accommodation party.**

accommodation party a person who signs a negotiable instrument in some capacity (maker, drawer, indorser, acceptor) to lend his/her credit status to another party to the instrument, which then becomes accommodation paper

accord and satisfaction an agreement by the parties to a contract to substitute a new performance in place of, and in satisfaction of, an existing obligation

account 1. for goods sold or leased or services rendered, a right to payment not evinced by an instrument or chattel paper 2. the concept of the individualized funds maintained by banks for each particular customer

account debtor a person obligated to pay on an account, contract right, chattel paper, or other intangible property right

accounting equitable proceeding/remedy, e.g., in partnership law, whereby the court directs an investigation of all potentially relevant transactions and all records to ascertain the rights and responsibilities (e.g., amounts owed and owing) of the parties

account stated an agreement on the final amount due between parties

accredited investors banks, insurance companies, and knowledgeable persons who may receive private sales offerings of securities under Regulation D of the Securities and Exchange Commission

accretion the gradual, natural accumulation of land (sediment) by, and next to, a river or other body of water; method by which a party on whose, or next to whose, real property this sediment (alluvium) accumulates, obtains title over the accumulation

act of God a natural event (e.g., hurricane, tidal wave) operating beyond the control of a party to a contract and excusing his/her performance; also, a tort defense, a type of superseding (intervening) cause

act of state doctrine the judicial doctrine that courts should refrain from inquiring into the validity of a foreign nation's actions within its own territory

actual authority the express or implied authority of an agent to act for a principal

actus reus (Latin) "a wrongful act"; if it is combined with *mens rea* ("guilty mind"), the actor is deemed to be criminally liable

adhesion contract a form of unconscionable contract between a merchant and consumer in which the superior party presses a printed-form contract upon the other

adjudication hearing or otherwise reviewing the claims of litigants and then rendering a judgment; an exercise of judicial power, just as legislation is an exercise of legislative power

administrative agency a governmental body (e.g., a board, a commission) created by the federal, state, or local government in order to implement and administer particular legislation

administrative law rules, regulations, orders, and decisions issued by administrative agencies. Generally, the term encompasses that body of law created and enforced by the agencies and, on occasion, reviewed by courts of law.

administrative process procedures governing an agency's exercise of administrative power, as well as a private party's right to advance rule-making proposals, present quasi-judicial claims or defenses, and otherwise take part in administrative proceedings

administrator the person named by a probate court to administer the decedent's estate. (Generally, either there was no will or the will did not designate an executor.)

admissions, requests for See requests for admissions

adverse possession ownership of real property acquired by openly, continuously, and exclusively occupying the property without the owner's permission and over a period of time established by state statute (varies from about 5 to 30 years). Some states require that the adverse possessor have had some claim of title beforehand. Governmental property cannot be acquired by adverse possession.

affectation doctrine doctrine whereby courts refuse to probe Congressional motives and uphold regulatory legislation enacted under the commerce clause, *if* the regulated activity affects, even in a minor way, interstate commerce

affidavit a voluntary, written statement of facts sworn to under penalty of perjury, usually before a notary public or another person authorized to administer oaths

affirmative defense a defense based not merely on denying the facts asserted by the plaintiff, but also on asserting additional facts or legal theories on the defendant's behalf. Generally, the defendant has the burden of proving his/her affirmative defenses.

agency a legal relationship whereby one person acts for another

agent a person authorized to act for another (principal)

agreement a meeting of the minds; the bargain reached by the parties

air rights the exclusive rights of a landowner to the air above his/her land, to that height over which control is reasonable

alien corporation a corporation formed under the laws of a foreign country

alienation voluntary, absolute transfer of title to, and possession of, real property from one person to another; owners in fee simple have a right to alienate

allegation an assertion of a claimed fact, particularly in a pleading

allonge a paper physically attached to, and made a part of, a negotiable instrument; this paper generally contains one or more additional indorsements

alter ego (Latin) "other self"; a person (e.g., an agent) who is legally the same as, and interchangeable with, another (e.g., the principal)

alteration See material alteration.

amended pleading a changed pleading, with added, altered, or removed allegations or legal arguments, that replaces a previous pleading of the same type (e.g., an amended complaint takes the place of the original complaint)

amicus curiae **brief** (Latin) "friend of the court" brief, filed by a nonparty interested in the law that an appellate court may decide and develop in a particular case

answer the defendant's response to the complaint; the answer usually admits or denies each of the various allegations in the complaint, and may include affirmative defenses

anticipatory breach a contract breach occurring if one party clearly states or implies that he/she cannot or will not perform the contract even though the time of performance has not yet arrived

antitrust law statutory, regulatory, and case law, the most important being federal, designed to prevent and correct unreasonable restraints on trade

apparent authority authority created by estoppel, that is, through conduct of a principal that causes a third party to believe that the agent has the authority to make contracts for the principal

appeal a request that a higher court review the decision of a lower court

appearance coming into court, whether in person or via a pleading; performed by the appearing party or the attorney

appellant the party that appeals a court decision

appellate jurisdiction the power of a court to hear appeals from other courts' decisions

appellee the party against whom an appeal is filed

appraisal rights the rights of shareholders (who object to certain corporate actions that may diminish the value of their stock) to compel the corporation to purchase their stock for its appraised value; sometimes called "dissenters' rights"

appropriation taking an item of tangible, personal property for one's own and/or using it for one's own interests. If wrongful, appropriation is a tort (e.g., conversion).

appurtenant easement an easement that is attached (appurtenant) to a parcel of real estate (the dominant estate) and "runs with the land" (passes to successive owners of the dominant estate). The dominant estate holds a negative or affirmative easement in the adjoining servient estate. See also **easement.**

arbitrary without rational basis, given the facts and/or law; such arbitrariness often must be proven to overturn decisions by juries, trial courts, or administrative bodies

arbitration an out-of-court procedure in which a dispute is presented to one or more persons (arbitrators), whose decision is binding on the parties

arbitration clause a provision in a contract for arbitration if a dispute develops between the contracting parties. Such a clause either makes arbitration mandatory or permits either party to choose arbitration in lieu of a lawsuit.

arguments statements (written and/or oral) to the court setting forth the opposing parties' positions on the facts and law. The oral arguments by the attorneys at the conclusion of a trial are called the "summation."

arson the act of willfully setting fire to and burning a building

articles of incorporation a formal document that creates a corporation; a charter

articles of partnership the written agreement by which a partnership is formed and its terms of operation stated; often called simply the "partnership agreement"

artisan's lien a possessory lien held by persons who have added value to (repaired or improved) another person's personal property. The lienholder retains as security the repaired or improved property to ensure payment for his/her service.

"as is" a disclaimer of warranty by asserting that goods are sold "as is," without warranty

assault the intentional tort (or crime) of unjustifiably arousing in another individual the apprehension of immediate harmful or offensive contact with his/her body

assault and battery the compound crime or tort of (a) assault (e.g., threat), and (b) carrying out the threatened harmful or offensive contact (battery)

assign to transfer legal rights from one person to another

assignee the party to whom an assignment is made

assignment the transfer of legal rights from one party to another

assignment for the benefit of creditors See **assignment to a trustee.**

assignment to a trustee an arrangement whereby (a) the debtor transfers to a trustee the title to some or most of the debtor's property, (b) the trustee sells or otherwise disposes of the property for cash and distributes the proceeds *pro rata* among the debtor's creditors, and (c) any creditor accepting such payment discharges the entire debt owed to him/her

assignor the party making an **assignment**

assumption of risk the tort defense that a plaintiff who knowingly and voluntarily faces a dangerous situation may not recover for an injury arising out of the known risks inherent to that situation

attachment court-ordered seizure of a debtor's property for payment of money owed to a creditor; may be accomplished before judgment (with property under the sheriff's control until a judgment is entered), in order to prevent depletion of assets pending the completion of a lawsuit

attempt the crime of intending to do a specific criminal act, and, in furtherance of that intent, taking action beyond mere preparation

attorney a representative or agent

attorney-at-law a legal representative; a person, trained in law, employed to represent others in lawsuits and other legal matters

attorney/client privilege privilege whereby disclosure of *confidential* communications solely between the attorney and the client cannot be compelled; the privilege can be waived by the client

attorney in fact a person named as a representative or agent in a power of attorney

"at-will" employee an employee without a set term for employment (i.e., he/she can quit at any time, for any reason)

"at-will" employment doctrine the common law principle that an "at-will" employee can be fired at any time, for any reason; now qualified by modern antidiscrimination statutes, the doctrine of abusive (wrongful) discharge, and the like

authorized stock the number of shares (common or preferred) that the charter permits the corporation to issue

avulsion sudden changing of course of a stream or river. Landowners retain the property lines as existed before the change; thus, distinct from property changes caused by accretion

bad faith purposely misleading another person or otherwise acting dishonestly and/or with ill will; willfully failing to act in accordance with statutory or contractual obligations. Compare **good faith.**

bail money or other security given to insure the appearance of a criminal defendant at all proceedings in his/her case; in return, the arrested person is freed ("out on bail") pending trial

bailee the party receiving a chattel for purposes of a bailment

bailment the transfer of possession, care, and/or control of a chattel to another person for a limited time for a special purpose

bailor the party transferring a chattel to another for purposes of a bailment

bank draft a check drawn by a bank either on its own funds within the bank or on funds it has on deposit at another bank

bankruptcy fraud a business crime and tort (fraud) involving the filing of false claims by creditors or debtors, fraudulent transfer or concealment of assets, or obtaining credit with the specific intent to avoid paying debts

bankruptcy proceeding a legal procedure for settling the debts of individuals or business entities unable to pay debts as they become due

battery the intentional tort (or crime) of unjustifiable contact with someone else's body or anything connected to the body

bearer the person in possession of bearer paper

bearer paper a negotiable instrument payable to "cash," indorsed in blank, or otherwise payable to "bearer," so that it can be negotiated merely by delivery (change in possession)

beneficiary one who benefits from the actions of another; a person for whose benefit a trust, a will, a contractual promise, or an insurance policy is made. See also **creditor, donee, "incidental,"** and **third-party beneficiary.**

bequest via a will, a gift of personal property (verb form: bequeath). See also **devise.**

bilateral contract a contract created by an exchange of promises

bill of attainder legislation intended to single out an individual and/or punish him/her without benefit of trial; forbidden by the U.S. Constitution, Article I, Sections 9 and 10

bill of exchange a form of negotiable instrument, commonly called a "draft." See also **draft.**

bill of lading document evincing receipt of goods for shipment, issued by a person engaged in the business of transporting goods

Bill of Rights the first ten amendments to the U.S. Constitution, all ratified in 1791

bill of sale a written document by which one person assigns or transfers his/her right or interest in goods and chattels to another

binder written, temporary insurance policy until a formal policy is issued or the insurer decides not to issue insurance and notifies the insured that the binder is terminated

blanket policy insurance covering (1) property at more than one location and/or (2) two or more types of property

blank (general) indorsement indorsement of a negotiable instrument by a holder whose indorsement lacks any accompanying instruction and does not indicate (e.g., by indorsing "Pay to the order of X") that any other indorser is necessary; thus the instrument is bearer paper, freely negotiable merely through delivery (change in possession)

blue laws laws that prohibit the making of certain contracts or the operation of certain businesses on Sundays

blue sky laws state laws regulating the intrastate issuance and sale of securities

board of directors the managers of a corporation, elected by the shareholders

bona fide (Latin) "in good faith"; genuine

bond a secured, long-term corporate debt security

book value the value of capital stock as calculated by the excess of assets over liabilities

breach nonperformance of a contract or of a condition in a contract

breach of duty failure to perform a legal duty owed to another person

bribery illegal payments to governmental officials or other persons for the purpose of receiving information, favorable treatment, or other assistance that the briber either is not entitled to receive or cannot lawfully receive by this method (e.g., kickbacks, payoffs)

brief a written argument supported by citations of court decisions, statutes, and/or other authorities

broker in securities law, a person who buys and sells stock as the agent for a customer but who does not retain for that purpose a supply of stock. Compare **dealer.**

bulk transfer a transfer made outside the ordinary course of the transferor's business and involving a substantial part of his/her equipment, supplies, and/or inventory. UCC Article 6 governs most bulk transfers.

burden of proof 1. the degree of proof necessary for a criminal conviction or for a successful civil suit. In a civil case, the plaintiff has a "preponderance of the evidence" burden of proof; his/her version of the facts must be considered, by the judge or jury, to be, at the very least, slightly more credible than the defendant's. In a criminal case, the prosecution must prove its case "beyond a reasonable doubt." 2. a party's obligation, when asserting a fact, to *come forward* with evidence supporting that fact

burglary breaking and entering (unlawful entry) into a building with the intent to commit a felony (e.g., larceny)

business judgment rule the legal rule requiring that directors and officers govern corporate affairs with reasonably good judgment

buy and sell agreement a contract, particularly appropriate for partnerships or closely held corporations, whereby the remaining owners or the entity are to buy the interest of a withdrawing or deceased owner

bylaws a comprehensive set of rules providing for the organization and operation of a corporation. Compare **charter.**

C & F "cost and freight"—the lump sum price of the goods includes the cost of shipping and freight, but not insurance

canceled stock stock that was issued but has been repurchased by the corporation and canceled

capacity a legally defined level of mental ability sufficient to reach an agreement. See also **insanity.**

capital; capital assets the total assets of a business; the owners' equity in a business

capital stock the class of shares that represent the owners' equity in the corporate business

capital surplus See **surplus.**

carrier person or business entity receiving consideration (e.g., money) for transporting passengers or goods. See also **common carrier.**

case law decisions of the courts, together with their rationale; the whole law as declared by the courts through cases decided before them

cashier's check a check drawn by a bank upon itself

causation in fact the relationship between an act or omission and an event (including alleged damages to the plaintiff) which would not have otherwise happened; that is, harm would not have occurred but for the defendant's wrongful conduct. Compare **proximate cause.**

cause of action the right to seek a remedy in a judicial proceeding. Prerequisites are the existence of a right and a violation of that right; facts that establish the two prerequisites constitute the cause of action.

caveat emptor (Latin) "Let the buyer beware."

caveat venditor (Latin) "Let the seller beware."

certificate of deposit a type of negotiable instrument, issued by a financial institution as an acknowledgment that the institution has received the deposit of a specified sum of money; the institution promises to pay the depositor the sum of money deposited, plus interest at a stated rate, at a specified time in the future

certificate of incorporation the state's official authorization for a corporation to commence to do business

certificate of stock physical evidence of share ownership in a corporation

certificated security a security for which a certificate has been issued

certified check a check marked as "accepted" by the drawee, thus certifying that there is money in the drawer's account to cover the check. Certification acts as a guarantee of payment and thus enhances the check's negotiability.

certified (certificated) stock a security (stock) for which a certificate has been issued

certiorari, **writ of** an appellate court's order that a lower court transmit to it for review the records of a case. The writ is requested by the appellant, and a grant or denial of the request is within the discretion of the higher court, as it is for the U.S. Supreme Court. (If the writ is denied, the appeal is denied.)

chancellor the judge in a court of equity

chancery an equity court

charter a formal document that creates a corporation; articles of incorporation

chattel an item of personal property; a movable piece of property

chattel paper a document evincing both a monetary obligation and a security interest in, or lease of, specific goods [UCC 9-105(1) (b)]

check a special type of draft in which the drawee is always a bank and the instrument is payable on demand. See also **cashier's, certified, stale,** and **traveler's check.**

checks and balances the governmental arrangement whereby powers of each governmental branch (executive, legislative, judiciary) check and/or balance powers of the other branches

C.I.F. "cost, insurance, freight"—the lump sum price of the goods includes the cost of insuring and shipping the goods

circumstantial evidence indirect evidence; circumstances or other secondary facts by which connected, principal facts may be rationally inferred

citation 1. a reference indicating where a relied-upon legal authority (e.g., statute, court decision) can be found 2. an order for a criminal defendant to appear in court and/ or answer charges; often used in minor cases (e.g., alleged traffic offenses); analogous to a summons in a civil case

civil action legal proceeding instituted to enforce a private, civil right or remedy, as distinguished from a criminal prosecution

civil law 1. codified law based on the Roman code of Justinian; the basis of the legal system of most western European countries 2. noncriminal law

class action a lawsuit in which a group of similarly situated persons, perhaps large in number, are represented by a few persons; the class is usually a plaintiff, but a defendant class is possible

clearinghouse an association of banks or other payors that exchanges drafts (e.g., checks) drawn on association members, determines balances, and otherwise "clears" (settles) these drafts

close corporation a stock corporation the shares of which are held by a relatively few persons, frequently members of a single family

closed shop an employment arrangement, outlawed by the Taft-Hartley Act (1947), requiring employees to belong to a union before being hired and to remain members throughout their employment

closely held corporation a corporation the stock of which is not freely circulated

cloud on title an outstanding claim or other evidence on record that, if true, would adversely affect the title or other interests of the presumed owner of real property. A quiet title action may be brought by the presumed owner against the claimant(s) who have thus "clouded" the owner's title.

code 1. civil law: a collection of laws into a single, organic whole; 2. common law: a collection of currently effective statutes enacted by legislative bodies, including Congress and state legislatures

codicil a change in, or addition to, a will, executed in the same formal manner as the will itself

collateral an interest in property given by a debtor to his/her creditor in order for the latter to secure payment of the debt. If the debt is paid, the creditor's interest in the property (collateral) generally ceases; if the debt is not paid, the creditor usually may sell or use the collateral to collect all or part of the debt.

collateral estoppel doctrine that issues decided in one lawsuit are conclusively resolved for other lawsuits between the same parties

collective bargaining negotiation between the employer's and employees' representatives

collegia in Roman law, nonprofit membership clubs, ancestors of modern corporations

comaker a person who joins one or more other persons, also called comakers, in the making of a negotiable instrument; the person thus becomes primarily liable (jointly and severally) with the other comakers for the instrument's payment

comity the recognition (deference, judicial restraint) that one nation gives to another nation's laws and judicial decrees

commerce clause the authority granted to Congress by Article I, Section 8, of the U.S. Constitution to regulate foreign and interstate commerce

commercial law the entire body of substantive law applicable to the rights and duties of persons engaged in commerce or mercantile pursuits

commercial paper in its broadest sense, documents used to facilitate the exchange of money or credit

commingling mixing the money or goods of another with one's own

common carrier a carrier that presents itself to the public as available (for hire) for transporting goods or passengers; it is subject to regulation as a public utility

common law law as developed and pronounced by the courts in deciding cases ("case law"), based on the common law of England and judicial precedent

common stock the class of shares that participate in the management of a corporation and also own the corporate equity

community property a system of joint ownership in some western and southwestern states whereby almost all property acquired by the husband or wife during the marriage, except for gifts or inheritances, is owned equally by both spouses

company (Co.) one of the words that indicate a business is incorporated; this word, however, may refer to a partnership or sole proprietorship

comparable worth doctrine a legal principle (not generally applied under existing federal law) that, if two different jobs (one held mainly by men; the other, by women) are essentially worth the same, there should not be a wage disparity or other difference in treatment between such comparably worthwhile jobs

comparative negligence a legal principle applied when the negligence of the plaintiff and the negligence of the defendant are concurrent causes of the plaintiff's damages; any damages awarded to the plaintiff are reduced by an amount proportionate to the degree of his/her fault. This rule for negligence cases has replaced the rule of contributory negligence in almost all states. See also **contributory negligence.**

compensatory damages the sum of money needed to compensate an injured party by making him/her "whole"

complainant 1. a plaintiff; a person who files a complaint 2. in criminal cases, a person who instigates a prosecution by making charges of criminal conduct

complaint the initial pleading in a lawsuit, sometimes called a "declaration," "petition," or "bill of complaint"; it includes a statement of facts, the legal basis of the suit (cause of action), and a request for one or more remedies

composition and/or extension agreement an arrangement whereby a debtor and his/her creditors agree that each creditor will receive a certain percentage (less than 100%) of the amount owed (the composition) and/or extend the payment period (the extension); the debtor's full compliance discharges the entire debt

composition of creditors See **composition and/or extension agreement.**

compounding a crime the crime of accepting money or something else of value in return for not reporting or prosecuting another crime

compromise an agreement to settle a dispute without resort to litigation or to settle litigation in progress

computer crime a crime committed by using a computer; e.g., to steal information, embezzle, or defraud

concurrent jurisdiction the simultaneous authority of two or more different courts (e.g., federal and state) to hear and decide a case

condition in the law of contracts, a fundamental requirement that must be met by one party before the other party has an obligation under a contract. See also **express** and **implied condition.**

condition concurrent a condition to be performed by both contracting parties simultaneously

condition precedent a condition that must be complied with, or occur, before the other contracting party becomes obligated

condition subsequent a condition the occurrence of which removes the obligation of one or both of the parties to the contract

conditional indorsement an indorsement in which the indorser places a present or subsequent condition (other than failure of prior parties to pay) that must be met before the indorser is liable on the instrument

condominium a form of real property featuring sole ownership of individual office or apartment units, with joint ownership (by all the sole owners) of the land and common areas

confession of judgment an admission of liability made by a creditor in the name of his/her debtor without the formality of the usual adversarial court hearing; instruments frequently contain such admissions, which are to take effect if the debtor fails to pay in accordance with the terms of the instrument

confiscation governmental seizure of private property and/or business without a proper purpose or just compensation; in international law, nationalization may be confiscation. Compare **expropriation.**

conflict of interest in agency law, an act of divided loyalty whereby the agent acts for him-/herself rather than for the principal

conflict of laws a body of law concerning the determination of which law should be applied to the facts of a particular case when the laws of more than one state or nation may be applicable

confusion commingling of two or more owners' personal property so that each owner's property (or property interest, e.g., a precise amount of fungible goods) can no longer be determined or distinguished from the property as a whole

conglomerate merger a merger between two or more business entities that are in different industries; not a horizontal or a vertical merger

consent the defense, to all torts and a few crimes, that the plaintiff agreed voluntarily to submit to the defendant's actions or proposals

consent decree a judgment in which the parties, having agreed on the disposition of a case, have their agreement approved and recorded by the court

consequential damages damages that include lost profits and other indirect injury caused by a faulty performance or other breach of a contract if the principles of foreseeability and certainty are met

conservator See **trustee.**

consideration something of value that is given in exchange for a promise or an act; one of the requirements for a valid contract

consignee the party receiving goods on consignment

consignment a delivery of goods, title remaining in the seller, for the buyer to sell. Risk of loss passes to the buyer.

consignor the party delivering goods on consignment

consolidation combining two corporations by a procedure under which a third corporation purchases the stock of both corporations

conspiracy an agreement between, or any combination of, two or more persons to commit an unlawful act

constitution a nation's or state's supreme set of laws, outlining the basic organization, powers, and responsibilities of the government and guaranteeing certain specified rights to the people

constructive the legal character or nature of a thing regardless of its actual character or nature

constructive bailment a bailment imposed by law rather than agreement; for example, a person who finds lost property or receives misdelivered property may be a constructive bailee

constructive eviction such material impairment by a landlord of the tenant's ability to enjoy the leased premises as to give the tenant a right to terminate the lease

constructive notice knowledge of a fact presumed or imputed by law, such as by recording an instrument, filing a document in court, or placing a legal advertisement in a newspaper or trade journal. Such "knowledge" is regardless of actual knowledge, which may never have been present or may have become forgotten

constructive trust a trust imposed by law against a person who wrongfully obtained and/or retains property; this trust is intended to correct fraud or other misconduct

contingent fee a charge permitted in some civil cases (e.g., negligence lawsuits) whereby the attorney's fee is dependent on successful outcome of the case; generally, the fee is a percentage of the client's recovery

contract a legally enforceable agreement, express or implied. See also **adhesion, bilateral, destination, executed, executory, express, implied, investment, option, output, quasi, requirements, shipment, unconscionable, unenforceable, unilateral, void,** and **voidable contract.**

contribution the right of a defendant liable for a loss to obtain a sharing of expenses (e.g., payments to the plaintiff) by other persons also responsible for that loss

contributory negligence an absolute defense to negligence by the defendant because the plaintiff's own negligence contributed to his/her injuries; replaced by the doctrine of comparative negligence in almost all states

conversion an intentional tort (or crime) involving unauthorized, unjustified exercise of control over another's personal property

convertible bond a bond that may be converted by its holder into other securities of a corporation, such as preferred or common stock

convertible stock stock that the corporation may convert from one class (preferred) into another class (common)

conveyance 1. an instrument (e.g., a deed) by which title or other interests in real property are transferred from one person to another 2. any transfer of property or interests in property

cooperative an association of individuals formed to carry out a common productive enterprise, the profits being shared in accordance with the capital or labor contributed by each individual or otherwise going to the members without gain to the cooperative itself; cooperatives may be for consumers, workers, labor unions, marketing or business purchasing, financial institutions, farmers, insurers, or others

copyright the exclusive right to print, sell, and exhibit written material, musical compositions, art works, photographs, movies, television programs, data systems, and other creations placed in a tangible, preserved medium of expression

corporate crime a crime committed by and thus chargeable to a corporation because of activities of its officers or other employees

corporate opportunity a business opportunity available to a corporation; an officer or director who takes personal advantage of a corporate opportunity violates his/her duty to the corporation

corporation 1. an artificial being created by operation of law, with an existence distinct from the individuals (shareholders) who are its "owners." See also **alien, close, closely held,** *de facto, de jure,* **domestic, federal, foreign, membership, parent, private, professional, public, quasi-public,** and **S corporation.** 2. a word that indicates a business is incorporated

costs in litigation, an award to the winning party for expenses incurred (but usually excluding attorney's fees), to be paid by the losing party

counterclaim a "reverse" complaint: one by the defendant against the plaintiff; sometimes called a "cross-complaint"

counteroffer a cross offer by the offeree that has the effect of rejecting the original offer and proposing a new one

course of dealing the customary method of doing business between two parties; it is a requirement of the Uniform Commercial Code that the course of dealing of the parties be a factor in determining their contractual intent

course of performance the conduct between the parties in the implementation of a contract. This conduct is useful in determining the meaning of the contract and the intent of the parties.

court a unit of the judiciary; a governmental body intended to apply the law to controversies brought before it and to administer justice

covenant an agreement or promise to do or not to do something; an express or implied promise incidental to a deed or contract

covenant of (for) quiet enjoyment a grantor's, landlord's, or other landowner's express or implied promise that the grantee or tenant will neither be evicted nor be disturbed in his/her use and enjoyment of real property (e.g., by hostile claimants of title)

convenant running with the land a convenant that concerns the land itself and binds (or benefits) all subsequent owners of that land

cover to seek a substitute performance of a contract; when seller S breaches, "covering" permits buyer B to purchase goods which conform to the S-B agreement and charge S for any portion of the substituted goods' price exceeding the S-B agreement price

cramdown confirmation of a bankruptcy reorganization plan over the objections of one or more class of creditors

creator See **trustor.**

creditor the party to whom a debtor owes money or another obligation

creditor beneficiary a person, not a party to a contract, who claims that he/she is owed the performance of the contract

crime a public wrong, committed with intent or (in a few cases) by negligence, for which the law provides punishment or recompense to society

crimes *per se* certain crimes that either presuppose or do not require criminal intent so that the act alone constitutes a crime

criminai fraud fraudulent conduct that is a crime (e.g., larceny by fraud, filing false tax returns)

criminal law a body of substantive law governing and defining crimes and punishments for crimes

cross-claim a claim filed against one or more parties on the same side of a lawsuit as is the claimant (e.g., by one defendant against another defendant)

cross-complaint See **counterclaim.**

cumulative preferred stock preferred stock that receives dividends accumulated for years in which no dividends were declared or paid

cumulative voting in the election of directors, a voting procedure whereby a shareholder may accumulate his/her votes and distribute them among the candidates as he/she wishes. Compare **straight voting.**

cure seller's right, under UCC 2-508, to correct a defective performance rather than be liable for breach of contract

curtesy See **dowry.**

custody concerning personal property, immediate charge and control of the property. Custody is not synonymous with possession or ownership; a person can have custody without owning or possessing.

customer Under UCC Article 4, any person or entity (including another bank) having an account with a bank or for whom a bank has agreed to collect on instruments.

damages in general, compensation designed to make an injured party "whole"; in the law of contracts, the compensation due to the nonbreaching party to recover any financial loss or injury caused by a breach of contract. See also **compensatory, consequential, direct, exemplary, incidental, indirect, liquidated, nominal, punitive,** and **special damages.**

d/b/a "doing business as" ·

dealer in securities law, a person engaged in the business of buying and selling securities for his/her account as a principal. Compare **broker.**

debenture an unsecured, long-term corporate debt security

debt a sum of money due, or obligation owed

debt security a security issued as evidence of a corporate debt

debtor a person who owes someone (a creditor) money or another obligation

deceit See **fraud.**

declaration See **complaint.**

decree a judgment, particularly in an equity court

deed a document by which title to property (usually real property) is transferred. See also **general warranty, quitclaim,** and **special warranty deed.**

deed of trust a document similar to a mortgage; when a debtor's purchase of real property is financed (i.e., he/she obtains a loan), a deed of trust conveys title to, but not possession of, the real property to a trustee (someone other than the debtor or creditor), who holds title as security for the debt

de facto **corporation** a corporation that has not been properly formed, even though the incorporators may have made a good-faith effort to do so. Compare **de jure corporation.**

defamation a tort; a false communication, oral (slander) or written or otherwise recorded (libel), by the defendant to a third person that harms the plaintiff's reputation

default failure to perform a duty as promised in a contract, negotiable instrument, deed, loan, or other transaction

default judgment judgment for the plaintiff because the defendant failed to respond to a summons or appear at trial. (Plaintiff's failure to appear may result in dismissal of the case.)

defendant the person against whom a criminal prosecution or civil action is filed

deficiency judgment a judgment against the debtor (mortgagor) for the remaining amount if a creditor (mortgagee) is still owed money on a secured debt (mortgage) after the collateral (mortgaged property) has been sold and the proceeds applied toward payment of the debt

defraud to deprive a person of his/her rights or property by use of deceit (fraud, misrepresentation)

de jure **corporation** a corporation formed in accordance with all the requirements of the law. Compare *de facto* **corporation.**

del credere agency an agency in which the agent holds harmless the principal against the default of those with whom contracts are made

delegated authority in administrative law, powers delegated by the legislature to administrative agencies

delegation transfer of duties under a contract from one person to another

delivery the actual or constructive (implied or inferred) transfer of goods or of an instrument from one person to another

demand a request by one person that another person perform an act (e.g., pay an instrument) the performance of which the first person is entitled to receive

demand paper an instrument payable on demand; a negotiable instrument that either (a) expressly states it is payable on demand, presentation, and/or sight, or (b) does not state a time for payment

de minimis part of the Latin phrase *de minimis non curat lex*, "the law does not concern itself with trifles"; thus, trifling, of no legal consequence

demurrer a motion to dismiss; an initial pleading by the defendant alleging that the complaint fails to state a cause of action

de novo (Latin) "new"; a new proceeding without regard to prior legal actions

deposition pretrial discovery involving sworn testimony by a party or any other witness, usually recorded and transcribed by a court reporter or notary public; testimony; ordinarily taken in response to oral questions from the parties' attorneys

derivative suit a suit brought by one or more shareholders on behalf of the corporation and for its benefit, claiming waste of corporate assets by directors or corporate principals

destination contract a contract that passes the risk of loss to the buyer when the goods are delivered to the specified destination

detriment in the law of contracts, forebearance serving as consideration or value

devise to bequeath property, usually real property, by a will

devisee person who receives devised property

dicta short for the Latin words *obiter dicta*, "statements in passing"; statements in a judicial opinion that are unnecessary for the decision of the case; dicta are not binding, nor do they carry the force of precedent, as do arguments intrinsic to a judicial holding (singular form: *dictum*)

direct damages damages immediately and directly caused by breach of contract

direct liability direct responsibility of a principal for torts committed by his/her agent under certain circumstances

directed verdict a judge's decision that one side has not presented evidence sufficient to support a verdict in its favor; thus the court renders a judgment in favor of the other party immediately before jury deliberations begin

director a person elected by the shareholders to manage a corporation

disaffirmance cancellation or rejection of a contract made by a person during his/her minority upon reaching the age of majority or within a reasonable time thereafter

discharge 1. the termination or completion of a contract   2. in commercial paper, the removal of parties' liability on an instrument, usually by payment   3. the release of an employee from his/her employment   4. in bankruptcy law, the release of a debtor from his/her debts

disclaimer 1. a denial of warranty   2. in negotiable instruments law, an indorsement phrase (most frequently, "without recourse") that places subsequent holders on notice that the indorser will not be liable if the instrument is not paid

disclosed principal a principal/agency relationship in which a third party knows, or should know, that the agent is acting for a principal, and the third party knows the identity of the principal. The agent thus has no personal responsibility.

discount shares shares issued for less than par or stated value; a shareholder who purchases shares at discount is liable to the corporation for the amount of the discount

discovery pretrial procedures by which the parties to a lawsuit obtain information from other parties and from potential witnesses

dishonor to refuse to pay (or accept for later payment) an instrument

disparagement trade libel; a business defamation that involves injurious falsehoods about a product or a competitor's reputation

dissenters' rights See appraisal rights.

dissolution 1. the termination of a corporation's existence   2. a change in partners' relationship caused when one partner ceases, generally because of death or voluntary or involuntary withdrawal, to be associated with the partnership business

distribution a distribution of a corporate asset to the shareholders

distribution of assets in the dissolution of a partnership, after winding up is completed, the distribution of partnership assets to creditors and partners

distributorship a business arrangement (e.g., franchise) in which a manufacturer licenses dealers to sell products

diversity jurisdiction the authority of federal courts to hear a civil case based on state law if the case involves parties from different states and the amount in controversy is more than $10,000

divestiture compulsory sale or other removal, by a business entity, of assets acquired in violation of antitrust laws

dividend a distribution of cash or stock to the shareholders of a corporation

division of powers the arrangement in which constitutions (e.g., the U.S. Constitution) give to each branch of government a different, major area of responsibility: legislative (law making), executive (law enforcement), judiciary (law interpretation)

docket in the court records of a case, a book or case jacket briefly stating all pleadings, hearings, and other actions in the case

doing business for a corporation, the maintenance of sufficient contacts in a foreign state, on a continuous and regular basis, to make it accountable to that state for its actions

domestic corporation a corporation carrying on business in the state of its creation; in that state, it is "domestic"

domicile an individual's permanent legal residence; for corporations, the central office, where its primary functions are discharged, according to law

donative intent language or circumstances indicating that the owner intended to give away a particular property; a necessary element of a gift

donee the recipient of a gift

donee beneficiary a person, not a party to a contract, who claims that the performance of the contract was a gift to him/her

donor the person who makes a gift

double jeopardy prohibition in the U.S. Constitution, Fifth Amendment, against trying a person twice for the same crime

dowry property or something else of value given as additional consideration for the obligation of marriage; the promise to give dowry is subject to the Statute of Frauds. "Dowry" is that which is given to the wife; "curtesy" is given to the husband.

draft a three-party instrument in which the drawer orders the drawee to pay a certain sum of money to the payee, or another person specified by the payee, either on demand or at a particular time in the future

drawee the person upon whom a draft is drawn by the drawer. The drawee, usually (always, when the draft is a check) a bank, is directed to pay the sum of money stated on the draft

drawer the person who draws (writes) a draft. The drawer directs the drawee to pay the sum of money stated on the draft.

due care the standard of care a person owes to others in the law of torts; usually that degree of care that a reasonable person would exercise in the same situation. Also referred to as "duty of care."

due process protection granted by the U.S. Constitution, Fifth and Fourteenth Amendments, against the government's depriving a person of "life, liberty, or property" without according that person fundamental procedural rights. (In some cases of "substantive due process," the deprivation is not permitted, no matter what procedure is followed.)

duress coercion, either physical or mental, that deprives a person of free will to make a contract

duty of care See **due care**

earned surplus undistributed net profits or income of a corporation

earnest (money) the payment of some part of the price of goods sold, or the delivery of some part of such goods, in order to bind the contract

easement a limited right to use (**affirmative easement**), or a prohibition of use of (**negative easement**), another person's land for a specific purpose

easement by necessity an implied easement that occurs when a land transfer makes an easement necessary to gain access to granted or retained land

easement by prescription an easement acquired in essentially the same manner as title to land is gained through adverse possession: here, actual, open, continual, and non-permissive easement of another's land for the required statutory period of time

easement in gross an express easement given for a specific purpose (e.g., for commerce or other public purposes such as placing utility lines). There is no adjoining dominant estate for this "personal easement" (i.e., not running with the land).

ecclesiastical courts early English courts of the Catholic church or other religious orders established to try matters pertaining to religion or offenses against religion; during the time of Henry VIII these courts were merged into the equity courts

eiusdem generis (Latin) "of the same class or kind"; a rule of contract or statutory construction indicating that in a series of words or phrases each word or phrase lends meaning to other words and phrases in the series. Compare *noscitur a sociis.*

ejectment 1. a civil action to recover possession of real property 2. a civil action to determine whether plaintiff or defendant has title to certain land

emancipation the act by which a minor is freed from the control of parent or guardian

embezzlement crime whereby a person lawfully possessing or having access to money or property belonging to another, unlawfully uses that money or property for his/her own purposes

eminent domain the power of, and its exercise by, the government to buy, at fair market value, privately owned real property for the public benefit

employee one who agrees to perform work under the control and supervision of another

employment a contractual relationship whereby one person agrees to perform work under the control and supervision of another; a master/servant relationship

employment law law pertaining to the individual rights of employees and employers (e.g., as to hiring, firing, promotion)

enabling act legislation by which an administrative agency is created and powers are delegated to it

encumbrance a burden on either title to property or on the property itself (e.g., a mortgage, a lien). Also spelled as "incumbrance."

enjoin to issue an injunction

entity a being, thing, or organization having a legal existence

entrapment the defense that a criminal act was induced by a governmental agency, with criminal intent originating from that agency (e.g., police)

environmental impact statement a comprehensive statement on the ecological effects, possible alternatives, etc., required by the National Environmental Policy Act (1969) for any action that may significantly affect environmental quality and that involves federal funds, approval, licensing, or supervision

environmental law statutory, regulatory, and case law, the most significant being federal, designed to protect and clean the environment

equal protection a provision in the U.S. Constitution, Fourteenth Amendment, that no person may be denied "the equal protection of the laws"; generally requires that any differences in treatment be reasonable and related to a permissible, governmental purpose (the "rational basis" test), but for cases involving "suspect" classifications (e.g., by race or religion) or fundamental rights (e.g., voting, marriage) differential treatment must be as narrow as possible and also necessary to achieve a compelling governmental interest (the "strict scrutiny" test)

equitable servitude a restriction on the use of land that is enforceable by a court

equity historically, in England and the United States, a parallel and independent legal system based on principles of "fair play" or equity; now merged into the general court system, with responsibility for (among other matters) family law, injunctions, and specific performance of contracts

equity of redemption the mortgagor's right, from the time of default until the foreclosure sale, to redeem (recover) the property by fully paying the debt, plus the foreclosure costs to date and any interest

equity securities securities issued to generate funds to operate the corporate enterprise; shares of common and preferred stock

escheat the passage of property to the state when a person dies intestate (without a will) and without any surviving relatives (heirs)

escrow placing a document, instrument, or funds in the hands of a third person, who holds the item or funds as a fiduciary, until the contract is performed or some other event occurs such that the escrow holder should then deliver the item or funds to the proper party (e.g., the grantee)

essence (of the) an expression stating that a certain thing (generally time of performance) is a condition of the contract

estate the sum total of a person's real and personal property

estate for years a tenancy (leasehold) for a definite period of time

estop to be blocked by one's previous actions from asserting certain legal claims or defenses

estoppel a legal circumstance in which a person, by reason of his/her actions, cannot assert certain legal defenses or rights that are contrary to these actions. See also **waiver.**

estray statutes state statutory procedures (including publication of notice) whereby the finder/holder of lost or mislaid property may claim title to it if it is not reclaimed by the owner within the statutory period

et al. Latin abbreviation meaning "and another" or "and others"

eviction action by the landlord to expel a tenant from the leased premises; eviction may be actual or constructive. See also **constructive eviction.**

evidence testimony, documents, and other relevant information presented at a trial, in accordance with the rules of evidence, so that the trier of fact (judge or jury) can determine the truth of facts at issue

exclusive jurisdiction the authority of only one type of court (e.g., state or federal) to decide a case

exculpatory clause a provision in a contract excusing one or both parties from the legal consequences of his/her or their actions or negligence

executed contract a contract fully performed by both parties

executor the person named in a will to administer the decedent's estate. Sometimes referred to as a "personal representative."

executory contract a contract that has not been fully performed by one or both parties

exemplary damages damages designed to make an example of the defendant. See also **punitive damages.**

exempt security a security not subject to the registration requirement of the Securities Act of 1933

exempted transaction a transaction in which the issuance of securities is not subject to the registration requirements of the Securities Act of 1933

exemption legal excuse from a duty imposed by law or from the operation of a law (e.g., property exempt from a bankruptcy proceeding)

exhaustion of remedies a doctrine whereby court appeals are not permitted until administrative remedies are exhausted; the appellants must use all available agency procedures before complaining to a court of law

ex parte (Latin) "on or from one side"; judicial proceeding requested by one party without notice to or attendance by an opposing party (e.g., a hearing to decide whether to impose a temporary restraining order)

ex post facto **law** (Latin) "from a thing done afterward"; a law making criminal a past action that was not defined as criminal when it occurred; forbidden by the U.S. Constitution, Article I, Sections 9 and 10

express condition a condition deliberately created by the parties at the time when the contract was made

express contract a conscious, specific contract; it must be written or oral, or partly written and partly oral

expropriation governmental seizure of private property and/or business for a proper, public purpose and with the payment of just compensation. Compare **confiscation.**

extradite to return an alleged criminal to the state in which his/her crime supposedly occurred, and where a trial should take place

factor an agent (a) employed to sell goods for a principal, usually in the agent's own name, and (b) given possession of the goods for that purpose

fair use an exception to the exclusivity of use generally given to copyrights; an example is limited reproduction, for classroom or other nonprofit purposes, of a small portion of a work in such a way as to have little effect on the market for the work

false arrest the intentional tort (or crime) involving detention of the plaintiff, without his/her permission, under the falsely asserted authority of the defendant

false imprisonment the intentional tort (or crime) involving wrongful use of force, physical barriers, or threats of force to restrain the plaintiff's freedom of movement

family law the law of divorce, adoption, and other family matters, transferred from the ecclesiastical courts of England to the equity court in the time of King Henry VIII

F.A.S. "free alongside ship"—seller's risk and cost of transport until delivered next to the ship

featherbedding an unfair labor practice, prohibited by the Taft-Hartley Act (1947), whereby employers pay for work not actually performed

federal corporation a corporation organized under the laws of the United States for a federal purpose

"federal questions" jurisdiction a type of subject-matter jurisdiction; the authority of federal courts to hear and decide cases involving the U.S. Constitution, federal statutes, or treaties

federalism a form of government in which power is divided between a national government and state (provincial) governments

fee simple absolute the highest form of ownership and possession; a fee simple estate includes all rights in real property

fee simple determinable ownership of an estate that automatically ends if a specified action occurs

fee simple subject to a condition subsequent ownership of an estate that is subject to a grantor's right of repossession if a specified action occurs

felony a serious crime punishable by imprisonment; a crime placed by a state's criminal code in a class more serious than the other main class of crimes, misdemeanors

fictitious payee a made-up payee whose account is actually controlled by a dishonest employee or other person, with the drawer/maker duped into drafting or making negotiable instruments payable to this fictitious person; under negotiable instruments law, negotiation is effective, and thus the drawer/maker may not have an effective defense against paying the instrument (except to those who actually duped him/her)

fiduciary a person occupying a position of trust in relationship to another

financing statement a document filed to perfect a security interest

firm offer an irrevocable, signed, written offer by a merchant to sell or buy goods, stating that the offer will not be withdrawn for a specified period (not to exceed 3 months)

fitness (warranty of) an implied warranty that the specified goods are fit for the buyer's use or purpose

fixture personal property that has become attached to real property (i.e., so incorporated into real property that it is difficult, costly, and/or impossible to remove); generally treated as part of the real property

F.O.B. "free on board"—risk and cost of loss pass to buyer at the designated point

force majeure an occurrence that is beyond the control of a party to a contract and therefore excuses his/her performance (e.g., an act of God)

forebearance refraining from acting when one has the right to act. In this sense, forebearance may be consideration.

foreclosure the proceeding whereby a mortgagee takes title to, or forces the sale of, mortgaged property in order to satisfy the mortgagor's debt

foreign corporation a corporation carrying on business in any state other than the state of its creation; in all such states, it is "foreign"

forgery 1. falsely making or materially altering a legal document (e.g., a negotiable instrument) in order to defraud another person and/or otherwise affect rights 2. without authority, writing another person's name (signature) on a legal document as if that person had done so

franchise a contractual arrangement in which the owner (franchisor) of a trademark, trade name, copyright, patent, trade secret, or some form of business operation, process, or system permits others (franchisees) to use that property, operation, process, or system in furnishing goods or services

franchisee a person who is granted a franchise

franchisor a person who grants a franchise

fraud an intentional tort (or crime) consisting of intentional misrepresentation of a material fact, made knowingly with intent to defraud, that is justifiably relied upon by the other party and causes injury to him/her. Also called "deceit" or "misrepresentation."

fraud against consumers a crime (or tort: fraud) involving such activities as fraudulent solicitation in the mail, false advertising about products, and false labeling

fraud in the execution a fraud pertaining to the execution or signing of an instrument or a contract

fraud in the inducement a fraud, pertaining to the value of goods to be sold or services to be obtained, thus inducing the execution of an instrument or a contract

fraudulent conveyance (transfer) a transfer of property or property rights made to defraud creditors. Such transfers may be challenged, and the creditor can reach (e.g., attach) the property by following the appropriate legal procedures.

freehold 1. real property held for life or in fee (e.g., fee simple)   2. an estate of uncertain duration, as opposed to a leasehold

"full faith and credit" clause a provision in the U.S. Constitution, Article IV, Section 1, requiring that, once a court with jurisdiction has rendered a judgment, other states honor that decision insofar as it affects the rights and duties arising between the parties to the judgment

fungible goods goods that, when mixed, cannot be separately identified, since each unit is basically like any other unit (e.g., grain, minerals, fruit)

garnishment a procedure whereby a court orders a third party holding property of a debtor (e.g., an employer holding wages due, a bank holding a customer's account) to transfer some or all of that property to a judgment creditor (person with an unpaid judgment against the debtor)

general agent one authorized to act for one's principal in all matters concerning a particular business

general partner a partner who has power to manage partnership business and has unlimited liability for partnership debts

general partnership a partnership in which there are no limited partners, and each partner has managerial power and unlimited liability for partnership debts

general warranty deed a deed wherein the grantor warrants title against defects or encumbrances arising before or during his/her ownership, and also makes any other covenants typically included in conveyances

gift a transfer of title to goods without consideration; the three elements of an effective gift are donative intent by the donor, delivery (actual or constructive) to the donee, and acceptance by the donee

gift *causa mortis* a conditional gift in which the donor, believing that his/her death is imminent, conveys property with the intent that the donee keep it after the donor's death; the gift is automatically revoked if the donor recovers

gift *inter vivos* a gift made during the donor's lifetime, when he/she is not facing imminent death

good faith 1. acting honestly, without knowledge of a legal defect; sincerely endeavoring to behave in accord with one's own agreements, ethical standards in the industry, and the law itself. Generally, the term denotes an honest intention to abstain from taking unfair advantage of another person. Compare **bad faith**.   2. in sales contracts, a UCC requirement that a merchant act with honesty and in accordance with reasonable commercial standards of fair dealing in the trade

goodwill the special favor or advantage enjoyed by a particular business because of its reputation for skill or judgment; hence, the capitalized value of the excess of estimated future profits over the rate of return on capital considered normal for that kind of business or industry

grand jury a body of jurors (larger in number than a petit jury) that, under the guidance of a prosecutor, decides whether a person or persons should be charged with a crime (indicted)

grandfather clause an exemption from a statute that, but for the exemption, would make certain acts or conditions illegal, provided that those acts or conditions took place before the statute was enacted

grant to bestow upon another person property, rights in property, an instrument, or some other right or privilege

grantee the person that receives a grant

grantor the person who makes a grant

gratuitous bailment a bailment to benefit solely the bailor, with no benefit passing to the bailee

gross negligence lack of even slight care; recklessness; extreme failure to comply with one's duty of care; conduct appreciably worse than ordinary negligence

guarantee(y) in contracts, a promise by one person to pay the debts of another

guarantor generally, a person who has expressly or implicitly agreed to be liable for another person's debts if the creditor cannot collect directly from the debtor; one who makes a guaranty; in negotiable instruments law, an indorser who guarantees payment or collection on the instrument

guilt beyond a reasonable doubt the burden of proof necessary for conviction of a crime

habeas corpus, writ of judicial order that a government official produce a detained or imprisoned person in an action testing the legality of that detention or imprisonment

hearsay evidence heard or otherwise learned from someone other than the person testifying in court; the truth of the matter rests on the credibility of someone not a witness (hence, not subject to cross-examination)

holder a person who possesses a negotiable instrument issued, drawn, or indorsed to that person or his/her order or to bearer

holder in due course a holder who takes a negotiable instrument (a) for value, (b) in good faith, and (c) without notice that it is overdue, has been dishonored, or is subject to defenses or claims

holding company a corporation that holds or owns the stock of another corporation or corporations

holographic deed or will an unwitnessed deed or will handwritten entirely by the grantor or testator, respectively; its validity depends upon state law

homestead exemption a provision in the law of most states that, when a home (debtor's residence, not rental property) is sold to pay a judgment, a specific amount may be retained by the debtor, free of the judgment debt; mortgages are not subject to this exemption

honor to pay (or to accept for payment) an instrument

horizontal merger a merger in which the merged business entities operated the same type of business at the same level (e.g., both were manufacturers); if monopolistic, usually illegal under antitrust law

horizontal privity privity among persons at the same level of the chain of distribution or consumption

hot-cargo contract an unfair labor practice, prohibited by the Taft-Hartley Act (1947), whereby an employer agrees with employees not to purchase, use, or handle products from a specified business

illusory promise a promise that appears to be real but in fact imposes no legal obligation upon the promisor

immunity an exemption from prosecution granted to an actual or a potential criminal defendant, usually to induce information and/or testimony from him/her

implied condition a condition implied from the nature of the transaction but not expressly specified by the parties

implied contract a contract implied from the conduct of the parties; sometimes referred to as an "implied-in-fact contract"

implied partnership a partnership implied from the conduct of the co-owners of a business

implied promise a promise implied from conduct

implied warranty a warranty implied by law, arising out of the buyer/seller relationship

impossibility such absolute factual impossibility as will discharge a contract; alternatively, commercial impracticability

impracticability commercial impracticability created by an unforeseen occurrence sufficient to discharge a contract (treated by some courts as impossibility)

imputed negligence negligence by another party for which one is held liable although he/she did not directly commit negligence. The negligence is imputed because of the relationship, privity, or other ties between the negligent party and the "imputed" one. A related term is "vicarious liability."

incapacity lack of mental capacity to make a contract

"incidental" beneficiary a person, not a party to a contract, who receives some slight or indirect benefit from the contractual promise

incidental damages the damages paid to a person to reimburse the cost of his/her minimizing the damages to which the person is entitled

incorporated (Inc.) one of the words that indicate a business is incorporated (i.e., is a corporation)

indemnify to hold harmless from, to guarantee against, loss or liability

indenture a contract stating the terms under which long-term debt securities (both bonds and debentures) are issued

independent contractor a person hired to undertake a contractually defined result without direct supervision (not an employee and usually not an agent)

indictment a criminal charge (or charges) issued by a grand jury

indirect damages damages not proximately caused by a breach of contract; remote damages

indorsee the person to whom a negotiable instrument is transferred by indorsement

indorsement the signature of the holder of a negotiable instrument, written on the instrument by or on behalf of the holder, with or without additional or qualifying words, so that title to the instrument and the holder's property interest in the instrument are transferred to a new holder. See also **blank, conditional, qualified, restrictive**, and **special indorsement**.

indorser a person who makes an indorsement

infancy the state of minority: in most states, under the age of 18

information a criminal charge (or charges) issued by a magistrate, prosecutor, or police officer

infringement an intentional tort (or crime) involving violation of another person's intellectual property rights (e.g., patents, copyrights, trademarks)

injunction a court order to do or to refrain from doing a specified act

innocent misrepresentation misrepresentation of a material fact without intent to deceive

in pari delicto (Latin) "equally at fault"

in rem **jurisdiction** the authority of a court to take action directly against the defendant's property; jurisdiction is thus based on the location of the property (i.e., the court is in the same state or county as is the property)

insanity mental impairment sufficient as to prevent a person from appreciating the nature of an agreement or the consequences of his/her actions; a defense to crimes and intentional torts

insider an owner of 10% or more of the corporate stock of an issuer listed on a national stock exchange, or a director or officer of such an issuer, as well as others, including employees, consultants and tippees, with inside information about corporate affairs

insolvency 1. inability to pay debts as they become due: this is the test for bankruptcy   2. a financial state in which liabilities exceed assets

instrument 1. a formal document or other writing that evinces a legal relationship (e.g., a deed, will, lease, mortgage)   2. under the UCC, a negotiable instrument, security, or other writing demonstrating a right to payment and not itself a security agreement or lease

insurable interest a legal or equitable interest in the subject matter such that the insured benefits from its preservation and/or incurs a loss if it is destroyed or damaged

insurance a contract whereby risks are transferred; the insurer issues a policy covering (paying compensation in the event of) certain occurrences (risks) that, if they occur, will result in a loss to the insured

intangible personal property property (rights in something) that lacks physical substance (e.g., stock, intellectual property)

intellectual property protected expressions of scientific, artistic or other creative, and/or commercial endeavors; a special type of intangible personal property, arising from the creative endeavors of the human mind, generally evinced by patents, copyrights, trademarks, and/or trade names

intent an express or implied desire to perform a particular act; a state of mind (to do the act) preceding or accompanying an act

intentional infliction of mental (emotional) distress an intentional tort involving disturbance of the plaintiff's peace of mind by the defendant's outrageous conduct

intentional misrepresentation See fraud.

intentional tort a tort in which the tortfeasor expressly or implicitly intends to do the act(s) causing the injury

inter alia (Latin) "among other things"

interference with contract an intentional tort with three requirements: (a) a valid contract exists, (b) a third party knows about the contract, and (c) the third party intentionally (and unjustifiably) causes one of the contracting parties to breach the contract, or otherwise unjustifiably prevents performance of the contract

interference with prospective economic advantage an intentional tort with essentially the same three requirements as the tort of interference with contract, except that the interference affects a prospective contract or other economic arrangement, not an existing contract

interlocking directorship a violation of antitrust laws whereby the same person serves as director of two or more competing companies, at least one of which has capital, surplus, and undivided profits altogether exceeding $1 million

international law law governing relations between nations; derived from custom, past court cases, treaties, texts, and all other sources used in national law

interrogatories a method of discovery: written questions, to be answered, in writing and under oath, by another party

intervening cause See superseding (intervening) cause.

intestacy laws state laws governing the administration and distribution of an intestate's estate.

intestacy succession the order in which an intestate's estate is divided among surviving relatives

intestate (to die) without leaving a valid will; the term also is a noun, designating a person who so dies

intoxication an impairment of the mind and will by alcohol or drugs so as to bring about contractual incapacity; if involuntary (occurring by force or mistake), it may be a defense to a crime or tort

intra vires (Latin) "within the powers" (of a corporation)

invasion of privacy an intentional tort involving interference with a person's right to be left alone

investment contract a contract that may be a "security" if it requires an investment of money in a common enterprise with the expectation of profits from the efforts solely of others

invitee person entering real property at the express or implicit invitation of the owner/possessor, generally to engage in business (e.g., to shop, to make repairs)

involuntary bankruptcy a proceeding initiated by one or more creditors against an insolvent debtor

issue in negotiable instruments law, the first delivery of a negotiable instrument to a holder; to issue securities; a decedent's lineal descendants (e.g., children, grandchildren)

issued shares shares in a corporation that have been sold to shareholders

issuer a person who issues securities, and any other persons or entities acting under his/her control or as part of a plan of sale or distribution of the securities

joint liability liability in which all parties are concurrently liable and all must be sued together

joint and several liability liability in which all parties are concurrently liable, but each is also individually liable; a plaintiff has the option of suing one of them, some of them, or all of them (i.e., any combination)

joint tenancy joint ownership of property, established when the instrument conveying the property states that the parties acquire the property as joint tenants; the co-owners must have received their property interest at the same time, from the same source, in equal interests, and with each owner having the right to possess the whole

joint tortfeasors two or more persons who commit a wrong with a common intent

joint venture an association of two or more entities to carry on a single business enterprise for profit

judgment a court's final decision on matters submitted to it; a pronouncement, holding, or decree by a court with competent jurisdiction

judgment creditor a creditor who has obtained a judgment against his/her debtor

judgment *non obstante veredicto (J.N.O.V.)* literally, a judgment notwithstanding the verdict; if, after the jury has rendered a verdict for one party, the judge finds that there is insufficient evidence to support the jury's decision, he/she enters a judgment for the other side

judgment proof having few, if any, assets that can be reached by a judgment creditor; thus, persons against whom money judgments are of no practical effect

judicial review a doctrine whereby courts, notably the federal courts (in particular, the U.S. Supreme Court), have the power to declare federal or state actions to be in violation of the constitution (unconstitutional)

judicial sale when the mortgagor is in default, the customary method of foreclosure on mortgaged property: after proper notice, the sheriff or other court official takes control of the property and sells it

jurisdiction the power of a court to hear and decide the issues in a case and to bind the parties. See also **appellate, concurrent, diversity, exclusive, "federal questions,"** *in rem,* **original, personal,** and **subject-matter jurisdiction.**

jurisprudence the science or philosophy of law

jury a body of persons charged with declaring the facts in a case and deciding (a) whether a criminal defendant is guilty, or (b) whether a civil defendant is liable; a petit jury usually has 12 members (jurors), although some states and the federal courts allow as few as six. See also **grand jury.**

justice the major goal of most legal systems; encompasses such ideals as impartiality, equity, and fairness

kite to secure temporary use of money by negotiating or issuing worthless paper and then redeeming such paper with the proceeds of similar paper

labor relations law statutory, administrative, and case law, almost exclusively federal, dealing with labor/management relations

laches an equity concept similar to statutes of limitations but with no stated period; serves to bar recovery for a claimant who waited too long to assert his/her rights

laissez-faire a political or legal doctrine favoring governmental restraint, if not outright abstention, from the regulation of business

landlord a lessor of real property

land-use restrictions governmental restrictions (e.g., zoning) on the use and disposition of real property

larceny the crime of unlawfully taking personal property with the intent to deprive the owner of it

lateral support, right to a right protecting a landowner by prohibiting his/her neighbors from excavating or otherwise changing their own land to such an extent that the landowner's land and/or buildings are damaged

law that which a judge will decide concerning matters properly brought before him/her; in a broader sense, any rule that society will enforce. See also **administrative, antitrust, commercial, criminal, environmental, employment, international, labor-relations, positive, procedural, public,** and **substantive law,** and **law merchant.**

law merchant the English system of commercial law, once enforced in special merchant courts, now merged into the common law; part of it was the basis for negotiable instruments law

lawsuit a broad, general term for an action or proceeding in a civil court

lease a transfer of possession of property (real or personal), but not title (ownership), for a period of time for a consideration (e.g., rent)

leasehold a real property estate held by a tenant, under a lease, for a set term

legacy personal property transferred (bequeathed) by will

legatee the person to whom a legacy is given

lessee the person to whom a lease is granted

lessor the person who grants a lease to another

letter of credit any instrument by which a drawer requests a particular person or people in general to give the bearer or a named person money or something else of value and to look for recompense from the drawer. Unlike most notes and drafts, letters of credit have no standard format; they are governed by UCC Article 5.

levy lawful seizure of property to obtain money owed

lex talionis (Latin) "the law of retaliation" (an eye for an eye)

libel written, photographic, or otherwise recorded defamation

license 1. freely revocable permission by a landowner to use his/her land for a limited, specific purpose (e.g., camping, hunting); persons given this right of use have a non-possessory interest in the real property   2. a revocable privilege granted by the government to do something (e.g., sell liquor, broadcast at a particular frequency) that would otherwise be illegal   3. a contractual arrangement whereby a party receives (in effect, purchases or leases) another party's right to manufacture, distribute, and/or sell goods or services

licensee a person entering real property with the permission of the owner/possessor (e.g., a guest invited to a party)

lien an encumbrance imposed on property to force payment of a debt; if the debt remains unpaid, the property (collateral) can be sold to satisfy the debt (lien). See also **artisan's lien** and **mechanic's lien.**

lien creditor a creditor who has a lien on the debtor's property

life estate a person's possessory interest in real property for the duration of one or more human lives as specified in the granting instrument

life estate *pur autre vie* a life estate measured by the life of a person other than the grantee (person holding the estate)

limitation of actions See **statute of limitations.**

limited (Ltd.) one of the words that indicate a business is incorporated (or a limited partnership)

limited partner a partner without power to manage partnership business and with liability for partnership debts only up to the amount of his/her contribution to the business

limited partnership a partnership conforming to state statutory requirements and having one or more general partners and one or more limited partners

limited warranty a warranty expressly limited as to duration and/or effect

liquidated damages the damages for breach of contract that are specified in the contract; these damages will be upheld in court if reasonable

liquidated debt an undisputed debt for a known or ascertainable sum of money

liquidation 1. conversion of assets to cash, usually in order to pay creditors; the procedure followed before distribution in a Chapter 7 bankruptcy proceeding   2. in partnership law, part of the "winding up" after dissolution; collection, preservation, and sale of partnership assets

litigants the parties to a lawsuit

living will instrument making known an individual's wishes concerning life-sustaining medical treatments

lobbying attempting to influence legislation

lockout a management tactic whereby employees are prevented from entering the work premises, generally in order for management to obtain better terms. Defensive lockout (permitted): when a single union bargains throughout an industry by striking one employer (or more), but not all employers, the struck employer responds by locking the workers out. Offensive lockout (sometimes allowed): management keeps workers out in anticipation of a strike.

long-arm statute a state law extending personal jurisdiction over out-of-state persons, including corporations, that do business in the state, own real property there, or have taken other relevant actions (e.g., committed an alleged tort, entered a contract) in a state

lost property personal property accidentally left somewhere; the owner does not intend to relinquish ownership

L.S. an abbreviation for *locus sigilli*, "place of the seal," that may serve as a seal

mailbox acceptance rule principle of contracts law that, unless the offer states otherwise, an acceptance using the same method of transmission as the offer is effective when the acceptance is *sent* (when the offeree places it in the mailbox or otherwise relinquishes control over it)

maker a person or institution that issues a promissory note or certificate of deposit (i.e., promises to pay)

malicious institution of civil proceedings the intentional tort of instigating civil proceedings against someone for an improper purpose and without good or probable cause, with those proceedings ending decisively in the defendant's favor

malicious prosecution an intentional tort involving the same factors as malicious institution of civil proceedings, except that the improperly instituted proceedings are criminal, not civil

malpractice suit a lawsuit alleging failure to exercise the standard of care expected of someone in a particular profession (e.g., law, medicine, accounting), that is, negligence by a professional during the course of his/her professional employment

margin the amount that must be paid in cash (not borrowed) in purchasing or investing in securities

master an employer. See **servant.**

material alteration substantial change in one or more terms of an instrument that gives the instrument a different legal effect (e.g., changes the liability, duties, and/or rights of one or more parties to the instrument)

material mistake a mistake that goes to the very heart of the agreement

maturity the date when an obligation to pay a debt (e.g., a note, a draft) becomes due

maxim a legal principle; an equity principle of fair play

mechanic's lien a statutory lien filed against a debtor's real property for materials or labor expended (but unpaid for) in repairing or improving that property

mediation an alternative method of dispute resolution, preceding or in lieu of litigation, whereby a third party (mediator) tries to help the disputing parties to settle their case

membership corporation a corporation owned by its members, such as a church or other nonstock corporation

memorandum the written evidence required by the Statute of Frauds for certain kinds of contracts

mens rea (Latin) "criminal intent"; usually a requirement for criminal liability

merchant one who deals in goods or has knowledge or skill with regard to goods

merchantability fitness for the ordinary purposes for which goods of a specific class are sold

merger concerning businesses and antitrust law, the combination of two or more business entities. Specifically, in corporate law, the combining of two corporations by a procedure under which one acquires the stock of the other. See also **conglomerate, horizontal,** and **vertical merger.**

metes and bounds a precise description of the territorial limits of a parcel of real property, including measured distances and angles

minor in most states, a person under the age of 18

misdemeanor a crime placed by a state's criminal code in a class less serious than the other main class of crimes, felonies, with lesser punishment than is generally accorded a felony

mislaid property personal property intentionally put somewhere, but then forgotten; the owner does not intend to relinquish ownership

misrepresentation a false statement of fact

mistake of fact in criminal law, ignorance of an important fact; this may negate *mens rea* and hence serve as a defense

mistake of law the criminal defense that a person honestly did not know that he/she was breaking the law *and* (a) the law was not published or otherwise made public, or (b) the person relied on an erroneous but official statement of the law; otherwise, ignorance of the law is no excuse

mitigation the requirement that an injured party reduce his/her damages to a minimum

monopoly exclusive or practically exclusive control of the supply and/or sale of a product or service

morality the body of self-imposed rules of conduct generally perceived to be right

mortgage a written agreement between a creditor (mortgagee) and debtor (mortgagor) whereby real property is given as security (mortgage) for a loan

mortgagee the creditor who has received a security interest in real property (a mortgage)

mortgagor the debtor who has given a security interest in real property (a mortgage)

motion a request that a court take a specified action in a case; motions can concern numerous matters

motion to dismiss a motion contending that, even if the plaintiff's allegations are true, there is no legal basis for finding the defendant liable. See also **demurrer.**

mutual mistake a mistake by both parties to an agreement concerning a fundamental fact

mutual rescission an agreement between the parties to a contract to terminate the contract

mutuality the reciprocal obligations of the parties to a contract, in the absence of which there is no legally binding agreement

nationalization the conversion of a private business into a government-owned business

necessaries goods or services considered essential to sustain existence (e.g., food, shelter) and/or to maintain a person's station in life

"necessary and proper" clause a provision in the U.S. Constitution, Article I, Section 8, granting to Congress the authority to make laws "necessary and proper" for carrying out any of the government's enumerated powers under the Constitution; hence, Congress has implied powers under this clause

negligence failure to exercise the standard of care that a reasonable person would exercise in like circumstances. To succeed in court, the plaintiff must show (a) duty of care, (b) breach of that duty, (c) causation, and (d) damages.

negligent misrepresentation a tort involving essentially the same elements as fraud, except that negligence replaces *scienter* (knowledge of falsity, or reckless disregard of truth or falsity); it applies mainly to special situations involving negligent opinions by supposed experts (e.g., lawyers, title examiners, accountants)

negotiable capable of being transferred by indorsement or delivery so that the subsequent holder has all the rights that, and possibly more, than, were held by the transferor, particularly the right to sue on the instrument in the holder's own name

negotiable instrument a type of commercial paper; specifically, a written, signed, unconditional promise or order to pay a certain sum of money to order or bearer either on demand or at a definite time

negotiation 1. contracts: the transaction of business; the usual setting for the formation of a contract   2. negotiable instruments: the process by which both possession of, and title to, an instrument are transferred from one party to another, with the transferee becoming a holder

nimble dividend a dividend to shareholders from current earnings, paid even though there are debts outstanding from previous years

nolo contendere (Latin) "I will not contest it"; a pleading by an accused criminal that does not admit guilt but is equivalent to a plea of guilt for sentencing purposes

nominal damages damages in the amount of $1 or some other token amount, awarded when the plaintiff has been legally wronged, but not actually injured

noncumulative preferred stock preferred stock that loses its dividend rights for years in which no dividend is declared or paid

no-par stock stock for which no dollar value is indicated on the share certificate; no-par stock is issued for any amount assigned by the board of directors

noscitur a sociis (Latin) "known by association"; a rule of statutory or contract construction meaning that words occurring together in a phrase are to be defined by their common relationship or their similarity of meaning. Compare *eiusdem generis.*

note See **promissory note.**

notice the formal presentation of information concerning matters of legal import. Notice is legally required in many situations (e.g., by service of process at the beginning of a lawsuit), regardless of whether the person receiving notice already has the information given in the notice.

novation an agreement among contracting parties and an outside third party that the third party will perform the duties (and receive the rights) of one of the original parties to the contract

NOW a negotiable order of withdrawal, treated the same as a check under the UCC; the federal Consumer Checking Account Equity Act (1980) permits savings and loan associations, mutual savings associations, credit unions, and banks to offer their savers NOW accounts

nudum pactum (Latin) "a naked promise"; a gratuitous promise for which there is no consideration; a promise to make a gift

nuisance the intentional tort (or crime) of substantially interfering with the plaintiff's right to use and enjoy his/her property (private nuisance) or with rights common to all (public nuisance)

obligee a person to whom an obligation is owed

obligor a person who owes an obligation to another

offer a proposal made by one person to another and intended to create a contract if the other party expresses his/her assent

offeree the person to whom an offer is made

offering circular information prepared by the issuer for distribution with a small public offering of securities under Regulation A of the Securities and Exchange Commission

offeror the person making an offer

officer (corporate) a person named by the board of directors to operate the corporate business

opinion the statement of reasons forming the basis for a court's judgment

option contract a contract to keep an offer open for a specified time

order paper a negotiable instrument payable to a specific person or to his/her order, so that it requires the proper indorsement(s) and delivery in order to be negotiated

ordinance a law passed by a governmental body below the state level and dealing with a local concern

organized crime crime committed by groups in the "business" of crime

original jurisdiction the authority to hear a case after it has first been filed, including holding a trial and passing judgment on the law and facts

output contract a contract whereby the seller (usually a manufacturer) agrees to sell all of his/her output or production of certain goods to a single, specific buyer

outstanding shares shares that have been issued, except those repurchased by the corporation after their original issuance

overdraft a check for more than the amount in the customer's account

overdraw to make an overdraft

P.A. an abbreviation for "Professional Association," indicating a professional corporation (e.g., doctors, accountants)

par value stock stock for which a specified dollar amount is indicated on the share certificate; the par value must be set out in the charter

parent corporation a corporation that owns all, or a majority of, the stock of another corporation

parol oral; in spoken words

parol evidence evidence concerning a written agreement that is not part of the writing

partnership the association of two or more persons who have expressly or implicitly agreed to carry on, as co-owners, a business for profit. See also **general, implied,** and **limited partnership.**

partnership agreement See **articles of partnership.**

partnership at will a partnership with no set term of duration

partnership by estoppel a partnership created by law because third parties were led to the reasonable belief that a partnership existed

past consideration an action completed in the past and claimed as consideration for a present promise

patent the 17-year exclusive right, granted by the U.S. government, to make, use, and sell a new and useful design, process, machine, manufactured item, or other composition, or any new and useful improvement on it; a patentable invention must be novel, useful, and nonobvious

pawn See **pledge.**

payee the party to whom a negotiable instrument is made payable

payor a party (e.g., drawee) directed to make a payment, generally pursuant to a negotiable instrument

P.C. an abbreviation for "Professional Corporation"

peremptory challenge See **voir dire.**

perfect tender rule the UCC rule that goods be tendered strictly in conformity with the contract

perfection See **perfection of security interest.**

perfection of security interest a procedure whereby a secured party obtains priority over other parties that seek, or may seek, to attach or otherwise use the collateral

performance discharge of a contract by substantial completion or by the performance of all of the conditions (essentials) of the contract

periodic tenancy (lease) tenancy for a definite period of time, which automatically renews until a timely notice to the contrary is given by the lessor or lessee

perpetual existence for most modern corporations, the period of corporate existence *per se* (Latin) "by itself"; this expression means "in and of itself, without looking (or having to look) to other persons or things"

per se **violations** agreements among competitors that are automatic violations of antitrust laws (e.g., concerning price fixing, production quotas, and some boycotts or tying arrangements)

personal (limited) defense any defense not a "real" defense; generally, insufficient against holders in due course

personal jurisdiction the authority of a court to bind the parties in a case

personal property all property, tangible and intangible, except real property; generally, property without a permanent location or property that may be easily moved without damage to real estate

personal representative See **executor.**

personal service contract a contract to perform services for another; generally not delegable

petit jury See **jury.**

petition See **complaint.**

petitioner the plaintiff; the term is often used in equity cases

pierce the corporate veil to disregard the corporate entity, and thus hold the shareholders liable for corporate actions; this is possible under circumstances involving fraud

plaintiff the person who initiates a lawsuit

plat a chart or map, usually filed in the local court or records office, delineating parcels (boundaries) of real property

plea bargain a deal between the criminal defendant and the prosecutor—typically, a trial is avoided as the defendant pleads guilty to a lesser charge; judges have the final authority over whether to approve these compromises

pleadings the papers filed in court, with copies to other parties concerned, in preparation for bringing or defending a lawsuit before the court

pledge the oldest and simplest type of secured transaction, whereby the debtor provides the creditor with physical possession of some of the debtor's property, which serves as collateral

plenary power authority not granted (expressly or implicitly) to the federal government, and thus reserved to the states and the people, by the U.S. Constitution, Tenth Amendment

police powers state power to promote or protect public health, safety, morals, and general welfare

positive law the aggregate of legal precepts specifically enacted or otherwise recognized by governments, as distinguished from natural law, moral principles, customs or ideal law

possibility of reverter a grantor's future right to retake real property if a specified action occurs; the right a grantor has under a fee simple subject to a condition subsequent

postdate to write on an instrument a date later than the one on which the instrument is actually executed

power of attorney an instrument authorizing a specified person to act as agent or attorney for the person executing the instrument

precedent a prior judicial decision relied on as authority or guide for resolving later, similar cases

preemption federal law expressly or implicitly covers a subject so completely that the states are barred from making their own laws on this subject

preemptive right the right of existing shareholders to preempt, or go ahead of, other purchasers of stock of the same class in order to protect their percentage interest in, or control of, the corporation

preferential transfer (preference) a transfer (of money or other property) that unfairly favors one creditor over others (i.e., the favored creditor gets more than he/she would under the bankruptcy laws); prohibited, and thus overturned, if to pay a preexisting debt and made during the 90-day period before the bankruptcy petition is filed

preferred stock the class of shares that take precedence over common shares as to (a) distribution of dividends, and (b) distribution upon liquidation

prejudgment attachment an attachment before a judgment, permitted if all statutory and constitutional (due process) requirements are met. See also **attachment.**

preponderance of the evidence the burden of proof necessary for civil liability

prescription See **easement by prescription.**

presentment the giving of a draft or note to a party (e.g., a bank) that is asked to transfer to the bearer the sum stated in the instrument

presentment warranty a warranty imposed both on the person who obtains payment of a negotiable instrument and on all prior transferors; it warrants title, signature authorization, and lack of material alteration and is given to any person who, in good faith, pays or accepts the instrument

president the chief executive officer of a corporation

prima facie (Latin) "on first face" or at first blush; creates a rebuttable presumption

prima facie **case** a presumptively good case that shifts the burden of proof to the opposing party; a case strong enough to require a jury's consideration

primary benefit under the holdings in some cases, the doctrine that an accountant is liable only to the party receiving the primary benefit of his/her services and not to all those to whom he could foresee injury because of his/her negligence

primary party in negotiable instruments law, the maker or acceptor (the party primarily liable on the instrument)

principal the person for whom an agent acts and from whom the agent derives authority

private corporation a corporation created for other than public or municipal purposes

private offering an offering of securities to a limited number of investors

privilege an immunity existing under law and constituting a defense in most tort cases (e.g., the privilege of self-defense can defeat the tort of battery)

privity in regard to contracts, the requirement that a person be one of the parties to a contract in order to have a legal interest in the contract. See also **horizontal** and **vertical privity.**

probable cause proper grounds for a search or arrest; reasonable grounds (something more than mere suspicion) to believe that a particular person committed a crime

probate a court procedure by which a will is held to be valid or invalid; broadly, all matters concerning the administration of estates and guardianships

procedural law the operating rules through which cases are presented, tried, and decided

process, service of in accordance with statutory, procedural requirements; formal notification to a civil defendant that he/she is being sued

professional corporation a corporation created by a professional or professionals in order to gain corporate tax advantages for traditional partnership or proprietary activities

proffer to tender

profit the right to obtain a possessory interest in some aspect of another's land (e.g., crops, timber, minerals)

promisee the person to whom a promise is made

promisor the person who makes a promise

promissory estoppel such reliance on the promise of another to make a gift, or on some other gratuitous promise, that the promisor is bound by his/her promise notwithstanding the absence of consideration. See also **estoppel.**

promissory note a two-party negotiable instrument in which one person (the maker) makes an unconditional, written promise to pay another person (the payee), or a person specified by the payee, a certain sum of money either on demand or at a particular time in the future

promoter a person who conceives of, organizes, and begins a corporation

property a collection of rights and interests, generally associated with the concept of ownership; anything subject to use, possession, transfer, and/or ownership. The two main types are real property and personal property. See also **intangible personal, intellectual, personal, real,** and **tangible personal property.**

pro rata (Latin) "in proportion"; division (e.g., of assets) according to the proportionate share held by each person

prospectus a statement or document describing securities to be offered or being offered; a statutory prospectus meeting the requirements of the Securities Act of 1933 must be prepared and submitted to the Securities and Exchange Commission before securities subject to the act may be advertised or offered

proximate cause an essential element for almost all tort cases, consisting of causation in fact and foreseeability; a tort defense can thus be that the plaintiff's damages were not the natural and probable consequence of the defendant's acts (i.e., the damages were unforeseeable—too remote in time, distance, or chain of events)

proxy a limited power of attorney whereby a shareholder names a proxy (agent or representative) to vote his/her shares

public corporation a corporation formed to meet a governmental or public purpose

public law the body of law dealing with the relationship between society (government) and individuals

public policy concepts of prevailing morality used by courts to determine the legality or illegality of contracts

public utility a private corporation created for certain public purposes, and governmentally controlled as to services and prices charged (rates)

puffing exaggerated statements of value that induce a party, usually a buyer, to enter into an agreement; usually not the basis of fraud or misrepresentation in the legal sense

punitive damages damages recovered in tort (not contract) cases to punish the defendant for outrageous or malicious conduct. See also **exemplary damages.**

purchase money security interest a security interest that is (a) held by the seller of the collateral in order to secure all or part of the sales price, or (b) held by a person lending money or otherwise giving value that the debtor uses to acquire or use the collateral (UCC 9-107)

qualified indorsement See **disclaimer, 2**

quantum meruit (Latin) "as much as he/she earned"; the compensation permitted by law to the actor in a quasi contract

quasi (Latin) "as if," "as if it were"

quasi contract a contract created by operation of law to prevent unjust enrichment

quasi-public corporation a privately owned corporation created for public purposes, such as a public utility

quid pro quo (Latin) "something for something (else)"; the thing sought; consideration

quiet title See **cloud on title.**

quitclaim deed a deed containing no warranty of title; it simply conveys all of the rights in the property that the grantor has, whatever those rights may or may not be

quorum for corporations: a majority of the outstanding shares of a corporation; the number of shareholders required to be present to conduct business at a shareholders' meeting

ratification a person's explicit or implicit approval or adoption of a prior act that did not bind him/her

reaffirmation agreement a debtor's written, signed agreement, filed in bankruptcy court, in which the debtor reaffirms (again agrees to pay) a dischargeable or already discharged debt

real (universal) defenses defenses to the enforcement of an instrument that are good against anyone, including holders in due course; examples are fraud in the execution (factum), forgery, discharge in bankruptcy, statute of limitations, material alteration, and defenses (e.g., duress, illegality) that render a contract void

real property land, whatever is growing or built on land, and the rights associated with ownership and use thereof

reasonable doubt See **guilt beyond a reasonable doubt.**

"reasonable person" standard a tort doctrine, used especially in negligence cases; the duty of care that a hypothetical, reasonable person would meet in the circumstances in question

receiver a fiduciary (for all parties) appointed by the court to take charge of property involved in a lawsuit and to manage and dispose of it as the court orders

recidivism repeated criminal conduct

red herring prospectus a preliminary prospectus, tentatively reviewed by the Securities and Exchange Commission, designated in red ink as such, and required to accompany a written offer of securities during the waiting period before the securities are formally offered for sale

redemption See **equity of redemption** and **statutory period of redemption.**

redemption right the right of a corporation to redeem (purchase) preferred shares, even over the objection of their owners

reformation an equity action used to revise a written contract so that it will state the actual agreement of the parties

registration statement a statement filed by an issuer with the Securities and Exchange Commission under the Securities Act of 1933 and containing all relevant information about the securities to be offered for sale

release an agreement by one party to a contract excusing the other party from performance

remainder an estate that commences upon the termination of a prior estate; for example, A gives B a life estate, with the remainder to C or C's heirs

remainderman the person entitled to a remainder

remand to return a case, by order of an appellate court, to the trial court for further action

reorganization rearrangement of a business under Chapter 11 of the Bankruptcy Code

replevin a court proceeding instituted to recover personal property wrongfully held by another person

repossession a creditor's taking possession of collateral after the debtor defaults (e.g., fails to make payments)

repudiation refusal to accept goods that have been tendered in accordance with a sales contract

requests for admissions a method of discovery; written requests that another party admit particular facts or acknowledge the genuineness of certain documents

requirements contract a contract whereby the buyer agrees to purchase all of his/her requirements of certain goods from a single, specified seller

res (Latin) "thing," "matter"; the subject matter of a legal action (e.g., the land involved in a quiet title action)

rescind to cancel

rescission cancellation

res ipsa loquitur (Latin) "the thing speaks for itself"; a principle in the law of torts excusing the requirement that a plaintiff prove the defendant negligent if, under certain conditions, the fact of the negligence is obvious

resident agent a person or other entity authorized to receive service of process and other official papers for a corporation

res judicata a doctrine prohibiting subsequent litigation between parties as to a dispute between those parties that has already been adjudicated (with final judgment entered and appeals either completed or not taken)

respondeat superior (Latin) "Let the superior respond"; liability of the principal for his/her agent's torts if committed while acting within the scope of the agent's authority

respondent a term for the defendant, often used in an equity case

restitution restoring the status quo; return of property; a tort or breach of contract remedy, such as for unjust enrichment; a criminal sentence requiring repayment of the victim

restraint of trade in a contract, a provision unreasonably restricting a person from making a livelihood after the sale of that person's business or that person's leaving his/her employment; any number of business practices that may violate antitrust laws

restricted security a security that has been issued under an exempted transaction, with further transfer being subject to limitations

restrictive covenant an express provision (e.g., placed in a deed) that attempts to restrict the transfer or use of property; also, a clause in an employment, partnership, or other agreement that limits or forbids the contracting party from performing the same or similar type of work (e.g., for a competitor) within a certain geographic area for a specified period of time after the contract ends

restrictive indorsement an indorsement that (a) is conditional, (b) attempts to prohibit further transfer of the instrument, (c) includes the words "for collection," "for deposit only," "pay any bank," or a similar term, or (d) states that it is for the benefit or use of the indorser or another person

resulting trust a trust that ensues when the person receiving property was not intended to receive it; he/she is made a resulting trustee for the intended beneficiary. This type of trust is intended to correct a mistake.

retaliatory eviction eviction or eviction proceedings initiated by a landlord because a tenant has complained or otherwise exercised contractual or statutory rights

reversion in effect, a remainder retained by the grantor of an estate; for example, A gives B a life estate, with reversion to A or his heirs

reversionary interest See reversion.

right a power, privilege, interest or immunity; a legally enforceable demand or claim; that which, upon its violation, affords one a remedy at law or in equity

right of contribution See contribution.

right of redemption See statutory period of redemption.

right of survivorship See survivorship, right of.

right to lateral support See lateral support, right to.

right-to-work law a state statute prohibiting union shops; that is, in that state, union membership cannot be required for continued employment

riparian rights a landowner's rights (use, accretion, etc.) in a natural waterway within his/her property

risk in insurance, a contingency, peril, or other area of potential exposure, which a policy may cover

robbery larceny accomplished by using force or threats of force

rule an established standard, guideline, principle, or doctrine; in administrative law, a regulation issued by a federal, state, or local administrative agency (or court) and governing procedure or conduct in a specific field

rule of reason the antitrust doctrine whereby most unintentional, reasonable restraints of trade are lawful if tied to a valid business purpose considering all facts and circumstances

S (formerly, Subchapter S) corporation a corporation organized to limit the effect of federal income taxes; taxes are not paid until corporate income has been distributed to shareholders

sale a transfer of title to goods for a consideration or price

sale on approval a delivery of goods for the buyer's inspection and approval; title and risk of loss remain with the seller until the buyer approves and accepts the goods

satisfactory performance a contractually stated measure of performance that is a condition of the contract if the satisfaction is subjective in nature, but is not a condition if satisfaction can be objectively tested

scienter (Latin) "knowingly," "with guilty knowledge" (i.e., with intent to deceive)

scope of employment conduct of an agent in furtherance of the business of his/her principal such that, if the agent commits a tort, the principal, as well as the agent, will be liable for the tort

seal a distinctive mark, wax impression, letters such as L.S. (*locus sigilli*), or the word "seal" itself, indicating an intention to sign a document with a seal

secondary boycott a boycott against businesses other than the one involved in the primary labor dispute; like secondary picketing and secondary striking, usually an unfair labor practice

secondary party in negotiable instruments law, the drawer or indorser (the party secondarily liable on the instrument)

secured party a secured creditor

secured transaction any transaction in which a creditor acquires a security interest in personal property or fixtures of the debtor; if the debtor fails to perform, the secured creditor can use the personal property or fixtures (known as collateral) as a substitute for, or a means to collect, the debtor's performance (e.g., payment)

securities notes, stocks, bonds, debentures, evidences-of-debt or other documents, certificates, or interests that represent a share in a corporation, business, or venture, or a debt owed by a corporation, business, or venture; any instrument or interest commonly known as a security and regulated by the Securities Act of 1933. See also **certificated, exempt, restricted,** and **uncertified security.**

security agreement an agreement granting a security interest

security interest an interest in the debtor's personal property (or fixtures) held by the creditor as a means to ensure payment or other performance of an obligation

self-defense a defense to criminal or tort liability that permits people to use the degree of force reasonably necessary to protect themselves (or others) from criminal force

self-proved will instrument recognized in states following the Uniform Probate Code, eliminating certain formalities of proof

servant an employee; subject to great control by the master (employer)

service mark a distinctive symbol, word, letter, number, picture, or combination thereof adopted and used by a business to identify its services (distinguish them from the services of others)

service of process See **process, service of.**

settlor See **trustor.**

share (of stock) a proportionate ownership interest in a corporation or in its equity. See also **stock.**

shareholder an owner of a share of a corporation through the ownership of its stock

shelter rule a doctrine of negotiable instruments law whereby, in the chain of title after a holder in due course, all transferees have the status and benefits of a holder in due course, except transferees who (a) were parties to fraud or illegality affecting the instrument, or (2) as prior holders, had notice of a claim or defense to the instrument [UCC 3-201(1)]

shipment contract a contract whereby the seller pays the cost of delivering goods to the carrier; upon delivery to the carrier, risk of loss passes to the buyer

short-swing profits profits made by an insider through the sale or other disposition of securities within 6 months after purchase

sight draft draft payable upon proper presentment

signature in commercial law, any name, word, or mark used for the purpose of executing or authenticating a document

slander oral defamation

sole proprietorship the simplest form of business, in which a sole owner and his/her business are not legally distinct entities, the owner being personally liable for business debts

sovereign immunity the doctrine under which a government (sovereign) may not be sued without its consent

special agent a temporary agent for a single transaction or some other limited purpose

special damages damages peculiar to the plaintiff in the situation or circumstance in question

special indorsement an indorsement specifying the person to whom, or to whose order, an instrument is payable. Compare **blank (general) indorsement.**

special warranty deed a deed that includes the general warranty deed's covenants, but warrants only against defects or encumbrances arising after the grantor acquired the property

specific intent crimes certain types of crimes (e.g., burglary, arson) requiring proof of an intent to commit that particular crime; otherwise, *mens rea* (criminal intent) can be transferred from the crime intended to the one that actually occurred

specific performance a court order to a breaching party to perform his/her contract

stale check an uncertified check drawn more than 6 months before presentation for payment

standing (to sue) requirement that a person have a sufficient stake in a dispute in order to sue. Plaintiffs generally must show that they have been either harmed or threatened with harm.

stare decisis (Latin) "Stand by the decision"; a requirement that a court follow its own and higher court precedents

stated capital the amount of money received by a corporation upon issuance of its shares, except capital surplus

statute a law passed by the U.S. Congress or a state legislature

Statute of Frauds the requirement that certain agreements be evinced by a memorandum in writing, and are not provable in court if entirely oral; based on a 1677 statute of the English Parliament and on the Uniform Commercial Code

statute of limitations a statute setting forth the period during which a lawsuit must be brought after a right to sue arises and after a person knows or should know of his/her right to sue

statute of repose See **statute of limitations.**

statutory period of redemption a brief, specified time after the foreclosure sale, in which mortgagors are allowed by statute in most states to redeem (recover) the mortgaged property; the mortgagor must pay all of the amounts necessary to redeem under a presale equity of redemption, and also (in most cases) the nonrefundable expenses incurred in the foreclosure sale

stock a term used synonymously with "share"; also, the physical evidence of share ownership, the share certificate; also, the aggregate of corporate shares. See also **authorized, canceled, capital, certified, common, convertible, cumulative preferred, noncumulative preferred, no-par, par, preferred,** and **treasury stock.**

stock certificate See **certificate of stock.**

stock option a right granted to the option holder to purchase stock at a time and price specified in the option

stock subscription a promise to buy shares of stock at a specified price

stock warrant a certificate sold to the public and entitling the owner to buy a specified amount of stock at a specified time for a specified price

stop-payment order an order, oral or written, by a depositor (drawer) directing his/her bank (drawee) not to honor a specified check

straight bankruptcy a Chapter 7 bankruptcy proceeding

straight voting the usual manner of election of directors in which each share of stock entitles its holder to cast one vote for as many different directors as there are vacancies being filled. Thus, if there are seven vacancies, the owner of 100 shares may vote 100 shares for each of seven persons. Compare **cumulative voting.**

street certificate a share certificate that has been transferred in blank, that is, without designating a transferee by name; this certificate may be further transferred by delivery only, without endorsement

strict liability a modern common law principle imposing liability (regardless of whether the defendant is at fault) as a matter of public policy

Subchapter S corporation See S corporation.

subject-matter jurisdiction the authority of a court to decide the issues in a particular case

sublease a lessee's lease of his/her leasehold interest to a third person; a sublease is for less than the full term of the leasehold (if not, it is an assignment rather than a sublease)

subpoena a court order requiring a person to appear as a witness, generally, at a deposition or at trial

subpoena *duces tecum* a court order requiring a person to appear as a witness and to bring specified documents

subrogation the right of an insurer, once it has paid the insured for a loss, to proceed against third parties responsible for that loss (exception: no subrogation on life insurance payments); a surety's or guarantor's right to reimbursement from the debtor for any amounts the surety or guarantor must pay the creditor

subscribe to agree to buy shares of stock at a specified price

substantive law a body of law defining rights and obligations within a single area, such as contracts or torts

subterranean rights the exclusive rights of a landowner to oil, minerals, and other substances found beneath his/her land, including reasonable use of percolating (subsurface) waters. (This last right is also often considered a riparian right.)

suit a lawsuit

summary judgment a pretrial judgment on behalf of a civil plaintiff or civil defendant; awarded if the judge decides that (a) there is no genuine issue as to material (potentially determinative) facts, *and* (b) when the law is applied to these facts, one party is clearly entitled to a judgment in his/her favor. Summary judgment is generally granted or denied in response to a motion for it; it may be awarded on all or just part of a lawsuit.

summons a document served on the defendant, along with the complaint, and notifying the defendant that he/she must file an answer or other response to the complaint within a certain time period (e.g., 30 days) or else be subject to a default judgment

superseding (intervening) cause a tort defense based on the lack of either causation in fact or proximate cause forseeability; an intervening cause, subsequent to and not resulting from the defendant's conduct, breaks the causal connection between the defendant's acts and the plaintiff's damages

"supremacy" clause a provision in the U.S. Constitution, Article VI, Section 2, stating that the federal Constitution, laws made in pursuit of the Constitution, and treaties are "the supreme law of the land"

surety a person who has expressly or implicitly agreed to be liable for another's debts even if the creditor has not exhausted all remedies for collection; the surety is primarily, not secondarily, liable (as is a guarantor)

surplus an excess of net assets over stated capital; capital surplus may be used in the calculation of dividends

survivorship, right of in certain types of joint ownership (e.g., joint tenancy, tenancy by the entireties), when a co-owner dies his/her interest passes equally to the surviving co-owner(s), who have a right of survivorship

sympathy strike a strike called, not to gain benefits for the strikers, but to assist other workers and/or unions

tangible personal property personal property that may be physically possessed

tenancy 1. the right to possess, and/or actual possession of, real property (a lease) without having title (ownership) 2. a form of co-ownership of property. See also **joint** and **periodic tenancy.**

tenancy at sufferance (lease) tenancy continuing after a lease has expired, with most states holding that the leasehold implicitly becomes a periodic tenancy

tenancy at will (lease) tenancy which either lessor or lessee may end at any time, although most states require a termination notice

tenancy by the entirety (co-ownership) no longer recognized in many states, tenancy held by a married couple; similar to a joint tenancy, with a right of survivorship and the four unities (owners received their interest at the same time, from the same source and in equal interests (e.g., amounts), with each having a right to possess the whole); however, unlike a joint tenancy, can be terminated only by death, divorce, or agreement by both owners

tenancy in common (co-ownership) tenancy in which each of two or more co-owners has a right to possess the whole; the three other unities (same time, same source, equal interests) are not required, and there is no right of survivorship (interests pass to one's heirs); if unclear, a conveyance to two or more persons is treated as creating this tenancy, not a joint tenancy

tenant 1. a person with a right to possess, and/or actual possession of, real property without having title (ownership); a lessee of real property   2. a co-owner of property owned by more than one person

tender to proffer or make available

tender of delivery to offer or make available goods conforming to a contract of sale

tender offer general invitation to all shareholders to purchase their shares at a specified price

testamentary gift a gift specified in a will, but effective (property is transferred) only upon death; hence, as with the will itself, this gift is revocable until death of the testator

testator a man who has executed a will

testatrix a woman who has executed a will

third-party beneficiary a person, not a party to a contract, who receives a benefit from the contractual promise

third-party claim a claim bringing a third party into an existing lawsuit; for example, A has sued B, who files a third-party claim against C for all or part of the damages A claims from B

tippee a person who receives special information about corporate affairs from an insider so that he/she may invest in its securities

title 1. a section of a code devoted to a single subject matter   2. legal, formal ownership rights—broadly, the right to possess, control, and benefit from property; other types of title (ownership) are more limited in scope

title insurance insurance against defects in title to real property

tombstone advertisement a limited informational notice of anticipation concerning an issuance of securities

tort a private wrong against a person or his/her property. Aside from certain limited circumstances, all torts arise from either an intentional, wrongful action or a negligent action.

tortfeasor a person who commits a tort

trade acceptance draft drawn by a seller of goods and presented to the buyer for his/her signature (acceptance)—its signing effectively makes the instrument a note receivable of the seller and a note payable of the buyer

trade fixture a fixture placed on leased premises by a tenant for use in his/her business; unlike the situation with other fixtures, the tenant can continue to treat a trade fixture as personal property

trade name a name that, while it may act as a trademark or service mark, is used in business and generally serves to designate the business entity itself

trade secret any formula, process, or method of operation used in the production of goods or services, needed by an employee to perform his/her job, and meant to be held in the employee's confidence

trademark a distinctive symbol, word, letter, number, picture, or a combination thereof adopted and used by a merchant or manufacturer to identify his/her goods (e.g., in the minds of consumers and potential consumers)

transfer warranty See **warranty on transfer.**

transferee the party to whom an instrument or other property or right has been transferred

transferor the party who has transferred to another an instrument or other property or right

traveler's check similar to a cashier's check (the same bank is both drawer and drawee); a negotiable instrument signed by the purchaser when obtained from the bank and later used as cash upon a second signature (indorsement) by the purchaser

treason the only crime defined in the U.S. Constitution: "treason against the United States shall consist only in levying war against them, or in adhering to their enemies, giving them aid and comfort" (Article III, Section 3)

treasure trove rule a common law principle, followed in most states, that a nontrespassing finder has title to money or other treasure buried for so long a time that it is unlikely a prior owner will return. (Otherwise, the landowner usually has the rightful claim.)

treasury stock shares issued and later repurchased by a corporation

trespass any wrongful encroachment on, or other offense against, real or personal property

trespass to personal property the intentional tort (and often a crime: e.g., conversion or criminal trespass) of unjustifiably interfering with the plaintiff's possessory interest (e.g., use) in personal property; not generally as serious as the intentional tort of conversion

trespass to real property the intentional tort (and usually a crime) of unauthorized entry onto the plaintiff's land, either by a person or by something the person caused to enter the land; also occurs when presence on the plaintiff's land becomes unauthorized, but continues

trial the proceedings before a competent tribunal in which a civil or criminal case is heard and adjudicated

trover a court action to recover damages for wrongfully converted property

trust 1. an arrangement whereby property is transferred to a trustee, who administers it for the benefit of another party, the beneficiary. Trusts can be *inter vivos* (taking effect during the trust creator's lifetime) or by will (testamentary trust). See also **constructive, resulting,** and **voting trust.** 2. a relationship requiring a high degree of loyalty

trustee 1. a person who administers property for the benefit of another party 2. a person occupying a position of trust; a fiduciary 3. in bankruptcy, a person who acquires title to the debtor's property (the estate) and administers the estate by collecting and liquidating assets, as well as deciding claims; the trustee has numerous powers and is in charge of distributing the estate to creditors

trustor a transferor of property to a trustee for the benefit of a third party. Also called a "settlor" or "creator."

tying arrangement an agreement requiring the purchase of one product in return for a contract involving another product; often a *per se* violation of antitrust laws *ultra vires* (Latin) "beyond the powers" (of a corporation)

unauthorized signature a signature indicating that the signer has authority to bind another person when such is not the case

uncertified security a security for which no certificate has been issued

uncertified share a share for which no certificate has been issued, but the ownership is shown on stock books maintained for that purpose by the issuer

unconscionability gross unfairness in favor of, and brought about because of, the superior position of one of the parties to the contract

unconscionable contract a grossly unfair contract brought about by the superior position of one of the parties

underwriter one who provides an outlet for the stock of an issuer and who may guarantee to furnish a definite sum of money by a definite date for an issue of bonds or stock; more than just someone whose sole interest in the sale of stock is an ordinary commission, the underwriter acquires securities intending their overall distribution. In insurance law, the insurer

undisclosed principal a principal/agency relationship in which neither the fact of agency, nor the identity of the principal, is disclosed to third parties acting in the belief that the agent is the real party in interest

undue influence taking advantage of another by reason of a position of trust in a close or confidential relationship

unenforceable contract an agreement that, for some legal reason, is not enforceable in a court of law

unfair competition broadly, an intentional tort encompassing such activities as infringement of intellectual property and interference with contracts or prospective economic advantage; more narrowly, the intentional tort of trying to "pass off" goods or services upon the public as if they were the goods or services of another, more reputable business or product; also, usually a crime

unfair labor practice any activity by a labor union or management that is prohibited by the National Labor Relations Act or an amendment to that act

Uniform Commercial Code a comprehensive uniform law covering most commercial transactions (e.g., banking, sale of goods)

uniform laws laws uniformly enacted in several, most, or all states; and designed to eliminate or at least to reduce (a) uncertainty about the law of other states, and (b) differing interpretations and enforcement of the law. An example is the Uniform Commercial Code.

unilateral contract a contract based on the exchange of a promise by one party for an action of the other

unilateral mistake a mistake by one of the parties, but not by both parties, to a contract; not grounds for rescission or cancellation

union shop a business entity that requires (e.g., because of union "rules") that a worker, in order to remain employed, become a union member within a specified period of time after being hired. Some states outlaw union shops. See also **right-to-work law**.

unlawful boycott 1. see **secondary boycott**. 2. a *per se* violation of antitrust laws: an agreement among supposed competitors that excludes other businesses from dealing in their product(s)

unliquidated debt debt about which there is a good faith dispute as to the amount due; an obligation not reduced to a specific amount due

unsecured creditor a creditor without security for a debt who has only the debtor's express or implied promise to pay

usage of trade a regular practice or method of dealing, observed with such frequency as to become part of the transaction or contract of the parties.

usury a charge of interest in excess of the rate allowed by law

vendee a person to whom something is sold; a buyer

vendor a person who sells something; a seller

venue the geographic district (e.g., a county) in which an action is tried and from which jurors are chosen

verbal in words, oral or written

verdict the formal decision reached by a jury in a civil or criminal case

vertical merger a merger in which the merged business entities operated the same type of business, but at different levels (e.g., a manufacturer merges with his/her supplier of raw materials); generally permitted under antitrust law

vertical privity privity among persons up and down, that is, on different levels, of the chain of distribution or consumption

vested settled; accrued; fixed; definite; more than an expectation based on a contingency; a present right or interest that is or will be definitely enforceable

vicarious liability responsibility for another party's actions because of the relationship between the two parties (the acting party and the vicariously liable party). *Respondeat superior* is the most important type of vicarious liability.

"victimless" crime a crime sometimes considered to have no specific victims, just society as a whole (e.g., prostitution, gambling)

void of no legal effect from the very beginning; not even susceptible to ratification

void contract an agreement having no legal force or effect; null from the very beginning

voidable capable of being made void; a voidable thing may have some validity until an appropriate action is taken declaring the thing to be void

voidable contract an agreement subject to being declared of no legal effect as a result of action (e.g., nullification, a lawsuit) by one of the parties

voidable title a title received by a buyer subject to cancellation by the seller

voir dire a jury selection process in which the judge and/or the attorneys for both sides question prospective jurors; the information provided may be used to determine whether persons can be kept off the panel "for cause" (e.g., bias) and whether a peremptory challenge (rejecting a potential juror without offering a reason) should be exercised

voluntary bankruptcy proceedings initiated by the debtor under Chapter 7, 9, 11, or 13 of the Bankruptcy Code

voluntary intoxication See intoxication. Generally, not a defense to crimes or torts.

voting trust a combination of shareholders accomplished through transfer of shares to a voting trustee for the limited purpose of voting on matters to come before a shareholders' meeting

waiver voluntary relinquishment of one or more of a person's known rights (e.g., rights in a contract). A written waiver does not require consideration; other waivers may. See also **estoppel.**

warehouseman a person engaged in the business of receiving and storing goods for hire (UCC Article 7)

warrant court order, such as a search or arrest warrant; see also **stock warrant.**

warranty a guarantee. See also **implied, limited,** and **presentment warranty.**

warranty deed a deed in which the grantor warrants good, clear title to the grantee. The usual covenants are possession, quiet enjoyment, right to convey, freedom from encumbrances, and defense of title as to all claims.

warranty of fitness an implied warranty that goods being sold are fit for the buyer's use or purpose

warranty of merchantability an implied warranty that goods being sold are fit for the ordinary purpose for which goods of that class or kind are sold

warranty on transfer a warranty made by any person who transfers a negotiable instrument and receives consideration; it covers title, signature genuineness, and authorization, lack of material alteration, lack of knowledge of insolvency proceedings (against maker, acceptor or—for unaccepted drafts—drawer), and lack of good defenses against the transferor (the last one can be qualified); it is given to the immediate transferee and, if the transfer is by indorsement, any subsequent holder who takes the instrument in good faith

waste property damage beyond ordinary wear and tear by a person in rightful possession of the property; the damage harms another with an interest in the property (e.g., a landlord, a co-owner)

watered stock stock issued without consideration or for cash, property, or services less than par value

white-collar crime a nonviolent crime, perpetrated by a person in a position of trust, against a business or government

will an instrument, executed by a testator/testatrix according to the formalities required by state statute, setting forth how that person's estate is to be distributed after his/her death

winding up 1. action by the corporation, after dissolution, to liquidate assets and distribute the proceeds—first, to creditors; second, to preferred shareholders (if any); finally, to common shareholders 2. in partnership law, the liquidation and termination process for a dissolved partnership. See **liquidation**, 2.

without recourse indorsement See **disclaimer**, 2.

without reserve the stipulation that an auctioneer may not withdraw goods from the auction

workers' compensation statute a law, found in all states, requiring many types of employees to relinquish their right to sue their employers for accidental death, injury, or disease arising from or during the course of their employment; in exchange, the employees gain the right to receive financial benefits (according to a statutory schedule of amounts) regardless of fault

writ a written court order requiring the performance of an act or giving authority to have it done

writ of attachment See **attachment**.

writ of *certiorari* See ***certiorari*, writ of**.

writ of execution after a judgment against the debtor, a court order that a sheriff or other authorized official seize and sell the debtor's nonexempt property

wrongful boycott See **unlawful boycott**, 2.

wrongful discharge See **abusive discharge**.

wrongful dishonor dishonoring, by a bank, of a customer's check without good cause (e.g., insufficient funds, improper or missing endorsements)

yellow dog contract an unlawful agreement in which the employee, as a condition of employment, agrees not to join or remain a member of a union

zoning legislative action, usually at the municipal level, regulating the use of real property, including the types of construction permitted within different zoning districts

INDEX

Abandoned property, 342
Abuse of process, 65
Abusive discharge, 63–64, 407–08
Acceptance, 90–92
Accession, 341, 390
Accommodation parties, 212
Accord and satisfaction, 140
Accountants, liability of, 330–32
Acts of God, 69,142
Actual authority, 235–36, 259
Actus reus, 56
Adequacy of consideration, 93
Adhesion contracts, 108
Administrative agencies
  administrative law of, 21–22
  judicial proceedings of, 47–48
Administrative Dispute Act, 45
Administrative law judges, 47
Administrative Procedure Act, 22, 47
Administrative rulings, 21
Adverse impact, 409
Adverse possession, 354
Advertisements as offers, 88
Advertising, deceitful, 64
Affectation doctrine, 16
Affirmative action, 409
Affirmative defenses, 38
Affirmative easement, 357
Age Discrimination in Employment Act
  (ADEA), 410
Agency, 229–42
  in corporations, 248, 283, 306
  of partners, 248, 258
Agent, 229
Agreement, 81–82, 85–86, 100
Air rights, 355
Aliens, contracts by, 116
Allonges, 189
Alterations, 223
Alternative dispute resolution, 45
Americans with Disabilities Act, 410–11
Amicus curiae brief, 43
Answer, 37
Anticipatory breach, 139–40
Antitrust law, 270, 398–402
  exemptions, 401–02
Apparent authority, 235–36, 241, 259
Appeals, 30–31, 43–44
Appellate jurisdiction, 23
Appraisal (dissenters') rights, 298
Appurtenant easement, 357
Arbitration, 46, 420
Arbitration Act, 46
Arson, 66
Articles of incorporation, 282
  (*see* Charters)
Artisan's liens, 371
"As is," 164
Assault, 63

Assent, 87
Assignee, 130, 187
Assignment of contract, 129–30, 187
Assignment of rights, 129–30
Assignment to a trustee, 373
Assignor, 130, 187
Assumption of risk, 69
Attachment, 384
  prejudgment, 371
Attempt, 66
Attorney-at-law, 230
Attorney/client privilege, 423, 424
Attorneys in fact, 230
Attorneys' roles, 423–24
Attractive nuisance, 360
At-will doctrine (employment), 63, 407–08
Authorized shares, 315
Auto Dealers' Day in Court Act, 270

Bailee, 158, 343–47
Bailments, 158,343–47,362
Bailor, 158, 343–45
Bank statements, 220
Bankruptcy, 143, 261–62, 376–82
  frauds, 66
Bankruptcy Code
  Chapter 7, 377–78
  Chapter 9, 377
  Chapter 11, 377–78
  Chapter 13, 377–78
Banks, 218–25
Battery, 63
Bearer paper, 186,188
Beneficiaries, 131–32
  creditor, 131–32
  donee, 132
  incidental, 132
  third-party, 131–32
Bilateral contract, 84
Bill of Rights, 17–18
Bill of attainder, 20
Blackstone, 3, 5
Blank indorsements, 190
Blue laws, 118
Blue sky laws, 330
Bonds
  corporate, 313
  performance and fidelity, 372–73
Boycotts, group (antitrust law), 399
Boycotts, secondary (labor law), 413
Breach of condition, 139
Bribery, 66–67
Briefs, 43
Bulk transfer, 372
Burden of proof, 42–43, 54, 57–58, 60
Burglary, 67
Business format franchises, 269
Business judgment rule, 303
Business organizations, comparisons of,
  246–54
Businessperson, with attorneys, 424
Bylaws, corporate, 284

C & F (cost and freight), 161
Call price, 315

Callable bonds, 313
Canceled shares, 315
Capacity, 87, 113–16, 209
Capital structure, 284
Capital surplus, 318
Case law, 4, 9, 23
Cases, citation of, 48–49
Cashier's check, 185
Causation, 60, 105
Caveat emptor, 102
Caveat venditor, 102
Certificate of incorporation, 278
Certificates of deposit(CDs), 178, 183–84
Certification elections (labor law), 414
Certified checks, 185, 222–23
Chain-style businesses, 269
Charitable corporations, 280
Charters, corporate, 278, 282–84, 295
Chattel, 155
Checking accounts, 218–25
Checks, 178,185,218,221–25
Checks and balances, 15
CIF (cost, insurance and freight), 161
Citations, 48–49
Civil law, development of, 4
Civil liberties, legislation to protect, 17–18
Civil Rights Act of 1964, 408
Civil Rights Law Amendments (1991), 411
Class action, 39
Clayton Act, 399–401
Clean Air Act, 404
Clean Water Act, 403–04
Close corporations, 280
Closed shop, 414
COD, 170
Code, 4
Codicil, 363
Collateral, 382–83, 386–87
Comity, 418
Commercial speech, 18
Commercial impracticability, 142–43
Commercial paper, 176–214
Commingling, 233–34
Common carriers, 346–47
Common law, 5–7
Common shares (stock), 314
Community property, 351
Comparable worth doctrine, 410
Comparative negligence, 69–70
Compensatory damages, 145–47
Complaint, 36–37
Composition/extension agreement, 373
Compounding a crime, 67
Comprehensive Environmental Response,
  Compensation and Liability Act
  (CERCLA—Superfund), 404
Compromise, 45
Computer crimes, 67
Computer Matching and Privacy Protection
  Act, 421
Computer Security Act, 421
Computer Software Act, 422
Computers, 67, 420–22
 funds transfer by, 224–25
Conditional indorsement, 190

Conditions, 137–39
Condominiums, 351
Confidential communications, 423
Confiscation (international law), 419
Conflict of interest, 234
Conflict of laws, 33–34
Confusion (of property), 341
Conglomerate, 400
Congress, 14, 16–19
Consent, 70
Consequential damages, 147
Consideration (in contracts) 81, 92–95
Consideration (corporate stock), 317
Consignment, 162
Consolidation, 295–96
Constitutions, 13–19
Constructive bailments, 343–44
Constructive eviction, 360
Constructive trust, 363
Consumer Credit Protection Act, 374–75
Consumer protection statutes, 375–76
Consumers
 HIDC and protection of, 205,206
 sales contracts and, 155–71
Contracts, 81–152
 applicable state law for, 34
 classification of, 83–84
 constitutional law, 18
 damages from breach of, 144–48
 destination, 161–62
 discharge of, 136–43
 illegality of, 117–20, 141–42
 impossibility of, 142–43
 injunction, 149
 interference with, 64
 liability of principals and agents for, 235–36,
  238–40
 mistakes in, 101–102
 negotiable instruments compared to,
  186–187
 parol evidence rule for, 128
 real estate, 149
 sales, 155–71
 shipment, 161
 specific performance of, 148–49
 time of performance, 138
 written evidence required for certain,
  124–28
Contributory negligence, 70
Convention on Contracts for the International
  Sale of Goods, 419
Conversion, 64, 212
Conversion of shares, 315
Convertible bonds, 313
Convicts, contracts by, 116
Cooling off period (labor law), 415
Copyrights, 348–49
 of computer software, 422
Corporate crime, 67
Corporate opportunity, 302
Corporations, 274–332
 alien, 280
 boards of directors of, 278, 301–06
 charters of. *See* Charters
 compared to proprietorships and

partnerships, 247–53
consolidation, 295–96
creation, 276
directors, 293–95,301–06
"doing business", 287
duration, 277, 283
employees, 306
financial structure, 313–16
foreign, 280, 287
formation, 277
gifts by, 299
management of, 293–94
merger, 295–96
name, 283
offers, 293, 305–06
perpetual existence, 277
powers of, 285–86, 294
purposes, 283–84, 294
sale of assets, 296
shareholders of, 293–301
termination of, 306–8
types of, 247, 279–82
Council of Environmental Quality, 403
Counterclaims, 39
Counterfeit Access Device and Computer
    Fraud and Abuse Act, 421
Counteroffer, 90
Course of dealing, 128, 159
Course of performance, 128
Court system (judiciary), 15,23,28–49
Covenants, 359
Covering (sales contracts), 171
Credit information, 421–22
Creditor beneficiary, 131–32
Creditors, 371–74
    priority of, 387–90
Creditors' rights, 371–73
Credit-reporting agencies, 421
Crimes, 54–59
    agent's, liability for, 240
    applicable state law for, 34
    business, with tort equivalents, 66–68
    general defenses to, 69–72
    organized, 56
    per se, 57
    torts compared to, 62, 66–67
    victimless, 56
    white-collar, 56, 68–69
Cross claims, 39
Cross-examination, 42
Cumulative voting, 297
Customer signature cards, 219

Damages
    compensatory, 145–47
    consequential, 147
    exemplary, 148
    from breach of contract, 144–48
    incidental, 147
    indirect, 147
    liquidated, 147
    mitigation, 146–47
    nominal, 145
    punitive, 148
Dartmouth College v. Woodward, 276

De facto corporation, 278
De jure corporation, 278
De minimis non curat lex, 145
Deadly force, 71
Dealers in goods, 160
Debentures, corporate, 313
Debit card, 225
Debt securities, 313
Debtors
    protection for, 364–76
    secured transactions by, 382–90
Debts
    collection of, 371–74
    in bankruptcy, 143,376–82
Deceit, 65
Decertification elections, 414
Deed of trust, 353
Deeds, 352
Defamation, 65
Default (secured transactions), 385–86
Defendants, 36
Defenses
    affirmative, 38
    to crimes and torts, 69–72
    to enforcing commercial paper, 202–4
Deficiency judgment, 373
Definiteness of offer, 88
Definitions of law, 2
Delegated authority (administrative law),
    21–22
Delegation of duties, 131, 231
Demand instruments, 199
Demurrer, 37
Depositions, 40
Derivative suits, 300
Destination contracts, 161
Differences in prices (antitrust law), 400
Direct examination, 42
Direct liability of principal, 236–37
Directed verdict, 42
Directors, 293–95, 301–6
Disabled or retired workers, 407, 410–11
Disaffirmance, 114
Discharge in bankruptcy, 377, 380–81
Discharge of contracts, 136–43
    breach of condition, 139
    by agreement, 140–41
    by anticipatory breach, 139–40
    by meeting conditions, 137–39
    by operation of law, 141–43
    by performance, 136–37
    satisfactory performance, 138
    time of performance, 138
Discharge of debt, 373
Discharge of negotiable instruments, 213–14
Disclaimers, 164–65, 191
Disclosed principal, 238–39
Discount shares, 318
Discovery, 40–41
Discrimination, protection vs., 408–12
Dishonoring an instrument, 199
Disparagement, 64
Disparate treatment, 409
Dissenters' rights, 298
Dissolution of corporations, 306–07

Dissolution of partnerships, 261–63
Distribution of bankrupt estate, 379–80
Distribution of corporate assets, 316
Distribution of partnership assets, 264 267
Distribution system franchises, 269
Diversity jurisdiction, 32, 418
Dividends and distributions, 298,316–17
Division of markets, 68, 399
Division of powers, 14–15
Domestic corporation, 280
Donee, 159, 340
Donee beneficiary, 132
Donor, 159, 340
Double taxation, 251, 253, 280–81
Dowry, 126
Drafts, 178,184
Drawee, 184–85
Drawer, 184–85
Due process, 17–18,55
Duress, 70,107–8
Duties, delegation of, 131
Duty (standard of care), 59–60

Easements, 357–58
  by necessity, 358
  by prescription, 358
  in gross, 357–58
Eighth Amendment, 55
Electronic Funds Transfer Act, 224–25, 421
Embezzlement, 67
Eminent domain, 18, 353–54
Emotional distress, 63
Employee bargaining unit, 414
Employee Polygraph Protection Act, 405
Employee Retirement Income Security Act
  (ERISA), 407
Employer free speech, 413
Employment law, 405–12
Enabling acts, 22
Endangered Species Act, 404
Enforcement of judgments, 44
English Bill of Rights, 5, 12
Entrapment, 70
Enumerated powers, 16–17
Environmental impact statement, 403
Environmental law, 403–05
Environmental Protection Agency, 403–04
Equal Credit Opportunity Act, 375
Equal Employment Opportunity Commission
  (EEOC), 408, 411
Equal Pay Act, 410
Equal protection, 18
Equity, 6–7
  illegal contracts, 120
  injunction, 149
  specific performance, 148–49
  titles of parties, 36
Equity of redemption, 373
Equity securities, 314
Escheat, 364
Estate for years (leasehold), 359
Estates, 361
Estoppel, 232
  partnership by, 256
  promissory, 95

Estray statutes, 342
Ethics (attorneys), 423–24. See morality.
Evidence, 47, 58
Ex post facto laws, 20
Exclusive dealing, 400
Exculpatory clauses, 119–20, 361
Executed contract, 84
Executor, 364
  contracts of, 126
Executory contract, 84, 127
Exemplary damages, 148
Exempt property (bankruptcy), 378–79
Exempted transactions (securities), 324
Exemption statutes, 374
Exhaustion of remedies, 48
Expedited Funds Availability Act, 219
Export Administration Act, 418
Export Trading Company Act, 418
Express authority, 236, 259
Express conditions, 137–38
Express contract, 83, 86
Express trusts, 363
Express warranties, 163
Expropriation (international law), 419
Ex-ship, 162
Extradition, 34

FAS (free alongside ship), 161
Fair Credit Billing Act, 375
Fair Debt Collection Practices Act, 375
Fair Credit Reporting Act, 375, 421–22
Fair Labor Standards Act (FLSA), 405, 406
Fair use exception (copyright), 348
False arrest or imprisonment, 63
False light, 63
Feather-bedding, 413
Federal constitution. See United States
  Constitution
Federal corporations, 279–80
Federal courts. See Court system
Federal Environmental Pesticide Control Act,
  404
Federal Insecticide, Fungicide and
  Rodenticide Act, 404
Federal Insurance Contributions Act (FICA),
  407
Federal mediation, 414
Federal questions, 32
Federal statutes, 16–19
Federal Trade Commission, 205, 270, 400–02
  franchises, 270
  rule as to instrument holders, 205
Federal Trade Commission Act, 399,400–01
Federal Water Pollution Control Act, 403
Fee simple determinable, 356
Fee simple estate, 356
Fee simple subject to a condition subsequent,
  356
Felonies, 56
Fictitious payees, 208
Fidelity bonds, 372
Fiduciary, 233, 258, 302
Fifth Amendment, 55
Financing statement, 384–85
Firm written offer, 90

First National Bank of Boston v. Bellotti, 27
"First to perfect" rule, 388–89
Fitness, warranty of, 164
Five percent shareholders, 328
Fixtures, 339,355,389–90
FOB (free on board), 161
Force majeure, 142
Foreclosure, 353, 373
Foreign corporations, 280, 287
Foreign Corrupt Practices Act, 418
Foreign Sovereign Immunities Act, 418
Foreseeability standard, 60,146,166,331–32
Forgery, 67,208–10,220
Four "unities" (joint ownership), 350
Fourteenth Amendment, 17,19
Fourth Amendment, 55
Franchise Agreement, 269
Franchises, 268–70
Franchisees, 268
Franchisors, 268
Fraud, 65, 100
  against consumers, 67
  businesspersons, 69
  in bankruptcy, 66
  in contracts, 103–06
  in the execution (factum), 202
  in the inducement, 203
  minor's liability for, 114–15
  in negotiable instruments, 202, 203
  silence, 65
  Statute of Frauds, 124–28,156–57
  in stock sales, 327, 329
  as tort, 65
Fraudulent conveyances, 372
Full faith and credit, 34–35
GAAP (Generally Accepted Accounting
  Principles), 331
GAAS (Generally Accepted Auditing
  Standards), 331
Garnishment, 219,373,374–75
GATT (General Agreement on Tariffs and
  Trade), 419
General indorsements, 190
General partners, 265
General partnerships, 254–64
  authority of partner to bind
  other partners, 259
  creation, 254–56
  distinct entity, 261
  liability of partners to third parties, 260
  mere aggregate, 261
  rights and duties of partners, 257–58
  termination, 261–64
General warranty deeds, 352
Gifts, 159, 299, 340
  causa mortis, 340
  corporate, 299
  inter vivos, 340
Good faith, 156, 198, 417
Grand jury, 41
Grandfather clause, 141
Gratuitous bailment, 343–44
Guarantors, 212–13,372
Guaranty agreements, 126, 372

Hammurabi, Code of, 4, 145, 254
Health and safety legislation, 406
Hearing examiners, 47
Holder, 188
Holder in due course (HIDC), 188,196–206
Homestead exemptions, 374,378–79
Horizontal privity, 165–66
"Hot cargo" contracts, 413
Hotelkeeper's liens, 371

Illusory promises, 93
Immigration Reform and Control Act, 419
Immunity, 70,71
Implied authority, 236, 259
Implied conditions, 138
Implied partnerships, 255–56
Implied powers, 16–17
Implied trusts, 363
Implied warranties, 163–64
Implied-in-fact contract, 83, 85
Implied-in-law contract, 83–84, 86
Impossibility, 142–43
Impostors (negotiable instruments), 208
Impracticability, 142–43
Incidental beneficiaries, 132
Incidental mistake, 101
Income protection, 406–07
Incorporators, 278, 283
Indentures, corporate, 313
Independent contractors, 230, 238
Indictment, 41, 57
Indirect liability of principal, 237–38
Indorsements, 189–91, 208
  forged, 209–10
Indorsers, 186
Infancy, 70
Information, 57
Infringement of intellectual property, 64
Inheritance, 354
Injunction, in law of contracts, 149
Innocent misrepresentations, 106
Insane persons
  contracts by, 116
  crimes and torts by, 71
  partners, 263
Insider (securities) transactions, 329
Inspection, buyer's right of, 170
Installment land contract, 353
Insurable interest, 416
Insurance, 416–17
Intangible personal property, 339
Intellectual property, 348–50
Intent
  in contracts, 82
  in crimes or torts, 56–57, 70
Intent to defraud, 105
Intentional infliction of mental distress, 63
Intentional misrepresentation, 103
Intentional torts, 59
Interference torts, 63–65
Interference with contract, 64
Interference with prospective economic
  advantage, 64
Interlocking directorships, 400
International Court of Justice, 420

International dispute resolution, 420
International law, 418–20
International Shoe Co. v. Washington, 33
Interrogatories, 40
Interstate commerce, 16,20
Intervening causes, 72
Intestate succession, 364
Intoxication, 71, 116
Intra vires, 286
Invasion of privacy, 63
Invitee, 360
Issued shares, 315

J.N.O.V., 43
Joint and several liability, 60, 240, 260
Joint ownership, 350–51
Joint tenancies, 350
Joint ventures, 247
Judgment by default, 37
Judgment creditor, 373
Judgment *non obstante veredicto*, 43
Judgment notwithstanding the verdict, 43
Judgment sale, 353
Judgments, 39–40,43,44
Judicial sale, 373
Judiciary, the. *See* Court system
Juries, 41–43
Jurisdiction, 23,29,32–33
Justifiable reliance, 105
Justinian Code, 4, 6

Labor-management relations, 412–16
Labor-Management Relations Act, 413
Labor-Management Reporting and Disclosure Act, 413
Labor relations law, 412–16
Landlords and tenants, 339, 358–60
Landrum-Griffin Act, 413
Land-use controls, 355–56
Lanham Act, 401
Larceny (theft), 67
Lateral and subjacent support, right to (land), 355
Law, 1–2
Law merchant, 177
Lawgivers, 3
Lawsuits, 35–45
  shareholders, 300–01
Leasehold, 357, 359
Leases, 159,357,359,362
Legal positivism, 2
Legality of subject matter, 117–20
Lender liability, 376
Length of offers, 88–89
Lessee, 159, 359
Lessor, 159, 359
Lex talionis, 1
Liability
  of accountants, 330–32
  of common carriers, 347
  of departing partners, 262
  of new partners, 262
  of parties on instruments, 207–13
  of partners to third parties, 260
  of principals and agents, 235–41

of shareholders, 300–301
on negotiable instruments, 207–10
under Securities Act, 326–27
Libel, 65
Licensee, 360
Licenses (real property), 358
Liens, 371, 388
Life estate, 357
Limited liability companies, 281
Limited liability of shareholders, 276, 300–01
Limited partners, 265–67
Limited partnerships, 265–68
Lingering apparent authority, 241
Liquidated damages, 147
Liquidation (bankruptcy), 377
Liquidation of corporations, 307
Liquidation of partnerships, 263
Lockouts, 415
Long-arm statutes, 33
Lost property, 342
Loyalty, duty of, 302, 350

MacPherson v. Buick Motor Co., 166
Magna Carta, 5, 12, 118
Magnuson-Moss Act, 165
Mail and wire fraud, 67
Maintenance of rented property, 360
"Make whole" principle, 170–71
Maker, 183, 185
Malice (in defamation), 65
Malicious institution of civil proceedings, 65
Malicious prosecution, 65
Malpractice, 330–31
Mansfield, Lord, 177
Manufacturing arrangements, 269
Marbury v. Madison, 48–49
Margin requirements, 329
Market divisions, 68, 399
Master/servant relationships, 230
Material alteration, 203
Material breach, 145
Material facts, 104
Material mistake, 101
McCulloch v. Maryland 16
Mechanic's liens, 371
Mediation, 45–46
Meeting of the minds, 100
Membership corporations, 280
Memorandum in writing, 127
Mens rea, 56–57, 71
Mental distress, 63
Merchant (under UCC), 156
Merchant protection laws, 63
Merchantability, warranty of, 164
Merger, 295–96, 400
Minimum wage, 405, 406
Minors
  contracts by, 114–16
  crimes and torts by, 70
Miranda v. Arizona, 55
Misappropriation of name or likeness, 63
Misappropriation of trade secrets, 68
Misdemeanors, 56
Mislaid property, 342
Misrepresentations, 65, 104–06

Mistake (contracts), 101–02
Mistake of fact or law, 71
Mitigation, 146–47
Model Business Corporation Act, 275, 285, 301, 317, 319
Monopolies, 398–400
Moral obligation, 94
Morality, 2–3
Mortgages, 353,373,374
Motion to dismiss, 37–38
Motions, 39
Motions after trial, 43
Motive, 57
Mutual agreement, 87, 100
Mutual mistake, 101–2

Napoleonic Code, 4
National Environmental Policy Act (NEPA), 403
National Labor Relations Act, 412–14
National Labor Relations Board, 412–14
Nationalization, foreign countries, 419
Natural law, 2
Necessaries, 115
Necessary and proper clause, 16
Necessity, agency by, 232
Negative easement, 357
Negligence
    defenses to, 69–70, 72
    in law of commercial paper, 208, 212
    in product liability, 167
    professional corporations and, 281
    torts arising from, 59–60, 62
Negligent misrepresentation, 66
Negotiability, 178–82
Negotiable instruments, 176–91
Negotiated Rulemaking Act, 22
Negotiation of contract, 85–87
Negotiation of instruments, 188–89
No arrival, no sale, 162
Noise, excessive, 64
Noise Control Act, 404
Nominal damages, 145
Nondischargeable debts, 380
Nonpossessory interests (land), 357–58
Nonprofit corporations, 280
No-par shares, 318
Norris-La Guardia Act, 412
Notice as to claims/defenses on negotiable instruments, 198–200
Notice of partnership dissolution, 263
Novation, 131
Nuisance, 64,355

Occupational Safety and Health Act, 406
Occupational Safety and Health Administration (OSHA), 406
Offer, 87–91
Offeree, 86
Offeror, 86
Office of Export Trade, 418
Officers (corporate), 293, 305–06
Oil Pollution Act, 405
Opening statements, 42
Opinion, 65, 104

Option contracts, 89
Oral condition, 128
Order paper, 181,189
Ordinances, 21
Organized crime, 56
Original jurisdiction, 23
Out-of-court settlements, 45–46
Output contracts, 94–95
Outstanding shares, 315
Overdrafts, 221
Overdue instruments, 199
Overseas Private Investment Corp., 419

Palsgraf v. Long Island R.R. Co., 60
Par shares, 317–18
Parol evidence rule, 128
Partially disclosed principal, 239
Partnerships
    agreements, 254–56
    by estoppel, 256
    compared to proprietorships and corporations, 247–53
    creditors, 262–64
    criminal law, 260
    duties of partners, 257–58
    general, 32, 254–64
    implied, 255–56
    liability of partners, 260
    limited, 265–68
    partners' property interests, 250
    rights of partners, 257–58
    termination, 261–64, 267
    "winding up," 263
"Pass off" goods, 64
Past consideration, 94
Patents, 348
    design patents, 348
    plant patents, 348
Pattern or practice (employment law), 409
Payable, 180–81
    at a definite time, 181
    on demand, 180
    to bearer, 181
    to order, 181
Payee, 183–85
Penalty provision in contract, 147
Pension Benefit Guaranty Corp., 407
Per se crimes, 5
Per se violations (antitrust law), 399
Peremptory challenge, 42
Perfect tender rule, 169
Perfection, 384–85
Performance bonds, 372
Performance of sales contracts, 168–70
Periodic tenancy, 359
Personal defenses, 203–04
Personal (in personam) jurisdiction, 32–33
Personal property, 338–43
Personal representative, 364
Petit jury, 41
Petitioners, 36
Petroleum Marketing Practices Act, 270
Pierce the corporate veil, 276–77
Plaintiffs, 33, 36
Pleadings, 36–40

Pledges, 383
Possession, 342
Possessory interests (land), 356–57
Power of attorney, 230
Precedent, 5–6
Preemptive rights, 300
Preexisting duty (contracts), 92–93
Preferential transfers, 379
Preferred stock (shares), 314–15
Pregnancy Discrimination Act, 411
Prejudgment attachments, 371
Prenuptial agreements, 126
Presentment warranties, 211
President, the, 14–15
Pretrial conference, 41
Price differentials, 400
Price restraints, 68
Price v. Neal, 211, 219, 220
Price-fixing, 399
Prima facie case, 168, 302
Primary benefit test (accountant's liability), 332·
Primary parties, 207
Principal, 229
Principals and agents, 229–42
Priorities
  bankruptcy, 376, 379–80
  payments to creditors of partners/partner-ships, 264
  secured transactions, 387–90
Privacy Act, 421
Private corporations, 279
Private law, 2
Private offerings, 324–25
Private property. See Property
Private restrictions (land use), 355–56
Privilege, 71
Privity of contract, 129–32, 165–66
Pro se plaintiff, 144
Probable cause, 57
Procedural law, 7–8, 35–44
Product liability, 163–68
Professional corporations, 281
Promissory estoppel, 95
Promissory notes, 178, 183
  corporate, 313
Promoter, 277–78
Property, 338–64
  compensation for taking of, 18
  joint ownership of, 350–51
  personal, 338–43
  real, 338, 351–61,373
  torts of interference with, 64–65
Probate, 364
Processing arrangements, 269
Production quotas, 399
Profits (real property), 358
Promoter, 277–78
Proprietorships, sole, 246–51
Prospectus (for securities), 323–24
Proxies, 297–98, 329
Proximate cause, 60
Public corporation, 279
Public enemy, 347
Public law, 1

Public offerings, 320
Public policy, 61, 118–20, 167
  contracts in violation of, 118–20
  strict liability, 61, 167
Public utilities, 279
Puffing, 65
Punitive damages, 148
Purchase-money security interest, 384, 388–89
Purchasers of collateral, 389

Quantum meruit, 84, 86, 137, 139
Quasi-contract, 83–84, 86, 115, 127–28, 137, 235
Quasi-public corporations, 279
Quid pro quo, 92
Quiet enjoyment, 359
Quitclaim deed, 352
Quotas, employment, 409–10
Quotas, production, 399

Racketeer Influenced and Corrupt
  Organizations (RICO) Act, 68
Railway Labor Act, 412
Ratification, 115–16, 232, 259
"Rational basis" test, 18
Reaffirmation agreement, 381
"Real" defenses, 202–04
Real property (real estate), 338,351–61,373
  Redemption, equity of, 373
  Redemption, statutory period of, 373
  Statute of Frauds, 125–26, 128
"Reasonable person," 59–60
Recording of deeds, 352
Recreational use statutes, 361
Red herring prospectus, 324
Redemption of shares, 315
Registered agent, 283
Registration of securities, 323–24, 328
Registration statement, 323
Reimbursement of partners, 258
Rejection of offers, 89
Release, 140–41
Remainder, 357
Remainderman, 357
Remedies for breach of sales contracts, 170–71
Rented property, 358–60
Representative elections (labor law), 414
Requests for admissions, 40–41
Requirements and output contracts, 94–95
Res ipsa loquitur, 60, 167
Rescission of contracts, 102, 106, 140
Rescission of notes, 210
Rescuer, 69
Researching the law, 8–9
Resource Conservation and Recovery Act
  (RCRA), 404
Respondeat superior, 61, 237–38, 260
Respondents, 36
Restatement (Second) of Torts §402A, 167
Restraint of trade, 118–19,399
Restrictive covenants, 357
Restrictive indorsement, 190–91
Resulting trust, 363
Retained earnings, 316

Reverse discrimination, 409–10
Revised Model Business Corporation Act,
    275, 285, 301, 317, 319
Revised Uniform Limited Partnership Act,
    265–67
Revocation of offers, 89–90
Right of survivorship, 350
Right-to-work laws, 414
Riparian rights, 355
Risk of loss, 160–62
Robbery, 68
Robinson-Patman Act, 399, 400, 401
Roman Law, 4, 254, 275
Rule, 12, 21
Rule of reason (antitrust law), 399
Rulings, administrative, 21

S corporations, 280–81
SEC Regulation A, 325
SEC Regulation B, 325
SEC Regulation C, 323, 325
SEC Regulation D, 325–26
SEC Rule 10b–5, 329
SEC Rule 14a–3, 329
SEC Rule 144, 326
SEC Rule 147, 323
SEC Rules 504–06, 325–26
SEC v. W. J. Howey Co., 322
Safety and health legislation, 406
Sale of goods, 159
Sale of real property, 352–53
Sale on approval/consignment, 162
Sales contracts, 155–71, 362
Satisfaction, 138
Scienter, 104, 240
Seals, 96
Secondary boycotts, 413
Secondary parties, 207
Section 1981, Civil Rights Act of 1866, 411
Secured creditor, 382
Secured transactions, 382–90
Securities, 313–30
    regulation of, 321–30
Securities Act of 1933, 321–27
    Section 3(a), 322
    Section 3(b), 325
    Section 4, 324, 325
    Section 11, 326–27, 330–31
    Section 12, 327
Securities and Exchange Comm'n, 321–29
Securities Exchange Act of 1934, 321, 327–29
    8-K report, 328
    Section 13(d), 328–29
    Section 16(b), 329
    10-K report, 328
    10-Q report, 328
Security interest, 362, 383
Self-defense, 71
Semiconductor Chip Protection Act, 422
Service marks, 349
Service of process, 37
Sexual harassment, 409
Share, 319
Share subscriptions, 318–19
Shareholders, 293–301

appraisal (dissenters') rights, 298
functions, 295–96
meetings, 296–98
inspection rights, 299
lawsuits, 300
limited liabilities, 276, 300–01
preemptive rights, 300
Shelter rule, 200–01
Sherman Act, 399, 400, 401
Shipment contracts, 161
Shipper, 346
"Short-swing" trading, 329
Signature, 179, 209
    unauthorized, 209
Silence as acceptance, 91–92
Sitdown strikes, 415
Sixth Amendment, 55
Slander, 65
Social Security Act, 407
Sole proprietorships, 246–51
Solon, Code of, 4
Special indorsements, 190
Special warranty deeds, 352
Specific performance, 148–49
Spend for general welfare, power to, 17
Stale checks, 221, 224
"Standing in the shoes" principle, 130
Stare decisis, 5
State action, 17
States
    blue sky laws of, 330
    conflict of laws of, 33–34
    constitutions of, 19
    courts of, 23, 28–29, 31–35
    full faith and credit to acts of, 34–35
    statutes of, 19–20, 143
    U.S. protection vs., 19
Statute of Frauds, 124–28, 156–57
Statutes, 6
    federal, 16–19
    state, 19–20
Statutes of limitations, 72, 94
    for a sales contract, 171
    on bank's liability for checks, 224
    revival (contracts), 143
Statutory law, 9,19–20
    contracts in violation of, 118
Statutory period of redemption, 373
Stock options, 315
Stock pooling, 298
Stock split, 316
Stocks, 314–30
Stolen instrument, 204
Stop-payment orders, 222,224
Street certificate, 320
Strict foreclosure, 373
Strict liability, 61,167–68
Strict scrutiny, 18
Strikes, 415
    as a privilege, 71
Subject-matter jurisdiction, 32
Subrogation, 372–73, 417
Subscriptions (shares), 318–19
Substantive law, 7,28
Subterranean rights, 354

Sum certain, 180
Summary judgment, 39–40
Summation, 42
Summons, 37
Superfund (environmental law), 404
Superseding causes, 72
Supremacy clause, 14
Surety, 126, 372
Surface rights, 354
Suspect classifications, 18

Taft-Hartley Act, 413–15
Tangible personal property, 338–39
Tax, power to, 17
Tenancies at sufferance, 359
Tenancies at will, 359
Tenancies by the entirety, 350
Tenancies in common, 351
Tenancies in partnership, 258
Tenants and landlords, 339, 358–60
Tender, 168–70
Termination of agency, 241–42
  by acts of the parties, 241
  by operation of law, 241–42
Termination of bailments, 345–46
Termination of corporations, 306–08
  dissolution, 306–07
  liquidation, 307
  winding up, 307
Termination of lease, 359–60
Termination of partnerships, 261–64, 267
  by acts of the parties, 262
  by court decree, 263
  by operation of law, 262
  dissolution, 261–63
  distribution of assets, 264
  limited partnerships, 267
  liquidation, 263
  notice of dissolution, 263
Termination statement (security interests), 387
Territorial limitations (antitrust law), 399
Testamentary gift, 340, 373
Testator, 363
Testatrix, 363
Theft (larceny), 67
Third-party beneficiaries, 131–32
Third-party claims, 39
Threats, 108
"Time" instruments, 199
Title VII of Civil Rights Act, 408–11
Titles, transfer of, 159–60
Tombstone advertisement, 324
Torts, 59–72
  agency and, 230, 236–38, 239–40
  applicable state law for, 34
  general defenses to, 69–72
  malpractice, 60, 330–31
  product liability from, 167–68
  real property, 360–61
Trade fixture, 339
Trade libel, 64
Trade secrets, 350
Trade unions, 419
Trade usage, 128, 159
Trademarks and trade names, 349

Transfer of securities, 320
Transmitting the acceptance, 91
Traveler's check, 185
Treason, 56
Treasure trove rule, 342
Treasury shares, 300, 315, 318
Treaties, 13, 418
Trespass, 65
Trespasser, 360
Trial
  in civil cases, 41–42
  in criminal cases, 57–58
Trustee (bankruptcy), 379–80, 389
Trusts, 361,363
Truth-in-Lending Act, 374–75
Tying arrangements, 399

UCC (Uniform Commercial Code)
  Article 2, 88, 155–57, 163, 168, 340, 419
  Atricle 2A, 159
  Article 3, 178,186,212,218,320,340
  Article 4, 178, 218, 221–22, 340
  Article 4A, 225
  Article 6, 372
  Article 8, 319–20
  Article 9, 382–83, 385
  Sections
    1-106, 170
    1-107, 141
    1-201, 179, 198
    2-103 to 2–104, 156
    2-106, 159
    2-201, 126, 156
    2-202, 128
    2-205, 90, 156
    2-206, 91
    2-207, 156
    2-208, 157
    2-312, 156. 211
    2-313, 163, 211
    2-314, 156, 164, 211
    2-315, 211
    2-316, 164
    2-324, 162
    2-507, 168–69
    2-509, 161–62
    2-511, 169–70
    2-513, 170
    2-601, 169
    2-613, 162
    2-615, 143
    2-706, 171
    2-712 to 2–713, 171
    2-718, 170
    2-719, 171
    2-725, 171
    3-103, 179
    3-104, 178–79, 190
    3-105 to 3–106, 180
    3-108, 180
    3-109, 180–81
    3-110 to 3–111, 181
    3-112, 180–81
    3-115, 181
    3-118, 181

3-119, 180
3-201, 200–01
3-206, 190
3-207, 209
3-302, 197–98
3-304, 198
3-305, 197
3-307, 179
3-401, 179
3-404, 179,209
3-405, 208–09, 220
3-406, 208–10, 212,220,223
3-410, 211
3-419, 212
3-805, 179,190
4-401 to 4-405, 224
4-406, 219–20,224
7-309, 347
3-102, 319
3-204, 320
4-207, 319
9-107, 385
9-204, 383
9-301, 388
9-307 to 9-309, 389
9-312, 388
9-313, 389–90
9-314, 390
9-401, 385
9-501, 386
9-503, 386
9-505, 386–87
Ultra vires doctrine, 286
Ultramares Corp v. Touche, 332
Ultramares principle, 332
Unauthorized completion of an instrument, 204
Unconditional, 179–80
Unconscionability,108
Undisclosed principal, 239
Undue influence, 106–07
Unemployment compensation/insurance, 406–07
Unenforceable contract, 84
Unfair competition, 64
Unfair labor practices, 412–14
Uniform Arbitration Act, 46
Uniform Commercial Code, 8, 86, 91, 94, 125, 127. *See also* UCC.
Uniform Consumer Credit Code, 205, 375–76
Uniform Gifts to Minors Act, 340
Uniform laws, 8
Uniform Limited Partnership Act, 265–67
Uniform Partnership Act, 256–58, 261–63
Uniform Securities Act, 330

Unilateral contract, 84, 90, 91
Unilateral mistake, 101–02
Union shop, 414
United States—Canada Free Trade Agreement, 419
United States Constitution, 14–19,55
    Article I—Section 8, 16, 377
    Article I—Section 9, 20
    Article I—Section 10, 18–20
    Article III, 23
    Article IV—Section 1, 34–35
    Article VI—Section 2, 14
    Eighth Amendment, 55
    Fifth Amendment, 18, 47, 55, 353–54
    First Amendment, 18
    Fourteenth Amendment, 17–19, 47, 55
    Fourth Amendment, 55
    Sixth Amendment, 55
United States v. Arthur Young & Co., 332
Unjust enrichment, 83
Usurpation of corporate opportunity, 302
Usury, 118

Valid contract, 84
Venue, 33
Verdict, 42
Vertical privity, 166
Victimless crimes, 56
Void contract, 84, 102, 107
Voidable contract, 84, 102, 106, 108
Voidable title, 159–60
Voir dire, 41–42
Voting rights (stock), 315
Voting trusts, 298

Wagner Act (NLRA), 412–14
Waiver, 141
Warnings, 168
Warranties, 163–66, 210–12, 359
    of habitability, 359
    on transfer, 211–12
Waste, 359
White-collar crimes, 56, 68–69
Wildcat strikes, 415
Wills, 363–64
Withdrawal of partners, 261
Worker Adjustment and Retraining Notification (WARN) Act, 407
Workers' compensation, 405, 417
Writs of execution, 373
Written confirmation (between merchants), 156
Wrongful (abusive) discharge, 63–64, 407–08
Wrongful dishonor, 219, 224

Zoning, 355

More selected BARRON'S titles:

TITLES THAT
GENERATE SUCCESS!

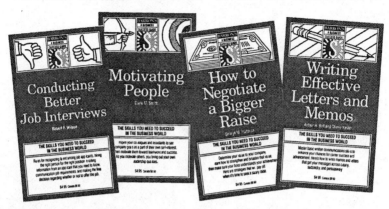

Business Success Series

Fourteen titles comprise Barron's innovative series designed to help the business person succeed! Seasoned professionals offer commonsense advice and facts on how to master job techniques that will generate success. Each book: Paperback, $4.95, Can. $6.50, 96 pp., 4 3/16" × 7"

Conduct Better Job Interviews (4580-7)
Conquering Stress (4837-7)
Creative Problem Solving (1461-8)
Delegating Authority (4604-8)
How To Negotiate a Bigger Raise (4604-8)
Making Presentations With Confidence (4588-2)
Maximizing Your Memory Power (4799-0)
Motivating People (4792-3)
Projecting a Positive Image (1455-3)
Running a Meeting That Works (4640-4)
Time Management (4792-3)
Using the Telephone More Effectively (4672-2)
Winning With Difficult People (4583-1)
Writing Effective Letters and Memos (4674-9)

Prices subject to change without notice. Books may be purchased at your bookstore or by mail from Barron's. Enclose check or money order for total amount plus sales tax where applicable and 10% for postage and handling (minimum charge of $3.75, Canada $4.00). ISBN PREFIX: 0-8120

Barron's Educational Series, Inc.
250 Wireless Blvd., Hauppauge, NY 11788
In Canada: Georgetown Warehouse
34 Armstrong Ave., Georgetown, Ont. L7G 4R9   R 9/94

More selected BARRON'S titles: